Life, Health and Variable Contracts

Study Manual

A License Preparation Manual
with Questions and Answers

Prepared by the National Association of Insurance
and Financial Advisors - Florida

National Association of
Insurance and Financial
Advisors - Florida

The Florida Department
of Financial Services

Florida

29th Edition

FLORIDA LIFE, HEALTH AND VARIABLE CONTRACTS STUDY MANUAL, 29TH EDITION
©2014 Kaplan, Inc.

The text of this publication, or any part thereof, may not be reproduced in any manner whatsoever without written permission from the publisher.

If you find imperfections or incorrect information in this product, please visit www.kfeducation.com and submit an errata report.

Published in September 2014 by Kaplan Financial Education.

Printed in the United States of America.

ISBN: 978-1-4754-2593-2 / 1-4754-2593-7

PPN: 3200-5222

Acknowledgments

The publisher would like to recognize and thank James C. Fogarty, CLU®, Legislative Vice President Emeritus of the Florida Association of Life Underwriters (FALU), Herbert F. Morgan (dec.), past CEO of the Florida Association of Insurance and Financial Advisors (FAIFA), Sharon G. Heierman, CAE, past CEO of the National Association of Insurance and Financial Advisors-Florida (NAIFA-FL), and Paul S. Brawner, AIP, QAS, current CEO of NAIFA-FL, for their contributions over the years in the development and content of this manual.

Founded in 1932, as the Florida Association of Life Underwriters, NAIFA-Florida, formerly the Florida Association of Insurance & Financial Advisors (FAIFA), is comprised of 19 local associations in the state of Florida representing nearly 3,000 insurance and financial advisors. The mission of NAIFA-Florida is to enhance the careers of its members through advocacy, professional development, and adherence to its code of ethics.

Preface

The life and health insurance industry is growing larger and more complex, and public demand for additional information and professional services has led to an increasing emphasis on insurance education. Florida, like other states throughout the nation, has instituted requirements for prelicensing education in insurance.

An insurance agent's career demands professionalism in dealing with the public. This is one reason why a license is required before an individual can sell insurance. This book will provide the necessary working knowledge of basic insurance principles. Future training and educational opportunities will be offered by insurance industry organizations and associations and by your own company or agency.

This text is designed to guide prospective licensees in preparing for the life (including variable contracts), health, or the combination life (including variable contracts) and health insurance exams in Florida. Use of the study aids included throughout this text will help the student make the best use of available study time, whether the book is used in a class or independently. The order of topics, as well as the overall scope of coverage, follows the recommended examination content outline.

The state licensing test is scored immediately, and the applicant who passes the test, is considered to be licensed as of that moment and may begin to sell after being appointed as an agent by the insurance company or companies that the applicant proposes to represent. For additional information on the examinations, consult the Department of Financial Services' publication, **Licensing Information Bulletin**. The purpose of the publication is to furnish guidelines and additional information to candidates regarding the Florida Insurance License Qualification Examinations. The most recent information should always be obtained from the Department of Financial Services, since changes and revisions are made periodically. The latest Licensing Information Bulletin may be obtained from:

Pearson VUE
3 Bala Plaza West. Ste. 300
Bala Cynwyd, PA 19004-3481
www.pearsonvue.com

Additional copies of this study manual may be obtained from:

National Association of Insurance and Financial Advisors – Florida
1836 Hermitage Blvd., Ste. 200
Tallahassee, FL 32308

Phone: (850) 422-1701 Fax: (850) 422-2762
www.naifa-florida.org

REPRESENTING

JEFF ATWATER
CHIEF FINANCIAL OFFICER
STATE OF FLORIDA

MEMORANDUM

TO: Prospective Insurance Professionals

FROM: Bureau of Licensing

DATE: November 2014

This study manual is designed to assist individuals interested in the insurance profession in obtaining a thorough knowledge of Florida's laws and rules and an accurate understanding of insurance and practice.

The manual is a basis for study, especially for those applying for a life (including variable contracts) or health insurance license, and a means for keeping up with the rapid changes taking place within the insurance industry. As in any profession, it is important that individuals working in insurance monitor changing trends, laws, regulations and services that affect their customers—the public.

The Department pledges to monitor the revisions to this publication to better serve those who use it. The Department welcomes suggestions for improvement from those who have chosen this manual as an important guide to insurance law and practice.

Table of Contents

Introduction

A successful career in insurance selling is achieved one step at a time. The first step is to become licensed, and it is the purpose of this book to help you prepare for the Florida Insurance License Qualification Examinations. This manual is revised every year to reflect changes in insurance trends and Florida laws.

■ This 29th edition of the *Florida Life, Health and Variable Contracts Study Manual* has been revised to reflect changes in the insurance industry and on the insurance licensing examinations.

This new edition includes industry statistics, updated deductibles for Medicare, current requirements for Medicare Supplement plans, and Florida rules on agency licensing, replacement, life insurance policy and annuity solicitation, and disclosure. Review questions have been revised at the end of each unit to reflect changes in the topics, and the Glossary has been updated.

The manual will provide you with a solid foundation of basic life and health insurance principles. Not only will it help you prepare for your licensing examinations, but it also offers you the most complete and up-to-date information on insurance topics.

HOW TO USE THIS STUDY MANUAL

Preparation for taking the exam should be based on a thorough reading and understanding of the material in this manual. The manual is organized into Parts I, II, III and IV.

Part I provides an introduction to the role and purpose of insurance in general and the principles that apply to both life and health insurance. It should be read by all students. Part II covers life insurance specifically, focusing on various types of life policies and their provisions, underwriting practices, and the many uses for life insurance. Part III is devoted to the subject of health insurance, covering types of policies and their provisions, providers of health insurance and services, underwriting standards, and uses of health insurance. Part IV focuses on Florida laws and regulations. Unit 26 explains Florida laws and rules pertinent to both life and health insurance, while Units 27 and 29 review more specific information on Florida life and health insurance regulation. Unit 28 discusses variable contracts and is especially important to those previously licensed life agents who want to add variable contracts to their licenses. Unit 30 explains how Health Maintenance Organizations operate in Florida and how they are regulated.

STUDY SUGGESTIONS

The following suggestions will help you develop a study plan and pass your licensing examination.

- Once you finish reading each unit, review the Key Concepts listed at the end of the unit. These indicate topics and concepts that frequently appear on the licensing exam.

- Answer the multiple-choice Questions for Review at the end of each unit. Check your answers against the Answer Key at the back of the book. If any of your responses are incorrect, review the pertinent material.

Florida Law States:
"F.S. 626.551—Every licensee shall notify the department in writing within 30 days after a change of name, residence address, principal business street address, mailing address, contact telephone numbers, including a business telephone number, or e-mail address. A licensed agent who has moved his or her residence from this state shall have his or her license and all appointments immediately terminated by the department. Failure to notify the department within the required time period shall result in a fine not to exceed $250 for the first offense and, for subsequent offenses, a fine of at least $500 or suspension or revocation of the license pursuant to FS 626.611 or 626.621."

Sample Test Questions for Florida Life, Health and Variable Contracts Examinations

The following sample questions illustrate the format of questions in the tests. They do not, however, represent the full range of content or levels of difficulty found in the tests.

1. A life insurance company that shares its surplus earnings with its insureds is known as

    A. a mutual insurance company
    B. a fraternal organization
    C. an association
    D. an admitted company

2. A beneficiary is NOT protected from creditors' claims if the beneficiary is the insured's

    A. estate
    B. spouse
    C. child
    D. business partner

3. Which of the following factors is NOT a primary consideration when a life insurance company computes the basic premium for a policy?

    A. Mortality factor
    B. Interest factor
    C. Expense factor
    D. Lien factor

4. All of the following groups would be eligible for group life insurance under Florida law EXCEPT

    A. a labor union
    B. a debtor group
    C. an employee-dependents group
    D. an employer-employee group

Answer Key

1. **A**

2. **A**

3. **D**

4. **C**

TEST PREPARATION

The knowledge you are responsible for and on which you will be tested is found in this study manual. You may use any other references you wish to help you prepare for the test. However, all test questions are referenced to a specific page and paragraph in these state-approved study manuals or reference materials. Following is a list of supplementary study materials.

Life Agent (including Variable Contracts), Health Agent, or Life (including Variable Contracts) and Health Agent

Florida Life, Health and Variable Contracts Study Manual. Available from the Florida Association of Insurance and Financial Advisors, 1836 Hermitage Blvd., #200, Tallahassee, FL 32308.
Tel: 1-850-422-1701.
www.faifa.org

Limited Variable Contracts Exam

To prepare for the limited variable annuity exam, study the following sections of the *Florida Life, Health and Variable Contracts Study Manual:*
    Part I: Unit 4
    Part II: Units 5 and 11
    Part IV: Units 26, 27, and 28

General Lines Agent and Customer Representative

Florida General Lines Agent and Customer Representative Study Manual. Available from the Florida Association of Insurance Agents, P.O. Box 12129, Tallahassee, FL 32317-2129.
Tel: 1-850-893-4155.
www.faia.com

Industrial Fire and Burglary Agent

Industrial Fire and Burglary Insurance Study Manual. Available from the Florida Association of Insurance and Financial Advisors, 1836 Hermitage Blvd., #200, Tallahassee, FL 32308.
Tel: 1-850-422-1701.
www.faifa.org

Crop Hail and Multiple-Peril Crop Insurance Agent

Study materials available from the Florida Department of Financial Services.
www.doi.state.fl.us

Surplus Lines Agent

Sections 626.901 through 626.939, Florida Statutes. A set of Florida Statutes is available at most local libraries.
www.leg.state.fl.us

Bail Bond Agent

Bail and Bail-Bond Insurance in Florida Study Guide. Accompanies the University of Florida Department of Independent Study correspondence course, *Insurance 3.* Available from the Division of Continuing Education, Department of Independent Study, University of Florida, Gainesville, FL 32611.
Tel: 1-352-392-1711.
www.correspondencestudy.ufl.edu

Adjusters—All Lines and Limited Lines

Florida Adjusters Study Manual.
Available from the Florida Association of Insurance Agents, P.O. Box 12129, Tallahassee, FL 32317-2129.
Tel: 1-850-893-4155.
www.faia.com

Source: Reproduced with permission of the Florida Department of Financial Services.

Notice to Test Takers

USE OF EXAMINATION CONTENT OUTLINES

State licensing exams are based on detailed content outlines of topics, subtopics, and references to applicable state laws, statutes, and regulations. The outlines are updated periodically to reflect changes in practice, state laws, and regulations. These outlines are provided to assist publishers of study materials, approved education providers, and exam candidates.

PROVIDERS AND CANDIDATES TAKE NOTE!

The content outlines provided in this 29th Edition have been revised by the Exam Provider, PearsonVUE, under the direction of the Department of Financial Services. Following is a *partial* list of potentially testable terms that were new in last year's outlines and that have new or amended definitions in the text:

- Life policy riders
    - Waiver of premium with disability income
    - Accidental death and dismemberment
    - Term riders
    - Long-term care
- Completing the application
    - Disclosures at the point of sale
    - USA PATRIOT Act
- Life underwriting
    - Investor-owned life insurance (IOLI)
- Department of Financial Services
- Office of Insurance Regulation
- Office of Financial Regulation
- Licensing
    - Background check

- Marketing practices
  - Coercion
  - Unfair discrimination
- Policy replacement
  - Duties of agent
  - Duties of insurer
- Medical expense insurance
  - Flexible spending accounts (FSAs)
  - Health reimbursement accounts (HRAs)
  - High deductible health plans (HDHPs)
- Long-term care (LTC)
  - Group/voluntary LTC contracts
- Limited benefit plans
  - Hospital indemnity plans
- Mandatory provisions
  - Misstatement of age
- Other provisions and clauses
  - Lifetime, annual, or per cause maximum
- Other insurance concepts
  - Modes of premium payments
  - Occupational vs. nonoccupational
  - Subrogation

The content outlines, which are provided on the following 11 pages, show the topics covered in each exam, the percentage of questions from each main topic, and page references showing where each topic is addressed in this manual. *In order to have the highest level of confidence in passing their licensing exam, candidates should be certain to cover all the topics listed in the appropriate content outline.*

Florida Insurance
Examination Content Outlines
Effective January 1, 2015

Florida Agent's Life Insurance and Annuity (including Variable Contracts)
85 scored questions plus 15 pretest questions
Time limit: 2 hours

GENERAL KNOWLEDGE

Florida Insurance
Examination Content Outlines
Effective January 1, 2015

Florida Insurance
Examination Content Outlines
Effective January 1, 2015

Florida Agent's Health Insurance
85 scored questions plus 15 pretest questions
Time limit: 2 hours

GENERAL KNOWLEDGE

Florida Insurance
Examination Content Outlines
Effective January 1, 2015

Florida Agent's Health and Life Insurance and Annuity (including Variable Contracts)
150 scored questions plus 15 pretest questions
Time limit: 2.75 hours

GENERAL KNOWLEDGE

Florida Insurance
Examination Content Outlines
Effective January 1, 2015

Florida Insurance
Examination Content Outlines
Effective January 1, 2015

Florida Insurance
Examination Content Outlines
Effective January 1, 2015

Florida Insurance
Examination Content Outlines
Effective January 1, 2015

Florida Examination for
Variable Insurance Contracts
40 scored questions plus 5 pretest questions
Time limit: 1 hour

1

Principles of Life and Health Insurance

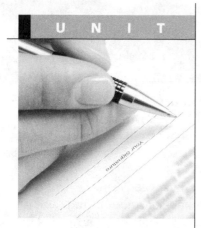

1

Purpose of Life and Health Insurance

- The Role of Insurance
- An Industry Overview
- The Nature of Insurance
- The Concept of Risk
- Economic Basis of Life and Health Insurance

The first step in the study of life and health insurance is to understand the purpose these instruments serve and the important role they play for individuals and for society. In this unit, we will take a look at this purpose and role by explaining the concept of risk and showing how insurance is uniquely designed to replace the uncertainties of risk with guarantees. ■

THE ROLE OF INSURANCE

Through the centuries, people have pursued financial security for themselves and those who depend on them. We all have a compelling need for security; security is peace of mind and freedom from worry. Insecurity is doubt, fear, and apprehension. Most economic actions we take are to satisfy some need and thus attain some degree of security.

Unfortunately, complete financial security has been elusive, in part because of certain universal problems: death, sickness, accidents and disability. These problems can strike at any time and without any warning. The emotional stress these problems bring is increased by the financial hardships that are almost certain to follow.

Death may strike anyone prematurely. When death takes the life of a family provider, surviving family members often suffer if they are left without an adequate income or the means to provide even basic necessities. However, some people face the unpleasant prospect of outliving their income. Retirement may be forced upon them before they have adequately prepared for a non-income-earning existence. Sickness and disability can also leave economic scars, often more intense than death. An accident or illness can easily result in catastrophic medical bills or the inability to work for months or even years.

Insurance evolved to produce a practical solution to such economic uncertainties and losses. **Life insurance**, which is based on actuarial or mathematical principles, guarantees a specified sum of money upon the death of the person who is insured. **Health insurance** also evolved from scientific principles to provide funds for medical expenses due to sickness or injury and to cover loss of income during a disability. **Annuities** provide a stream of income by making a series of payments to the annuitant for a specific period of time or for his lifetime. *The true significance of insurance is its promise to substitute future economic certainty for uncertainty and to replace the unknown with a sense of security.*

ILLUSTRATION 1.1

Life Insurance Purchases in the United States, by Year, at Five-Year Intervals

| | Policies and certificates in thousands/Amounts in millions | | | | | |
| | Individual | | Group | | Total | |
Year	Policies	Amount	Certificates	Amount	Policies/ Certificates	Amount
1940	17,872	$10,039	285	$691	18,157	$10,730
1945	16,212	13,289	681	1,265	16,893	14,554
1950	20,203	22,728	2,631	6,068	22,834	28,796
1955	21,928	37,169	2,217	11,258	24,145	48,427
1960	21,021	59,763	3,734	14,645	24,755	74,408
1965	20,429	90,781	7,007	51,385	27,436	142,166
1970	18,550	129,432	5,219	63,690	23,769	193,122
1975	18,946	194,732	8,146	95,190	27,092	289,922
1980	17,628	389,184	11,379	183,418	29,007	572,602
1985	17,637	911,666	16,243	319,503	33,880	1,231,169
1990	14,199	1,069,880	14,592	459,271	28,791	1,529,151
1995	12,595	1,039,258	19,404	537,828	31,999	1,577,086
2000	13,345	1,593,907	21,537	921,001	34,882	2,514,908
2005	11,407	1,796,384	23,112	1,039,878	34,519	2,836,262
2010	10,123	1,673,216	18,498	1,135,354	28,621	2,808,570

Sources: ACLI tabulations of National Association of Insurance Commissioners (NAIC) data, used by permission; LIMRA-International. NAIC does not endorse any analysis or conclusions based on use of its data.

AN INDUSTRY OVERVIEW

The insurance industry plays an important role in our society. A snapshot of insurance statistics at five-year intervals illustrates this point. (See Illustration 1.1.) The majority of American households own some form of life insurance. In 2010, the average face amount of a newly purchased individual life insurance policy was $165,300. Premiums for life insurance policies totaled $105 billion in 2010, a 16% decrease from the previous year. Bucking the negative economic and industry trends, annuity premium receipts increased 27% in 2010 to $294 billion. The amount paid out—benefits, dividends, annuity payments, and surrender values—exceeded $365 billion.

Most new life insurance policies are purchased by individuals from life insurance agents. According to the American Council of Life Insurers 2011 Life Insurers Fact Book, Americans purchased $2.87 trillion of new life insurance coverage in 2010, 3.1% less than in 2009. Life insurance in force in the United States at the end of 2010 totaled over $18.4 trillion, a 2% increase from 2009.

The health insurance industry is also vital to our national well-being. In 2010, US Census Bureau statistics indicate that 260 million Americans, 85% of the population, had some form of health coverage. 196 million, or 64% of the insured, had private insurance, and 88%, or 176 million, participated in employer-based health programs. The number of those covered by government-based insurance programs (principally Medicare) increased in 2010 to over 95 million.

Despite these impressive coverage statistics, according to the Census Bureau, the uninsured in America continue to increase and now total 47.2 million, or 15.5% of the population. There is no simple profile for the uninsured; 10.8 million, or 23%, are non-US citizens; 29 million, or 61%, have family incomes below $50,000 per year; and 13 million, or 28%, are eligible for state or federal health benefits but have not enrolled.

Paying for health care remains a challenge for both individuals and the nation. According to the Centers for Medicare and Medicaid Services, while health care costs in 2010 increased just under a modest 4%, the slowest rate in half a century, it is also true that health care spending accounted for 17.9% of the nation's GDP in 2010, compared to 17.6% in 2009, and averaged $8,402 per person.

Finally, we should note that the insurance industry makes a substantial contribution to our nation's economy. It is a significant source of investment funds because insurance companies invest the billions of premium dollars they receive annually in a wide range of investments.[1]

---

[1] As we will see, one of the basic factors in life and health premiums is the interest earned by the insurance company on the premiums it receives and subsequently invests.

THE NATURE OF INSURANCE

We are exposed to many perils. The purpose of insurance—any insurance—is to provide economic protection against losses that may be incurred due to a chance happening or event, such as death, illness, or accident. This protection is provided through an **insurance policy**, which is simply a device for accumulating funds to meet these uncertain losses. The policy is a legally binding contract that sets forth the company's promise and obligations as follows:

Whereby, for a set amount of money (the premium)*, one party (the* insurer*) agrees to pay the other party (the* insured *or the insured's* beneficiary*) a set sum (the* benefit*) upon the occurrence of some event.*

In the case of life insurance, for example, the benefit is paid when the insured dies. In the case of health or disability insurance, the benefit is paid if and when the insured incurs certain medical expenses or becomes disabled, as defined by the contract.

Basic Insurance Principles

Insurance is based on two fundamental principles: the **spreading** or **pooling of risks** (also known as "loss sharing") and the **law of large numbers**. To understand these principles, consider the following example.

Risk Pooling

Assume that 1,000 individuals in the same social club agree that if any member of their group dies, all of the members will pitch in to provide the deceased's family with $10,000. This $10,000, it was determined, would provide the family with enough funds to cover the immediate costs associated with death and to provide a cushion for at least a few months. Because it is not known when any one individual within the group will die, the decision is made to "pre-fund" the benefit by assessing each member $10. Each individual contributes $10, thus creating the $10,000 fund. As you can see, without the agreement to help provide for each other's potential loss, each group member (and the member's family) would have to face the economic cost of death alone. But by sharing the burden and spreading the risk of death over all 1,000 group members, the most any one member pays is $10.

This is, of course, a simplified example, but it explains the basic concept of loss sharing. By spreading a risk, or by sharing the possibility of a loss, a large group of people can substitute a small certain cost ($10) for a large unknown risk (the economic risk of dying). In other words, the risk is transferred from an individual to a group, each member of which shares the losses and has the promise of a future benefit. Insurance companies pool risks among thousands and thousands of insureds and apply certain mathematical principles to guarantee policyowners that the money will be there to pay a claim when it arises.

Law of Large Numbers

In addition to the spreading of risks, insurance relies on the principle that the larger the number of individual risks (or "exposures") that are combined into a group, the more certainty there is as to the amount of loss incurred in any given period. In other words, given a large enough pool of risks, an insurer can predict with reasonable accuracy the number of claims it will face during any given time. No one can predict when any one person will die or if any one person will become disabled. However, it is possible to predict the approximate *number* of deaths or the *likelihood* of disability that will occur among a certain group during a certain period. This principle, known as the **law of large numbers**, is based on the science of probability and the experience of mortality (death) and morbidity (sickness) statistics. The larger and more homogeneous the group, the more certain the mortality or morbidity predictions will be.

For example, statistics may show that among a group of 100,000 40-year-old males, 300 will die within one year. While it is not possible to predict who the 300 will be, the number will prove very accurate. However, with a small group, an accurate prediction is not possible. Among a group of 100 40-year-old males, it is not statistically feasible to predict if any in the group will die within one year. Because insurers cover thousands and thousands of lives, it is possible to predict when and to what extent deaths and disabilities will occur and, consequently, when claims will arise.

All forms of insurance—life, health, accident, property, and casualty—rely on risk pooling and the law of large numbers. These principles form the foundation upon which insurance is based and allow for its successful operation.

THE CONCEPT OF RISK

As we have learned, insurance replaces the uncertainty of risk with guarantees. But what exactly does the word *risk* mean? And how does insurance remove the uncertainty and minimize the adverse effects of risk?

Risk Defined

Risk can be defined as uncertainty regarding loss. Property loss, such as the destruction of a home due to fire, is an example of risk. Negligence or carelessness can give rise to a liability risk if there is potential injury to an individual or damage to property. The inability to work and earn a living due to a disability is another example of risk, as is loss of a family's income due to the death of the breadwinner. The loss that is involved with all of these risks is characterized by a lessening (or disappearance) of value.

Risks can be divided into two classes: *speculative risks* and *pure risks*.

1. **Speculative risks.** Speculative risks involve the chance of both loss and gain. Betting at the race track or investing in the stock market are examples of speculative risks. There is a chance for gain and a chance for loss.

2. **Pure risks.** Pure risks involve only the chance of loss; there is never a possibility of gain or profit. The risk associated with the chance of injury from an accident is an example of pure risk. There is no opportunity for gain if the event does not occur—only the opportunity for loss if it does occur. *Only pure risks are insurable.*

With life insurance, the risk involved is *when* death will occur. It can be tomorrow, next week, next year, or well into the future. Loss can result if death is premature or comes too late. With health insurance, the risk is not when, but *if* illness or disability will strike. Losses associated with health risks include medical costs and loss of income. With annuities, the risk is living too long and outlasting one's income. Annuities cover this risk by paying a guaranteed income to the annuitant for life.

Perils and Hazards

In conjunction with risk are the concepts of *perils* and *hazards*. Perils and hazards are factors that cause or give rise to risk.

A **peril** is defined as the immediate specific event causing loss and giving rise to risk. A peril is the *cause* of a risk. For example, when a building burns, fire is the peril. When a person dies, death is the peril. When an individual is injured in an accident, the accident is the peril. When a person becomes ill from a disease, the disease is the peril.

A **hazard** is any factor that gives rise to a peril. For purposes of life and health insurance, there are three basic types of hazards: *physical*, *moral*, and *morale*.

- **Physical hazards.** Physical hazards are individual characteristics that increase the chance of peril. For example, physical hazards may exist because of a person's physical condition, past medical history, or condition at birth. Blindness and deafness are physical hazards.

- **Moral hazards.** Moral hazards are tendencies that people may have that increase risk and the chance of loss. Alcoholism and drug addiction are considered moral hazards.

- **Morale hazards.** Morale hazards are also individual tendencies, but they arise from an attitude or state of mind causing indifference to loss. For example, a person may have a habit of driving recklessly, with no fear of death or injury. This indifference is a morale hazard, increasing the chance of death or injury.

Treatment of Risk

How risks are treated varies greatly, depending on the situation, the degree of potential loss and the individual. Basically speaking, there are four options: *avoid the risk*, *reduce the risk*, *retain the risk* or *transfer the risk*. Let's consider each.

Risk Avoidance

One method of dealing with risk is **avoidance**—simply avoiding as many risks as possible. By choosing not to drive or own an automobile, one could avoid the risks associated with driving. By never flying, one could eliminate the risk of being in an airplane crash. By never investing in stocks, one could avoid the risk of a market crash. Clearly, risk avoidance is effective, but it is not always practical. Few risks can be handled in this manner.

Risk Reduction

Risk reduction is another means of dealing with risk. Since we cannot avoid risk entirely, we often attempt to lessen the possibility of loss by taking action to reduce the risk. Installing a smoke alarm in a home will not lessen the possibility of fire, but it may reduce the risk of loss from fire.

Risk Retention

Risk retention is another method of coping with risk. This means accepting the risk and confronting it if and when it occurs. One way to handle a retained risk is self-insurance. Setting up a fund to offset the costs of a potential loss is regarded as self-insurance.

Risk Transference

The most effective way to handle risk is to **transfer** it so that the loss is borne by another party. Insurance is the most common method of transferring risk (i.e., from an individual or group to an insurance company). Though purchasing insurance will not eliminate the risk of death or illness, it relieves the insured individual or group of the losses these risks bring. Insurance satisfies both economic and emotional needs. It replaces the uncertainty surrounding risk with the assurance of guarantees, and it transfers the financial consequences of death, illness, or disability to the insurer.

Elements of Insurable Risk

Though insurance may be one of the most effective ways to handle risks, not all risks are insurable. As noted earlier, insurers will insure only pure risks or those that involve only the chance of loss. However, not all pure risks are insurable. Certain characteristics or elements must be evident before a pure risk can be insured.

- **The loss must be due to chance.** In order to be insurable, a risk must involve the chance of loss that is fortuitous and outside the insured's control.

- **The loss must be definite and measurable.** An insurable risk must involve a loss that is definite as to cause, time, place, and amount. An insurer must be able to determine how much the benefit will be and when it becomes payable.

■ **The loss must be predictable.** An insurable risk must be one whose occurrence can be statistically predicted. This enables insurers to estimate the average frequency and severity of future losses and set appropriate premiums. Death, illness, and disability are all events whose rates of occurrence can be projected, based on statistics.

■ **The loss cannot be catastrophic.** Insurers typically will not insure risks that will expose them to catastrophic losses. There must be limits that insurers can be reasonably certain their losses will not exceed. This is why an insurer would not issue a policy for $1 trillion on a single life. That one death would create a catastrophic loss to the company.

■ **The loss exposures to be insured must be large.** An insurer must be able to predict losses based on the law of large numbers. Consequently, there must be a sufficiently large pool to be insured, and those in the pool (the "exposures") must be grouped into classes with similar risks. Individuals, for example, are grouped according to age, health, sex, occupation, and other classifications.

■ **The loss exposures to be insured must be randomly selected.** In addition, the group to be insured must be randomly selected. Insurers must have a fair proportion of good risks and poor risks. A large proportion of poor risks would financially threaten the insurance company because there would be many claims without sufficient premiums to offset them. Keep in mind that there is a tendency, called **adverse selection**, for less favorable insurance risks (i.e., people in poor health) to seek or continue insurance to a greater extent than other risks.

ECONOMIC BASIS OF LIFE AND HEALTH INSURANCE

To fully appreciate the purpose and function of insurance, it is important to understand that its roots lie in economics and the concept of the **human life value**.

It has long been recognized that individuals have an economic value that can be measured in part by their future earning potential. This earning potential is the sum of one's net future earnings or, more precisely, the dollar value of an individual's future earning capability. The true significance of this earning potential extends beyond the individual to those who depend on that individual for their financial security. Thus, by definition, human life value is the value today of an individual's future earnings that are devoted to that individual's dependents.

In the abstract, human life value is the means by which homes are purchased, college educations provided, monthly bills paid—in short, it is the essence of an individual's or family's economic existence. Yet, this value is subject to loss through death, retirement, disability, or poor health. Any one of these perils affects earning capacity to one degree or another and, consequently, diminishes human life value. It is for this purpose—to conserve and protect human life value—that life and health insurance exist.

SUMMARY

Life and *health insurance* evolved to provide a practical solution to the economic losses associated with death, sickness, and accidents. It does so through an *insurance policy*, which is a device to accumulate funds to meet these losses. Insurance is based on *risk pooling* and the *law of large numbers*, the principles that allow insurers to spread risks among thousands of individuals and to predict losses with reasonable accuracy.

Insurance transfers risk, which is one of the most effective ways to deal with *risk* and its losses. Not all risks are insurable, however. There are certain elements every risk must contain before it can be insured. For example, it must be a pure risk; the loss it entails must be due to chance; the loss must be definite and measurable; the loss must be predictable; the loss cannot be catastrophic; and the loss exposure must be part of a large randomly selected group.

The true worth of insurance lies in its ability to protect *human life values*—the value associated with an individual's earning potential—and to provide financial security.

KEY CONCEPTS

Students should be familiar with the following concepts:

speculative risk	peril
pure risk	risk pooling
law of large numbers	methods of handling risk
elements of insurable risk	adverse selection
hazard	

UNIT TEST

1. Which of the following insurance concepts is founded on the ability to predict the approximate number of deaths or frequency of disabilities within a certain group during a specific time?
   A. Principle of large loss
   B. Quantum insurance principle
   C. Indemnity law
   D. Law of large numbers

2. The owner of a camera store is worried that her new employees may help themselves to items from inventory without paying for them. What kind of hazard is described?
   A. Physical hazard
   B. Ethical hazard
   C. Morale hazard
   D. Moral hazard

3. All of the following actions are examples of risk avoidance EXCEPT
   A. Bill won't fly in an airplane
   B. Wendy keeps her money out of the stock market
   C. Pat pays his insurance premium
   D. John never drives a car

4. Which of the following statements is CORRECT?
   A. Only speculative risks are insurable.
   B. Only pure risks are insurable.
   C. Both pure risks and speculative risks are insurable.
   D. Neither pure risks nor speculative risks are insurable.

5. Which of the following statements does NOT describe an element of an insurable risk?
   A. The loss must not be due to chance.
   B. The loss must be definite and measurable.
   C. The loss cannot be catastrophic.
   D. The loss exposures to be insured must be large.

6. In the insurance business, risk can best be defined as
   A. sharing the possibility of a loss
   B. uncertainty regarding the future
   C. uncertainty regarding financial loss
   D. uncertainty regarding when death will occur

7. Buying insurance is one of the most effective ways of
   A. avoiding risk
   B. transferring risk
   C. reducing risk
   D. retaining risk

8. Which of the following best describes the function of insurance?
   A. It is a form of legalized gambling.
   B. It spreads financial risk over a large group to minimize the loss to any one individual.
   C. It protects against living too long.
   D. It creates and protects risks.

9. A tornado is an example of
   A. a physical hazard
   B. a speculative risk
   C. a peril
   D. a moral hazard

10. Tom buys his wife Mary a $50,000 diamond ring. When she is not wearing the ring, she keeps it in a safe deposit box at a local bank. This is an example of risk
    A. avoidance
    B. reduction
    C. retention
    D. transference

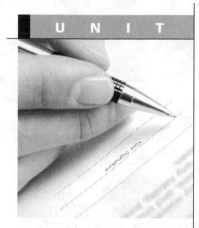

2

The Insurance Industry

- Types of Insurers
- How Insurance Is Sold
- Evolution of Industry Oversight

The insurance industry is one of the most efficiently organized and effectively operated industries in our country today. The purpose of this unit is to provide a broad overview of the insurance industry, how it operates, and how it is regulated. Please note that Florida, like every other state, has its own laws and regulations regarding insurance, and a review of Florida's state laws is recommended. ■

TYPES OF INSURERS

There are many ways to classify organizations that provide insurance. In the broadest of terms, there are two classifications: private and government. Within these two classes are many categories of insurance providers as well as insurance plans and insurance producers.

Private Insurers

Private insurers offer many lines of insurance. Some sell primarily life insurance and annuities, some sell accident and health insurance, and some sell property and casualty insurance. Companies that write more than one line of insurance are known as **multi-line insurers**.

Within this broad category of private insurers are specific types of insurance companies. A discussion of each type follows.

Stock Insurers

A **stock insurance company** is a private organization, organized and incorporated under state laws for the purpose of making a profit for its stockholders. It is structured the same as any corporation. Stockholders may or may not be policyholders. When declared, stock dividends are paid to stockholders. In a stock company, the directors and officers are responsible to the stockholders. A stock company is referred to as a **nonparticipating company** because policyholders do not participate in dividends resulting from stock ownership.

Mutual Insurers

Mutual insurance companies are also organized and incorporated under state laws, but they have no stockholders. Instead, the owners are the policyholders. Anyone purchasing insurance from a mutual insurer is both a customer and an owner. She has the right to vote for the board of director members. By issuing participating policies that pay **policy dividends**, mutual insurers allow their policyowners to share in any company earnings. Essentially, policy dividends represent a "refund" of the portion of premiums that remains after the company has set aside the necessary reserves and has made deductions for claims and expenses. Policy dividends can also include a share in the company's investment, mortality, and operating profits. Mutual companies are sometimes referred to as **participating companies** because the policyowners participate in dividends.

Occasionally, a stock company may be converted into a mutual company through a process called **mutualization**. Likewise, some mutuals are **demutualizing** by converting to stock companies. Stock and mutual companies are often referred to as **commercial insurers**. They both can write life, health, property, and casualty insurance.

Assessment Mutual Insurers

Assessment mutual companies are typified by the way in which they charge premiums. A **pure assessment mutual company** operates on the basis of loss sharing by group members. No premium is payable in advance; instead, each member is assessed an individual portion of losses that actually occur. An **advance premium assessment mutual** charges a premium in advance, at the beginning of the policy period. If the original premiums exceed the operating expenses and losses, the surplus is returned to the policyholders as dividends. However, if total premiums are not enough to meet losses, additional assessments are levied against the members. Normally, the amount of assessment that may be levied is limited, either by state law or simply as a provision in the insurer's bylaws. Assessment insurance companies are not permitted in Florida.

Reciprocal Insurers

Similar to mutuals, **reciprocal insurers** are organized on the basis of ownership by their policyholders. However, with reciprocals, it is the policyholders themselves who insure the risks of the other policyholders. Each policyholder assumes a share of the risk brought to the company by others. Reciprocals are managed by an attorney-in-fact.

Lloyd's of London

Contrary to popular opinion, **Lloyd's of London** is not an insurer but rather an association of individuals and companies that individually underwrite insurance. Lloyd's can be compared to the New York Stock Exchange, which provides the arena and facilities for buying and selling public stock. Lloyd's function is to gather and disseminate underwriting information, help its associates settle claims and disputes and, through its member underwriters, provide coverages that might otherwise be unavailable in certain areas.

Reinsurers

Reinsurers are a specialized branch of the insurance industry because they insure insurers. Reinsurance is an arrangement by which an insurance company transfers a portion of a risk it has assumed to another insurer. Usually, reinsurance takes place to limit the loss any one insurer would face should a very large claim become payable. Another reason for reinsurance is to enable a company to meet certain objectives, such as favorable underwriting or mortality results. The company transferring the risk is called the **ceding** company; the company assuming the risk is the **reinsurer**.

Risk Retention Group

A **risk retention group (RRG)** is a mutual insurance company formed to insure people in the same business, occupation, or profession (e.g., pharmacists, dentists, or engineers).

Fraternal Benefit Societies

Fraternal benefit societies, as insurers, are organized under a special section of the Insurance Code. Fraternal benefit societies have existed in the United States for more than a century. Fraternal societies, noted primarily for their social, charitable, and benevolent activities, have memberships based on religious, national, or ethnic lines. Fraternals first began offering insurance to meet the needs of their poorer members, funding the benefits on a pure assessment basis. Today few fraternals rely on an assessment system, most having adopted the same advanced funding approach other insurers use.

To be characterized as a fraternal benefit society, the organization must be nonprofit, have a lodge system that includes ritualistic work, and maintain a representative form of government with elected officers. Most fraternals today issue insurance certificates and annuities with many of the same provisions found in policies issued by commercial insurers.

Home Service Insurers

Insurance is also sold through a special branch of the industry known as **home service** or **"debit" insurers**. These companies specialize in a particular type of insurance called **industrial insurance**, which is characterized by relatively small face amounts (usually $1,000 to $2,000) with premiums paid weekly.

Service Providers

Service providers offer benefits to subscribers in return for the payment of a premium. Benefits are in the form of services provided by the hospitals and physicians participating in the plan. They sell medical and hospital care services, not insurance. These services are packaged into various plans, and those who purchase these plans are known as **subscribers**.

Another type of service provider is the **health maintenance organization (HMO)**. HMOs offer a wide range of health care services to member subscribers. For a fixed periodic premium paid in advance of any treatment, these subscribers are entitled to the services of certain physicians and hospitals contracted to work with the HMO. Unlike commercial insurers, HMOs are distinct because they provide financing for health care plus the health care itself. HMOs are known for stressing preventive health care and early treatment programs.

A third type of service provider is the **preferred provider organization (PPO)**. Under the usual PPO arrangement, a group desiring health care services (e.g., an employer or a union) will obtain price discounts or special services from certain select health care providers in exchange for referring its employees or members to them. PPOs can be organized by employers or by the health care providers themselves. The contract between the employer and the health care professional, be it a physician or a hospital, spells out the kind of services to be provided. Insurance companies can also contract with PPOs to offer services to insureds. (Service providers are discussed in detail in Unit 16.)

Government as Insurer

As noted at the beginning of this unit, federal and state governments are also insurers, providing what are commonly called **social insurance programs**. Ranging from crop insurance to bank and savings and loan deposit insurance, these programs have far-reaching effects because millions of people come under these plans. The major difference between these government programs and private insurance programs is that the government programs are funded with taxes and serve national and state social purposes. Social insurance programs include the following:

- Old-Age, Survivors, and Disability Insurance (OASDI), commonly known as Social Security

- Social Security Hospital Insurance (HI) and Supplemental Medical Insurance (SMI), commonly known as Medicare

- Medicaid

Each of these programs is discussed in Unit 12 and 20. The federal government has also established life insurance programs to benefit active members of the armed services and veterans. Three of the most notable programs are *Servicemembers' Group Life, Veterans' Group Life, and National Service Life*.

The government plays a vital role in providing social insurance programs. These programs pay billions of dollars in benefits every year and affect millions of people.

Self-Insurers

Though **self-insurance** is not a method of transferring risk, it is an important concept to understand. Rather than transfer risk to an insurance company, a self-insurer establishes its own reserves to cover potential losses. Self-insurance is often used by large companies for funding pension plans and some health insurance plans. Many times a self-insurer will look to an insurance company to provide insurance above a certain maximum level of loss. The self-insurer will bear the amount of loss below that maximum amount.

HOW INSURANCE IS SOLD

Insurance is sold by a variety of companies through a variety of methods. Most consumers purchase insurance through licensed **producers** who present insurers' products and services to the public via active sales and marketing methods. Insurance producers may be either **agents,** who represent a particular company, or **brokers**, who are not tied to any particular company and can represent many companies' products. In a sales transaction, agents represent the insurer, and brokers represent the buyer. An agent has an agent's contract; a broker must have a broker's contract.

Florida law does not provide for licensure of brokers. Properly licensed and appointed agents may broker under certain circumstances, as provided in the Florida statutes. (Review Unit 26 regarding Florida law on agents' licensing and appointment for specific provisions.)

Agents are also classified as **captive** or **career agents** and **independent agents**. A captive or career agent works for one insurance company and sells only that company's insurance policies. An independent agent works for himself or for other agents and sells the insurance products of many companies.

The agent who solicits an insurance application represents the insurer and not the insured or beneficiary in any dispute between the insured or beneficiary and the insurer. In most states, however, the agent may represent as many insurers as will appoint him.

There are three systems that support the sale of insurance through agents and brokers. These are the *career agency system*, the *personal producing general agency system*, and the *independent agency system*.

Career Agency System

Career agencies are branches of major stock and mutual insurance companies that are contracted to represent the particular insurer in a specific area. In career agencies, insurance agents are recruited, trained, and supervised by either a manager-employee of the company or a general agent (GA) who has a vested right in any business written by the GA's agents. GAs may operate strictly as managers, or they may devote a portion of their time to sales. The career agency system focuses on building sales staffs.

Personal Producing General Agency System

The **personal producing general agency (PPGA)** system is similar to the career agency system. However, PPGAs do not recruit, train, or supervise career agents. They primarily sell insurance, although they may build a small sales force to assist them. PPGAs are generally responsible for maintaining their own offices and administrative staff. Agents hired by a PPGA are considered employees of the PPGA, not the insurance company, and are supervised by regional directors.

Independent Agency System

The **independent agency system**, a creation of the property and casualty industry, does not tie a sales staff or agency to any one particular insurance company; rather, independent brokers represent any number of insurance companies through contractual agreements. They are compensated on a commission or a fee basis for the business they produce. This system is also known as the *American agency system*.

Other Methods of Selling Insurance

While most insurance is sold through agents or brokers under the systems previously described, a large volume is also marketed through *direct selling* and *mass marketing methods*.

With the **direct selling** method, the insurer deals directly with consumers, selling its policies through vending machines, advertisements, or salaried sales representatives; no agent or broker is involved. Insurers that operate using this method are known as "direct writers" or "direct response insurers."

A large volume of insurance also is sold through **mass marketing** techniques, such as direct mail or newspaper, magazine, radio, and television ads. Mass marketing methods provide exposure to large groups of consumers, often using direct selling methods with occasional follow-up by agents.

Take note that in Florida, the law specifies that no life or health insurance policy may be issued for delivery unless the application is taken by, and the policy delivered through, a licensed agent who will receive the usual commission.

EVOLUTION OF INDUSTRY OVERSIGHT

The insurance industry is regulated by a number of authorities, including some inside the industry itself. The primary purpose of this regulation is to promote the public welfare by maintaining the solvency of insurance companies. Other purposes are to provide consumer protection and ensure fair trade practices as well as fair contracts at fair prices. It is very important insurance agents understand and obey the insurance laws and regulations.

History of Regulation

A brief overview of the history of insurance regulation will show a seesaw between the authority of the states and the federal government. Though a balance between these two bodies has been reached and maintained for many years, arguments favoring control by one governing authority over another are still being waged.

■ *1868—Paul v. Virginia.* This case, which was decided by the U.S. Supreme Court, involved one state's attempt to regulate an insurance company domiciled in another state. The Supreme Court sided against the insurance company, ruling that the sale and issuance of insurance is not interstate commerce, thus upholding the right of states to regulate insurance.

■ *1944—United States v. Southeastern Underwriters Association (SEUA).* The decision of *Paul v. Virginia* held for 75 years before the Supreme Court again addressed the issue of state versus federal regulation of the insurance industry. In the SEUA case, the Supreme Court ruled that the business of insurance is subject to a series of federal laws, many of which were in conflict with existing state laws, and that insurance is a form of interstate commerce to be regulated by the federal government. This decision did not affect the power of states to regulate insurance, but it did nullify state laws that were in conflict with federal legislation. The result of the SEUA case was to shift the balance of regulatory control to the federal government.

■ **1945—The McCarran-Ferguson Act.** The turmoil created by the SEUA case prompted Congress to enact Public Law 15, the McCarran-Ferguson Act. This law made it clear that continued regulation of insurance by the states was in the public's best interest. However, it also made possible the application of federal antitrust laws ". . . to the extent that [the insurance business] is not regulated by state law." This act led each state to revise its insurance laws to conform to the federal law. Today, the insurance industry is considered to be state regulated.

■ **1958—Intervention by the FTC.** In the mid-1950s, the Federal Trade Commission (FTC) sought to control the advertising and sales literature used by the health insurance industry. In 1958, the Supreme Court held that the McCarran-Ferguson Act disallowed such supervision by the FTC, a federal agency. Additional attempts have been made by the FTC to force further federal control, but none have been successful.

■ **1959—Intervention by the SEC.** In this instance, the issue was variable annuities: Are the insurance products to be regulated by the states or securities to be regulated federally by the Securities and Exchange Commission (SEC)? The Supreme Court ruled that federal securities laws applied to insurers that issued variable annuities and, thus, required these insurers to conform to both SEC and state regulation. The SEC also regulates variable life insurance.

■ **1970—Fair Credit Reporting Act.** In an attempt to protect an individual's right to privacy, the federal government passed the Fair Credit Reporting Act, which requires fair and accurate reporting of information about consumers, including applications for insurance. Insurers must inform applicants about any investigations that are being made. If any consumer report is used to deny coverage or charge higher rates, the insurer must furnish to the applicant the name of the reporting agency conducting the investigation. Any insurance company that fails to comply with this act is liable to the consumer for actual and punitive damages. (For specific provisions of this act, refer to the section entitled "The Fair Credit Reporting Act of 1970" in Unit 9.)

■ **1999—Financial Services Modernization Act.** The Glass-Steagall Act of 1933, which barred common ownership of banks, insurance companies, and securities firms and erected a regulatory wall between banks and nonfinancial companies, came under repeated attack in the 1980s. In 1999, Congress passed the Financial Services Modernization Act, which repealed the Glass-Steagall Act. Under this new legislation, commercial banks, investment banks, retail brokerages, and insurance companies can now enter each other's lines of business.

■ **2001—USA PATRIOT Act.** Congress passed the Uniting and Strengthening America by Providing Appropriate Tools Required to Intercept and Obstruct Terrorism (USA PATRIOT) Act to give various agencies of the federal government broad powers to curtail attempts to launder money and finance terrorism.

— The act specifically provides the following:

  - Guidance to financial institutions

- Forfeiture of laundered assets

- Increased regulation of financial services

- Increased ability for financial institutions to maintain employee integrity

- Required reporting of potential money-laundering actions

- Interception of attempts by corrupt officials to use U.S. financial system for personal gain

— As part of this act, insurers and other financial institutions must:

- develop new compliance systems and training;

- designate anti-money laundering officers;

- share information with other financial institutions and enforcement entities; and

- adopt robust procedures to verify the identity of any person opening an account.

The chronology cited reflects the roles the courts and the federal government have played in regulating the insurance industry. Let's now take a look at how individual states regulate this business and how the industry practices self-regulation.

State Regulation of the Insurance Industry

In addition to federal laws, the insurance industry is regulated at the state level by state *offices of insurance regulation*, *divisions*, or *boards*. These in turn are headed by an *officer*, *commissioner*, *director*, or *superintendent*, depending on the state. Though specific laws will vary from state to state, in Florida, insurance regulation includes:

■ issuing rules and regulations to enforce the state's insurance laws;

■ licensing and supervising insurance companies formed within the state;

■ licensing and supervising insurance agents and brokers;

■ controlling the kinds of insurance contracts and policies that may be sold in the state;

■ determining the amount of reserves an insurer must maintain;

■ regulating the investment activity of insurers; and

■ overseeing insurance companies' marketing practices and investigating consumer complaints.

See Unit 26 for specific Florida laws and regulations.

All insurance companies doing business within a given state must be **licensed** or **certified** by that state. Thus, insurance companies are referred to as "licensed" or "nonlicensed." (In some states, the terms used to designate whether or not a company is licensed are "authorized" and "unauthorized" or "admitted" and "nonadmitted.") In addition, the following terms are frequently used to describe insurance companies and their site of incorporation:

■ **Domestic insurers.** A company is a domestic insurer when doing business in the state in which it is incorporated.

■ **Foreign insurers.** A foreign insurer is one licensed and doing business in states other than the one in which it is incorporated.

■ **Alien insurers.** Insurers incorporated in a country other than the United States, when doing business in the United States, are referred to as alien insurers.

Whether companies are considered domestic, foreign, or alien, they must be licensed in each state where they conduct business. State laws restrict insurance companies that are not licensed or not authorized from doing business within their borders.

Insurance Producers

Every state requires that individuals who sell insurance have a license from the state. However, before the Department of Financial Services will issue such a license—whether it's to a prospective agent or broker—the candidate must pass a **producer licensing exam** administered by the Department. In Florida, an agent's license is perpetual unless suspended or revoked. Agents must complete at least 24 hours of continuing education courses every two years. Agents who have been licensed for six or more years must complete 20 hours every two years. An agent's license terminates if the agent allows four years to elapse without being appointed for each class of insurance listed on the license.

Agent Marketing and Sales Practices

Marketing and selling financial products, such as life insurance and annuities, require a high level of professionalism and ethics. Every state requires its licensed producers to adhere to certain standards designed to protect consumers and promote suitable sales and application of insurance products. Among these standards are the following.

■ **Selling to needs.** The ethical agent determines what needs the client has and then determines the product best suited to address those needs. Two principles of needs-based selling include the following:

— Fact-find (learn the client's situation and understand the client's goals, needs, and concerns)

— Educate (teach the client about insurance as a financial tool)

■ **Suitability of recommended products.** The ethical agent assesses the correlation between a recommended product and the client's needs and capabilities by asking and answering the following questions.

— What are the client's needs?

— What product can help meet those needs?

— Does the client understand the product and its provisions?

— Does the client have the capability, financially and otherwise, to manage the product?

— Is this product in the client's best interest?

■ **Full and accurate disclosure.** The ethical agent makes it a practice to inform clients fully about all aspects of the products the agent recommends—their limitations as well as their benefits. There never is any attempt to hide or disguise the nature or purpose of the product nor the company that is being represented. Insurance products are highly effective financial planning tools. They should be presented clearly, completely, and accurately.

■ **Documentation.** The ethical agent documents each client meeting and transaction. The agent uses fact-finding forms and obtains the client's written agreement as to the needs determined, the products recommended, and the decisions made. Some documentation is required by state law. Ethical agents know these laws and follow them precisely.

■ **Client service.** The ethical agent knows that a sale does not mark the end of a relationship with a client, but the beginning. Routine follow-up calls are recommended to ensure that the client's needs always are covered and the products in place still are suitable. When clients contact their agents for service or information, these requests are given top priority. Complaints are handled promptly and fully.

Buyers' Guides and Policy Summaries

To help ensure that prospective insurance buyers select the most appropriate plan or plans for their needs and to improve their understanding of basic product features, most states require agents to deliver a buyer's guide to consumers whenever they solicit insurance sales. These guides explain the various types of life insurance products (including variable contracts) in a way that the average consumer can understand. In addition, a policy summary containing information about the specific policy being recommended must be given to a potential buyer. It identifies the agent, the insurer, the policy, and each rider, and includes information about premiums, dividends, benefit amounts, cash surrender values, policy loan interest rates, and life insurance cost indexes of the specific policy being considered. Most states require this to be done before the applicant's initial premium is accepted.

The policy summary also contains cost indexes that help the consumer evaluate the suitability of the recommended product. The **net payment cost comparison index** gives the buyer an idea of the cost of the policy at some future point in time compared to the death benefit. The **surrender cost comparison index** compares the cost of surrendering the policy and withdrawing the cash values at some future time.

Because all states are interested in protecting the interests of the buying public, the actions of individuals soliciting insurance sales are strictly regulated. However, the laws regarding insurance marketing and trade practices vary from state to state. As a result, it is very important that you examine and understand your state's laws.

National Association of Insurance Commissioners

All state insurance commissioners or directors are members of the **National Association of Insurance Commissioners (NAIC)**. This organization has standing committees that work regularly to examine various aspects of the insurance industry and to recommend appropriate insurance laws and regulations.

Basically, the NAIC has four broad objectives:

1. To encourage uniformity in state insurance laws and regulations

2. To assist in the administration of those laws and regulations by promoting efficiency

3. To protect the interests of policyowners and consumers

4. To preserve state regulation of the insurance business

The NAIC has been instrumental in developing guidelines and model legislation that help ensure that the insurance industry maintains a high level of public trust by conducting its business competently and fairly. This group also develops standards for policy provisions, helping ensure that policies are more uniform than disparate across the country. Notable among the NAIC's accomplishments was the creation of the *Advertising Code* and the *Unfair Trade Practices Act*, which have been adopted by virtually every state.

Advertising Code

A principal problem of states in the past was regulating misleading insurance advertising and direct mail solicitations. Many states now subscribe to the **Advertising Code** developed by the NAIC. The Code specifies certain words and phrases that are considered misleading and are not to be used in advertising of any kind. Also required under this code is full disclosure of policy renewal, cancellation, and termination provisions. Other rules pertain to the use of testimonials, statistics, special offers, and the like.

Unfair Trade Practices Act

Most jurisdictions have also adopted the NAIC's **Unfair Trade Practices Act**. This act gives chief financial officers the power to investigate insurance companies and producers, to issue cease and desist orders, and to impose penalties on violators. The act also gives officers the authority to seek a court injunction to restrain insurers from using any methods believed to be unfair or deceptive. Included in the context of unfair trade practices are misrepresentation and false advertising, coercion and intimidation, unfair discrimination, and inequitable administration or claims settlements.

State Guaranty Associations

All states have established **guaranty funds** or **guaranty associations** to support insurers and to protect consumers if an insurer becomes insolvent. Should an insurer be financially unable to pay its claims, the state guaranty association will step in and cover the consumers' unpaid claims. These state associations are funded by insurance companies through assessments.

NAIFA and NAHU

The **National Association of Insurance and Financial Advisors (NAIFA)** and the **National Association of Health Underwriters (NAHU)** are organizations of life and health insurance agents that are dedicated to supporting the life and health insurance industries and advancing the quality of service provided by insurance professionals. Each organization issues a Code of Ethics that stresses the high professional duty expected of underwriters toward their clients, as well as to their companies, and emphasizes that only by observing the highest ethical balance can conflict between these two obligations be avoided. (See the Appendix for both the NAIFA and NAHU Codes of Ethics.)

Rating Services

The financial strength and stability of an insurance company are two vitally important factors to potential insurance buyers and to insurance companies themselves. Guides to insurance companies' financial integrity and claims-paying ability are published regularly by various **rating services**, such as A.M. Best, Inc., Standard & Poor's, Moody's, and Fitch's. For instance, in *Best's Insurance Reports*, companies are rated A++ to A+ (superior), A to A– (excellent), B++ to B+ (very good), B to B– (good), C++ to C+ (fair), C to C– (marginal), D (below minimum standards), E (under state supervision), and F (in liquidation). Experts generally recommend that insurance buyers purchase policies from companies that have a rating of A++ to A– because these ratings indicate a strong ability to meet obligations to policyowners. (See Illustration 2.1.)

ILLUSTRATION 2.1

Insurance Company Rating System

A.M. Best Company

A++, A+	Superior; very strong ability to meet obligations
A, A–	Excellent; strong ability to meet obligations
B++, B+	Very good; strong ability to meet obligations
B, B–	Good; adequate ability to meet obligations
C++, C+	Fair; reasonable ability to meet obligations
C, C–	Marginal; currently has ability to meet obligations
D	Below minimum standards
E	Under state supervision
F	In liquidation
S	Suspended

S&P

AAA	Superior; highest safety
AA	Excellent financial security
A	Good financial security
BBB	Adequate financial security
BB	Adequate financial security; ability to meet obligations, may not be adequate for long-term policies
B	Currently able to meet obligations, but highly vulnerable to adverse conditions
CCC	Questionable ability to meet obligations
CC, C	May not be meeting obligations; vulnerable to liquidation
R	Under a court order of liquidation; in receivership

Moody's

Aaa	Exceptional security
Aa	Excellent security
A	Good security
Baa	Adequate security
Ba	Questionable security; moderate ability to meet obligations
B	Poor security
Caa	Very poor security; elements of danger regarding payment of obligations
Ca	Extremely poor security; may be in default
C	Lowest security

Fitch

AAA	Highest claims-paying ability; negligible risk
AA+, AA, AA–	Very high claims-paying ability; moderate risk
A+, A, A–	High claims-paying ability; variable risk over time
BBB+, BBB, BBB–	Below average claims-paying ability; considerable variability in risk over time
BB+, BB, BB–	Uncertain claims-paying ability
CCC	Substantial claims-paying ability risk; likely to be placed under state supervision

SUMMARY

There are many types of insurance providers. *State* and *local governments* provide insurance, as do private insurers. Private insurers include *stock companies*, *mutual companies*, *reciprocals*, *assessment mutuals*, *fraternal societies*, *home service insurers*, and *service providers*. Special categories of insurers include *reinsurers* and *Lloyd's of London*.

Insurance is sold through a variety of methods, the most common being through licensed *producers*. The systems that support the sale of insurance through agents and brokers are the *career agency system*, the *personal producing agency system*, and the *independent agency system*.

To promote public welfare, the insurance industry is regulated by a number of authorities. These authorities include:

- the states and their departments of insurance;

- the NAIC and its model legislation; and

- the federal government through the application of antitrust laws and the Fair Credit Reporting Act.

All states have enacted various laws and regulations that affect the business of insurance, always with consumer interest in mind. Insurance companies, as well as agents and brokers, are bound by these laws.

KEY CONCEPTS

Students should be familiar with the following concepts:

types of insurers	Financial Services Modernization Act
NAIC	federal regulation
NAIFA/NAHU	state regulation
Fair Credit Reporting Act	prohibited practices
McCarran-Ferguson Act	insurance company rating systems
types of marketing/distribution	organization and ownership of insurers
U.S. v. Southeastern Underwriters Association	

UNIT TEST

1. Producers are expected to adhere to all of the following standards to protect consumers and promote suitable sales EXCEPT

    A. selling to customers' needs
    B. determining the suitability of recommended products
    C. assessing prospects' financial ability to pay commissions
    D. full and accurate disclosure

2. An insurance company organized and headquartered in Florida can be described as what type of company in Florida?

    A. Alien
    B. Home-based
    C. Foreign
    D. Domestic

3. Which of the following statements regarding types of insurers is NOT correct?

    A. Reinsurers usually deal with group policyowners.
    B. Mutual insurance companies are "owned" by their policyowners.
    C. Stock insurance companies seek a profit for their shareholders.
    D. Fraternal benefit societies must be nonprofit organizations.

4. Regarding landmark cases and laws involving the regulation of insurance, which of the following statements is NOT correct?

    A. Insurers are required to disclose when an applicant's consumer/credit history is being investigated.
    B. The Securities and Exchange Commission (SEC) may regulate insurers that sell variable annuities and variable life insurance.
    C. The Federal Trade Commission (FTC) directly supervises all insurance marketing activities.
    D. The McCarran-Ferguson Act (1945) led directly to our current understanding that the insurance industry is predominantly regulated by state governments.

5. Which of the following statements regarding the National Association of Insurance Commissioners (NAIC) is NOT correct?

    A. The NAIC is empowered to prosecute and punish criminal violators in the insurance industry.
    B. The NAIC seeks to preserve state rather than federal regulation of the insurance industry.
    C. The NAIC promotes uniformity in state insurance laws and regulations.
    D. The NAIC seeks to promote efficient administration of insurance laws and regulations.

6. In an insurance transaction, licensed agents legally represent which of the following?

    A. Insurer
    B. Applicant and insured
    C. State office of insurance regulation
    D. Themselves

7. In Florida, properly licensed and appointed agents may act as brokers in insurance transactions, in which case they may legally represent

    A. the insurer
    B. the applicant and insured
    C. the state office of insurance regulation
    D. themselves

8. A life insurance company organized in Illinois, with its home office in Philadelphia, is licensed to conduct business in Florida. In Florida, this company is classified as

    A. a domestic company
    B. an alien company
    C. a foreign company
    D. a regional company

9. Which of the following is NOT a service provider?

    A. HMO
    B. Benefit plans offering medical services to subscribers
    C. Lloyd's of London
    D. PPO

10. A reinsurer is a company that
    A. accepts all the risk from another insurer
    B. assumes a portion of the risk from another insurer
    C. cedes the risk
    D. does not take any risk

11. The head of a state office of insurance regulation is generally responsible for all of the following EXCEPT
    A. licensing and supervising agents and brokers
    B. overseeing insurance companies' marketing practices
    C. issuing rules and regulations
    D. making insurance laws

12. In addition to the state, the organization that regulates variable life and variable annuities is the
    A. Federal Trade Commission (FTC)
    B. National Association of Insurance Commissioners (NAIC)
    C. Securities and Exchange Commission (SEC)
    D. Federal Communications Commission (FCC)

13. The *Buyer's Guide* is intended to accomplish all of the following EXCEPT
    A. help buyers choose the most suitable plan
    B. explain basic product features
    C. provide information about the recommended policy
    D. ensure that buyers obtain the lowest price for insurance

14. The State Guaranty Association guarantees
    A. that a policy will be issued
    B. that a claim will be paid if an insurer becomes insolvent
    C. that dividends will be paid
    D. the rate of return on a policy

15. All of the following methods support the sale of insurance through agents and brokers EXCEPT
    A. independent agency system
    B. personal producing general agency system
    C. career agency system
    D. direct selling system

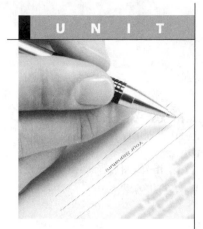

3

Law and the Insurance Contract

- General Law of Contracts
- Special Features of Insurance Contracts
- Agents and Brokers
- Other Legal Concepts

Life and health insurance policies are legal contracts. As such, they are governed by many of the same legal principles that are applicable to the formation of any contract, plus specific principles that are pertinent to insurance only. In this unit, we will first review the general principles of contract law, then look at insurance contracts. ■

GENERAL LAW OF CONTRACTS

A **contract** is an agreement enforceable by law. It is the means by which one or more parties bind themselves to certain promises. With a life insurance contract, the insurer binds itself to pay a certain sum upon the death of the insured. In exchange, the policyowner pays premiums.

For a contract to be legally valid and binding, it must contain certain elements—an *offer and acceptance, consideration, legal purpose*, and *competent parties*. Let's consider each.

Offer and Acceptance

To be legally enforceable, a contract must be made with a definite, unqualified **offer** by one party and the **acceptance** of its exact terms by the other party. In many cases, the offer of an insurance contract is made by the applicant when she submits the application with the initial premium. The insurance company accepts the offer when it issues the policy as applied for. In other cases, the insurance company will not issue the policy as applied for; instead, it may **counteroffer** with the issuance of another policy at different premium rates or with different terms. In these situations, the applicant has the right to accept or reject the counteroffer.

If an applicant does not submit an initial premium with the application, the applicant is simply inviting the insurance company to make the contract offer. The insurer can respond by issuing a policy (the offer) that the applicant can accept by paying the premium when the policy is delivered.

Until an offer has been accepted, the person making the offer has the right to rescind it. Thus, for example, if an applicant wishes to withdraw her application before the insurer accepts it, the offer is terminated, even if the initial premium has been submitted. The insurer must return the premium.

Consideration

For a contract to be enforceable, the promise or promises it contains must be supported by **consideration**. Consideration can be defined as the value given in exchange for the promises sought. In an insurance contract, consideration is given by the applicant in exchange for the insurer's promise to pay benefits, and it also consists of the application and the initial premium. This is why the offer and acceptance of an insurance contract are not complete until the insurer receives the application and the first premium.

Legal Purpose

To be legal, a contract must have a **legal purpose**. This means that the object of the contract and the reason the parties enter into the agreement must be legal. A contract in which one party agrees to commit murder for money would be unenforceable in court because the object or purpose of the contract is not legal. In all jurisdictions, insurance is considered to possess a legal purpose.

Competent Parties

To be enforceable, a contract must be entered into by **competent parties**. With a contract of insurance, the parties to the contract are the applicant and the insurer. The insurer is considered competent if it has been licensed or authorized by the state (or states) in which it conducts business. The applicant, unless proven otherwise, is presumed to be competent, with three possible exceptions:

■ Minors

■ The mentally infirm

■ Those under the influence of alcohol or narcotics

Each state has its own laws governing the legality of minors and the mentally infirm entering into contracts of insurance. These laws are based on the principle that some parties are not capable of understanding the contract they agree to.

It should be noted that beneficiaries and insureds (if different from the applicant) are not parties to an insurance contract. As such, they do not have to have contractual capability.

Other competent parties that may enter into contracts of insurance with an insurance company include business entities, trusts, and estates.

SPECIAL FEATURES OF INSURANCE CONTRACTS

The elements just discussed must be contained in every contract for it to be enforceable by law. In addition to these, insurance contracts have distinguishing characteristics that set them apart from many other legally binding agreements. Some of these characteristics are unique to insurance contracts. Let's review these distinctions.

Aleatory

Insurance contracts are **aleatory** in that (1) there is an element of chance for both of the contracting parties and (2) the dollar values exchanged may not be equal. An aleatory contract is conditioned upon the occurrence of an event. Consequently, the benefits provided by an insurance policy may or may not exceed the premiums paid. For example, an individual who has a disability insurance policy will collect benefits if she becomes disabled; if no disability strikes, no benefits are paid.

The opposite of an aleatory contract is a commutative contract, where there is no element of chance and the parties exchange goods of equal value. A real estate transaction is a commutative contract—the seller agrees to sell property for a certain sum and the buyer agrees to buy the property for the same sum.

Adhesion

Insurance contracts are contracts of **adhesion**. This means that the contract has been prepared by one party (the insurer); it is not the result of negotiation between the parties. In effect, the applicant "adheres" to the terms of the contract when she accepts it.

In contract law, and notably with respect to contracts of adhesion, the contract is to be viewed or interpreted most favorably for the party that did not draft it. The purpose is to overcome or balance any advantage that may result for the party that prepared the contract. Consequently, if there are any ambiguities in the contract, they will be construed in favor of the party that did not create the contract. For insurance contracts, this means that any ambiguous provisions will be given the interpretation most favorable to the insured or beneficiary, not the insurer.

Unilateral

Insurance contracts are **unilateral** in that only one party, the insurer, makes any kind of enforceable promise. Insurers promise to pay benefits upon the happening of a certain event, such as death or disability. The applicant makes no such promise—she does not even promise to pay premiums—and the insurer cannot require that they be paid. Of course, the insurer has the right to cancel the contract if premiums are not paid.

A unilateral contract can be contrasted to a bilateral contract, in which each contracting party makes enforceable promises.

Not a Personal Contract

Life insurance is not a **personal contract** or **personal agreement** between the insurer and the insured. The owner of the policy has no bearing on the risk the insurer has assumed. For this reason, people who buy life insurance policies are called policyowners rather than policyholders. These people actually own their policies and can give them away if they wish. Such a transfer of ownership is known as **assignment**. To assign a policy, a policyowner simply notifies the insurer in writing. The company will then accept the validity of the transfer without question. The new owner is then granted all of the rights of policyownership.

Most other insurance contracts are personal contracts. They constitute a personal agreement between the insured and the insurer, and they cannot be transferred to another person without the insurer's approval. Because of this personal nature of most insurance contracts, they cannot be freely assigned by the policyholder to other parties. To permit a fire insurance contract to be assignable without the insurer's approval, for example, would be unfair to the insurer. Only by knowing and investigating each applicant for insurance can an insurance company accurately appraise the risk it is accepting.

Conditional

An insurance contract is **conditional** in that the insurer's promise to pay benefits is dependent on the occurrence of the risk insured against. If the risk does not materialize, no benefits are paid. Furthermore, the insurer's obligations under the contract are conditioned on the performance of certain acts by the insured or the beneficiary. For example, the timely payment of premiums is a condition of the continuance of the contract. If premiums are not paid, the company is relieved of its obligation to pay a death benefit (though it would be bound by other promises contained in the contract's surrender and reinstatement provisions). Providing proof of death (or proof of disability or medical expenses) would be another condition. Until the insurer receives such proof, it is not liable for payment.

The significance of a condition is that if the policyowner or beneficiary satisfies the condition, it legally binds the insurer to its obligations under the contract. If the condition is not met, the insurer is released from its obligations. However, conditions upon a policyowner or beneficiary are not legally binding or enforceable. An insured who does not meet a contractual condition simply gives up the right to make a claim under the contract. If a policyowner stops paying premiums, for example, the insurance company cannot compel further payment. It can only cancel the policy. By contrast, an insurance company that does not meet its contractual obligations once the policyowner or beneficiary satisfies the conditions for making a claim may be liable to the insured for damages.

Valued or Indemnity

An insurance contract is either a **valued contract** or an **indemnity contract**. A valued contract pays a stated sum, regardless of the actual loss incurred, when the contingency insured against occurs. Life insurance contracts are valued contracts. If an individual acquires a life insurance policy insuring her life for $1 million, that is the amount payable at death. There is no attempt to value actual financial loss.

An indemnity contract, however, is one that pays an amount equal to the loss; it attempts to return the insured to her original financial position. Fire and health insurance policies are examples of indemnity contracts. An insured that owns a $100,000 fire insurance policy and suffers a $5,000 loss due to fire will be able to collect up to $5,000, not $100,000.

Inherent to indemnity contracts is the doctrine of **subrogation**. This means that in the event a claim is paid, the insurer acquires the insured's right to action against any negligent third party that may have caused or contributed to the loss. The right of subrogation does not exist with life insurance contracts. An auto insurer has the right to action against an individual who caused damage to one of the company's insured vehicles (up to the amount of the loss payment); a life insurer has no such recourse if the death of one of its insureds was caused by a negligent third party.

Utmost Good Faith

Insurance is a contract of **utmost good faith**. Both the policyowner and the insurer must know all material facts and relevant information. There can be no attempt by either party to conceal, disguise, or deceive. A consumer purchases a policy based largely on what the insurer and its agent claim are its features, benefits, and advantages. An insurer issues a policy based primarily on what the applicant reveals in the application.

Associated with this are the concepts of *warranties*, *representations*, and *concealment*. These represent grounds through which an insurer might seek to avoid payment under a contract.

Warranty

A **warranty** in insurance is a statement made by the applicant that is *guaranteed* to be true. It becomes part of the contract and, if found to be untrue, can be grounds for revoking the contract. Warranties are presumed to be material because they affect the insurer's decision to accept or reject an applicant.

Representation

A **representation** is a statement made by the applicant that she *believes* to be true. It is used by the insurer to evaluate whether or not to issue a policy. Unlike warranties, representations are not a part of the contract and need be true only to the extent that they are material and related to the risk. Most states require that life insurance policies contain a provision that all statements made in the application be deemed representations, not warranties. If an insurance company rejects a claim on the basis of a representation, the company bears the burden of proving materiality.

The practical distinction between a warranty and a representation is this: if a warranty is untrue, the insurer has the right to cancel the contract; if a representation is untrue, the insurer has the right to cancel the contract only if the representation was material to the creation of the contract.

Concealment

The issue of **concealment** is also important to insurance contracts. Concealment is defined as the failure by the applicant to disclose a known material fact when applying for insurance. If the purpose for concealing information is to defraud the insurer (that is, to obtain a policy that might not otherwise be issued if the information were revealed), the insurer may have grounds for voiding the policy.[1] Again, the insurer must prove concealment and materiality.

---

[1]   In most instances, life insurers have only a limited period of time to uncover false warranties, misrepresentations, or concealment. After that time period passes, usually two years from policy issue, the contract cannot be voided or revoked for these reasons. (See "Incontestable Clause," Unit 6.) Health insurance contracts follow slightly different rules. (See "Time Limit on Certain Defenses," Unit 22.)

ILLUSTRATION 3.1

Elements of an Insurance Contract

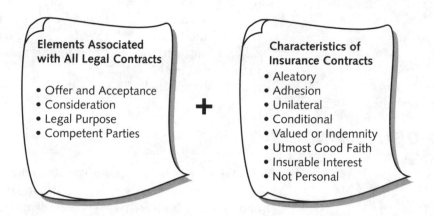

Insurable Interest

Another element of a valid insurance contract is **insurable interest**. This means that the person acquiring the contract (the applicant) must be subject to loss upon the death, illness, or disability of the person being insured. A policy obtained by a person not having an insurable interest in the insured is not valid and cannot be enforced.

Thus, insurable interest must exist between the applicant and the individual being insured. When the applicant is the same as the person to be insured, there is no question that insurable interest exists; individuals are presumed to have insurable interest in themselves. Questions tend to arise when the applicant is not the person to be insured. As a general rule, the consent of the person to be insured is required before a policy is issued, even if the applicant has an insurable interest. Insurers have a legal responsibility to verify insurable interest and obtain the insured's consent. (See also "Does Insurable Interest Exist?" in Unit 9.)

One important point to note about insurable interest with life and health contracts is that the interest must exist at the *inception* of the policy. It does not have to continue throughout the duration of the policy nor does it have to exist at the time of claim. This is in contrast to property and casualty insurance policies where insurable interest must exist at the time of the claim.

Stranger-Originated Life Insurance (STOLI or IOLI)

Stranger-Originated Life Insurance (STOLI) transactions, which are also called Investor-Originated Life Insurance (IOLI), are life insurance arrangements where investors persuade individuals, typically seniors, to take out new life insurance with the investors named as beneficiary.

Generally, the investors loan money to the insured to pay the premiums for a defined period (usually two years based on the life insurance policy's contestability period).

After two years, the insured assigns ownership to the investors, who make the premium payments and will receive the death benefit when the insured dies. The seniors receive some financial inducement for this: an upfront payment, a loan, or a small continuing interest in the policy death benefit.

Many regulators believe STOLI arrangements are not consistent with the intended purposes of insurable interest. States are increasingly banning STOLI transactions, and purchasers risk invalidation of the policy if it is identified as such.

AGENTS AND BROKERS

Because contracts of insurance are binding and enforceable, certain legal concepts extend to those who bring together the contract parties: the applicant and the insurer. In most cases, bringing the parties together is done by an agent or a broker. In Unit 2, we discussed some of the more important regulations that states impose on those who solicit and sell insurance; here we will focus on legal aspects of negotiating and placing contracts of insurance.

The Concept of Agency

As noted earlier, an agent is an individual who has been authorized by an insurer to be its representative to the public and to offer for sale its goods and services. Specifically, this role entails:

- describing the company's insurance policies to prospective buyers and explaining the conditions under which the policies may be obtained;

- soliciting applications for insurance;

- in some cases, collecting premiums from policyowners; and

- rendering service to prospects and to those who have purchased policies from the company.

The authority of an agent to undertake these functions is clearly defined in a "contract of agency" (or agency agreement) between the agent and the company. Within the authority granted, the agent is considered identical with the company. The relationship between an agent and the company he represents is governed by **agency law**.

Principles of Agency Law

By legal definition, an agent is a person who acts for another person or entity (known as the *principal*) with regard to contractual arrangements with third parties. Implicit in this definition is the concept of **power**—an authorized agent has the power to bind the principal to contracts (and to the rights and responsibilities of those contracts). With this in mind, we can review the main principles of agency law.

- The acts of the agent (within the scope of his authority) are the acts of the principal.

- A contract completed by an agent on behalf of the principal is a contract of the principal.

- Payments made to an agent on behalf of the principal are payments to the principal.

- Knowledge of the agent regarding business of the principal is presumed to be knowledge of the principal.

Agent Authority

Note the parenthetical limitation "within the scope of his authority" in the previous section. **Authority**—that which an agent is authorized to do on behalf of his company—is another important concept in agency law. Technically, only those actions for which an agent is actually authorized can bind a principal. In reality, however, an agent's authority can be quite broad. In essence, there are three types of agent authority: *express*, *implied*, and *apparent*. Let's take a look at each.

1. **Express authority.** Express authority is the authority a principal intends to, and actually does, give to its agent. Express authority is granted by means of the agent's contract, which is the principal's appointment of the agent to act on its behalf. For example, an agent has the express authority to solicit applications for insurance on behalf of the company.

2. **Implied authority.** Implied authority is authority that is not expressly granted but which the agent is assumed to have in order to transact the business of the principal. Implied authority is incidental to express authority because not every single detail of an agent's authority can be spelled out. For example, an agent's contract may not specifically state that he can print business cards that contain the company's name, but the authority to do so is implied.

3. **Apparent authority.** Apparent authority is the appearance of, or the assumption of, authority based on the actions, words, or deeds of the principal or because of circumstances the principal created. For example, by providing an individual with a rate book, application forms, and sales literature, a company creates the impression that an agency relationship exists between itself and the individual. The company will not later be allowed to deny that such a relationship existed.

The significance of authority—whether express, implied, or apparent—is that it ties the company to the acts and deeds of its agent. The law will view the agent and the company as one and the same when the agent acts within the scope of his authority.

Agent as a Fiduciary

Another legal concept that governs the activity of an agent is that of fiduciary. A fiduciary is a person who holds a position of special trust and confidence. Agents act in a fiduciary capacity when they accept premiums on behalf of the insurer or offer advice that affects people's financial security.

Agents have fiduciary responsibilities to both their clients and the insurance companies they represent. Acting as a fiduciary requires that an agent:

- be fit and proper;
- be honest and trustworthy;
- have a good business reputation;
- be qualified to perform insurance functions;
- have knowledge of, and abide by, state laws and regulations; and
- act in good faith.

Brokers Versus Agents

As noted earlier, brokers, unlike agents, legally represent the insureds. A broker solicits and accepts applications for insurance and then places the coverage with an insurer. The business is not in force and the insurance company is not bound until it accepts the application. Technically speaking, a broker does not represent anyone until a prospect or client requests coverage; then the broker represents the buyer.

In practice, the legal distinction between brokers and agents is not significant. As noted before, Florida does not issue separate licenses for brokers. Instead, licensed agents may act as brokers under certain circumstances. Brokers and agents are insurance **producers** and are subject to insurance laws and regulations. In fact, in some states any individual who solicits insurance and places a policy will be considered an agent of the insurer with regard to that policy.

Professional Liability Insurance

Just as doctors should have malpractice insurance to protect against legal liability arising from their professional services, insurance agents need **errors and omissions (E&O) professional liability insurance**. Under this insurance, the insurer agrees to pay sums that the agent legally is obligated to pay for injuries resulting from professional services that he rendered or failed to render. Under E&O policies, the insurer will defend any suits covered by the policy, even if the suits are groundless, false, or fraudulent. Any claim arising from injuries, real or alleged, comes within the scope of this coverage.

OTHER LEGAL CONCEPTS

In addition to the principles of contract law and agency law, there are other legal concepts that are applicable to insurance and the power of agents. These are *waiver*, *estoppel*, *the parol evidence rule*, *void versus voidable contracts*, and *fraud*.

Waiver

A **waiver** is the voluntary giving up of a legal, given right. If an insurer voluntarily waives a legal right it has under a contract, it cannot later deny a claim based on a violation of that right. For example, assume a life insurance contract specifies that premium payments are to be made by the policyowner directly to the company at the home office address. John, one of the company's insureds, has instead made his payments over the years to his agent and the company has accepted this arrangement. In so doing, the company has effectively "waived" the direct payment provision and cannot later deny payment of claim on John's policy on the grounds that premiums were not remitted directly to the company.

Estoppel

The concepts of waiver and **estoppel** are closely related. Whereas a waiver involves a company voluntarily giving up a right, estoppel involves a company being forbidden (estopped) by legal action from exercising a right. Using the example above, if the insurer has waived its right to have premiums remitted to it directly, it will be *estopped* from denying John's claim because he gave his premium payments to his agent. Another example of estoppel is if a company severs its agency relationship with an agent but later accepts an application from this individual, thereby reasserting the agency relationship, the company will be estopped from claiming an agency relationship did not exist at the time it entered into the contract with the insured.

Parol Evidence Rule

Parol evidence is oral or verbal evidence, or that which is given verbally in a court of law. The **parol evidence rule** states that when parties put their agreement in writing, all previous verbal statements come together in that writing, and a written contract cannot be changed or modified by parol (oral) evidence.

Void Versus Voidable Contracts

The terms *void* and *voidable* are often incorrectly used interchangeably. A **void contract** is simply an agreement without legal effect. In essence, it is not a contract at all, for it lacks one of the elements specified by law for a valid contract. A void contract cannot be enforced by either party. For example, a contract having an illegal purpose is void, and neither party to the contract can enforce it.

A **voidable contract**, however, is an agreement which, for a reason satisfactory to the court, may be set aside by one of the parties to the contract. It is binding unless the party with the right to reject it wishes to do so. Say that a situation develops under which the policyholder has failed to comply with a condition of the contract: the policyholder ceased paying the premium. The contract is then voidable, and the insurance company has the right to cancel the contract and revoke the coverage.

This raises another possibility under a voidable contract. In the situation previously described, the insurance company may choose *not* to exercise its right to cancel the contract after the policyholder fails to pay the premium. The same possibility does not exist under a void contract.

Fraud

In the event of **fraud**, insurance contracts are unique in that they run counter to a basic rule of contract law. Under most contracts, fraud can be a reason to void a contract. With life insurance contracts, an insurer has only a limited period of time (usually two years from date of issue) to challenge the validity of a contract. After that period, the insurer cannot contest the policy or deny benefits based on material misrepresentations, concealment, or fraud. (This is explained in more detail in "Incontestable Clause," Unit 6 and "Time Limit on Certain Defenses," Unit 22.)

SUMMARY

An insurance policy is a legally binding *contract* between the applicant or owner and the insurance company. As such, it must contain an *offer and acceptance, consideration, a legal purpose,* and *competent parties*—elements required of all enforceable contracts. In addition, contracts of insurance are distinguished by other features unique to the purpose and scope of insurance. Among these special features is the element of *insurable interest*.

Agents and brokers, and the companies they conduct business with, operate under the concept of "agency" and the principles of *agency law*. One of the most important aspects of agency law is that it gives the agent the power to act on behalf of the principal-insurer and to bind it to contracts. Agents are empowered by three types of authority: *express, implied,* and *apparent*.

Finally, there are additional legal concepts that have direct application to insurance and insurance contracts. These include *waiver, estoppel,* the *parol evidence rule, void versus voidable contracts,* and *fraud*.

KEY CONCEPTS

Students should be familiar with the following concepts:

offer and acceptance	consideration
legal purpose	competent parties
aleatory	adhesion
unilateral	conditional
valued versus reimbursement	insurable interest
warranties	representations
concealment	waiver
estoppel	parol evidence rule
fraud	void versus voidable contract
express authority	implied authority
apparent authority	personal contract

UNIT TEST

1. The authority that an insurer gives to its agent by means of the agent's contract is known as
   A. implied authority
   B. express authority
   C. fiduciary responsibility
   D. general authority

2. "An insurance contract is prepared by one party, the insurer, rather than by negotiation between the contracting parties." Which of the following statements explains this characteristic of insurance contracts?
   A. The insurance contract is an aleatory contract.
   B. The insurance contract is a contract of acceptance.
   C. The insurance contract is a contract of adhesion.
   D. The insurance contract names only the insurer as the competent party.

3. Which of the following statements regarding insurable interest is NOT correct?
   A. Insurable interest exists when the applicant is the insured.
   B. A policy obtained by a person without an insurable interest in the insured can be enforced.
   C. The applicant must be subject to loss upon the death, illness, or disability of the insured.
   D. Generally, the person to be insured must give consent before a policy is issued, even if the applicant has an insurable interest.

4. Which of the following statements about authority is NOT correct?
   A. Express authority is granted by means of the agent's contract.
   B. Express authority is determined by a principal's conduct.
   C. Implied authority is not overtly extended in the agent's contract but does permit many of the agent's operations.
   D. Apparent authority can be assumed from the actions of the principal.

5. Which of the following statements regarding utmost good faith in insurance contracts is CORRECT?
   A. The concept of utmost good faith—that there is no attempt to conceal, disguise, or deceive—applies only to the insurer.
   B. Although a warranty is a statement, it is not technically part of the contract.
   C. A representation is a statement that the applicant guarantees to be true.
   D. Most state insurance laws consider statements made in an application for an insurance policy to be representations, not warranties.

6. Which of the following statements describes an insurable interest?
   A. The policyowner must expect to benefit from the insured's death.
   B. The policyowner must expect to suffer a loss when the insured dies or becomes disabled.
   C. The beneficiary, by definition, has an insurable interest in the insured.
   D. The insured must have a personal or business relationship with the beneficiary.

7. Which of the following statements describes the parol evidence rule?
   A. A written contract cannot be changed once it is signed.
   B. An oral contract cannot be modified by written evidence.
   C. A written contract cannot be changed by oral evidence.
   D. An oral contract takes preference over any earlier written contracts.

8. Which of the following is a distinguishing characteristic of an insurance contract?
   A. Offer and acceptance
   B. Conditional
   C. Consideration
   D. Competent parties

9. An insurer is considered competent if it

    A. is registered with the NAIC
    B. is licensed or authorized by the state
    C. follows the Code of Ethics of the state Office of Insurance Regulation
    D. is registered with the Securities and Exchange Commission

10. Competent parties who can enter into insurance contracts are

    A. applicants
    B. trusts and estates
    C. business entities
    D. all of the above

11. Which of the following is an example of legal consideration?

    A. Politeness
    B. Initial premium
    C. Legal purpose
    D. Offer and acceptance

12. With life and health contracts, when must an insurable interest exist?

    A. After the policy is issued
    B. Before the beneficiary is named
    C. While the policy is in force
    D. At the inception of the policy

13. An insurance company has how many years to challenge the validity of a life insurance contract?

    A. One
    B. Two
    C. Three
    D. Four

14. Which of the following terms is used for the voluntary relinquishment of a known right?

    A. Estoppel
    B. Adhesion
    C. Waiver
    D. Unilateral

15. Bob and Tom enter into a contract in which Bob agrees to fraudulently induce sick people to sell their insurance contracts to Tom's company. Bob and Tom's contract can best be described as

    A. void
    B. competitive
    C. voidable
    D. conditional

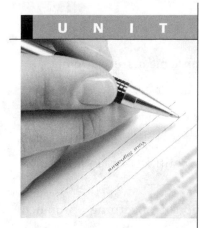

4

Licensure, Ethics, and the Insurance Producer

■ Ethical Business Practices

■ Overview of Ethics and the Insurance Producer

■ A View from the Field

■ Public Perceptions of the Insurance Industry

■ Presenting Recommendations to Clients

■ Ethics and the Law

In addition to information on Florida licensure and appointment, this unit will provide insurance producers with the basic knowledge they need to function ethically in the insurance industry. Producers have ethical duties to insurers, policyowners, clients, and the general public, as well as to the state. Therefore, the state has mandated ethical standards that include specific guidelines on what is considered acceptable and unacceptable ethical behavior.

Florida law requires any individual who solicits insurance to hold a valid license issued by the Department of Financial Services. Then, the licensed individual must be properly appointed by an insurer or employer to transact insurance or adjust claims on behalf of the insurer or employer. For purposes of this requirement, *solicitation of insurance* means any attempt to persuade any person to purchase an insurance product by:

- describing the benefits or terms of insurance coverage, including premiums or rates of return;

- inviting prospective purchasers to enter a contract for an insurance product;

- making general or specific recommendations concerning insurance products;

- completing orders or applications for insurance products; or

- comparing insurance products, advising on insurance matters, or interpreting policies or coverages.

An individual employed by a life or health insurer as an officer or other salaried representative may solicit and effect contracts of life insurance or annuities or contracts of health insurance, without being licensed as an agent, only when he is accompanied by, and solicits for and on the behalf of, a licensed and appointed agent.

In addition, a licensed agent is prohibited from transacting any kind of insurance for which he is not properly appointed. An **appointment** is defined as the authority given by an insurer or employer to a licensee to transact insurance or adjust claims on behalf of an insurer or employer. An individual may not be appointed until that individual has been licensed for the same kind of insurance. [Secs. 626.015(3), F. S.; 626.112, F.S.] ■

ETHICAL BUSINESS PRACTICES

Why should an insurance producer study ethics? Studying ethics helps producers make the right decision when they find themselves, as they often do, in ambiguous, confusing, or otherwise difficult situations, situations that present them with conflicts of interest, or situations that may be perfectly legal but not necessarily ethical. Such situations are so common that many clients say ethical behavior is the number one characteristic they want in their insurance producer. Strong ethical behavior is an invaluable characteristic to an insurance producer's success. Ethical insurance producers quickly gain the trust, respect, and loyalty of their clients. Such clients provide additional business and valuable referrals. Ethical behavior is a key ingredient of success in the insurance industry.

Most financial services companies today have made ethical practices a priority and are teaching their sales representatives how to act ethically in selling insurance and other financial products. In addition, compliance and market conduct now play a central role in virtually all insurance sales activities. Because these terms are in such common use today, it's important to understand the distinction between them.

Compliance

Compliance means conducting business in accordance with current rules and laws set by government regulatory agencies and the courts. It means following the rules, making sure life insurance producers and companies go by the book when conducting business. Laws and regulations set the minimum standard by which producers are expected to behave. Laws and regulations tell them what they must do.

Ethics

Ethics are standards of conduct and moral judgment. Ethics is the moral framework within which decisions are made. Codes of ethics identify and encourage desirable activities by formally establishing a high standard against which each individual may measure performance. An ethical insurance producer is honest, loyal, fair, compassionate, has integrity and respect for others, and a sense of personal responsibility and accountability.

Market Conduct

Market conduct is a combination of both ethics and compliance. It refers to how insurance companies and producers conduct themselves in accordance with ethical standards and in compliance with rules and laws governing insurance policy sales, marketing and underwriting practices, as well as policy issuance, service, complaints, and terminations. Market conduct is synonymous with professional behavior.

The ethical insurance producer knows and acts in accordance with ethical principles as well as in compliance with rules and laws governing the sale and servicing of insurance policies.

OVERVIEW OF ETHICS AND THE INSURANCE PRODUCER

Ethical behavior helps insurance producers gain professional satisfaction and the respect and loyalty of clients. A code of ethics also helps a producer avoid controversy, misunderstandings, and legal entanglements and increases personal efficiency as an insurance producer. Good clients usually refer good clients to ethical producers. However, success should be defined not just by financial gain but also by serving insurers and the public.

Under the law, ethical conduct is generally defined as that which a reasonable person is expected to do under any circumstances. However, not all actions that are unethical (such as selling a prospect more life insurance than he can afford) are illegal. A producer must pay attention to both the legal requirements and the ethical standards of business.

Insurance producers have ethical responsibilities to insurers, policyowners, the public, and the state. As the insurer's **producer**, the producer owes an insurer honesty, good faith, and loyalty. As the insurer's **representative**, the producer's day-to-day activities are a reflection of the insurer's image within the community. A producer meets the major responsibilities to insured policyowners by filling their insurance needs and providing them with quality service. The producer also owes the policyowner the same degree of loyalty he owes to the insurer. The producer has two main ethical responsibilities to the public. The first responsibility is to inform the public about insurance with the highest level of professional integrity. The second is to display a high level of professionalism in all public contacts in order to convey a strong, positive image of the industry.

Although the insurance industry has taken a more active role in this area in the past few decades, through mandatory provisions such as the expanded Unfair Trade Practices Act, producers fulfill responsibilities to the public through their day-to-day, routine interaction with prospects and clients. A producer must adhere to the ethical standards mandated by the state as marketing practices or unfair trade practices.

The principles of agency law, the responsibilities of the producer to the insurer, and the duties of the producer as a fiduciary were discussed in Unit 3, "Law and the Insurance Contract." This unit will now turn to the duties of the insurer to the producer.

Responsibilities to the Principal

The principal must select honest, loyal, and hard-working producers to protect itself from potential liability. In return the principal gives the producer compensation for the business brought in and employment. The principal also reimburses the producer for any damages or expenses incurred in defending against claims that the producer may be held liable for in the course of fulfilling agency obligations.

Perhaps the greatest source of ethical concern for many producers is the feeling that they are caught in the middle between two parties who have conflicting interests. On the one hand, a producer's primary responsibility is to serve the insurer. On the other hand is the consumer, to whom the producer also owes dedication, loyalty, and service. How can a producer reconcile this conflict?

Responsibilities to the Policyowners

A producer must sell the kind of policies that best fit the prospect's needs and in amounts that the prospect can afford. This involves problem analysis, action planning, product recommendation, and plan implementation. The producer has two important commitments:

1. A commitment to obtain and maintain the knowledge and skills necessary to carry out those tasks.

2. A commitment to educate the prospect or client about the products and plans that the producer recommends.

The policyowner relies on the producer to provide informed options and trusts that the producer's recommendations for insurance are in the policyowner's best interest. To ensure that this trust is justified, a producer has an ethical responsibility to obtain the knowledge and skills needed to evaluate and service the insurance needs of clients. The producer must keep his base of knowledge and skills current by committing to a program of continuing education.

Client trust must be earned, nurtured, and constantly reinforced. The producer who remembers this basic rule will communicate to the client the reasons *why* a particular insurance policy or program is being recommended and *how* it will serve.

This communication and education continues long after the particular policy or program is sold and becomes part of the overall insurance program designed for that client. The producer will review each client's needs annually and meet with the client to explain and discuss the programs put in place to meet those needs.

Service the Sale

Service, during and after the sale, is just as important as selling to needs in meeting a producer's ethical responsibilities. One of the most important aspects of business ethics is that the characteristics one associates with an ethical person—fairness, honesty, and personal responsiveness—also affect the level of service that a company provides. For the purposes of this discussion, service means:

■ educating the client before, during, and after the sale, ensuring that the client fully understands the application and underwriting processes, the policy purchased, and any attached rider;

■ treating all information with confidentiality;

■ disclosing all information so that the policyowner or applicant can make an informed decision;

■ keeping the prospect or client informed of any rejection, exclusion, or cancellation of coverage; and

■ showing loyalty to prospects and clients.

Service Begins with the Application

A producer's primary responsibility in the application process is to the insurer. However, a producer also has an ethical duty to educate the prospective insured about the application process, including:

■ why the information is required;

■ how it will be evaluated;

■   the need for accuracy and honesty in answering all questions; and

■   the meaning of such terms as *waiver of premium, automatic premium loan, nonforfeiture options, policy loans,* and *conditional receipt.*

A **conditional receipt** normally is given when the applicant pays the initial premium at the time the application for a policy is signed. This means that the applicant and the company have formed what might be called a "conditional contract," one contingent upon conditions that existed at the time of application or when a medical examination is completed. It provides that the applicant is covered immediately from the date of application as long as she passes the insurer's underwriting requirements. It is the producer's ethical responsibility to explain that the applicant is covered on the condition that she proves to be insurable and passes the medical exam, if required.

Another ethical responsibility the producer owes the client is to briefly explain the **underwriting process** that the application will undergo. This explanation should include a description of the checks and balances that apply to underwriting a risk, such as the Medical Information Bureau, the inspection report, and the credit report. These will be discussed in Unit 9.

Precision and accuracy in completing the application are in the best interest of both the insurer and the prospective insured. It is vital that a producer understands this and explains the need for full disclosure to an applicant.

Insurance producers have access to a client's personal and financial information. Ethics require that the producer respect the sensitive nature of this information and keep it confidential. Personal information about a client should never be released without prior approval from the client.

In this context, **full disclosure** means informing the prospect or client of all facts involving a specific policy or plan so that an informed decision can be made. Two forms that many producers use as educational tools and in sales presentations are the *NAIC Buyer's Guide* and the *Policy Summary*. In Florida, an agent is required to deliver to the applicant a *Life Insurance Buyer's Guide* and a *Policy Summary*. These documents are usually delivered before the agent accepts the applicant's initial premium.

The underwriting process for an insurance application can be time consuming. All information on an applicant has to be analyzed so the applicant can be classified accurately and so appropriate rates are charged for the risks involved. A producer's ethical responsibilities to the client during the underwriting process center on promptness and policy delivery. An insurance producer needs to ensure that there are no unnecessary delays in the underwriting process. This means making sure that all information on the application is complete, accurate, and clear before it is submitted. It also means submitting the application without delay. If a producer has reason to believe the underwriting process may take longer than anticipated, the producer should notify the applicant of the delay.

Policy Delivery

Most policies are issued as applied for. In such cases, the producer owes the new policyowner prompt delivery of the policy and a review of its features and benefits. Not only does this help solidify the sale, it represents a step toward making the policyowner a lasting client.

Unfortunately, some policies will be rated or rejected. When this happens, the producer has two responsibilities:

1. **Personally review the rating or rejection.** Was it medical? Was there an unfavorable medical report? Was something overlooked or not made known to the underwriter? Should additional information be submitted? Is the rating or rejection proper? Should the application be reconsidered? In any event, the producer should have as much information as possible and be able to explain the rating or rejection to the applicant.

2. **Assuming the rating or rejection was valid, the producer has the responsibility to notify the applicant promptly.** To withhold this information in an effort to prevent the applicant from seeking insurance elsewhere is a breach of ethics and could actually harm the applicant and the applicant's family.

Special Situations. In most cases, an insurance producer needs only common sense to avoid an unethical situation with a policyowner. However, in some specialized areas, such as the sale of estate or business planning insurance, the ethical guidelines are clearly defined by professional organizations chartered to monitor the activities of their practitioners.

The insurance producer who works the estate or business planning market works with other professionals, such as lawyers and accountants. The insurance producer understands that his ability to help meet the client's objectives depends on the involvement of these other professionals and encourages their participation.

The producer understands that each member of the estate or business planning team serves a specific function. The *attorney* drafts the documents necessary to accomplish the client's objectives and advises the client of any legal consequences, while the *accountant* determines the accounting and tax implications and procedures. On the other hand, the producer recommends specific insurance policies or plans in an appropriate amount and ensures that ownership and beneficiary designations conform to the legal agreements prepared by the attorney.

Once the policy is issued and an applicant becomes a policyowner and client, service becomes more than the producer's ethical responsibility; service now forms the basis for a lasting relationship. All policyowners should receive periodic reviews to ensure that their insurance programs are in step with their plans and objectives.

Responsibilities to the Public

Insurance plays a key role in people's lives. Life insurance supports families in times of crises, pays for children's education, and carries out businesses. Health insurance gains access to health care services that are so expensive that consumers couldn't pay for them otherwise. Insurance plays a major role in the lives of most people in the United States. Yet most people are woefully ignorant of how insurance plans work and how insurance can benefit them, a situation that offers opportunities for unethical producers. The producer has a duty to provide the public with a fair and honest representation of the policies and services offered.

Insurance professionals have been aware of ethical problems within the industry and have been re-examining and raising their ethical standards since the 1970s. As one step in this direction, the National Association of Insurance Commissioners (NAIC) began amending and expanding the model Unfair Trade Practices Act (created in the 1940s) to deal with the inappropriate use of advertising. More states adopted all or portions of the model act. At the same time, a number of initiatives were undertaken to assure the proper use of policy illustrations.

Advertising

The potential for deceptive advertising or promotion by insurance companies and producers alike is significant, and the consequences to the consumer can be grave. Accordingly, all states regulate insurance advertising. The basis for many of these state statutes is the NAIC's model Unfair Trade Practices Act, which covers not only advertising but also such acts as coercion, unfair discrimination, and rebating.

The NAIC has also created a model regulation more specifically directed at advertising: the Rules Governing the Advertising of Life Insurance. This model regulation, adopted itself or through related regulation in 31 states, defines advertising and attempts to address those actions that have caused trouble in the industry. It also mandates the proper identification of insurance professionals and companies, a system of control over its advertisements, a description of the type of policy advertised, the disclosure of graded or modified benefits over time, and so forth.

In practice, most of the advertising and sales literature a producer uses is prepared by the insurer under the careful eye of its legal staff. For a producer, the ethical issue isn't necessarily the material itself but how the material is used and the deceptive sales presentation that may result.

Deceptive Sales Presentations

Deceptive sales presentations have probably generated more complaints of unethical behavior than any other activity. A deceptive sale is any presentation that gives the prospect or client the wrong impression about any aspect of an insurance policy or plan, that does not provide complete disclosure, or that includes any misleading or inconclusive product comparisons. Deceptive sales presentations can be blatant, but even subtle misrepresentations are unethical. Even if the deception is unintentional, the producer has done the client a great disservice.

Policy Illustrations

Policy illustrations are based on certain expectations of what will or might happen. When premiums, rates of returns, and death benefits are fixed and guaranteed as in whole life, this is not a large problem. When these things become variable and contingent, however, as they are in many newer products, the projected numbers are not guaranteed. The new products are also more risky for the insured. The more flexible the policy and the more aggressive the assumptions, the more sensitive the product will be to changes in mortality, expense, and interest rates.

Insurance companies have redesigned their disclosures to promote better consumer understanding of policy pricing, company and product performance, and illustration assumptions. Probably the most significant initiatives, given their combined impact and reach, come from the NAIC and the Society of Financial Service Professionals (SFSP, formerly the American Society of CLU® & ChFC®). The NAIC has drafted model legislation on policy illustrations; the SFSP has developed illustration questionnaires to help producers understand the assumptions that are used to design and create sales illustration.

A VIEW FROM THE FIELD

Skill and Competence Issues

Many ethical problems producers face or create for themselves can be traced to a simple lack of *skill* and *competence*. For example, failure to identify prospects' needs and recommend appropriate products is a problem, as are producers who misrepresent their abilities to provide competent service. It is obvious that these problems would not exist if producers were knowledgeable and competent. A knowledgeable, competent producer would not fail to identify a prospect's needs nor would a competent producer have to misrepresent his capabilities.

Skill and competence are prerequisites to selling insurance. These qualities are the means by which an insurance producer provides informed options and recommendations that are in the client's best interest. Therefore, a producer has the ethical responsibility to do the following.

■ *Develop and maintain a high level of knowledge and skill through concentrated study and dedicated work.* Skill can be mastered and knowledge can be acquired, but only through dedication and a willingness to work. All producers should be committed to a program of continuing education and participate in industry organizations, such as the National Association of Insurance and Financial Advisors – Florida (NAIFA-Florida).

■ *Acknowledge those cases or situations that are beyond the producer's skill level.* No one can be an expert at everything. When a case is clearly beyond a producer's expertise, the producer should seek help from a more experienced colleague or other professional.

Professional Obligations

A number of ethical issues can develop when a producer lacks a commitment to **professionalism**. A lack of professionalism can lead to disparaging the competition, not being objective with others in business dealings, failing to provide prompt and honest answers to clients' questions, and failing to provide products and services of the highest quality in the eyes of the customers. Producers who make a true commitment to professionalism will not be hampered by these conflicts. Professionalism requires a producer to do the following.

- *Place the client's interest beyond one's self-interest.* Professionals are loyal to their clients and are dedicated to protecting their clients' welfare. This means they remain independent and objective in their judgment and evaluations and recommend plans or policies that most benefit the client. When a policyowner asks for help or advice, the producer is quick to follow up, embracing client service as an important responsibility.

- *Be dedicated to the industry and supportive of all its member companies and representatives.* A true professional aligns himself with colleagues and competitors alike, knowing that all represent the same products and services and that all should share a commitment to the purpose and goals of these products and services.

- *Offer quality plans and represent quality companies.* A professional producer represents only those companies with solid financial standings and accurately informs prospects and clients of an insurer's financial position as part of the sales process. The lure of additional commission incentives a company might offer should be ignored if the company cannot deliver quality products backed by a sound financial base.

Moral Issues

Finally, there are moral issues, such as making false or misleading representations of products or services and the temptation that exists between opportunities for financial gain (or other personal benefit) and the proper performance of producer responsibilities.

While many questionable practices can be condemned outright as being immoral or unethical, maybe the cause of the problem is a lack of knowledge or understanding on the producer's part. The producer who misrepresents a policy may not recognize that what he is doing is unethical. After all, if a prospect needs insurance, does it matter how it is sold? If a client needs a specific type of plan but is willing to purchase a higher-priced alternative, should the producer redirect the focus to the policy that is more appropriate? The answers, of course, are "yes." If a sale cannot be made with honesty, fairness, and objectivity, it must not be made at all. If there is an opportunity for personal gain, but it comes at the expense of another person or company, it must be ignored. Thus, the ethical producer does the following.

- *Learns very early the difference between right and wrong in the business and practices and acts accordingly.* The ethical producer develops high ethical standards through training with experienced professionals and association with industry groups.

- *Consistently adheres to his values and maintains this integrity throughout his sales career.* The ethical producer resists conflicts of interest, real or perceived, in all business dealings. Ethics means emphasizing the interests of clients and company over one's self.

■ *Willingly assumes the obligation to perform his duties in a way that reflects the highest degree of dignity on the industry and best serves the interests of the client or prospect.* This means that the producer must put service above sales.

PUBLIC PERCEPTIONS OF THE INSURANCE INDUSTRY

An insurance producer represents his insurance company to the general public and prospective insureds. A producer's actions help shape the public's perceptions of the insurance industry. A producer's primary ethical duty to the public and each prospective insured is to provide accurate information regarding insurance policies and benefits in a fair and unbiased manner. That information should be complete in every way, providing the prospect with the details of any deductibles, waiting periods, benefit limitations, exclusions, or qualification requirements for the policy.

A producer's ethical duties to the public and prospects are quite demanding. In addition to the responsibilities the surveys indicated—skill, competence, professionalism, and moral integrity—let's review other ways in which producers can help (or hinder) the public's perception of insurance and the insurance industry.

Communication

A prospect's lack of understanding of what benefits an insurance policy will and will not provide is usually the result of poor communication. Sometimes the source of this problem is that a producer attempts to sell a new product without fully understanding the policy's features and benefits.

Attempting to sell a new policy, or any policy, without adequate knowledge and training is unethical because it is a producer's responsibility to determine if and how a policy will fit the prospect's needs. Understanding how policies work will help the producer determine that fit and also help the producer compare them to those of the competition.

Complete and Honest Representation

A producer has a duty to present each policy with complete honesty and objectivity. This means pointing out any limitations or drawbacks the product may have, along with its features and benefits. In all cases, a simple, straightforward explanation of the policy and how it will help fill the prospect's needs is always the proper ethical course.

Selling to Fit Needs

A prime violation of a producer's ethical duty to a prospect is deliberately selling to fit the needs of the *producer* rather than the needs of the prospect.

The typical result is a prospect being sold insurance with the highest premium (and the greatest commission) instead of the proper coverage.

Insurance producers have faced a number of complex ethical issues over the past several years, ranging from misleading advertising and policy illustrations to lack of knowledge needed to perform in a professional manner. These issues are not likely to go away. As competition increases, insurance producers may find themselves faced with even more ethical challenges. However, by committing themselves to professionalism and the needs of the client, insurance producers can act both responsibly and ethically.

PRESENTING RECOMMENDATIONS TO CLIENTS

There are two principles that form the foundation for an effective sales presentation. The first is that its purpose is to *uncover the needs of the prospect and eventually show how life insurance satisfies those needs.* Everything a producer does and says during the presentation is part of the strategy to influence the prospect to make a decision that, before the presentation, she had no thought of making.

The second principle is that the function of the life insurance producer is *to help people solve financial problems.* It is likely that many people a producer talks to will not recognize these problems or, if they do, they will be inclined to ignore them. People are engrossed in the task of taking care of today's needs; if they think of the future at all, they are inclined to put it in second place because today's pressures consume their attention. A producer's role is to isolate these problems and present them to prospects in such a way that they will want to do something about them. A life insurance producer does not create problems; he helps people solve problems. A producer does not approach people to interfere with their plans but to help them organize their plans.

These two principles—to uncover needs and to solve problems—are at the heart of all sales presentations.

The Organized Sales Presentation

The steps in an organized sales presentation are not theoretical concepts but proven, time-tested methods. In many cases, the entire sales process can be accomplished in one interview or one meeting. Other times, it will require two or more meetings because the producer will need to spend some time assessing the information received in the initial meeting before recommending the appropriate life insurance solution. The organized sales presentation proceeds according to six steps:

1. The approach

2. Establishing the general problem

3. Establishing the specific problem

4. Assessing the need

5. Presenting the life insurance solution

6. The close

This section focuses on presenting the life insurance solution. This step is the most enjoyable part of the organized sales presentation for many producers because it involves selling. However, during this step, serious problems of misrepresentation can occur as producers warm to the task of talking about products they believe will meet their clients' needs. Therefore, producers must use special care to provide full and accurate disclosure when presenting products to clients and motivating them to buy those products.

This section looks at the importance of full disclosure when presenting recommendations and examines how to make sure that requirement is met. It also looks at specific ways to avoid making misrepresentations when presenting, including what constitutes a misrepresentation. Some specific problem areas that traditionally have caused misunderstandings are also addressed. This includes a review of the correct use of policy illustrations and a thorough discussion of the subject of policy replacement: when it is appropriate, when it is not appropriate, and how to carry out a by-the-book replacement when necessary.

Informed Decisions

Once facts have been gathered and analyzed and suitable products have been identified that will help a client achieve her objectives, the next step in the selling process is the presentation. In days gone by, at this step in the sales process, the prospect was convinced—using virtually any means available—to buy the recommended product and pay the first premium. This was often accomplished by scare tactics in which the client was reminded, often with the help of fictitious motivational stories, that death was inevitable, if not imminent.

Today, such hard-sell tactics are not acceptable. The only proper approach is needs-based, with the focus on the client. Needs-based selling means selling products that meet identified needs of clients. The objective is to educate clients so they can make informed decisions about what is best for them, not to sell them or convince them that the producer's recommendations are best. It is the producer's role to provide clients with complete and accurate information under the ethical and legal requirements of full disclosure. When a client asks questions or expresses concerns, the producer must treat the client with respect and address her directly and honestly. Questions should not be treated as objections to be overcome. Rather, producers should consider client questions concerns to be addressed, signs of interest, and opportunities to further explain a certain feature or benefit of the policy.

This approach to selling involves a partnership between producer and client that enables the client to make informed decisions based on facts. It also is recognized in this day of diverse product options that a producer may offer more than one way to help a client meet objectives. This is one reason many producers present several alternatives, all of which may be suitable. The idea is to provide clients with choices that allow them to make their own decisions about what's best for them.

Ethical producers see this method of doing business as liberating. Not only does it take the sales pressure off clients, it also removes it from producers. If they have taken the time to establish relationships, conduct quality fact-finding interviews, and select products that reflect genuine needs, this next step, the product presentation, is simply the logical progression in the client's decision-making process. It involves discussion and disclosure, not pressure and manipulative selling tactics.

If the client disagrees with the recommendations, the producer may suggest alternatives. It is also possible that no sale will result; the client simply may not be ready to act. Ideally, however, the door will remain open for future contacts. With this approach, producers may meet and work with a smaller number of prospects and clients. The emphasis is not on quantity, but quality. This low-pressure approach to selling also may yield fewer initial sales than a high-pressure, take-the-money-and-run sales method. Still, the business that comes in will be more likely to remain. Relationship-based selling tends to reduce lapses and generate more repeat business in the future.

Overview of the Presentation

The product presentation may take just a few minutes, or it may require an hour, depending on the complexity of the product or products under discussion. Regardless, the presentation will flow through the following four steps:

1. First, the producer reviews and reestablishes the relationship. A week or longer may have elapsed between the fact-finding interview and this next meeting. The producer also should take a few minutes to review his credentials. As with the initial meeting, it is important to make sure that all information is accurate.

2. The producer then reviews the client's needs and priorities. Clients are busy. Odds are that the details of a conversation that took place several days ago will be vague at best. It is in everyone's best interests to review the priorities discussed and any decisions made at that first meeting. This step helps ensure that you and the client agree about the facts and that all relevant information has been disclosed.

3. Next, the producer introduces one or more specific product solutions and provides an overview of how the policies work. This usually involves a description of policy features and benefits. (Note: There will be occasions when no product should be recommended. At these times, the producer should schedule an appointment, nonetheless, to confirm this with the client. This not only ensures that the client understands and agrees with the decision, it also leaves the door open for future business.)

4. Finally, if the producer uses a product illustration, he should review and explain the illustration in detail as part of the product presentation process.

The producer is responsible for meeting all disclosure rules, being careful to avoid even the impression of misrepresentation. Now, let's look at the presentation process and identify areas where possible problems may occur and discuss how to deal with them.

Full Disclosure

Full and accurate disclosure is the cornerstone of the product presentation. This means more than just serving up the facts about a particular policy. The producer also must explain these facts so the client understands the ramifications of a given decision in relation to her particular situation and objectives. The producer is responsible for communicating relevant information in an understandable manner. The goal is to explain and educate, not to sell. The producer must be careful not to go from an accurate presentation of factual information to an overenthusiastic and inaccurate song of praise for a particular policy. It is easy for a producer who believes in a company's products to be so positive and motivated that he crosses the line to misrepresentation.

At the same time, the producer should not be afraid to motivate. The producer never should forget that his role is to motivate by educating and informing. The client makes the decision to buy or not to buy. In this respect, the producer is a teacher and facilitator. The producer presents the facts; the client makes the decision. Nonetheless, the more conscientiously the producer has built a relationship, listened carefully to the client, analyzed needs accurately and with the client's best interests always in mind, and conscientiously tried to make only appropriate product recommendations, the greater the likelihood that the client's decision will be to buy.

This means full disclosure. When presenting recommendations, many producers prefer to start with a general overview of how a particular product meets identified needs, followed by a detailed explanation of specific features and benefits. This presentation may include the use of policy illustrations, company-approved product brochures and other support materials. (The use of preprinted materials is recommended because they generally have been reviewed for compliance, so they meet requirements of full disclosure and market conduct.)

Full disclosure also means discussing a policy's limitations openly. Most consumers welcome being given the complete picture as candidly as possible.

A simple way to help explain today's more complex products is to describe their features and benefits. The producer can identify the feature clearly and then explain it in terms of its benefits. The producer should also be sure to note possible limitations of a particular feature. Here is an example of possible features of a variable universal life policy, along with a summary of the product's benefits and limitations:

> *One of this policy's features is that it offers 12 separate account options as well as a fixed account. This gives you flexibility and control over how your policy's cash values are allocated. It also gives you the opportunity to adjust the level of risk. Now, keep in mind that these cash values are not guaranteed. A level of risk is involved.*

You also can switch accounts as often as you want without fees or charges. I can do this for you, or you can do it yourself by telephone. The idea is to keep transfers as convenient as possible.

Plus, like every cash value life insurance policy, this policy offers tax-deferred accumulation. This allows your policy's cash values to enjoy maximum growth without being subject to current income taxes. Of course, if you terminate the policy or make withdrawals, it is possible that all or a portion of the cash value may become taxable.

This policy also includes loan provisions, which provide liquidity and access to funds. Policy loans are provided at a floating rate but cannot exceed ___ percent. Keep in mind that when cash value is borrowed from the policy, it may affect the policy's performance.

These separate accounts also provide professional fund management. Each mutual fund is managed by the fund's professional investors. This means that while you are in control of how your cash values are allocated, you need not make daily investment decisions.

Positioning the policy with the client.   With certain policies, it may take some time to provide full and accurate disclosure. Here is one way to position the policy with the client:

Henry, based on everything we discussed last week, it is my recommendation that one of my company's variable universal life policies has the potential to meet your needs. This type of policy, called VUL for short, has some unique features that I want to go over with you. This policy offers life insurance protection, tax-favored accumulation, competitive returns on account values, allocation control of cash value accounts, death benefit flexibility, premium flexibility, access to cash values, and more.

At this point, the producer should go through each key feature and its benefits, being sure to explain the potential drawbacks as well. The key is to be accurate and balanced in the presentations.

The most important point producers should remember when discussing a product is that while its features and benefits are familiar to the producer, they may confuse the client. The producer must be sure to explain the policy clearly and completely.

It is important that producers respond in an honest and straightforward manner to questions and concerns. They should not view questions as objections to be overcome. Instead, questions should be treated as signs of interest. They present producers with the opportunity to further explain a particular feature or benefit to the client.

Avoiding Misrepresentation

Perhaps the biggest market conduct danger producers face during the presentation is that of misrepresentation. Sometimes, it is the result of over-enthusiasm, of selling the benefits of a policy too strongly. It may also be the result of a willingness to stress the advantages of a particular product and sidestep any drawbacks. Providing vague or elusive responses is just as serious a form of misrepresentation as is deliberately lying about a policy's features or expected performance.

What Constitutes a Misrepresentation?   Producers must be sure to avoid creating a false impression about themselves, their companies, their products, or their services. A misrepresentation can be a verbal statement, a brochure or policy illustration that has been altered, or some other written communication with a prospect or client. Some of the most common examples of misrepresentation follow.

- **Misrepresenting a policy's provisions or benefits or how the policy can be expected to perform over time.** This includes referring to a policy as anything other than insurance (i.e., a wealth-building plan or an insured investment). It may consist of making inaccurate statements or providing inadequate disclosure. Some clients do not understand the tax and other consequences of decisions regarding insurance policies. It is the producer's job to explain these things to them. This is why it is important today to be particularly familiar with the withdrawal penalties and tax consequences of all decisions and recommendations. Clients must understand them.

- **Overstating promises and guarantees.** Sometimes just a few words make the difference between a projection and a guarantee. When explaining dividends or vanishing premiums to clients, for example, producers should be very clear that they are discussing projections, not guaranteeing the figures. There is a big difference between stating that earnings "are guaranteed" and "are possible." Clients must clearly understand that difference.

- **Giving the impression that policy dividends or cash value projections (other than those that are, in fact, guaranteed, as stated in the policy) are guaranteed.** Producers should be sure to distinguish between projections and guarantees and make sure that clients understand the distinction.

- **Using inaccurate or misleading information or numbers that misrepresent the financial condition of an insurance company, a broker-dealer, or another producer.** When producers venture into discussions about a company's financial stability, they must be sure to stick to the facts. The fact that a company is in receivership is public information; however, producers should use caution in explaining the ramifications of a company's financial condition. It is equally important not to spread rumors about another producer, agency, or broker-dealer.

- **Making any statements or giving reassurances of any kind about coverage, the policy, or premiums that are not true or that cannot be supported clearly by the policy.** One of the most serious examples of this practice would be to tell an applicant that she is insured when this is not the case or coverage is only conditional.

- **Engaging in the most serious type of misrepresentation—intentional fraud.** This criminal act can lead to a fine and loss of license, possibly even criminal proceedings. The agency, manager, broker-dealer, and home office may be held liable as well. This is why it is important for producers to make sure they remain within the legal limits of their state laws, as well as their companies' ethical guidelines.

Misrepresentation accounts for the majority of complaints insurers and regulatory agencies receive. In most cases, this misrepresentation is not intentional. For example, a client might not completely understand a producer's explanation because the producer could not define certain industry terms. Most of these misrepresentations result from inexperience, lack of knowledge, or just plain carelessness, all of which can harm clients and damage the credibility of the producer, the company, and the industry. These are the reasons why it is so important for producers to know their products and sales materials and be able to present and explain them clearly. This is also why it is so critical for producers to be able to determine whether their clients completely understand what they have been told and are making informed decisions in purchasing products.

Knowledge—The Key to Avoiding Misrepresentation. Knowledge of a company's products can help producers avoid many problems involving misrepresentation. However, the producers' understanding is only the first step. They also must be willing and able to communicate this information clearly to clients. The following two steps can help producers use their knowledge to benefit clients and themselves.

- **Learn the products and the industry.** Producers should read their policies to make sure they understand them. A producer's knowledge and ability to explain policy provisions clearly can help protect clients from costly mistakes. Knowledge truly is power in that it increases the producer's confidence, which in turn enhances selling effectiveness and overall productivity.

- **Plan sales presentations carefully.** Producers must be sure to make complete and accurate sales presentations, disclosing all relevant information about their products to clients. The best guideline is to make sure the clients understand all information from the outset so no surprises or misunderstandings occur later.

Common Dangers of Misrepresentation

Some specific topics consistently cause the most problems when it comes to misrepresentation. These areas, which often are fairly complex in nature and difficult to explain, include the following.

Vanishing premiums. This term, which has fallen into disfavor because of past abuses, should no longer be used. During the early days of interest-sensitive and variable products, when interest rates generated double-digit returns, companies began to realize that under ideal conditions, some policies could become self-paying. This realization went from *could happen* to *will happen* in the collective mind of the entire industry. It wasn't long before the vanishing premium was touted as a major feature of policies, complete with specific (if only implied) vanishing premium dates.

That these vanish points were not guaranteed or that they depended on unrealistic rates of return was often ignored. When projected or promised vanish dates came and went and policyowners continued to pay premiums, lawsuits and complaints multiplied.

Today producers recognize that the best course of action is to steer clear of the words *vanishing premiums* with clients. While it is possible for premiums in some policies to vanish under certain conditions, producers should make no guarantees. The vanishing premium concept allows for a policyowner to make cash payments to a point at which future dividend and other cash values may be sufficient to pay all future premiums. However, the vanishing premium is not a contractual provision or part of the policy, and it is not guaranteed. Growth can often be projected but it cannot be guaranteed, and this is an important distinction producers must make to clients. Under no condition should a producer state or imply that premiums will vanish or that premiums may end on a specific date.

One way of presenting the concept is as follows:

> Under one policy option, it is possible, after the policy has been in force for a number of years, to allow your dividends and cash value accumulations to pay your premiums, possibly for good but not necessarily. Whether the premium ends depends entirely on several factors, including policy dividends the company declares.

Flexible premiums.   In many of today's policies, once the initial premium has been paid, the amount of additional premiums in the future is flexible or even optional to some degree for the policyowner. Although a recommended or guideline premium exists, the policyowner has the option to pay more premium, less premium, or even skip premiums completely. While this is a valuable option for policyowners, it never should be implied that after the initial premium has been paid, a policy generally will fund itself.

Instead, this feature should be presented as a tool to help clients achieve financial objectives, such as the option to suspend premiums temporarily during times of financial stress or high expenses, perhaps when children are in college. Clients must be informed of the potential consequences of skipping premiums in terms of how this course of action may affect policy values.

Insurance presented as a savings or retirement plan.   While cash value life insurance does have an accumulation element, producers should not give the impression that life insurance is anything other than life insurance, even when it has cash value features. In fact, producers must make sure that the cash value is identified and described as just that: cash value.

Guaranteed versus potential cash value accumulations.   When the cash value growth is guaranteed by the insurance company, as it is in fixed-return policies, it can be stated as such. In all other cash value policies, however, including universal life (which has a declared rate of return) and variable universal life (which features competitive returns based on market performance), clients should be made aware how cash values are credited.

Dividend misrepresentation. When dividends are possible in participating policies, it is common for clients to believe that the dividends are earnings similar to those associated with stocks. Producers must explain that dividends are a return of premium, which is why they are not taxed. Most of all, producers must make sure they never give clients the impression that dividends are guaranteed. Producers should make this especially clear when giving cash value projections. Also, a company's past dividend performance must be presented as just that—a history of past performance, which in no way can be interpreted as a projection of future dividends.

Insurance described as investments. If the product is life insurance (even if the cash value depends on securities), producers must not imply that the product is an investment or describe it as such. The emphasis should be on life insurance as a means of protection with accumulation features that receive favorable tax treatment. Producers should also not describe cash values as investments, investment returns, equity, savings, or emergency accounts.

Premiums referred to as other than premiums. Producers should always refer to premiums as just that, premiums. They should not be described as payments, contributions, or some other similar term.

Failure to distinguish between tax-free and tax-deferred accumulations. While it is recommended that producers tell clients that the cash value increases in their policies are tax deferred, producers should not imply or state that cash value growth is tax free because this is not always the case. It is acceptable to remind clients, however, that beneficiaries receive proceeds tax free in most situations.

Failure to divulge risks. In addition to the positive aspects, producers have an obligation to divulge the risks associated with insurance policies, especially when discussing variable-rate products. Clients must understand that they, not the insurance companies, bear the full risk of loss with the cash values in variable products.

Failure to explain product differences. Producers should help clients understand the differences between policies under discussion. For instance, it would be grossly unfair to compare premiums and cash values between a traditional whole life policy and a variable universal life policy without also pointing out the other differences. This information would be critical in helping the client make an informed buying decision.

Policy Illustrations

One of the best ways to explain policies clearly and completely is to use policy illustrations. Traditional fixed-value policies could be explained with one or two pages showing guaranteed values. With the development of interest-sensitive and variable policies, however, that was no longer possible. As a result, computer-generated life insurance policy illustrations, illustrating policy performance under a handful of possible scenarios, were developed to explain potential policy performance. Many producers began to build all their policy presentations around these illustrations. Although these educational sales tools were intended to help clients better understand guaranteed and projected policy values, they were also the cause for many complaints about their misuses in marketing and sale of life insurance.

Today's policy illustrations.   Today, as a result of the NAIC's Life Insurance Illustrations Model Regulation and efforts by individual companies, illustrations have become somewhat standardized. Most important for insurance producers, so have the rules and requirements for presenting and explaining policy illustrations.

The NAIC's Model Regulation sets the following guidelines.

- Each policy illustration must have a written explanation or policy summary.

- Each policy illustration must show that cash values and coverage will vary depending on changes in an insurer's costs and dividends.

- Each policy illustration must be labeled "life insurance illustration" and contain such basic information as the names and addresses of both the insurer and the producer as well as other relevant identifying information about the source of the illustration.

- Each policy illustration must describe nonguaranteed elements in a straightforward manner and must not give the impression that they are in any way guaranteed.

- Each policy illustration must be complete. The illustration cannot be altered or marked up in any way to highlight any particular area.

- No policy illustration can represent or imply that premium payments are not required, unless that is the case.

- No policy illustration can contain the word *vanish* or *vanishing premium* or similar wording that could mislead the applicant into believing the policy will become paid up through the use of nonguaranteed or projected elements.

- No policy illustration can represent that the policy is anything other than life insurance.

- No policy illustration can show projections of elements (such as reduced expenses or mortality gains) that have not yet occurred.

- Each policy illustration must follow a specific basic illustration format.

Finally, when using an illustration, producers must obtain a signed and dated statement from the applicant. A signed and dated statement from the applicant with wording similar to the following would suffice as proper notice:

> *I have received a copy of this illustration and understand that any nonguaranteed elements illustrated are subject to change and could be either higher or lower. The producer has told me that they are not guaranteed.*

When using policy illustrations. When using illustrations as part of the presentation, producers should take a proactive approach. Illustrations cannot stand by themselves; they make little sense (or, worse, are open to gross misinterpretation) unless they are explained. For this reason, producers should not give illustrations to clients without explanation and discussion. To best use illustrations to help clients make informed buying decisions, producers should take the following nine steps.

1. **Become knowledgeable.** Producers need to understand how insurers develop policy illustrations, how illustrations work, and how they should be presented. Producers must understand the assumptions underlying illustrations and how these assumptions affect a policy's future performance. This understanding will help producers avoid errors in communicating information about the policy to the client.

2. **Make only credible and realistic assumptions.** When requesting illustrations from insurers or creating original ones from compliance-approved software, use credible and realistic assumptions. For example, introducing 20% projected rates of return in a 5% current environment simply is not ethical.

3. **Illustrations are not predictions.** Take time to make sure applicants understand clearly that illustrations are not predictions but simply scenarios that indicate what could take place based on the assumptions used.

4. **Make clear distinctions between guaranteed and nonguaranteed cash values.** Guaranteed cash values are just that, the policy's guaranteed values. Provided the applicant pays all premiums and assumes no policy loans, this is the amount of guaranteed cash value in the policy each year. It often is referred to as the minimum cash value. Other values, including dividends and account value increases, are projected based on present assumptions and can change over time based on performance.

5. **Encourage applicants to ask questions.** When applicants have questions about illustrations, answer those questions candidly.

6. **Review the illustration with the applicant.** Starting with the proposal page, review the entire illustration. This page identifies the type of policy, face amount, premiums, and other relevant information. Note that the rest of the illustration consists of columns that show changing values year by year.

7. **Point out that total cash value includes nonguaranteed values.** This number is a projection of how policy values could look over time. The figure is based on the company's current dividend scale continued into the future. It should not be presented as or implied to be a guarantee or prediction of future performance.

8. **Be aware of the assumptions used in illustrations.** No policy loans may be taken against cash value, and dividends are used to purchase paid-up additions, for example. These affect future values.

9. **Ask questions.** An illustration can be fairly complicated, so the producer should encourage applicants to ask questions if necessary to understand the illustration.

ILLUSTRATION 4.1

Life Insurance Policy Cost
Comparison Methods

Insurance producers sometimes encounter a competitive situation in which a prospect is considering two or more policies. In a situation like this, producers who can accurately compare the true costs of each policy may have an advantage.

Rarely are two policies so closely alike that a true "apples to apples" comparison can be made (one company may provide a free waiver of premium provision, for example). Fortunately, however, there are some established methods of comparing policy costs. While it is beyond the scope of this book to provide an in-depth review of each, producers should be familiar with the two primary methods: **traditional net cost** and **interest adjusted net cost**.

Traditional Net Cost Method

Under the **traditional net cost method**, projected premiums for a certain time period (say, 20 years) are totaled. Projected policy dividends (if any) and the cash value at the end of that period are subtracted from the total. The resulting number, divided by the number of years in the comparison, yields the net cost per thousand per year.

This method is no longer permitted in many states because of one significant flaw—it ignores the time value of money. Money placed in an investment vehicle (like insurance) earns interest. Different companies apply different interest rates to their policies. By ignoring this fact, traditional net cost comparison falls short in projecting the real cost of a policy.

Interest Adjusted Net Cost Method

The **interest adjusted net cost method** is widely used today to compare policy costs. It is calculated in much the same way as the traditional net cost method, except that it adds the extra component of *interest* to the formula. The interest factor used is based on each company's projected interest rate. In this way, the cost estimates more accurately reflect the actual cost of a policy.

Policy Replacement

Perhaps one of the biggest challenges a producer faces is deciding when it is appropriate to replace an existing policy with another. On one hand, due to the rapid evolution of new (and, in many cases, improved) products in recent years, a replacement may be in the client's best interests. On the other hand, a replacement often exposes the client to undue financial loss and risk.

Generally, replacement results from one of two possible motives. First, the producer genuinely may believe canceling one policy (or reducing its values) to replace it with another benefits the client. This can occur when an existing policy appears to be completely inappropriate or no longer meets client needs, such as in a divorce or the death of beneficiaries. The second motive, the one that has resulted in investigations into the abuse of replacements, is the result of a producer's desire to generate new first-year commissions without regard to the client's needs. Producers are paid high first-year commissions, followed by lower subsequent renewal commissions. It is not unusual for a producer to receive up to 80% of the first-year premiums as commission on life insurance policies.

Definition of replacement. The legal definition of **replacement** varies from state to state, so it is important that each producer knows the law in the state in which he does business. Producers should be aware that replacement, by its broadest definition under the Society of Financial Services Professionals, may involve "an action which eliminates the original policy or diminishes its benefits or values. Examples of this are policy loans, taking reduced paid-up insurance, or withdrawing dividends."

Therefore, the producer who recommends that a client borrow cash value from an existing policy to pay premiums on a new policy may be engaging in replacement just as much as the producer who encourages a client to drop one policy and replace it with another.

Traditionally, improper replacement is divided into two categories: twisting and churning:

- **Twisting** also is referred to as external replacement. It involves illegally inducing a person to drop existing insurance to buy similar coverage with another producer or company. This often is associated with making false statements about another insurer or producer, an illegal act that also runs contrary to ethical market conduct.

- **Churning** also is known as internal replacement. It involves replacing policies within the same company, often by the same producer who sold the original policies.

When in doubt. As a rule, producers should avoid replacement unless it is obviously so appropriate that they cannot in good conscience think it best to leave an existing policy in force. Most of all, they should not look for opportunities to replace existing coverage. They never should initiate replacement to generate commissions for themselves.

Indeed, it may sometimes be advisable to replace a client's policy with another. However, the litmus test must be how well the action serves the best interests of the client, not the producer. All too often, replacement—especially when cash value policies are involved—is not clearly in the client's favor. Before executing a policy replacement, producers should make sure it is appropriate. Also, they should not assume that it is automatically acceptable to replace a policy with another one from the same company.

In most situations, reports the National Association of Insurance and Financial Advisors in its consumer publication *Points to Ponder If You're Considering Replacing Your Life Insurance*, "the life insurance you already own is your best buy." This generally is true for the following reasons.

- **Changes in health and age.** The risk always exists that the client has become uninsurable or insurable only at a higher rate. Even if the client's health is sound, a whole life policy purchased at age 20 almost always carries a lower premium than one purchased at age 48.

- **New contestable period.** A company's right to challenge a death claim or other information, usually within two years from the date of policy issue, may expose the client to the risk of dying without coverage or may subject beneficiaries to legal conflicts.

- **New policy fees and expenses.** The new policy often comes with new sales loads, policy fees, and other expenses, which may mean that it could take years before the client breaks even in terms of total policy values.

■ **Possible loss of policy upgrades or automatic improvements that may meet the policyowner's objectives.** Many companies are introducing unilateral policy improvements to existing policies. These also should be considered before a replacement is initiated.

■ **Loss of grandfathered rights.** For example, if the original policy was purchased when tax laws were more favorable, replacement may entail the loss of "grandfathered" income tax benefits.

When a replacement may be appropriate.   At times, recommending that one policy be canceled and replaced by another is best for the client. Here are some situations in which replacement may be appropriate.

■ The client's health has improved. For instance, a man diagnosed with childhood leukemia at an early age survived; however, because traces of the disease were evident for the next 30 years, the insurance he was able to obtain was rated steeply. Finally, at age 45, he was declared completely free of the disease. In this case, a policy he could obtain at age 30 may no longer be appropriate for his needs, especially if he can obtain new coverage at a rate half that for the existing policy. Of course, it might be possible to convince the existing carrier to reconsider the rating and reduce the premium.

■ A female client originally was underwritten with unisex rates in compliance with the laws of her state. When she moves to another state, one that allows sex-based rates, it may be possible that a new policy will reduce her coverage cost.

■ A policy that was issued at a young age and features a small death benefit for an inappropriately large premium no longer meets the client's needs.

■ The purpose of the replacement is to undo a bad replacement. For example, this may occur when a middle-aged client who had whole life insurance was induced to replace this policy with term insurance. The recommendation to replace the temporary coverage with a permanent policy may indeed be appropriate.

The above examples do not automatically warrant replacement. It is crucial to replace policies conscientiously. Replacement is a serious action. Before recommending replacement, even if it appears to be ethical at first glance, producers should make sure it is in their clients' best interests to do so.

Before recommending a replacement.   When it appears that replacement may be in a client's best interests, a producer should conduct a rigorous series of tests. If even one of these is not carried out or fails to conclude that replacement is ethically and legally appropriate, the producer should not recommend replacement. Following are some of the steps involved.

■ Make sure the replacement is legal according to state regulations. If the replacement fails to meet state law, discontinue all replacement activities. Note that even when the replacement is not illegal, this does not necessarily mean that it is appropriate.

■ Conduct a self-check to ensure that the replacement is ethical.

■ Give the client a form called a "Notice Regarding Replacement," which provides up-to-date information about the client's existing coverage so she can compare it with the new, proposed policy.

■ Provide the client with a completed and signed comparison statement that fairly and accurately allows the client to compare the two policies.

■ Notify the existing carrier of the proposed replacement. Where external replacement is involved, this enables the policyowner to meet with the original selling producer. Where internal replacement is involved, this also enables the company to ensure that all internal replacement rules are being met.

■ Make full and fair disclosure of all facts concerning the new coverage and the existing insurance. Policyowners who consider replacement should be aware of how changing coverage will affect cash values, incontestability provisions, and other features of their existing policies.

■ Give a follow-up letter to the client that summarizes the meeting with the producer, including what they talked about regarding replacement, what the producer recommended, and what the client decided.

■ Complete all other appropriate forms properly. By signing these forms, the insured acknowledges that she is fully aware of which benefits are being given up and which benefits are being accepted when she purchases the new coverage.

How replacement rules benefit the producer. The regulations on replacement involve a great deal of work because they are designed to reduce the number of inappropriate replacements. In this respect, they assist ethical producers by reducing the incidence of replacements of their policies. Just as producers have a responsibility not to replace a policy without carrying out due diligence, they have the opportunity to stop inappropriate replacement of their own coverage by other producers.

To avoid inappropriate replacement, producers should do the following.

■ **Maintain close contact with clients.** At the minimum, the producer should conduct an annual review. Client contact is crucial if the producer intends to respond to clients' changing needs and concerns. The producer does not give clients a reason to discuss their insurance needs with any other insurance professional.

■ **Educate clients about how the policies they purchase suit their needs.** The producer should periodically remind clients why they purchased coverage and how it benefits them and their families.

■ **Ask clients to call if they're ever asked to consider replacing their policies.** The producer should explain that part of his service is to review other plans and help clients make informed decisions.

ETHICS AND THE LAW

Once an insurance producer understands and embraces a personal and professional code of ethics, he must also find ways to avoid the temptation to use illegal, unethical, or questionable practices that could provide short-term profit at the expense of compromising his integrity.

The responsibility to regulate the insurance industry is shared jointly by the federal government and the various state governments. States carry the major burden of regulating insurance affairs, including the ethical conduct of agents licensed to conduct business within their borders. This regulation of ethical conduct in some states is called **marketing ethics**.

Regulation of an insurance agent's ethical conduct is conducted through the Department of Financial Services to oversee the marketing practices of both producers and insurance companies in Florida. Many of the regulations governing ethical conduct are derived from model legislation developed by the National Association of Insurance Commissioners (NAIC), such as the Unfair Trade Practices Act.

Marketing Ethics

Though state laws regarding sales and marketing practices by insurance producers vary, there is a great deal of uniformity in the principle and intent of these laws. All are designed to protect the interests of consumers by ensuring fair, reasoned, and ethical conduct by a producer.

Unauthorized Insurers

By law, only insurers that have been authorized or licensed by a state may issue policies in that state. Consequently, a producer must make sure that the insurers he represents are licensed to do business where solicitation is made. In general, a state's guaranty fund only covers the liabilities of authorized insurers, so anyone purchasing policies from unauthorized or unlicensed companies would be at risk if those insurers could not meet their claims. Some states will hold the producer personally liable on any insurance contract he or she places for an unauthorized insurer.

Misrepresentation

Any written or oral statement that does not accurately describe a policy's features, benefits, or coverage is considered a misrepresentation. The states have enacted laws that penalize producers who engage in this practice. Keep in mind that it is unlawful to make any misleading representations or comparisons of companies or policies to insured persons to induce them to forfeit, change, or surrender that insurance. As we have stressed throughout this course, producers have an ethical duty to present their policies in a truthful and open manner.

Defamation

Defamation is any false, maliciously critical, or derogatory communication, written or oral, that injures another's reputation, fame, or character. Individuals and companies both can be defamed. Unethical producers practice defamation by spreading rumors or falsehoods about the character of a competing producer or the financial condition of another insurance company.

Rebating

Rebating occurs if the buyer of an insurance policy receives any part of the producer's commission or anything else of significant value as an inducement to purchase a policy. State regulations are very strict in this respect and are designed to prohibit discrimination in favor of, or against, policyowners.

In Florida, rebating is allowed if the agent adheres to the following rules.

- The rebate has to be available to all insureds in the same actuarial class.

- The rebate must be in accordance with a rebating schedule filed by the agent with the insurer issuing the policy to which the rebate applies.

- The rebating schedule must be uniformly applied so that all insureds who purchase the same policy through that producer for the same amount of insurance receive the same rebate percentage.

- Rebates should not be given to an insured who purchases a policy from an insurer that prohibits its producers from rebating commissions.

- The rebate schedule must be prominently displayed in public view at the producer's place of business and a free copy made available to insureds on request.

- The age, sex, place of residence, race, nationality, ethnic origin, marital status, occupation, or location of the risk cannot be used in determining the percentage of the rebate or whether a rebate will be available.

Twisting and Churning

Twisting is the unethical act of persuading a policyowner to drop a policy solely for the purpose of selling another policy without regard to possible disadvantages to the policyowner. By definition, twisting involves some kind of misrepresentation by the producer to convince the policyowner to switch insurance companies or policies. In some states, persuading a policyowner to surrender a whole life policy and use the cash value to make other investments falls under the category of twisting.

Directly related to twisting is **churning**, a practice in which the policy values in an insurance policy are used to purchase another policy with the same insurer for the sole purpose of earning additional premiums or commissions. In cases involving churning, there is no demonstrable benefit to the insured with the new policy.

Coercion

Coercion is an unfair trade practice that occurs when someone in the insurance business applies physical or mental force or threat of force to persuade another to transact insurance. While most agents will understand the illegality of using force to make a sale, remember that coercion can often be much more subtle. If agents suggest, for example, that they can interfere with or injure a client's reputation or business unless a policy is purchased, it would be coercion. Any activity by an agent that seeks to limit the client's free choice regarding transacting insurance is coercion.

Unfair Discrimination

Making a distinction, in sales, underwriting, pricing, claims handling, or any other insurance applicant function, between two different individuals of substantially the same underwriting classification and expectation of life or health is **unfair discrimination**. Agents should offer their insurance products and services to all members of the public equally, without regard to race, gender, age, ethnicity, or any other characteristic that is not a legitimate underwriting distinction. The Florida code specifically cautions insurers and agents against unfair discrimination against victims of domestic violence or abuse (Sec. 626.9541, F.S.). Agents should also remember that unfair discrimination may either be in favor of or against particular applicants.

License Suspension and Termination

An unethical act can have severe repercussions. This is because what states consider unethical, they have usually made illegal. A producer's license can be suspended or terminated for any of the following unethical actions:

- Making a materially untrue statement in the application for a producer's license

- Stating or implying that a policy is self-supporting or that projected dividends under a participating policy will be sufficient to assure any benefits without any further payment of premiums

- Implying that a policy is being sold or issued by the investment department of a life insurance company

- Conveying the idea that by purchasing a policy, the applicant will become a member of a limited group of persons who will receive special advantages or favored treatment by the insurance company

- Describing a premium as a deposit unless the payment establishes a debtor-creditor relationship and clearly shows when and how the deposit may be withdrawn

- Giving any indication that future policy dividends are guaranteed

- Stating that an insured will be guaranteed certain benefits should a policy lapse without giving an adequate explanation of nonforfeiture benefits

- Stating that a policy contains certain benefits not found in any other insurance contract

- Stating that a prospect must buy a policy immediately or lose the opportunity to purchase it

- Avoiding any clear and unequivocal statement that insurance is the subject of the solicitation

- Using such terms as *financial planner, financial consultant, investment counselor,* or *financial counselor,* implying that the producer is in an advisory business in which compensation is unrelated to sales, unless such is actually the case

- Using amounts and numbers in such a way as to mislead the prospect with regard to the cost of the policy or any other significant aspect of the contract

- Disparaging a competitive producer or insurer or their policies, services, or business methods

- Using any method of policy cost comparison that does not take into account the time value of money

Knowledge and calculated awareness can help the honest and ethical producer avoid many of the traps described in this unit.

SUMMARY

While laws set the minimum standard by which producers are expected to behave, a person's personal values or ethics provide a guidance system to help him choose the right answer or alternative to ethical dilemmas when several choices are available.

Historically, certain codes of ethics developed as a covenant among peers. However, modern codes of ethics have been based as well on considerations of the public interest, especially with regard to trade and commercial relationships. Codes of ethics identify and encourage desirable activities by formally establishing a high standard against which each individual may measure his performance.

Most professions have written codes of ethics that pledge the members of the profession to certain standards of conduct. For example, in addition to having a broad understanding of accounting and tax laws, Certified Public Accountants (CPAs) must pass a series of rigorous examinations and are expected to adhere to a code of ethics. Many other professional codes of conduct, such as the American College of CLU® & ChFC®, National Association of Insurance and Financial Advisors, National Association of Fraternal Insurance Counsellors, and the Certified Financial Planner Board of Standards, Inc., address the issue of ethics by establishing strict codes of ethics. These professional ethics are designed to guide, advise, and regulate behavior on the job.

However formal the process is to establish the rules for ethical conduct, the rules still do not go beyond common sense and natural integrity. These attributes, plus knowledge and calculated awareness, can help the ethical producer steer clear of many temptations.

KEY CONCEPTS

Students should be familiar with the following concepts:

ethics	inspection report
compliance	credit report
market conduct	policy illustrations
Medical Information Bureau	policy replacement

UNIT TEST

1. An insurance salesperson who offers a $100 gourmet dinner in exchange for the purchase of a life insurance policy would be considered to have violated ethical sales practices by

    A. twisting
    B. replacement
    C. churning
    D. rebating

2. In what phase of the selling process are serious problems of misrepresentation likely to occur?

    A. Approach
    B. Presentation of recommendations
    C. Fact finding and needs analysis
    D. Policy delivery and ongoing service

3. Which of the following phrases should agents avoid using when explaining policies to prospective applicants or clients?

    A. Cash value
    B. Vanishing premium
    C. Flexible premium
    D. Death benefit

4. All of the following are involved in a product presentation EXCEPT

    A. pressure
    B. education
    C. discussion
    D. disclosure

5. Which of the following is NOT part of the home office underwriting process?

    A. Credit report
    B. Medical Information Bureau report
    C. Applicant's analysis report
    D. Inspection report

6. The basis for many state statutes regulating insurance advertising is the NAIC's

    A. McCarran-Ferguson Act
    B. Fair Credit Reporting Act
    C. Ethics in Advertising Act
    D. Unfair Trade Practices Act

7. *Ethics* is best described as

    A. laws and statutes enacted by duly elected representatives
    B. religious rituals and ceremonies
    C. instructions on how to interact with fellow members of a group or community
    D. a society's laws and regulations

8. Which of the following is the goal of a sales presentation?

    A. To educate the client so the client can make her own decisions about what's right for her
    B. To sell the client as many products as possible
    C. To convince the client that the producer's recommendations are best
    D. To explain the rules and regulations governing particular insurance products

9. Which of the following is NOT part of a sales presentation?

    A. Review and re-establish the client-producer relationship
    B. Introduce the recommended policy
    C. Review the product application
    D. Review the client's needs and priorities

10. Which of the following should a producer NOT do during a presentation?

    A. Explain and educate
    B. Sell a policy
    C. Motivate the client
    D. Openly discuss a policy's limitations

11. All of the following are reasons why it is seldom in the best interest of a policyholder to replace a life insurance policy with a new one EXCEPT

    A. most of the first-year premium is swallowed up in commission
    B. replacement policies are never in the best interest of the policyowner
    C. the premium is higher because the insured is older
    D. waiting periods begin anew

12. Diverting insurance funds for personal use is an example of
    A. replacement
    B. rebating
    C. misuse of premiums
    D. misrepresentation

13. Selling variable universal life insurance policies as mutual funds is an example of a prohibited practice called
    A. twisting
    B. misrepresentation
    C. replacement
    D. rebating

14. When an agent spreads a false story that damages a competing agent's reputation, the offense is called
    A. twisting
    B. defamation
    C. disclosure
    D. rebating

15. When values of an insurance policy are used to purchase another policy with the same insurer for the sole purpose of earning additional premiums or commissions, this practice is called
    A. replacement
    B. misalliance
    C. rebating
    D. churning

16. Which of the following is an objective of the NAIC?
    A. To promote federal legislation of the insurance industry
    B. To encourage uniformity in state insurance laws and regulations
    C. To develop continuing education courses for insurance producers
    D. To develop model insurance policies for adoption by insurers

17. Which of the following is NOT a provision of NAIC's Life Insurance Illustrations Model Regulation?
    A. Each policy illustration must be accompanied by a written explanation or policy summary.
    B. Each policy illustration should use the words vanish and vanishing premium sparingly.
    C. Each policy illustration must show that cash values and coverage vary depending on changes in an insurer's costs and dividends.
    D. Each policy illustration must be complete.

18. Which of the following is NOT part of a product presentation?
    A. Explaining policies
    B. Asking for referrals
    C. Motivating the client
    D. Discussing a policy's limitations

19. The use of preprinted material in a sales presentation is recommended for which of the following reasons?
    A. The agent doesn't have to know exactly how a product works.
    B. It saves a lot of time and explanations.
    C. Such material generally has been reviewed for compliance.
    D. The agent can give it to the client instead of answering the client's questions.

20. The purpose behind full disclosure requirements is to
    A. make sure a client is told everything there is to know about a product
    B. help a client make an informed decision
    C. make sure agents comply with the letter of the law
    D. help a client distinguish one insurer's product from a similar offering from another insurer

21. Jim gives Bill a couple of tickets to a baseball game to thank him for purchasing a policy. This is an example of
    A. rebating
    B. twisting
    C. replacement
    D. churning

22. Which of the following is an example of churning?
    A. Illegally inducing a person to drop existing insurance to purchase similar coverage with another agent or company
    B. Rephrasing a policy provision in such a way that it says just the opposite of the original
    C. Replacing a policy for another with the same insurer with the intent of earning additional premiums or commissions
    D. Representing an insurance policy as a retirement plan

23. Melanie is a newly licensed producer. A customer calls and asks for some product recommendations, but Melanie thinks that she is not yet qualified to help the customer. Therefore, Melanie has an ethical responsibility to
    A. answer the customer's questions on the basis of her current knowledge and then send a letter confirming their conversation
    B. assure the customer that because she is licensed, there is a presumption that the advice Melanie gives is reliable
    C. refuse to speak to the customer
    D. seek help from a more experienced colleague or other professional before responding to the customer's questions

24. Solicitation of insurance includes
    A. inviting prospective purchasers to enter a contract for an insurance product
    B. making general or specific recommendations concerning insurance products
    C. comparing insurance products, advising on insurance matters, or interpreting policies or coverages
    D. all of the above

2

Principles of Life Insurance

5

Life Insurance Policies

- Categories of Life Insurance
- Term Life Insurance
- Whole Life Insurance
- Endowment Policies
- Special Use Policies
- Nontraditional Life Policies

There are many types of life insurance policies, all of which are designed to serve different needs. This unit will introduce you to these various policies. We will begin by defining the general categories of life insurance coverage and then move to the basic kinds of life insurance plans today's insurers provide. From there, we will focus on special types of policies as well as some of the newer, nontraditional policies. ■

CATEGORIES OF LIFE INSURANCE

Life insurers issue three basic kinds of coverage: **ordinary insurance**, **industrial insurance**, and **group insurance**. Many companies offer all; some companies specialize in one or another. These coverages are distinguished by types of customers, amounts of insurance written, underwriting standards, and marketing practices.

Ordinary Life

Ordinary life insurance is individual life insurance that includes many types of temporary (term) and permanent (whole life, endowment, universal life, variable universal life, and other interest-sensitive cash value plans) insurance protection plans written on individuals with premiums paid monthly, quarterly, semiannually, or annually. Ordinary life insurance is the principal type of life insurance purchased in the United States.

Industrial Insurance

Industrial life insurance is characterized by comparatively small issue amounts, such as $1,000, with premiums collected on a weekly or monthly basis by the agent at the policyowner's home. Quite often it is marketed and purchased as burial insurance.

Years ago, industrial life insurance accounted for a significant amount of life insurance in force. Today, however, this amount has fallen to less than 1%. The decline has been due, in part, to rising incomes, increased awareness of the need for adequate life insurance, and the expansion of employer-provided group life insurance.

Group Insurance

Group life insurance is written for employer-employee groups, associations, unions, and creditors to provide coverage for a number of individuals under one contract. Underwriting is based on the group, not the individuals who are insured. Group insurance, which has grown tremendously over the past few decades, will be discussed in detail in Unit 10.

Keep in mind that the coverages previously described are general categories of insurance. Let's turn our attention now to the various life insurance plans: **term**, **whole life** (or **permanent**), and **endowment**.

TERM LIFE INSURANCE

Term life insurance is the simplest type of life insurance plan. It provides insurance protection for a specified period (or term) and pays a benefit only if the insured dies during that period. For example, assume Harry purchases a five-year $50,000 level term policy on his life, naming his sister, Joan, the beneficiary. If Harry dies at any time within the policy's five-year period, Joan will receive the $50,000 death benefit. If Harry lives beyond that period, nothing is payable. The policy's term has expired. If Harry cancels or lapses the policy during the five-year term, nothing is payable: there are no cash values in term policies.

Term life is also called temporary life insurance since it provides protection for a temporary period of time.

The period for which these policies are issued can be defined in terms of years (1-year term, 5-year term, or 20-year term, for example) or in terms of age (term to age 45, term to age 55, term to age 70, for example). Term policies issued for a specified number of years provide coverage from their issue date until the end of the years so specified. Term policies issued until a certain age provide coverage from their date of issue until the insured reaches the specified age.

Basic Forms of Term Life

There are a number of forms of term life insurance that insurers offer. These forms, distinguished primarily by the amount of benefit payable, are known generally as **level term**, **decreasing term**, and **increasing term**.

Level Term Insurance

Level term insurance provides a level amount of protection for a specified period, after which the policy expires. A $100,000 10-year level term policy, for example, provides a straight, level $100,000 of coverage for a period of 10 years. A $250,000 term to age 65 policy provides a straight $250,000 of coverage until the insured reaches age 65. If the insured under the $100,000 policy dies at any time within those 10 years, or if the insured under the $250,000 policy dies prior to age 65, the insured's beneficiaries will receive the policy's face amount benefits. If the insured lives beyond the 10-year period or past age 65, the policies expire and no benefits are payable.

ILLUSTRATION 5.1

Level Term Insurance

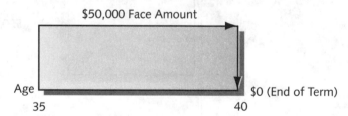

The term insurance plan illustrated is a $50,000 five-year level term policy. The insured has a level $50,000 worth of coverage for a period of five years, after which the policy—and its benefits—expire.

Decreasing Term Insurance

Decreasing term policies are characterized by benefit amounts that decrease gradually over the term of protection. A 20-year $50,000 decreasing term policy, for instance, will pay a death benefit of $50,000 at the beginning of the policy term; that amount gradually declines over the 20-year term and reaches $0 at the end of the term.

Decreasing term insurance is best used when the need for protection declines from year to year. For example, a family breadwinner who has a $100,000 30-year mortgage could purchase decreasing term mortgage insurance that would retire the mortgage balance should the breadwinner die during the 30-year mortgage paying period. Credit life insurance, sold to cover the outstanding balance on a loan, is also based on decreasing term.

Increasing Term Insurance

Increasing term insurance is term insurance that provides a death benefit that increases at periodic intervals over the policy's term. The amount of increase is usually stated as specific amounts or as a percentage of the original amount. Or it may be tied to a cost of living index, such as the Consumer Price Index. Increasing term insurance may be sold as a separate policy; however, it is usually purchased as a **cost of living rider** to a policy. (See "Cost of Living Rider," Unit 6.)

Features of Term Life

Though term policies are issued for a specified period, defined in terms of years or age, most contain two options that can extend the coverage period, if the policyowner desires. These are the **option to renew** and the **option to convert** the policy.

ILLUSTRATION 5.2

Level Term Versus Decreasing Term

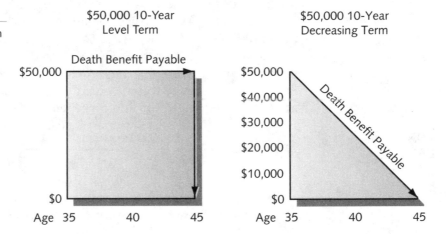

A level term policy provides a straight, level benefit amount over the entire term of the policy. A decreasing term policy pays a gradually decreasing benefit over the term of the policy.

Option to Renew

A **guaranteed renewable policy** allows the policyowner to renew the term policy before its termination date, without having to provide evidence of insurability (that is, without having to prove good health). For example, a five-year renewable term policy permits the policyowner to renew the same coverage for another five years at the end of the first five-year term. The premiums for the renewal period will be higher than the initial period, reflecting the insurer's increased risk (see "Term Life Premiums" later in this unit). Renewal options with most term policies typically provide for several renewal periods or for renewals until a specified age. The advantage of the renewal option is that it allows the insured to continue insurance protection, even if the insured has become uninsurable.

A common type of renewable term insurance is **annually renewable term (ART)**—also called **yearly renewable term**, or YRT. Essentially, this type of policy represents the most basic form of life insurance. It provides coverage for one year and allows the policyowner to renew coverage each year, without evidence of insurability. Again, most insurers limit the number of times such a policy can be renewed or specify an age limit. However, it is not uncommon for ART policies to be renewable to age 65 or beyond.

Some renewable term plans offer a *re-entry option*. With reentry term policies, the policyowner is guaranteed, at the end of the term, to be able to renew coverage without evidence of insurability, at a premium rate specified in the policy. However, this policy also provides that, at periodic intervals, the insured may submit evidence of insurability and, if found acceptable by the insurer, qualify for renewed protection at a rate lower than what the contract states.

Option to Convert

The second option common to most term plans is the **option to convert.** The option to convert gives the insured the right to convert or exchange the term policy for a whole life (or permanent) plan without evidence of insurability. This exchange involves the issuance of a whole life policy at a premium rate reflecting the insured's age at either the time of the exchange (the **attained age method**) or at the time when the original term policy was taken out (the **original age method**). For example, if Sharon was 35 years old when she converted her term policy to whole life insurance, and she paid the whole life premium for age 35, she converted at her attained age. But if Sharon was 30 years old when her term policy was issued and, at age 35, she converted to whole life insurance at the age-30 premium rate, she made the conversion on the basis of her original age.

If a conversion is made on the original age basis, the premium for the new policy will naturally be lower. However, the policyowner may have to pay an additional amount to make up the difference between the term and permanent insurance from the date of the term policy's original issue to the time of conversion. By paying the difference, the policyowner enjoys a lower premium and builds cash values more rapidly in the new policy than if conversion had been at the attained age.

The option to convert generally specifies a time limit for converting, such as 10 years in force or at age 55, whichever is later.

The option to convert and the option to renew can be (and typically are) combined into a single term policy. For instance, a 10-year convertible renewable policy could provide for renewals until age 65 and be convertible any time prior to age 55.

Term Life Premiums

Though a detailed discussion of premiums appears in Unit 8, a simplified introduction is appropriate here. To begin, understand that the amount of premium any insurance plan entails reflects, in part, the degree of risk the insurer accepts when it issues a policy. With life insurance, age is a significant risk factor: the higher the age, the more likely the death. Consider two males, one age 25, the other age 55. Both make an application to purchase a 10-year $50,000 term policy. Statistically speaking, it's more likely that the 55-year-old man will die within the 10-year period than the 25-year-old; consequently, it's more likely that the insurance company will pay benefits on the older man's policy than the younger man's. Due to this increased risk (and assuming all other factors are equal), the 55-year-old will pay a higher premium for his protection than will the 25-year-old.

Because the probability of death increases with age, premiums also increase gradually with age. At older ages, this increase becomes quite sharp, reflecting the higher death rates at advanced ages. Few people could afford the premium rates that would be charged at higher ages; therefore, insurance companies offer term insurance plans on a *level-premium basis*—premiums are calculated and charged so that they remain level throughout the policy's term period. If the policy is renewed, the premium is adjusted upward, reflecting a higher rate for the increased age and will remain level at that amount for the duration of the renewed term. The phrase used to describe this method of premium payments is **step-rate**.

ILLUSTRATION 5.3

Level Term Premium Versus Renewable Term Premium

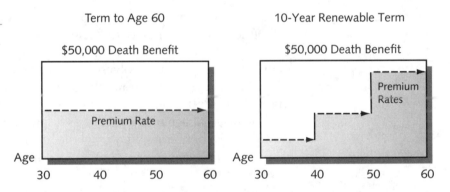

A term to age 60 policy, issued at the insured's age 30, has premiums that are fixed and level over the 30-year term period. A 10-year renewable policy, issued at the insured's age 30, will have premium increases at each of the renewal periods.

If you picture a staircase, the first step represents the premium amount payable for the initial term; at the end of the term, the premium "steps up" to a higher amount for the second term and remains at that level until the second term expires, and so on.[1] (See Illustration 5.3.)

Term policies that include the option to renew, the option to convert, or both will carry a higher premium than those policies that do not have these features.

---

1   An exception to the level premium approach is **deposit term insurance**. This type of term policy requires a premium payment in the first year that is much higher than the level premiums required in the second and subsequent years. At the end of the policy's term, the policyowner receives some of the premium back; the amount returned is typically a multiple of the difference between the higher first-year premium and the lower second-year premium. Deposit term insurance accounts for a very small percentage of the term insurance sold today.

WHOLE LIFE INSURANCE

A second type of life insurance plan is **whole life insurance** (also known as permanent or cash value insurance). Whole life insurance is so called because it provides permanent protection for the whole of life—from the date of issue to the date of the insured's death, provided premiums are paid. The benefit payable is the face amount of the policy, which remains constant throughout the policy's life. Premiums are set at the time of policy issue, and they too remain level for the policy's life.

Features of Whole Life

In addition to its permanence, there are certain other features of whole life insurance that distinguish it from term insurance: cash values and maturity at age 100. These two features combine to produce living benefits to the policyowner.

Cash Values

Unlike term insurance, which provides only death protection, whole life insurance combines insurance protection with a savings or accumulation element. This accumulation, commonly referred to as the policy's **cash value**, builds over the life of the policy. This is because whole life insurance plans are credited with a certain guaranteed rate of interest; this interest is credited to the policy on a regular basis and grows over time.

Though it is an important part of funding the policy, the cash value is often regarded as a savings element because it represents the amount of money the policyowner will receive if the policy is ever cancelled. It is often called the **cash surrender value**. This value is a result of the way premiums are calculated and interest is paid, as well as the policy reserves that build under this system.

The amount of a policy's cash value depends on a variety of factors, including:

■ the face amount of the policy;

■ the duration and amount of the premium payments; and

■ how long the policy has been in force.

Generally speaking, the larger the face amount of the policy, the larger the cash values; the shorter the premium-payment period, the quicker the cash values grow; and the longer the policy has been in force, the greater the build-up in cash values. The reason for these things can be clarified with an understanding of the maturity of a whole life policy.

Maturity at Age 100

Whole life insurance is designed to mature at age 100. The significance of age 100 is that, as an actuarial assumption, every insured is presumed to be dead by then. (While some people live beyond age 100, the number of people who do live that long is not a statistically significant portion of the population.) Consequently, the premium rate for whole life insurance is based on the assumption that the policyowner (usually the insured) will be paying premiums for the whole of life, to the insured's age 100. At age 100, the cash value of the policy has accumulated to the point that it equals the face amount of the policy, as it was actuarially designed to do. At that point, the policy has completely matured or endowed. No more premiums are owed; the policy is completely paid up.

For those lucky insureds who live to age 100, the insurance company will issue checks for the full value of their policies. At that point, the policy expires; the contract has been completed. Thus, when whole life is defined as a policy that provides a death benefit "whenever death occurs," some qualification is required. Whole life insurance provides a death benefit if death occurs before age 100; if the insured has not died by age 100, the full maturity value of the policy is paid out to the policyowner (usually the insured) or a beneficiary as a living benefit and the policy terminates. In either event, age 100 defines the point at which the cash value of the policy equals the face amount (or death benefit amount) of the policy. (See Illustration 5.4.)

Practically speaking, very few people live to age 100. It's far more likely that a whole life policy will be cashed in for its surrender value or that its face amount will be paid out as a death benefit prior to maturity.

ILLUSTRATION 5.4

Whole Life Insurance

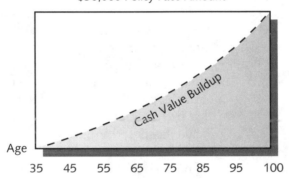

$50,000 Policy Face Amount

At the insured's age 100, the cash value of a whole life policy equals the face amount and will be paid to the policyowner (usually the insured) or a beneficiary as a "living benefit," if the beneficiary is still living.

Living Benefits

Another unique feature of whole life insurance is the **living benefits** it can provide. Through the cash value accumulation build-up in the policy, a policyowner has a ready source of funds that may be borrowed at reasonable rates of interest. These funds may be used for a personal or business emergency; for example, they could be used to help pay for a child's education or to pay off a mortgage. It is not a requirement of the policy that the loan be repaid. However, if a loan is outstanding at the time the insured dies, the amount of the loan plus any interest due will be subtracted from the death benefit before it is paid. Indeed, policy loans are more like benefit advances than loans.

In addition, because life insurance is considered property with a quantifiable cash value, it may be used as collateral or security for loans. Also, the policyowner may draw on the cash value to supplement retirement income.

Cash values belong to the policyowner. The insurance company cannot lay claim to these values. This concept is discussed in more detail in Unit 6, under "Nonforfeiture Values."

Whole Life Premiums

As noted, whole life is actuarially designed as if the insured will live to age 100. Accordingly, the amount of premium for a whole life policy is calculated, in part, on the basis of the number of years between the insured's age at issue and age 100. This time span represents the full premium-paying period, with the amount of the premium spread equally over that period. This is known as the **level premium approach**. As is the case with level premium term insurance, this approach allows whole life insurance premiums to remain level rather than increase each year with the insured's age. To put it simply, the premium amount is calculated so that in the early years it is more than necessary to meet anticipated claims and expenses and is less than adequate in the later years when the claims will likely be paid. The balanced result is a level amount payable over the entire period.

Basic Forms of Whole Life

Just because whole life premiums are calculated as if they were payable to age 100, they do not necessarily have to be paid this way. Whole life is flexible and a number of policy types have been developed to accommodate different premium-paying periods. Three notable forms of whole life plans are **straight whole life**, **limited pay whole life**, and **single-premium whole life**.

Straight Whole Life

Straight whole life is whole life insurance providing permanent level protection with level premiums from the time the policy is issued until the insured's death (or age 100).

Limited Pay Whole Life

Limited pay whole life policies have level premiums that are limited to a certain period (less than life). This period can be of any duration. For example, a 20-pay life policy is one in which premiums are payable for 20 years from the policy's inception, after which no more premiums are owed. A life paid-up at 65 policy is one in which the premiums are payable to the insured's age 65, after which no more premiums are owed.

The names of the policies denote how long the premiums are payable. For example, a 30-year-old applicant who purchases a life paid-up at 65 policy will pay premiums for 35 years and then have a paid-up policy. If the same applicant buys a "20-pay life" policy, the applicant will pay premiums for 20 years and have a paid-up policy at age 50.

Keep in mind that even though the premium payments are limited to a certain period, the insurance protection extends until the insured's death, whenever that may be, or to age 100.

Single-Premium Whole Life

The most extreme form of limited pay policies is a single-premium policy. A **single-premium whole life** policy involves a large one-time-only premium payment at the beginning of the policy period. From that point, the policy is completely paid for.

Premium Periods

The shorter the premium-paying period, the higher the premium. It's the same principle that applies when a person purchases an item on a credit installment plan—the shorter the payment period, the higher each payment will be. As Illustration 5.5 shows, the premium rates at age 35 for a 20-pay life policy are over one and a half times those for a straight life policy, per $1,000 of insurance coverage. This is because the 20-pay life policy has a premium-paying period of 20 years, while the straight life policy assumes a premium-paying period of 65 years, or until age 100.

ILLUSTRATION 5.5

Premium Rate per $1,000 of Insurance

Issue Age	One-Year Term	Straight Whole Life	Life Paid-up at 65	20-Pay Life
35	$1.35	$16.29	$21.07	$26.00
45	$3.10	$23.17	$32.16	$32.16
55	$12.68	$36.44	$70.01	$50.12

The length of the premium-paying period also affects the growth of the policy's cash values. The shorter the premium-paying period (and consequently, the higher the premium), the quicker the cash values grow. This is because a greater percentage of each payment is credited to the policy's cash values. By the same token, the longer the premium-paying period, the slower the cash values grow. Illustration 5.6 shows how the cash values grow in a 20-pay, a 30-pay, and a straight whole life policy.

As this illustration also shows, the cash values build up in the limited pay policies faster during the premium-paying years than during the non-premium-paying years. After the premium-paying period, the cash values continue to grow, but more slowly, until the policy matures and the cash value equals the face amount, again, at age 100.

ILLUSTRATION 5.6

How Cash Values Grow

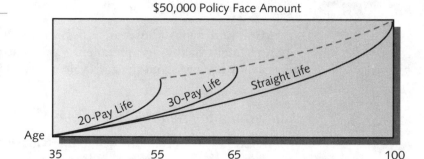

The diagonal lines represent increasing cash values. These are shown as solid lines during the premium-paying period and as a dotted line thereafter.

It should be noted that life insurance policies must meet certain statutory definitions and tests, which are primarily aimed at limited pay policies and single-premium policies.

These rules are explained in a later section of this unit, titled "Modified Endowment Contracts."

Other Forms of Whole Life

There are many other forms of whole life insurance, most of which are characterized by some variation in the way the premium is paid. Let's review these policies next.

Modified Whole Life

Modified whole life policies are distinguished by premiums that are lower than typical whole life premiums during the first few years (usually five) and then higher than typical thereafter. During the initial period, the premium rate is only slightly higher than that of term insurance. Afterwards, the premium is higher than the typical whole life rate at age of issue.

The purpose of modified whole life policies is to make the initial purchase of permanent insurance easier and more attractive, especially for individuals who have limited financial resources, but the promise of an improved financial position in the future. Actuarially, the premiums are equivalent to standard whole life policies.

Graded Premium Whole Life

Similar to modified whole life, **graded premium policies** also redistribute the premiums. Premiums are lower than typical whole life rates during the preliminary period following issue (usually five to ten years) and increase each year until leveling off after the preliminary period. Again, the premium rates are actuarially equivalent to standard whole life.

Minimum Deposit Whole Life

Minimum deposit insurance begins building cash values immediately upon payment of the first premium. From that point, the policyowner systematically borrows from the cash value to pay some or all of the premium.

Indeterminate Premium Whole Life

Indeterminate premium whole life policies are those in which the premium rate can be adjusted based on the insurance company's anticipated future experience. The maximum premium that the insurer can charge is stated in the contract, though the premium payable at issue is much lower and is fixed at the lower rate for a specified initial period (typically two to three years). After the initial period, and based on the company's expected mortality, expense, and investment projections, the premium may be raised, kept the same, or lowered.

Indexed Whole Life

The face amount of **indexed whole life insurance** automatically increases as the Consumer Price Index (CPI) increases. Two basic pricing methods are used with this type of policy:

■ the policyowner assumes the risk of future increases and thus must pay additional premium with each face amount increase; or

■ the insurer assumes the risk and thus the policyowner does not pay a higher premium with face amount increases.

Regardless of the method used, the policyowner is not required to furnish evidence of insurability to obtain the face amount increase.

ENDOWMENT POLICIES

Besides term and whole life insurance, life insurers also issue **endowment policies**. An endowment policy is characterized by cash values that grow at a rapid pace so that the policy matures or endows at a specified date (that is, before age 100). An endowment policy provides benefits in one of two ways:

■ as a death benefit to a beneficiary if the insured dies within the specified policy period (known as the **endowment period**); or

■ as a living benefit to the policyowner if the insured is alive at the end of the endowment period, at which time the policy has fully matured.

Because an endowment policy pays a death benefit if the insured dies during a certain period, it can be compared to level term insurance. The new concept presented here is that of **pure endowment**. Pure endowment insurance is a contract that guarantees a specified sum payable only if the insured is living at the end of a stated time period—nothing is payable in the case of prior death. These two elements—level term insurance and endowment—together provide the guarantees endowment contracts offer.

Endowment policies can be compared to whole life policies with accelerated maturity dates; age 65 is a common maturity age. At the maturity age, the cash value has grown to match the face amount, just like what occurs at age 100 with a whole life policy.

Illustration 5.7 shows some of the more common endowment policies insurers offer. The name of each policy indicates how long premiums are payable, how long the insurance lasts, and when the policy endows. A 20-year endowment policy, for example, calls for premiums to be paid for 20 years. During this period, the insured will have insurance protection. If the insured lives for 20 years and the policy remains in force, the policy will endow and the company will pay the policyowner the full face amount.

ILLUSTRATION 5.7

Types of Endowment Policies

Description	Type of Policy
These policies will all endow for the face amount at the end of the premium-paying period. That is, premiums are paid to the time of endowment.	10-Year Endowment 20-Year Endowment 25-Year Endowment 30-Year Endowment Endowment at Age 55 Endowment at Age 60 Endowment at Age 65
In these policies, the premium payments are completed before the time of endowment. After premiums stop, the cash value increases from interest earnings and equals the face amount at the time of endowment. Insurance protection extends to the time of endowment.	20-Pay Endowment at Age 60 20-Pay Endowment at Age 65 Single Premium Endowment

Because they are designed to build cash values quickly, endowment policies are typically purchased to provide a living benefit for a specified future time—for retirement, for example, or to fund a child's college education.

Endowment Premiums

Due to their rapid cash value build-ups to provide early policy maturity, endowment policies have comparatively high premiums. Remember that the shorter the policy term, the higher the premiums. Illustration 5.8 shows some typical premium costs for a 20-year endowment and an endowment at age 65, issued at various ages. Compare these premium costs to those shown for term and whole life policies in Illustration 5.5.

ILLUSTRATION 5.8

Premium Rates per $1,000 of
Endowment Insurance

Issue Age	Endowment at Age 65	20-Year Endowment
20	$15.20	$43.59
30	$22.35	$44.03
40	$36.14	$45.74

It should be noted that the purchase of endowment policies has been on the decline for several years. This is because they no longer meet the income tax definition of "life insurance," and consequently, they no longer qualify for the favorable tax treatment life insurance is given. Essentially, the Tax Code specifies that life insurance products cannot endow before age 95. Because one objective of endowment policies is to provide a living benefit by building an endowment fund for a definite future objective (presumably before the insured reaches age 95), they generally do not qualify as life insurance. Though a number of endowment policies are still in force today, very few new policies are being sold.

Modified Endowment Contracts

In 1988, Congress enacted the Technical and Miscellaneous Revenue Act, commonly referred to as TAMRA. Among other things, this act revised the tax law definition of a "life insurance contract," primarily to discourage the sale and purchase of life insurance for investment purposes or as a tax shelter. By redefining life insurance, Congress effectively created a new *class* of insurance, known as **modified endowment contracts**, or MECs.

For the producer who sells life insurance and for the consumer who purchases life insurance, the significance of this is the way a life policy, if it is deemed an MEC, will be taxed. Historically, life insurance has been granted very favorable tax treatment, as showing in the following.

■ Cash value accumulations are not taxed to the policyowner as they build inside a policy.

■ Policy withdrawals are not taxed to the policyowner until the amount withdrawn exceeds the total amount the policyowner paid into the contract.

■ Policy loans are not considered distributions and are not taxed to the policyowner unless or until a full policy surrender takes place, and then, only to the extent that the distribution exceeds what was paid into the policy.

However, for those policies that do not meet the specific test (described below) and consequently are considered MECs, the tax treatment is different—and it is the policyowners who pay.

If a policy is deemed an MEC and the policyowner receives any amount from it in the form of a loan or withdrawal, that amount will be taxed first as ordinary income and second as return of premium, if there is any gain in the contract over premiums paid. There may also be a 10% penalty tax imposed on these amounts if they are received before the policyowner's age 59½.

How does a life insurance policy become an MEC? More importantly, how does a policy avoid being classified as an MEC? It must meet what is known as the **7-pay test**. This test states that if the total amount a policyowner pays into a life contract during its first years *exceeds* the sum of the net level premiums that would have been payable to provide paid-up future benefits in seven years, the policy is an MEC. And once a policy is classified as an MEC—which it can be at any time during the first seven years—it will remain so throughout its duration.

Let's look at a very simple example. Suppose a policyowner purchased a $100,000 seven-year limited pay whole life policy. The scheduled premiums are $7,500 a year, payable for seven years. At the end of that period, the policy will be completely paid up. The first year, the policyowner pays $7,500. The second year, the policyowner pays $8,000. At that point, the policy would become an MEC because the policyowner paid more into the policy than the net level premiums required to provide paid-up benefits in seven years. From that point on, any withdrawals or loans the policyowner takes from that policy will be taxed as income, to the extent there is gain in the policy.

Now let's assume that this policyowner paid $7,500 in the first year and $7,000 in the second year. In the third year, the policyowner can make an $8,000 payment and not run afoul of the 7-pay test—the policyowner is still within the guidelines of the sum of the net level premiums payable. However, if that sum total limit is ever exceeded in those first seven years, the policy will become an MEC.

Making sure that policies meet the definition of life insurance and comply with the 7-pay test is the responsibility of insurers and their actuaries. Agents do not have the time or resources; consumers do not have the knowledge or understanding. However, because the potential for misuse—or even abuse—exists with single-pay, limited pay, and universal life policies, and because consumers may be lured into purchasing insurance for its tax benefits instead of its protection guarantees, producers must be alert to this law and its implications.

SPECIAL USE POLICIES

In addition to the basic types of life insurance policies—term, whole life and endowment—there are a number of "special use" policies insurers offer. Many of these are a combination or "packaging" of different policy types, designed to serve a variety of needs.

Family Plan Policies

The **family plan policy** is designed to insure all family members under one policy. Coverage is sold in units. A typical plan would insure the family breadwinner for, say, $10,000 or $15,000, the spouse for $3,000, and each child for $1,000. Usually the insurance covering the family head is permanent insurance; that covering the spouse and children is level or decreasing term. These plans generally cover all children presently in the family within certain age limits—for example, older than 14 days and younger than 21. Children who are born later are covered automatically at no extra premium. The children's coverage is usually convertible without evidence of insurability.

Multiple Protection Policies

A **multiple protection policy** pays a benefit of double or triple the face amount if death occurs during a specified period. If death occurs after the period has expired, only the policy face amount is paid. The period may be for a specified number of years—10, 15, or 20, for example—or to a specified age, such as 65. These policies are combinations of permanent insurance and, for the multiple protection period, level term insurance.

Joint Life Policies

A **joint life policy** is one policy that covers two or more people. Using some type of permanent insurance (as opposed to term), it pays the death benefit when one of the insureds dies. The survivors then have the option of purchasing a single individual policy without evidence of insurability. The premium for a joint life policy is less than the premium for separate, multiple policies. The ages of the insureds are "averaged" and a single premium is charged for each life.

A variation of the joint life policy is the **last survivor policy**, also known as a "second-to-die" policy. This plan also covers two lives, but the benefit is paid upon the death of the last surviving insured.

Juvenile Insurance

Insurance written on the lives of children (ordinarily age one day to age 14 or 15 years) is called **juvenile insurance**. Application for insurance and ownership of the policy rest with an adult, such as a parent or guardian. The adult applicant is usually the premium-payor as well, until the child comes of age and is able to take over the payments. A **payor provision** is typically attached to juvenile policies. It provides that, in the event of death or disability of the adult premium-payor, the premiums will be waived until the insured child reaches a specified age (such as 25) or until the maturity date of the contract, whichever comes first. (See "Payor Rider," Unit 6.)

A special form of juvenile insurance is the **jumping juvenile** or **junior estate builder** policy. These policies are typically written on children ages 1 to 15 in units of $1,000, which automatically increase to $5,000—or five times the face amount—at age 21. Although the face amount increases automatically, the premium remains the same and no evidence of insurability is required.

Note that some states limit the amount of life insurance that can be written on a child at the early ages. They do so by specifying a maximum that can be in force on a child's life during the child's early years, such as up to 5, 10, or 15 years old.

Credit Life Insurance

Credit life insurance is designed to cover the life of a debtor and pay the amount due on a loan if the debtor dies before the loan is repaid. The beneficiary of such a policy is usually the lender. The type of insurance used is decreasing term, with the term matched to the length of the loan period (though usually limited to 10 years or less) and the decreasing insurance amount matched to the declining loan balance.

Credit life is sometimes issued to individuals as single policies, but most often it is sold to a bank or other lending institution as group insurance that covers all of the institution's borrowers. (See "Group Life Insurance," Unit 10.)

NONTRADITIONAL LIFE POLICIES

In the 1980s, insurance companies introduced a number of new policy forms, most of which are more flexible in design and provisions than their traditional counterparts. The most notable of these are interest-sensitive whole life, **adjustable life, universal life, variable life**, and **variable universal life**.

Interest-Sensitive Whole Life

Also known as **current-assumption whole life**, this policy is characterized by premiums that vary to reflect the insurer's changing assumptions with regard to its death, investment, and expense factors. In this respect, it is similar to indeterminate premium whole life. However, interest-sensitive products also provide that the cash values may be greater than the guaranteed levels, if the company's underlying death, investment, and expense assumptions are more favorable than expected. In this way, policyowners have two options: lower premiums or higher cash values.

If underlying assumptions turn out to be less favorable than anticipated, which otherwise would call for a higher premium than that at policy issue, the policyowner may either pay the higher premium or choose to reduce the policy's face amount and continue to pay the same premium.

Adjustable Life

Adjustable life policies are distinguished by their flexibility that comes from combining term and permanent insurance into a single plan. The policyowner determines how much face amount protection is needed and how much premium the policyowner wants to pay. The insurer then selects the appropriate plan to meet those needs. Or the policyowner may specify a desired plan and face amount, and the insurer will calculate the appropriate premium. As financial needs and objectives change, the policyowner can make adjustments to the coverage, such as:

- increasing or decreasing the premium, the premium-paying period, or both; or

- increasing or decreasing the face amount, the period of protection, or both.

Consequently, depending on the desired changes, the policy can be converted from term to whole life or from whole life to term, or from a high premium contract to a lower premium or limited pay contract.

Most adjustable life policies contain limits that restrict the changes in face amounts or premium payments to specified minimums and maximums. Typically, increases in the face amounts on these policies require evidence of insurability. Moreover, due to its design and flexibility, adjustable life is usually more expensive than conventional term or whole life policies.

Universal Life

Universal life is a variation of whole life insurance, characterized by considerable flexibility. Unlike whole life, with its fixed premiums, fixed face amounts, and fixed cash value accumulations, universal life allows its policyowners to determine the amount and frequency of premium payments and to adjust the policy face amount up or down to reflect changes in needs. Consequently, no new policy need be issued when changes are desired.

Universal life provides this flexibility by "unbundling" or separating the basic components of a life insurance policy—the insurance (protection) element, the savings (accumulation) element, and the expense (loading) element. As with any other life policy, the policyowner pays a premium. Each month, a mortality charge is deducted from the policy's cash value account for the cost of the insurance protection. This mortality charge may also include an expense, or loading, charge.

Like term insurance premiums, the universal life mortality charge steadily increases with age. Actually, universal life is technically defined as term insurance with a policy value fund. Even though the policyowner may pay a level premium, an increasing share of that premium goes to pay the mortality charge as the insured ages.

As premiums are paid and as cash values accumulate, interest is credited to the policy's cash value. This interest may be either the **current interest rate**, declared by the company (and dependent on current market conditions) or the **guaranteed minimum rate**, specified in the contract. As long as the cash value account is sufficient to pay the monthly mortality and expense costs, the policy will continue in force, whether or not the policyowner pays the premium. Of course, premium payments must be large enough and frequent enough to generate sufficient cash values. If the cash value account is not large enough to support the monthly deductions, the policy terminates.

A specific percentage of all premiums must be used to purchase death benefits or the universal life policy will not receive favorable tax treatment on its cash value.

At stated intervals (and usually upon providing evidence of insurability), the policyowner can increase the face amount of the policy. Or a decrease in face amount can be requested. A corresponding increase (or decrease) in premium payment is not required, again as long as the cash values can cover the mortality and expense costs. By the same token, the policyowner can elect to pay more into the policy, thus adding to the cash value account, subject to certain guidelines that control the relationship between the cash values and the policy's face amount.

ILLUSTRATION 5.9

Universal Life Death Benefit
Options

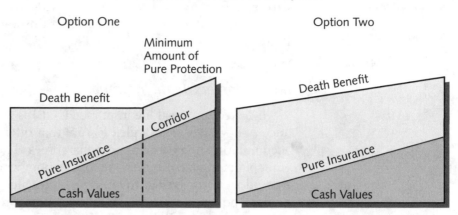

Universal Life Death Benefit Options

Another factor that distinguishes universal life from whole life is the fact that **partial withdrawals** can be made from the policy's cash value account. (Whole life insurance allows a policyowner to tap cash values only through a policy loan or a complete cash surrender of the policy's cash values, in which case the policy terminates.) Also, the policyowner may surrender the universal life policy for its entire cash value at any time. However, the company probably will assess a surrender charge unless the policy has been in force for a certain number of years.

Universal life has other features in common with traditional cash value insurance policies, including an accidental death benefits rider that provides a multiple of the death proceeds (i.e., "double indemnity") if the cause of death is a covered accidental event, an accelerated benefit rider that pays a portion of the death benefit if the insured person is diagnosed with a terminal illness, a no-lapse guarantee rider that guarantees a death benefit for life so the insured is covered even if premium payments lapse or fall behind, an additional insured rider that provides a death benefit on the lives of family members, a children's insurance rider that extends a death benefit to the insured's child up to age 25, and more.

UL Death Benefit Options

Universal life insurance offers two death benefit options. Under **Option One**, the policyowner may designate a specified amount of insurance. The death benefit equals the cash values plus the remaining pure insurance (decreasing term plus increasing cash values). This level death benefit is composed of the increasing cash values and the remaining pure insurance (decreasing term). If the growing cash value-to-total death benefit ratio exceeds a certain percentage fixed by federal law, an additional amount of pure insurance, called the "corridor," is added to maintain the minimum death benefit requirement. (Illustration 5.9 illustrates Option One.)

Under **Option Two**, the death benefit equals the face amount (pure insurance) plus the cash values (level term plus increasing cash values). To comply with the Tax Code's definition of life insurance, the cash values cannot be disproportionately larger than the term insurance portion. (Illustration 5.9 illustrates Option Two.)

Index Universal Life Insurance

Indexed universal life insurance (IUL) is an indexed universal life insurance policy offering an index feature that offers the potential for cash value accumulation and basic interest guarantees. These features help the policyowner plan for family security and offer a number of interest crediting strategies that allow the potential to build up cash value in the policy. These choices give the policyowner more flexibility as compared to traditional universal life insurance policies. Policy cash value can be transferred from a fixed account that offers traditional fixed interest rates to an indexed account. The indexed account uses an outside index like the Standard & Poor's 500 Index or the Nasdaq-100 Index in the calculation of interest credits. Although the impact of negative index returns is limited by a growth floor (typically 0% to 2%), the maximum interest crediting rate for an IUL policy is limited by a growth cap. The cap varies among insurers from 7% to 12%. Each index is made up of different companies and measures a slightly different mix of industries. The policyowner should examine and select the index account that meets the policyowner's overall objectives.

Variable Insurance Products

Introduced in the 1970s, **variable insurance product**s added a new dimension to life insurance: the opportunity for policyowners to achieve higher-than-usual investment returns on their policy cash values by accepting the risk of the policy's performance. This concept is best explained by a comparison to traditional whole life plans.

Under traditional whole life insurance policies, the insurer *guarantees* a certain minimum rate of return will be credited to the policies' cash values. This is accomplished because the insurer invests the policyowner's premiums in its **general account**—an investment account that is composed of investments that are carefully selected to match the liabilities and guarantees of the contracts they back. (These investments are usually quite conservative: US government securities and investment-grade bonds are common.) Actually, the premiums paid for life insurance are not, in and of themselves, sufficient to cover the benefits promised in the contract. Rather, they will be sufficient *only* if the insurer can earn a certain interest rate on the invested values. This makes earnings of crucial importance; the insurer is bound to provide the contractually guaranteed values and benefits whether or not it earns its assumed rate of return. Consequently, with traditional whole life policies, it is the insurer that bears the investment risk. That is why the guaranteed rate of return for traditional whole life policies is quite conservative—typically 3–5%.

In contrast, variable insurance products do not guarantee contract cash values, and it is the policyowner who assumes the investment risk. Variable life insurance contracts do not make any promises as to either interest rates or minimum cash values. What these products do offer is the potential to realize investment gains that exceed those available with traditional life insurance policies. This is done by allowing policyowners to direct the investment of the funds that back their variable contracts through *separate account* options. By placing their policy values into separate accounts, policyowners can participate directly in the account's investment performance, which will earn a variable (as opposed to a fixed) return. Functioning on much the same principle as mutual funds, the return enjoyed—or loss suffered—by policyowners through their investment in a separate account is directly related to the performance of the assets underlying the separate account. Separate accounts are *not* insured by the insurer and the returns on their investments are *not* guaranteed. For the insurer, this presents a means of transferring the investment risk from itself to the policyowner. The insurer can offer policyowners the *possibility* (though not the *guarantee*) of competitively high returns without facing the investment risk posed by its guaranteed fixed policies.

Because of the transfer of investment risk from the insurer to the policyowner, variable insurance products are considered **securities contracts** as well as insurance contracts. Therefore, they fall under the regulatory arm of both state offices of insurance regulation and the Securities and Exchange Commission (SEC). To sell variable insurance products, an individual must hold a life insurance license and a Financial Industry Regulatory Authority (FINRA) registered representative's license. Some states may also require a special variable insurance license or special addendum to the regular life insurance license. In Florida, agents who have fully satisfied the requirements for a life insurance license, including successful completion of a licensing exam that covers variable annuities, may sell or solicit variable annuity contracts.

ILLUSTRATION 5.10

General Accounts Versus Separate
Accounts

Understanding the distinctions between an insurer's general account and its separate account is key to understanding the differences between traditional guaranteed contracts and variable contracts.

General account assets are used to support the contractual obligations of an insurer's fixed, traditional policies; they represent the general assets of the company. Though they are the foundation of the insurer's policy reserves, they are also subject to the claims of creditors. If an insurer's general account assets ever fail to support its reserve liability, the company is said to be insolvent and the assets become subject to the claims of the company's creditors—including policyowners. To reduce the likelihood of this occurring, insurers typically invest their general account assets in conservative investment instruments.

Separate accounts are just as their name implies: accounts separate from the insurer's general accounts. Separate accounts are maintained solely for the purpose of allowing policyowners to participate directly in the account's investment performance and contract values earn a variable, rather than a fixed, return. Also, because they are separate from the insurer's general account, separate accounts are not subject to the claims of the insurer's general creditors. This means that policyowners cannot lose the physical assets underlying their variable contracts in the event of the company's insolvency (though the assets' value can be "lost" by changes in market conditions). Many consumers today purchase variable contracts for this reason. In addition to being able to participate in the investment performance of the assets underlying their contracts, variable contract holders are assured that their share of those assets will never be compromised, even in the event of company insolvency.

Some contracts have features that seem similar to those of variable contracts, but no separate account is established for them. One relatively new type is equity index contracts. The cash values of an equity index contract are generally designed to follow changes in the stock market. However, such contracts are almost never invested directly in stocks. Although a small proportion of the funds may be invested in stock options or derivatives (i.e., as a hedge), those investments often are done through the general account; the bulk of the assets backing the cash values are usually similar to those for non-indexed products. Equity index contracts often are supported by general account assets, although they may be placed in separate accounts.

Indexed cash values are more commonly used for annuities than life insurance. Some of these contracts are issued with separate accounts, which makes them variable products (i.e., by state law definition). Some insurers have felt a need to set up separate accounts for indexed contracts to comply with SEC rules and Florida law. The SEC has not yet clarified whether this is required.

Because variable insurance policies are securities, full and fair disclosure must be provided to the prospective policyowner. Therefore, by law, a variable insurance sales presentation cannot be conducted unless it is preceded or accompanied by a **prospectus**, prepared and furnished by the insurance company and reviewed by the SEC. A prospectus contains information about the nature and purpose of the insurance plan, the separate account, and the risk involved. It is a significant source of information for the prospect. Also, all other materials used in selling and promoting variable insurance products—direct mail letters, brochures, advertising pieces—must also have prior approval of the SEC. These requirements provide consumer protection and promote meaningful communication between agents and consumers.

With this introduction in mind, let's look at two types of variable insurance products: **variable life insurance** and **variable universal life insurance**.

Keep in mind that while these policies involve investment management and offer the potential for investment gains, they are primarily life insurance policies, not investment contracts. The primary purpose of these plans, like any life insurance plan, is to provide financial protection in the event of the insured's death.

Variable Life Insurance

Variable life insurance is permanent life insurance with many of the same characteristics of traditional whole life insurance. The main difference, as explained above, is the manner in which the policy's values are invested. With traditional whole life, these values are kept in the insurer's **general accounts** and invested in conservative investments selected by the insurer to match its contractual guarantees and liabilities. With variable life insurance policies, the policy values are invested in the insurer's **separate accounts** which house common stock, bond, money-market, and other securities investment options. Values held in these separate accounts are invested in riskier, but potentially higher-yielding, assets than those held in the general account.

As with any permanent insurance product, the growth of the policy's cash values support the death benefit. In traditional whole life products, that benefit is fixed and guaranteed; with variable life insurance, the benefit rises (and falls) in relation to the performance of the policy's values. There is a minimum guaranteed death benefit; this is equal to the face amount at policy issue and is based on an assumed rate of return, usually 3–4%. However, if the separate account growth (and by extension, the cash value growth) exceeds this assumed rate, the result is an elevated death benefit.

Illustration 5.11 shows the effect over time of increases—and decreases—in a variable life insurance policy's separate account rate of return. Each year that the actual return *exceeds* the assumed rate of return (shown in this example as 4%), there is a positive net investment return and the death benefit is increased. In years where the actual return or growth is less than the assumed, the effect is to decrease the death benefit from any previously attained levels. Note, however, that the death benefit will never drop below the face amount guaranteed at policy issue.

Like traditional whole life insurance, variable life insurance requires the payment of set premiums on a scheduled basis. Failure to make these premium payments results in policy lapse.

Variable life insurance policyowners can access their policy values through policy loans. However, the amount of the loan is limited—usually 75–80% of the cash value. (Compare this to conventional whole life policies which typically permit loans up to 100% of the cash value.) The reason for this restriction is to reduce the possibility that falling returns will cause an outstanding policy loan to become greater than the policy's cash value.

ILLUSTRATION 5.11

Variable Life Death Benefit

The following graph shows how the investment performance of a variable life insurance policy's values affect the death benefit. Here, the assumed rate of return is 4%. If the net investment results were equal to 4% throughout the life of the policy, the death benefit would remain the same—that is, the face amount of the policy at issue. However, as is more likely, the actual investment results will vary. A return greater than 4% produces a rise in the death benefit; a return less than 4% produces a drop in the death benefit from the previous year.

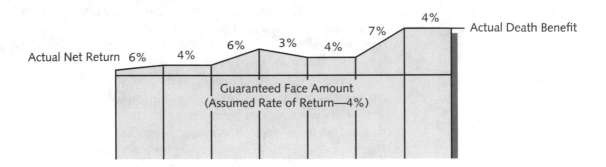

Variable Universal Life

Variable universal life (VUL) is a product that blends many features of whole life, universal life, and variable life. Key among these features are premium flexibility, cash value investment control, and death benefit flexibility. These features give VUL its unique characteristics and make it responsive to policyowners' needs.

Every variable universal life insurance policy is issued with a minimum scheduled premium based on an initial specified death benefit. This initial premium establishes the plan, meets first-year expenses, and provides funding to cover the cost of insurance protection. Once this initial premium has been paid, policyowners can pay whatever premium amount they wish, with certain limitations. Provided adequate cash value is available to cover periodic charges and the cost of insurance, they can suspend or reduce premium payments. Policyowners may even be able to "vanish" their premiums indefinitely if their cash values realize consistently strong investment returns.

Conversely, policyowners wishing to increase death benefits or take advantage of tax-favored accumulation of cash values can pay additional premiums into their plans. However, most policies contain maximum limits, and if the increase is above a certain amount, proof of insurability may be required. These maximum limits are imposed to maintain the corridor between the cash value and the death benefit. This corridor must exist for the policy to qualify as life insurance and retain its tax-sheltered cash value accumulation status.

ILLUSTRATION 5.12

Loan or Withdrawal?

Partial cash value distributions may be classified as "loans" or "withdrawals"; which of the two is chosen depends on several factors.

A **loan** is just that—a loan against one's own money. It is withdrawn with either the presumption that it will be repaid (with accrued interest) or the understanding that by not repaying it the amount of future benefits—including the death benefit—will be reduced by the loaned amount (plus accrued interest).

A **withdrawal** has generally the same impact on policy benefits, but there is no presumption that it will be repaid. The withdrawn amount is treated as a permanent withdrawal, thus immediately reducing the death benefit and, of course, the cash value. The withdrawn amount does not accrue interest against future policy values, as it does with a loan. However, from an actuarial perspective, the impact on future policy values is identical with either approach.

Generally, only universal life and variable universal life policies, with their inherent policy flexibility, permit withdrawals. Traditional whole life and variable life do not lend themselves to this type of flexibility and, though there may be a few exceptions, they typically provide only for loans.

Because cash value withdrawals (versus loans) are recognized as taxable income to the extent they exceed the policyowner's cost basis in the contract, most sizeable withdrawals are technically regarded as "withdrawals" up to the owner's basis; withdrawn amounts above basis are regarded as "loans," which are not taxable. By recognizing withdrawn amounts that exceed basis merely as loans and not permanent withdrawals, this technique defers and possibly avoids income taxation of the full withdrawn amount.

Cash value in a VUL plan is maintained separately from the rest of the plan. At the time of application, the policyowner elects to have the net premiums and cash values allocated to one or more separate account investment options. These accounts are usually mutual funds created and maintained by the insurance company or provided through arrangements between the insurance company and other investment companies. These funds are kept in separate accounts and function independently of the insurance company's assets. Earnings or losses accrue directly to the policyowner's cash value, subject to stated charges and management fees. Policyowners can redirect future premiums and switch accounts periodically, generally once a year, without charge. The result is a life insurance policy that provides policyowners with their own self-directed investment options.

VUL policies generally offer both a **level** death benefit, which provides for a fixed death benefit (until the policy values reach the corridor level) and potential higher cash value accumulation, or a **variable** death benefit, which provides a death benefit that fluctuates in response to the performance of investments.

Under the level death benefit, the policyowner specifies the total death benefit in the policy. This amount remains constant and does not fluctuate as cash values increase or decrease. Instead, cash values build up within the policy until they reach the **corridor**, at which time the death benefit will increase to corresponding increases in the cash value. Until that point is reached, however, the cash value simply accumulates, with each increase replacing a corresponding amount of pure insurance needed to keep the death benefit at the specified amount.

Under the variable death benefit, the policyowner selects a specified amount of pure insurance coverage. This specified amount remains constant. The death benefit payable at any time is a combination of the specified (or face) amount and the cash value within the policy. Essentially, the cash value is added to the specified amount to create the total death benefit. Under this option, the emphasis is on the potential for both cash value and death benefit growth. This option is often recommended for policyowners who want favorable investment results and additional premiums reflected directly in increased death benefits.

Like universal life, VUL policies permit partial withdrawals, allowing the owner to tap the cash value without incurring any indebtedness. Policyowners don't have to repay those funds, and no interest is incurred on the amount withdrawn. Withdrawals, of course, affect the policy's future earnings, and their effect on the death benefit depends on the death benefit option in force. Partial withdrawals taken in a policy's early years may be subject to surrender charges (when the insurer is trying to recover the costs of issuing the policy).

SUMMARY

Today's life insurers offer a vast array of life insurance plans, which are designed to serve various functions and meet different needs. *Term insurance*, the simplest type of plan, provides pure protection only, for a specified temporary period or term. At the end of the term, the protection expires. If a policyowner desires, the coverage can be extended through two options: the *option to renew* the term policy for another term and/or the *option to convert* the term policy to a whole life, or permanent, plan.

Whole life insurance provides protection for the whole of life and pays a death benefit if the insured dies at any time prior to age 100. Whole life insurance is characterized by *cash values* that accumulate over time, eventually reaching a level equal to the policy's face amount at the insured's age 100. At that point, the policy has *matured* or *endowed*. Premiums for whole life insurance are level throughout the policy's period and are calculated as though the insured were to pay them until age 100. A large percentage of whole life policies, known as *straight life policies*, are purchased on this basis. However, if a policyowner desires, the premium-paying period can be limited to a certain age or for a specified number of years; these policies are known as *limited pay life policies*. The most extreme example of limited pay life is *single-premium whole life*. Other types of whole life plans—such as modified whole life, graded premium whole life, minimum deposit whole life, and indeterminate premium whole life—also provide permanent protection but vary the way in which premiums are paid.

Endowment insurance combines the principles of term insurance and pure endowment. If the insured dies at any time within the endowment period, the policy pays a death benefit. If the insured lives to the end of the endowment period, the policy matures and is paid off as a completely endowed policy.

Various *special use* plans, which combine features of term and whole life into single policies, are available to fit different needs. These include *family policies*, *multiple protection policies*, *joint life policies*, *juvenile insurance*, and *credit life insurance*.

Finally, there are a number of newer, nontraditional life policies that have been introduced over the past decade or so. These policies are characterized in part by increased flexibility and current market returns. Most notable of these newer policy forms are *interest-sensitive whole life*, *adjustable life*, *universal life*, *variable life*, and *variable universal life*.

█ KEY CONCEPTS

Students should be familiar with the following concepts:

ordinary insurance	industrial insurance
group insurance	level term
decreasing term	increasing term
whole life	graded premium whole life
modified whole life	single-premium whole life
enhanced whole life	indexed whole life
limited pay whole life	endowment policies
modified endowment contract	joint and last survivor policy
minimum deposit	credit life
juvenile insurance	multiple protection plan
adjustable life	interest-sensitive whole life
universal life	variable life
variable universal life	

U N I T   T E S T

1. Which of the following terms best describes a life insurance policy that provides a straight $100,000 of coverage for a period of five years?

   A. Permanent level
   B. Whole term
   C. Level term
   D. Variable term

2. All of the following statements regarding term life insurance are correct EXCEPT

   A. a 3-year renewable policy allows a term policyowner to renew the same coverage for another 3 years
   B. a 3-year renewable policy allows a term policyowner to increase coverage for the next 3 years
   C. an option to convert provides that a term life insurance policy can be exchanged for a permanent one
   D. both the option to renew and the option to convert relieve the insured from furnishing evidence of insurability

3. "When level premium insurance is renewed, the premium amount rises to reflect the increased mortality risk of the insured's older age." What phrase best describes this approach to increasing premiums?

   A. Variable rate
   B. Targeted rate
   C. Step rate
   D. Seniority rate

4. Which of the following statements describing whole life insurance is CORRECT?

   A. The face amount of the policy gradually increases the longer the policy remains in force.
   B. The shorter the premium period, the slower the cash value will grow.
   C. Whole life insurance is designed to mature at age 100.
   D. The policy's cash value decreases each year the policy is in force.

5. The cash values of life insurance policies belong to which of the following?

   A. Policyowner
   B. Insured
   C. Insurer
   D. Beneficiary

6. All of the following statements regarding basic forms of whole life insurance are correct EXCEPT

   A. generally, straight life premiums are payable, at least annually, for the duration of the insured's life
   B. the owner of a 30-pay life policy will owe no more premiums after the 30th year the policy is in force
   C. limited payment life provides protection only for the years during which premiums are paid
   D. a single-premium life policy is purchased with a large one-time only premium

7. Which of the following statements regarding modified endowment contracts (MECs) is CORRECT?

   A. A 1988 revenue act, commonly known as TAMRA, greatly increased the popularity of MECs.
   B. Congress has granted the MEC the most favorable tax status among all life insurance policies.
   C. To avoid being classified as an MEC, a life insurance policy must satisfy the "7-pay test."
   D. According to the "7-pay test," if the total amount a policyowner pays into a life contract during its first 7 years is less than the sum of the net level premiums that would have been payable to provide paid-up future benefits in 7 years, the policy is an MEC.

8. Which of the following whole life insurance policies attempts to make insurance premiums more manageable by offering lower premiums during the first few years following issue?

   A. Minimum deposit whole life
   B. Indexed whole life
   C. Modified whole life
   D. Indeterminate premium whole life

9. What type of policy would be best used when the need for protection declines from year to year?

   A. Level term
   B. Decreasing term
   C. Whole life
   D. Universal life

10. All of the following statements about term insurance are correct EXCEPT

    A. it pays a benefit only if the insured dies during a specified period
    B. level, decreasing, and increasing are basic forms of term insurance
    C. cash values build during the specified period
    D. it provides protection for a temporary period of time

11. Bob purchases a $50,000 5-year level term policy. All of the following statements about Bob's coverage are correct EXCEPT

    A. the policy provides a straight, level $50,000 of coverage for 5 years
    B. if the insured dies at any time during the 5 years, his beneficiary will receive the policy's face value
    C. if the insured dies beyond the specified 5 years, only the policy's cash value will be paid
    D. if the insured lives beyond the 5 years, the policy expires and no benefits are payable

12. Mrs. Williamson purchases a 5-year $50,000 level term policy with an option to renew. At the end of the 5-year term, she renews the policy. Which of the following statements is CORRECT?

    A. The premium for the renewal period will be the same as the initial period.
    B. The premium for the renewal period will be higher than the initial period.
    C. The premium for the renewal period will be the same as the initial period, but a one-time service charge will be assessed upon renewal.
    D. The premium for the renewal period will be lower than the initial period.

13. All of the following statements about variable insurance policies are correct EXCEPT

    A. sales presentations must be preceded or accompanied by a prospectus
    B. state laws protect consumers and promote meaningful communication
    C. materials used in selling variable policies must be approved only by the state Office of Insurance Regulation
    D. full and fair disclosure must be provided to prospective policyowners

14. In contrast to traditional whole life insurance policies, with variable life insurance products

    A. premiums are invested in an insurer's general account
    B. investments match the insurer's contractual guarantees and liabilities
    C. contract cash values are not guaranteed
    D. the insurer assumes the investment risk

15. All of the following statements about variable insurance are correct EXCEPT

    A. they are considered insurance contracts
    B. sellers must hold a state insurance license
    C. they are not considered securities contracts
    D. sellers must hold a registered representative license from FINRA

16. A policy covering 2 lives that only pays a death benefit when the second insured person dies is

    A. a joint life policy
    B. a family policy
    C. a double indemnity policy
    D. a joint and last survivor policy

17. A policy that pays double or triple the face amount if death occurs during a specified period is

    A. a multiple protection policy
    B. a credit life policy
    C. a family policy
    D. a joint policy

6

Life Insurance Policy Provisions, Options, and Riders

- Rights of Policy Ownership
- Standard Policy Provisions
- Policy Exclusions
- Nonforfeiture Values
- Policy Dividends
- Policy Riders

It is easy to think of a life insurance policy as little more than a piece of paper. Unfortunately, this attitude diminishes the true value of a life insurance contract. Life insurance is property, and policyowners have important rights, as well as responsibilities, inherent in this special type of property. The policy provisions spell out the owner's rights, responsibilities, and limitations. In addition, life insurance, like many other forms of property, can be customized to meet the specific needs of the owner through policy riders and options. This unit will look at policy rights, provisions, riders, and options that give the life insurance contract its form and flexibility. ■

RIGHTS OF POLICY OWNERSHIP

Generally, the person who pays the premium for an insurance contract is designated as the **policyowner** or **policyholder**. Although there are no provisions in a life insurance policy specifically titled "Rights of Ownership," the fact is, owning a life insurance policy does entail important rights. These rights are woven throughout the policy in various clauses and provisions. The most significant rights of ownership include the following:

- The right to designate and change the beneficiary of the policy proceeds

- The right to select how the death proceeds will be paid to the beneficiary

- The right to cancel the policy and select a nonforfeiture option

- The right to take out a policy loan, assuming the policy is a whole life or other permanent plan, and a cash value exists

- The right to receive policy dividends and select a dividend payment option, if it is a participating policy

- The right to assign ownership of the policy to someone else

The clauses and provisions that set forth these rights will be examined in this and later units.

STANDARD POLICY PROVISIONS

Despite efforts by insurance companies to offer products distinct from their competitors, insurance policies are more notable for their many similarities than differences. This high degree of uniformity is rooted in the state-level regulation of the industry and the adoption of NAIC guidelines.

As discussed in Unit 2, regulators in each state protect consumers by establishing strict guidelines as to what must and must not be included in an insurance policy. Furthermore, in an effort to promote state-by-state uniformity of insurance industry regulation, most states have adopted, to one degree or another, the standard wording of NAIC Model Regulations. Accordingly, policy language is strikingly similar among the many different life insurance contracts available to consumers.

We will begin this section with a discussion of the *standard provisions* that appear in most life insurance contracts, then take a look at some of the common *exclusions*. It should be noted that while the provision names used here are commonly accepted terms, individual contracts may use different wording. For example, the "Entire Contract" clause falls under the heading "The Contract" in one company's policy, "Entire Contract" in another's, and "General" in a third. (It may be helpful to review the sample policy in the Appendix as you read this section.)

Entire Contract Provision

The **entire contract provision**, found at the beginning of the policy, states that the policy document, the application (which is attached to the policy), and any attached riders constitute the entire contract. Nothing may be "incorporated by reference," meaning that the policy cannot refer to any outside documents as being part of the contract. For example, a company could not claim that a special rider, not attached to the policy but on file in the home office, is part of the policy.

The entire contract clause has another important function—it prohibits the insurer from making any changes to the policy, either through policy revisions or changes in the company's bylaws, after the policy has been issued.

This clause does not prevent a mutually agreeable change from being made to the policy if the policy specifically provides a means for modifying the contract after it has been issued (for example, changing the face amount of an adjustable life policy).

Insuring Clause

The **insuring clause** or provision sets forth the company's basic promise to pay benefits upon the insured's death. Generally, this clause is not actually titled as such, but appears on the cover of the policy.

One company's insuring clause reads:

The Insurance Company agrees, in accordance with the provisions of this policy, to pay to the beneficiary the death proceeds upon receipt at the Principal Office of due proof of the insured's death prior to the maturity date.

Further, the Company agrees to pay the surrender value to the owner if the insured is alive on the maturity date.

The insuring clause is typically undersigned by the president and secretary of the insurance company.

Free-Look Provision

The **free-look provision**, required by most states, gives policyowners the right to return the policy for a full premium refund within a specified period of time, if they decide not to purchase the insurance. In Florida, the free-look period for life insurance contracts (and annuities) is 14 days from policy delivery.

Consideration Clause

As we learned in Unit 3, **consideration** is the value given in exchange for a contractual promise. The **consideration clause** or provision in a life insurance policy specifies the amount and frequency of premium payments that the policyowners must make to keep the insurance in force. Often, the amount and frequency of required premiums are listed on the "Schedule" or "Specifications" page. A separate page will provide details on the manner in which premiums must be paid (as well as the consequences of not making a premium payment).

Grace Period Provision

The **grace period provision** undoubtedly has saved many life insurance policies from lapsing. If policyowners forget or neglect to pay their premiums by the date they are due, the grace period allows an extra 30 days (four weeks for industrial policies) during which premiums (after the first) may be paid to keep policies in force. (See Unit 27 for Florida law regarding the policy grace period for persons 64 years of age and older.) In policies for which the premiums are paid monthly, the grace period is one month, but no less than 30 days. If an insured dies during the grace period and the premium has not been paid, the policy benefit is payable. However, the premium amount due is deducted from the benefits paid to the beneficiary.

Reinstatement Provision

It is always possible that, due to nonpayment of premiums, a policy may lapse, either deliberately or unintentionally. In cases where a policyowner wishes to reinstate a lapsed policy, the reinstatement provision allows the policyowner to do so, with some limitations. With reinstatement, a policy is restored to its original status and its values are brought up to date.

Most insurers require the following to reinstate a lapsed policy:

- All back premiums must be paid

- Interest on past-due premiums may be required to be paid

- Any outstanding loans on the lapsed policy may be required to be paid

- The policyowner may be asked to prove insurability

In addition, there is a limited period of time in which policies may be reinstated after lapse. This period is usually three years, but may be as long as seven years, in some cases. A new contestable period usually goes into effect with a reinstated policy, but there is no new suicide exclusion period. (See "Incontestable Clause" and "Suicide Provision," in the following.)

Policy Loan Provision

State insurance laws require that cash value life insurance policies include a **policy loan provision**. This means that, within prescribed limits, policyowners may borrow money from the cash values of their policies if they wish to do so.

Actually, a policy loan is more an advance on proceeds than a true loan. As such, these "loans" may not be "called" by the company and can be repaid at any time by the policyowners. If not repaid by the time the insured dies, the loan balance and any interest accrued are deducted from the policy proceeds at the time of claim. If the policy is surrendered for cash, the cash value available to the policyowner is reduced by the amount of any outstanding loan plus interest.

Interest rates on policy loans vary, but most states stipulate a maximum allowable rate (in Florida, that maximum is 10%). Some newer policies are issued with a variable interest rate tied to the Moody's corporate bond index; older policies still in force stipulate a flat rate of interest, such as 5–8%.

Loan values and cash surrender values are shown as identical amounts in a policy and are often listed under the single column heading of "Cash or Loan Value." (See Illustration 6.1.)

Incontestable Clause

The **incontestable clause** or provision specifies that after a certain period of time (usually two years from the issue date and while the insured is living), the insurer no longer has the right to contest the validity of the life insurance policy so long as the contract continues in force. This means that after the policy has been in force for the specified term, the company cannot contest a death claim or refuse payment of the proceeds even on the basis of a material misstatement, concealment, or fraud. Even if the insurer learns that an error was deliberately made on the application, it must pay the death benefit at the insured's death if the policy has passed the contestable period.

ILLUSTRATION 6.1

Table of Guaranteed Values

| Face Amount: $100,000 | | Annual Premium: $2,000 | |
| End of Policy Year | Cash or Loan Value | Reduced Paid-Up | Extended Term | |
			Years	Days
1	$0	$0	0	0
2	$50	$210	0	66
3	$960	$3,600	2	290
4	$2,150	$7,250	6	9
5	$4,000	$12,000	8	111
6	$5,975	$16,110	10	147
7	$7,210	$19,880	12	22
8	$9,340	$23,800	14	18
9	$11,415	$27,620	15	312
10	$13,005	$30,990	16	362
11	$14,770	$34,010	17	202
12	$16,785	$37,880	18	116
13	$19,430	$40,940	18	1
14	$23,000	$43,985	17	144
15	$26,990	$47,010	16	302
16	$30,215	$50,600	15	347
17	$34,600	$53,815	15	88
18	$38,910	$56,910	14	117
19	$43,020	$60,010	13	361
20	$47,910	$63,715	13	47
Age 65	$56,770	$78,700	11	36

This table shows how the guaranteed ("nonforfeitable") values are presented in a life insurance policy. These figures reflect the values available to the policy-owner at different points in the policy's life for purposes of surrendering the policy for cash, taking out a loan against the policy, purchasing a reduced paid-up policy, or purchasing an extended term policy. (See also the sample policy in the Appendix.)

Although the incontestable clause applies to death benefits, it generally does *not* apply to accidental death benefits or disability provisions if they are part of the policy. Because conditions relating to accidents vary and are often uncertain, the right to investigate them usually is reserved by the company.

The incontestable clause applies to the policy face amount, plus any additional death benefit added by rider that is payable in the case of normal death.

It should be noted that there are three situations to which the incontestable clause does not apply. A policy issued under any of these circumstances would not be considered a valid contract, which gives the insurer the right to contest and possibly void the policy at any time:

■ **Impersonation.** When application for insurance is made by one person but another person signs the application or takes the medical exam, the insurer can contest the policy and its claim.

■ **No insurable interest.** If no insurable interest existed between the applicant and the insured at the inception of the policy, the contract is not valid to begin with; as such, the insurer can contest the policy at any time.

■ **Intent to murder.** If it is subsequently proven that the applicant applied for the policy with the intent of murdering the insured for the proceeds, the insurance company can contest the policy and its claim. Since the policy did not have a legal purpose from the start, the insurance company may simply deny coverage. The policyowner is powerless to enforce such a claim as no court of law will force an insurer to provide coverage under these circumstances.

Assignment Provision

People who purchase life insurance policies are commonly referred to as policyowners rather than policyholders because they actually own their policies and may do with them as they wish. They can even give them away, just as they can give away any other kind of property they own. This transfer of ownership is known as **assignment**.

The **assignment provision** in a life insurance contract sets forth the procedure necessary for ownership transfer. This procedure usually requires that the policyowner notify the company in writing of the assignment. The company will then accept the validity of the transfer without question. A policyowner does not need the insurer's permission to assign a policy.

The new owner is known as the **assignee**. If, for example, an individual gave a policy to his church as a donation, the church would be the assignee. An insurable interest does not have to exist between the insured and the assignee.

As the owner of the policy, the assignee is granted all the rights of policy ownership, including the right to name a beneficiary. If the assignee does not change the beneficiary designation, the proceeds will be paid to the beneficiary named by the original owner. Note, however, the assignee does have the right to change the beneficiary as long as the original beneficiary designation was revocable.[1] If a policyowner names an **irrevocable beneficiary** (meaning the beneficiary cannot be changed), the policyowner must get the beneficiary's agreement to any assignment. (See Unit 7.)

There are two types of assignments: **absolute** and **collateral**.

1. **Absolute assignment.** Under an absolute assignment, the transfer is complete and irrevocable, and the assignee receives full control over the policy and full rights to its benefits.

2. **Collateral assignment.** A collateral assignment is one in which the policy is assigned to a creditor as security, or collateral, for a debt. If the insured dies, the creditor is entitled to be reimbursed out of the benefit proceeds for the amount owed. The insured's beneficiary is then entitled to any excess of policy proceeds over the amount due the creditor. Once the debt is repaid, the policyowner is entitled to the return of the rights assigned.

---

[1]   Though there may be exceptions, most jurisdictions will not allow an assignee to change the beneficiary designation if it was originally designated irrevocable. (See "Changing a Beneficiary," Unit 7.)

Accelerated Benefits Provision

Until recently, traditional whole life insurance policies provided cash benefit payments in the event of the insured's death (or in the rare case of an insured living to a contract's maturity date). The only way an insured could access the policy's cash value while living was through a policy loan or policy surrender. If an insured was faced with a life-threatening medical condition, the life insurance policy, by design, could provide no immediate financial relief.

Today, **accelerated benefits provisions** are standard in life insurance policies. They provide for the early payment of some portion of the policy face amount should the insured suffer from a terminal illness or injury. The death benefit, less the accelerated payment, is still payable. For example, a $250,000 policy that provides for a 75% accelerated benefit would pay up to $187,500 to the terminally ill insured, with the remaining $62,500 payable as a death benefit to the beneficiary when the insured dies. Accelerated payment can be made in a lump sum or in monthly installments over a special period, such as one year.

This provision is given without an increase in premium. There are some companies that deduct an interest charge from the proceeds paid out to make up for what the company would have earned had the money not been withdrawn from the contract.

Suicide Provision

The **suicide provision**, found in most life policies, protects the company and its policyowners against the possibility that a person might buy an insurance policy and commit suicide to provide a sum of money for the beneficiary. With this provision, a life insurance policy discourages suicide by stipulating a period of time (usually one or two years from the date of policy issue) during which the death benefit will not be paid if the insured commits suicide. If that happens, however, the premiums paid for the policy will be refunded.

Of course, if an insured takes his own life after the policy has been in force for the period specified in the suicide clause, the company will pay the entire proceeds, just as if death were from a natural cause.

Because of the instinct for self-preservation, most courts will assume a death was unintentional unless there is strong evidence to the contrary. So even if death occurs during the suicide exclusion period and suicide is suspected, the company must prove it beyond a reasonable doubt; otherwise, the policy proceeds generally must be paid to the beneficiary.

Misstatement of Age or Sex Provision

The **misstatement of age or sex provision** is important because the age and sex of the applicant are critical factors in establishing the premium rate for a life insurance policy. To guard against a misunderstanding about the applicant's age, the company reserves the right to make an adjustment at any time. Likewise, an adjustment is made if an applicant's sex is incorrectly indicated in a policy because, age for age, premium rates for females generally are lower than for males. Normally, such adjustments are made either in the premium charged or in the amount of insurance.

Assume an error in age is discovered after the death of an insured. If the insured was younger than the policy showed, the amount of proceeds would be increased to a sum the premium paid would have bought at the correct age. However, if the insured was older than the policy indicated, the amount of proceeds would be decreased to whatever the premium paid would have purchased at the correct age.

If an error is discovered while the insured is living, the premium will be adjusted downward if the insured is younger than the policy shows and a refund of the premium overpayments will be made. By the same token, if the insured is older than the policy indicates, the company will either adjust the premium upward and require the difference in premium or it will reduce the amount of insurance to what it should be for the amount of premium being paid.

Automatic Premium Loan Provision

A provision that is now commonly added to most cash value policies is the **automatic premium loan**. This provision authorizes the insurer to withdraw from the policy's cash value the amount of premium due if the premium has not been paid by the end of the grace period. The amount withdrawn becomes a loan against the cash value, bearing the rate of interest specified in the contract. In time, if the loan is not repaid, the interest will also be deducted from the cash value. Should the insured die, the loan plus the interest will be deducted from the benefits payable.

Depending on the insurer, this provision may be standard to the contract or added as a rider, with no additional charge to the policyowner.

Note that this provision may be very beneficial for a policyowner who forgets to pay the premium within the grace period or who cannot pay the current premium because of financial difficulties. Most importantly, the policy does not lapse and coverage continues. If the policyowner allows the automatic premium loan to continually pay the premiums, of course, the policy eventually will lapse when the cash value is reduced to nothing. The owner then would have to reinstate the policy and pay back the loans.

Other Policy Provisions

There are two additional provisions that appear in all policies: the **beneficiary designation**, whereby the policyowner indicates who is to receive the proceeds, and **settlement options**, whereby the ways in which the proceeds can be paid out, or "settled," are explained. Beneficiaries are discussed in Unit 7; settlement options are discussed in Unit 8.

POLICY EXCLUSIONS

Most life insurance policies contain restrictions that exclude from coverage certain types of risks. If there were no **exclusions**, premium rates would be much higher. Exclusions can be stated in the policy itself or attached as riders. The most common types of exclusions include:

■ **War.** This exclusion provides that the death benefit will not be paid if the insured dies as a result of war.

■ **Aviation.** This exclusion is commonly found in older policies; very few policies issued today exclude death as a result of commercial aviation. However, some insurers will exclude aviation deaths for other than fare-paying passengers.

■ **Hazardous occupations or hobbies.** Individuals who have hazardous occupations, such as stunt people, or who engage in hazardous hobbies, such as auto racing, may find that their life insurance policies exclude death as a result of their occupation or hobby. Or, these risks may be covered, but an increased (or "rated") premium will be charged.

■ **Commission of a felony.** Some contracts will exclude death when it results from the insured committing a felony.

■ **Suicide.** As previously noted, almost all policies exclude payment of the benefit if the insured commits suicide during the specified time period. After that period passes, death by suicide is covered.

Because these exclusions are allowed by state regulators to be included in policies at the discretion of the insurance company, they are also called "optional provisions." Note, however, the term "exclusions" more precisely defines their purpose.

NONFORFEITURE VALUES

In Unit 5 we learned that an important feature of whole life insurance is its cash value, which is created in part by the level premium funding method. As a policy matures, cash values grow until, when the policy endows, the cash value equals the face amount of the policy. Ownership of a policy's cash value rests solely with the policyowner. Even though the cash value is an important part of the underlying funding of the policy, the policyowner is entitled to receive the accrued cash value at any time. When a policy is active, the owner can borrow from the cash value. If a policy is lapsed or surrendered, the owner is entitled to the cash surrender value.

Until the beginning of the 20th century, it was common for insurers to keep part or all of the cash value in a surrendered policy. The idea that it was the policyowner, not the insurer, who was entitled to a policy's cash value did not gain universal acceptance until the 1905 Armstrong Investigation looked at a number of insurer abuses, including the practice of keeping policy cash values upon policy surrender.

Today every state has legislated laws, modeled after the NAIC Standard Nonforfeiture Law, assuring policyowners that they are fully entitled to the accrued cash values of their policies. The term **nonforfeiture value** refers to the fact that a policy's cash value is not forfeitable. **Nonforfeiture options** are the ways in which cash values can be paid out to or used by policyowners, if they choose to lapse or surrender their policies. Cash value policies will contain a page in the contract illustrating the nonforfeiture values at various policy anniversaries. (See Illustration 6.1.)

Nonforfeiture Options

There are three nonforfeiture options from which policyowners can select: **cash surrender, reduced paid-up insurance**, and **extended term insurance**.

Cash Surrender Option

If they desire, policyowners may request an immediate **cash payment** of their cash values when their policies are surrendered. A table of cash surrender values is included in every permanent life insurance policy, as illustrated in Illustration 6.1, under the heading "Cash or Loan Value." The amount of cash value the policyowner receives is reduced by any outstanding policy indebtedness.

Insurers are required to make cash surrender values available for ordinary whole life insurance after the first three policy years and, for industrial insurance, after five years. In practice, however, most policies begin to generate cash values in as little as one year.

Most states permit insurers to postpone payment of cash surrender values for up to six months after policyowners request payment. This **delayed payment provision** is a protective measure for companies should an economic crisis arise, but such delays are rarely invoked.

Reduced Paid-up Option

A second nonforfeiture option is to take a paid-up policy for a reduced face amount of insurance. By doing this, the policyowner does not pay any more premiums but still retains some amount of life insurance. In essence, the cash value is used as the premium for a single-premium whole life policy, at a lesser face amount than the original policy.

When this option is exercised, the paid-up policy is the same kind as the original, but for a lesser amount of coverage. For example, if the original policy was a participating whole life policy, the paid-up policy also will be a participating whole life policy. The paid-up policy is computed as a single-premium policy at the attained-age rate. Any term insurance rider and disability or accidental death benefits from the original policy are excluded when the amount of paid-up life insurance is calculated.

Once the paid-up policy has been issued, the new face value remains the same for the life of the policy, which also builds cash values. (See Illustration 6.2.)

ILLUSTRATION 6.2

Reduced Paid-Up Option

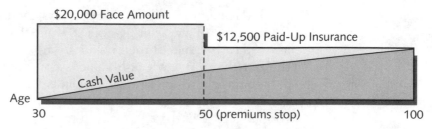

Using the above diagram as an example, assume Lyman purchased a $20,000 whole life policy at age 30 and now, at age 50, decides to discontinue premium payments and use the accumulated cash value to make a single payment to purchase a reduced amount ($12,500) of permanent paid-up insurance. Lyman has exercised the reduced paid-up nonforfeiture option. (Amounts shown are illustrative only.)

ILLUSTRATION 6.3

Extended Term Option

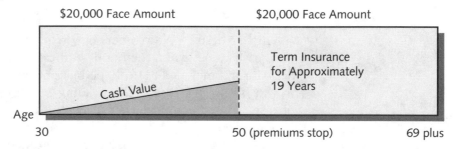

Using the above diagram as an example, assume Lyman purchased a $20,000 whole life policy at age 30 and now, at age 50, decides to discontinue premium payments and use the accumulated cash value to purchase a $20,000 term policy. The cash value will provide $20,000 of protection for approximately 19 years, until Lyman is about 69. Lyman has exercised the extended term nonforfeiture option. (Extended term shown is illustrative only.)

Extended Term Option

The third nonforfeiture option is to use the policy's cash value to *purchase a term insurance policy* in an amount equal to the original policy's face value, for as long a period as the cash value will purchase. When the term insurance expires, there is no more protection. Moreover, all supplemental benefits included with the original policy, such as a term rider or accidental death or disability benefits, are dropped. (See Illustration 6.3.)

In the case of endowment insurance, the extended term insurance will not be provided beyond the maturity date of the original endowment policy. The cash value of an endowment policy will eventually exceed the amount needed to buy extended term insurance so, in that case, the excess cash value is used to purchase a pure endowment policy with the same maturity date as the original policy.

▍POLICY DIVIDENDS

As noted previously, life insurance policies may be either participating or nonparticipating, and it is important to distinguish between the two to understand the source of *policy dividends*. At any given age, people who buy participating (par) policies normally pay premiums that are slightly higher than premiums paid by those who purchase nonparticipating (nonpar) policies. This is because an extra charge to cover unexpected contingencies is built into premiums for par policies.

At the end of each year, the insurance company analyzes its operations. If fewer insureds have died than was estimated, a divisible surplus results and the company can return to the policyowners a part of the premiums paid for participating policies. A company also can issue returns stemming from positive operating or investment income. These payments are called dividends but should not be confused with the dividends paid on stocks. Policy dividends are really a return of part of the premiums paid. As such, policy dividends are generally not taxable income, unlike corporate dividends, which are reportable for income tax purposes. However, policy dividends can be taxed when they exceed the cost of the policy.

ILLUSTRATION 6.4

Paid-Up Additions: A Popular Option

The **paid-up additions dividend option** is popular with many policyowners. A close look at the benefits of this option will explain why.

When a dividend is declared, it is used in effect as the premium for a single-payment whole life policy of the same type as the base policy under which the dividend is declared. The face amount of this paid-up addition is generally small, but over time the sum of these additions can be substantial.

The paid-up addition enjoys all the advantages of any whole life policy. It will accrue a cash value. It possesses all the tax advantages of whole life insurance. Most significantly, it is issued to the policyowner without any additional premium requirement beyond the premium being paid for the base policy.

Consider the example of a policyowner with a $100,000 par policy who is paying a level premium of $1,300 annually. As each year passes, a paid-up addition is added. In time, the total face amount of the policy will grow as more paid-up additions are added; perhaps after 10 years the total face amount may be $115,000. The cash value of this policy will increase at an ever-faster rate as the paid-up additions' cash values are added to the base policy's cash value. And all of this will occur with the same $1,300 annual outlay as was required when the policy was first purchased.

The payment of policy dividends hinges on several "ifs" (unexpected contingencies, as noted). And because all of those conditions will affect the amount of the dividend, policy dividends normally will vary from year to year and cannot be guaranteed.

Thus, when an insurance company gives a policy illustration that includes dividends, it is purely an estimate or approximation of what future dividends might be. To protect life insurance buyers against the misuse of dividend illustrations, most states require life insurance proposals containing a dividend illustration to state clearly that future dividends are not guaranteed.

Dividends usually become payable at the end of the first or second policy year. A provision in each participating policy states when the policyowner can expect to begin receiving any dividends.

Stock companies can issue either participating policies or nonparticipating policies. If a stock company issues both types of policies, it is said to be doing business on a **mixed plan**. Mutual companies can issue only participating policies.

Dividend Options

Policyowners are generally permitted by insurers to utilize their dividends through one of five options:

- **Take dividends in cash.** When dividends become payable, they usually are paid on policy anniversary dates. Policyowners who elect to take their dividends in cash automatically receive their dividend check after the company approves a dividend.

- **Apply dividends against premium payments.** Dividends can also be applied directly to the policyowner's premium payments, lowering the owner's out-of-pocket expense.

- **Allow dividends to accumulate at interest.** A third option is to leave the dividends with the company to accumulate with interest, for withdrawal at any time. Note that while policy dividends are not taxable, any interest paid on them is taxable income in the year the interest is credited to the policy, whether or not it is actually received by the policyowner.

- **Use dividends to buy paid-up additions.** Dividends can also be used to purchase paid-up additions of life insurance, of the same kind as the original or base policy. The premium rate is based on the attained age of the insured at the time the paid-up additions are purchased.

- **Use dividends to purchase one-year term insurance.** A fifth option, though not utilized as frequently as the others, is to use dividends to purchase as much one-year term insurance as possible or to purchase one-year term insurance equal to the base policy's cash value. This is done through specific application for and issue of a separate rider. Sometimes called the "fifth dividend option," this provision allows for any excess dividend portions to be applied under any of the other regular options.

POLICY RIDERS

The flexibility of life insurance policies is well demonstrated by the ability policyowners have to customize a policy to meet their specific needs. Imagine buying a new car without being able to purchase optional features, such as air conditioning or GPS. Chances are good you might not even buy that car. Insurers offer their applicants the privilege of adding options—in the form of policy riders—to their policies to meet their unique needs. Like new car options, policy riders are available at an extra cost (through increased premiums) but are justified because of the increased value the riders give to the base policy.

Most of the optional riders described below must be selected at the time the policy is applied for. The automatic premium loan rider (if it is an option and not a standard policy feature) is the only optional rider available at no cost to the policyowner. It can sometimes be added after the policy is in force.

Guaranteed Insurability Rider

For an extra premium, the **guaranteed insurability rider** may be attached to a permanent life insurance policy at the time of purchase. It permits the insured, at specified intervals in the future, to buy specified amounts of additional insurance **without evidence of insurability**.

Typically, this option allows the insured to purchase additional life insurance at stated policy intervals or at stated ages. The amount of insurance that can be purchased at each option date is subject to minimums and maximums specified in the rider, but the insurance is available at **standard premium rates**, whether or not the insured is still insurable.

These riders generally allow the insured to buy additional life insurance at three-year intervals, beginning with the policy anniversary date nearest the insured's 25th birthday and terminating at the anniversary date nearest the insured's 40th birthday. (Guaranteed insurability options usually do not extend past age 40.) Thus, the option dates listed in the rider are for the insured when the insured is ages 25, 28, 31, 34, 37 and 40. The insured normally has 90 days in which to exercise an option to purchase. If no purchase is made within that time, the option for that particular age expires automatically. The expiration of one option will not affect the exercise of future options.

Company practice varies, but if a waiver of premium or accidental death benefit (both are explained below) is included with the original policy, most companies allow these benefits to be added to the additional life insurance purchased under the guaranteed insurability option, if the policyowner wants to pay the additional premium.

Waiver of Premium Rider

The **waiver of premium rider** provides valuable added security for policyowners. It can prevent a policy from lapsing for nonpayment of premiums while the insured is disabled and unable to work. The waiver of premium rider is available on both permanent and term insurance policies.

Under the waiver of premium, if the company determines that the insured is totally disabled, the policyowner is relieved of paying premiums as long as the disability continues. Some companies include the waiver of premium as part of the contract, with the cost built into the overall premium. In other companies, the waiver may be added to a policy by rider or endorsement for a small, additional premium.

Some policies specify that an insured must be totally and permanently disabled for the waiver to take effect. It does not apply to short-term illnesses or injuries. In fact, an insured generally must be seriously disabled for a certain length of time, called the "waiting period" (usually 90 days or six months). The policyowner continues paying premiums during the waiting period. If the insured is still disabled at the end of this period, the company will refund all of the premiums paid by the policyowner from the start of the disability.

The company then continues to pay all premiums that become due while the insured's disability continues. If the insured recovers and can start back to work, premium payments then must be resumed by the policyowner. No premiums paid by the company, however, have to be repaid by the policyowner.

For the waiver to become operative, the insured must meet the policy's definition of "totally disabled." **Totally disabled** may be defined as the insured's inability to engage in any work for which the insured is reasonably fitted by education, training, or experience. Or, as with some policies, the definition is worded in terms of the insured's inability to work at the insured's own occupation for a stated period (for example, 24 months) and at any occupation thereafter.

A waiver of premium rider generally remains in effect until the insured reaches a specified age, such as 60 or 65. When the provision expires, the policy premium is reduced accordingly. If an insured becomes disabled prior to the specified age, all premiums usually are waived while the disability continues—even those premiums falling due after the insured passes the stipulated age.

ILLUSTRATION 6.5

Which Rider to Purchase?

Riders can work in tandem. Consider the insured policyowner who has both a **guaranteed insurability** and **waiver of premium** rider on her policy. At age 29, she becomes totally and permanently disabled. Because she meets the definition of total disability in her policy, her premiums will be waived and in two years, when she is 31, she can increase the face amount of her policy to the maximum permitted under the guaranteed insurability rider—all without paying any premiums.

Although premiums are waived for a disabled insured, the death benefit remains the same, cash values increase at their normal rate, and dividends for a participating policy are paid as usual. In fact, cash values continue to be available to the policyowner at all times while the insured's disability continues.

Disability Income Rider

Similar to and sometimes paired with the Waiver of Premium rider is the **Disability Income Rider**. In the event that the insured is disabled and unable to work, this rider provides a monthly income payment to the insured for the duration of the disability. The income paid by this rider is not tied to the earnings of the insured. Rather, it is defined as a small percentage of the face amount of the life insurance policy to which the rider is attached. As with waiver of premium, this rider normally has a waiting period of 90 days or six months, and the insured must meet the insurer's standard of totally disabled.

Automatic Premium Loan Rider

The **automatic premium loan** feature, discussed earlier in this unit, is a standard feature in some life insurance policies; in others, its provisions are added to the policy by rider. In either case, it is available to the policyowner at no additional charge. As previously noted, it allows the insurer to pay premiums from the policy's cash value if premiums have not been paid by the end of the grace period. These deductions from cash values are treated as "loans" and are charged interest; in time, if the loan is not repaid, the interest will also be deducted from the cash value. Should the insured die, the loan plus interest will be deducted from the benefits payable.

Automatic premium loans provide that, as long as premiums are not paid, the loan procedure will be repeated until the cash value of the policy is exhausted. When the cash value is depleted, the policy lapses.

An automatic premium loan option can be elected at the time of application or, with some insurers, added after the policy is issued.

Payor Provision or Rider

As noted earlier in the discussion of juvenile insurance, a **payor provision** is usually available with such policies, providing for waiver of premiums if the adult premium-payor should die or, with some policies, become totally disabled.

Typically, this payor provision, also known as a "death and disability payor benefit," extends until the insured child reaches a specified age, such as 21 or 25. It is available for a small extra premium but, before it is issued, the adult who is to pay the premium usually must show evidence of insurability.

Accidental Death/Dismemberment Benefit Rider

The **accidental death benefit rider** (sometimes called a "double indemnity" provision) provides an additional amount of insurance, usually equal to the face amount of the base policy, if death occurs under stated conditions. Consequently, if the insured died as a result of the stated circumstances, and the insured had a double indemnity rider, the total benefit paid would be double the policy's face—the benefit payable under the policy plus the same amount payable under the rider. A "triple indemnity" provision would provide a total death benefit of three times the face amount. Any policy loans are subtracted from the policy's face amount and not from the accidental death riders.

"Accidental death" is strictly defined. It does *not* include accidents resulting, directly or indirectly, from an ailment or physical disability relating to the insured. The additional proceeds are paid only if the insured dies as a result of bodily injury from some external, violent, and purely accidental cause. Also, death must occur within a specified time (usually 90 days) following the accident. Deaths that might be considered accidental, such as those resulting from self-inflicted injury, war, or private aviation activities, are excluded.

When sold as **accidental death and dismemberment**, this rider adds an additional lump sum payable in the event that the insured does not die, but instead loses a qualifying body part (eye, arm, or leg) in a qualifying accident. The dismemberment benefit is usually half of the amount paid for accidental death.

Many companies do not offer the accidental death/dismemberment benefit to anyone older than age 55 or 60, and the extra protection generally expires after the insured reaches age 60 or 65. While in effect, the additional insurance does *not* build any cash value.

The extra premium for this benefit is not payable beyond the date when the additional benefit expires, nor does the benefit apply to any paid-up additions that may be purchased with policy dividends. The benefit also drops off in the event the policyowner surrenders the policy and selects one of the nonforfeiture options.

Long-Term Care Rider

A life policy rider that allows the insured to receive a set monthly income to help pay the cost of confinement in a nursing home or other long-term care facility is called the **long-term care rider**. In order to receive the rider benefit, the insured must meet all the requirements to qualify for long-term care (see Long-Term Care Insurance, Unit 21). The benefit paid will be a small percentage of the face amount of the policy to which the rider is attached, and it may or may not cover the actual costs of care. The rider income amount will be selected when the life insurance policy is purchased and, if paid, will be an acceleration of the death benefit. This means that any long-term care benefits paid reduce the face amount of the policy, and the total benefits paid cannot exceed the policy face amount. If the rider benefit is not used or does not consume the entire policy, any remaining death benefit is paid to the beneficiary at the death of the insured.

Return of Premium Rider

A **return of premium rider** provides that in the event of the death of the insured within a specified period of time, the policy will pay, in addition to the face amount, an amount equal to the sum of all premiums paid to date. In actuality, this rider does not return premiums but pays an additional benefit equal to premiums paid upon the date of death. The policyowner is simply purchasing term insurance that increases as the total amount of premiums paid increases. Many insurers now also offer a return of premium to a living policyowner after a specified time.

There are also Return of Premium (ROP) term life insurance policies that return 100% of premiums paid at the end of the term if no death benefit has been paid, and the returned money may be tax free. Generally speaking, the longer the term, the less an insured will pay in premiums. So, a 30-year ROP term life policy could cost less money, at the end of the term, than a 15-year ROP policy. If a ROP term life policy is surrendered, the insured will get some premiums returned based on a sliding scale, provided the insured has held the policy for a few years. Many companies will not return premiums if the policy is surrendered within the first few years. The longer the policy is held, the higher the percentage of premiums that will be returned, up to 100% at the end of the term. If the insured dies during the term, beneficiaries will receive the death benefit without any premium return.

Cost of Living Rider

Some companies offer their applicants the ability to guard against the eroding effects of inflation. A **cost of living (COL)** or **cost of living adjustment (COLA)** rider can provide increases in the amount of insurance protection without requiring the insured to provide evidence of insurability. The amount of increase is tied to an increase in an inflation index, most commonly the Consumer Price Index (CPI). Depending on the type of base policy, these riders can take several different forms.

For standard whole life policies, a COL rider is usually offered as an **increasing term insurance rider** that is attached to the base policy. The COL rider provides for automatic increases in the policy death benefit in proportion to increases in the CPI. Generally there is a maximum percentage increase, such as 5%, allowed in any one year. When the increase becomes effective, the policyowner is billed for the additional coverage. It is important to note that declines in the CPI are not matched by a decline in the amount of coverage; instead, future increases are held off until the CPI again exceeds its prior high point.

Adjustable life insurance, which is characterized in part by giving the policyowner limited freedom to increase and decrease the policy's face amount, frequently includes a COL agreement. The COL agreement waives the need for evidence of insurability for limited face amount increases that are intended to match increases in the CPI. The face amount increase is accompanied by an increase in premium, although the agreement itself is usually offered at no charge to the policyowner.

The COL agreement can also be used, with certain restrictions, with term and whole life policies. They are not practical with universal life policies, however, because of the high degree of flexibility already present in UL policies.

Other Insureds/Term Rider

A rider that is useful in providing insurance for more than one family member is the **other insureds rider**. Usually this rider is offered as a term rider, covering a family member other than the insured, and is attached to the base policy covering the insured. Sometimes this is called a **children's rider** if it covers only the children; otherwise, it is often referred to as a **family rider**. This type of rider is used in family plan policies, discussed in Unit 5. When the policy provides level term insurance in addition to whole life and both coverages are on the primary insured, the term coverage is simply called a **term rider**, not an other insured rider.

SUMMARY

All life insurance policies are characterized by standardized *policy provisions* that identify the rights and obligations of the policyowner and the insurance company. There are many standard provisions that are required by state insurance regulators to be included in policies. Other provisions, dealing with *exclusions* and *restrictions* of coverage, are optional and can be included at the discretion of the insurer.

Whole life policies generate cash values to which policyowners are entitled. Policyowners may borrow from a policy's cash value or, upon lapse or surrender of the policy, may select one of three possible *nonforfeiture options*.

Participating policies share in the divisible surplus of company operations by returning part of the premium to the owner as a policy dividend. There are five *dividend options* available to policyowners in deciding how to use their policy dividends.

Policyowners can customize their policy to meet their specific insurance needs by including, generally at a cost, one or more *policy riders*.

KEY CONCEPTS

Students should be familiar with the following concepts:

owner's rights	entire contract provision
insuring clause	free look
consideration clause	grace period
reinstatement	policy loans
incontestable clause	assignment provision
suicide provision	misstatement of age or sex clause
policy exclusions (optional) provisions	nonforfeiture options
policy dividends and options	guaranteed insurability rider
waiver of premium	automatic premium loan
payor benefit	accidental death benefit
cost of living adjustments	other insureds rider
accelerated benefits rider	

UNIT TEST

1. In which of the following situations does the incontestable clause apply?

   A. Impersonation of the applicant by another
   B. No insurable interest
   C. Intent to murder
   D. Concealment of smoking

2. An error in age is discovered after the death of an insured but before any policy death proceeds are distributed. The insured was older than previously assumed. How would an insurance company handle such a situation?

   A. No adjustment would be made because the contestable period had passed.
   B. The amount of death proceeds would be reduced to reflect the statistically diminished mortality risk.
   C. The amount of death proceeds would be reduced to reflect whatever benefit the premium paid would have purchased at the correct age.
   D. The beneficiary would be required to pay all underpaid back premiums before the death benefit is received.

3. Which of the following allows 30 days during which premiums may be paid to keep policies in force?

   A. Grace period
   B. Reinstatement clause
   C. Incontestable clause
   D. Waiting period

4. Which of the following statements regarding the assignment of a life insurance policy is NOT correct?

   A. Absolute assignment involves a complete transfer, giving the assignee full control over the policy.
   B. Under a collateral assignment, a creditor is entitled to be reimbursed out of the policy's proceeds only for the amount of the outstanding credit balance.
   C. Under a collateral assignment, policy proceeds in excess of the collateral amount pass to the insured's beneficiary.
   D. All beneficiaries must expressly approve any assignments of life insurance policies.

5. Which of the following is(are) a common life insurance policy exclusion?

   A. Death from war
   B. Death by accidental means
   C. Death by commercial aviation
   D. All of the above

6. All of the following are standard life insurance policy nonforfeiture options EXCEPT

   A. cash surrender option
   B. 1-year term insurance option
   C. extended term insurance option
   D. reduced paid-up (permanent) insurance option

7. Which of the following statements best describes life insurance policy dividends?

   A. Policy dividends represent earnings to shareowners who hold stock in insurance companies.
   B. Policy dividends affect the costs of virtually all insurance policies issued today.
   C. Policy dividends are an intentional return of a portion of the premiums paid.
   D. Policy dividends provide policyowners with a level, known annual cash inflow.

8. The most common guaranteed insurability riders allow additional life insurance to be purchased on the insured within a range of ages. The common age range in which guaranteed insurability is available is from

   A. 16 to 65
   B. 21 to 59½
   C. 25 to 40
   D. 30 to 70½

9. Which life insurance provision allows the policyholder to inspect and, if dissatisfied, to return the policy for a full refund?

   A. Waiver of premium
   B. Facility of payments
   C. Probationary period
   D. Free look

10. Which of the following statements regarding a cost of living (COL) rider on a life insurance policy is CORRECT?

    A. A cost of living rider provides for a level premium even if the cost of living increases.
    B. An inflation index, usually the Consumer Price Index, determines the amount of inflation adjustment that is made to the policy up to a maximum percentage increase.
    C. To acquire additional amounts of life insurance under a COL rider, evidence of insurability must be provided.
    D. Declines in the CPI cause corresponding declines in the amount of insurance coverage.

11. "If an insurance company determines that the insured is totally disabled, the policyowner is relieved of paying the policy premiums as long as the disability continues." This statement describes

    A. the premium suspension clause
    B. the waiting period exemption
    C. the disability income rider
    D. the waiver of premium rider

12. To what period would a 14-day free-look provision apply in Florida?

    A. The first 14 days after the application has been signed by the applicant
    B. The first 14 days after the application has been received by the insurer
    C. The first 14 days after the policy has been issued by the insurer
    D. The first 14 days after the issued policy has been received by the insured

13. All of the following statements regarding assignment of a life insurance policy are correct EXCEPT

    A. to secure a loan, the policy can be transferred temporarily to the lender as security for the loan
    B. the policyowner must obtain approval from the insurance company before a policy can be assigned
    C. the life insurance company assumes no responsibility for the validity of an assignment
    D. the life insurance company must be notified in writing by the policyowner of any assignment

14. Which provision of a life insurance policy states that the application is part of the contract?

    A. Consideration clause
    B. Insuring clause
    C. Entire contract clause
    D. Incontestable clause

15. Ron, the insured under a $100,000 life insurance policy, dies during the grace period. What happens, considering that the premium on the policy has not been paid?

    A. The premium is cancelled because the insured died during the grace period.
    B. The amount of the premium is deducted from the policy proceeds paid to the beneficiary.
    C. The premium due, plus a 10% penalty, is charged against the policy.
    D. The beneficiary must pay the premium after the death claim is paid.

16. Which of the following is stated in the consideration clause of a life insurance policy?

    A. Insured's risk classification
    B. Insured's general health condition
    C. Amount and frequency of premium payments
    D. Benefits payable upon the insured's death

17. John stopped paying premiums on his permanent life insurance policy 8 years ago though he never surrendered it. He is still insurable and has no outstanding loan against the policy. The company probably will decline to reinstate the policy because the time limit for reinstatement has expired. The limit usually is

    A. 6 months
    B. 1 year
    C. 2 years
    D. 3 years or as long as 7 years

18. All of the following statements pertaining to reinstatement of a life insurance policy are correct EXCEPT

    A. a suicide exclusion period is renewed with a reinstated policy
    B. when reinstating a policy, the insurer will charge the policyowner for past-due premiums
    C. when reinstating a policy, the insurer will charge the policyowner for interest on past-due premiums
    D. a new contestable period becomes effective in a reinstated policy

19. Leland elects to surrender his whole life policy for a reduced paid-up policy. The cash value of his new policy will

    A. continue to increase
    B. decrease gradually
    C. remain the same as in the old policy
    D. be forfeited

20. If error is discovered after an insured dies and the insured was younger than the insurance policy stated, the insurance company will

    A. reduce the death benefits
    B. reduce premiums
    C. waive the difference
    D. increase the death benefits

21. Each of the following statements about the incontestable clause in a life insurance policy is correct EXCEPT

    A. the clause gives people assurance that when their policies become claims, they will be paid without delays or protests
    B. the incontestable clause means that after a certain period, an insurer cannot refuse to pay the proceeds of a policy or void the contract
    C. incontestable clauses usually become effective 2 years from the issue date of the policy
    D. insurers can void a contract even after the specified period, provided they can prove the policy was purchased fraudulently

22. If an error is discovered while an insured is living and the insured is older than the policy states, the insurance company can

    A. increase the premium
    B. reduce the premium
    C. waive the difference
    D. increase the benefits

23. The rider that provides for a waiver of premiums on a juvenile policy if the adult payor dies or becomes disabled is

    A. a guaranteed insurability rider
    B. a payor rider
    C. a waiver of premium rider
    D. an automatic premium loan rider

24. Which of the following statements about a life insurance policy's cash value is CORRECT?

    A. In many states (but not all), policyowners are entitled to the accrued cash values of their whole life policies.
    B. When a whole life insurance policy is active, the owner can borrow from the cash value.
    C. Owners of both term and whole life insurance are entitled to the cash surrender value when a policy is lapsed or surrendered.
    D. If a policyowner lets her whole life policy lapse, the beneficiary will be entitled to part of the policy's cash value.

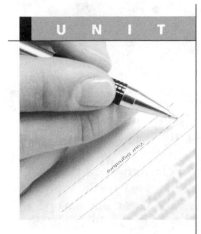

7

Life Insurance Beneficiaries

■ Who Can Be a Beneficiary?

■ Types of Beneficiary Designations

■ Special Situations

In Unit 6, we noted that a right involved with owning a life insurance policy is the right to name a beneficiary. The beneficiary is the party designated to receive the policy's proceeds upon the insured's death. Determining the proper beneficiary is a matter of utmost importance. To counsel their clients competently, life insurance agents must fully understand the laws and the practices involved with naming policy beneficiaries. ■

WHO CAN BE A BENEFICIARY?

Life insurance companies place very few restrictions on who may be named the beneficiary of a life insurance policy. The decision rests solely with the owner of the policy. However, in some cases, the insurer must consider the issue of **insurable interest**.

As we have learned, insurable interest is not a concern when the applicant for a policy is also the insured. In those cases, a person can apply for as much life insurance as the company will issue and can name anyone as beneficiary, whether or not insurable interest exists between the applicant-insured and the beneficiary. This is because, by law, individuals are presumed to have an unlimited insurable interest in their own lives.

The situation is different when the policy applicant is not the insured (that is, a **third-party applicant**). When a third-party applicant names himself as beneficiary, insurable interest must exist between the applicant and insured. When a third-party applicant names yet another as beneficiary, most states require that insurable interest must exist between that beneficiary and the insured. For example, if Bill were to apply for life insurance coverage on Sue and name himself as beneficiary, insurable interest would have to exist between Bill and Sue. If Bill were to apply for life insurance coverage on Sue but name Jason as beneficiary, insurable interest would probably have to exist between Jason and Sue.

With this in mind, let's take a look at what kinds of entities are commonly designated beneficiaries. (See Unit 27 for Florida law concerning agents as beneficiaries.)

Individuals as Beneficiaries

In most cases, an individual is selected to be the sole or proportional beneficiary of a life insurance policy. There may be one named individual or more than one. For example, a policyowner could designate his wife as the sole beneficiary or designate that she receive half the proceeds of his policy, with the remainder to be split equally between his two children.

Businesses as Beneficiaries

There is no question that insurable interest exists in business relationships. For example, professional sports clubs have an insurable interest in the lives of their best players. Partnerships have an insurable interest in the lives of their partners. Small corporations have an insurable interest in the lives of their key employees. Creditors have an insurable interest in the lives of people who owe them money. Life insurance policies may designate businesses as beneficiaries.

Trusts as Beneficiaries

A trust is a legal arrangement for the ownership of property by one party for the benefit of another. Designating a trust as the beneficiary of a life insurance policy means that the proceeds will be paid to the trust for the ultimate benefit and use by another. Trusts are managed by trustees, who have the fiduciary responsibility to oversee and handle the trust and its funds for its beneficiaries.

Estates as Beneficiaries

In the event that no beneficiary is designated on a life insurance policy or if any or all beneficiaries predecease the insured before a new beneficiary is designated, proceeds from the life insurance policy will go to the estate of the insured.

Policyowners may intentionally designate their estates as beneficiaries, so that, upon death, the proceeds can be used to meet federal estate taxes, debts, and other administrative costs, leaving other assets intact to pass on to heirs.

Charities as Beneficiaries

Naming a charity as the beneficiary of a life insurance policy is another commonly accepted practice. Life insurance is one of the most attractive and flexible ways to make a contribution to a church, educational institution, hospital, public welfare agency, or similar nonprofit organization. One of the benefits of making a contribution of life insurance proceeds—in contrast to leaving a bequest in a will—is that the gift cannot be contested by disgruntled heirs. This is because life insurance proceeds are not part of the insured-donor's probate estate.

Minors as Beneficiaries

Naming minors as life insurance beneficiaries can present some legal and logistical complications. For instance, the minor may not have the legal capacity to give the insurance company a signed release for receipt of the policy proceeds. (Some states have adopted special laws that only allow minors of minimum specified ages, such as 15, to sign a valid receipt.) If an insurer were to pay out the proceeds and not receive a receipt, the minor could legally demand payment a second time, once the minor has reached the age of majority. Furthermore, the minor may simply lack the judgment or expertise to properly manage the proceeds.

Nonetheless, insurers recognize that policyowners may want minors to benefit from an insurance policy. In those cases, and in accordance with the laws of the particular state, insurers may:

- make limited payments to an adult guardian for the benefit of the minor beneficiary;

- retain the policy proceeds at interest and pay them out when the child reaches majority or when an adult guardian is appointed; or

- place the proceeds in a trust for the present or future benefit of the minor, as determined by the trustee.

Classes as Beneficiaries

There is also a beneficiary designation known as a **class designation**. This means that rather than specifying one or more beneficiaries by name, the policyowner designates a class or group of beneficiaries. For example, "children of the insured" and "my children" are class designations.

TYPES OF BENEFICIARY DESIGNATIONS

There are a number of ways to classify beneficiary designations: by the order of succession (or preference), by the number named, by line of descent, or by whether or not the designation(s) can be changed. A discussion of these various types of designations follows. In any event, it is important to select and arrange beneficiary designations carefully, because once they are in effect, the insurance company must follow them to the letter.

Order of Succession

It is always possible that a beneficiary to a life insurance policy may predecease the insured. To meet this contingency, policyowners are encouraged to designate **primary**, **secondary**, and, occasionally, **tertiary** beneficiaries.

Primary Beneficiaries

A **primary beneficiary** is the party designated to receive the proceeds of a life insurance policy when they become payable. There may be more than one primary beneficiary, and how the proceeds are to be split is up to the policyowner.

Secondary (Contingent) Beneficiaries

A **secondary beneficiary** may also be named and stands second in line to receive the proceeds of a life insurance policy if the primary beneficiary dies before the insured. Secondary beneficiaries are entitled to policy proceeds only if no primary beneficiaries are living. Secondary beneficiaries are also known as "contingent" or "successor" beneficiaries.

Tertiary (Contingent) Beneficiaries

A **tertiary beneficiary** stands third in line to receive the proceeds of a life insurance policy, in cases where all primary and secondary beneficiaries predecease the insured.

Example of Beneficiary Succession

For example, assume that Deborah takes out a $150,000 policy on her life and establishes the beneficiary designations as follows: her husband, Rob, is to receive the full benefit; if he predeceases her, her two children are to share equally in the benefit; and if her husband and both her children predecease her, the benefit is payable to Homestate College, her alma mater. In this situation, Rob is the primary beneficiary, the children are contingent secondary beneficiaries, and Homestate College is the contingent tertiary beneficiary.

If no beneficiary is named, or if all primary and contingent beneficiaries are deceased at the time of the insured's death, the proceeds are paid to the policyowner or to the policyowner's estate, if the policyowner is deceased.

More than One Beneficiary per Category

Policyowners may name more than one beneficiary in any category, whether the category is primary, secondary, or tertiary. When they do so, however, they should specify the percentage or dollar amount of the proceeds that each is to receive. Most companies recommend that each beneficiary's share be indicated as a fraction. For instance, assume Harry specifies that the proceeds of his $50,000 life insurance policy are to be paid out as follows: $25,000 to his wife, Louise, and the remaining $25,000 to his son, Jack. When Harry dies, there is a $20,000 loan against the policy. Consequently, in accordance with the way Harry designated his beneficiaries, Louise will receive $25,000 and Jack will receive $5,000. Had Harry specified that his wife and his son were to share equally (50%) in the proceeds, the remaining death benefit would have been distributed more equitably—$15,000 to each—which probably was Harry's intent.

Following is an example of a beneficiary designation that properly takes the proportioning of the proceeds into account:

> *One-half to my wife, Shirley Dawn Brown; one-fourth to my son, Curtis Rodney Brown; and one-fourth to my daughter, Mary Lee Brown. In the event of the death of any beneficiary, his or her share shall be divided equally between the survivors or all shall go to the sole survivor.*

Distribution by Descent

When life insurance policy proceeds are to be distributed to a person's descendents, a *per stirpes* or a *per capita* approach is generally used.

Per Stirpes

The term **per stirpes** means "by way of" or "by branches." A per stirpes distribution means that a beneficiary's share of a policy's proceeds will be passed down to the beneficiary's living child or children in equal shares should the named beneficiary predecease the insured.

Per Capita

The term **per capita** means "per person" or "by head." A per capita distribution means that a policy's proceeds are paid only to the beneficiaries who are living and have been named in the policy.

Example of Per Stirpes Versus Per Capita

To illustrate the difference between per stirpes and per capita distributions, assume that Arthur names his wife as primary beneficiary and his two married children, Sam and Linda, as secondary beneficiaries to share equally per stirpes. If Arthur's wife died before her husband, Sam and Linda would share equally in the proceeds, if they were living. But if Sam also were to predecease his father, leaving three children of his own, his share of the proceeds would be divided equally among his three children. Linda's share would remain the same.

Had Arthur used a per capita designation, naming Sam and Linda secondary beneficiaries, the full proceeds would be paid to Linda—her mother, the primary beneficiary, had already died and the only other named beneficiary, Sam, had also died. Sam's children would not be entitled to his share of the proceeds under a per capita distribution.

In short, the per capita beneficiary claims in his own right, while the per stirpes beneficiary receives the proceeds through the rights of another. Today, the per stirpes method of distribution is by far the more common approach. (See Illustration 7.1.)

Changing a Beneficiary

Beneficiary designations are classified according to whether they can be changed after a policy is issued. Recall that the right to change beneficiary designations is a right of ownership. It is a right the policyowner may retain or relinquish by designating either a revocable beneficiary or irrevocable beneficiary.

Revocable Beneficiary

When beneficiaries are designated **revocable**, the policyowner may change the designation at any time. It also means that the policyowner remains the complete owner of the policy. The policyowner can make policy changes whenever needed or desired. A revocable beneficiary has no vested claim on the policy or its proceeds as long as the insured (or policyowner, if different) is living.

ILLUSTRATION 7.1

Per Stirpes and Per Capita
Distributions

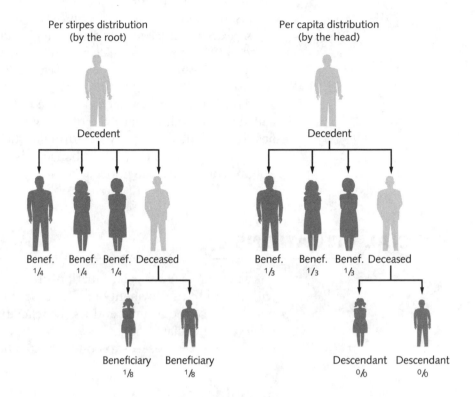

Per stirpes distribution
(by the root)

Per capita distribution
(by the head)

Irrevocable Beneficiary

When a beneficiary is designated **irrevocable**, the policyowner gives up the right to change the beneficiary. For all practical purposes, the policy is owned by both the policyowner and the beneficiary. An irrevocable beneficiary has a vested right in the policy and the policyowner cannot exercise any right that would affect the vested rights of the beneficiary without the beneficiary's consent. For example, a policyowner cannot borrow from the policy, assign the policy, or surrender it without the written consent of the beneficiary. If an irrevocable beneficiary agrees in writing, control of the policy may be retained by the policyowner.

Irrevocable clauses can be **absolute** or **reversionary**. When absolute, the beneficiary has an absolute vested interest in the life insurance contract even if the beneficiary predeceases the policyowner. When reversionary, the right to modify the beneficiary clause as well as all other rights of ownership revert to the policyowner if and when the beneficiary predeceases the policyowner.

Procedure for Changing Beneficiaries

Each life insurance policy describes the procedure for changing a beneficiary. Here, for example, is the beneficiary change clause that appears in the sample life insurance policy in Appendix A (assuming the policyowner is the insured):

> *A change of beneficiary may be made by written request while the insured is living. The change will take place as of the date the request is signed, even if the insured is not living on the day the request is received. Any rights created by the change will be subject to any payments made or actions taken by Superior Mutual before the written request is received.*

This is the common method in use today for changing beneficiaries. It's called the **recording method**. Following this method, the policyowner notifies the insurance company in writing of the beneficiary change. When the insurance company records the change, it becomes effective as of the date the policyowner signed the notice.

SPECIAL SITUATIONS

There are a few special situations that insurers must occasionally address with regard to the payment of policy proceeds. These include the simultaneous deaths of the insured and the beneficiary, how to prevent the proceeds paid to a beneficiary from being attached by creditors, and situations in which insurers can pay proceeds to nondesignated beneficiaries.

Simultaneous Death

When an insured dies and the death benefit is payable to a named beneficiary, usually there is nothing to complicate the transaction. But what if the insured and the primary beneficiary die in the same accident and there is no evidence to show which one died first? How and to whom does the insurer pay the proceeds?

To address this problem, the *Uniform Simultaneous Death Act* has been enacted in most states. This law stipulates that if the insured and the primary beneficiary are killed in the same accident and there is not sufficient evidence to show who died first, the policy proceeds are to be distributed *as if the insured died last*. This law allows the insurance company to pay the proceeds to a secondary or other contingent beneficiary. If no contingent beneficiary has been named, the insured's estate will receive the proceeds.

The Uniform Simultaneous Death Act is only a partial solution to the problem, however. There are situations in which the primary beneficiary clearly outlives the insured, but only for the briefest time—minutes, hours, or a few days. In these cases where the beneficiary obviously outlived the insured, if the provisions of the insurance contract were strictly followed, the insurer would pay the proceeds to the estate of the recently deceased primary beneficiary. Chances are, this would be contrary to the policyowner's wishes. The policyowner likely would have preferred that the proceeds be paid to a secondary beneficiary or to the policyowner's own estate.

The problems resulting from the proximate but not (proven) simultaneous death of both the insured and the primary beneficiary prompted insurance companies to develop and offer a **common disaster provision** that gives policyowners greater control over payment of the policy proceeds. This provision, which may be part of the policy itself or incorporated into the beneficiary designation, activates only when the insured and the primary beneficiary die as a result of the same accident. It provides that:

- if the insured and primary beneficiary die in the same accident, it is presumed that the insured died last (consistent with the Uniform Simultaneous Death Act); and

- the primary beneficiary must outlive the insured by a definite period of time, as stipulated by the policyowner—14 days or 30 days are typical choices—or it is still assumed that the insured died last.

Thus, with a common disaster provision operating, a policyowner can be sure that if both the insured and the primary beneficiary die within a short period of time, the death benefits will be paid to the secondary beneficiary (if there is one) or to the insured's estate. Let's look at an example.

Burt and Carol, his wife by a second marriage and primary beneficiary of his $100,000 life insurance policy, are both killed in a single auto accident. Carol survives Burt by only 24 hours. Without a common disaster clause, the proceeds of Burt's policy would be paid to Carol's estate and possibly go to her children by her first marriage. Burt's children by his first marriage could be left out entirely. But because a common disaster provision was in effect in Burt's policy, the proceeds were instead paid to his estate, and distribution of the estate's assets made according to his wishes by virtue of his will.

Spendthrift Trust Clause

The **spendthrift trust clause** is another commonly used clause in life insurance policies. Its purpose is to help protect beneficiaries from the claims of their creditors. More precisely, it shelters life insurance proceeds that have not yet been paid to a named beneficiary from the claims of either the beneficiary's or policyowner's creditors.

The spendthrift clause does not apply to proceeds paid in one lump sum. As we will learn in the next unit, proceeds may be held in trust by the insurer and paid to the beneficiary in installments over a period of time. The spendthrift clause pertains to these installment payment arrangements. Generally, the clause states that policy distributions payable to the beneficiary after the insured dies are not assignable or transferable and may not be attached in any way.

For example, assume Al is receiving monthly installment income payments from the proceeds of his late wife's life insurance policy. He buys an expensive sports car and later finds out that he cannot meet the payments on the car. If the finance company is awarded a judgment when it sues Al, his unpaid life insurance proceeds are protected against the claim. Of course, the finance company can still go after Al's other assets.

The spendthrift trust clause does not operate to protect proceeds that belong to the policyowner and are payable as income to the policyowner. It applies only to money held in trust by the insurance company that is earmarked to be paid to the named beneficiary at some future time. Spendthrift trust clauses are valid in the majority of states and are found in many life insurance policies.

Facility-of-Payment Provision

There are a few limited situations in which an insurer must pay proceeds to someone not designated as a beneficiary. A **facility-of-payment provision**, most typically found in industrial policies, permits an insurer to pay all or a portion of the proceeds to someone who, though not named in the policy, has a valid right. These situations include cases in which:

- the named beneficiary is a minor;

- the named beneficiary is deceased;

- no claim is submitted within a specified period of time; or

- costs were incurred by another party for the deceased insured's final medical expenses or funeral expenses.

SUMMARY

Designating an individual or entity as the *beneficiary* of a life insurance policy is one of the policyowner's most important rights. Insurance companies place very few conditions on this right, but care must be taken because the insurer is bound to follow the designation once it is established.

There are many ways to classify beneficiary designations: by *order of succession*—primary, secondary or tertiary; by the *number named* within each order; and by *descent—per stirpes* or *per capita*. Whether or not a beneficiary designation can be *changed* is also a consideration.

There are a few special situations insurers must address regarding the payment of life insurance proceeds. Should the insured and the primary beneficiary die simultaneously or within a short time of each other, the appropriate and fair disbursement of proceeds could be compromised. The *Uniform Simultaneous Death Act* and the *common disaster provision* help assure that the proceeds will be paid in line with the insured's wishes, as far as possible. The *spendthrift trust clause* protects unpaid insurance proceeds from claims by the beneficiary's creditors. Finally, the *facility-of-payment provision* allows an insurer to pay proceeds to someone not named in the policy but, due to special circumstances, has a right to them.

KEY CONCEPTS

Students should be familiar with the following concepts:

beneficiary designation options	classifications of beneficiaries
per stirpes	per capita
revocable beneficiary	irrevocable beneficiary
Uniform Simultaneous Death Act	common disaster provision
spendthrift trust clause	facility-of-payment provision

UNIT TEST

1. Sandra has a life insurance policy that states her husband, Gerald, is to receive the full death benefit. If he predeceases her, their 3 children are to share the benefit equally. If her husband and all 3 children predecease her, the benefit is payable to the First Community Church. All of the following statements are correct EXCEPT

   A. Gerald is the primary beneficiary
   B. the 3 children are all secondary beneficiaries
   C. the First Community Church is the tertiary beneficiary
   D. the designation of the First Community Church can be contested by any of Sandra's relatives who survive the children

2. The beneficiary on Walter's life insurance policy reads, "Children of the Insured." Which of the following phrases best describes this type of beneficiary designation?

   A. Juvenile beneficiaries
   B. Class beneficiaries
   C. Generational beneficiaries
   D. Attractive nuisance beneficiaries

3. Which of the following statements is CORRECT?

   A. A per capita distribution is the most common method of distributing proceeds to beneficiaries.
   B. If a policyowner designates a per stirpes distribution of the proceeds, the designation becomes irrevocable once a beneficiary predeceases the policyowner.
   C. A per stirpes distribution means that a beneficiary's share of a policy's proceeds will be passed down to the beneficiary's living child or children if the named beneficiary predeceases the insured.
   D. A per capita distribution ensures that an insured's surviving family will share in the insurance proceeds.

4. If an irrevocable beneficiary dies before the policyowner, who of the following gains control of a life insurance policy with a reversionary irrevocable clause?

   A. Insured
   B. Irrevocable beneficiary's children
   C. Policyowner
   D. Insurer

5. Christine's policy has a clause that reads as follows: "Should the primary beneficiary and the insured die in the same accident and the primary beneficiary fails to survive the insured by 14 days, it will be assumed that the beneficiary predeceased the insured." Which of the following phrases best describes this clause?

   A. Secondary beneficiary provision
   B. Facility-of-payment provision
   C. Uniform Simultaneous Death Act
   D. Common disaster provision

6. Kevin, the insured under a $200,000 life insurance policy, and his sole beneficiary, Lynda, are killed instantly in a car accident. Under the Uniform Simultaneous Death Act, to whose estate will the policy proceeds be paid?

   A. Lynda's estate
   B. Kevin's estate
   C. Both Kevin's and Lynda's estate, equally
   D. The proceeds will escheat to the state

7. When a policyowner cannot exercise his rights of ownership without the policy beneficiary's consent, the beneficiary is designated

   A. vested
   B. contractual
   C. irrevocable
   D. primary

8. Mr. Williams names his son John a beneficiary of his life insurance policy. What designation should he use if he wants to make sure that John's children would receive John's share of the life insurance policy proceeds should John predecease his father?

   A. Per capita
   B. All my children
   C. Per stirpes
   D. Grandchildren

9. What is the beneficiary designation that can only be changed with the beneficiary's written agreement?

   A. Revocable beneficiary
   B. Wife of the insured
   C. Per stirpes
   D. Irrevocable beneficiary

10. All of the following statements concerning a *common disaster provision* are correct EXCEPT

   A. the provision activates when the insured and primary beneficiary die as a result of the same accident
   B. the provision stipulates that if the insured and primary beneficiary die in the same accident, it is presumed that the insured died last
   C. the provision gives a policyowner assurance that proceeds will be distributed according to the policyowner's wishes
   D. the provision stipulates that if the primary beneficiary outlives the insured by more than 48 hours, then the proceeds will be paid to the primary beneficiary's estate

11. A clause that states that policy distributions payable to a beneficiary after the insured dies are not assignable or transferable and may not be attached in any way is called

   A. a facility-of-payment clause
   B. a debtors protection clause
   C. a spendthrift trust clause
   D. an assignment clause

12. All of the following statements about facility of payment provisions are correct EXCEPT

   A. they are often found in group life policies
   B. they permit an insurer to pay all or part of the proceeds to a party who is not named in the contract
   C. they are typically found in industrial policies
   D. they permit insurance proceeds to be paid to someone not named in the policy when the named beneficiary is a minor

13. Mary names her husband, Rick, as primary beneficiary of her life insurance policy and her two children, Pam and Matt, as contingent beneficiaries. Rick dies in March. Pam and Matt are killed simultaneously in a car accident later that month. Hearing the news, Mary has a fatal heart attack. In this case, Mary's life insurance proceeds will be paid

   A. one-half to Rick's estate and one-quarter each to Pam and Matt's estates
   B. to Rick's estate
   C. to Mary's estate
   D. in equal shares to Rick, Pam, and Matt's estates

14. All of the following statements about beneficiary designations are correct EXCEPT

   A. when a charity is named beneficiary, the policyowner's heirs cannot contest the gift
   B. minors cannot be named life insurance beneficiaries
   C. a business may be designated as a beneficiary
   D. when a trust is named beneficiary, a trustee will manage the insurance proceeds

15. The method used today to change beneficiaries is known as

   A. the recording method
   B. the beneficiary alteration method
   C. the assignment method
   D. the change of designation method

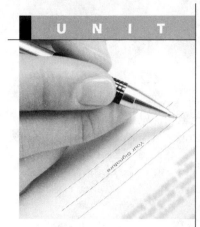

8

Life Insurance Premiums and Proceeds

- Life Insurance Premiums
- Primary Factors in Premium Calculations
- Mortality Factor
- Life Insurance Policy Proceeds
- Tax Treatment of Proceeds

People buy life insurance for the same basic reason they buy any product—it satisfies a need. In the case of life insurance, the need is financial security. Policyowners pay for this product through premiums. Upon the insured's death, policy proceeds (the "death benefit") are payable to the beneficiary in any one of a variety of ways, depending on the unique situation and needs of the beneficiary. This unit examines these two important aspects of life insurance—premiums and proceeds—and reviews their tax treatment. ■

LIFE INSURANCE PREMIUMS

The task of determining an insurance company's **premium rates** rests with the company's actuaries. Actuaries are mathematicians by education who are responsible for bringing together the financial and statistical data that have an influence on life (and health) insurance premium rates. Establishing realistic premium rates is a critical function in any life insurance company. Rates must be high enough to cover the costs of paying claims and doing business, yet low enough so that they are competitive with other insurers' rates.

Life insurance premium rates are generally expressed as an annual cost per $1,000 of **face amount**. For example, one company's rate for a male, age 35, is $13.73. What exactly does this mean? It means that for the particular policy in question (say, a $50,000 participating straight whole life policy), the policyowner, a male who was 35 when he purchased the policy, pays an annual premium of $13.73 for every $1,000 of face amount he purchased, or $686.50 ($13.73 × 50). Because it is a straight whole life policy, this policyowner will pay $686.50 per year for his life (or to age 100, if he is fortunate enough to live that long).

ILLUSTRATION 8.1

How the Life Insurance Premium Dollar Is Used

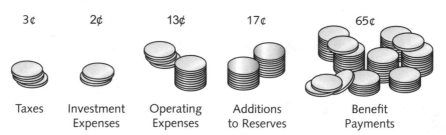

3¢	2¢	13¢	17¢	65¢
Taxes	Investment Expenses	Operating Expenses	Additions to Reserves	Benefit Payments

Source: 2007 ACLI Life Insurers Fact Book

PRIMARY FACTORS IN PREMIUM CALCULATIONS

Three primary factors are considered when computing the basic premium for life insurance: mortality, interest, and expense. Of these, the **mortality factor** has the greatest effect on premium calculations (commonly termed "rate-making"). That is, while an insurer's interest and expense factors are generally the same for all of its policyholders, the mortality factor can vary greatly, depending on personal characteristics of individual insureds.

MORTALITY FACTOR

A basic principle of life insurance is that it must be based on an accurate prediction of mortality, that is, the average number of deaths that will occur each year in each age group. Throughout the years, statistics have been compiled, showing how many and at what ages people can generally be expected to die. Compiled, these statistics become mortality tables, which reflect **death rates** at each age.

For a mortality table to be accurate, it must be based on two things: a **large cross section of people** and a **large cross section of time**.

Illustration 8.2 is a sample mortality predictions table taken from the 2001 Commissioner's Standard Ordinary (CSO), Mortality Table. The Florida Department of Financial Services has adopted the Commissioners' 2001 Standard Ordinary Mortality Table. Only 10-year age intervals are shown, and the ages in between (except age 99) are not included.

ILLUSTRATION 8.2

2001 CSO Mortality Table

Age	Male	Female
0	76.62	80.84
10	66.88	71.03
20	57.23	61.26
30	47.79	51.56
40	38.33	42.00
50	29.18	32.69
60	20.64	24.08
70	13.32	16.40
80	7.49	9.92
90	3.81	5.29
99	2.19	2.82
100	2.07	2.61

The figures above are a sampling from the 2001 CSO Mortality Table. The age at the left is the insured age at this time. The numbers under Male and Female are the number of years of life remaining. For example, an 80-year-old male is expected to live to 87.49, and an 80-year-old female should live to be 89.92.

Two primary purposes of a mortality table are to indicate:

- the **expectation of life** at given ages—the average number of years remaining for a group of persons of the same age; and

- the **probability of death**—the average number of deaths for a group of persons in given years.

Obviously, the significance of mortality predictions to an insurance company is that they provide a basis to estimate how long its insureds will live, how long they will be paying premiums, and at what future dates the company will have to pay out benefits. Consequently, the portion of the premium associated with mortality reflects the pure cost of providing death protection. Large insurance companies typically base their rates on their own statistics and experience or construct their own mortality tables from a "data pool" based on the experience of many insurers. Actuaries use the experience of several years to determine the mortality data that will be incorporated into premium rates.

Interest Factor

When policyowners pay premiums to a life insurance company, the funds do not sit idle in the insurer's vaults. They are combined with other funds and invested to earn **interest**. Among other things, this interest earned helps hold down the cost of life insurance premiums.

An insurer makes two assumptions with regard to interest. First, it assumes that a *specific net rate of interest will be earned* on all its investments. Actually, some investments will earn more than the assumed rate and some will earn less, so the company selects an average rate for its assumption. The assumed interest rate may seem low (generally, 3–4%), but it directly affects the premium levels that are guaranteed to policyowners for years into the future. Thus, the assumed rates must be reasonably conservative.

The second assumption made by the company is that one full year's interest will be earned by each premium policyowners pay. Therefore, it must be assumed that *all premiums are paid at the beginning of the year.*

Because there is no reliable basis for predicting future interest rates or trends, a company must remain conservative in its interest assumptions because it is committed to the interest rate guaranteed in its life insurance policies for as long as those policies remain in force. Interest earnings on invested premiums is the second consideration in premium rate calculations; the higher the assumed rate of interest, the lower the premium rate charged to policyowners.

Expense Factor

The third factor affecting premium rates is *expenses*. As does any business, an insurance company has various operating expenses. Personnel must be hired and paid; sales forces must be recruited, trained, and compensated; supplies must be purchased; rent must be paid; and buildings must be maintained. In addition, local, state, and federal taxes must be paid. Each premium must carry its small proportionate share of these normal operating costs.

Thus, an expense factor is computed and included in the premium rates for life insurance. Sometimes the expense factor is called the "loading charge."

Net Versus Gross Premiums

The factors basic to premium calculations—mortality, interest, and expense—are only a portion of the equation. Actuaries use the assumptions underlying these factors and translate them into **net single premium, net level premiums**, and **gross premiums.**

The **net single premium** can be defined as the single amount needed today to fund the future benefit. Basically, it is the amount of premium, when combined with interest, that will be sufficient to pay the future death benefit. However, only rarely do people purchase life insurance with a single premium because of the large cash outlay required. Most pay premiums over a number of years. Thus, the net single premium is converted into **net annual level**

premiums, with some adjustments due to a lesser amount of interest these smaller premiums will earn. Finally, the **gross premium** is determined, which reflects the addition of the expense factor. The gross premium is what the policyowners are required to pay.

In very general terms, actuaries deduct the assumed interest earnings from the mortality cost. The mortality cost less the assumed interest earnings equals the net premium. The expense factor then is added to the net premium to arrive at the gross premium.

The two key formulas to keep in mind are:

$$\text{Net single premium} = \text{Mortality cost} - \text{Interest}$$

$$\text{Gross premium} = \text{Net single premium} + \text{Expenses}$$

Other Premium Factors

The preceding discussion focused on the three primary factors underlying all life insurance premiums. When evaluating individual applications for life insurance, other premium factors come into play, all of which influence mortality to one degree or another.

■ **Age.** As we have seen, the age of an individual has a direct bearing on mortality, and mortality is figured directly into premium calculations. The older the insured, the greater the mortality risk.

■ **Sex.** The sex of the applicant also has a bearing on mortality. Experience has shown that, on the average, women live five or six years longer than men. Statistically, then, they are considered better life insurance risks than men, and their premium rates have usually been lower than those for men.[1]

■ **Health.** Another factor influencing mortality is the health of the applicant. Obviously, those in poorer health represent a higher risk than those in good health.

■ **Occupation or avocation.** An applicant's occupation or avocation can also affect mortality. Those employed in hazardous occupations pose a greater risk to an insurer, as do those who engage in dangerous hobbies.

■ **Habits.** An individual's personal habits may also influence the premium rate that individual will be assessed. Habits such as smoking or overeating adversely affect health and may increase the risk of death.

Factors such as these are considered carefully by insurance company underwriters, whose job it is to evaluate and select risks. The three risk classifications typically used are preferred, standard, and substandard. In those cases where an individual applicant represents a higher-than-normal risk to the insurer due to one or more of the personal characteristics listed above, the individual is known as a "substandard risk." Of course, insurers can reject a substandard risk, and some applicants are denied. However, another way to

---

[1]   It should be noted that many insurance companies have adopted unisex rating tables, which effectively disregard the difference in mortality rates between men and women of the same age.

treat a substandard case is to adjust the premium to reflect the increased risk. This approach is known as **rating**.

Methods of Rating Substandard Risks

There are a number of approaches insurance companies use to set or adjust premiums for substandard cases. These methods include **extra percentage tables, permanent flat extra premiums, temporary flat extra premiums, rate-up in age**, and **liens.** Let's briefly review each.

Extra Percentage Tables

Although the **extra percentage tables** rating system varies somewhat from company to company, it is the one used most extensively today. This method involves a numerical system for rating substandard cases, so the premium charged, for example, may be from 125–500% of standard. A number of premium rates usually are established for each age and type of policy. The system assumes there are a certain number of extra deaths per thousand that will increase with age for all kinds of cases.

Permanent Flat Extra Premiums

The **permanent flat extra premiums** rating system adds a fixed charge of so many dollars per $1,000 of insurance for substandard cases. This additional charge is assessed for the extra risk, which is measured in extra deaths per thousand. The flat extra premiums do not increase the policy's cash or nonforfeiture values. Any extra premium may be removed when the insured's condition is believed to have changed to a point where the risk is reduced.

Temporary Flat Extra Premiums

The **temporary flat extra premiums** rating system is identical to the permanent flat extra premium system, except that the fixed additional premium is charged for a specified number of years. With either permanent or temporary flat extra premiums, the amount of the additional charge generally will vary with the type of policy. A temporary extra premium may be charged when most of the extra risk is anticipated during the early years the policy is in force (e.g., perhaps the first few years following surgery).

Rate-up in Age

Though the **rate-up in age** system of rating substandard cases is no longer widely used, it warrants mention. Under this method, the proposed insured is assumed to be a number of years older than the insured really is, and the policy is issued with a correspondingly higher premium.

Lien System

Under the **lien system**, a policy is issued at standard rates on a substandard applicant, but with a lien against the policy. This lien reduces the amount of insurance automatically in the event the insured dies from a cause cited in the policy (and which resulted in the rating). Generally, this system is used now only with some money purchase pension plans where premiums are uniform. However, this system has had major drawbacks, primarily because insureds have not understood that they are getting less protection than is shown as the face amount of their policies.

Level Premium Funding

As mentioned earlier, the age of an insured has direct influence on the mortality charge—the higher the age, the higher the mortality charge. Since the mortality charge has a direct impact on the amount of premium, it stands to reason that as a person ages, the premium rate for that person should increase.

In Unit 5, it was pointed out that term insurance is characterized, in part, by steadily increasing premiums. The most dramatic example of this is annually renewable term (ART) insurance. With ART policies, policyowners are paying for one year of pure insurance protection only, meaning that they will pay, in any given year, the cost of insurance for that year. The older an insured becomes, the higher the mortality charge becomes and, thus, the higher the premium becomes.

In Unit 5, the concept of *level premiums* was also introduced. As we discussed, life insurance is issued with premiums calculated and payable on a level basis for the policy's life. If the policy is a term policy, the premiums are level for the duration of the term; if the policy is a whole life policy, the premiums are level for life or, in the case of a limited pay policy, for the duration of the premium-paying period.

How is this possible? If the mortality rate (and consequently the mortality charge) for an insured increases each year, how can any type of life insurance permit its premiums to remain level for the life of the policy? The answer lies in the funding method underlying the policy.

All forms of permanent insurance (and those types of term whose periods extend beyond one year) are based on the **level premium funding method.** A full explanation of this complex actuarial concept is beyond the scope of this book; however, it is possible to simplify the explanation. Under the level premium funding method, the insured pays more than the insurance protection requires in the policy's early years; in the policy's later years, when the increasing mortality charge would normally increase the premium to a very high level, the excess paid in the early years is used to help fund the additional cost now required.

Interest plays an important role in this process. The "excess" funds paid in the early years will earn interest, thus making it possible to keep the actual premium level lower than if interest were not considered. In essence, *the level premiums collected under a permanent policy are actuarially (that is, mathematically) equivalent to the sum of the increasing annual renewable term rates for the same insured risk and for the same period of time.* Because of the "time value of money" (that is, the influence of interest), the actual sum of out-of-pocket premiums paid under a permanent policy (or a term policy that extends for a number of years) will be significantly less than those paid under an ART policy, all other factors (for example, age and policy face amount) being equal.

Reserves Versus Cash Values

What happens to those excess funds that are paid in the early years of a permanent policy? Because they are not actually required to cover the insurance risk at that time, they are set aside for the future time when they will be required. As one might guess, the unused funds belong to the policyowner; they constitute the policy's **cash value**. It is easy to see how important these funds are to the overall funding of the policy, especially in the policy's later years. This also explains why any loan against the cash value must be offset by a reduction in the proceeds paid out of the policy, unless the policyowner returns the borrowed funds, with interest.

People sometimes confuse the term *policy cash value* with *policy reserve*. While the two are similar in concept, there are some important differences. Basically, the cash value is a tangible amount that represents the additional funds paid in the early years of a whole life policy. It is, quite literally, the savings element of a whole life policy. The policy reserve is more intangible; it is a fund required by each state's insurance laws to be set aside to ensure that money will be available to pay future claims.

Literally, the policy reserve is the amount which, when added to the present value of future *net* premiums, will equal the present value of future claims. A very simple example will better illustrate this. Note that the term "present value" simply means the value *today* of a sum which will be larger in the future, after it accrues interest.

Assume the policyowner is 38 years old, owns a $50,000 permanent policy, and is actuarially expected to live to age 78. The annual net premium is $450, and the company is using an assumed interest rate of 4%.

Present value of the future claim	$10,400
Present value of the future premiums	− 8,900
Reserve liability	$ 1,500

This example shows that, with a 4% interest rate assumption, the present value of the $50,000 death benefit is $10,400. In other words, if $10,400 were invested at 4% interest for the next 40 years, it would grow to $50,000. The present value of future premiums is $8,900. If this amount were set aside to earn 4% interest, it would accumulate to an amount actuarially equivalent to the $450 premium the owner is paying each year. The difference, $1,500, is the required policy reserve.

Reserves are treated as a liability, meaning that companies must keep the reserve amount as a liability, not an asset, on their books. It is money that must be set aside to assure policyowners (and state regulators) that sufficient funds will be available when a claim arises.

Modes of Premium Payment

Policyowners ordinarily may pay their premiums under one of four modes: annually, semiannually, quarterly, or monthly. On any policy anniversary date (or at other times, if company rules permit) a policyowner may change from one payment mode to another, provided the payment is not less than a minimum specified by the company. There is a slight extra charge when premiums are not paid annually, as all gross premiums are calculated on an annual basis. The extra charge is to cover the additional paperwork and to make up for interest lost by the company because it does not have the full annual premium in advance to invest.

All premiums are payable in advance. The first premium is due on the day the policy is issued. Subsequent premiums become payable at the end of the period for which the preceding premium was paid. The first premium usually is paid to the agent at the time of application. If not paid then, it must be paid at the time of policy delivery. Premiums have to be paid to keep a policy in force, although policyowners have the right to stop paying premiums at any time.

ILLUSTRATION 8.3

The Claims Process

It is the duty of the insurance company's *claims office* to make sure that a death claim is handled promptly and properly. At the very least, the claims examiner will require a certified death certificate, which states in part the cause of the insured's death. The examiner will review the policy to determine if there is a reason to contest the claim. For example, if the cause of death was suicide, the claims examiner will want to know if the policy is still within the suicide exclusion period. If the insured was murdered, the laws of most states prevent life insurance proceeds from being paid to the beneficiary if the beneficiary was an accomplice to the murder.

Even if death resulted from natural causes, the examiner will review the policy carefully, especially if it is within the contestable period, to determine if the insured's application contained any misrepresentations that could void the contract. At the very least, the claims examiner will make sure that the actual age and sex of the insured agree with company records. Assuming that there is no reason to contest the claim (which is true in the majority of cases), the examiner will authorize payment of the death benefit to the policy beneficiary.

The next question the examiner will seek to answer is this: Did the policyowner wish the proceeds to be paid in any particular manner, or can the beneficiary select the manner of proceeds distribution (more properly called the *settlement option*)? If the policyowner did not specify a particular option, and if the beneficiary does not wish to select any settlement option, the claim will be paid as a lump sum. Often, though, either the policyowner or the beneficiary will select a settlement option.

Tax Treatment of Premiums

As a general rule, premiums paid for personal life insurance policies by individual policyowners are considered to be personal expenses and, therefore, are not deductible from gross income. Also, premiums paid for business life insurance usually are not deductible. For example, if the ABC Corporation purchased a key-person life insurance policy on the life of its president, the premiums are not deductible by the corporation.

There are a few exceptions to this rule.

- Premiums paid for life insurance owned by a qualified charitable organization *are* deductible.

- Premiums paid for life insurance by an ex-spouse as part of an alimony decree *are* deductible (as alimony).

- Premiums paid by a business creditor for life insurance purchased as collateral security for a debt *are* deductible.

- Premiums paid by an employer for employee group life insurance *are* deductible as an employee benefit business expense, as long as certain conditions are met.

Tax Treatment of Cash Values

The yearly increase in the cash value of a whole life insurance policy is not taxed during the period it accumulates inside the policy. If the cash value is taken out while the insured is still living—for example, as retirement income—a portion of each retirement income payment is received tax free because it represents a return of principal. Let's look at this in more detail.

With regard to the taxation of surrendered cash values, a policyowner is allowed to receive, tax free, an amount equal to what the policyowner paid into the policy over the years in the form of premiums. The sum of the premiums paid is known as the policyowner's *cost basis*. However, when the accumulated cash value exceeds the premiums paid—when the cash value is greater than the policyowner's cost basis—the difference is taxable. For example, assume that at the age of 65, Mel decides to surrender his whole life policy and take the $28,000 accumulated cash value in a lump sum. He paid a total of $19,000 in premiums over the years. The difference between his cost basis and the accumulated value ($28,000 − $19,000 = $9,000) will be treated as taxable income in the year Mel actually receives it.

As long as a policy is not surrendered, the cash value continues to accumulate tax free. There is never a tax imposed on the policyowner, even if the cash value exceeds the cost basis, as long as the cash value remains in the policy.

LIFE INSURANCE POLICY PROCEEDS

One thing that distinguishes life insurance from other forms of insurance is that a life insurance policy kept in force long enough is inevitably going to pay a benefit. When this benefit is payable due to the death of the insured, it is known as the policy's **death proceeds**. Certainly, the payment of death proceeds is how many policies deliver their benefit; however, today life insurance policy proceeds are also available to the living through such means as accelerated benefits and viatical settlements as well as through traditional policy surrenders.

Death Benefits

The death proceeds of a life insurance policy can be paid out in a variety of ways. The choice is up to the policyowner, as a right of ownership, or the policyowner may leave the decision to the beneficiary. These payment options are known as **settlement option**s. The selection of the appropriate settlement option should be based on the wishes of the insured and the needs of the beneficiary. The variety of options insurers offer makes the selection fairly easy, since the decision usually rests on whether the beneficiary will need the entire amount at once or as income, payable over time. There are five settlement options available: lump-sum, interest only, fixed period, fixed amount, and life income.

Lump-Sum Cash Option

Many years ago, all life insurance policy proceeds were paid out in single **lump-sum cash** settlements. Today, this option is still available, though not used to the extent of some of the others.

Interest-Only Option

Under the **interest-only option,** the insurance company holds the death proceeds for a specified period of time and, at regular intervals, pays the beneficiary the interest earned on the proceeds. The proceeds themselves are then paid out at the end of the specified period, either in cash or under one of the other settlement options.

Because the interest is paid out rather than accumulated, the proceeds of the policy remain the same and intact. Interest payments to the beneficiary may be made monthly, quarterly, semiannually, or annually. The interest rate will never be lower than the guaranteed rate specified in the policy, but it can be higher. If the company has sufficiently high earnings, it might pay additional interest over and above the guaranteed minimum. (See Illustration 8.4.)

ILLUSTRATION 8.4

Interest-Only Option

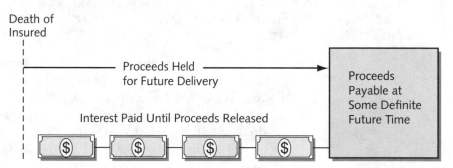

Death of
Insured

Proceeds Held
for Future Delivery

Proceeds
Payable at
Some Definite
Future Time

Interest Paid Until Proceeds Released

The interest-only option provides that the insurance company hold the death proceeds in trust for a specified time, during which the interest earned on the proceeds is paid to the beneficiary at stated intervals. For example, a policyowner may direct that upon his death, the beneficiary is to receive interest payments until age 60, and then the proceeds should be paid out as monthly income from then on, under a life income plan.

It is also possible for the interest payments and policy proceeds to be paid to different beneficiaries. A common use of the interest-only option is to have the interest payments made to a surviving spouse for the remainder of that spouse's life, and the proceeds then divided among the children at that spouse's death.

Fixed-Period Option

Under the **fixed-period** (or fixed-time) **option**, the company pays the beneficiary equal amounts of money at regular intervals over a specified period of years. This option pays out both principal (proceeds) and the interest earned. The amount of each installment payment is determined by the length of the desired period of income. Thus, the longer the period of income, the smaller each payment will be. Conversely, the shorter the period, the larger each payment amount.

If company earnings are large enough to permit paying excess interest, the excess interest will be used to make each payment larger. It will *not* be used to extend the payment period. If company earnings are lower than expected, the guaranteed payments to the beneficiary cannot be reduced. Guaranteed life insurance payments may always be more but may never be less. (See Illustration 8.5.)

ILLUSTRATION 8.5

Fixed-Period Option

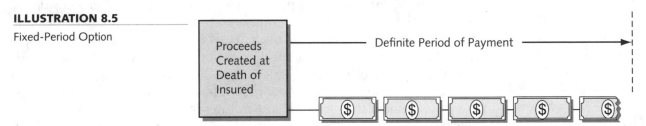

A fixed-period settlement option provides for equal payments of an amount that will exhaust the principal and interest by the end of the fixed period.

Fixed-Amount Option

Under a **fixed-amount option**, the policy proceeds plus interest are used to pay out a specified amount of income at regular intervals for as long as the proceeds last. The policyowner or beneficiary requests the size of payment desired. The amount of each income payment is fixed, and the duration of the payment period varies according to the payment amount. If excess interest is credited, it will be used to extend the payment period; the amount of each payment remains the same. (See Illustration 8.6.)

ILLUSTRATION 8.6

Fixed-Amount Option

The fixed-amount option involves the payment of equal installments of a stated amount, payable until the principal and interest are exhausted. For example, if the proceeds of a $25,000 policy were paid out under this option at a guaranteed 3% rate and the monthly income amount selected was $200, the duration of the payment period would be longer than if the monthly payments were $300.

Life Income Options

Under a **life income option,** of which there are many, the beneficiary receives a guaranteed income for life—no matter how long the beneficiary lives. This unique concept is successful because the principal and interest of life insurance proceeds are paid out together, with the amount of payment actuarially calculated and guaranteed to last a lifetime. Even if the principal is depleted, income payments will continue, so long as the primary beneficiary lives. Essentially, the insurance company uses the death benefit to purchase a single payment immediate annuity for the beneficiary. As you will learn in Unit 11, the purpose of annuities is to provide an income stream for the duration of an individual's life.

Because the life income settlement options are the same as annuity income options, a detailed discussion is reserved for Unit 11. For now, note that these options are:

- straight life income option;

- cash refund option;

- installment refund option;

- life with period certain option;

- joint and survivor option; and

- period certain option.

Living Benefits

In addition to the cash surrender option discussed earlier in Unit 6 under "Nonforfeiture Options," policy benefits are available to living insureds through accelerated benefits and viatical settlements.

Accelerated Benefits

Accelerated benefit provisions are standard in most individual and group life insurance policies. Through these provisions, people who are terminally or chronically ill have tax-free access to policy death benefits. People suffering from AIDS, cancer, heart disease, Alzheimer's disease, or other terminal or severe chronic illnesses often experience devastating financial hardship. During such times, funds from accelerated benefits help them maintain their independence and dignity. These funds are usually used for such necessities as rent, food, and medical services.

A person is considered terminally ill when a physician certifies that the person has an illness or condition that can be reasonably expected to result in death within two years. To be considered chronically ill, a licensed health care practitioner must have certified within the previous 12 months that the person:

■ is unable to perform, without substantial assistance, at least two activities of daily living for at least 90 days, due to a loss of functional capacity;

■ has a similar level of disability as defined by regulations; or

■ requires substantial supervision to protect the person from threats to health and safety because of severe cognitive impairment.

Viatical Settlements

Through **viatical settlements**, individuals with a terminal illness or severe chronic illness sell their life insurance policies to viatical companies. The policies, of course, must have been in force beyond the contestable period. The price viatical companies pay for policies depends on the insured's life expectancy and the cost of future premiums. The NAIC has adopted model guidelines for fair payment. Under these guidelines, insureds receive anywhere from 50–80% of the policy face value. When a viatical company purchases a policy, it becomes the policyowner and is responsible for paying premiums. The company receives the death benefit when the insured dies.

Before the enactment of the Health Insurance Portability and Accountability Act of 1996 (HIPAA), the amount a chronically or terminally ill individual received after selling or assigning a life insurance contract was treated as a sale of property. This meant that the gain—the amount received that was more than the person's basis in the contract—was subject to federal income tax. However, under HIPAA, the proceeds from the sale of life insurance by a chronically or terminally ill individual to a qualified viatical settlement provider are exempt from federal income tax, as are accelerated death benefits.

This exclusion from gross income applies only if the policy is sold to a qualified viatical settlement provider. A provider will be considered qualified if it regularly engages in the business of buying or accepting assignment of life insurance contracts on the lives of insured individuals who are terminally or chronically ill.

Life Settlements

Life settlements are similar to viatical settlements, except the policyowner is not necessarily terminally or chronically ill. Many states are reclassifying viatical settlements as a type of life settlement.

A life settlement transaction is a transfer of an ownership interest in a life insurance policy to a third party for compensation less than the expected death benefit under the policy or the sale of a life insurance policy for a dollar amount that is less than the policy's face.

It is important that the life settlement broker ensure that the transaction is suitable and appropriate for the seller, and the broker should perform due diligence to obtain and evaluate offers from multiple providers.

When a policyowner applies for a life settlement transaction, it is important that the following disclosures be made.

- There are possible alternatives to the life settlement (i.e., accelerated benefits).

- The transaction may have tax implications and advice should be sought from a qualified tax advisor.

- The transaction may affect creditors' rights.

- There may be an effect on conversion rights and waiver of premium benefits.

- A life settlement transaction may limit ability to purchase future life insurance.

- Rescission rights exist.

- The date by which funds will be available must be disclosed.

- The owner will be required to disclose medical, financial, and personal information.

- The insured will be contacted periodically to determine health status.

When the life settlement contract is executed, the following disclosures should be made:

- Affiliations between broker and provider and affiliations between provider and issuer

- Provider disclosures

- Gross purchase price paid for policy

- The amount to be paid to the policyowner

- Full disclosure of compensation to a broker or any party involved in the life settlement transaction

- Contact information for broker

- Broker disclosures

- Complete description of all offers, counteroffers, acceptances, and rejections

- Affiliation between broker and person making an offer on a proposed life settlement contract

- All estimates of life expectancy of the insured

Privacy Concerns

For life settlement transactions, the insured's identity and personal financial and medical information should not be disclosed unless it is:

■ necessary to put the life settlement contract in place and the owner and insured have provided prior written consent;

■ necessary in order to sell the life settlement contracts as investments, provided the applicable securities laws are followed and the owner and insured have provided prior written consent;

■ provided in response to an investigation/examination by the Commissioner;

■ a condition to the transfer of a settled life insurance policy by one provider to another provider, and the receiving provider agrees to comply with the Insurance Code's confidentiality provisions; or

■ necessary to allow the provider, life settlement broker, or their authorized representative to make contact for purposes of determining health status of the insured.

TAX TREATMENT OF PROCEEDS

To understand the taxation of life insurance proceeds, remember one basic principle—*death benefits* paid under a life insurance policy to a named beneficiary are generally free of federal income taxation. However, *interest* paid by an insurance company on death benefit proceeds left with the company is taxable income, just as interest payments made by any financial institution are taxable. Proceeds paid in installments are taxable because they include interest earned on the proceeds. The same principle applies in the case of life insurance policy *dividends*; the dividends themselves are generally free of income taxation, but *interest* under a dividend option is taxable in the year the interest is paid.

Proceeds Paid at the Insured's Death

When an insured dies, proceeds of a life insurance policy paid as a lump-sum death benefit to a beneficiary are exempt from federal income tax. The amount paid under a double indemnity provision and the benefits from any paid-up additions to a life insurance policy also are tax exempt.

When proceeds to an individual are paid out on any kind of installment basis—as would be the case with the fixed-amount, fixed-period, or life income options—a portion of each payment consists of principal and a portion consists of interest. The portion of the proceeds attributed to interest is taxable; the remaining portion of the proceeds is received tax free. This method of taxing life insurance proceeds is consistent with what is known as the **annuity rule.**

Under the annuity rule, a fixed, unchanging fraction of each payment is considered a return of principal and so is excluded from gross income for tax purposes. Thus, that portion of the proceeds representing principal is received tax free. The balance of each payment representing interest income is taxable as ordinary income. The percentage of each payment to be exempted is determined by dividing the insured's investment in the contract by the expected return. The expected return is based on the insured's life expectancy.

However, when the death proceeds of a policy are held by the insurance company under the interest-only option (the company holds the proceeds for a specified period of time and, at regular intervals, pays the beneficiary interest on the proceeds), the interest payments are taxable as ordinary income to the beneficiary. The principal amount, when it is finally paid out, still represents tax-free income.

Accumulated **dividends**, which are not properly classed as life insurance proceeds, also are exempt from federal income tax. The interest element in installment payments, as previously explained, is taxable income.

Transfer for Value Rule

Another tax provision applies in certain cases. This is the transfer for value rule. If a policy is transferred by assignment or otherwise for "valuable consideration" (i.e., the policy is sold to another party) and the insured dies, the person who then owns the policy will be taxed on the excess of the proceeds over the consideration paid, including any premiums paid by the transferee. However, the rule does not apply to certain transfers, including transfers for value to the insured, to a partner (or partnership) of the insured, or to a corporation in which the insured is a shareholder or an officer.

Proceeds Paid During the Insured's Lifetime

There are three reasons why an insured policyowner might receive proceeds from (or by reason of) a life insurance policy while the policyowner is still living: as a result of a policy surrender, as accelerated benefits, or as payment received in a viatical settlement. Let's review the tax treatment of such proceeds paid during the insured's lifetime.

Policy Surrender

As noted earlier in this unit, under "Tax Treatment of Cash Values," the taxation of accumulated values received when a policyowner surrenders a policy is determined by the policyowner's cost basis. Only the excess of such proceeds over the cost of the policy is taxable. (The policyowner's cost basis is figured as total premiums paid, less policy dividends received, less any policy loan, and less extra premiums paid for supplementary benefits, such as waiver of premium or accidental death benefits.) In other words, a policyowner who receives the cash value for a surrendered policy must pay taxes on any gain.

Endowment policy proceeds, even though left with the company at maturity under an interest-only option, will be partially taxable under the rule of constructive receipt. The taxable amount will be the excess of the proceeds over the premiums paid, the rationale being that the insured has the right to withdraw the endowed proceeds and so has them in "constructive receipt."

The policyowner has 60 days after the policy maturity date to exercise an annuity option before the rule of constructive receipt takes effect.

Accelerated Death Benefits and Viatical Arrangements

As noted, with the passage of the Health Insurance Portability and Accountability Act of 1996, accelerated death benefits terminally or chronically ill insureds receive from life insurance policies may be tax free.

For chronically ill insureds, there is a limit on the maximum amount of accelerated benefits that can be excluded from income. In 2011, this limit was $300 per day ($109,500 annually) and is adjusted annually for inflation. Any amounts received that exceed this dollar limit must be included in gross income. This limit does not apply, however, to accelerated death benefits paid to terminally ill insureds.

Although accelerated death benefits are not included in a terminally ill insured's income and are partially tax free for chronically ill insureds, there is an exception. This exclusion does not apply to any amount paid to a person other than the insured if that other person has an insurable interest in the life of the insured because the insured:

- is a director, officer or employee of the other person; or

- has a financial interest in the business of the other person.

A terminally or chronically ill person can also assign or sell a life insurance policy to a viatical settlement provider and not pay federal taxes on amounts received. These provisions remove tax barriers for policyowners who need access to policy values because of terminal or chronic illness.

The income tax treatment of viaticals varies by state. California and New York, for example, treat viatical settlements as tax-free transactions for viators. With the passage of the Health Insurance Portability and Accountability Act, other states are expected to adopt similar legislation. Florida insurance law requires viatical settlement brokers and providers to inform viators that the proceeds of a viatical settlement could be taxable, and that the services of a professional tax advisor should be sought. [Sec. 626.991, F.S.]

1035 Policy Exchanges

Another provision of the Internal Revenue Code pertains to life insurance policies that are exchanged or transferred for another "like-kind" policy. Typically, when an individual realizes a gain on a financial transaction, that gain is taxed. For example, as we just learned, if a policyowner surrenders a life insurance policy and receives the cash value, the policyowner will realize a gain to the extent that the cash value exceeds the amount of premiums paid. That gain is considered ordinary income and is fully taxable. However, if a policy is exchanged for another, Section 1035 of the Tax Code stipulates that no gain (or loss) will be recognized. Consequently, the transaction is not subject to any tax. The following kinds of exchanges are allowed under this provision:

- A life insurance policy for another life insurance policy, endowment policy, or annuity contract

- An endowment policy for an annuity contract

- An annuity contract for another annuity contract

Life Insurance and the Insured's Estate

When an insured dies, the value of life insurance covering the insured is included in the insured's gross estate for federal estate tax purposes. State death taxes must also be payable. However, proceeds payable at death to a beneficiary, as explained previously, are not subject to federal income tax.

Any accumulated policy dividends, although exempt from income tax, are also included in the insured's gross estate for federal estate tax purposes.

SUMMARY

There are three primary factors in a life insurance premium. The *mortality charge* has the greatest influence in making one insured's premium different from another insured's, assuming the two people represent different risks to the insurance company. The mortality charge is reduced by expected *interest earnings*, which is the second premium factor; these two factors constitute the *net premium*. The insurer's cost of doing business is partly recouped through an *expense charge*, the third premium factor which, when added to the net premium, equals the *gross premium*.

Generally, life insurance premiums are not tax deductible unless the premiums qualify as some other form of expense that is tax deductible (for example, alimony payments or charitable contributions).

Life insurance proceeds can be paid out in a variety of ways. The standard means of paying a death benefit is in a lump sum. However, either the policyowner or the beneficiary can select another *settlement option* as an alternate method of paying a policy's proceeds.

Life insurance death benefits are paid with no income tax consequence, with one exception. If the *transfer for value* rule applies, the recipient of the proceeds will be taxed on a portion of the proceeds that exceeds the amount paid for the policy.

Federal income taxes are payable on interest earnings credited to a policy on either death benefit proceeds or policy dividends that have been left with the company.

KEY CONCEPTS

Students should be familiar with the following concepts:

level premium funding	viatical settlement
premium factors	cash value
settlement options	tax treatment of premiums, cash values, and proceeds
policy reserves	1035 exchange
accelerated benefits	

UNIT TEST

1. A mortality table reveals which of the following?

   A. There is no death rate for persons age 99.
   B. It specifies the people who will die in any given year.
   C. It shows the average number of deaths that are expected each year in any age group.
   D. The death rate normally is higher in the lower age groups.

2. All of the following are primary premium factors EXCEPT

   A. expense
   B. interest
   C. dividends
   D. mortality

3. Which of the following statements pertaining to life insurance premiums is CORRECT?

   A. Premium rates usually are lower for men than women.
   B. Harold and Billy, both age 25, each buy a whole life policy from the same company. However, Harold has a participating policy, while Billy's policy is nonparticipating. Harold will pay a higher premium.
   C. The most significant factor in premium rate calculation is interest.
   D. Lucy, who is substantially overweight, has applied for a life insurance policy. Her weight may affect her insurability, but not the amount of premium on her policy.

4. Which of the following statements pertaining to life insurance premiums is CORRECT?

   A. The premiums for a policy that insures a spouse are tax deductible.
   B. A company may purchase key-person life insurance and deduct the premiums as a business expense.
   C. Premiums for group term insurance covering employees are tax deductible, assuming certain requirements are met.
   D. Premiums for policies in which the insured is someone other than the policyowner are tax deductible.

5. Art, the owner and insured under a $75,000 life policy, is killed in an accident. He had paid total premiums of $26,000. How much of the death benefit will be included in his gross estate for estate tax purposes?

   A. $0
   B. $26,000
   C. $49,000
   D. $75,000

6. With regard to the situation described in Question 5, how much of the $75,000 death benefit that was paid to Art's wife in a lump sum is taxable income to her?

   A. $0
   B. $26,000
   C. $49,000
   D. $75,000

7. Which of the following statements pertaining to life insurance policy settlement options is NOT correct?

   A. By using the interest-only option, two or more settlement options can be combined for added flexibility.
   B. Payments under the interest-only option may be made at a rate higher than the guaranteed minimum.
   C. Diane and Rhonda each are receiving monthly income from their deceased husbands' identical life insurance policies under the fixed-period option. Diane's payments are to be made for 15 years and Rhonda's for 20 years. Diane receives the larger monthly payments.
   D. Under the fixed-period option, the payment of excess interest will lengthen the payment period.

8. Assume the following persons buy identical life insurance policies from the same company. Generally speaking, who will pay the lowest premium, if all have standard ratings?

   A. Linda, age 28
   B. Thomas, age 28
   C. Louise, age 40
   D. Joe, age 45

9. Sarah, age 65, the owner of a $150,000 whole life policy, decides to surrender the policy and take the $90,000 cash value in a lump sum. Over the years, she has paid a total of $54,000 in premiums. How much, if any, of the payment will be taxed?

   A. $0
   B. $36,000
   C. $54,000
   D. $90,000

10. Beth, age 50, the beneficiary of her late husband's life insurance policy, has elected to receive the proceeds in monthly installments over the next 5 years. Due to the insurer's interest earnings, Beth notices that the amount of the payments is often more than what she was guaranteed. What kind of settlement option did Beth select?

    A. Life-income
    B. Fixed-amount
    C. Cash value
    D. Fixed-period

11. Under which option does the insurer hold the death proceeds for a specified period of time and, at regular intervals, pay the beneficiary interest on the proceeds?

    A. Fixed-period
    B. Interest-only
    C. Fixed-amount
    D. Life-income

12. Bill names his church as the beneficiary of his $300,000 life insurance policy. When Bill dies, who is responsible for the income taxes payable on the lump-sum proceeds received by the church?

    A. His estate is responsible.
    B. His church is responsible.
    C. No income tax is payable on the death proceeds.
    D. His estate and the beneficiary share the tax liability equally.

13. Which of the following factors is most important when computing basic premiums for life insurance?

    A. Expense
    B. Interest
    C. Mortality
    D. Reserves

14. All of the following statements about accelerated death benefits and viatical settlements are correct EXCEPT

    A. a terminally ill person receives accelerated death benefits tax-free
    B. an insured who sells an insurance policy to a viatical company usually receives 100% of the policy's face value
    C. the maximum amount of accelerated benefits that a chronically ill person can exclude from income is limited
    D. accelerated benefit provisions are standard in most individual and group life insurance policies

15. All of the following statements about the taxation of insurance proceeds are correct EXCEPT

    A. interest earned on policy dividends is exempt from income tax
    B. a beneficiary will not be taxed on insurance proceeds paid as a lump sum death benefit
    C. a policyowner who receives the cash value for a surrendered policy must pay taxes on any gain
    D. generally, no gain or loss is recognized when one insurance policy is exchanged for another

16. Life insurance premiums are typically based on what increment of the face value?

    A. $10
    B. $100
    C. $1,000
    D. $10,000

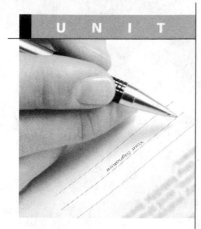

9

Life Insurance Underwriting and Policy Issue

- The Purpose of Underwriting

- The Underwriting Process

- Field Underwriting Procedures

- Policy Issue and Delivery

Who is qualified to purchase life insurance and who is not? The process of answering this question is called *risk selection*, a function that is performed by insurance company underwriters. Sales representatives are sometimes called field underwriters, indicating the important role they also play in helping the company decide if an applicant is an insurable or uninsurable risk. This unit looks at the overall underwriting process, as well as the important processes of policy issue and policy delivery. ■

THE PURPOSE OF UNDERWRITING

Insurance companies would like nothing more than to be able to sell their policies to anyone wishing to buy them. However, they must exercise caution in deciding who is qualified to purchase insurance. Issuing a policy to someone who is uninsurable is an unwise business decision that can easily mean a financial loss for the company.

Each insurer sets its own standards as to what constitutes an insurable risk versus an uninsurable risk, just as each insurer determines the premium rates it will charge its policyowners. Every applicant for insurance is individually reviewed by a company underwriter to determine if the applicant meets the standards established by the company to qualify for its life insurance coverage.

Underwriting, another term for risk selection, is the process of reviewing the many characteristics that make up the risk profile of an applicant to determine if the applicant is insurable and, if so, at standard or substandard rates. There are two basic questions underwriters seek to answer about an applicant:

■ Is the applicant *insurable*?

■ If the applicant and insured are two different people, *does an insurable interest exist* between the two of them?

ILLUSTRATION 9.1

What Constitutes Insurable Interest?

Though laws differ slightly from state to state, in general the following types of relationships automatically carry insurable interest.

■ An individual has an insurable interest in his or her life.
■ A husband or wife has an insurable interest in a spouse.
■ Parents have an insurable interest in their children.
■ A child has an insurable interest in a parent or grandparent.
■ A business has an insurable interest in the lives of its officers, directors, and key employees.
■ Business partners have an insurable interest in each other.
■ A creditor has an insurable interest in the life of a debtor (but only to the extent of the debt).

Does Insurable Interest Exist?

As discussed in Unit 3 and Unit 7, insurable interest is extremely important in life insurance. Without this requirement, people could purchase life insurance and the policy would be nothing more than a wagering contract. As we have established, an insurable interest exists when the death of the insured would have a clear financial impact on the policyowner. Individuals are presumed to have an insurable interest in themselves; therefore, when the applicant and proposed insured are the same person, there is no question that insurable interest exists. Questions are raised, however, with third-party contracts—those in which the applicant is not the insured. Some relationships are automatically presumed to qualify as an insurable interest—spouses, parents, children, and certain business relationships. (See Illustration 9.1.) In most other cases, the burden is upon the applicant to show that an insurable interest exists.

It bears repeating that with life insurance, an insurable interest must exist only at the policy inception; it does not necessarily have to exist when the policy proceeds are actually paid. Thus, for example, a policyowner could assign a life policy to someone who has no insurable interest in the insured, and the assignment would nonetheless be valid.

Is the Applicant Insurable?

Once the underwriter determines that insurable interest exists, the next question is, "Is the applicant insurable?" The answer lies in the underwriting process.

THE UNDERWRITING PROCESS

The underwriting process is accomplished by reviewing and evaluating information about an applicant and applying what is known of the individual against the insurer's standards and guidelines for insurability and premium rates.

Underwriters have several sources of underwriting information available to help them develop a risk profile of an applicant. The number of sources checked usually depends on several factors, most notably the size of the requested policy and the risk profile developed after an initial review of the application. The larger the policy, the more comprehensive and diligent the underwriting research. Regardless of the policy size, if the application raises questions in the underwriter's mind about the applicant, that, too, can trigger a review of other sources of information. The most common sources of underwriting information include the application, the medical report, an attending physician's statement, the Medical Information Bureau, special questionnaires, inspection reports, and credit reports.

The Application

The application for insurance is the basic source of insurability information. Regardless of what other sources of information the underwriter may draw from, the application—the first source of information to be reviewed—will be evaluated thoroughly. Thus, it is the agent's responsibility to see that an applicant's answers to questions on the application are recorded fully and accurately. (A sample application appears in the Appendix.) There are three basic parts to a typical life insurance application: Part I—General, Part II—Medical, and Part III—Agent's Report.

Part I—General

Part I of the application asks general questions about the proposed insured, including name, age, address, birth date, sex, income, marital status, and occupation. Also to be indicated here are details about the requested insurance coverage, including:

- type of policy;

- amount of insurance;

- name and relationship of the beneficiary;

- other insurance the proposed insured owns; and

- additional insurance applications the insured has pending.

Other information sought may indicate possible exposure to a hazardous hobby, foreign travel, aviation activity, or military service. Whether the proposed insured smokes is also indicated in Part I.

Part II—Medical

Part II focuses on the proposed insured's health and asks a number of questions about the health history, not only of the proposed insured, but of the proposed insured's family, too. This medical section must be completed in its entirety for every application. Depending on the proposed policy face amount, this section may or may not be all that is required in the way of medical information. The individual to be insured may be required to take a medical exam.

Part III—Agent's Report

Part III of the application is often called the **agent's report**. This is where the agent reports personal observations about the proposed insured. Because the agent represents the interests of the insurance company, the agent is expected to complete this part of the application fully and truthfully.

In this important section, the agent provides first-hand knowledge about the applicant's financial condition and character, the background and purpose of the sale, and how long the agent has known the applicant.

The agent's report also usually asks if the proposed insurance will replace an existing policy. If the answer is "yes," most states demand that certain procedures be followed to protect the rights of consumers when policy replacement is involved.

The Medical Report

Quite often a policy is issued on the basis of the information provided in the application alone. Most companies have set nonmedical limits, meaning that applications for policies below a certain face amount (perhaps $50,000 or even $100,000) will not require any additional medical information other than what is provided by the application. However, for larger policies (or smaller policies when the applicant is older than a certain age) a medical exam may be required to provide further underwriting information. If the application's medical section raises questions specific to a particular medical condition, the underwriter may also request an attending physician's statement (APS) from the physician who has treated the applicant. The statement will provide details about the medical condition in question.

Medical exams must be completed by a qualified person, but that person does not necessarily have to be a physician. Many companies accept exams that are completed by a paramedic or a registered nurse. Usually the applicant can select the physician or paramedic facility to perform the exam; insurers are also prepared to recommend paramedic facilities where the exam can be given. In almost all cases, the expense for the exam is borne by the insurance company.

When completed, the medical report is forwarded to the insurance company, where it is reviewed by the company's medical director or a designated associate.

The Medical Information Bureau

Another source of underwriting information that specifically focuses on an applicant's medical history is the **Medical Information Bureau** (MIB). The MIB is a nonprofit central information agency that was established years ago by a number of insurance companies to aid in the underwriting process. The bureau is supported by more than 700 member insurance companies.

Its purpose is to serve as a reliable source of medical information concerning applicants and to help disclose cases where an applicant either forgets or conceals pertinent underwriting information, or submits erroneous or misleading medical information with fraudulent intent. The MIB operations help to hold down the cost of life insurance for all policyowners through the prevention of misrepresentation and fraud.

This is how the system works. If a company finds that one of its applicants has a physical ailment or impairment listed by the MIB, the company is pledged to report the information to the MIB in the form of a code number. By having this information, home office underwriters will know that a past problem existed should the same applicant later apply for life insurance with another member company. The information is available to member companies only and may be used only for underwriting and claims purposes.

Each member company and its medical director sign a pledge to follow the rules and principles of the MIB. The basic requirements are:

- applicants for life insurance must be notified in writing that the insurance company may make a brief report on their health to the MIB;

- applicants must be advised that, should they apply to another MIB company for coverage or if a claim is submitted to such a company, the MIB will supply any requested information in its files to the company;

- applicants must sign authorization forms for information from the MIB files to be given to a member company; and

- the MIB will arrange the disclosure of any information it has concerning an applicant upon request by the applicant. Medical information, however, will be disclosed only to the individual's physician, who then can interpret best the facts for the applicant (patient).

Special Questionnaires

When necessary, **special questionnaires** may be required for underwriting purposes to provide more detailed information related to aviation or avocation, foreign residence, finances, military service, or occupation. For example, if an applicant has a hobby of skydiving, the insurance company needs detailed information about the extent of the applicant's participation to determine whether or not the insurance risk is acceptable. The most common of these special questionnaires is the **aviation questionnaire** required of any applicant who spends a significant amount of time flying, such as an airline pilot.

Inspection Reports

Inspection reports usually are obtained by insurance companies on applicants who apply for large amounts of life insurance. These reports contain information about prospective insureds, which is reviewed to determine their insurability. Insurance companies normally obtain inspection reports from national investigative agencies or firms.

The purpose of these reports is to provide a picture of an applicant's general character and reputation, mode of living, finances, and any exposure to abnormal hazards. Investigators or inspectors may interview employees, neighbors, and associates of the applicant, as well as the applicant.

Inspection reports ordinarily are not requested on applicants who apply for smaller policies, although company rules vary as to the sizes of policies that require a report by an outside agency.

Credit Reports

Some applicants may prove to be poor credit risks, based on information obtained before a policy is issued. Thus, **credit reports** obtained from retail merchants' associations or other sources are a valuable underwriting tool in many cases.

Applicants who have questionable credit ratings can cause an insurance company to lose money. Applicants with poor credit standings are likely to allow their policies to lapse within a short time, perhaps even before a second premium is paid. An insurance company can lose money on a policy that is quickly lapsed, because the insurer's expenses to acquire the policy cannot be recovered in a short period of time. It is possible, then, that home office underwriters will refuse to insure persons who have failed to pay their bills or who appear to be applying for more life insurance than they reasonably can afford.

The Fair Credit Reporting Act of 1970

To protect the rights of consumers for whom an inspection report or credit (or consumer) report has been requested, Congress in 1970 enacted the **Fair Credit Reporting Act.** As previously mentioned, this federal law applies to financial institutions that request these types of consumer reports, including insurance companies.

The Fair Credit Reporting Act, or FCRA, established procedures for the collection and disclosure of information obtained on consumers through investigation and credit reports; it seeks to ensure fairness with regard to confidentiality, accuracy, and disclosure. The FCRA is quite extensive. Included in it are the following important requirements pertaining to insurers.

■ Applicants must be notified (usually within three days) that the report has been requested. The insurer must also notify applicants that they can request disclosure of the nature and scope of the investigation. If the applicants request such disclosure, the insurer must provide a summary within five days of the request.

■ The consumer must be provided with the names of all people contacted during the preceding six months for purposes of the report. People contacted who are associated with the consumer's place of employment must be identified as far back as two years.

■ If, based on an inspection or consumer report, the insurer rejects an application, the company must provide the applicant with the name and address of the consumer reporting agency that supplied the report.

■ If requested by the applicant (more formally, the "consumer"), the consumer reporting agency—not the insurance company—must disclose the nature and substance of all information (except medical) contained in the consumer's file. Note that the file may be more extensive than the actual report that was provided to the insurer. The Fair Credit Reporting Act does not give consumers the right to see the actual report, although most reporting agencies do routinely provide copies of the report, if requested.

■ If the consumer disagrees with information in the file, the consumer can file a statement giving an opinion on the issue.

HIPAA Disclosures

The Heath Insurance Portability and Accountability Act (HIPAA) imposes specific requirements on health care providers with respect to the disclosure of patients' health and medical information. Health care providers must preserve patient confidentiality and protect this information. If this information is inadvertently disclosed, providers must mitigate harm to the patients.

Insurers and agents are under similar requirements when dealing with protected health information. When examining an applicant for underwriting purposes, all medical information is to remain confidential, and the agent and insurer must protect the applicant's privacy. If the insurer needs to share this information (such as with medical professionals), including information related to possible HIV infection, the applicant must be given full notice of the insurer's practices with respect to the treatment of this information, the applicant's right to maintain privacy, and an opportunity to refuse permission for the dissemination of the information.

Classification of Applicants

Once all the information about a given applicant has been reviewed and evaluated, the underwriter seeks to classify the risk that the applicant poses to the insurer. In a few cases, an applicant represents a risk so great that the applicant is considered uninsurable, and the application will be rejected. However, the vast majority of insurance applicants fall within an insurer's underwriting guidelines and accordingly will be classified as a **preferred risk**, **standard risk**, or **substandard risk**.

Preferred Risk

Many insurers today reward exceptionally good risks by assigning them to a **preferred risk** classification. Preferred risk premium rates are generally lower than standard risk rates. Personal characteristics that contribute to a preferred risk rating include not smoking, weight within an ideal range, and favorable cholesterol levels.

Standard Risk

Standard risk is the term used for individuals who fit the insurer's guidelines for policy issue without special restrictions or additional rating. These individuals meet the same conditions as the tabular risks on which the insurer's premium rates are based.

Substandard Risk

A **substandard risk** is one below the insurer's standard or average risk guidelines. An individual can be rated as substandard for any number of reasons: poor health, a dangerous occupation, or attributes or habits that could be hazardous. Some substandard applicants are rejected outright; others will be accepted for coverage but with an increase in their policy premium.

FIELD UNDERWRITING PROCEDURES

As noted earlier, an agent plays an important role in underwriting. As a **field underwriter,** the agent initiates the process and is responsible for many important tasks: proper solicitation, completing the application thoroughly and accurately, obtaining appropriate signatures, collecting the initial premium, and issuing a receipt. Each of these tasks is vitally important to the underwriting process and policy issue.

Proper Solicitation

As a representative of the insurer, an agent has the duty and responsibility to solicit good business. This means that an agent's solicitation and prospecting efforts should focus on cases that fall within the insurer's underwriting guidelines and represent profitable business to the insurer. At the same time, the agent has a responsibility to the insurance-buying public to observe the highest professional standards when conducting insurance business. All sales solicitations should be open and aboveboard, with the agent clearly identifying the insurer that the agent represents and the reason for the call. In addition, good sales practices avoid high pressure tactics and are aimed at helping applicants select the most appropriate policies to meet their needs.

False advertising is prohibited as an unfair trade practice in all states. In this context, advertising encompasses almost any kind of communication used to promote the sale of an insurance policy. It includes, for example, descriptive literature, sales aids, slide shows, prepared group talks, brochures, sales illustrations, and policy illustrations. All advertising must be truthful. Insurance products should be described properly and accurately, without exaggerating benefits or minimizing drawbacks.

Sales presentations must not be deceptive. What is a deceptive sale? Any presentation that gives a prospect or client the wrong impression about any aspect of an insurance policy or plan is deceptive. Any presentation that does not provide complete disclosure to a prospect or client is deceptive. Any presentation that includes misleading or inconclusive product comparisons is deceptive. Even if the deception is unintentional, the agent has done the consumer a disservice. In addition, it's likely the agent has violated some aspect of the state insurance code.

In Florida, as in many states, an agent is required to deliver to the applicant a **Life Insurance Buyer's Guide** and a **Policy Summary.** These documents are usually delivered before the agent accepts the applicant's initial premium. Typically, the buyer's guide is a generic publication that explains life insurance in a way that average consumers can understand. It speaks of the concept in general and does not address the specific product or policy being considered.

The policy summary addresses the specific product being presented for sale. It identifies the agent, the insurer, the policy, and each rider. It includes information about premiums, dividends, benefit amounts, cash surrender values, policy loan interest rates, and life insurance cost indexes of the specific policy being considered.

Completing the Application

The application is one of the most important sources of underwriting information, and it is the agent's responsibility to see that it is completed fully and accurately. Statements made in the application are used by insurers to evaluate risks and decide whether or not to insure the life of the applicant. Such statements are considered representations: statements an applicant represents as being substantially true to the best of the applicant's knowledge and belief, but which are not warranted to be exact in every detail. Representations must be true only to the extent that they are material to the risk. In most states, statements made in insurance applications are considered representations, not warranties. Warranties are statements that are considered literally true. A warranty that is not literally true in every detail, even if made in error, is sufficient to render a policy void. If an insurer rejects a claim based on a representation, it bears the burden of proving materiality. Representations are considered fraudulent only when they relate to a matter material to the risk and when they were made with fraudulent intent.

Several signatures are required to complete an application, and to overlook a needed signature will cause delay in issuing a policy. Note that in Florida, a child must be a minimum age of 15 years to sign a life insurance application; otherwise, an adult, such as a parent or legal guardian, must sign.

Each application requires the signatures of the **proposed insured,** the **policyowner** (if different from the insured), and the **agent** who solicits the application. If the policyowner is to be a firm or corporation, one or more partners or officers, other than the proposed insured, generally must sign the application.

If additional questionnaires regarding an applicant's aviation or avocation activities are required for underwriting purposes, they also need the signatures of the applicant and the agent.

Where required by state law, the agent also must sign a form attesting that a disclosure statement has been given to the applicant. Moreover, a form authorizing the insurance company to obtain investigative consumer reports or medical information from investigative agencies, physicians, hospitals, or other sources generally must be signed by the proposed insured and the agent as witness.

In Florida, the name of the insurance company and the agent's name and license identification number must appear on the application. It may be printed, typed, stamped, or handwritten, if legible.

When premiums are to be paid according to an automatic check plan, forms for that purpose also must be signed by the applicant.

Changes in the Application

The application for insurance must be completed accurately, honestly, and thoroughly, and it must be signed by the insured and witnessed. The completed application is important because the information in it is used, sometimes exclusively, to evaluate risks and determine whether or not to issue a policy. When attached to the insurance policy, the application becomes part of the legal contract between the insurer and the insured. Consequently, the general rule is that no alterations of any written application can be made by any person other than the applicant without the applicant's written permission.

When an applicant makes a mistake in the information given to an agent in completing the application, the applicant can have the agent correct the information, but the applicant must initial the correction. If the company discovers a mistake, it usually returns the application to the agent, and the agent corrects the mistake with the applicant and has the applicant initial the change. If the company accepts an application and then, before the policy's incontestable clause takes effect, discovers incorrect or incomplete information in it, the company may rescind or cancel the contract.

Some states permit insurers to make insertions in applications for administrative purposes, provided the insurer clearly indicates that those insertions are not to be ascribed to the applicant.

Initial Premium and Receipts

It is generally in the best interests of both the proposed insured and the agent to have the initial premium (or a portion of it) paid with the application. For the agent, this will usually help solidify the sale and may accelerate the payment of commissions on the sale. The proposed insured benefits by having the insurance protection become effective immediately, with some important restrictions.

However, if a premium deposit is not paid with the application, the policy will not become valid until the initial premium is collected. Recall from the discussion in Unit 3 that one of the requirements for a valid contract is **consideration.** In the case of an insurance contract, the consideration is the first premium payment plus the application. An insurer will not allow an applicant to possess a policy without receipt of the initial premium. There is one exception to this rule. The applicant may be allowed to sign an **inspection receipt** and obtain the policy for inspection purposes. However, the 14-day free-look policy provision required in Florida makes this generally unnecessary today.

Applicants who pay a premium deposit with the application are entitled to a **premium receipt**. It is the type of receipt given that determines exactly when and under what conditions an applicant's coverage begins. The two major types of receipts are **conditional receipts** and **binding receipts** (sometimes called **temporary insurance agreements**).

Conditional Receipts

The most common type of premium receipt is the **conditional receipt.** A conditional receipt indicates that certain conditions must be met in order for the insurance coverage to go into effect. Some companies refer to a conditional receipt as a temporary receipt.

There are two types of conditional receipts: the **insurability type** and the **approval type.** Both specify what conditions are required for coverage; the primary distinction between the two is when the coverage goes into effect.

- **Insurability Receipt.** The insurability type of receipt provides that when the applicant pays the initial premium, coverage is effective—on the condition that the applicant proves to be insurable—either on the date the application was signed or the date of the medical exam, if one is required. For instance, with this type of receipt, if the applicant dies between the date of application or of the medical exam and the date the insurer actually approves the application, the coverage is retroactively effective, as long as the applicant proved to be insurable on the specified date. However, with the insurability type of receipt, if the applicant proves to be uninsurable as of the date of application or of the medical exam, no coverage takes effect and the premium is refunded.

- **Approval Receipt.** The approval type of receipt is more restrictive than the insurability type. In general, with the approval type, coverage is effective only after the application has been approved by the insurer (and before the policy is actually delivered to the policyowner). Because they offer only a short period of special protection and are usually frowned upon by the courts, approval types of receipts are rarely used today.

With conditional receipts, if the applicant is found to be insurable, but only on a substandard or rated basis, no retroactive protection is provided. This is because the applicant did not qualify for the policy applied for (and to which the receipt pertains); instead, the insurer will counter with an offer of another policy at a different rate. Consequently, if an applicant who has a conditional receipt is found to be substandard, and dies prior to accepting the rated policy counteroffered by the insurer, there would be no coverage.

Companies usually impose a limit on the amount of coverage provided under a conditional receipt (generally $100,000 or less). Therefore, even if the applicant is applying for a policy with a much higher face amount, the insurer will usually restrict the conditional coverage to a specified limit.

ILLUSTRATION 9.2

Conditional Receipts

When a conditional receipt is given, the applicant and the company form what might be called a **conditional contract**—contingent upon conditions that exist at the time the application is signed (or when the medical exam is completed, if required). In providing early coverage, the insurer conditionally assumes the risk and will provide coverage from the specified date, on the condition that the applicant is approved for policy issue.

For example, assume an agent sells a $50,000 nonmedical life insurance policy to Matthew, who hands the agent his signed application with a check for the first premium. In turn, Matthew receives from the agent a conditional receipt for the premium. Two days later, Matthew becomes seriously ill and enters the hospital. So long as the company finds that Matthew qualifies for the policy as applied for, the company will issue the policy regardless of his condition in the hospital. In fact, if Matthew died before the policy was issued, but qualified at the time of application, his beneficiary still would receive the $50,000 death benefit.

However, in this example, if the company's underwriter determined that Matthew was uninsurable, and thus rejected the application, then there is no coverage, even during the period when the receipt was effective.

Binding Receipts

Under the **binding receipt** (or temporary insurance agreement), coverage is guaranteed, even if the proposed insured is found to be uninsurable, until the insurer formally rejects the application. Since the underwriting process can often take several weeks or longer, this can place the company at considerable risk; accordingly, binding receipts are often reserved only for a company's most experienced agents.

Like the conditional receipt, a binding receipt typically stipulates a maximum amount that would be payable during the special protection period.

The provisions a binding receipt contains can vary slightly from company to company. Generally, however, upon payment of the initial premium at the time of application, the receipt provides the following provisions.

■ The applicant is covered at the time of application (or on the date a later medical examination is completed, if required) for the amount of insurance applied for, but usually not to exceed a maximum of $100,000 under all outstanding receipts. The temporary coverage continues until the policy is issued as requested, until the company offers a different policy or until the company rejects the application, but in no event for more than 60 days from the date the agreement was signed.

■ If a medical examination is required, the temporary insurance coverage does not begin until the examination has been completed. But, if death accidentally occurs within 30 days from the date of the agreement, the death benefit is paid even though the medical examination was not taken.

■ The applicant must pay in advance at least one month's premium for the policy being applied for. Furthermore, there must be no material misrepresentations in the application, and the death must not result from suicide.

Policy Effective Date

An important question that must be addressed in any life insurance sale is this: when does the policy become effective? The effective date is important for two reasons: not only does it identify when the coverage is effective, but also it establishes the date by which future annual premiums must be paid.

If a receipt (either conditional or binding) was issued in exchange for the payment of an initial premium deposit, the date of the receipt will generally be noted as the policy effective date in the contract.

If a premium deposit is *not* given with the application, the policy effective date is usually left to the discretion of the insurer. Often, it will be the date the policy is issued by the insurance company. However, the policy will not be truly effective until it is delivered to the applicant, the first premium is paid, and a Statement of Continued Good Health is obtained.

Backdating

As we have learned, the premiums required to support a life insurance policy are determined, in part, by the insured's age. If an applicant can be treated by the insurance company as being a year younger, the result can be a lifetime of slightly lower premiums. Thus, it is understandable that applicants might want to **backdate** a policy, making it effective at an earlier date than the present, in order to save age.

As surprising as it may seem, many insurers are willing to let an applicant back date a policy. As one might guess, though, there are some important conditions that must be met before this step can be taken.

First of all, the insurer must allow backdating. Second, the company will usually impose a time limit on how far back a policy can be backdated (typically six months, the limit imposed by most states' laws). More important, the policyowner is required to pay all back-due premiums and the next premium is due at the backdated anniversary date (which can be as close as six months in the future).

Preliminary Term for Interim Coverage

Some applicants for life insurance desire immediate protection but, for one reason or another, want to defer the issue dates of their policies for several months or to some specific date in the future. This usually can be accomplished by using **preliminary** (or **interim**) **term insurance**.

Companies ordinarily allow preliminary term to be used to defer the effective date of the original policy from 1 to 11 months. Premiums for preliminary term are based on the age of the insured at the time of application. The premium for the principal policy involved is based on the age of the insured at the end of the interim period.

By using preliminary term, the applicant can be insured without delay and still postpone payment of premium on the principal policy for one or more months.

POLICY ISSUE AND DELIVERY

After the underwriting is complete and the company has decided to issue the policy, other offices in the company assume the responsibility for issuing the policy. Once issued, the policy document is sent to the sales agent for delivery to the new policyowner. The policy usually is not sent directly to the policyowner since, as an important legal document, it should be explained by the sales agent to the policyowner.

Constructive Delivery

From a legal standpoint, policy delivery may be accomplished without physically delivering the policy into the policyowner's possession. **Constructive delivery,** which satisfies the legal interpretation, is accomplished technically if the insurance company intentionally relinquishes all control over the policy and turns it over to someone acting for the policyowner, including the company's own agent. Mailing the policy to the agent for unconditional delivery to the policyowner also constitutes constructive delivery, even if the agent never personally delivers the policy. However, if the company instructs the agent not to deliver the policy unless the applicant is in good health, there is no constructive delivery.

Mere possession of a policy by the client does not actually establish delivery if all conditions have not been met. For example, a policy may be left with an applicant for inspection and an **inspection receipt** obtained to indicate that the policy is neither in force during the inspection period nor will it be in force until the initial premium has been paid.

Explaining the Policy and Ratings to Clients

Most applicants will not remember everything they should about their policies after they have signed the application. This is another reason agents should deliver policies in person. Only by personally delivering a policy does the agent have a timely opportunity to review the contract and its provisions, exclusions, and riders. In fact, some states (and most insurers) insist that policies be delivered in person for this very reason. The agent's review is especially important, for it helps to reinforce the sale. It can also lead to future sales by building the client's trust and confidence in the agent's abilities and desire to be of genuine service.

Explaining the policy and how it meets the policyowner's specific objectives helps avert misunderstandings, policy returns, and potential lapses. Agents sometimes may have a chance to prepare applicants in advance when it appears that policies may be rated as substandard. And sometimes both agent and policyowner may be surprised when the policy is issued as a rated contract. In either case, the agent usually can stress reasons why the insured has an even greater need for insurance protection because of the physical impairment or condition. Indeed, it may be the policyowner's last chance to purchase such coverage because a worsening of the condition responsible for the rating could render the person completely uninsurable.

Obtaining a Statement of Insured's Good Health

In some instances, the initial premium will not be paid until the agent delivers the policy. In such cases, common company practice requires that, before leaving the policy, the agent must collect the premium and obtain from the insured *a signed statement attesting to the insured's continued good health*.

The agent then is to submit the premium with the signed statement to the insurance company. Because there can be no contract until the premium is paid, the company has a right to know that the policyowner has remained in reasonably good health from the time the policyowner signed the application until receiving the policy. In other words, the company has the right to know if the policyowner represents the same risk to the company as when the application was first signed.

ILLUSTRATION 9.3

From Application to Policy Delivery

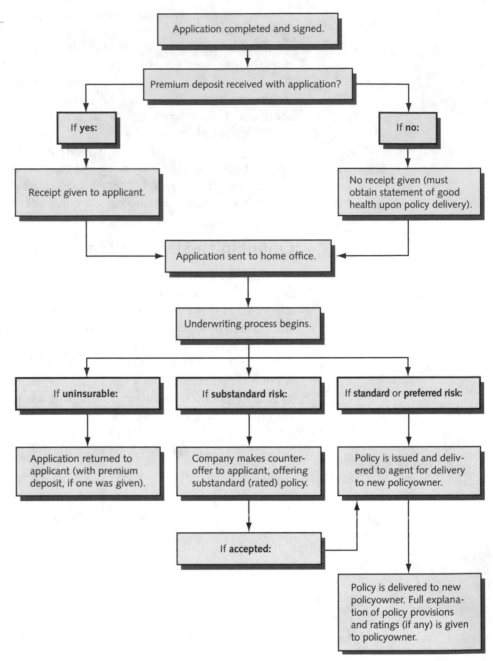

SUMMARY

It is during the *underwriting process* that an insurance company decides if it is going to issue a policy to an applicant. The underwriter seeks to determine if the proposed insured is *insurable*, and if so, at *standard*, *substandard*, or *preferred* rates. Underwriters *assign* rates to proposed insureds, based on the risks the applicants represent to the insurers.

The effective date of the policy depends on whether or not an initial premium deposit was paid with the application (thus requiring the agent to issue either a *conditional* or *binding receipt*) as well as the date requested by the applicant (policies can be *backdated* in some situations).

Policy delivery is an important responsibility of the sales agent.

KEY CONCEPTS

Students should be familiar with the following concepts:

underwriting process	standard versus substandard (rated) policies
insurable interest	Medical Information Bureau
consumer and investigative reports	Fair Credit Reporting Act
application	standard risk
substandard risk	preferred risk
required signatures	initial premium deposits
conditional receipts	binding receipts
policy delivery	effective date of coverage
statement of good health	explanation of the policy to the client
proper solicitation	

UNIT TEST

1. Underwriting is a process of
   A. selection and issue of policies
   B. evaluation and classification of risks
   C. selection, reporting, and rejection of risks
   D. selection, classification, and rating of risks

2. Which of the following statements pertaining to a life insurance policy application is CORRECT?
   A. The names of both the insured and the beneficiary are indicated on the application.
   B. If an applicant's age is shown erroneously on a life insurance application as 28 instead of 29, the result may be a premium quote that is higher than it should be.
   C. The size of the policy being applied for does not affect the underwriting process.
   D. The agent's report in the application must be signed by the agent and the applicant.

3. If a medical report is required on an applicant, it is completed by
   A. a home office underwriter
   B. a paramedic or examining physician
   C. the agent
   D. the home office medical director

4. Which of the following statements pertaining to the Medical Information Bureau (MIB) is CORRECT?
   A. The MIB is operated by a national network of hospitals.
   B. Information obtained by the MIB is available to all physicians.
   C. The MIB provides assistance in the underwriting of life insurance.
   D. Applicants may request that MIB reports be attached to their policies.

5. Which of the following statements regarding the Fair Credit Reporting Act (FCRA) is CORRECT?
   A. Applicants must be notified within a short period of time that their credit report has been requested.
   B. If an applicant for insurance is rejected based on a consumer report, the name of the reporting agency must be kept confidential.
   C. If requested to do so, the insurance company must provide the actual consumer report to the applicant.
   D. Consumer reports are final in nature and cannot be disputed by an applicant.

6. All of the following statements about the classification of applicants are correct EXCEPT
   A. a substandard applicant can never be rejected outright by the insurer
   B. applicants who are preferred risks have premium rates that are generally lower than standard rate risks
   C. an individual can be rated as a substandard risk because of a dangerous occupation
   D. a standard applicant fits the insurer's guidelines for policy issue without special restrictions

7. Which of the following statements about the Fair Credit Reporting Act is CORRECT?
   A. It prohibits insurance companies from obtaining reports on applicants from outside investigative agencies.
   B. It provides that consumers have the right to question reports made about them by investigative agencies.
   C. It applies to reports about applicants that are made by insurance agents to their companies.
   D. It prohibits insurance companies from rejecting an application based on a credit report.

8. Elaine signs an application for a $50,000 nonmedical life policy, pays the first premium, and receives a conditional insurability receipt. If Elaine were killed in an auto accident two days later

   A. the company could reject the application on the basis that death was accidental
   B. her beneficiary would receive $50,000, if Elaine qualified for the policy as applied for
   C. the premium would be returned to Elaine's family because the policy had not been issued
   D. the company could reject the death claim because the underwriting process was never completed

9. Generally, the party who delivers an insurance policy to the new policyowner is

   A. the insurance company's home office
   B. the sales agent
   C. the state's chief financial officer
   D. the underwriter

10. The primary distinction between the insurability and approval types of conditional receipts is when

   A. the applicant pays the initial premium
   B. the coverage goes into effect
   C. the medical exam is given
   D. the applicant proves insurable

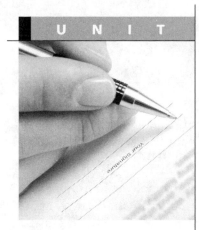

10

Group Life Insurance

- Principles of Group Insurance
- Features of Group Insurance
- Eligible Groups
- Group Life Insurance
- Other Forms of Group Life Coverage

Up to this point, the focus of our discussion has been individual life insurance plans, policies, and underwriting. However, as noted in Unit 5, one of the general categories of insurance is **group insurance**. Group insurance is a way to provide life insurance, health insurance, or both kinds of coverage for a number of people under one contract. Typically, group insurance is provided by an employer for its employees; however, it is available to other kinds of groups, as we will see. In this unit, we will take a look at the principles of group insurance in general, focusing specifically on group life insurance plans. Group health and disability plans are also available and will be discussed in detail in Unit 24. ■

PRINCIPLES OF GROUP INSURANCE

The basic principle of **group insurance** is that it provides insurance coverage for a number of people under a single **master contract** or **master policy**. Because a group policy insures a group of people, it is the group—not each individual—that must meet the underwriting requirements of the insuring company.

Group insurance is most typically provided by an employer for its employees as a **benefit**. In these cases, the employer is the applicant and contract policyholder; the employees, as group members, are not parties to the contract: in fact, they are not even named in the contract. Instead, each employee who is eligible to participate in the plan fills out an enrollment card and is given a **certificate of insurance**, which summarizes the coverage terms and explains the employee's rights under the group contract. A list of individual employees covered under the contract is maintained by the insurer.

In most cases, it is the policyholder—the employer—that selects the type of insurance coverage the group will have and determines the amount of coverage the contract will provide for covered group members. In addition, it is typical for the employer to pay all or a portion of the premium. When an employer pays all of the premium, the plan is a **noncontributory plan** since the employees are not required to contribute to premium payments. If a group plan requires its members to pay a portion of the premium, it is a **contributory plan**.

FEATURES OF GROUP INSURANCE

To individual members covered by a group life or group health insurance plan, the function the insurance serves is identical to an individual plan. In the case of group life, should the covered member die, the covered member's beneficiary will receive a stated amount in death proceeds. In the case of group health, should the covered member become ill or disabled, the plan will provide a stated benefit amount to help cover the corresponding medical costs or replace income lost due to the disability. Thus, the purpose of group life and health plans is the same as individual life and health plans. However, there are a number of features of group plans that set them apart from individual plans.

Master Contract

As noted, the foremost distinction of a group plan is that it insures a number of people under one contract. Because of this, individual underwriting and individual evidence of insurability are generally not required. When it comes to underwriting, the insurer looks at the group as a whole, not at the health or habits or characteristics of individual members. Group insurance involves **experience rating**, which is a method of establishing a premium for the group based on the group's previous claims experience. The larger and more homogeneous the group, the closer it comes to reflecting standard mortality and morbidity rates.

Low Cost

Another characteristic of group insurance is that, per unit of benefits, it is available at lower rates than individual insurance, due primarily to the lower administrative, operational, and selling expenses associated with group contracts. And because most employers pay all or part of the group premium, individual insureds are able to have insurance coverage for far less than what they would normally pay for an individual or personal plan.

Flow of Insureds

Finally, group insurance is distinguished by a **flow of insureds**, entering and exiting under the policy as they join and leave the group. In fact, in order for it to operate effectively, group insurance requires a constant influx of new members into the group to replace those who leave and to keep the age and health of the group stable.

ELIGIBLE GROUPS

What kinds of groups are eligible for group insurance coverage? Generally, almost any kind of **natural group**—those formed for a purpose other than to obtain insurance—will be considered by an insurer.

Insurable groups most typically fall into one of the following categories:

- Single-employer groups

- Multiple-employer groups

- Labor unions

- Trade associations

- Creditor/debtor groups

- Fraternal organizations

In years past, only groups of a certain size, such as 50 or more, were eligible for group insurance. Today, in accordance with NAIC guidelines that do not set a minimum size limit, insurers often issue coverage to groups with as few as 10 (or fewer) members.[1] It is important to note, however, that once a group policy is issued, insurers usually require that a certain number or percentage of eligible members participate in order to keep the coverage in force. See Unit 29 for a discussion of the major types of groups eligible for group insurance under Florida law.

---

[1]   Remember that most states impose their own regulations on group insurance and often stipulate a minimum number of participants, usually 10, that constitute an eligible group. However, in Florida, there is no minimum number of participants as long as the organization is eligible for group insurance.

Eligibility of Group Members

By its very nature, group insurance provides for participation by virtually all members of a given insured group. Whether or not an individual member chooses to participate usually depends on the amount of premium that individual must pay, if the plan is contributory. If the plan is noncontributory and the employer pays the entire premium, full participation is the general rule.

However, employers and insurers are allowed some latitude in setting minimum eligibility requirements for employee participants. For example, employees must be full-time workers and actively at work to be eligible to participate in a group plan. If the plan is contributory, the employee must authorize payroll deductions for the employee's share of premium payments. In addition, a probationary period may be required for new employees, which means they must wait a certain period of time (usually one to six months) before they can enroll in the plan. The probationary period is designed to minimize the administrative expense involved with those who remain with the employer only a short time. The probationary period is followed by the **enrollment period**: the time during which new employees can sign up for the group coverage. If an employee does not enroll in the plan during the enrollment period (typically 31 days), the employee may be required to provide evidence of insurability if enrollment is desired at a later date. This is to protect the insurer against adverse selection.

With these basics in mind, let's turn our attention to group life insurance plans. As noted, group health plans are discussed in Unit 24.

GROUP LIFE INSURANCE

Today, approximately 44% of life insurance in force in the United States is group life insurance and billions of dollars more are purchased every year. In fact, as far as coverage amounts go, group life has been the fastest growing life insurance line. According to the American Council of Life Insurers *2009 Life Insurers Fact Book*, at the end of 2008, group life insurance in force in the United States totaled more than $8.7 trillion. This represents a 5% decrease from the previous year. Many employees look to their group coverage to provide the foundation for their life insurance programs.

Group life plans may be contributory or noncontributory. If the employer pays the entire premium, the plan is noncontributory. If the employees pay part of the premium, the plan is contributory. Florida law requires 100% participation by eligible employees in noncontributory group life insurance plans. There is no requirement for minimal participation in contributory group life insurance plans. [Sec. 627.552(2), F.S.]

Types of Group Life Plans

There are many types of group life plans that insurers offer employers. The appropriate choice depends on the employer's objectives, needs, and resources. Group life can be either term or permanent.

Group Term Life

Most group life plans are term plans, which use **annual renewable term (ART) insurance** as the underlying policy. This gives the insurer the right to increase the premium each year (based on the group's experience rating), and it gives the policyholder the right to renew coverage each year. As is characteristic of ART policies, coverage can be renewed without evidence of insurability. The prevalent use of ART insurance is another reason why the cost of group insurance is fairly low.

Group Permanent Life

Some group life plans are permanent plans, using some form of permanent or whole life insurance as the underlying policy. The most common types of permanent group plans are **group ordinary**, **group paid-up**, and **group universal life**.

Group ordinary insurance is any type of group life plan—and there are many variations—that uses cash value life insurance in the plan. In some cases, the employees are allowed to own the cash value portion of the policy if they contribute to the plan. In other instances, an employee's termination results in the forfeiture of the cash value, which is then used to help fund the plan for the remaining employees.

With **group paid-up plans**, a combination of term and whole life insurance is used. Usually the employer pays for the term portion of the plan and employee contributions are used to purchase units of single-premium whole life. The sum of the employees' paid-up insurance and the employer-paid term insurance (usually decreasing term, to offset the annually increasing amount of paid-up insurance) equals the amount of life insurance the employees are entitled to under the plan. At retirement or termination, employees possess their paid-up policies.

A growing number of group life plans are using **universal life insurance policies** due to the flexibility these policies provide. The underlying policy contains the same features as individual universal life, but the policy is administered in much the same way as any group ordinary policy. Characteristic of group universal life plans is that the employees pay most of the premium; however, they are given certain rights to policy ownership that are not found in ordinary group life plans.

ILLUSTRATION 10.1

Taxation of Group Life Premiums and Proceeds

To encourage employers to provide employee benefits—such as a group life insurance plan—the federal government has granted these plans favorable tax treatment. To begin with, an employer may deduct the group plan premiums as a business expense. Secondly, the employee does not have to report the employer-paid premiums as income, as long as the insurance coverage is $50,000 or less. (Employees who are provided with more than $50,000 of coverage must declare as taxable income the premiums paid by the employer for the excess coverage.)

Proceeds paid under a group life plan to a deceased employee's beneficiary are exempt from income taxation if they are paid in a lump sum. If the proceeds are paid in installments, consisting of principal and interest, the interest portion is taxed.

For a group life insurance plan to receive favorable tax treatment, the government imposes some requirements to ensure that rank-and-file employees are not discriminated against in favor of select key employees. Basically, these requirements apply to eligibility and the type and amount of benefits provided.

Regarding eligibility, the requirements are that:
- the plan must benefit at least 70% of all employees; or
- at least 85% of all participating employees must not be key employees.

Regarding benefits, the requirements state that, again, the plan cannot discriminate in favor of key employees. For example, the amount of life insurance provided to all employees must bear a uniform relationship to their level of compensation or position. If a group life insurance plan fails to meet these nondiscriminatory requirements, the cost of the first $50,000 of coverage—normally excluded from gross income—will be included in a key employee's gross income for tax purposes. Rank-and-file employees are not so penalized.

How Benefits Are Determined

The type and amount of benefits provided to each insured member under a group life plan are typically predetermined by the employer as policyholder. Most employers will establish benefit schedules according to **earnings**, **employment position**, or as a **flat benefit**. A set schedule, such as one of these, helps protect the insurer against adverse selection, since the employees do not have the option to insure themselves for any more or any less than the schedule allows.

- **Earnings.** Under an earnings schedule, the amount of life insurance provided to individual employees is based on each employee's salary or earnings. It can be a flat amount per earnings level or a percentage of earnings. For instance, an earnings schedule could provide an employee with life insurance coverage equal to 1½ times that particular employee's salary.

- **Employment position.** An employment position schedule sets the amount of life insurance according to an employee's position with the company. For example, general staff employees may be provided with $30,000 of life insurance, managers with $50,000, account supervisors with $75,000, and vice presidents with $100,000.

- **Flat benefit.** A flat benefit schedule provides the same amount of life insurance to all employees, regardless of their earnings or position. Flat benefit schedules are most frequently used when the employer wants to provide only a small amount of insurance to its employees.

Conversion to Individual Plan

Once coverage becomes effective for an individual under a group life plan, it remains effective until the individual leaves the employer group (or the plan is terminated). In Florida, group life policies must contain a **conversion provision** that allows individual insured members to convert to an individual plan without evidence of insurability, if their employment is terminated. Usually, the employee has a limited period of time following termination (typically 31 days) in which to exercise the conversion privilege. This means that the group coverage will continue in force for the terminated employee for the duration of the conversion period, even if no conversion takes place. Thus, if a group-insured ex-employee were to die within 31 days after termination of employment, the group insurance death benefit would be payable to the employee's beneficiary.

Most group conversion provisions require the individual to convert to a whole life policy, as opposed to term. The premium for the new policy is based on the individual's attained age at the time of conversion.

There is a growing trend among employers to offer more than just a conversion privilege. Many employers now are offering portable group term life insurance. This means that employees can take (or **port**) their insurance with them when they leave the employer. The insurance coverage remains a term life benefit with no cash value.

With portable group term life insurance, all of the ported policies are pooled together rather than remaining in the employer's plan. The rates, therefore, are more like group rates and are much lower than individually sold coverage. In contrast, most group conversion provisions require the individual to convert to a whole life policy, as opposed to term. As a result, the policy's rates will mirror individual rates and generally will be much higher.

OTHER FORMS OF GROUP LIFE COVERAGE

There are a number of other kinds of group life insurance plans, two of which should be noted—**credit life insurance plans** and **blanket life insurance plans**. In addition, as alternatives to traditional insured plans, **multiple employer trusts** and **multiple employer welfare arrangements** are becoming popular options.

Group Credit Life Insurance

Group credit life insurance is another form of group insurance. A type of decreasing term insurance, it is issued by insurance companies to creditors to cover the lives of debtors in the amounts of their respective loans. Typically, it is provided through commercial banks, savings and loan associations, finance companies, credit unions, and retailers.

If an insured dies before the insured's loan is repaid, the policy proceeds are paid to the creditor to settle the remaining loan balance. Unlike regular group life insurance, premiums for group credit life may be paid wholly by the individual insureds. State laws, which vary, generally set a maximum amount of group credit life insurance per individual creditor (generally the creditor must have a minimum of 100 debtors per year) and limit the amount of insurance per borrower, which may not exceed the amount of indebtedness. Debtors cannot be forced to take the coverage from any particular insurance company. They have the right to choose their insurers.

Blanket Life Insurance

Blanket life insurance covers a group of people exposed to a common hazard. Individuals do not need to apply for blanket coverage and insurers do not need to provide each person with a certificate of coverage. Insureds are not specifically named in the policy because coverage is temporary. In fact, individuals may be covered for only a few hours at a time. Members of the group are automatically covered, but only while participating in the specific hazards named in the policy. For example, a blanket policy can be issued to the owner of an airline to cover its passengers. A person is covered by the blanket policy only while a passenger on that airline.

State insurance laws generally allow a number of groups to hold blanket life insurance policies. Some common policyholders include the following:

■ A college, a school, or a principal of a school, covering students, teachers, or employees

■ Religious, recreational, or civic organization, covering its members while participating in specific hazards as part of an activity sponsored by the organization

■ Employer, covering any group of employees who participate in specified hazards of employment

■ Sports team, covering members while they are participating on the team

■ Volunteer fire department, covering its firefighters while participating in specific hazards related to membership (such as fighting fires)

■ Newspaper, covering its carriers

Multiple Employer Trusts and Multiple Employer Welfare Arrangements

A method of marketing group benefits to employers who have a small number of employees is the **multiple employer trust (MET)**. METs may provide either a single type of insurance (such as health insurance) or a wide range of coverages (for example, life, medical expense, and disability income insurance). In some cases, alternative forms of the same coverage are available (such as comprehensive health insurance or basic health insurance).

An employer who wants to get coverage for employees from an MET must first become a member of the trust by subscribing to it. The employer is issued a joinder agreement, which spells out the relationship between the trust and the employer and specifies the coverages to which the employer has subscribed. It is not necessary for an employer to subscribe to all the coverages offered by an MET.

An MET may either provide benefits on a self-funded basis or fund benefits with a contract purchased from an insurance company. In the latter case, the trust, rather than the subscribing employers, is the master insurance contract holder. In either case, the employees of subscribing employers are provided with a benefit description (certificates of insurance) in a manner similar to the usual group insurance agreement.

In addition to alternative methods of funding benefits, METs can be categorized according to how they are administered, that is, whether by an insurance company or a third-party administrator.

A **multiple employer welfare arrangement (MEWA)** is a type of MET for union employees that is self-funded and has tax-exempt status. Employees covered under an MEWA are required by law to have an employment-related common bond.

SUMMARY

Group insurance is a way to provide insurance coverage for a number of individuals under one *master policy*. It is generally purchased by an employer as a benefit for employees. Usually the employer pays all or a portion of the premium on behalf of its employees. Employer-pay-all plans are known as *noncontributory* plans; plans that require partial premium contributions from employees are *contributory* plans.

When a group plan is initially installed, all employees who meet the *eligibility requirements* are eligible for coverage. Individual underwriting is usually not done; instead, the insurer looks at the characteristics of the group as a whole. New employees who are hired after the plan is in effect are usually subject to a *probationary period* before they are allowed to enroll.

Most group life insurance plans are term plans that use *annually renewable term insurance* as the underlying policy. Permanent group life plans include *group ordinary*, *group paid-up*, and *group universal life*. The amount of life insurance coverage individual employees receive is determined by the employer, based on earnings, employment position, or flat benefit schedule.

Other types of group plans are *franchise life*, *group credit life*, *blanket life*, *multiple employer trusts*, and *multiple employer welfare arrangements*.

KEY CONCEPTS

Students should be familiar with the following concepts:

master policy	certificate of insurance
experience rating	probationary period
enrollment period	annually renewable term
group ordinary	group paid-up
group universal life	blanket life insurance
group credit life insurance	multiple employer welfare arrangements
multiple employer trusts	

UNIT TEST

1. With regard to group insurance plans, which of the following statements is CORRECT?

   A. Employees generally pay for the entire premium.
   B. The sponsoring employer of a group insurance plan is given a master certificate of insurance that lists the names of all employees covered by the plan.
   C. Per unit of benefits, group insurance generally is available at rates lower than those for individual plans.
   D. Group insurance plans are a means for employers to provide a benefit for their key employees, without having to include all employees.

2. Group insurance plans that require employees to pay a portion of the premium are called

   A. underwritten
   B. contributory
   C. participatory
   D. shared

3. All of the following statements pertaining to the conversion privilege of group term life insurance are correct EXCEPT

   A. an insured employee typically has 31 days following termination of employment in which to convert the group insurance
   B. an insured employee must convert to the same type of coverage as was provided under the group plan (that is, term)
   C. insureds who convert their coverage to individual plans pay a premium rate according to their attained age
   D. an insured employee may exercise the conversion privilege regardless of that employee's insurability

4. The type of insurance most frequently used in group life plans is

   A. annually renewable term
   B. 10-year renewable term
   C. limited pay whole life
   D. single-premium whole life

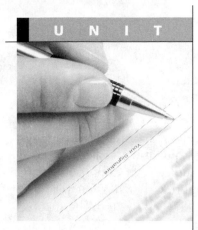
11

Annuities

- Purpose and Function of Annuities
- Annuity Basics
- Structure and Design of Annuities
- Income Taxation of Annuity Benefits
- Uses of Annuities

As noted in Unit 8, there are several options available when it comes to deciding how the proceeds of a life insurance policy are to be paid out or "settled." One such option is the life income option. This option (which actually consists of about half a dozen choices) gives beneficiaries an important guarantee: they can never outlive the income provided under the contract.

When individuals select a life income option, they are actually using the proceeds to purchase an **annuity** and selecting an **annuity payout option**. Annuities are a means of providing a stream of income for a guaranteed period of time, a period which is most typically defined in terms of the recipient's life. The value of this concept should be apparent to anyone in the business of providing financial advice. ■

PURPOSE AND FUNCTION OF ANNUITIES

An **annuity** is a mathematical concept that is quite simple in its most basic application. Start with a lump sum of money, pay it out in equal installments over a period of time until the original fund is exhausted, and you have an annuity. An annuity is simply a vehicle for liquidating a sum of money. Of course, in practice the concept is more complex. An important factor not mentioned above is interest. The sum of money that has not yet been paid out is earning interest, and that interest is also passed on to the income recipient (the annuitant).

Anyone can provide an annuity. By knowing the original sum of money (the **principal**), the **length of the payout period**, and an assumed **rate of interest**, it is a fairly simple process to calculate the payment amount. Actuaries have constructed tables of annuity factors that make this process even easier.

For example, the table in Illustration 11.1 shows that the factor for a 20-year annual payment of $1, based on a 7% interest factor, is $10.59. This means that if a person set aside $10.59 and could earn 7% interest while the fund was being depleted, an annual income of $1 could be paid for 20 years. The income recipient would receive a total of $20 for the original $10.59 invested in the annuity.

ILLUSTRATION 11.1

Present Value of $1 Payable

The following is a present value annuity table that shows the amount that, if deposited today at 7% interest, would produce an annual income of $1 for the specified number of years. In other words, this table reflects the value today of a series of payments tomorrow. For example, the present value of $1 payable for 25 years, at 7% interest, is $11.65. This means that $11.65 deposited today at 7% interest would generate a payment of $1 for 25 years.

Years	Present Value (at 7%)	Years	Present Value (at 7%)
5	$4.10	30	$12.40
10	$7.02	35	$12.94
15	$9.10	40	$13.33
20	$10.59	45	$13.60
25	$11.65	50	$13.80

In more practical terms, suppose you wanted to know how much money you should have on hand at age 65 that would generate $10,000 a year in income for 10 years, assuming you could earn 7% interest while the fund was being paid out. The present value of $1 payable for 10 years is $7.02; therefore, the present value of $10,000 payable for 10 years is $70,200 ($10,000 × $7.02).

There are other tables similar to this that solve for related problems (for example, how long income can be paid for any given amount of principal). The basic underlying principle, however, is the same in every case—the amount of an annuity payment is dependent upon three factors: starting principal, interest, and income period.

There is one important element absent from this simple definition of an annuity, and it is the one distinguishing factor that separates life insurance companies from all other financial institutions. While anyone can set up an annuity and pay income for a stated period of time, only life insurance companies can do so and guarantee income for the life of the annuitant.

Because of their experience with mortality tables, life insurance companies are uniquely qualified to combine an extra factor into the standard annuity calculation. Called a survivorship factor, it is, in concept, very similar to the mortality factor in a life insurance premium calculation. Thus, it provides insurers with the means to guarantee annuity payments for life, regardless of how long that life lasts.

Annuities Versus Life Insurance

It is important to realize that annuities are not life insurance contracts. In fact, it can be said that an annuity is a mirror image of a life insurance contract: they look alike but are actually exact opposites. Whereas the principal function of a life insurance contract is to create an estate (an "estate" being a sum of money) by the periodic payment of money into the contract, an annuity's principal function is to liquidate an estate by the periodic payment of money out of the contract. Life insurance is concerned with how soon one will die; life annuities are concerned with how long one will live.

It is easy to see the value of annuities in fulfilling some important financial protection needs. Their role in retirement planning should be obvious; guaranteeing that an annuitant cannot outlive the payments from a life annuity has brought peace of mind to countless numbers of people over the years. Annuities can play a vital role in any situation where a stream of income is needed for only a few years or for a lifetime.

ANNUITY BASICS

An annuity is a cash contract with an insurance company. Unlike life insurance products where policy issue and pricing are based largely on mortality risk, annuities are primarily investment products. Individuals purchase or fund annuities with a single sum amount or through a series of periodic payments; the insurer credits the annuity fund with a certain rate of interest, which is not currently taxable to the annuitant. In this way, the annuity grows. The ultimate amount that will be available for payout is, in part, a reflection of these factors. Most annuities guarantee a death benefit payable in the event the annuitant dies before payout begins; however, it is usually limited to the amount paid into the contract plus interest credited.

With any annuity, there are two distinct time periods involved: the accumulation period and the payout or annuity period. The accumulation period is that time during which funds are being paid into the annuity, in the form of payments by the contract holder and interest earnings credited by the insurer. The payout or annuity period refers to the point at which the annuity ceases to be an accumulation vehicle and begins to generate benefit payments on a regular basis. Typically, benefits are paid out monthly, though a quarterly, semiannual, or annual payment arrangement can be structured.

STRUCTURE AND DESIGN OF ANNUITIES

Annuities are flexible in that there are the following options available to purchasers that will enable them to structure and design the product to best suit their needs:

- **Funding method.** Single lump-sum payment or periodic payments over time

- **Date annuity benefit payments begin.** Immediately or deferred until a future date

- **Investment configuration.** A fixed (guaranteed) rate of return or a variable (nonguaranteed) rate of return

- **Payout period.** A specified term of years or for life, or a combination of both

ILLUSTRATION 11.2

Annuities Classification Chart

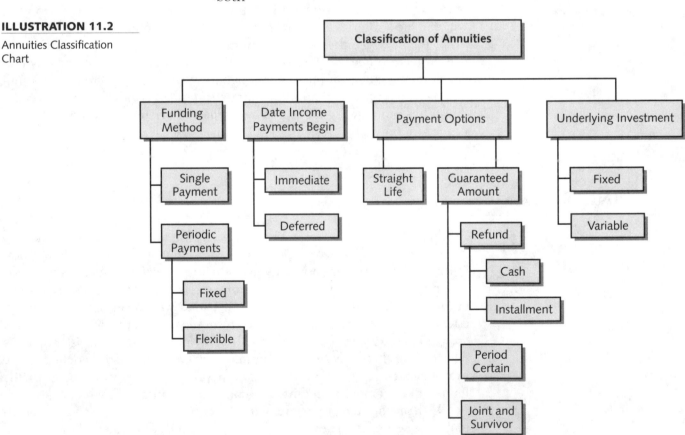

Let's take a closer look at each of these options. (They are illustrated in graphic form in Illustration 11.2.)

Funding Method

An annuity begins with a sum of money, called the principal sum. Annuity principal is created (or funded) in one of two ways: immediately with a single premium or over time with a series of periodic premiums.

Single Premium

Annuities can be funded with a **single, lump-sum premium**, in which case the principal sum is created immediately. For example, individuals nearing retirement whose financial priority is retirement income could surrender their whole life policies and use the cash value as a lump-sum premium to fund an annuity.

ILLUSTRATION 11.3

Types of Annuities

FPDA	Flexible-premium deferred annuity
SPIA	Single-premium immediate annuity
SPDA	Single-premium deferred annuity
TSA	Tax-sheltered annuity

Flexible (and Periodic) Payments

Today, it is more common to allow annuity owners to make **flexible premium** payments. A certain minimum premium may be required to purchase the annuity, but after that, the owner can make premium deposits as often as is desired. With flexible premium annuities, the benefit is expressed in terms of accumulated value. For instance, a contract might specify that it will provide for guaranteed lifetime monthly payments of $5.06 per $1,000 at the annuitant's age 65. This means that a contract that has grown to $100,000 upon the annuitant's age 65 would generate $506 a month for life.

Annuities can also be funded through a series of **periodic premiums** that, over time, will create the annuity principal fund. At one time, it was common for insurers to require that periodic annuity premiums be fixed and level, much like insurance premiums. The purpose of this type of funding is to create a certain amount of periodic annuity income. In other words, the contract defines what premium is required to generate a specified amount for a specified period of time upon contract maturity.

Date Annuity Income Payments Begin

Annuities can be classified by the date the income payments to the annuitant begin. Depending on the contract, annuity payments can begin immediately or they can be deferred to a future date.

Immediate Annuities

An **immediate annuity** is designed to make its first benefit payment to the annuitant at one payment interval from the date of purchase. Since most annuities make monthly payments, an immediate annuity would typically pay its first payment one month from the purchase date. Thus, an immediate annuity has a relatively short accumulation period.

As you might guess, immediate annuities can only be funded with a single payment, and are often called single-premium immediate annuities, or SPIAs. An annuity cannot simultaneously accept periodic funding payments by the annuitant and pay out income to the annuitant.

Deferred Annuities

Deferred annuities are those that provide income payments at some specified future date. Unlike immediate annuities, deferred annuities can be funded with periodic payments over time. Periodic payment annuities are commonly called **flexible premium deferred annuities (FPDAs)**. Deferred annuities can also be funded with single premiums, in which case they're called **single-premium deferred annuities**.

Most insurers charge contract holders for liquidating deferred annuities in the early years of the contract. These **surrender charges** cover the costs associated with selling and issuing contracts as well as costs associated with the insurer's need to liquidate underlying investments at a possibly inappropriate time. Surrender charges for most annuities are of limited duration, applying only during the first five to eight years of the contract. However, for those years in which surrender charges are applicable, most annuities provide for an annual "free withdrawal," which allows the annuity owner to withdraw up to a certain percentage, usually 10%, of the annuity account with no surrender charge applied. Additionally, some annuities may offer a **bailout provision**, which allows the annuity owner to surrender the annuity without surrender charges if interest rates drop a specified amount within a specified time period.

Annuity Payout Options

Just as life insurance beneficiaries have various settlement options for the disposition of policy proceeds, so too do annuitants have various **income payout options** to specify the way in which an annuity fund is to be paid out. In fact, as noted in Unit 8, selecting any of the life income options as a life insurance settlement (see the section titled "Life Income Options" in Unit 8) is the same as using the policy proceeds to purchase a single-premium immediate annuity and selecting an annuity income option.

There are a number of annuity income options available: **straight life income, cash refund, installment refund, life with period certain, joint and survivor,** and **period certain.**

Straight Life Income Option

A **straight life income** annuity option (often called a **life annuity** or a **straight life annuity**) pays the annuitant a guaranteed income for the annuitant's lifetime. When the annuitant dies, no further payments are made to anyone. If the annuitant dies before the annuity fund (i.e., the principal) is depleted, the balance, in effect, is forfeited to the insurer. It is used to provide payments to other annuitants who live beyond the point where the income they receive equals their annuity principal. (See Illustration 11.4.)

ILLUSTRATION 11.4

Life Income Option

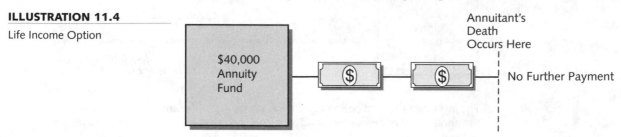

A straight life annuity income option provides for annuity payments to the annuitant for as long as the annuitant lives. Upon the annuitant's death, no further payments are made.

Cash Refund Option

A **cash refund** option provides a guaranteed income to the annuitant for life and, if the annuitant dies before the annuity fund (i.e., the principal) is depleted, a lump-sum cash payment of the remainder is made to the annuitant's beneficiary. Thus, the beneficiary receives an amount equal to the beginning annuity fund less the amount of income already paid to the deceased annuitant. (See Illustration 11.5.)

ILLUSTRATION 11.5

Cash Refund Option

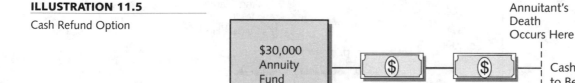

A cash refund option provides for payments to the annuitant for life and, if the annuitant dies before the principal fund is depleted, the remainder is to be paid in a single cash payment to the annuitant's beneficiary. Thus, the total annuity fund is guaranteed to be paid out.

Installment Refund Option

Like the cash refund, the **installment refund** option guarantees that the total annuity fund will be paid to the annuitant or to the annuitant's beneficiary. The difference is that under the installment option, the fund remaining at the annuitant's death is paid to the beneficiary in the form of continued annuity payments, not as a single lump sum. (See Illustration 11.6.)

Under either the cash refund or installment refund option, if the annuitant lives to receive payments equal to the principal amount, no future payments will be made to a beneficiary.

ILLUSTRATION 11.6

Installment Refund Option

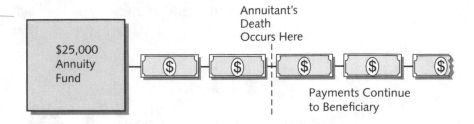

The installment refund option guarantees payments to the annuitant for life and, if the annuitant dies before the principal fund is depleted, the same annuity payments will continue to the beneficiary until the fund is paid out.

Life with Period Certain Option

Also known as the **life income with term certain** option, this payout approach is designed to pay the annuitant an income for life, but guarantees a definite minimum period of payments. For example, if an individual has a life and 10-year certain annuity, the individual is guaranteed payments for life or 10 years, whichever is longer. If the individual receives monthly payments for six years and then dies, the individual's beneficiary will receive the same payments for four more years. Of course, if the annuitant died after receiving monthly annuity payments for 10 or more years, the annuitant's beneficiary would receive nothing from the annuity. (See Illustration 11.7.)

ILLUSTRATION 11.7

Life With Period Certain Option

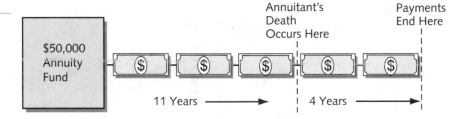

The life with period certain annuity option provides income to the annuitant for life but guarantees a minimum period of payments. Thus, if the annuitant dies during the specified period, benefit payments continue to the beneficiary for the remainder of the period. For example, if an individual has a 15-year life with period certain annuity, receives monthly benefit payments for 11 years and then dies, the individual's beneficiary will receive the same payments for the remainder of the period certain, or four years.

Joint and Full Survivor Option

The **joint and full survivor** option provides for payment of the annuity to two people. If either person dies, the same income payments continue to the survivor for life. When the surviving annuitant dies, no further payments are made to anyone. (See Illustration 11.8.)

ILLUSTRATION 11.8

Joint and Survivor Option

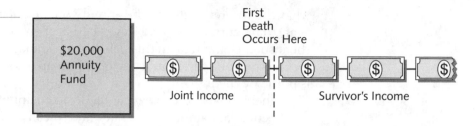

A joint and survivor annuity option provides for benefit payments to two people. If either dies, benefit payments continue to the survivor for the remainder of the survivor's life. A full survivor option pays the same benefit amount to the survivor; a two-thirds survivor option pays two-thirds of the original joint benefit; and a one-half survivor option pays one-half of the original joint benefit.

There are other joint arrangements offered by many companies:

■ **Joint and two-thirds survivor.** This is the same as the joint and full survivor arrangement, except that the survivor's income is reduced to two-thirds of the original joint income.

■ **Joint and one-half survivor.** This is the same as the joint and full survivor arrangement, except that the survivor's income is reduced to one-half of the original joint income.

Period Certain Option

The period certain income option is not based on life contingency; instead, it guarantees benefit payments for a certain period of time, such as 10, 15, or 20 years, whether or not the annuitant is living. At the end of the specified term, payments cease.

Investment Configuration

Annuities can also be defined according to their investment configuration, which affects the income benefits they pay. The two classifications are **fixed annuities**, which provide a fixed, guaranteed accumulation or payout, and **variable annuities**, which attempt to offset inflation by providing a benefit linked to a variable underlying investment account. **Indexed annuities**, a form of fixed annuity, are fairly new but have become quite popular.

Fixed Annuities

Fixed annuities provide a guaranteed rate of return. During the period in which the annuitant is making payments to fund the annuity (the **accumulation period**), the insurer invests these payments in conservative, long-term securities (typically bonds). This, in turn, allows the insurer to credit a steady interest rate to the annuity contract. The interest payable for any given year is declared in advance by the insurer and is guaranteed to be no less than a minimum specified in the contract. In this way, a fixed annuity has two interest rates: a minimum guaranteed rate and a current rate. The current rate is what the insurer credits to the annuity on a regular schedule (typically each year). The current rate will never be lower than the minimum rate, which the insurer guarantees. In this way, the accumulation of funds in a fixed annuity is certain and the contract owner's principal is secure. The investment risk is borne by the insurer.

When converted to a payout mode, fixed annuities provide a guaranteed fixed benefit amount to the annuitant, typically stated in terms of dollars per $1,000 of accumulated value. This is possible because the interest rate payable on the annuity funds is fixed and guaranteed at the point of annuitization. The amount and duration of benefit payments are guaranteed. Because they provide a specified benefit payable for life (or any other period the annuitant desires), fixed annuities offer security and financial peace of mind. However, since the benefit amount is fixed, annuitants may see the purchasing power of their income payments decline over the years due to inflation. For many, a variable annuity is preferable.

Variable Annuities

In the early 1950s, a group of people representing a teacher's association reviewed the annuity principle that was the foundation of their pension plan. The question of protection against inflation arose; it was noted that someone who retired with a given amount of income (say, $200 per month) would find that after a decade or so of inflation, the real purchasing power of that income would diminish. Attention then turned to solving the problem, and the solution was the birth of the **variable annuity**.

In Unit 5, we discussed variable life insurance. The same underlying principles of variable life insurance apply to variable annuities. As is true with variable life, variable annuities shift the investment risk from the insurer to the contract owner. If the investments supporting the contract perform well (as in a bull market), the owner will probably realize investment growth that exceeds what is possible in a fixed annuity. However, the lack of investment guarantees means that the variable annuity owner can see the value of the annuity decrease in a depressed market or in an economic recession.

Variable annuities invest deferred annuity payments in an insurer's separate accounts, as opposed to an insurer's general accounts (which allow the insurer to guarantee interest in a fixed annuity). Because variable annuities are based on non-guaranteed equity investments, such as common stock, a sales representative who wants to sell such contracts must be registered with the Financial Industry Regulatory Authority, or FINRA, as well as hold a state insurance license.

Not only can the value of a variable annuity fluctuate in response to movements in the market, so too will the amount of annuity income fluctuate, even after the contract has annuitized. It was for that reason the product was developed in the first place. In spite of inevitable dips in the amount of benefit income, the theory is that the general trend will be an increasing amount of income over time as inflation pushes up the price of stocks—a theory that has generally held true.

To accommodate the variable concept, a new means of accounting for both annuity payments and annuity income was required. The result is the accumulation unit (which pertains to the accumulation period) and the annuity unit (which pertains to the income payout period).

Accumulation Units

In a variable annuity, during the accumulation period, contributions made by the annuitant, less a deduction for expenses, are converted to **accumulation units** and credited to the individual's account. The value of each accumulation unit varies, depending on the value of the underlying stock investment.

For example, assume that the accumulation unit is initially valued at $10, and the holder of a variable annuity makes a payment of $200. This means she has purchased 20 accumulation units. Six months later, she makes another payment of $200, but during that time, the underlying stocks have declined and the value of the accumulation unit is $8. This means that the $200 payment will now purchase 25 accumulation units.

The value of one accumulation unit is found by dividing the total value of the company's separate account by the total number of accumulation units outstanding. Thus, if a company had $20 million in its separate account, and a total of 4 million accumulation units outstanding, the value of one accumulation unit would be $5. As the value of the account rises and falls, the value of each accumulation unit rises and falls.

Annuity Units

At the time the variable annuity benefits are to be paid out to the annuitant, the accumulation units in the participant's individual account are converted into **annuity units**. At the time of initial payout, the annuity unit calculation is made and, from then on, the number of annuity units remains the same for that annuitant. The value of one annuity unit, however, can and does vary from month to month, depending on investment results.

For instance, let's say that our annuitant has 1,000 accumulation units in her account by the time she is ready to retire and these units have been converted into 10 annuity units. She will always be credited with 10 annuity units—that number does not change. What does change is the value of the annuity units, in accordance with the underlying stock. Assume when she retired, each annuity unit was valued at $40. That means her initial benefit payment is $400 (10 × $40). As long as the value of the annuity unit is $40, her monthly payments will be $400. But what if the value of the stock goes up and her annuity unit value becomes $45? Her next monthly payment will be $450 (10 × $45).

The theory has been that the payout from a variable annuity over a period of years will keep pace with the cost of living and thus maintain the annuitant's purchasing power at or above a constant level. As with fixed annuities, the variable annuity owner has various payout options from which to choose. These options usually include the life annuity, life annuity with period certain, unit refund annuity (similar to a cash refund annuity), and a joint and survivor annuity.

Indexed Annuities

A fairly recent innovation, **indexed annuities (IA)** are a type of fixed annuity that offer the potential for higher credited rates of return than their traditional counterparts but also guarantee the owner's principal. The interest credited to an IA is tied to increases in a specific equity or stock index. Underlying the contract for the duration of its term is a minimum guaranteed rate (ordinarily 3 or 4%), so a certain rate of growth is guaranteed. When the increases in the index to which the annuity is linked produce gains that are greater than the minimum rate, that gain becomes the basis for the amount of interest that will be credited to the annuity. At the end of the contract's term—which is usually five to seven years—the annuity will be credited with the *greater* of the guaranteed minimum value or the indexed value. The index to which most IAs are tied is the Standard & Poor's 500 Composite Stock Price Index.

It is easy to understand why indexed annuities have become popular. They offer potential for market-linked rates of return with a guarantee that the owner's principal is protected. In this way, IAs bridge the gap between traditional guaranteed fixed annuities (which are subject to inflation risk) and variable annuities (which are subject to market risk). With an IA, individuals who do not want to risk principal can still receive market-based earnings, which are likely to be higher than those offered by traditional fixed products.

The primary purpose of indexed annuities is accumulation. When it comes time to access the funds, the owner can select a lump-sum distribution or annuitization. Annuitization can be either fixed or variable.

The basic principles of equity index contracts are explained in Unit 5 in Illustration 5.10, "General Accounts Versus Separate Accounts." To understand index products, it is helpful to know some of the special terminology used in the industry. Some common terms follow:

■ **Participation rates.** The participation rate refers to the percentage of the index growth that is credited to the annuity's values. The cash values in most contracts don't change as much or as fast as stock market indices. When the stock market index moves, many indexed contracts change the values by a percentage of the change in the stock index. For example, if the participation rate is 80% and the stock market moves up 10%, the amount credited to the cash value is 8%. This may also be subject to other factors, such as spreads, floors, and caps (see below), all of which may change every year (or even more often).

■ **Spread.** This feature is sometimes used in combination with participation rates. This amount, often expressed as an interest rate, is subtracted from the percentage increase in the stock index. For example, if the index goes up 20%, but the spread is 4%, the contract cash values would go up 20% − 4%, or 16%. The maximum spread is usually guaranteed, but a smaller current spread may be declared each year.

■ **Cap.** A limit, usually expressed as a percentage, on the increase in cash value. For example, if the stock index rises 25% but there is a 20% cap, the cash value will rise a maximum of 20%.

- **Floor.** A limit, often shown as a percentage per year (but sometimes expressed as a table of fixed-dollar minimums), on the decrease in cash values over a specific period. For example, if the stock index drops 15% but there is a 10% floor, the cash value will drop a maximum of 10%.

- **Ratcheting.** This guarantees that past increases in accumulated cash value (e.g., from previous years) will not be lost. Suppose the stock index drops 10%. If the contract is ratcheted year to year, it may guarantee that the values will not go down due to the drop in stock index. (In fact, many will guarantee a minimum increase of 3%.) The ratcheting effectively sets the previous value as a minimum floor, which limits the drop in values; sometimes it precludes all drops, allowing only gains.

- **Point-to-point.** This method of crediting interest or changing values ignores the average changes in the stock index and changes contract values according to the change in index from one point in time (often the anniversary) to another. For example, a point-to-point crediting method may ignore all the values between anniversaries and base the credited interest entirely upon the change from one anniversary to the next. Contracts that do not use point-to-point usually use averages of stock market indices (e.g., the average of all the index values at the first of each month) which would be compared with the average of the first-of-month values from the previous year to determine the change.

Some contracts offer multiple funds simultaneously. These are often a combination of indexed and declared-rate funds, often called "cash value strategies" contracts. Allocations of premiums to the different funds may be done automatically by the insurer as part of the contract, or it may be left to the discretion of the contract owner. Some allow the allocation to be changed after issue, and often operate similarly to variable contracts with multiple fund choices, but are commonly set up in the general account (i.e., without a separate account).

Retirement Income Annuities

While all annuities are well suited to provide retirement income, there is one type of annuity that is especially designed for retirement planning uses. Called the retirement income annuity, this plan is basically a deferred annuity policy to which a decreasing term life insurance rider is added.

If the policyowner reaches retirement age (usually age 65), the term insurance expires and the deferred annuity is used to provide retirement income under standard annuity principles. The unique feature of this plan is the death protection it provides. If the insured dies before retirement, the combination of the deferred annuity values and the term insurance benefits are paid to the beneficiary. The beneficiary may use the combined benefits to select any settlement option.

INCOME TAXATION OF ANNUITY BENEFITS

Annuity benefit payments are a combination of principal and interest. Accordingly, they are taxed in a manner consistent with other types of income: the portion of the benefit payments that represents a return of principal (i.e., the contributions made by the annuitant) are not taxed; the portion representing interest earned on the declining principal is taxed. The result, over the benefit payment period, is a tax-free return of the annuitant's investment and the taxing of the balance.

The unique advantage of annuity taxation as compared with other financial products is that it accumulates earnings on a tax-deferred basis; that is, no taxes are imposed until benefits are distributed.

The payout option selected by the annuitant (discussed earlier) also affects the way benefits are taxed. Lump sums, partial withdrawals, and period certain distributions are treated first as gain (taxed as ordinary income). Only after all the earnings have been withdrawn and taxed, may the annuitant retrieve the tax-free principal. This method of taxation is called last in, first out (LIFO). In addition, to discourage early withdrawal from annuities, a 10% penalty tax is imposed on withdrawals from a deferred annuity made before age 59½.

Annuity distributions that involve payments for life (straight life income, refund, life with period certain, or joint and survivor) are called annuitized settlements. Such settlements are not taxed using the LIFO and penalty method discussed previously. Rather, they are taxed using an exclusion ratio which is applied to each payment the annuitant receives.

$$\frac{\text{Investment in the contract}}{\text{Expected return}} = \text{Exclusion ratio}$$

The investment in the contract is the amount of money paid into the annuity by the annuitant (basis); the expected return is the annual total of the benefit payments multiplied by the remaining years of the annuitant's life expectancy as found in the mortality tables. The resulting ratio is applied to the benefit payments. At the end of each year, the insurer calculates and reports to the annuitant (IRS Form 1099) how much basis (not taxable) and how much gain (taxable) the insured received during the year. Note that because some of each payment is a return of basis, this method results in lower taxes in the early years than the LIFO approach. Also, there is no tax penalty imposed regardless of the annuitant's age, so this approach is particularly useful for annuitants under age 59½.

1035 Contract Exchanges

As discussed in Unit 8, Section 1035 of the Internal Revenue Code provides for tax-free exchanges of certain kinds of financial products, including annuity contracts. Recall that no gain will be recognized (meaning no gain will be taxed) if an annuity contract is exchanged for another annuity contract or if a life insurance or endowment policy is exchanged for an annuity contract. An annuity contract *cannot* be exchanged tax free for a life insurance contract. This is not an acceptable exchange under Section 1035.

USES OF ANNUITIES

Annuities have a variety of uses. They are suited to a variety of circumstances that require a large sum of money to be converted into a series of payments over a set time, particularly a lifetime. Let's now look at some of the common uses of annuities.

Individual Uses

The principal use of an annuity is to provide income for retirement. The advantage of the structured, guaranteed life income provided by annuities for retirement purposes is obvious and is one of the primary reasons the annuity is so popular. Many individuals, especially those in retirement, may be reluctant to use the principal of their savings, fearing it may become depleted. However, if they choose to conserve the principal, they run the risk of never deriving any benefit from it at all and ultimately are obliged to pass it on to others at their deaths. An annuity is designed to liquidate principal, but in a structured, systematic way that guarantees it will last a lifetime.

Besides being able to guarantee a lifetime income, annuities make excellent retirement products because they are conservative in nature, reliable and flexible enough to meet nearly all needs. As accumulation vehicles, they offer safety of principal, tax deferral, diversification, competitive yields (enhanced by tax deferral), and liquidity. As distribution vehicles, they offer a variety of payout options, which can be structured to conform to certain payment amounts or certain payment periods. They can cover one life or two. They can be arranged so that a beneficiary will receive a benefit if the annuitant dies before receiving the full annuity principal.

While annuities are designed to create and accumulate income for retirement, they can be used for other purposes as well. For example, they can be used to create and accumulate funds for a college education. Annuities serve a variety of purposes for which a stream of income is needed for a few years or a lifetime.

Qualified Annuity Plans

A qualified plan is a tax-deferred arrangement established by an employer to provide retirement benefits for employees. The plan is qualified by reason of having met government requirements. A qualified annuity is an annuity purchased as part of a tax-qualified individual or employer-sponsored retirement plan, such as an individual retirement account (IRA), which will be discussed in Unit 13, a tax-sheltered annuity (TSA) or other IRS-recognized plans.

A TSA is a special type of annuity plan reserved for nonprofit organizations and their employees. It's also known as a 403(b) plan or a 501(c)(3) plan because it was made possible by those sections of the Tax Code. For many years, the federal government, through its tax laws, has encouraged specified nonprofit charitable, educational, and religious organizations to set aside funds for their employees' retirement. Regardless of whether the money is actually set aside by the employers for the employees of such organizations or the funds are contributed by the employees through a reduction in salary, such funds may be placed in TSAs and are excludable from the employees' current taxable income.

Upon retirement, payments received by employees from the accumulated savings in taxsheltered annuities are treated as reportable income. However, as the total annual income of the employees is likely to be less after retirement, the tax to be paid by such retirees is likely to be less than while they were working. Furthermore, the benefits can be spread out over a specified period of time or over the remaining lifetime of the employee so that the amount of tax owed on the benefits in any one year generally will be small.

In addition to TSAs and IRAs, annuities are an acceptable funding mechanism for other qualified plans, including pensions and 401(k) plans.

Structured Settlements

Annuities are also used to distribute funds from the settlement of lawsuits or the winnings of lotteries and other contests. Such arrangements are called **structured settlements**.

Court settlements of lawsuits often require the payment of large sums of money throughout the rest of the life of the injured party. Annuities are perfect vehicles for these settlements because they can be tailored to meet the needs of the claimant. Annuities are also suited for distributing the large awards people win in state lotteries. These awards are usually paid out over a period of several years, usually 10 or 20 years. Because of the extended payout period, the state can advertise large awards and then provide for the distribution of the award by purchasing a structured settlement from an insurance company at a discount. The state can get the discounted price because a one million dollar award distributed over a 20-year period is not worth one million dollars today. Trends indicate that significant growth can be expected from both these markets for annuities.

A Note About Annuity Investments

The Florida Legislature has established standards and procedures for recommendations made to consumers relating to annuities. Section 627.4554 is intended to ensure that such recommendations appropriately address the insurance needs and financial objectives of a consumer at the time of the transaction. This law applies to any recommendation to purchase or exchange a fixed or variable annuity whether the product is classified as an individual or group annuity.

An agent must have an objectively reasonable basis for believing that the recommendation is suitable for the consumer based upon the facts disclosed regarding the consumer's investments, other insurance products, and the senior's financial situation. An agent is required to make reasonable efforts to obtain information concerning financial status, tax status, and investment objectives, among other specified information relevant to determining suitability. An agent is not responsible for any transaction wherein a consumer refuses to provide relevant information required by the agent, fails to provide accurate or complete information, or decides to enter into a transaction that is not based on the agent's recommendation. If the consumer refuses to provide relevant information requested by the agent, the agent must obtain a signed verification from the consumer that the consumer has refused to provide the requested information and may be limiting protections regarding the suitability of the sale.

Agents are required to maintain procedures that are reasonably designed to detect or prevent violations of this law. Agents are also required to maintain records relating to such transactions for five years. The insurer may maintain these records on behalf of the agent.

Any person who is registered with a member of the Financial Industry Regulatory Authority, who is required to make a suitability determination, and who makes and documents the determination is deemed to satisfy the requirements under this law for the recommendation of annuities. [Sec. 627.4554, F.S.]

SUMMARY

Annuities are ideally suited for providing peace of mind to anyone who is concerned about receiving income for life. The exact opposite of the life insurance concept, annuities start with a large fund and reduce it through a series of payments. Life insurance companies are the only financial institutions that can guarantee annuity payments will be made to the annuitant for life. Like beneficiaries of life insurance policies, annuitants have a variety of *payout options* as to how they can receive their annuity benefit payments.

While many annuitants find comfort in the guarantees of a traditional *fixed annuity*, many others prefer the potential investment gains possible with *equity indexed annuities* or *variable annuities*. Because variable annuities are recognized by the Securities and Exchange Commission as an investment, sales people who want to sell them must be licensed by and registered with FINRA. All states also require salespeople to hold a valid life insurance license to sell any type of annuity.

KEY CONCEPTS

Students should be familiar with the following concepts:

single-premium annuities	equity indexed annuities
immediate and deferred annuities	fixed and variable annuities
annuity payout options	taxation of annuities
tax-sheltered annuities	exclusion ratio
periodic payment annuities	

UNIT TEST

1. All of the following statements regarding annuities are correct EXCEPT
   A. generally, annuity contracts issued today require fixed, level funding payments
   B. annuities are sold by life insurance agents
   C. an annuity is a periodic payment
   D. annuitants can pay the annuity premiums in lump sums

2. What annuity payout option provides for lifetime payments to the annuitant but guarantees a certain minimum term of payments, whether or not the annuitant is living?
   A. Installment refund option
   B. Life with period certain
   C. Joint and survivor
   D. Straight life income

3. Which of the following statements regarding annuity payout options is NOT correct?
   A. Under a straight life annuity option, all annuity payments stop when the annuitant dies.
   B. In a cash refund annuity, the annuitant's beneficiary always receives an amount equal to the beginning annuity fund plus all interest.
   C. A period certain annuity guarantees a definite number of payments.
   D. Joint and survivor annuities guarantee payments for the duration of two lives.

4. James died after receiving $180 monthly for six years from a $25,000 installment refund annuity. His wife Lucy, as beneficiary, now will receive the same monthly income until her payments total
   A. $2,160
   B. $12,040
   C. $12,960
   D. $25,000

5. "Annuity payments are taxable to the extent that they represent interest earned rather than capital returned." When an annuitized payout option is chosen, what method is used to determine the taxable portion of each payment?
   A. Exclusion ratio
   B. Marginal tax formula
   C. Surtax ratio
   D. Annuitization ratio

6. Before he died, Gary received a total of $9,200 in monthly income payments from his $15,000 straight life annuity. He also was the insured under a $25,000 life insurance policy that named his wife, Darlene, as primary beneficiary. Considering the two contracts, Darlene would receive death benefits totaling
   A. $15,000
   B. $25,000
   C. $30,800
   D. $40,000

7. When a cash value life insurance policy is converted into an annuity in a nontaxable transaction, that event is generally known as
   A. a rollover
   B. a 1035 exchange
   C. a modified endowment
   D. a pension enhancement

8. Joanna and her husband, Tom, have a $40,000 annuity that pays them $200 a month. Tom dies and Joanna continues receiving the $200 monthly check as long as she lives. When Joanna dies, the annuity payments cease. This is an example of
   A. an installment refund annuity
   B. a joint and full survivor annuity
   C. a life annuity
   D. a cash refund annuity

9. All of the following statements about variable annuities are correct EXCEPT

   A. individuals who sell variable annuities must be registered with FINRA
   B. the contract owner bears the investment risk rather than the insurance company
   C. once a variable annuity has been annuitized, the amount of monthly annuity income cannot fluctuate
   D. during the accumulation period, the contract owner's contributions to the annuity are converted to accumulation units and credited to the owner's account

10. Albert has purchased an annuity that will pay him a monthly income for the rest of his life. If Albert dies before the annuity has paid back as much as he put into it, the insurance company has agreed to pay the difference to Albert's daughter. What annuity payout option did Albert select?

    A. A straight-life income
    B. A life income with period certain
    C. A cash refund
    D. A fixed period

11. Which of the following statements regarding equity index contract factors is most CORRECT?

    A. Equity index contracts usually follow all stock market changes exactly.
    B. All equity index contracts guarantee that cash values will grow a minimum amount each year.
    C. Most equity index contracts are backed by separate accounts and are variable products.
    D. Cash values of equity index contracts usually grow at a minimum interest rate.

12. Which of the following statements best describes equity index contracts?

    A. Equity index contracts are always backed by investments in stocks.
    B. Selling equity index contracts always requires a license for variable products.
    C. Most of the investments backing equity index contracts are similar to those for non-indexed contracts.
    D. Cash values of equity index contracts mirror all changes in stock market values.

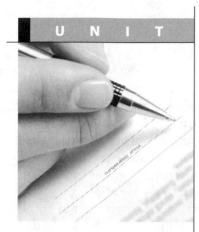

12

Social Security

- Purpose of Social Security
- Who Is Covered by Social Security?
- How Social Security Benefits Are Determined
- Types of OASDI Benefits

How does one judge the justness of a society? One test is its willingness to provide its citizens with a floor of protection against the financial loss that often accompanies death, disability, or old age—events beyond people's control. The Social Security program, enacted in 1935, offers Americans just such a foundation of protection. This unit reviews this important government-sponsored program. ■

PURPOSE OF SOCIAL SECURITY

There is much confusion and misunderstanding surrounding the Social Security program and the role it serves in our society. This misunderstanding has led to unrealistic expectations of Social Security benefits and what they mean to an individual's overall financial plan. Life insurance producers have the important duty to make sure their clients understand the true function of Social Security and recognize the purpose for which it was designed.

The Social Security system provides a basic floor of protection to all working Americans against the financial problems brought on by death, disability, and aging. Social Security augments but does not replace a sound personal insurance plan. Unfortunately, too many Americans have come to expect Social Security will fulfill all their financial needs. The consequence of this misunderstanding has been disillusionment by many who found, often too late, they were inadequately covered when they needed life insurance, disability income, or retirement income.

The Social Security program, enacted in 1935 and administered at the federal level by the Social Security Administration, is more formally called OASDI. This acronym aptly identifies the types of protection provided under the program: "Old Age" (retirement), "Survivors" (death benefits), and "Disability Insurance."[1] Social Security is an entitlement program, not a welfare program; Americans are entitled to participate in the program's benefits, provided they meet basic eligibility requirements. With few exceptions, most gainfully employed people are covered by Social Security today and are, or will be, eligible for the program's benefits. It is estimated that over 58 million Americans are currently receiving benefits under the system and with the retirement of the baby boom generation starting, this number is expected to rise rapidly through the next several decades.

WHO IS COVERED BY SOCIAL SECURITY?

With only a few exceptions, Social Security extends coverage to virtually every American who is employed or self-employed. Those not covered include:

- most federal employees hired before 1984 who are covered by Civil Service Retirement or another similar pension plan;

- approximately 25% of state and local government employees who are covered by a state pension program and who have elected not to participate under the Social Security program (each state and local government unit decides for itself whether or not to participate); and

- railroad workers who are covered under a separate federal program, the Railroad Retirement System.

It is easy to see that Social Security is quite broad in its reach, excluding only a small fraction of the working population. In addition to cover-

---

1　　Social Security also provides health insurance (HI) through its Medicare program.

ing workers, Social Security provides for spouses, dependent children and, in some cases, dependent parents of covered workers. It is important to note that a basic condition for coverage is that a person must **work**; OASDI is funded by a payroll tax (called the FICA tax) and eligibility for benefits is contingent upon a person contributing to the system during his or her working years.

Coverage Versus Eligibility

There is a significant difference between being covered by Social Security and being eligible for Social Security benefits. Being **covered** means that a worker is actively participating in the program through FICA tax contributions, but he or she may or may not be eligible for benefits. **Eligibility** for benefits is based on a person's insured status, which can be described as either fully insured or currently insured. Being **fully insured** entitles a worker and the worker's family to full retirement and survivor (that is, death) benefits. A **currently insured** status qualifies a worker for a limited range of survivor benefits.

Quarters of Coverage

A person's insured status—currently or fully—is based on that person's accrued **credits**. A credit is earned for a set amount of annual earnings on which FICA taxes are paid. This amount, which was $1,110 in 2010, is generally increased each year based on inflation. No matter how much a taxpayer earns, however, a maximum of four credits may be accumulated in a single year.

Fully Insured Versus Currently Insured

Workers are **fully insured** if they have accumulated the required number of credits based on their age. For most people, the required number of credits is 40 (representing approximately 10 years of work). Again, fully insured status provides eligibility for full retirement and survivor benefits.

To be considered **currently insured** and thus eligible for limited survivor (such as death) benefits, a worker must have earned six credits during the 13-quarter period ending with the quarter in which the worker died.

HOW SOCIAL SECURITY BENEFITS ARE DETERMINED

The amount of benefits to which a worker is entitled under Social Security is based on the worker's earnings over the years. There is a direct relationship between the amount of FICA taxes paid and the level of benefits earned. Workers who pay the maximum FICA tax over their lifetimes will receive higher benefits than those who pay less than the maximum. However, the FICA tax is not necessarily applied to all of a worker's earnings; the FICA tax is assessed only up to a maximum amount of earnings (known as the **maximum taxable wage base**, discussed later). Accordingly, Social Security benefits actually bear an inverse relationship to earnings: the more the person makes over a lifetime in excess of the maximum taxable wage base, the less Social Security provides in benefits as a proportion to total earnings. Conversely, a person who earned relatively little will receive a higher level of benefits in proportion to that person's total earnings.

Critics of Social Security sometimes complain of the apparent unfairness of a system in which the rich do not have to pay taxes above the maximum taxable wage base. These critics fail to point out, however, that those same wealthy people will receive benefits no greater than a worker who earned only the amount of the maximum taxable wage base.

Social Security Taxes

To understand Social Security, one must understand the basis upon which it is funded. Social Security is a pay-as-you-go system; the taxes paid by workers today are used to provide benefits today. Excess contributions are placed in a fund for future benefits, but they are not earmarked for individual contributors. As noted, OASDI is supported by a payroll tax, paid by employees, employers, and self-employed individuals.

This payroll, or FICA tax, is applied to employees' incomes up to a certain limit, called the **taxable wage base**. A portion of the FICA tax funds OASDI benefits; the other portion funds Medicare benefits. Employers pay an equal amount on behalf of each employee. Self-employed workers pay a higher rate (roughly equal to the sum of an employee's plus an employer's rate), but on annual income up to the same taxable wage base. When a worker's salary exceeds the taxable wage base in a calendar year, no more FICA tax is deducted from the worker's salary for the remainder of that year.

The maximum taxable wage base was, until 1971, quite stable. However, since 1972, the wage base has increased every year, meaning that more and more of a worker's earning are subject to FICA taxes. Up until 1991, the same wage base was used to calculate FICA taxes for both OASDI and Medicare; now, however, the wage base to which the Medicare portion of the tax applies has been greatly extended. In 2010, for example, the taxable wage base for OASDI was $106,800. This means that up to $106,800 of earned income was subject to being taxed for OASDI. There is no cap on earnings for Medicare, so all earned income is subject to the Medicare portion of the FICA tax.

The FICA tax rate is also subject to increases, though not as often as the wage base. For more than 20 years, the rate for employers and employees alike has been 7.65%, of which 6.20% is applied to OASDI and 1.45% is applied to Medicare. The tax rate for self-employed persons is the total of the employer and employee rates, or 15.30%.

Calculating Benefits

Social Security benefits were computed on a worker's **average monthly wage (AMW)** if the person became eligible for benefits before 1979. For people becoming eligible in 1979 or later, the calculation is based on the worker's **average indexed monthly earnings (AIME)**. The AIME, like its predecessor the AMW, is an average of the worker's lifetime earnings that were subject to the FICA tax. The AIME adds the additional, and critical, step of "weighting" a worker's past earnings to take inflation into account and to bring them up to current economic standards; failure to do so would result in exceptionally small benefits.

Consider, for example, the worker now retiring who never earned any more than the taxable wage base in, say, 1970. At the time, the taxable wage base was $7,800. If the worker's retirement benefit today were directly based on earnings of $7,800 in 1970 (and so on), it is easy to see how painfully small the worker's level of retirement income would be by today's economic standards. Through weighting, the AIME adjusts past earnings to equal what they would be worth by current economic standards.

The averaged monthly earnings figure derived by the AIME is next applied to a formula to yield the **primary insurance amount (PIA).** The PIA is actually the amount equal to the worker's full retirement benefit at age 65 (benefits are reduced for early retirement) or benefits to a disabled worker. Benefits payable to workers and their spouses and dependents are usually expressed as a percentage of the worker's PIA. For example, a person who elects to retire at age 62 with Social Security retirement benefits will receive benefits equal to 80% of that person's PIA. It should be noted that this reduced amount does not increase to 100% of the PIA when the worker reaches full retirement age; the reduction stays in effect for the remainder of the worker's life.

TYPES OF OASDI BENEFITS

Now that you have a basic understanding of how Social Security benefits are determined, let's take a closer look at the benefits themselves. Specifically, we will review the **death**, **retirement**, and **disability** benefits provided under Social Security. (Medicare benefits will be discussed in Unit 20.)

Death Benefits

Upon the death of an eligible worker, Social Security provides death benefits to a surviving spouse, dependent children and dependent parents. These death benefits are more commonly called **survivor benefits**.

Lump-Sum Death Benefit

Social Security provides a one-time lump-sum death benefit to a deceased worker's surviving spouse or children. The amount of this benefit is equal to three times the worker's PIA, up to a maximum of $255. This benefit is designed to help defray funeral expenses. The benefit is surprisingly low because it is one of the few Social Security benefits that has never been increased or indexed for inflation. Only surviving spouses or eligible children may receive this benefit.

Surviving Spouse's Benefit

The eligible surviving spouse of a fully insured deceased worker is entitled, at age 65, to a monthly life income equal to the worker's PIA at death.

Or, if the worker wishes to receive these benefits early, the surviving spouse can elect reduced benefits, starting as early as age 60.

A surviving spouse can be entitled to benefits on the deceased worker's record if the surviving spouse cares for a child entitled on the deceased spouse's record and the child is either under age 16 or over age 15 and disabled. In the case of the physically disabled child, the spouse must render personal services for the child. In the case where the child is mentally disabled, the spouse simply must have the child in his care.

Child's Benefit

A child who is under age 18 (or disabled before age 22) whose parent is a deceased worker may receive a benefit equal to 75% of the worker's PIA until the child turns 18 (19 if still in high school). If the child marries before age 18, the benefit terminates.

Parents' Benefits

Beginning at age 62, each parent of a deceased fully insured worker is eligible to receive a monthly benefit if the parent was at least one-half supported by the worker at the time of death. When two parents are eligible, each receives 75% of the worker's PIA; if only one parent is eligible, that parent receives 82.5% of the worker's PIA.

Maximum Survivor Benefits

Social Security has placed limits on the total amount of survivor benefits that any one family may receive. This limit is known as the **maximum family benefit**, and it varies according to the PIA. If the sum of the individual benefits paid to members of one family exceeds this maximum limit, they will be reduced proportionately to bring the total within the limit.

Retirement Benefits

Social Security also provides **old age** or **retirement** benefits to qualified (fully insured) workers and their families. These benefits are paid monthly.

Worker's Retirement Benefit

Fully insured workers are eligible for full retirement income benefits (i.e., 100% of the PIA) at their **full retirement age (FRA)**. This is age 65 for those born before 1938. Permanently reduced benefits are available from age 62 for those who elect to retire early and draw benefits; slightly greater benefits are available for those who delay retirement beyond their FRA.

It should be noted that, as a result of federal legislation passed in the 1980s, the age of eligibility for full retirement benefits (FRA) began to increase starting in 2000. Acknowledging the increased longevity of retired workers, Congress gradually raised the FRA from 65 to 66 between 2000 and 2006. It will remain at 66 through 2016, but from 2017 through 2022, the

FRA will again increase from 66 to 67. Although the FRA is being increased, the eight-year window between earliest retirement age (62) and latest age when benefits increase (70) is not changing.

Spouse's Benefit

The spouse of any worker eligible for retirement benefits is entitled to an old age income at the spouse's FRA, or a reduced benefit at age 62. At FRA, the spouse's benefit is 50% of the retired worker's PIA; at age 62, a spouse may receive permanently reduced benefits.

If there is a dependent child under age 16 (or disabled before age 22), the spouse is eligible to receive the 50% spousal benefit, regardless of the spouse's age.

Child's Benefit

An unmarried child of a worker on retirement income is generally eligible to receive a monthly benefit of 50% of the worker's PIA until the child turns 18. If the child is disabled before age 22, the child's benefit will continue indefinitely.

Maximum Retirement Benefits

As is the case with survivor benefits, a maximum family benefit amount also applies to Social Security retirement benefits. If the total benefits due to a spouse and children exceed this limit, their benefits will be reduced proportionately.

Earnings Test

Under prior law, people under age 70 who were receiving Social Security retirement benefits but continued to work could earn only so much each year without having their benefits reduced. However, this law was repealed in 2000. Under the current rules, starting with the month a person reaches full retirement age, that person can continue working and receive Social Security benefits, with no limit on earnings. However, if a person is under the full retirement age when she begins receiving Social Security benefits and continues to work, her benefits still will be reduced.

In this case, $1 in benefits will be deducted for each $2 earned above the annual limit. However, in the year a worker reaches full retirement age, $1 in benefits will be deducted for each $3 earned above a different limit. Only earnings received before the month the worker reaches the full benefit retirement age will be counted.

Disability Benefits

A fully insured worker who becomes disabled is entitled to **disability benefits** under Social Security, as are the worker's spouse and dependent children.

Disabled Worker's Benefit

A disabled worker is entitled to a monthly benefit equal to the worker's PIA at the time the disability occurred. There is no reduction in benefits if they begin prior to age 65; however, if the worker becomes disabled after age 63 and had been receiving a reduced retirement benefit, the worker's disability benefits will be reduced to take into account the retirement benefits already received.

Spouse's Benefit

The spouse of a qualified disabled worker may also receive benefits from Social Security, depending on the spouse's age. If the spouse is 65, the benefit is equal to 50% of the worker's PIA. A spouse who is 62 can elect reduced benefits.

If there is a dependent child under age 16 (or who is disabled, regardless of age), the spouse can receive the 50% spousal benefit, regardless of the spouse's age.

Child's Benefit

An unmarried dependent child of a disabled worker who is under 18 (or a child who was disabled prior to age 22) is eligible for monthly benefits equal to 50% of the worker's PIA.

Maximum Disability Benefits

Again, a maximum family benefit applies, limiting the amount of disability benefits one family can receive on the worker's earnings record. The earnings test is also applicable and pertains individually to each family member.

It should be noted that qualification for Social Security disability benefits is subject to rigid requirements. To begin with, the worker must meet Social Security's definition of disability, which is the inability to engage in any substantial gainful work. The disability must be the result of a medically determinable physical or mental impairment that can be expected to last at least 12 months or to result in an earlier death.

Disability benefits begin after the worker has satisfied a waiting period of five consecutive months, during which the worker must be disabled. The benefits may be paid retroactively for as long as 12 months (excluding the waiting period) preceding the date an application for benefits is filed.

Taxation of Social Security Benefits

Until 1984, all Social Security benefits were exempt from federal income taxes. Today, however, up to 85% of Social Security benefits may be treated as taxable income for recipients whose income exceeds certain base amounts. Certain step-rate thresholds determine the amount on which a worker's benefits might be taxed.

SUMMARY

The federally managed *Social Security program*, more formally called Old Age, Survivors, and Disability Insurance (OASDI), is the government's attempt to provide a basic floor of financial protection to all working Americans. It is a pay-as-you-go system funded by a mandatory FICA *payroll tax* on almost all workers. While Social Security benefits do provide an important source of income for retirees and the surviving spouses and children of covered workers, these benefits alone are not sufficient to maintain a meaningful standard of living. Social Security benefits augment, but do not replace, a well-founded personal insurance program.

KEY CONCEPTS

Students should be familiar with the following concepts:

OASDI benefits	FICA tax
fully insured status	currently insured status credits
taxable wage base	average indexed monthly earnings (AIME)
PIA earnings test	
full retirement age (FRA)	taxation of Social Security benefits

UNIT TEST

1. Ellen works part time to supplement her family's income. Last year she earned $6,500 and worked at least part of every month. With how many quarters of coverage will she be credited?

   A. 1
   B. 2
   C. 3
   D. 4

2. Which of the following statements regarding Social Security survivor benefits is NOT correct?

   A. A surviving widow, age 66, will be entitled to a life income equal to her husband's PIA.
   B. A healthy dependent child of a deceased worker will be entitled to an income benefit until age 18, or to age 22, if the child attends college.
   C. A surviving widower, age 47, has a 13-year-old child who was also a dependent of the deceased worker. The widower is entitled to monthly income until the child reaches age 16, at which time benefits will cease to the widower until the widower reaches at least age 60.
   D. A deceased covered worker was providing one-half of the support for a 62year-old parent who is confined to a nursing home. The parent is entitled to a survivor's benefit.

3. Which of the following examples pertaining to Social Security benefits is CORRECT?

   A. Simon has a Social Security PIA of $700 at the time of his death. His surviving spouse will receive a lump-sum death benefit of $2,250.
   B. Lola, age 30, has a daughter, age 10. Her husband, who is covered under Social Security, died unexpectedly last month following surgery. Both Lola and her daughter are entitled to receive monthly survivor benefits until her daughter reaches age 18.
   C. Mason, who is married with one son, age 16, is a fully insured retired worker receiving Social Security benefits. In addition, his spouse is eligible for benefits at age 62 and his son, is eligible for benefits until he is 18 years old.
   D. Arlene, the 20-year-old daughter of a fully insured retired worker, becomes totally and permanently disabled from injuries received in a car accident. Because her disability occurred after age 16, Arlene is not eligible for her father's Social Security benefits.

4. In determining Social Security retirement benefits, which of the following statements is CORRECT?

   A. Average monthly wages (AMW) are adjusted for inflation.
   B. The primary insurance amount (PIA) determines the worker's average indexed monthly earnings (AIME).
   C. The PIA is a determination of the amount equal to the worker's full retirement benefit at the worker's full retirement age.
   D. Workers retiring past age 59½ can receive 100% of their PIA.

5. Rudy is eligible for full death, retirement, and disability benefits under Social Security. His worker status is

   A. completely insured
   B. currently insured
   C. fully insured
   D. partially insured

6. All of the following statements correctly describe the purpose of Social Security EXCEPT
    A. it provides a source of income for a meaningful standard of living during retirement
    B. it provides basic protection against financial problems accompanying death, disability, and retirement
    C. it augments a sound personal insurance plan
    D. it provides retirement and survivor benefits to a worker and the worker's family

7. Bill is self-employed. The FICA tax rate for Bill is
    A. 6.2%
    B. 7.65%
    C. 15%
    D. 15.3%

8. Jan, a single, working mother, dies at age 40. Dave, her only son, would receive a one-time lump-sum benefit of
    A. $255
    B. $500
    C. $1,000
    D. $2,555

13

Retirement Plans

■ Qualified Versus Nonqualified Plans

■ Qualified Employer Retirement Plans

■ Qualified Plans for the Small Employer

■ Individual Retirement Plans

As stated in the last unit, Social Security benefits should be regarded as a basic floor of financial protection and not as a source that alone can provide a meaningful standard of living. Individuals must take the initiative if they want full security in meeting financial challenges. This means maintaining adequate life insurance to meet the costs of death, health insurance to cover the expenses of becoming ill, and a well-planned retirement program to maintain a desired standard of living when employment income ceases. In this unit, we will discuss the broad topic of retirement plans. Although this subject is complex and can be covered only superficially here, life insurance professionals should recognize this as an important part of the overall insurance concept and should be prepared to learn more about retirement planning as they progress through their careers. ■

QUALIFIED VERSUS NONQUALIFIED PLANS

The field of retirement planning has grown tremendously in both scope and significance. In various ways, the federal government encourages businesses to set aside retirement funds for their employees and provides incentives for individuals to do likewise. There are many kinds of **retirement plans**, each designed to fulfill specific needs. Life insurance companies play a major role in the retirement planning arena, as the products and contracts they offer provide ideal funding or financing vehicles for both individual plans and employer-sponsored plans.

Broadly speaking, retirement plans can be divided into two categories: **qualified plans** and **nonqualified plans**. Qualified plans are those that, by design or by definition, meet certain requirements established by the federal government and, consequently, receive favorable tax treatment.

- Employer contributions to a qualified retirement plan are considered a deductible business expense, which lowers the business's income taxes.

- The earnings of a qualified plan are exempt from income taxation.

- Employer contributions to a qualified plan are not currently taxable to the employee in the years they are contributed, but they are taxable when they are paid out as a benefit (and, typically, when the employee is retired and in a lower tax bracket).

- Contributions to an individual qualified plan, such as an individual retirement account or annuity (IRA), are deductible from income under certain conditions (which will be discussed shortly).

If a plan does not meet the specific requirements set forth by the federal government, it is termed a **nonqualified plan** and, thus, is not eligible for favorable tax treatment. For example, Bill, age 42, decides he wants to start a retirement fund. He opens a new savings account at his local bank, deposits $150 a month in that account, and vows not to touch that money until he reaches age 65. Although his intentions are good, they will not serve to "qualify" his plan. The income he deposits and the interest he earns are still taxable every year. Our discussion in this unit will focus on qualified retirement plans, both individual and employer-sponsored.

QUALIFIED EMPLOYER RETIREMENT PLANS

An **employer retirement plan** is one that a business makes available to its employees. Typically, the employer makes all or a portion of the contributions on behalf of its employees and is able to deduct these contributions as ordinary and necessary business expenses. The employees are not taxed on the contributions made on their behalf, nor are they taxed on the benefit fund accruing to them until it actually is paid out. By the same token, contributions made by an individual employee to a qualified employer retirement plan are not included in the individual's ordinary income and therefore are not taxable.

Basic Concepts

Many of the basic concepts associated with qualified employer plans can be traced to the **Employee Retirement Income Security Act of 1974**, commonly called **ERISA**. The purpose of ERISA is to protect the rights of workers covered under an employer-sponsored plan. Before the passage of ERISA, workers had few guarantees to assure them that they would receive the pension benefit they thought they had earned. A sad but common plight was the worker who had devoted many years to one employer, only to be terminated within a few years of retirement—and not be entitled to a pension benefit.

ILLUSTRATION 13.1

General Qualification Requirements for Employer-Sponsored Retirement Plans

- A plan must be written.
- A plan must be in effect.
- A plan must be communicated to employees.
- A plan must be established by the employer.
- Contributions must be made by the employer, the employees, or both.
- A plan must be for the exclusive benefit of the employees.
- A plan must be permanent.
- Any life insurance benefits must be incidental to retirement benefits.
- Minimum participation standards must be met.
- A plan must not discriminate in coverage.
- A plan must not discriminate in contributions or benefits on the basis of income or gender.
- Annuity payments under a plan must be available in the form of a joint and survivor annuity.
- Comprehensive vesting standards concerning the vesting of an employee's benefits must be followed.
- Minimum funding standards must be met.
- A plan must comply with limitations on contributions and benefits.
- There must be no assignment or alienation of benefits.
- A plan must meet Social Security integration rules.
- A plan must meet rules for mergers and consolidations.
- A plan must meet rules for multi-employer plans.
- A plan must meet rules pertaining to the reduction of benefits because of Social Security.
- A plan must fulfill plan termination requirements.
- A plan must fulfill special requirements for particular plans.
- A top-heavy plan must contain contingency provisions.

ERISA imposes a number of requirements that retirement plans must follow to obtain IRS approval as a qualified plan eligible for favorable tax treatment. (See Illustration 13.1.) While an in-depth discussion of these requirements is beyond the scope of this text, the basic concepts of **participation**, **coverage**, **vesting**, **funding**, and **contributions** should be noted.

Participation Standards

All qualified employer plans must comply with minimum **participation standards** designed to determine employee eligibility. In general, employees who have reached age 21 and have completed one year of service must be allowed to enroll in a qualified plan. Or, if the plan provides for 100% vesting upon participation, they may be required to complete two years of service before enrolling.

Coverage Requirements

The purpose of **coverage requirements** is to prevent a plan from discriminating against rank-and-file employees in favor of the "elite"—shareholders, officers, and highly compensated employees—whose positions often enable them to make basic policy decisions regarding the plan. The IRS will subject qualified employer plans to **coverage tests** to determine if they are discriminatory. A qualified plan cannot discriminate in favor of highly paid employees in its coverage provisions or in its contributions and benefits provisions.

Vesting Schedules

All qualified plans must meet standards that set forth the employee vesting schedule and nonforfeitable rights at any specified time. **Vesting** means the right employees have to their retirement funds; benefits that have "vested" belong to each employee even if the employee terminates employment prior to retirement. For all plans, an employee always has a 100% vested interest in benefits that accrue from the employee's own contributions. Benefits that accrue from employer contributions must vest according to vesting schedules established by law. (See Illustration 13.2.)

Funding Standards

For a plan to be qualified, it must be **funded**. In other words, there must be real contributions on the part of the employer, the employee, or both, and these funds must be held by a third party and invested. The **funding vehicle** is the method for investing the funds as they accumulate. Federal minimum funding requirements are set to ensure that an employer's annual contributions to a pension plan are sufficient to cover the costs of benefits payable during the year, plus administrative expenses.

Contributions

Qualification standards regarding the amount and type of **contributions** that can be made to a plan vary, depending on whether the plan is a **defined contribution plan** or a **defined benefit plan**, discussed later. Suffice it to say, all plans must restrict the amount of contributions that can be made for or accrue to any one plan participant.

With these basics in mind, let's turn to the two major categories of qualified employer retirement plans, used primarily by corporate employers. They are the **defined contribution plan**, which obligates the plan sponsor to make periodic contributions for each participant per a defined formula, and the **defined benefit plan**, which defines the amount of retirement income each participant will receive.

ILLUSTRATION 13.2

Vesting Schedules for Qualified Plans

An employer may chose between two types of vesting schedules: cliff vesting or graded vesting.

Cliff Vesting

Under a cliff-vesting schedule for employer contributions, such as profit-sharing contributions and employer matching contributions, the employee becomes fully vested at specified time, such as after five years of service. If the employee leaves the company before that time, the employee would not receive any of the employer contributions.

Graded Vesting

Under a graded-vesting schedule for employer matching contributions, the employee is 20% vested in employer contributions after completing two years of vesting service. For each subsequent year, the vesting is increased by 20% until it reaches 100%, which occurs after six years of service.

The vesting schedules are summarized in the following tables:

Regular Employer Contributions			
Five-Year Cliff Vesting		Seven-Year Graded Vesting	
Years of Vesting Service	Vested %	Years of Vesting Service	Vested %
1	0	1	0
2	0	2	0
3	0	3	20
4	0	4	40
5+	100	5	60
		6	80
		7+	100

Employer Matching Contributions			
Two-Year Cliff Vesting		Six-Year Graded Vesting	
Years of Vesting Service	Vested %	Years of Vesting Service	Vested %
1	0	1	0
2+	100	2	20
		3	40
		4	60
		5	80
		6+	100

Defined Contribution Plans

The provisions of a **defined contribution plan** address the amounts going into the plan currently and identify the participant's vested (nonforfeitable) account. These predetermined amounts contributed to the participant's account accumulate to a future point (i.e., retirement) and the final fund available to any one participant depends on total amounts contributed, plus interest and dividends earned.

There are three types of defined contribution plans: **profit-sharing plans**, **stock bonus plans**, and **money purchase plans**.

Profit-Sharing Plans

Profit-sharing plans are established and maintained by an employer and allow employees to participate in the profits of the company. They provide for a definite predetermined formula for allocating plan contributions among the participants and for distributing the funds upon retirement, death, disability, or termination. Since contributions are tied to the company's profits, it is not necessary that the employer contribute every year or that the amount of contribution be the same. However, the IRS states that to qualify for favorable tax treatment, the plan must be maintained with "recurring and substantial" contributions.

Stock Bonus Plans

A **stock bonus plan** is similar to a profit-sharing plan, except that contributions by the employer do not depend on profits, and benefits are distributed in the form of company stock.

Money Purchase Plans

Money purchase plans provide for fixed contributions with future benefits to be determined and thus most truly represent a defined contribution plan. A money purchase plan must meet the following three requirements:

- Contributions and earnings must be allocated to participants in accordance with a definite formula.

- Distributions can be made only in accordance with amounts credited to participants.

- Plan assets must be valued at least once a year, with participants' accounts being adjusted accordingly.

Defined Benefit Plans

In contrast to a defined contribution plan that sets up predetermined contributions, a **defined benefit plan** establishes a definite future **benefit**, predetermined by a specific formula. When the term *pension* is used, the reference is typically to a defined benefit plan. Usually the benefits are tied to the employee's years of service, amount of compensation, or both. For example, a defined benefit plan may provide for a retirement benefit equal to 2% of the employee's highest consecutive five-year earnings, multiplied by the number of years of service. Or the benefit may be defined as simply as $100 a month for life.

To qualify for federal tax purposes, a defined benefit plan must meet the following basic requirements.

- The plan must provide for **definitely determinable benefits**, either by a formula specified in the plan or by actuarial computation.

- The plan must provide for **systematic payment of benefits** to employees over a period of years (usually for life) after retirement. Thus, the plan has to detail the conditions under which benefits are payable and the options under which benefits are paid.

■ The plan must provide **primarily retirement benefits**. The IRS will allow provisions for death or disability benefits, but these benefits must be incidental to retirement.

■ The **maximum annual benefit** an employee may receive in any one year is limited to an amount set by the tax law and is periodically adjusted for inflation.

The appropriate choice of qualified corporate retirement plan—defined contribution or defined benefit—requires an understanding of the operation and characteristics of each plan as they relate to the employer's objectives.

Cash or Deferred Arrangements (401(k) Plans)

Another form of qualified employer retirement plan is known as the **401(k) plan**, whereby employees can elect to take a reduction in their current salaries by deferring amounts into a retirement plan. These plans are called *cash or deferred arrangements* because employees cannot be forced to participate; they may take their income currently as cash or defer a portion of it until retirement with favorable tax advantages.

The amounts deferred are not included in the employees' gross income and earnings credited to the deferrals grow tax free until distribution. Typically, 401(k) plans include matching employer contributions: for every dollar the employee defers, for example, the employer will contribute $.50. The maximum annual amount an employee can defer is set by tax law and indexed for inflation periodically.

A cash or deferred arrangement must be part of a profit-sharing or stock bonus plan. In addition to meeting the qualification rules applicable to defined contribution plans, 401(k) plans also must qualify under the following special set of rules.

■ Amounts deferred can be distributed penalty-free because of retirement, death, disability, separation from service, or attainment of age 59½.

■ Employee deferred contributions are nonforfeitable.

■ Special nondiscrimination requirements must be met to prevent highly compensated employees from deferring disproportionately higher amounts of their salaries.

Employer matching contributions to a qualified cash or deferred profit-sharing plan are not currently taxed to the employee.

Tax-Sheltered Annuities (403(b) Plans)

Another type of employer retirement plan is the **tax-sheltered annuity** or **403(b) plan**. This was explained in Unit 11, but it is appropriate to review it here.

A tax-sheltered annuity is a special tax-favored retirement plan available only to certain groups of employees. Tax-sheltered annuities may be established for the employees of specified nonprofit charitable, educational, religious, and other 501(c)(3) organizations, including teachers in public school systems. Such plans generally are not available to other kinds of employees.

Funds are contributed by the employer or by the employees (usually through payroll deductions) to tax-sheltered annuities and, thus, are excluded from the employees' current taxable income. The maximum annual salary reduction for an employee under a 403(b) plan is the same as that for a 401(k) plan.

IRC Section 457 Deferred Compensation Plans

Deferred compensation plans for employees of state and local governments and nonprofit organizations became popular in the 1970s. Congress enacted Internal Revenue Code Section 457 to allow participants in such plans to defer compensation without current taxation as long as certain conditions are met.

If a plan is eligible under Section 457, amounts deferred will not be included in gross income until they are actually received or made available. Life insurance and annuities are authorized investments for these plans.

The annual amounts an employee may defer under a Section 457 plan are similar to those available for 401(k) plans. For the three years preceding retirement, the deferral limit in each year will be twice the applicable limit.

QUALIFIED PLANS FOR THE SMALL EMPLOYER

Before 1962, many small business owners found that their employees could participate in, and benefit from, a qualified retirement plan, but the owners themselves could not. Self-employed individuals were in the same predicament. The reason was that qualified plans had to benefit "employees." Because business owners were considered "employers," they were excluded from participating in a qualified plan.

The **Self-Employed Individuals Retirement Act**, signed into law in 1962, rectified this situation by treating small business owners and self-employed individuals as "employees," thus enabling them to participate in a qualified plan, if they chose to do so, just like their employees. The result was the Keogh or HR-10 retirement plan.

Keogh Plans (HR-10s)

A **Keogh plan** is a qualified retirement plan designed for unincorporated businesses that allows the business owner (or partner in a business) to participate as an employee. These plans may be set up as either defined contribution or defined benefit plans.

In the first years following enactment of the Keogh bill, there was a great deal of disparity between the rules for Keogh plans and those for corporate plans. However, various laws have eliminated most of the rules unique to

Keogh plans, thereby establishing parity between qualified corporate employer retirement plans and noncorporate plans. This change means that Keogh plans:

■ are subject to the same maximum contribution limits and benefit limits as qualified corporate plans;

■ must comply with the same participation and coverage requirements as qualified corporate plans; and

■ are subject to the same nondiscrimination rules as qualified corporate plans.

Simplified Employee Pensions (SEPs)

Another type of qualified plan suited for the small employer is the **simplified employee pension (SEP) plan**. Due to the many administrative burdens and the costs involved with establishing a qualified defined contribution or defined benefit plan as well as maintaining compliance with ERISA, many small businesses have been reluctant to set up retirement plans for their employees. SEPs were introduced in 1978 specifically for small businesses to overcome these cost, compliance, and administrative hurdles.

Basically, an SEP is an arrangement whereby an employee (including a self-employed individual) establishes and maintains an **individual retirement account (IRA)** to which the employer contributes. Employer contributions are not included in the employee's gross income. A primary difference between an SEP and an IRA is the much larger amount that can be contributed each year to an SEP. The maximum amount that can be contributed to an employee's SEP plan is 25% of the employee's annual compensation, subject to a dollar-limit set by tax law and indexed for inflation.

In accordance with the rules that govern other qualified plans, SEPs must not discriminate in favor of highly compensated employees with regard to contributions or participation.

Salary Reduction SEP Plans

A variation of the SEP plan is the **salary reduction SEP (SARSEP)**. SARSEPs incorporate a deferral/salary reduction approach in that the employee can elect to have employer contributions directed into the SEP or paid out as taxable cash compensation. The limit on the elective deferral to a SARSEP is the same as a 401(k).

SARSEPs are reserved for small employers—those with 25 or fewer employees—and had to be established before 1997. As a result of tax legislation, no new SARSEPs can be established; however, plans that were already in place at the end of 1996 may continue to operate and accept new employee participants.

SIMPLE Plans

The same legislation that did away with SARSEPs also created a new form of qualified employer retirement plan. Known as a **Savings Incentive**

Match Plan for Employees, or a **SIMPLE** plan, these arrangements allow eligible employers to set up tax favored retirement savings plans for their employees without having to address many of the usual (and burdensome) qualification requirements.

SIMPLE plans are available to small businesses (including tax exempt and government entities) that employ no more than 100 employees who received at least $5,000 in compensation from the employer during the previous year. In addition, to establish a SIMPLE plan, the employer must not have a qualified plan in place.

SIMPLE plans may be structured as an IRA or as a 401(k) cash or deferred arrangement. Under these plans, employees who elect to participate may defer up to a specified amount each year and the employer then makes a matching dollar-for-dollar contribution, up to an amount equal to 3% of the employee's annual compensation. All contributions to a SIMPLE IRA or SIMPLE 401(k) plan are nonforfeitable; the employee is immediately and fully vested. Taxation of contributions and their earnings is deferred until funds are withdrawn or distributed.

In place of dollar-for-dollar matching contributions, an employer can choose to make nonelective contributions of 2% of compensation on behalf of each eligible employee.

Catch-Up Contributions

Both SARSEP and SIMPLE plans allow participants who are at least 50 years old by the end of the plan year to make additional "catch-up" contributions.

INDIVIDUAL RETIREMENT PLANS

In much the same way that it encourages businesses to establish retirement plans for their employees, federal tax law provides incentives for *individuals* to save for their retirement by allowing certain kinds of plans to receive favorable tax treatment. Individual retirement accounts (IRAs) are the most notable of these plans. Available IRAs include the traditional tax-deductible IRA and the traditional non-tax-deductible IRA, as well as the Roth IRA (named after IRA advocate William Roth, Jr., Chairman of the Senate Finance Committee). The Roth IRA was created by the Taxpayer Relief Act of 1997. This IRA requires nondeductible contributions but offers tax-free earnings and withdrawals.

Traditional IRA

An **individual retirement account**, commonly called an IRA, is a means by which individuals can save money for retirement and receive a current tax break. Basically, the amount contributed to an IRA accumulates and grows tax deferred. IRA funds are not taxed until they are taken out at retirement. In addition, depending on the individual's earnings and whether or not the individual is covered by an employer-sponsored retirement plan, the amount the individual contributes to a traditional IRA may be fully or partially deducted from current income, resulting in lower current income taxes.

IRA Participation

Anyone under the age of 70½ who has earned income may open a traditional IRA and contribute up to the contribution limit or 100% of compensation each year, whichever is less. (The limit is $5,500 in 2013.) A non-wage-earning spouse may open an IRA and contribute up to the limit each year.

A Roth IRA has the same contribution limits as the traditional IRA, but no maximum age limit.

Since 2002, persons who are age 50 and older have been allowed to make "catch-up" contributions to their IRAs, above the scheduled annual limit, enabling them to save even more for retirement. These catch-up payments can be either deductible or made to a Roth IRA. The additional catch-up amount allowed in 2011 and after is $1,000.

Deduction of IRA Contributions

In many cases, the amount an individual contributes to a traditional IRA can be deducted from that individual's income in the year it is contributed. The ability of an IRA participant to take a deduction for her contribution rests on two factors:

- Whether or not the participant is covered by an employer-sponsored retirement plan

- The amount of income the participant makes

Individuals who are *not* covered by an employer-sponsored plan may contribute up to the annual limit to a traditional IRA and deduct from their current income the full amount of the contribution, no matter what their level of income is. Married couples who both work and have no employer-sponsored plan can each contribute and deduct up to the maximum each year.

Individuals who *are* covered by an employer-sponsored plan are subject to different rules regarding deductibility of traditional IRA contributions. For them, the amount of income they make is the determining factor: the more they make, the less IRA deduction they can take.

Do not confuse deductibility of contributions with the ability to make contributions. Anyone under age 70½ who has earned income (as well as a non-wage-earning spouse) can *contribute* to a traditional IRA. However, level of income and participation in an employer plan may affect the traditional IRA owner's ability to deduct the contributions.

Traditional IRA Withdrawals

Because the purpose of an IRA is to provide a way to accumulate retirement funds, there are a number of rules that discourage traditional IRA owners from withdrawing these funds prior to retirement. By the same token, traditional IRA owners are discouraged from perpetually sheltering their accounts from taxes by rules that mandate when the funds must be withdrawn.

- Traditional IRA owners must begin to receive payment from their accounts no later than April 1 following the year in which they reach age 70½. The law specifies a minimum amount that must be withdrawn every year. Failure to withdraw the minimum amount can result in a stiff penalty tax in the difference between the amount that should have been withdrawn and the amount that was actually withdrawn.

- With few exceptions, any distribution from a traditional IRA before age 59½ will have adverse tax consequences. In addition to income tax, the taxable amount of the withdrawal will be subject to a 10% penalty (similar to that imposed on early withdrawals from deferred annuities). Early distributions taken for any of the following reasons or circumstances will not be assessed the 10% penalty

  — if the owner dies or becomes disabled,

  — if the owner is faced with a certain amount of qualifying medical expenses,

  — to pay for higher education expenses,

  — to cover first-time home purchase expenses (up to $10,000),

  — to pay for health insurance premiums while unemployed,

  — if the distribution is taken in equal payments over the owner's lifetime, or

  — to correct or reduce an excess contribution.

- At retirement, or any time after age 59½, the IRA owner can elect to receive either a lump-sum payment or periodic installment payments from his or her fund. Traditional IRA distributions are taxed in much the same way as annuity benefit payments are taxed. That is, the portion of an IRA distribution that is attributed to nondeductible contributions is received tax free; the portion that is attributed to interest earnings or deductible contributions is taxed. The result is a tax-free return of the IRA owner's cost basis and a taxing of the balance.

- If an IRA owner dies before receiving full payment, the remaining funds in the deceased's IRA will be paid to the named beneficiary.

- If the IRA owner is a military reservist called to active duty (between September 11, 2001 and December 31, 2007) for more than 179 days or for an indefinite period, the 10-percent early-withdrawal penalty does not apply; however, regular income taxes will apply.

- If the IRA owner is a firefighter, a policeman or woman, or an emergency medical technician (EMT) with a pension or retirement plan who retires after age 50, he or she is also exempt from the penalty tax.

IRA Funding

An ideal funding vehicle for IRAs is a **flexible premium fixed deferred annuity**. Other acceptable IRA funding vehicles include bank time deposit open accounts, bank certificates of deposit, insured credit union accounts, mutual fund shares, face amount certificates, real estate investment trust units, and certain US gold and silver coins.

Roth IRA

The 1997 Taxpayer Relief Act introduced a new kind of IRA: the **Roth IRA**. Roth IRAs are unique in that they provide for back-end benefits. No deduction can be taken for contributions made to a Roth, but the earnings on those contributions are entirely tax free when they are withdrawn.

An amount up to the annual contribution limit can be contributed to a Roth IRA for any eligible individual. Active participant status is irrelevant; an individual can open and contribute to a Roth regardless of whether the individual is covered by an employer's plan or maintains and contributes to other IRA accounts. It should be noted, however, that the annual limit on contributions applies collectively to both traditional and Roth IRAs. No more than this amount can be contributed in any year for any account or combination of accounts.

Unlike traditional IRAs, which are limited to those under age 70½, Roth IRAs impose no age limits. At any age, an individual with earned income can establish a Roth IRA and make contributions. However, Roth IRAs subject participants to earnings limitations that traditional IRAs do not. High income earners may not be able to contribute to a Roth IRA since the maximum annual contribution that can be made begins to phase out for individuals whose modified adjusted gross incomes reach certain levels. Above these limits, no Roth contributions are allowed.

Qualified Roth Withdrawals

Withdrawals from Roth IRAs are either qualified or nonqualified. A qualified withdrawal is one that provides for the full-tax advantage that Roths offer—tax-free distribution of earnings. To be a qualified withdrawal, the following two requirements must be met:

- The funds must have been held in the account for a minimum of five years.

- The withdrawal must occur because

  — the owner has reached age 59½,

  — the owner dies,

  — the owner becomes disabled, or

  — the distribution is used to purchase a first home.

If these requirements are met, no portion of the withdrawal is subject to tax.

ILLUSTRATION 13.3

Tax Consequences of IRA Distributions

Reason for Distribution	Roth IRA Held Fewer Than 5 Years		Roth IRA Held 5 Years or More		Traditional IRA	
	Earnings Taxed	10% Penalty	Earnings Taxed	10% Penalty	Earnings Taxed	10% Penalty
Pre-59½	Yes	Yes	Yes	Yes	Yes	Yes
Death	Yes	No	No	No	Yes	No
Disability	Yes	No	No	No	Yes	No
First-time home purchase	Yes	No	No	No	Yes	No
Substantially equal payments	Yes	No	Yes	No	Yes	No
Medical payments	Yes	No	Yes	No	Yes	No
Health insurance while unemployed	Yes	No	Yes	No	Yes	No
Higher education expenses	Yes	No	Yes	No	Yes	No
Post 59½	Yes	No	No	No	Yes	No

Nonqualified Roth Withdrawal

A **nonqualified withdrawal** is one that does not meet the previously discussed criteria. The result is that distributed Roth **earnings** are subject to tax. This would occur when the withdrawal is taken without meeting the above requirements and the amount of the withdrawal exceeds the total amount that was contributed. Since Roth contributions are made with after-tax dollars, they are not subject to taxation again upon withdrawal. The only portion of a Roth withdrawal that is subject to taxation is earnings and only when those earnings are removed from the account without having met the above requirements. If the owner of the Roth IRA is younger than age 59½ when the withdrawal is taken, it will be considered premature and (if it does not qualify as an exception to the premature distribution rule) the earnings portion will also be assessed a 10% penalty.

No Required Distributions

Unlike traditional IRAs, Roth IRAs do not require mandatory distributions. There is no minimum distribution requirement for the account owner; the funds can remain in the account as long as the owner desires. In fact, the account can be left intact and passed on to heirs or beneficiaries.

Spousal IRA

Persons eligible to set up IRAs for themselves may create a separate spousal IRA for a nonworking spouse and contribute up to the annual maximum to the spousal account, even if the working spouse is in an employer-sponsored plan. However, there are a number of limitations. If the spousal account is a traditional IRA, the amount of the deduction that can be taken for contributions may be reduced or eliminated if the partner is an active participant and the couple's adjusted gross income exceeds certain amounts. If the spousal account is a Roth IRA, the maximum contribution may be reduced or eliminated if the couple's adjusted gross income exceeds certain thresholds. The spousal IRA contribution must be reported on the couple's joint tax return, as would the IRA contribution for the working spouse.

Rollover IRA

Normally, benefits withdrawn from any qualified retirement plan are taxable the year in which they are received. However, certain tax-free "rollover" provisions of the tax law provide some degree of portability when an individual wishes to transfer funds from one plan to another, specifically to a **rollover IRA**.

Essentially, rollover IRAs provide a way for individuals who have received a distribution from a qualified plan to reinvest the funds in a new tax-deferred account and continue to shelter those funds and their earnings from current taxes. Rollover IRAs are used by individuals who, for example, have left one employer for another and have received a complete distribution from their previous employer's plan or by those who had invested funds in an individual IRA of one kind and want to roll over to another IRA for a higher rate of return.

A distribution received from an employer-sponsored retirement plan or from an IRA is eligible for a tax-free rollover if it is reinvested in an IRA within 60 days following receipt of the distribution and if the plan participant does not actually take physical receipt of the distribution. The entire amount need not be rolled over; a partial distribution may be rolled over from one IRA or eligible plan to another IRA. However, if a partial rollover is executed, the part retained will be taxed as ordinary income and subject to a 10% early distribution penalty.

Only the person who established an IRA is eligible to benefit from the rollover treatment—with one exception. A surviving spouse who inherits IRA benefits or benefits from the deceased spouse's qualified plan is eligible to establish a rollover IRA in the surviving spouse's own name. Note that tax law now allows non-spousal beneficiaries to take IRA proceeds over their lifetimes, plus the lifetimes of their oldest named beneficiary.

Pension Protection Act of 2006

The Pension Protection Act of 2006 embodied the most sweeping reform of America's pension laws in over 30 years. It improves the pension system and increases opportunities to fund retirement plans.

The act encourages workers to increase their contributions to employer-sponsored retirement plans and helps them manage their investments. For example, automatic enrollment is a means of increasing participation in 401(k) plans, especially among young workers entering the workforce. The act also provides for automatic deferrals into investment funds and automatic annual increases in employees' salary deferral rates beginning in 2008. Since 2007, plan sponsors can offer fund-specific investment advice to participants through their retirement plan providers or other fiduciary advisers. Counseling in person is also allowed under strict guidelines.

Significant changes in the rules for funding defined benefit plans took effect in 2008. Sponsors of plans that are *at risk* (meaning less than 80% funded) are subject to special requirements that include additional funding obligations and prohibitions on lump-sum distributions.

The provisions of the act carry out its intent on two fronts, addressing employers' pension funds and assisting employees who are saving for retirement.

It addresses employers' responsibilities to their plans by:

- requiring additional contributions from employers with underfunded pension plans;

- continuing a requirement that employers that terminate their pensions pay more into the pension insurance system;

- requiring that employers obtain more accurate assessments of their pension plans' financial obligations;

- closing loopholes by which underfunded plans have skipped pension payments;

- raising limits on the amount that employers can pay into their pension plans, thereby allowing them to increase funding during economic growth to build a cushion for solvency during lean economic times; and

- preventing employers with underfunded plans from promising extra benefits to employees without first funding those benefits.

It helps employees who save for their retirement through defined contribution plans like IRAs and 401(k) plans by:

- allowing employers to automatically enroll employees in defined contribution plans so that employees must affirmatively opt out to not participate;

- ensuring that employees have more information about account performance;

- increasing employees' access to personalized, professional advice about investing for retirement;

- giving employees more control over the investment of their accounts;

- allowing for direct deposit of income tax refunds from the IRS into an IRA;

■ allowing individuals entering active military duty to make early withdrawals from their IRAs, 401(k) plans, and other similar plans without incurring a penalty;

■ waiving the 10% penalty on early distributions from a governmental plan for some public safety employees;

■ allowing 401(k) plan withdrawals for hardships and financial emergencies for anyone who is a beneficiary of the 401(k) plan; and

■ allowing a rollover of a deceased person's interest in a qualified retirement plan, government plan, or tax-sheltered annuity into an IRA without taxation for the benefit of a person who is not the deceased's spouse.

For distributions after December 31, 2007, the law permits direct rollovers from qualified retirement plans, tax-sheltered annuities, or governmental plans directly to a Roth IRA. These rollovers will be treated as a Roth conversion if they would otherwise qualify as such. Note that the Pension Protection Act also eliminates the Roth IRA income limits for rollovers starting in 2010. The rollover income limits prevented a person earning over $100,000 in modified adjusted gross income from converting to a Roth IRA. Starting in 2010, anyone, regardless of income, can convert funds from a 401(k) plan to a traditional or Roth IRA.

The act makes permanent increased limits on tax-qualified retirement plans that were created by the Economic Growth and Tax Relief Reconciliation Act of 2001 (EGTRRA) but due to expire in 2010. These include:

■ increased limits on contributions to Roth 401(k) and 401(k) plans of $5,000 in 2010;

■ increased catch-up contribution limits for employees age 50 and over, at $1,000 for IRAs, $2,500 for SIMPLE plans, and $5,500 for 401(k) plans;

■ permanent higher limits on defined contribution plans;

■ full vesting in employer-matching contributions under three- or six-year vesting schedules;

■ permanent better portability for 403(b) and 457 plans; and

■ permanent higher deductible amounts for employer contributions to employee retirement plans.

The act also continues the Saver's Credit, which was scheduled to end at the end of 2006. This credit allows eligible persons to contribute to a 401(k) plan, qualified pension plan, or IRA and receive a federal matching contribution in the form of an income tax credit for the first $2,000 of their annual contributions.

SUMMARY

Individuals prepare for the financial challenges of retirement in a variety of ways. They may be covered under any one (or more) of a variety of employer-sponsored qualified retirement plans, including defined benefit and defined contribution pension plans, 403(b) plans, 457 deferred compensation plans, simplified employee pension (SEP) plans, SIMPLE plans, Keogh plans, and 401(k) plans. Even if they are not covered under an employer-sponsored plan, individuals can save for retirement with a traditional or Roth individual retirement account or annuity (IRA).

KEY CONCEPTS

Students should be familiar with the following concepts:

qualified versus nonqualified retirement plans	Coverdell education savings accounts
defined benefit plans	tax-sheltered annuity plans—403(b) plans
minimum participation standards	defined contribution plans
457 plans	401(k) plans
SEP plans	Keogh plans
traditional IRAs	vesting
Roth IRAs	spousal IRAs
rollover IRAs	SIMPLE plans

UNIT TEST

1. All of the following employed persons who have no employer-sponsored retirement plan would be eligible to set up and contribute to a traditional IRA EXCEPT

A. Miriam, age 26, secretary
B. Brent, age 40, medical technician
C. Edna, age 72, nurse
D. Jack, age 60, plumber

2. If David sets up a traditional IRA, what is the maximum contribution he can make and deduct from adjusted gross income for 2013?

A. $1,000
B. $3,000
C. $4,000
D. $5,500

3. Herbert and Olga, both age 48, have been married for 10 years. They have no children, and each has a well-paying job. However, neither is covered by an employer retirement plan. What is the maximum amount they may set aside together in tax-deductible, traditional IRA funds in 2013?

A. $4,000
B. $5,000
C. $8,000
D. $11,000

4. Which of the following scenarios pertaining to IRAs is NOT correct?

A. June has accumulated $30,000 in her IRA. At age 53 she withdraws $2,500 to take a vacation. She will have to include the $2,500 in her taxable income for the year and pay a $250 penalty.
B. Bradley, age 72, is covered by an employer-sponsored retirement plan. He cannot establish a traditional IRA.
C. Peter inherits $15,000 in IRA benefits from his father, who died in 2008. Peter can set up a tax-favored rollover IRA with the money and defer current income tax on the benefits received.
D. Walter is age 60. He may take a distribution from his IRA without having to worry about an early withdrawal penalty.

5. All of the following statements regarding Roth IRAs are true EXCEPT

A. they provide for tax-free accumulation of funds
B. they limit contributions each year
C. they mandate distributions no later than age 70½
D. they are not available to those in the upper-income tax brackets

6. Which of the following statements correctly describes the tax advantage of a qualified retirement plan?

A. Employer contributions are not taxed when they are paid out to the employee.
B. Earnings of the plan are taxable to the employee only when the employee receives benefits.
C. Earnings of the plan are only taxable if the employee voluntarily terminates participation in the plan.
D. Employer contributions are deductible business expenses when the employee receives benefits.

7. Which of the following phrases best describes vesting?

A. The time at which a worker meets the eligibility requirements for plan participation
B. The age at which an employee must begin to make withdrawals from retirement plans
C. The right of a worker's spouse to be considered in retirement income needs
D. The employee's right to funds or benefits, contributed by the employer, should the employee leave that employer

8. All of the following should be eligible to establish a Keogh retirement plan EXCEPT

A. a dentist in private practice
B. partners in a furniture store
C. a sole proprietor of a jewelry store
D. a major stockholder-employee in a family corporation

9. All of the following types of plans are reserved for small employers EXCEPT

   A. 401(k)s
   B. SARSEPs
   C. SIMPLE IRAs
   D. SIMPLE 401(k)s

10. A distribution received from an employer-sponsored retirement plan or from an IRA is eligible for a tax-free rollover if it is reinvested in an IRA within how many days after the distribution?

    A. 20
    B. 30
    C. 45
    D. 60

11. All of the following statements about SIMPLE plans are correct EXCEPT

    A. an employer may establish a SIMPLE plan if another qualified plan is not already in place
    B. they can be structured as an IRA or as a 401(k) cash or deferred arrangement
    C. an employer must make a nonelective contribution of 2% of compensation on behalf of each eligible employee
    D. only employers with no more than 100 employees can establish SIMPLE plans

12. Which of the following statements about 401(k) plans is CORRECT?

    A. All of a company's employees must participate in the plan.
    B. An employee's deferred contributions become nonforfeitable according to the plan's vesting schedule.
    C. Employer contributions are included in the employee's income for the year.
    D. There is a limit on employee deferrals.

13. Bob, age 43, owns a traditional IRA and a Roth IRA. What is the maximum amount that he can contribute to both accounts in 2013 without being penalized?

    A. $2,000
    B. $4,000
    C. $5,500
    D. $6,000

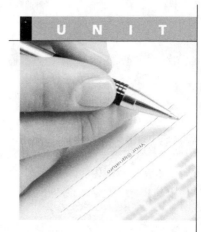
14

Uses of Life Insurance

- Determining Proper Insurance Amounts
- Individual Uses for Life Insurance
- Business Uses for Life Insurance

The valuable role life insurance plays in providing a death benefit is easily recognized. What is often overlooked or not understood are the many "living benefits" of life insurance—especially whole life insurance. The cash value feature of permanent insurance and the owner's right to borrow from the cash value make these policies an important source of funds to meet living needs. This unit reviews the more common uses of life insurance in meeting individual needs as well as business needs, not only at the death of the policyowner but during the owner's life, too. ■

DETERMINING PROPER INSURANCE AMOUNTS

There are many uses for life insurance, some of which are easily recognized, others of which aren't so apparent. A family's desire to provide protection against the loss of its breadwinner (or breadwinners) is certainly understood to involve life insurance. A small business's need to protect itself against the death of a key employee is also easily solved with life insurance. But how many people recognize whole life insurance as a means of saving for retirement or a child's education? The uses of life insurance extend far beyond the realm of "death benefits."

How much life insurance is enough? Professional insurance producers know that the answer is not, "How much can the owner afford?" Determining the proper amount of life insurance depends on a number of factors. The ability of the policyowner to comfortably afford the premium payments is, of course, an important consideration. Other questions must be asked, though. What are the planned uses for the insurance? What are the owner's long-range goals and can life insurance help meet those goals? These are just a few of the questions that the insurance producer should ask before recommending the purchase of a policy.

There are two basic approaches used today to help insurance buyers and producers determine the proper amount of life insurance. The older method, known as the **human life value approach**, has since been largely replaced by the more practical **needs approach**, but both methods can be effective in answering the primary question, "How much life insurance is needed?"

Human Life Value Approach

The concept of **human life value** was first mentioned in Unit 1, where we discussed the purpose and function of insurance. This concept was formulated by the late Dr. Solomon S. Heubner in 1924 as a philosophical framework for understanding the services that can be performed by life and health insurance, for people both in and out of the insurance business. The result of Dr. Heubner's work is that everyone can have a better idea of how an insurance plan can be tailor-made to meet specific objectives.

Dr. Heubner pointed out that the value of a human life can and should be expressed as a **dollar valuation**; that is, determining the economic value of a person by **discounting estimated future net earnings** used for family purposes at a reasonable rate of interest.

A relatively simple method of accomplishing this is to:

- estimate an individual's average annual future earnings after deducting taxes and personal living costs;

- estimate the number of years the individual expects to work until retirement;

- select a reasonable interest rate (comparable to current rates paid on insurance proceeds held by insurers) at which future earnings should be discounted; and

- multiply the present value of one dollar payable annually for the number of years until expected retirement, using the selected interest rate, by the estimated average future annual earnings. The result is a reasonably accurate estimate of the individual's economic value to his or her family. (Tables are available that show the present value of one dollar at various interest rates.)

Example of the Human Life Value Approach

As a simple example of the human value approach, take 35-year-old George who estimates that he will earn an average of $40,000 a year until retirement at age 65. Of that $40,000, $25,000 is devoted to the care and maintenance of his family; the remaining $15,000 goes for taxes and his personal living costs.

Based on these assumptions, we can see that George's family will need and use $750,000 over George's working lifetime ($25,000 per year × 30 years). Essentially, this is George's economic value to his family over the next 30 years. However, what if today George were to die or become so severely disabled that he could not work? What source could his family rely on to continue to provide them with $25,000 a year for the next 30 years? What George needs today is a fund that, when compounded at a certain rate of interest, will produce a constant $25,000 a year for the next 30 years.

Illustration 14.1 shows the amount of money that must be on hand today to produce annual incomes of $10,000, $15,000, $20,000, and $25,000 for various terms, assuming a 4% interest factor. For George, who needs a fund that will generate $25,000 a year for 30 years, the amount needed today is $432,300. Thus, George's human life value to his family is $432,300—the amount required today that, at 4% interest, would produce the same annual income his family consumes over the same length of time that George plans to work. This $432,300 is a measurement of how much financial protection—insurance—George's family needs to replace the income that will be lost if he dies or becomes disabled.

ILLUSTRATION 14.1

Amount Necessary to Produce Future Income Streams

This table illustrates the amounts of capital that must be on hand today to produce various annual incomes for specified time periods. The assumed interest rate is 4%.

Number of Years of Income	Annual Income Streams (4% Interest)			
	$10,000	**$15,000**	**$20,000**	**$25,000**
20	$135,903	$203,855	$271,306	$339,758
25	$156,221	$234,332	$312,442	$390,553
30	$172,920	$259,380	$345,840	$432,300
35	$186,646	$279,969	$373,292	$466,615
40	$197,928	$296,892	$395,856	$494,820

For example, to generate $25,000 a year for 30 years, one needs $432,300 on hand today, earning 4% interest.

Calculating human life value is one method of determining the amount of life insurance an individual should have. The modern approach now takes into account inflation or the likelihood of increases in wages or standards of living. However, some industry experts point out that it may overstate the amount of insurance needed if it does not take into consideration other sources of income or family situations changing. Consequently, the method most typically used today is the *needs approach*.

Needs Approach

Fundamentally, the **needs approach** for determining how much insurance protection a person should have requires first analyzing the family's (or business's) financial needs and objectives should the breadwinner (or businessperson) die or become disabled. Then, those needs are weighed against the ability of the family (or business) to meet them out of current or anticipated assets. For example, the death of a family's breadwinner will necessitate a new source of funds to replace the earnings that are now lost. The obvious answer is life insurance. However, the amount of life insurance required must take into account the amount of monthly benefits the family will be receiving from Social Security, from the deceased's pension plan, from personal savings, and any other source. The difference between what is now owned (or will ultimately be available) and what is needed in terms of funds is then used to help the insurance producer recommend an insurance program that may involve the use of term insurance, permanent insurance, annuities, or a combination of all three.

The needs approach is not limited to fulfilling objectives in the event of death only. It also considers a family's (or business's) living needs, such as providing for a child's education and planning for retirement. Again, the amount of life insurance required to meet these needs is coordinated with other assets that may be available.

In the remainder of this unit, we will look at the many uses for life insurance. Insurance producers should consider all these concerns when helping a person or a business determine the proper insurance program to meet anticipated needs. In some cases, such as planning for education or retirement, the producer must consider the need for funds not only if the insured dies, but lives, as well. A whole life policy, in this example, can provide funds either in the form of a death benefit or cash value when those funds are needed. If the insured should die prematurely, the beneficiary can take comfort in knowing that funds will be available to meet the planned objectives. If the insured lives, the policy's cash value can be used to meet the same objectives.

A family's or business's ability to pay for the insurance deemed necessary to meet its objectives is, of course, an important consideration. It may be decided that only part of the insurance plan can be purchased immediately and the rest will be put into effect at a later date. For this reason, and because a family's or business's needs change over time, a needs approach insurance program usually includes plans for periodic reviews (usually annually) to update the program as needed.

INDIVIDUAL USES FOR LIFE INSURANCE

The number of uses for life insurance in meeting personal and family financial needs is really quite impressive. The following list of common uses can be met with *term insurance* if the need is temporary (such as providing an additional protection fund while the children are growing up and living at home), with *whole life insurance* if the need is permanent (such as meeting estate planning objectives and for any "living" financial need), or with *annuities* if the need is for future income (such as retirement income).

In some cases, different products can be mixed to strengthen the protection. For example, a person may use a deferred annuity to plan for retirement but also use a whole life policy to provide protection before retirement and additional retirement funds, through the policy's cash value, at retirement. Health insurance, covered later in this text, also plays an important role in a balanced insurance program.

When working with a client, the insurance producer should consider the following individual needs.

Final Expense Fund

A **final expense fund** is the amount of cash that is required (and should be on hand) at death to pay for a deceased breadwinner's last illness and funeral costs, outstanding debts, federal and state death taxes, and any other unpaid taxes, legal fees, court costs, executor's fees, and so on. These last expenses usually will total at least several thousand dollars. Social Security provides only a very small amount—a maximum lump sum of $255—and only to an eligible surviving spouse or child.

Housing Fund

In the case of a breadwinner's death, there may be the need for a **home mortgage** or **rental allowance fund**. With this cash fund, a surviving family can, for example, pay off the mortgage or continue mortgage payments. If the family rents its home, the need may be for a monthly amount that will continue rental payments for a certain number of years.

Education Fund

How much, where, and how expensive a child's *education* will be—together with how it is to be paid for—are goals that vary widely from family to family. However, most people want their children to obtain a good education, and studies prove that a college education is vitally important for today's young people.

The cost of college educations have continued to increase in recent years, currently ranging from about $105,000 or more for four years in state universities to approximately $150,000 or more in private institutions. An adequate education fund is a typical family need.

Monthly Income

The income a breadwinner provides for a family will obviously cease upon the breadwinner's death. However, the income needs of the surviving family continue. Monthly income will be needed during the years that the children are growing and living at home and then for the surviving spouse after the children are self-supporting. Thus, there are two distinct income needs periods: the **dependency period** and the **blackout period**. Ensuring a source of monthly income during these two critical periods is another use for life insurance.

Dependency Period

The **dependency period** refers to that period following the death of a breadwinner during which the children are living at home. The need for family income is greatest while the children are growing up. When a breadwinner dies, a surviving spouse with small children usually will be eligible for Social Security benefits. However, as we have seen, Social Security benefits, while helpful, generally will not meet the total family need.

Moreover, an eligible spouse with an eligible child receives Social Security income only while the child is under age 16 (or disabled). Once the child turns 16, the child's Social Security benefits will continue another two years, but income to the spouse ceases and will not resume until, at the earliest, the spouse reaches age 60.

Blackout Period

The period in which there are no Social Security benefits for the surviving spouse is known as the **blackout period**. Again, the blackout period begins when the youngest child turns 16. If there are no eligible children with the surviving spouse when the breadwinner dies, the blackout period starts immediately and continues until, at the earliest, the spouse reaches age 60.

Emergency Fund

Every family faces emergencies from time to time, so a fund is needed to provide money for various miscellaneous costs and expenses that may arise, but cannot be foreseen.

Coverdell Education Savings Accounts

Coverdell Education Savings Accounts are special investment accounts that allow individuals and families to fund formal education expenses on a tax-favored basis.

Education savings accounts are designed to fund education expenses of a designated beneficiary by allowing after-tax (nondeductible) contributions to accumulate on a tax-deferred basis. When distributions are taken from an education savings account, the earnings portion of the distribution is excluded from income to the extent it is used to pay qualified education expenses. Earnings are taxed when they are not used to pay qualified education expenses, and then they are also subject to a 10% penalty.

Contributions to education savings accounts are not deductible, are limited to $2,000 each year per child, and must be made before the beneficiary turns 18 years of age. Single taxpayers whose adjusted gross incomes are $95,000 or less and joint filers with adjusted gross incomes of $190,000 or less can take full advantage of the maximum contribution. As income exceeds these levels, the amount of allowable education savings account contribution is phased down until it is eliminated at $110,000 for single taxpayers and $220,000 for joint filers.

If the child for whom an account has been established does not use the funds for education, or if there are any amounts remaining in an account when the beneficiary reaches age 30, remaining funds can be rolled over to another education savings account benefiting another family member with no penalty. Any account distributions that are not used to pay for a beneficiary's education expenses will be included in the recipient's income and will be subject to a 10% penalty.

Nothing prevents more than one individual from contributing to an education savings account. The annual limit applies to each beneficiary only. Consequently, parents and grandparents can contribute to a single account, so long as the annual limit is not exceeded in any year. Excess contributions will still be subject to a 6% excise penalty.

Income Needs if Disabled or Ill

Basically, the same cash (except a final expense fund) and monthly income needs that arise at the death of a breadwinner exist when disability strikes a breadwinner. In both cases, the family loses the breadwinner's earnings. However, the need for income is often greater with disability because most of the disabled person's expenses continue and the family is generally faced with additional medical expenses. Medical expense insurance and disability income insurance (discussed in Units 17 and 18) should also be considered in a personal insurance program.

Life-threatening or severe chronic diseases, such as Alzheimer's disease, cancer, heart disease, and AIDS, can wipe out a person's life savings in a short time and have other devastating effects on a person's life. People suffering such illnesses often face the loss of their job and their home as well as their independence and dignity. Funds from a life insurance policy under an accelerated death benefits provision can relieve the immediate financial hardships and help people preserve their possessions and lifestyle. Care must be taken, however, to ensure that the financial well-being of dependents is not compromised.

Retirement Income

The happy eventuality is that both spouses will live to a ripe old age. If so, they also will need income to supplement their Social Security or other retirement benefits. The same holds true for single individuals as well.

Universal life, variable life, and adjustable life are permanent forms of contracts, and therefore could be used as a basis for retirement. Term life should not be used as a basis for retirement.

BUSINESS USES FOR LIFE INSURANCE

Continued financial well-being for families depends not only upon income from breadwinners, but also upon the continued good health of the businesses in which they are engaged. So life insurance also plays an important role in the business world. The reasons for buying life insurance for business uses are the same as those for buying personal insurance: in one word, protection. Businessowners wish to protect the condition of their businesses in order to provide security for their families. When people buy insurance for personal reasons, their families are concerned; when they buy it for business reasons, their employees, their associates, and their families are involved.

Life insurance is used in businesses in a variety of ways.

■ **As a funding medium.** For example, life insurance can be used to fund a business continuation (buy-sell) agreement to transfer ownership between partners or stockholders or to fund a deferred compensation plan.

■ **As a form of business interruption insurance.** Life insurance cannot prevent the interruption of business activity caused by death or disability; however, it can indemnify the business for losses created by these interruptions.

■ **As an employee benefit.** Life insurance can protect employees and their families from the financial problems of death, disability, illness, and retirement.

Health insurance also plays a vital role in the business arena, primarily as an employee benefit. In this unit, we will focus on business uses of life insurance; Unit 25 covers business (and personal) uses of health insurance.

A Funding Medium

When a businessowner dies, the business itself may terminate, or at least its ownership and management personnel will change. The death of a businessowner often creates havoc—not only with the business, but also with the deceased owner's estate.

Insured buy-sell agreements can ensure the orderly continuation of a business, while family survivors receive a fair cash settlement for a deceased owner's interest in the business. Such an agreement guarantees that cash will be available at the owner's death to purchase the deceased owner's interest, so the business can continue without financial disruption. Buy-sell plans may be used in any form of business—sole proprietorship, partnership, or close corporation—so long as there are potential buyers.

Sole Proprietor Buy-Sell Plans

When a sole proprietor dies, the proprietor's business generally comes to a sudden halt unless some arrangement has been made beforehand to continue the business. There are three alternatives. First, a member of the proprietor's family may be willing and able to pick up the reins and operate the business at the proprietor's death. If so, the proprietor may wish to leave the business to one or more family survivors as a gift. Second, there may be no interested taker, so the only thing to do is close down the business at the proprietor's death. The third, and often most desirable alternative, is for the business to be sold to a competent and faithful employee.

Employees who have been active in the operation or the management of the business are the most likely buyers. Many times, the employee's talent is recognized by customers, creditors, and suppliers, and it is obvious that the employee has helped build the good reputation enjoyed by the business. As a result, there is every indication that the business can continue successfully under the employee's direction.

A **two-step buy-sell plan** then can be arranged to sell the business to the employee at the proprietor's death:

1. A **buy-sell agreement** is drafted by an attorney, setting forth the employee's obligation to buy and the responsibility of the proprietor's estate to sell the business interest at an agreed-upon price.

2. An **insurance policy** is purchased by the employee on the life of the proprietor. The employee is the owner, premium-payor, and beneficiary of the policy, the proceeds from which will be used to buy the business at the proprietor's death.

In addition, when cash value life insurance is used to fund the agreement, the plan may call for a transfer of ownership should the proprietor prefer to retire at some future time. The employee then could use the policy's cash value to make a substantial down payment toward the purchase of the business. The balance of the purchase price might be paid in installments over a period of years.

Partnership Buy-Sell Plans

By law, *partnerships* are dissolved automatically upon the death of a partner. Thus, it is vital that a binding buy-sell agreement be established by the partners while they are living. Under such an agreement, the interest of any partner who dies will be sold to and purchased by the surviving partners. The price (or a formula to determine one) is agreed upon in advance and stipulated in the buy-sell plan.

When properly executed—and funded with life insurance—a partnership buy-sell plan benefits all parties involved and there is no uncertainty as to the outcome. The deceased has agreed beforehand to the sale of his interest. The surviving partners know they will have a legal right to buy, and the deceased's family and heirs are certain that the partnership interest will be disposed of at a fair price. Furthermore, with life insurance as the funding vehicle, the money needed to purchase the deceased partner's interest will be available at precisely the moment it is needed. So, at the death of any partner, the surviving partners are able to maintain the business while the deceased partner's estate receives full value for the deceased's interest.

ILLUSTRATION 14.2

Partnership Cross-Purchase Buy-Sell Plan

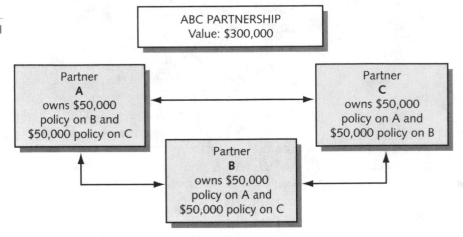

There are two kinds of partnership insured buy-sell agreements: the **cross-purchase plan** and the **entity plan**.

Partnership Cross-Purchase Plan

Under the **cross-purchase buy-sell plan**, which is the more common approach to a buyout, the partners individually agree to purchase the interest of a deceased partner, and the executor of the deceased partner's estate is directed to sell the interest to the surviving partners. The partnership itself is not a party to the agreement.

With these plans, each partner owns, is the beneficiary of and pays the premiums for life insurance on the other partner or partners in an amount equal to his or her share of the purchase price. For example, assume that a partnership worth $300,000 is owned equally by Partners A, B, and C. Under an insured cross-purchase plan, each partner insures the life of each of the other partners for $50,000. As a result, the total insurance on each partner's life equals each partner's share—$100,000—which would approximate the total purchase price the surviving partners would pay to the deceased's estate. (See Illustration 14.2.)

Partnership Entity Plan

Under the **entity buy-sell plan**, the business itself—the partnership—owns, pays for and is the beneficiary of the policies that insure the lives of the individual partners. The partnership is a party to the buy-sell agreement.

With an entity plan, when a partner dies, that partner's interest is purchased from her estate by the partnership. This interest is then divided among the surviving partners in proportion to their own interest. For example, assume the XYZ Partnership is worth $600,000 and each partner has an equal interest. The partnership purchases a $200,000 insurance policy on the life of each partner. If Partner X dies first, the partnership buys X's interest from his estate with the $200,000 insurance proceeds and divides this interest equally between Partners Y and Z. The proportionate share of Y and Z would then be increased from 33 1/3% to 50%. (See Illustration 14.3.)

ILLUSTRATION 14.3

Partnership Entity Buy-Sell Plan

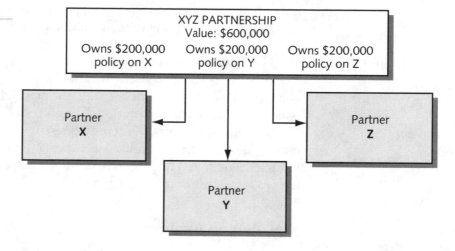

Close Corporation Buy-Sell Plans

In a **close corporation** (generally an incorporated family business), an insured buy-sell agreement can provide multiple advantages for all concerned. Unlike a partnership, a corporation does not cease to exist after the death of one of its owners. It is, by law, a separate entity apart from its owners, the stockholders. Nevertheless, problems are certain to develop if an agreement is not made in advance as to the disposition of a deceased stockholder's interest.

So buy-sell agreements are every bit as important to a close corporation as to a partnership. Just as in partnerships, the corporate insured buy-sell plan can take one of two forms: **cross-purchase** or **entity.** In a corporate plan, however, the entity type of agreement is known as a **stock redemption plan**. It does not matter which plan—cross-purchase or stock redemption—is used, although a close corporation with a relatively large number of stockholders usually will find the stock redemption plan more suitable. The decision about the type of plan should be left to the stockholders themselves, their attorney and their accountant.

Close Corporation Cross-Purchase Plan

The **close corporation cross-purchase agreement** is similar to that used in a partnership. The agreement calls for the surviving stockholders, as individuals, to purchase the interest of the deceased stockholder and for the estate of the deceased stockholder to sell the interest directly to the surviving stockholders. The corporation itself is not a party to the agreement. To fund a cross-purchase plan, each stockholder owns, pays for, and is the beneficiary of insurance on the life of each of the other stockholders in amounts equivalent to his or her share of the purchase price.

Close Corporation Stock Redemption Plan

The **close corporation stock redemption plan** operates in much the same manner as an entity plan in a partnership. The corporation, rather than the individual stockholders, is owner, premium-payor, and beneficiary of policies on the lives of the stockholders. The corporation is a party to the agreement.

The amount of insurance carried by the corporation on the lives of the stockholders is equal to each stockholder's proportionate share of the purchase price. When a stockholder dies, the proceeds of the policy insuring that person are paid to the corporation. The corporation then uses the proceeds to buy the deceased's business interest represented by the stock in the deceased's estate. As with other life insurance, the premiums paid by the corporation are not tax deductible. The proceeds, however, are generally received income tax free, as is the case in a partnership plan.

Key-Person Insurance

Another important use of life insurance is to protect a business against interruptions caused by the loss of one of its valuable assets: a **key employee** or **key executive**.

When an individual dies, the primary function of life insurance is to offset the economic loss. We have noted how important life insurance is to the family. Key-employee or key-executive life insurance provides similar benefits—not to the family, but to the business. For example, when an insured key person dies, the insurance beneficiary is the business itself.

A key person is any person in an organization whose contribution to the operation and success of the business is essential. Therefore, an owner-executive or highly skilled employee generally may be considered a key person.

With key-person insurance, the owner, premium-payor, and beneficiary of the policy is the business organization. Complete control of the policy rests with the business, which means key-person insurance can be considered a company-owned asset not earmarked for any specific purpose. The death proceeds, or even the policy's cash value, may be used for a variety of business purposes. In fact, flexibility is one of the outstanding features of this type of insurance. However, it usually is employed for some major purposes that, rather than being distinct from one another, actually work together to make the life insurance a practical company investment.

Generally speaking, the following are the primary purposes that key-person insurance serves:

- **Business indemnification.** Key-person insurance indemnifies a business; that is, it compensates a business for any financial loss caused by the death of a valuable key person. For example, the death of a key person—whether an owner or employee—may result in less liberal credit terms from suppliers; banks may be less willing to lend the business money; valuable accounts once served by the key person may be lost. The proceeds from a key-person policy can be utilized to avoid some or all of these problems before they occur or to ease the financial burden they bring about.

- **A reserve fund.** Key-person life insurance also provides a business with a "living benefit." When a business purchases key-person insurance, it automatically acquires an asset that can perform valuable services for the business while the key person is still alive. For example, when whole life insurance is purchased, the cash values increase steadily to provide a cash reserve fund for the business, which appears each year as an asset on the company's balance sheet.

- **Business credit.** Disruption of a business by the death of a key person can seriously affect a business's credit. Key-person life insurance, however, can offset this danger in two ways: as tangible evidence of business character and as a guarantee of loan repayment at the death of the key person.

- **Favorable tax treatment.** Finally, key-person life insurance receives favorable tax treatment. The death proceeds received by the business are not taxable. Premiums, of course, are not deductible for income purposes.

Employee Benefit Plans

Life insurance also serves an important role in the area of **employee benefits**. Basically, employee benefits are plans established by employers who pay all or a portion of the cost of the plans to benefit their employees and, in some cases, to obtain favorable tax treatment. Let's review a few of these plans.

Split-Dollar Plans

Many business organizations have found **split-dollar life insurance plans** to be an effective and economical way to encourage young employees to join the organization and to discourage the established executive from taking his talents and knowledge elsewhere.

Split-dollar insurance plans enable an employer and any employee of the employer's choosing to share premium payments toward the purchase of insurance on the employee's life. Therefore, the split-dollar policy is a method of buying life insurance rather than a reason for buying it. The employee already has determined the need for the insurance, but cannot afford the entire premium. The employer has the funds to help finance the purchase of the insurance and has a specific reason for doing so—the desire to attract and hold key employees.

The split-dollar plan is informal in nature; it requires no qualification or approval by the Internal Revenue Service. A split-dollar plan has a low premium outlay. It is a single contract that uses cash value whole life and term insurance protection (generally dividends are used to purchase one-year term; any dividend excess is applied to the year's premium) to guarantee the return of the premium money to one party while ensuring a death benefit to the policy beneficiary.

In a typical split-dollar plan, the employer and the employee share the premium cost. Though there are variations, generally the employer contributes to the premium each year the amount equal to the increase in the policy's cash value. The employee pays only the balance of the premium. Upon the insured employee's death, the amount of death proceeds equal to the cash value generally goes to the employer, and the balance of the proceeds goes to the insured's beneficiary. However, if the plan is terminated while the insured is living, the cash value generally goes to the employer to compensate for the portion of premiums paid.

This method permits a financially able person or entity to help another person buy insurance, generally in the favorable interest of both parties. For example, split-dollar may be used as an incentive plan by an employer for an employee, by an employer for a stockholder/employee, for business partners, for business co-owners, or by a parent for a child or child-in-law.

Deferred Compensation Plans

Deferred compensation plans are a popular way for businesses to provide an important benefit for their owners or for select employees. Basically speaking, a deferred compensation plan is an arrangement whereby an employee (or owner) agrees to forgo some portion of her current income (such as annual raises or bonuses) until a specified future date, typically retirement. Life insurance is a popular funding vehicle for deferred compensation plans, in that the amounts deferred are used to pay premiums on cash value life insurance. At retirement, the cash values are available to the employee to supplement income. If the employee dies prior to retirement, the employee's beneficiary will receive the policy's proceeds. Deferred compensation plans can be employer-motivated or established at the employee's request.

A deferred compensation plan is an example of a *nonqualified plan*. Recall that a nonqualified plan does not receive favorable tax treatment by the IRS. Because it is nonqualified, a company can pick and choose who among its employees and owners may participate in the plan, without regard to years of service, salary levels, or any other criteria. A nonqualified plan allows a business to provide proportionate benefits for officers, executives, and other highly paid employees; a qualified plan is not nearly as flexible.

Salary Continuation Plans

Deferred compensation and **salary continuation plans** appear similar in nature but, in fact, are quite different. Deferred compensation gives employees deferred benefits in lieu of a current raise or bonus. Salary continuation, however, is an additional fringe benefit, rather than a "salary reduction" type plan. In simple terms, the *employee* funds the deferred compensation plan; the *employer* funds the salary continuation plan.

A salary continuation plan may be set up between an employer and its employees or between a business and an independent contractor. Typically, the employer agrees to pay the employee (or the employee's assignee) continuing payments at retirement, death, or disability. This is subject to the condition that the employee continues employment with the employer. Or the plan may require that the employee provide continuing consulting-type services after retirement. The plan is informally funded through life insurance.

Other Employee Benefit Plans

There are many other types of employee benefit plans and programs. These programs include **retirement plans** (pensions, profit-sharing plans, employer-sponsored IRAs, 401(k) and 403(b) plans), **group life and health plans, child care plans, educational assistance programs, disability plans, survivor benefit plans**, and **wellness programs**, to name just a few. Some might even argue that an employer's FICA contributions to the Social Security system and payments to workers' compensation programs, though they are mandatory, are forms of employee benefits.

Throughout this text, we have discussed many of these benefit plans and, in the next section, we will focus specifically on health and disability programs; therefore, we will not go into any additional detail here, other than to emphasize that insurance helps make a lot of these employee benefits possible, either as the funding vehicle or as the benefit itself.

SUMMARY

Beyond the obvious use for life insurance—to provide a source of funds for an insured's beneficiary—there are a number of other uses for this versatile product in meeting individual needs as well as business needs. Some producers find that they are most comfortable working in the individual or family market, while others prefer the business market.

An important duty of the professional insurance producer is to determine the proper amount of insurance needed to meet a client's needs. The two most common methods used in answering the question "How much?" are the *human life value* and the *needs* approaches.

Life insurance can be used in a variety of ways to meet personal and family financial needs. The cash values of a *whole life insurance policy* make it especially helpful in meeting permanent insurance needs such as estate planning objectives as well as financial needs that arise at death. However, *term insurance* is ideally suited for meeting temporary needs. *Annuities* are the perfect answer to a future income need, such as retirement.

Businesses also have many needs for life insurance. It can provide the foundation for *business continuation agreements* or *buy-sell plans*, for *key-person protection*, or for any number of *employee benefit programs*.

KEY CONCEPTS

Students should be familiar with the following concepts:

human life value approach	key-person insurance
needs approach	split-dollar life insurance
individual uses for life insurance	deferred compensation plans
business uses for life insurance	employee benefits
buy-sell plans	salary continuation plans

UNIT TEST

1. Which of the following statements regarding ways to determine the proper amount of life insurance is CORRECT?

    A. The most popular method today for determining the proper amount of life insurance is the human life value approach.

    B. When using the needs approach to determine the proper amount of life insurance to purchase non-insurance-type assets, such as pension benefits or personal savings, are not factors in the calculation.

    C. The needs approach considers only the most immediate financial concerns, without regard for family financial goals such as college education for children or retirement income for a surviving spouse.

    D. There are two basic approaches to determining the amount of life insurance that is needed: the human life value approach and the needs approach.

2. All the following statements regarding survivor financial needs are correct EXCEPT

    A. the term dependency period refers to the 20-year period immediately following the insured's death during which the widowed spouse must depend on Social Security

    B. the period for which there are no Social Security benefits for the surviving spouse is known as the blackout period

    C. a final expense fund addresses a deceased breadwinner's last illness and funeral costs, death taxes, outstanding debts, and more

    D. a housing fund addresses a family's rental or home mortgage needs

3. Three business partners individually agree to acquire the interest of a deceased partner and own life insurance on each of the other partners in the amount of his or her share of the business's buyout value. What is described here is

    A. an entity buy-sell plan

    B. a stock redemption buy-sell plan

    C. a cross-purchase buy-sell plan

    D. a 401(k) plan

4. Which of the following statements regarding key-person insurance is NOT correct?

    A. Key-person life insurance indemnifies a business for financial loss caused by the death of a key employee or key executive.

    B. The business may borrow from the cash value of a permanent key-person life insurance policy.

    C. The policy's death proceeds received by the business are not taxable.

    D. Premiums for a key-person life insurance policy are a tax-deductible expense to the business.

5. Which of the following statements regarding deferred compensation plans is CORRECT?

    A. A deferred compensation plan must always be designed as a qualified plan.

    B. Life insurance is not a permissible funding vehicle, but annuities are.

    C. They permit a business to provide extra benefits to officers, executives, and other highly paid employees.

    D. A deferred compensation plan must be made available to all employees who are at least 21 years old and have 1 year of service to the business.

6. With three partners in a business, how many life insurance policies would be required to insure a cross-purchase buy-sell plan?

    A. 3

    B. 6

    C. 9

    D. 12

7. Robert and his employer agree on the purchase of a split-dollar life insurance policy and the usual split-dollar approach to premium payments. Each year, the employer will contribute to the premium an amount equal to

    A. one-half the premium

    B. the annual dividend

    C. the increase in the policy's cash value

    D. two-thirds of the premium

8. Roland is 45 years old and married. He has a son, age 19, a freshman at a local university and a daughter, age 8. Decreasing term insurance could be recommended for Roland in order to accomplish which of the following reasons?

   A. Supplement retirement income
   B. Guarantee a college education for the son
   C. Provide payment protection
   D. Provide a college education fund for the daughter

9. A partnership owns, pays for, and is the beneficiary of the life insurance policies on the lives of its individual partners. This is known as

   A. an entity buy-sell plan
   B. a stock redemption plan
   C. a cross purchase plan
   D. a Keogh plan

10. Which of the following statements about key-person insurance is CORRECT?

    A. The key employee's family is the beneficiary of the policy.
    B. The death proceeds are taxable.
    C. The business may take a tax deduction for premiums paid.
    D. Because the business has complete control over the policy, it can be considered a business asset.

3

Principles of Health Insurance

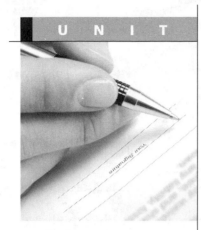

15

Introduction to Health Insurance

- Basic Forms of Health Insurance Coverage
- How Health Insurance Is Purchased
- Characteristics of Health Insurance
- Health Care Reform Act

The terms "health and accident insurance," "accident and sickness insurance," and "health insurance" are used interchangeably in the health insurance industry, from state to state and company to company. No matter what it is called in the industry, it all means the same thing to consumers—a critically important type of insurance that provides financial protection from the high costs of illness and injury.

The remainder of this text is devoted to the principles of health insurance. We will take a look at the types of health insurance plans, including plans for the elderly; the providers of health insurance coverages; policy provisions; underwriting standards; and more. This unit is designed to provide an overview of the broad field of health insurance, focusing on the basics. ■

BASIC FORMS OF HEALTH INSURANCE COVERAGE

Health insurance refers to the broad field of insurance plans that provide protection against the financial consequences of illness, accidents, injury, and disability. Coverage is provided by commercial insurers, self-funded plans, and prepayment plans such as Health Maintenance Organizations (HMOs). In addition, many individuals receive health coverage through public or government-sponsored health insurance (e.g., Medicaid, Medicare, or military health care).

There are three distinct categories of health coverage within the broad field of health insurance: **medical expense insurance, disability income insurance,** and **accidental death and dismemberment insurance.** Each of these coverages will be discussed in detail in subsequent units, but an introduction is appropriate here.

ILLUSTRATION 15.1

Health Coverages and
What They Provide

Type of Coverage	Provisions and Benefits
Medical Expense Insurance	Provides benefits for the cost of medical care. Depending on the type of policy (and its specific provisions), coverage can range from limited (e.g., coverage for hospital costs only) to very broad (e.g., coverage for all aspects of medical services and care).
Disability Income Insurance	Provides a specified periodic income to the insured—usually on a monthly basis—in the event he becomes disabled.
Accidental Death and Dismemberment Insurance	Provides a lump-sum payment in the event the insured dies due to an accident or suffers the loss of one or more body members due to an accident.

Medical Expense Insurance

Medical expense insurance provides financial protection against the cost of medical care by reimbursing the insured, fully or in part, for these costs. It includes many kinds of plans that cover hospital care, surgical expenses, physician expenses, medical treatment programs, outpatient care, and the like. Medicare supplement insurance and long-term care insurance, two types of health insurance coverage designed for the elderly, are also examples of medical expense insurance plans. They are discussed in detail in Unit 21.

Disability Income Insurance

Disability income insurance is designed to provide a replacement income when wages are lost due to a disability. As such, it does not cover the medical expenses associated with a disability; rather, it provides the disabled insured with a guaranteed flow of periodic income payments while she is disabled.

Accidental Death and Dismemberment Insurance

Accidental death and dismemberment insurance, commonly referred to as AD&D insurance, is the purest form of accident insurance, providing the insured with a lump-sum benefit amount in the event of accidental death or dismemberment under accidental circumstances. Typically, AD&D coverage is a part of a group insurance plan.

Within each of the previous three categories are many forms and variations of coverage that have evolved to meet unique insurance needs. Even the type of health insurance provider—of which there are many—can make a difference in the basic makeup of any of these kinds of coverages. Each of these basic coverages, as well as the many types of health insurance providers, will be discussed in later units. They are introduced here to help acquaint you with the health insurance field in general.

HOW HEALTH INSURANCE IS PURCHASED

As is the case with life insurance, health insurance is available to individuals and families through individual plans and policies or group plans and policies, including blanket policies and franchise policies.

Individual health insurance is issued by commercial insurers and service organizations as contracts between the insured and the company. Though all companies have standard policies for the coverages they offer, most allow an individual to select various options or benefit levels that will most precisely meet his needs. Individual health contracts require an application, and the proposed insured usually must provide evidence of insurability.

Group health insurance, also issued by commercial insurers and service organizations, provides coverage under a master contract to members of a specified group. Like group life, group health plans are available to employers, trade and professional associations, labor unions, credit unions, and other organizations. Insurance is extended to the individuals in the group through the master contract, usually without individual underwriting and usually without requiring group members to provide evidence of insurability. The employer or the association is the policyowner and is responsible for premium payments. The employer may pay the entire premium or may require some contribution from each member to cover the insurance cost. Generally speaking, the provisions and coverages of group health insurance contracts are more liberal than individual health contracts.

Health insurance is also provided through **state and federal government programs**. At the state level, **Medicaid** is available to assist low-income individuals in meeting the costs of medical care. The federal government offers health insurance protection through **Medicare** and **OASDI disability provisions**, components of the Social Security system.

CHARACTERISTICS OF HEALTH INSURANCE

Though closely related to life insurance in purpose, health insurance differs from its life cousin in several important ways. A review here of the distinguishing characteristics of health insurance will set the stage for the more in-depth discussion to follow in later units.

Renewability Provisions

Life insurance (particularly whole life insurance) and annuities are characterized by their permanence; the policies cannot be cancelled by the insurer unless the policyowner fails to make a required premium payment. Even term life policies are guaranteed effective for the duration of the term, as long as premiums are paid. Health insurance is not as permanent in nature. Health insurance policies may contain any one of a wide range of renewability provisions, which define the rights of the insurer to cancel the policy at different points during the life of the policy. There are five principal renewability classifications: *cancellable*, *optionally renewable*, *conditionally renewable*, *guaranteed renewable*, and *noncancellable*. The distinguishing characteristics of each type will be covered in Unit 22, but generally speaking, the more advantageous the renewability provisions to the insured, the more expensive the coverage.

Premium Factors and Modes

Like life insurance, health insurance is funded by the regular payment of premiums. Unlike life insurance, however, there are relatively few payment options available with a health policy. For example, health policies do not offer any sort of limited payment option, as one would find with, say, a 10-pay or paid-up at 65 life policy. Health insurance policies are paid for on a year-by-year basis. Furthermore, except for the noncancellable type of policy cited previously, health insurance premium rates *are* subject to periodic increases.

Health premiums can be paid under one of several different payment modes, including annual, semiannual, quarterly, monthly, and even weekly. As with life insurance, the least expensive premium mode is annual. Monthly premiums are often paid through some form of preauthorized check method, by which the insurer automatically obtains the premium directly from the policyholder's checking account.

There are various factors that enter into premium calculations for health insurance. These include interest, expense, types of benefits, and **morbidity**. Morbidity is the expected incidence of sickness or disability within a given age group during a given period of time; it is to health insurance what mortality is to life insurance. Other health insurance premium factors are claims experience and the age, sex, and occupation of the insured. All of these factors are discussed in detail in Unit 23.

Participating Versus Nonparticipating Policies

Health insurance policies may be written on either a **participating** or **nonparticipating** basis. Most individual health insurance is issued on a non-participating basis. Group health insurance, however, is generally participating and provides for **dividends** or **experience rating**.

Group health plans issued by mutual companies usually provide for dividends, while stock companies frequently issue experience-rated plans. A group policy that is experience-rated may make premium reductions retroactive for 12 months. Premium increases for such policies are not retroactive. Experience-rated refunds may be contingent upon renewal of the master policy, but the payment of dividends usually is not contingent upon renewal.

Cost-accounting formulas are complex and vary from insurer to insurer; however, the two major factors that influence whether or not dividends or experience-rated refunds are payable are **expenses** and **claims costs** of the insurer. If these cost items are less than anticipated, the group policyowner benefits by receiving a dividend or refund credit. If expenses and claims costs are higher than expected, the group policyowner may not qualify for a dividend or refund credit.

Reserves

Reserves are set aside by an insurance company and designated for the payment of future claims. Part of each premium is designated for the reserves.

Two types of health insurance reserves are **premium reserves** and **loss (or claims) reserves**. Premium reserves reflect the liability of the insurer for losses that have not occurred but for which premiums have been paid. Reserves earmarked as loss (or claims) reserves represent the insurer's liability for losses that have occurred but for which settlement is not yet complete. The details of how reserves are handled and recorded by the company are very technical. State laws dictate the minimum requirements for reserves for both life and health insurance. The annual statements required by state insurance departments break down a company's reserves in considerable detail.

Claims

The role of the health insurance claims examiner differs somewhat from that of the life insurance claims examiner. In the case of life insurance, most **claims** are fairly well defined: the amount of insurance coverage is readily determined by the policy, and benefits are payable if the insured has died. With health insurance, though, the claims process is not as clearly defined. Medical expense insurance, for example, is typically based on a **contract of reimbursement**, meaning that the benefit an insured receives is not fixed but instead is dependent on the amount of the loss. Its purpose is to reimburse the insured for the amount of loss sustained (within limits). This is in contrast to life insurance, AD&D, and disability income insurance that are all **valued contracts**—they pay the amount stated in the contract if a defined event, such as death or disability, occurs.

The health claims examiner must also decide if, in fact, a loss has actually occurred. This is especially challenging in disability income cases, where a subjective assessment of "disabled" can create misunderstandings.

HEALTH CARE REFORM ACT

Subsidies

Individuals and families who make between 100–400% of the Federal Poverty Level (FPL) and want to purchase their own health insurance on an exchange are eligible for subsidies. They cannot be eligible for Medicare and Medicaid and cannot be covered by an employer. Eligible buyers receive premium credits, and there is a cap for how much they have to contribute to their premiums on a sliding scale.

This health reform will close the Medicare prescription drug "donut hole" by 2020. Seniors who hit the donut hole by 2010 will receive a $250 rebate.

Beginning in 2011, seniors in the gap will receive a 50% discount on brand name drugs. The bill also includes $500 billion in Medicare cuts over the next decade.

Medicaid

In regards to Medicaid, the Health Care Reform Act will:

- expand Medicaid to include 133% of federal poverty level, which is $29,327 for a family of four;

- require states to expand Medicaid to include childless adults starting in 2014; and

- require the federal government to pay 100% of costs for covering newly eligible individuals through 2016.

Illegal immigrants are not eligible for Medicaid.

Insurance Reforms

The following insurance reforms have occurred as a result of the Health Care Reform Act.

- Six months after enactment, insurance companies could no longer deny children coverage based on a preexisting condition.

- Starting in 2014, insurance companies cannot deny coverage to anyone with preexisting conditions.

- Insurance companies must allow children to stay on their parent's insurance plans until age 26.

- In 2014, everyone must purchase health insurance or face a $695 annual fine. There are some exceptions for low-income people.

Employer Mandate

Employers with more than 50 employees must provide health insurance or pay a fine of $2,000 per worker each year if any worker receives federal subsidies to purchase health insurance. Fines are applied to entire number of employees, minus some allowances.

SUMMARY

This unit introduced the important field of health insurance. There are many hybrid plans that offer health protection in three different forms: **medical expense**, **disability income**, and **accidental death and dismemberment**. Health insurance is available to individuals and families on an **individual basis**, through a **group plan** or by the **federal government**. It is distinguished by many factors, including its provisions for renewability, premium factors, whether or not the contract is participating, reserves, and its claims procedures. In the following units, we'll review the different types of health insurance and health insurance providers in greater detail.

KEY CONCEPTS

Students should be familiar with the following concepts:

accidental death and dismemberment insurance	participating versus nonparticipating policies
disability income insurance	reserves
valued versus reimbursement contracts	morbidity
medical expense insurance	renewability provisions

UNIT TEST

1. Which of the following statements pertaining to health insurance policy premium factors is CORRECT?

   A. A "policy fee" is another term for policy premium.
   B. A policyowner has an individual health plan; therefore, the policy is most likely a participating policy.
   C. Age and sex of the individual insureds would have the most influence on a group health insurance policy's experience rating refund credit.
   D. Health insurance policies are paid for on a year-by-year basis and are subject to periodic increases.

2. All of the following are basic forms of health insurance coverage EXCEPT

   A. medical expense
   B. limited pay health
   C. disability income
   D. accidental death and dismemberment

3. Which of the following premium factors is unique to health insurance (as opposed to life insurance)?

   A. Age
   B. Sex
   C. Morbidity
   D. Interest

4. Which of the following statements regarding health insurance is CORRECT?

   A. Once issued, health insurance policies cannot be cancelled by the insurer.
   B. There are many premium-payment options available with health insurance policies.
   C. Medical expense policies reimburse the insured for the costs of medical care.
   D. Disability income policies are designed to pay hospital expenses associated with a disability.

5. Assume a health insurance contract states that it will pay $350 a month to the insured, should she become totally disabled. Which term most aptly defines this kind of contract?

   A. Participating
   B. Valued
   C. Inclusive
   D. Reimbursement

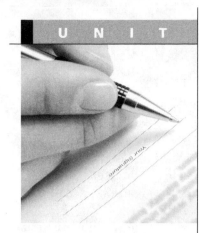

16

Health Insurance Providers

- Commercial Insurance Providers
- Service Providers
- Government Insurance Programs
- Alternative Methods of Providing Health Insurance

Most Americans regard medical insurance as the most important form of insurance protection to own, and with good reason. As the cost of medical care increases, an uninsured illness or injury could result in financial disaster for many families.

A number of sources are available for individuals seeking health insurance protection. In general, health insurance providers can be divided into three main categories: commercial insurers, service providers, and state and federal government. In all cases, the objective is the same: to provide protection against the financial costs associated with illness, injury, or disability. In this unit, we will look at some of the specific types of providers in each of these groups. We will also introduce Medicare and Medicaid, which play an important role in providing health insurance for a large segment of our population. ■

COMMERCIAL INSURANCE PROVIDERS

Health insurance may be written by a number of **commercial insurers**, including life insurance companies, casualty insurance companies, or mono-line companies that specialize in one or more types of medical expense and disability income insurance. This includes both individual and group insurance policies. Among life insurance companies, health insurance is offered by *ordinary* companies as well as *debit* (or home service) companies. (Recall that debit companies sell what are known as *industrial* policies.)

Commercial insurance companies function on the **reimbursement approach**; that is, policyowners obtain medical treatment from whatever source they feel is most appropriate and, per the terms of their policy, submit their charges to their insurer for reimbursement. The **right of assignment** built into most commercial health policies lets policyowners assign benefit payments from the insurer directly to the health care provider, thus relieving the policyowner of first having to pay the medical care provider. The right to assign a policy's benefits, however, does not change the fact that the policy is reimbursing the insured for covered medical expenses.

SERVICE PROVIDERS

Service providers offer benefits to subscribers in return for the payment of a premium. Benefits are in the form of services provided by hospitals and physicians in the plan.

Blue Cross and Blue Shield are the dominant health insurers of the United States. The nation's Blue Cross and Blue Shield plans are loosely affiliated through the national Blue Cross and Blue Shield Association but are independently managed. The Blues provide the majority of their benefits on a service basis rather than on a reimbursement basis. This means that the insurer pays the provider directly for the medical treatment given the subscriber, instead of reimbursing the insured.

The Blues have contractual relationships with the hospitals and doctors. As participating providers, the doctors and hospitals contractually agree to specific costs for the medical services provided to subscribers. Thus, there is no contractual arrangement between the Blues and the subscribers as there would be between the insurer and the insured.

Traditionally, the Blues have operated as nonprofit organizations, which means any net gain realized from company operations is eventually returned to the subscribers in the form of reduced premiums or increased benefits. A few plans have been allowed to become for-profit companies, or form for-profit subsidiaries, to allow them to raise money for expansion and compete in the health care marketplace.

Blue Cross traditionally has been a hospital service plan and Blue Shield a physician service plan, but these distinctions are becoming blurred.

Members of Blue Cross and Blue Shield are known as subscribers. Subscribers can transfer their membership from one Blues organization to another in other areas of town or to other cities or states. Subscribers may also change their coverage from individual to family, from family to group. When transfers or changes are made, the subscriber's coverage continues without interruption.

Blue Cross and Blue Shield plans are called **prepaid** plans because the plan subscribers pay a set fee, usually each month, for medical services covered under the plan.

The Blues have also been strongly influenced by managed care. Many Blues subscribers are now covered by a Blues-affiliated HMO or PPO, or **point-of-service (POS) plan**, which is a type of health plan allowing the covered person to choose to receive a service from a participating or a nonparticipating provider, with different benefit levels associated with the use of in-plan and out-of-plan providers.

Health Maintenance Organizations

A **health maintenance organization**, or HMO, is another type of organization offering comprehensive prepaid health care services to its subscribing members. HMO participants can be members under a group insurance plan or they can be individual or family members.

HMOs are distinguished by the fact that they not only finance health care services for their subscribers on a prepayment basis, but they also organize and deliver the health services as well. Subscribers pay a fixed periodic fee to the HMO (as opposed to paying for services only when needed) and are provided with a broad range of health services, from routine doctor visits to emergency and hospital care. This care is rendered by physicians and hospitals who participate in the HMO. HMOs are known for stressing preventive care, the objective being to reduce the number of unnecessary hospital admissions and duplication of services. Unlike commercial insurers, HMOs rarely assess deductibles; when they do, the charges are nominal.

Health maintenance organizations may be self-contained and self-funded based on dues or fees from their subscribers, or they may contract for excess insurance or administrative services provided by insurance companies. In fact, some HMOs are sponsored by insurance companies.

The Health Maintenance Act of 1973, which provided some federal funding for these organizations, spurred the HMO movement forward. One of its provisions requires employers with 25 or more employees to offer enrollment in an HMO if they provide health care benefits for their workers. A complete explanation of HMOs with reference to Florida law appears in Unit 30.

Preferred Provider Organizations

Another type of health insurance provider is the **preferred provider organization**, or PPO. A preferred provider organization is a collection of health care providers, such as physicians, hospitals, and clinics, who offer their services to certain groups at prearranged prices. In exchange, the group refers its members to the preferred providers for health care services.

Unlike HMOs, preferred provider organizations usually operate on a fee-for-service-rendered basis, not on a prepaid basis. Members of the PPO select from among the preferred providers for needed services. Also in contrast to HMOs, PPO health care providers are normally in private practice. They have agreed to offer their services to the group and its members at fees that are typically less than what they normally charge. In exchange, because the group refers its members to the PPO, the providers broaden their patient/service base. One of the features that attracts groups to PPOs is the discounted fees that are negotiated in advance.

Groups that contract with PPOs are very often employers, insurance companies, or other health insurance benefits providers. While these groups do not mandate that individual members must use the PPO, a reduced benefit is typical if they do not. For instance, individuals may pay $100 coinsurance if they use PPO services and $500 coinsurance if they go outside the PPO for health care services.

GOVERNMENT INSURANCE PROGRAMS

For many people, health care cost protection is made available through a state or federal government program. At the federal level, **Medicare** is the primary source of health insurance. It is a part of the Social Security program that also provides **disability income** to qualified workers under OASDI. At the state level, Medicaid offers protection to financially needy individuals, and **state workers' compensation programs** provide benefits for workers who suffer from occupational injuries or illnesses. Let's take a brief look at each. Because of their significance to the health care needs of seniors, a detailed discussion of Medicare and Medicaid is included in Unit 20.

Medicare

The federally administered Medicare program took effect in 1966. Its purpose is to provide hospital and medical expense insurance protection to those aged 65 and older, to those of any age who suffer from chronic kidney disease, or to those who are receiving Social Security disability benefits.

Social Security Disability Income

In addition to Medicare, the federal government also provides **disability-related benefits** through the Social Security OASDI program. Though this subject was covered in Unit 12, let's review some of the important points here.

Disability income benefits are available to covered workers who qualify under Social Security requirements. One of the requirements is that the individual must be so mentally or physically disabled that he cannot perform any substantial gainful work. In addition, the impairment must be expected to last at least 12 months or result in an earlier death. The determination of disability for Social Security purposes is usually made by a government agency. In addition to meeting the definition of disabled, the individual must have earned a certain minimum number of quarters of coverage under Social Security.

A five-month waiting period is required before an individual will qualify for benefits, during which time she must remain disabled. For example, if Jerry became disabled in January, he must wait five full months—February through June—before he will qualify for disability benefits. His first benefit payment would be for July, and it would be paid in August. No second five-month waiting period is required if the disabled worker recovers and then is disabled again within five years.

Medicaid

Medicaid is Title XIX of the Social Security Act, added to the Social Security program in 1965. Its purpose is to provide matching federal funds to states for their medical public assistance plans to help needy persons, regardless of age. If family income is below a specified level, Medicaid benefits generally are available. Although each state has some leeway in establishing eligibility requirements, Medicaid benefits are generally payable to low-income individuals who are blind, disabled, or under 21 years of age. The benefits may be applied to Medicare deductibles and co-payment requirements.

State Workers' Compensation Programs

All states have **workers' compensation laws**, which were enacted to provide mandatory benefits to employees for work-related injuries, illness, or death. Employers are responsible for providing workers' compensation benefits to their employees and do so by purchasing coverage through state programs, private insurers, or by self-insuring.

Although each state's laws differ with regard to procedures, requirements, and minimum benefits, there is uniformity to the following extent:

- If a worker is killed in an industrial accident, the law provides for payment of burial expenses, subject to a maximum amount, and compensation for the surviving spouse or other dependents of the worker at the time of death.

- Regardless of any negligence or due care by the employer, he is liable for work-related disabilities that employees suffer.

- Under the law, a disabled employee is entitled to benefits as a matter of right, without having to sue the employer for benefits. However, in return for the benefits provided under the law, the employee gives up the right to sue the employer.

- Under most laws, a disabled employee is paid benefits on a weekly or monthly basis, rather than in a lump sum.

- The employer must provide the required benefits; the employee does not contribute to the plan.

The law provides for a schedule of benefits, the size of which is based on such factors as the severity of the disability and the employee's wages.

ALTERNATIVE METHODS OF PROVIDING HEALTH INSURANCE

As the cost of health insurance has increased, business and individuals have turned to nontraditional methods of providing health insurance. These include self-insured plans, multiple employer trusts (METs), and multiple employer welfare arrangements (MEWAs).

Self-Insurance

For businesses and individuals, an alternative to a commercial or service health insurance plan is **self-insurance**. Large corporations especially will self-insure their sick-leave plans for their employees. Labor unions, fraternal associations, and other groups often self-insure their medical expense plans through dues or contributions from members. Others may self-insure part of a plan and use insurance to protect against large, unpredictable losses.

Many of these self-insured plans are administered by insurance companies or other organizations that are paid a fee for handling the paperwork and processing the claims. When an outside organization provides these functions, it is called an **administrative-services-only (ASO)** or **third-party administrator (TPA) arrangement**.

To bolster a self-insured plan, some groups adopt a **minimum premium plan (MPP)**. These plans are designed to insure against a certain level of large, unpredictable losses, above and beyond the self-insured level. As the name implies, MPPs are available for a fraction of the insurer's normal premium.

Multiple Employer Trusts

As mentioned in Unit 10, a method of marketing group benefits to employers who have a small number of employees is the **multiple employer trust (MET)**. METs can provide a single type of insurance (e.g., health insurance) or a wide range of coverages (e.g., life, medical expense, and disability income insurance). In some cases, alternative forms of the same coverage are available (e.g., comprehensive health insurance or basic health insurance).

An employer who wants to get coverage for employees from an MET must first become a member of the trust by subscribing to it. The employer is issued a joinder agreement, which spells out the relationship between the trust and the employer and specifies the coverages to which the employer has subscribed. It is not necessary for an employer to subscribe to all the coverages offered by an MET.

An MET may either provide benefits on a self-funded basis or fund benefits with a contract purchased from an insurance company. In the latter case, the trust, rather than the subscribing employers, is the master insurance contract holder. In either case, the employees of subscribing employers are provided with benefit descriptions (certificates of insurance) in a manner similar to the usual group insurance agreement.

In addition to alternative methods of funding benefits, METs can be categorized according to how they are administered, that is, whether by an insurance company or a third-party administrator.

Multiple Employer Welfare Arrangements

A **multiple employer welfare arrangement (MEWA)** is a type of MET. It consists of small employers who have joined to provide health benefits for their employees, often on a self-insured basis. They are tax-exempt entities. Employees covered by a MEWA are required by law to have an employment-related common bond.

SUMMARY

A number of sources are available for people seeking health insurance protection. **Commercial insurance companies**, which include life insurance companies as well as monoline and casualty insurance companies, are one source. **Service providers**, including **health maintenance organizations**, are others. **Preferred provider organizations** provide an additional option by contracting their services with employer groups or insurers.

For many people, health insurance protection is obtained through a **government-sponsored program**. At the federal level, the Social Security program (OASDI) provides both disability income benefits and medical expense protection, the latter through the **Medicare** program.

At the state level, medical expense insurance is provided through the Medicaid program to financially needy citizens who are blind, disabled, or under age 21. Because Medicaid is state-administered (and only partially federally supported), each state has some leeway in setting the qualification standards for its program. All states have also enacted workers' compensation programs, which provide benefits to workers for occupational illnesses and disabilities.

Some large employers prefer to retain the risk of covering their employees' medical care expenses, or at least part of the expenses, and thus self-insure their plan.

KEY CONCEPTS

Students should be familiar with the following concepts:

commercial health insurers	preferred provider organizations (PPOs)
health maintenance organizations (HMOs)	administrative-services-only (ASO) plans
third-party administrator (TPA) plans	Medicare
self-insured plans	Medicaid
Social Security disability income	multiple employer trusts (METs)
workers' compensation	service providers
multiple employer welfare arrangements (MEWAs)	

UNIT TEST

1. HMOs are known for stressing
   A. preventive medicine and early treatment
   B. state-sponsored health care plans
   C. in-hospital care and services
   D. health care services for government employees

2. Which of the following organizations would make reimbursement payments directly to the insured individual for covered medical expenditures?
   A. Administrative-services-only plan
   B. Commercial insurer
   C. Preferred provider organization
   D. Health maintenance organization

3. Marty just received his first Social Security disability payment. From this, we can assume
   A. he had previously applied for Medicaid
   B. he is at least 65 years of age
   C. his disability is expected to last at least 12 months
   D. his disability commenced 3 months ago

4. Which of the following statements pertaining to health maintenance organizations is CORRECT?
   A. An insurance company that also markets group health insurance is known as an HMO.
   B. If a person joins an HMO and undergoes a physical examination, she will be billed for the exam and each subsequent medical service as it is performed.
   C. An insurance company may sponsor an HMO or assist an HMO by providing contractual services.
   D. Like commercial insurers, HMOs generally assess deductibles.

5. The waiting period before qualifying for Social Security disability benefits is how many months?
   A. 3
   B. 5
   C. 6
   D. 12

6. Which of the following individuals would probably qualify for Social Security disability benefits?
   A. George, a ski instructor who breaks his leg
   B. Carl, who becomes ill with a viral infection and is not expected to be able to work for the next 6 months
   C. Mike, a mechanic who loses his dominant hand in an accident
   D. John, who experiences serious early-onset Alzheimer's and is unable to remember how to get to work

7. Which of the following statements pertaining to Medicaid is NOT correct?
   A. It provides federal matching funds to states for medical public assistance plans.
   B. Its purpose is to help eligible needy persons with medical assistance.
   C. Medicaid benefits may be used to pay the deductible and coinsurance amounts of Medicare.
   D. It limits financial assistance to persons age 65 or over who are in need of medical services they cannot afford.

8. Jerry is injured while working. Under state workers' compensation laws, we can assume that
   A. his employer will not be liable for Jerry's work-related disabilities if the employer's negligence did not contribute to the injuries
   B. Jerry will probably receive workers' compensation benefits on a monthly or weekly basis
   C. Jerry must sue his employer to receive workers' compensation benefits
   D. both Jerry and his employer are required to contribute to the cost of workers' compensation coverage

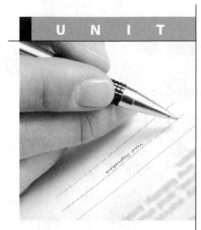

17

Medical Expense Insurance

- Purpose of Medical Expense Insurance
- Basic Medical Expense Plans
- Major Medical Expense Plans
- Other Types of Medical Expense Coverage

When people speak of their health insurance, they are usually referring to insurance that protects against the costs of medical care. Medical expense insurance, which is available in several different forms, reimburses policyowners for part or all of the costs of obtaining medical care. It is a vital form of insurance considered by many to be the one type of insurance they cannot do without. ■

PURPOSE OF MEDICAL EXPENSE INSURANCE

Medical expense insurance provides financial protection against the cost of medical care for accidents and sickness. In this broad context, "medical care" includes hospital care, physician services, surgical expenses, drugs, nursing and convalescent care, diagnostic treatment, laboratory services, rehabilitative services, dental care, physical therapy—in short, all medical treatment and services. To what extent a given medical expense policy covers medical care—the specific types of services and treatments covered and the benefits provided—depends on the policy. Generally speaking, medical expense insurance is available through one of two different policy plans: **basic medical insurance** or **major medical insurance**. **Basic medical insurance** limits coverage to select types of medical care. **Major medical insurance**, which can work either as a supplement to a basic plan or as a comprehensive stand-alone plan, provides broader, more complete coverage. The limits of coverage for medical expense or major medical policies may be expressed on a "per cause," "per year," or "lifetime" basis, or as some combination of several or all of these.

Reimbursement Versus Fixed-Rate Approach

Medical expense plans typically pay benefits as a **reimbursement** of actual expenses, although some benefits are paid at a fixed rate, regardless of the actual loss. The distinction can be clarified with an example.

Assume Karl owns a reimbursement-type medical expense policy that pays a maximum benefit of $200,000. He is hospitalized for 10 days and incurs covered medical expenses totaling $10,000. The policy would provide benefits of $10,000—the **expenses incurred**.

Assume Doris owns a medical expense policy that provides a fixed rate of $100 per day for each day of hospitalization. She is hospitalized for 10 days, incurring medical expenses of $10,000. Her policy will provide benefits of $1,000: 10 days at $100 per day. Medical expense policies that pay a fixed rate provide the insured with a stated benefit amount for each day he is confined to a hospital as an inpatient. The money may be used by the insured for any purpose.

With this foundation, we're ready to take a look at the two kinds of medical expense insurance policies: **basic** and **major medical**. Within these two categories are many types of plans.

BASIC MEDICAL EXPENSE PLANS

Basic medical expense insurance is sometimes called "first dollar insurance" because, unlike major medical expense insurance, it provides benefits up front, without requiring the insured to first satisfy a deductible. For many years it was the leading type of medical expense insurance sold, but today it is overshadowed by major medical insurance. This is due largely to the fact that basic medical expense policies limit the type and duration of services covered and dollar amounts that will be paid (or reimbursed) to the insured. Major medical plans are not as limiting.

Basic medical expense policies classify their coverages according to general categories of medical care: **hospital expense, surgical expense,** and **physicians' (nonsurgical) expense.** Additional plans cover **nursing expenses** and **convalescent care.** While it is common to find all categories contained under the umbrella of one policy, they can be written as separate coverages.

Basic Hospital Expense

Basic hospital expense insurance reimburses policyowners for the cost of hospital confinement. (Many policies today also provide coverage for outpatient care if it is provided in lieu of hospitalized care.) Basic hospital policies cover costs associated with daily room and board and other miscellaneous expenses.

Daily Room and Board

Basic hospital expense policies cover the daily cost of **room and board.** There are no set standards these policies follow; they vary by daily amount payable and by the length of time the benefits are payable. For example, some policies will pay an in-hospital benefit for as long as 365 days, while others pay benefits for only 90 days or 30 days. Some policies reimburse the insured for the daily room and board charge up to a specified dollar amount. Others provide a service type of benefit, paying an amount equal to the hospital's daily charge for a semiprivate room.

Miscellaneous Expenses

In addition to room and board, basic hospital expense policies cover **hospital "extras"** or **miscellaneous charges,** up to a specified limit. Covered miscellaneous expenses include drugs, x-rays, anesthesia, lab fees, dressings, use of the operating room, and supplies.

Generally, the maximum miscellaneous expense benefit is expressed as a multiple of the daily room and board benefit (e.g., 10 times room and board or 20 times room and board) or it may be a stated dollar amount. Some policies may even specify individual maximums for certain expenses within the maximum miscellaneous benefit. For example, the overall maximum for miscellaneous expenses may be $1,000, with maximums of $150 for use of the operating room, $125 for anesthesia, $75 for drugs, and so on. But the total miscellaneous benefit would be limited to $1,000.

It is important to note that physicians' services are not covered under a basic hospital expense policy, even in the case of surgery. The cost for a physician is covered under a basic surgical expense or basic physicians' (nonsurgical) expense policy.

Basic Surgical Expense

Basic surgical expense policies provide coverage for the cost of a surgeon's services, whether the surgery is performed in or out of the hospital. Generally included in the coverage is the surgeon's fees as well as the fees of the anesthesiologist and any post-operative care.

There are three different approaches used by insurers in providing this type of coverage and determining the benefits payable. These are the **surgical schedule** approach, the **reasonable and customary** approach, and the **relative value scale** approach.

Surgical Schedule

Under the **surgical schedule** method, every surgical procedure is assigned a dollar amount by the insurer. Although the policy itself will only contain a representative sampling of common surgical procedures and their prices, a complete listing of all established surgical procedures is maintained in the insurer's claims office, for use by its claims examiners. When a claim is submitted to the insurer, the claims examiner reviews the policy to determine what amount is payable; if the surgeon's bill is more than the allowed charge set by the insurer, it is up to the insured to pay the surgeon the difference. If the surgeon's bill is less than the allowed charge, the insurer will pay only the full amount billed; the claim payment will never exceed the amount charged.

Reasonable and Customary Approach

Whereas the surgical schedule method pays up to a stated dollar amount regardless of the actual charge, the **reasonable and customary approach** is more open in its determination of benefits payable. Under this approach, the surgical expense is compared to what is deemed reasonable and customary for the geographical part of the country where the surgery was performed. If the charge is within the reasonable and customary parameters, the expense is paid, usually in full. If the charge is more than what is reasonable and customary, the patient must absorb the difference.

Relative Value Scale

The **relative value scale** is similar to the surgical schedule method, except that instead of a flat dollar amount being assigned to every surgical procedure, a set of **points** is assigned.

The number of points assigned to any one procedure is relative to the number of points assigned to a **maximum procedure**. Typically, something like a triple heart bypass would be considered a maximum procedure and assigned a high number of points (usually 500 or 1,000). Every other procedure is also assigned a set of points relative to that; an appendectomy, which is a major procedure but not as serious as a triple bypass, might be assigned 200 points. Setting a broken finger might rate five points.

How are benefit amounts determined? The policy will carry a stated dollar-per-point amount, known as the **conversion factor**, to determine the benefit. For example, a plan with a $5-per-point conversion factor would pay $1,000 for a 200-point procedure. Generally, the larger the conversion factor, the larger the policy's premium.

Basic Physicians' (Nonsurgical) Expense

Basic physicians' expense insurance provides benefits for nonsurgical physicians' services. Examples of services covered include office visits and the care by a physician while the insured is hospitalized for a nonsurgical reason. Benefits are usually based on the indemnity approach; for example, a plan might pay a flat fee of $50 per visit (but not to exceed the actual charge, if less). These policies typically carry a number of exclusions, such as x-rays, drugs, and dental treatment.

Other Basic Plans

Two other basic medical expense plans are worth noting: **nurses' expense benefits** and **convalescent care facility benefits**.

ILLUSTRATION 17.1

Basic Medical Expense Coverages

Medical Expense Category	What Is Covered
Hospital expense	Daily room and board Miscellaneous expenses
Surgical expense	Cost of surgeon's services Anesthesiologist
Physicians' expense	Office visits Nonsurgical care by a physician while hospitalized
Nurses' expense	Private duty nursing care
Convalescent care expense	Skilled nursing facility expenses

Basic medical expense policies provide coverage according to general categories of medical care. Policies covering all categories are available, as are policies that cover only select categories.

Nurses' expense coverage generally is limited to private duty nursing care arranged in accordance with a doctor's order while the insured is a hospital patient. It may cover both registered professional and licensed practical nurses.

Convalescent care facility coverage provides a maximum daily benefit for confinement in a skilled nursing facility for a specified recovery period following discharge from a hospital. Rest cures and normal custodial care are not covered.

MAJOR MEDICAL EXPENSE PLANS

Major medical expense insurance, often called **major medical**, has made it possible for many people to achieve substantial protection against the high cost of medical care. It offers broad coverage under one policy, typically paying benefits for hospital room and board, hospital extras, nursing services in hospital or at home, blood, oxygen, prosthetic devices, surgery, physicians' fees, ambulance services, dental as a result of accidental injury, and more. In addition, it provides for high benefit limits. It generally is available on both an individual basis and a group basis.

The services and supplies covered under a major medical policy must be performed or prescribed by a licensed physician and are necessary for the treatment of an insured's illness or injury. The benefit period may be defined on a calendar-year basis or may be specified as a two-year to five-year period. In contrast to basic medical expense insurance, major medical policies provide total maximum lifetime benefits to individual insureds from about $250,000 to $1,000,000 or more.

Major medical expense insurance usually picks up where basic medical expense insurance leaves off, in one of two ways: as a **supplement** to a basic plan or as a **comprehensive stand-alone plan**.

Supplementary Major Medical

A **supplementary major medical plan** covers expenses not included at all under a basic plan. It also provides coverage for expenses that are in excess of the dollar maximums specified in the basic policy as well as those expenses no longer covered by the basic plan because the benefits have been exhausted.

With a supplemental plan, major medical coverage is coordinated with various basic medical expense coverages, picking up where the basic plan leaves off. For example, a basic plan may provide for hospital room and board for a maximum of 45 days. If that basic plan were supplemented with a major medical plan, the supplementary major medical plan would cover hospital room and board expenses beginning on the 46th day. Or, if a basic plan provides a maximum of $1,500 for a specific surgical procedure and the actual cost of the procedure was $2,000, a major medical supplement would cover the additional $500. In addition, because of the broad coverage associated with most major medical supplements, a supplement will likely cover expenses that are either beyond the scope of the basic plan or excluded from its coverage.

Comprehensive Major Medical

The second type of major medical plan is the **comprehensive major medical plan**. Comprehensive plans are distinguished by the fact that they cover virtually all medical expenses—hospital expenses, physician and surgeon expenses, nursing care, drugs, physical therapy, diagnostic x-rays and laboratory services, medical supplies and equipment, transfusions, and more—under a **single policy**.

Major medical plans, whether supplementary or comprehensive, typically include two important features: **deductibles** and **coinsurance**. Both of these features require the insured to absorb some of the cost of her medical expenses, thus allowing the insurer to avoid small claims and keep the cost of premiums down. In contrast, a basic medical plan usually does not include either of these features; instead it imposes limitations in the form of maximum benefit amounts that will be paid.

Deductibles

A **deductible** is a stated initial dollar amount that the individual insured is required to pay before insurance benefits are paid. For example, if a plan has a flat $250 annual deductible, the insured is responsible for the first $250 of medical expenses every year. Covered expenses in excess of $250 are then paid by the major plan (subject to any coinsurance).

Depending on the type of major medical policy, the deductible may be one of three kinds: **flat**, **corridor**, or **integrated**.

Flat Deductible

A **flat deductible** is a stated amount that the insured must pay before policy benefits become payable. For example, if an insured has a policy with a $500 deductible and incurs $2,000 of covered medical expenses, he must pay $500 toward the total. The insurer will then base its payments on the remaining $1,500. Quite often, policies will include a **family deductible**, usually equal to three times the individual deductible amount. In a family of four, for example, if three members each satisfied the individual deductible in one year, no deductible would be applied to medical expenses incurred by the fourth member.

Corridor Deductible

A **corridor deductible** is typical for a supplementary major medical policy that works in conjunction with a basic medical expense policy. The first covered medical expenses the insured incurs are paid by the basic policy. After the basic policy benefits are exhausted, the insured pays the full deductible, and then the major medical benefits are payable.

For example, Lynda has a supplementary major medical policy that provides for a corridor deductible of $500. The deductible applies after full payment of up to $2,000 by the basic medical expense policy and before additional expenses are shared on a coinsurance basis by the insurer and Lynda (see *Coinsurance* later in this unit). Let us suppose that Lynda incurs a medical bill of $8,500. Responsibility for payment is as follows:

Total expenses:	$8,500
Basic medical expense pays:	−$2,000
	$6,500
Corridor deductible paid by Lynda:	− $500
Basis for major medical expense payment and coinsurance:	$6,000

As you can see, the basic medical expense policy paid for the first $2,000 of Lynda's medical bills. The corridor deductible, which the insured is responsible for, is applied next. To the extent that additional medical expenses remain—in this case, $6,000—they become the basis for the major medical payment. This is usually accomplished on a coinsurance or co-payment basis, whereby the insured shares some percentage of the cost. This is explained in the following section.

Integrated Deductible

An **integrated deductible** is also used with a supplementary major medical plan, but it is *integrated* into the amounts covered by the basic plan. For example, if a supplementary plan carries a $500 deductible and the insured incurs $500 or more of covered expenses under the basic plan, the deductible is satisfied. If the basic policy benefits do not cover the entire deductible amount specified in the major medical policy, the insured is compelled to make up the difference.

Each of the preceding deductibles may be figured on one of two bases. If a major medical plan provides for a **calendar year deductible**, the deductible amount is applied only once during each calendar year. Once the deductible has been met in a calendar year, all claims submitted will be treated for the balance of the year without regard to any deductibles.

If a major medical plan has a **per cause deductible**, separate deductibles are required for each separate illness or each separate accident. Per cause deductibles are common in policies that define causes of loss as "each sickness or each injury."

ILLUSTRATION 17.2

Types of Major Medical Deductibles

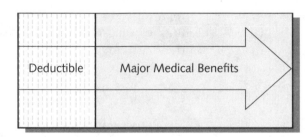

Flat Deductible

Typically used with comprehensive policies, a flat deductible is a stated amount that the insured must pay before any policy benefits are paid.

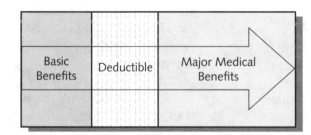

Corridor Deductible

Typically used with supplemental plans, a corridor deductible is the deductible imposed after all basic benefits have been paid but before any major medical benefits will be paid.

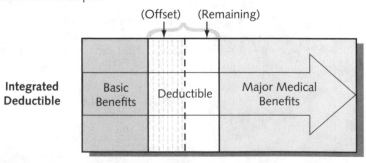

Integrated Deductible

Occasionally used with supplemental plans, this deductible is the amount that must be satisfied before major medical benefits are paid, but it is offset dollar-for-dollar by any benefits paid under the basic plan.

Coinsurance

Coinsurance, or percentage participation, is another characteristic of major medical policies. It is, simply, a sharing of expenses by the insured and the insurer. After the insured satisfies the deductible, the insurance company pays a high percentage of the additional (covered) expenses—usually 75% or 80%—and the insured pays the remainder. For example, Joe has an 80%/20% major medical policy, with a $200 flat annual deductible. This year, he incurs $1,200 in medical expenses, all of which are covered by his policy. The responsibility for payment would be as follows:

Total expenses:	$ 1,200
Deductible Joe pays:	$ 200
Basis for insurer's payment:	$ 1,000
	× .80
Amount insurer pays:	$ 800
Coinsurance amount Joe pays:	$ 200

Thus, the insurer will pay 80% of the charges after the deductible has been satisfied, or $800. Joe must pay the $200 deductible and 20% of the remaining expenses, for a total cost share of $400.

Now let's assume that Joe experiences two separate medical problems this year. The first, which required hospitalization and surgery, totaled $7,500. Under his major medical policy, Joe submitted his claim and paid his $200 deductible. The policy would pay 80% of the charges above the deductible, or $5,840; Joe is responsible for the remaining $1,460. Three months later, Joe incurs another round of medical expenses amounting to $900. Because his policy stipulates a flat annual deductible, which Joe has already paid, the policy will base its 80% payment on the full $900; Joe must pay the remaining 20%, or $180.

Coinsurance provisions are effective throughout the duration of a policy.

Stop-Loss Feature

To provide a safeguard for insureds, most major medical policies contain a **stop-loss feature** that limits the insured's out-of-pocket expenses. This means that once the insured has paid a specified amount toward her covered expenses—usually $1,000 to $2,000—the company pays 100% of covered expenses after that point.

How a stop-loss cap is defined depends on the policy. For example, one policy may stipulate that the contract will cover 100% of eligible expenses after the insured incurs $1,000 in out-of-pocket costs. Another policy may specify that the coinsurance provision applies only to the next $5,000 of covered expenses after the deductible is paid, with full coverage for any remaining expenses.

Let's use this last policy as an illustration. Assume Bill has such a policy. It calls for a $500 deductible, followed by an 80%/20% coinsurance on the next $5,000 in covered expenses. Amounts above that are fully absorbed by the policy. If Bill were to incur hospital and surgical bills of $20,000 this year, this is how payment would be assigned:

Total expenses:	$20,000
Deductible Bill pays:	−$500
Remaining:	$19,500
Coinsurance Bill pays (20% of the next $5,000 in expenses):	− $1,000
Amount insurer pays:	$18,500

Thus, with a $500 deductible and $1,000 in coinsurance for the next $5,000, Bill's plan provides for a maximum out-of-pocket expenditure by the insured of $1,500.

Preexisting Conditions

Another feature characteristic of most major medical policies is the exclusion for **preexisting conditions**. For individual plans, a preexisting condition is an illness or physical condition that existed before the policy's effective date and one that the applicant did not disclose on the application. (A condition that is noted on the application may be excluded by rider or waiver.) Consequently, medical costs incurred due to a preexisting condition are excluded from coverage under plans that contain this exclusion. However, the exclusion applies for only a limited time. After that time limit passes, any existing conditions are no longer considered *preexisting* and will be covered in full, subject to any other policy limitations. (See also *Time Limit on Certain Defenses*, Unit 22.)

The exclusion for preexisting conditions is designed to protect insurers against adverse selection by those who know they have a medical ailment and are facing certain medical costs.

(The rules regarding preexisting conditions are different for group insurance plans. The Health Insurance Portability and Accountability Act, or HIPAA, limited the ability of employer-sponsored groups and insurers to exclude individuals from health insurance coverage due to preexisting conditions. These rules will be discussed in more detail in Unit 24.)

High Deductible Health Plans (HDHP)

A high deductible health plan (HDHP) is a health plan that offers very low premiums but requires the insured to pay a relatively high deductible. For an individual, a qualified HDHP has a minimum deductible of $1,250 and a cap on out-of-pocket expenses of $6,250. A family HDHP has a minimum deductible of $2,500 and a cap of $12,500. (These limits are for 2013. They are indexed for inflation and change annually.) Because HDHPs require substantial deductibles and co-payments from participants, they are usually paired with one of the health savings accounts discussed in the following. These accounts allow employers or employees to put aside contributions that are tax free and grow tax free so long as they are used to pay qualified medical expenses.

Health Savings Accounts (HSAs)

The Medicare Prescription Drug and Modernization Act of 2003 also established a new way for consumers to pay for medical expenses—health care savings accounts (HSAs). An HSA is a tax-favored vehicle for accumulating funds to cover medical expenses. Individuals under age 65 are eligible to establish HSAs if they have a qualified high-deductible health plan.

For 2013, annual, pretax contributions of up to $3,250 for an individual or $6,450 for a family could be made to an HSA. Individuals with HSAs who are age 55 and older may make additional annual contributions of $1,000 in 2009 and after.

Earnings in HSAs grow tax free, and account beneficiaries can make tax-free withdrawals to cover current and future qualified health care costs. Qualified health care expenses include amounts paid for doctors' fees, prescription and non-prescription medicines, and necessary hospital services not paid for by insurance. They also include retiree health insurance premiums, Medicare expenses (but not Medigap), qualified long-term care services, and COBRA coverage. Qualified medical expenses are those expenses incurred by the HSA owner and the HSA owner's spouse and dependents. Nonqualified withdrawals are subject to income taxes and a 10% penalty tax. HSAs are fully portable, and assets can accumulate over the years. Upon death, HSA ownership may be transferred to a spouse tax free.

Flexible Spending Accounts (FSAs)

The **flexible spending account** (FSA) is a cafeteria plan that is funded with pretax employee contributions called salary reductions; the employee agrees to a reduction in compensation, and these funds are set aside to pay certain medical expenses. When paired with an HDHP, this results in lower employer costs for the health care plan, and the employees are provided with a convenient, tax-advantaged way to meet their higher plan obligations. FSAs are usually found in medium- to large-sized employers.

Health Reimbursement Accounts (HRAs)

Another variation in health care funding is the **health reimbursement account** (HRA). In this arrangement, the employer sets aside pretax contributions for each employee to pay deductibles, coinsurance, and co-payments. The employer sets plan limits and authorized uses of these funds, and typically unused funds may roll over from year to year. HRAs are the dominant funding form for HDHPs.

OTHER TYPES OF MEDICAL EXPENSE COVERAGE

As we've discussed, basic medical expense plans and major medical expense plans are the two primary kinds of health policies that provide coverage for accidents and illness. However, a discussion of medical expense plans would not be complete without mentioning a couple of other plans, most notably **hospital indemnity policies** and **limited risk** (or **dread disease**) **policies**.

Hospital Indemnity or Fixed-Rate Policies

A **hospital indemnity or fixed-rate policy** simply provides a daily, weekly, or monthly payment of a specified amount based on the number of days the insured is hospitalized. For example, such a plan may provide the insured $100 a day for every day he is confined in a hospital. This insurance has been available for many years but has been promoted more heavily in recent years largely due to skyrocketing health care costs. Many companies can offer high benefit fixed-rate plans at reasonable premiums because underwriting and administration are greatly simplified and claim costs are not affected by increases in medical costs.

Benefits may run as high as $4,500 per month, based on a daily hospital confinement benefit of $150, and some are even higher. Maximum benefit periods range from about six months to several years or up to a lifetime. Benefits are payable directly to the insureds and may be used for any purpose. Hospital fixed-rate policies usually are exempt from most state laws that apply to specific kinds of insurance contracts.

Limited Risk Policies

Policies that provide medical expense coverage for specific kinds of illnesses are known as **limited risk, dread disease,** or **critical illness** policies. They are available primarily due to the high costs associated with certain illnesses, such as cancer or heart disease. Such policies will frequently pay a single, lump sum amount to help defray medical costs associated with a specific medical diagnosis. It should be noted, however, that some states prohibit the sale of these policies because they invite questionable sales and marketing practices that take advantage of people's fear of these diseases.

Limited risk policies that cover specified accidents are also available and are discussed in Unit 19.

SUMMARY

The need for medical expense insurance—*health care insurance* in current vernacular—is greater today than at any time in the past because of the high cost of medical care. **Basic medical expense insurance**, once the predominant form of health insurance, is now overshadowed by **major medical insurance** in terms of premium dollars and total coverage. Offered as individual and group policies, medical expense insurance is an indispensable part of a total insurance portfolio.

KEY CONCEPTS

Students should be familiar with the following concepts:

deductibles

preexisting condition

basic medical expense policies

basic surgical expense

basic physicians' (nonsurgical) expense

basic hospital expense

stop-loss feature

limited risk policy

coinsurance

supplementary and comprehensive major medical expense policies

UNIT TEST

1. The miscellaneous expense benefit in a basic hospital expense policy normally will cover
   A. physicians' bedside visits
   B. the administering of anesthesia
   C. drugs and medicine administered in the hospital
   D. hospital room and board

2. Clarence is to enter the hospital for a thyroidectomy. His basic medical expense policy includes a relative value schedule for surgical expense. The schedule lists 55 units for a thyroidectomy and a conversion factor of $8. How much will the policy pay?
   A. $400
   B. $440
   C. $540
   D. $550

3. Which of the following statements about deductible provisions in medical insurance policies is NOT correct?
   A. They help to eliminate small claims.
   B. They provide that initial expenses up to a specified amount are to be paid by the insured.
   C. They are most common in basic medical expense policies.
   D. They help to hold down premium rates.

4. An insured has a basic hospital/surgical expense policy, which provides benefits of $50 per day for up to 30 days of hospitalization and $750 for miscellaneous charges. It bases its surgical benefits on a schedule approach. The insured is hospitalized for a severely broken leg that requires surgery. The surgical procedure has been assigned $500 by the policy, though the customary charge in the area is $600. The insured incurs the following covered expenses:

   $80 per day for seven days hospital charge

   $675 for the surgical procedure

   $800 for miscellaneous expenses

   The insured's policy will pay
   A. $1,600
   B. $1,700
   C. $1,810
   D. $2,035

5. When a medical expense policy pays benefits on a fixed-rate basis, it pays
   A. a certain percentage of whatever the hospital room charges are
   B. for total hospital expenses, less a deductible
   C. a flat amount per day for hospital room and board
   D. only for surgery and miscellaneous hospital expenses

6. Wilbur's basic medical expense policy limits the miscellaneous expense benefit to 20 times the $90 daily room and board benefit. During his recent hospital stay, miscellaneous expenses totaled $2,100. How much, if any, of this amount will Wilbur have to pay?
   A. $0
   B. $210
   C. $300
   D. $2,100

7. Which of the following examples pertaining to major medical policy deductibles is CORRECT?

   A. Eric's major medical policy has a $500 flat deductible provision. He incurs covered expenses totaling $350. He will pay nothing and his major medical policy will pay $350.

   B. Sarah has a major medical policy with a $500 flat deductible and an 80/20 coinsurance provision. Her covered expenses total $1,800. Of that amount, she will pay $500 and her insurance will pay $1,300.

   C. Valerie incurs a hospital bill of $8,300. Her basic medical expense insurance pays $2,400. Valerie pays a $200 deductible and her major medical plan takes care of the balance of covered expenses. Her deductible would be classified as a corridor deductible.

   D. An integrated deductible amount is $2,000. With this deductible, after the basic policy benefits are exhausted, the insured pays the full $2,000 deductible and then the major medical benefits are payable.

8. Arthur incurs total hospital expenses of $9,500, all of which are covered by his major medical policy. The policy includes a $500 deductible and a 75/25 coinsurance feature. Of the total expense, how much will Arthur have to pay?

   A. $2,375
   B. $2,750
   C. $2,875
   D. $6,675

9. All of the following are types of deductible provisions associated with major medical policies EXCEPT

   A. corridor
   B. integrated
   C. flat
   D. stop-loss

10. If the coinsurance feature in a major medical insurance policy is 75/25 with a $100 deductible, how much of a $2,100 bill would the insured pay?

   A. $100
   B. $500
   C. $600
   D. $1,500

18

Disability Income Insurance

- Purpose of Disability Income Insurance
- Disability Income Benefits
- Disability Income Policy Provisions
- Disability Income Policy Riders

All too often, what is thought to be a well-planned insurance program—a program consisting of life insurance, annuities, and medical expense coverage—is proven completely inadequate when disability, the one risk not covered, materializes. The risk associated with disability is not merely the loss of income; there is also the additional cost of caring for a disabled breadwinner who no longer can earn an income. Because a disability can be permanent, the financial consequences rank in severity with the death of the wage earner. The sudden loss of income resulting from a disabling accident or illness would, in most cases, lead to serious financial consequences. Fortunately, protection is available. The purpose of this unit is to describe the important role disability income insurance serves and to explain the different features found in these types of policies. ■

PURPOSE OF DISABILITY INCOME INSURANCE

Disability income insurance is designed to provide an individual with a stated amount of periodic income in the event she cannot work due to a disabling illness or accident. Statistics prove that the probability of disability greatly exceeds the probability of death during an individual's working years. The need for protection against the **economic death** of a wage earner cannot be overemphasized and it is this need that disability income insurance fills.

Disability income policies provide coverage for disabilities resulting from either accidents alone or from accidents and sickness. Because sickness-related disabilities represent only a small fraction of all disabilities, it is not economically feasible to issue sickness-only disability policies. To obtain sickness income protection, one normally has to purchase accident income coverage as well.

Disability income policies are available as individual plans and group plans. They also serve a very important function for businesses and businessowners. In this unit, we will focus on the basics of individual disability policies; group disability is discussed in Unit 24 and business uses of disability income insurance are discussed in Unit 25.

DISABILITY INCOME BENEFITS

The benefits paid under a disability income policy are in the form of monthly **income payments**. Unlike life insurance, which insurers will issue for almost any amount the applicant applies for (and qualifies for), disability income insurance is characterized by benefit limits. Insurers typically place a ceiling on the amount of disability income protection they will issue on any one applicant, defined in terms of the insured's earnings. And with few exceptions, this benefit ceiling is less than the insured's regular income. Without such restrictions, a disabled insured could conceivably receive as much income as he did while working, with little incentive to return to work and much incentive to prolong the disability.

Insurers use two methods to determine the amount of benefits payable under their disability income policies. The first method determines the benefit using a percentage of the insured's predisability earnings and takes into account other sources of disability income. For example, an individual earning $2,000 a month may be limited by Company A to a monthly benefit of 60% of income, or $1,200. If that individual already has an existing disability income policy from Company X that provides for $400 in monthly income, the amount payable by Company A would be limited to $800 a month. Some policies that use the percent-of-earnings formula provide a benefit that varies with the length of the disability. For instance, the benefit amount may equal 100% of the insured's predisability earnings for the first month and then reduce the benefit amount to 70% thereafter.

The second method used to establish disability benefits is the flat-amount method. Under this approach, the policy specifies a flat income benefit amount that will be paid if the insured becomes totally disabled. Normally, this amount is payable regardless of any other income benefits the insured may receive.

The percent-of-earnings approach is typically used in group disability income plans; the flat-amount method is more common in individual plans.

Occupational vs. Nonoccupational Coverage

Some people work in occupations that are considered extremely hazardous, where insurers are reluctant to provide disability coverage for occupational risks. In such cases, a **nonoccupational policy** may be written that only covers disabling injuries that occur off-the-job. Such policies are logically less expensive so insureds may seek this type of coverage. In such cases, they are relying on employer-provided workers' compensation benefits to cover them if they are injured on the job.

For disability benefits for both job-related and non-job-related injuries, an **occupational policy** would be sought. Note that off-the-job injuries would be covered by either an occupational or nonoccupational policy.

Disability Defined

With one exception (partial disability), an insured must be **totally disabled** before benefits under a disability income policy are payable. What constitutes total disability varies from policy to policy. The insured must meet the definition set forth in her policy. Basically, there are two definitions: **any occupation** or **own occupation**.

Any Occupation

The "any occupation" definition of total disability requires the insured to be unable to perform any occupation for which he is reasonably suited by reason of education, training, or experience in order to qualify for disability income benefits.

Own Occupation

The "own occupation" definition of total disability requires that the insured be unable to work at her *own* occupation as a result of an accident or sickness. Obviously from a policyowner's point of view, an "own occupation" disability income policy is more advantageous—it is also more expensive and difficult to qualify for. Often, disability income policies qualify total disability in two stages, using both the own occupation and any occupation definitions. These policies will provide initial benefits based on the own occupation definition for a specified period of time (e.g., during the first two years of the disability), then change the qualifying basis to the any occupation definition.

Presumptive Disability

Most policies today contain a **presumption of disability** provision. Basically, this provision specifies certain conditions that automatically qualify the insured for the full benefit because the severity of the conditions **presumes** the insured is totally disabled even if he is able to work. Presumptive disabilities include blindness, deafness, loss of speech, and loss of two or more limbs. For example, if an insured has a stroke and loses the ability to speak, she has suffered a presumptive disability and would be entitled to total disability benefits for the rest of the policy's benefit period. Presumptive disability benefits are often paid in a lump-sum settlement with the insured.

Partial Disability

The exception to the "total disability" requirement is a policy that also pays benefits in the event of a **partial disability**. It is not uncommon for disability income policies to make provisions for **partial disability**, either as part of the basic coverage or as an optional rider for an additional premium. By most definitions, partial disability is the inability of the insured to perform *one or more important duties of the job* or the inability to work at that job on a *full-time basis*, either of which results in a decrease in income.

Normally, partial disability benefits are payable only if the policyowner has first been totally disabled. This benefit is intended to encourage disabled insureds to get back to work, even on a part-time basis, without fear that they will lose all their disability income benefits. The amount of benefit payable when a policy covers partial disabilities depends on whether the policy stipulates a **flat amount** or a **residual amount**.

Flat Amount Benefit

A **flat amount benefit** is a set amount stated in the policy. This amount is usually 50% of the full disability benefit. For example, let's assume Helen, who has a disability income policy with an own-occupation definition, is severely injured after falling down a flight of stairs. She is unable to work for four months, during which time her disability income policy pays a full benefit. After four months she is able to return to work, but only on a part-time basis, earning substantially less than she did before her injury. If her policy did not contain a partial disability provision, her benefits would cease entirely because she no longer meets the definition of totally disabled. However, if her policy provides for partial disability benefits to be paid as a flat amount, she will be able to work on a part-time basis and continue to receive half of her disability benefits.

Residual Amount Benefit

A **residual amount benefit** is based on the proportion of income actually lost due to the partial disability, taking into account the fact that the insured is able to work and earn some income. The benefit is usually determined by multiplying the percentage of lost income by the stated monthly benefit for total disability. For example, if the insured suffered a 40% loss of income because of the partial disability, the residual benefit payable would be 40% of the benefit that the policy would provide for total disability. This percentage is subject to change as the disabled insured's income varies. Generally, residual benefits are provided through a rider to the policy, which specifies that no residual benefits are paid if the loss of income is less than either 20% or 25%. Usually, residual benefits are payable even if the insured was not first totally disabled.

Let's look at an example. Larry, a printer, suffered a severe back injury following a car accident. Though he was able to continue working, it was on a limited part-time basis, at only 60% of his predisability salary. If Larry's disability income policy provided for residual disability benefits, he would receive monthly payments from the insurer equal to 40% of the total disability benefit.

Insurers require proof of an insured's total or partial disability before they will pay benefits. To be eligible for benefits, the disabled insured must be under the care of a physician.

Cause of Disability

Another important aspect of disability income policies is the way in which they define the **cause** of disability. As noted previously, disability income insurance policies cover accidents only or accidents and sickness. Thus, how a disability occurs is an important consideration for disability income policies, as well as any other kind of policy covering injury due to accident.

Generally, disability income policies state that benefits are payable when injuries are caused by either external, violent, and accidental means or result in accidental bodily injury.

Policies that use the **accidental means** provision require that the cause of the injury must have been unexpected and accidental. Policies that use the **accidental bodily injury provision** require that the **result** of the injury—in other words, the injury itself—has to be unexpected and accidental. This is also known as the results provision.

For example, assume Jim, the insured, took an intentional dive off a high, rocky ledge into a lake. He struck his head on some rocks and ended up partially paralyzed. If his policy had an accidental means provision, the benefits would probably not be payable because the cause of his injury—the dive—was intentional. However, if his policy had an accidental bodily injury (or results) provision, benefits would be payable because the result of the accident—his injury—was unintentional and accidental.

Today, most disability income policies (and other policies providing accident protection) use the accidental bodily injury or results provision, which is far less restrictive than the accidental means provision. In fact, many states now require all accident-based insurance benefits to be based on the accidental bodily injury provision.

DISABILITY INCOME POLICY PROVISIONS

In addition to specifying the amount of benefit payable and the circumstances under which a benefit is payable (plus complying with required provisions standards), disability income policies contain a number of other important provisions. The most notable of these are as follows.

Probationary Period

The **probationary period** specified in a disability insurance policy is the period of time that must elapse *following the effective date of the policy* before benefits are payable. It is a one-time-only period that begins on the policy's effective date and ends 15 or 30 days after the policy has been in force. The purpose of the probationary period is to exclude **preexisting sicknesses** from coverage and provide a guidepost in borderline cases when there is a question as to whether an insured became ill before or after the effective date of the policy. Just as important, it helps protect the insurer against adverse selection because those who know they are ill are more likely to try to obtain insurance coverage.

Note that a disability income probationary period applies to sickness only; it does not apply to accidents. Whereas a person may be able to anticipate a sickness-related disability (after a visit to the doctor, for example), it is not possible to anticipate an accident.

Elimination Period

Similar in concept to a deductible, the **elimination period** is the time *immediately following the start of a disability* when benefits are *not* payable. Elimination periods eliminate claims for short-term disabilities for which the insured can usually manage without financial hardship and save the insurance company from the expense of processing and settling small claims. This, in turn, helps keep premiums down. The longer the elimination period, the lower the premium for comparable disability benefits. An elimination period can be compared to a deductible because both are cost-sharing devices that can have a direct bearing on the amount of premium required of the policyowner.

Depending on the policy, elimination periods may apply only to disabilities caused by sickness and not to disabilities caused by accident. In either event, elimination periods usually range from one week to one year or longer, but most are at least 30 days.

Benefit Period

The **benefit period** is the maximum length of time that disability income benefits will be paid to the disabled insured. The longer the benefit period, the higher the cost of the policy. For individual policies, there are basically two types of benefit periods and accordingly they serve to classify a disability income policy as either "short term" or "long term." Individual short-term policies provide benefits for six months to two years, after which payments cease. Individual long-term policies are characterized by benefit periods of more than two years, such as 5, 10, or 20. In some cases, a long-term policy will provide for benefits until the insured reaches age 65. The classifications of short term and long term are not necessarily the same for individual and group plans. See Unit 24 for a discussion of group disability plans.

Delayed Disability Provision

In some cases, total disability does not occur immediately after an accident but develops some days or weeks later. Most policies allow a certain amount of time during which total disability may result from an accident and the insured will still be eligible for benefits. The amount of time allowed for a delayed disability may be 30, 60, or 90 days, for example.

Recurrent Disability Provision

It is not unusual for a person who experienced a total disability to recover and then, weeks or months later, undergo a recurrence of the same disability. Most policies provide for **recurrent disabilities** by specifying a period of time during which the recurrence of a disability is considered a continuation of the prior disability. If the recurrence takes place after that period, it is considered a new disability and will be subject to a new elimination period before benefits are again payable.

For example, Rachel has a short-term disability policy that stipulates a new benefit-paying period begins if the insured is disabled, recovers, and returns to work for six months and then becomes disabled again. Rachel is totally disabled and off work from January 15 to April 15, when she returns to work. She is stricken again the same year and is off work from September 1 to November 10. Rachel's policy would resume paying benefits, classifying her recurrence as a continuation of her prior disability because her return to work did not last six months. She would not be subject to a new elimination period.

Nondisabling Injury

Frequently, a person covered by a disability income policy will suffer an injury that does not qualify for income benefits. Many such policies include a provision for a medical expense benefit that pays the actual cost of medical treatment for **nondisabling injuries** that result from an accident.

The benefit is generally limited to a percentage of the weekly or monthly income benefit specified in the policy. It is payable to eligible insureds in lieu of other benefits under the policy.

Elective Indemnity

Some short-term disability income policies provide for an optional lump-sum payment for certain named injuries. The insured may sometimes select this **elective indemnity** option when applying for the policy.

DISABILITY INCOME POLICY RIDERS

As is true with life insurance policies, disability income policies may be purchased with riders or options that will enhance their value to the insured. Some of the more common riders are discussed in the following section.

Waiver of Premium Rider

A **waiver of premium rider** generally is included with guaranteed renewable and noncancellable individual disability income policies. It is a valuable provision because it exempts the policyowner from paying the policy's premiums during periods of total disability. To qualify for the exemption, the insured must experience total disability for more than a specified period, commonly three or six months. In some cases, the waiver retroactively applies to the original date of disability and any premiums paid for that period are refunded. The trend is to have the waiver apply to the entire period of total disability, rather than to just the benefit period.

The waiver of premium generally does not extend past the insured's age 60 or 65. When the waiver is added, policy premiums are adjusted upward to cover the additional risk. Premiums then are reduced when the waiver is dropped due to the insured reaching the specified age limit.

Social Security Rider

The **Social Security rider**, sometimes called the social insurance substitute rider, provides for the payment of additional income when the insured is eligible for social insurance benefits but those benefits have not yet begun, have been denied, or have begun in an amount less than the benefit amount of the rider. Usually covered under the definition *social insurance* are disability benefits from Social Security as well as state and local government programs or workers' compensation programs.

When applying for the rider, the applicant states the amount of benefit expected from Social Security and any other programs for which he might be eligible. Of course, the level of expected benefits must be realistic in light of the applicant's earnings level. When total disability strikes, the applicant must show that social insurance benefits have been applied for. After the Social Security Administration (or comparable administrative body of a state or local program) determines the benefit payable, the **difference** between the actual benefit and the "expected" benefit listed in the rider is payable as an additional disability income benefit.

Cost-of-Living Adjustment (COLA) Rider

The **cost-of-living adjustment (COLA) rider** provides for indexing the monthly or weekly benefit payable under a disability policy to changes in the Consumer Price Index (CPI). Typically, the benefit amount is adjusted on each disability anniversary date to reflect changes in the CPI (though often a minimum CPI change, such as 4%, is required to trigger a disability income benefit increase). When the disability ceases, the policyowner can elect to maintain the policy at the new (increased) benefit level by paying additional premiums or can choose to let the benefit return to the originally scheduled amount for the same premium as was paid before the disability commenced.

Guaranteed Insurability Rider

A disability income policy is the only type of health insurance policy to which a **guaranteed insurability rider** may be attached. This option guarantees the insured the right to purchase additional amounts of disability income coverage at predetermined times in the future *without evidence of insurability*. The guarantee may be contingent upon the insured meeting an earnings test prior to each purchase—a condition stipulated by the insurer to avoid over-insurance.

Most guaranteed insurability riders require the insured to exercise the option for additional coverage prior to a specific age.

SUMMARY

Often called "the forgotten need," disability income insurance is an important part of a complete insurance program. Monthly or weekly benefits are paid when the insured is **totally disabled**, as determined by either the "any occupation" or the more liberal "own occupation" definition. If the policy has a **partial disability provision**, benefits may be payable if the insured is able to work only part time or suffers a less-than-total disability. Another feature of disability income policies is that they define the cause of a disabling accident on an **accidental means** or **accidental results** basis.

Disability income contracts are characterized by **probationary periods**, which exclude preexisting sickness from immediate coverage, and **elimination periods**, which specify the time after the start of a disability when benefits are not payable, thereby excluding very short-term disabilities from coverage. Like life insurance, disability income policies may be purchased with policy riders that can increase their value to the insured.

Disability income coverage may be purchased as individual or group policies. Its uses for businesses and businessowners will be discussed in Unit 25.

KEY CONCEPTS

Students should be familiar with the following concepts:

total disability	any occupation
own occupation	partial disability
presumptive disability	residual disability
probationary period	elimination period
waiver of premium rider	Social Security rider
cost-of-living adjustment rider	guaranteed insurability rider

UNIT TEST

1. Assume an insurer will issue a maximum monthly disability income benefit of $5,000, provided the total of such benefits payable by all companies does not exceed 60% of the insured's regular monthly income. Ted earns $4,500 per month and has no existing disability income policy. The maximum monthly disability income benefit this insurer would issue to Ted is

   A. $2,500
   B. $2,700
   C. $4,500
   D. $5,000

2. Which of the following is NOT a basis for occupational suitability when determining total disability?

   A. Education
   B. Training
   C. Experience
   D. Job interest

3. Which of the following statements about elimination periods in disability income policies is NOT correct?

   A. Elimination periods may apply to disabilities due to sickness and not accidents.
   B. Benefits are not payable during an elimination period but are paid retroactively to the beginning of the period if the insured remains disabled throughout the period.
   C. An elimination period follows the start of a disability.
   D. Elimination periods help keep premiums down.

4. Which of the following riders provides for changes in the benefit payable based on changes in the Consumer Price Index (CPI)?

   A. Guaranteed insurability rider
   B. Cost-of-living adjustment rider
   C. Social Security rider
   D. Waiver of premium rider

5. Benefit periods for individual short-term disability policies typically vary from

   A. 1 to 12 months
   B. 3 months to 3 years
   C. 6 months to 2 years
   D. 1 to 5 years

6. Which of the following statements about waiver of premium in health insurance policies is NOT correct?

   A. It exempts an insured from paying premiums during periods of permanent and total disability.
   B. It may apply retroactively.
   C. It generally drops off after the insured reaches age 60 or 65.
   D. It normally applies to both medical expense and disability income policies.

7. Which of the following terms relates to disability income insurance?

   A. Service basis
   B. First-dollar
   C. Residual amount benefit
   D. Coinsurance

8. Which definition of total disability is more favorable to the insured?

   A. "Own occupation" is more favorable.
   B. "Any occupation" is more favorable.
   C. They are the same in terms of benefits to the insured.
   D. There is no way to determine from the information provided.

9. Sidney has a monthly benefit of $2,500 for total disability under a residual disability income policy. If Sidney suffers a 40% loss of his predisability income, how much will his benefit be?

   A. $0
   B. $1,000
   C. $1,500
   D. $2,500

10. What is the initial period of time specified in a disability income policy that must pass, after a policy is in force, before a loss due to sickness can be covered?

A. Preexisting term
B. Probationary period
C. Temporary interval
D. Elimination period

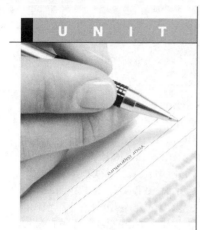

19

Accidental Death and Dismemberment Insurance

- Nature of AD&D Policies
- AD&D Benefits
- Other Forms of AD&D

The third major type of health insurance coverage is accidental death and dismemberment (AD&D) insurance. It pays benefits in the event of a fatal accident or if dismemberment results from an accidental injury. Although the circumstances under which benefits are paid are somewhat limited, it is a widely used form of insurance protection and often is attached as a rider on a basic life or health insurance policy. AD&D policies are widely used in group insurance plans as well. In this unit, we will examine the typical features of and benefits provided by AD&D policies and some of the other more specific forms of AD&D policies. ■

NATURE OF AD&D POLICIES

Accidental death and dismemberment insurance is the primary form of pure **accident coverage**. As such, it serves a somewhat limited purpose: it provides a stated lump-sum benefit in the event of accidental death or in the event of loss of body members due to accidental injury. This latter includes loss of hands or feet or the loss of sight in one or both eyes. ("Loss of body member" is typically defined as actual severance from the body, though it may include loss of use, depending on the policy.) Separate benefits for hospital, surgical, and other medical expenses are generally not included in AD&D policies, although some may pay a medical reimbursement benefit up to a stated amount.

AD&D BENEFITS

Because an AD&D policy pays a specified benefit to the insured in the event of accidental death or dismemberment due to accidental injury, it is necessary for the policy to make distinctions between these two contingencies and to define the benefits accordingly. Consequently, AD&D policies make benefits payable in two forms of payment.

- *Principal Sum.* The principal sum under an AD&D policy is the amount payable as a death benefit. It is the amount of insurance purchased—$10,000, $25,000, $50,000, $100,000, or more. The principal sum represents the maximum amount the policy will pay.

- *Capital Sum.* Another form of payment payable under an AD&D policy is the amount payable for the accidental loss of sight or accidental dismemberment, or the capital sum. It is a specified amount, usually expressed as a percentage of the principal sum, that varies according to the severity of the injury. For example, the benefit for the loss of one foot or one hand is typically 50% of the principal sum. The benefit for the loss of one arm or one leg is usually two-thirds of the principal sum. The most extreme losses, such as both feet or sight in both eyes, generally qualify for payment of the full benefit, which is 100% of the principal sum.

Let's say, for example, Kevin has an accidental death and dismemberment policy that pays $50,000 for accidental loss of life and the same for accidental loss of two limbs or the sight in both eyes. Thus, $50,000 is the policy's principal sum. The same policy pays $25,000 for accidental loss of sight of one eye or dismemberment of one limb. Therefore, $25,000 is the policy's capital sum.

Some AD&D policies provide for payment of double, triple, or even quadruple the principal sum if the insured dies under specified circumstances. A double payment is referred to as **double indemnity**. If three times the principal sum is payable, it is called **triple indemnity**. However, do not let these terms confuse you. AD&D policies, because they pay a stated benefit, are **valued contracts**. They are not contracts of indemnity.

Accidental Means Versus Accidental Results

As we learned in the last unit, an insurance policy that provides benefits in the event of an injury due to an accident must define "accident." In all cases, an accident is "external and violent," but accidental death and dismemberment policies (like disability income policies) make a distinction between injuries due to **accidental means** and those due to **accidental results** (or accidental bodily injury).

By way of a review, policies that base their benefit payments on accidental means require that both the cause and the result of an accident must be unintentional. Policies that use the more liberal accidental results definition stipulate that only the injury resulting from an accident must be unintentional. If Ted, the insured under an AD&D policy, intentionally jumps from the roof of his house after fixing his antenna (instead of climbing down the ladder) and so severely injures his leg that it must be amputated, he would be paid the appropriate percentage of the capital sum only if his policy used the "results" definition. If his policy used the "means" definition, no benefit would be payable because Ted intentionally performed the action (i.e., the jump) that resulted in the injury.

As noted in the discussion of disability income policies, most states require that policies that provide any form of accident benefit, as do AD&D policies, base the definition of "accident" on the results definition, not the means definition.

OTHER FORMS OF AD&D

Accidental death and dismemberment coverage is made available in a variety of ways. It can be purchased by individuals as a single policy or it may be a part of an individual disability income policy. Quite typically, however, it is an aspect of a group insurance plan—either group life or group health—or it may in and of itself constitute a group plan. Usually, AD&D benefits are payable whether the injury resulted on or off the job.

By their very nature, AD&D policies are somewhat narrow, providing benefits only in the event of death or dismemberment due to an accident. There is another type of AD&D coverage, even more narrow in scope, that provides protection against accidental death or dismemberment only in the event of certain *specified* accidents. These are **limited risk policies** and **special risk policies**.

Limited Risk Policies

As noted in Unit 17, **limited risk policies** set forth a specific risk and provide benefits to cover death or dismemberment due to that risk. For example, an **aviation policy** provides benefits for accidental death or dismemberment if death or injury results from an aviation accident during a specified trip. An **automobile policy** provides benefits for accidental death or injury while riding in a car. **Travel accident** covers most kinds of travel accidents, but only for a specified period of time, such as one year.

Special Risk Policies

A distinction should be made between limited risk and special risk policies. A special risk policy covers unusual hazards normally not covered under ordinary accident and health insurance. An actress who insures her legs for $1 million or a pilot test-flying an experimental airplane who obtains a policy covering his life while flying that particular plane are both purchasing special risk policies. But a traveler who purchases an accident policy at the airport to provide coverage while she is a passenger on a commercial airlines flight is purchasing a limited risk policy.

SUMMARY

Accidental death and dismemberment insurance, known as AD&D, represents the purest form of accident coverage. It provides a stated sum benefit in the event of accidental death, accidental loss of one or more body members, or accidental loss of sight. The benefit payable in the event of death is known as the **principal sum**; the benefit payable in the event of dismemberment or loss of sight is the **capital sum**.

Like all policies that provide accident benefits, AD&D policies must define the term "accident" on either a **means basis** (in which both the cause and the result of the accident must be unintentional) or on a **results basis** (requiring only that the injury itself be accidental). Florida, like most states, stipulates the use of the results definition.

AD&D coverage may be purchased as an individual policy but usually is part of a larger group life or health plan. In some cases, it is offered as a separate group plan. Specialized forms of AD&D coverage, known as **limited risk** and **special risk insurance**, provide accident protection in the event of specified limited risks, such as travel or aviation.

KEY CONCEPTS

Students should be familiar with the following concepts:

capital sum	principal sum
special risk policies	limited risk policies
accidental death and dismemberment coverage	accidental means versus accidental results

UNIT TEST

1. The amount payable as a death benefit in an accidental death and dismemberment policy is known as the

   A. primary amount
   B. capital sum
   C. indemnity amount
   D. principal sum

2. Theodore received a $15,000 cash benefit from his $50,000 accidental death and dismemberment policy for the accidental loss of one eye. The amount he received could be identified as the policy's

   A. principal sum
   B. secondary sum
   C. capital sum
   D. contingent amount

3. Which of the following examples pertaining to accidental death and dismemberment insurance is CORRECT?

   A. Merrill is the insured under a $50,000 AD&D policy and dies unexpectedly of a heart attack. His beneficiary will receive $50,000 as the death benefit.
   B. Linda has a $40,000 AD&D policy that pays triple indemnity. If she should be killed in a train wreck, her beneficiary would receive $120,000.
   C. Paula has an AD&D policy that pays $15,000 for the loss of one hand or foot or the sight of one eye. That benefit is called the principal sum.
   D. Eric has an AD&D policy. He is killed in an auto accident. The $30,000 his beneficiary receives as a death benefit is the policy's capital sum.

4. Agnes purchases a round-trip travel accident policy at the airport before leaving on a business trip. Her policy would be which type of insurance?

   A. Limited risk
   B. Business overhead expense
   C. Credit accident and health
   D. Industrial health

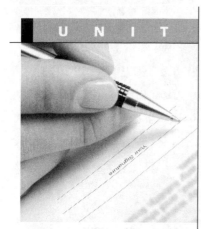

20

Government Health Insurance Programs

- Medicare
- Medicaid
- State Workers' Compensation Programs

Many people receive health care cost protection through federal or state government programs. As the longevity of the U.S. population has increased, more people than ever are faced with paying health care bills. Government officials have long struggled to find a solution to the problem of affordable health care. In the mid-1960s, the problem of providing medical care for the poor and elderly was solved, in part, by the passage of the Social Security Amendments of 1965. Part of that legislation, called Title XIX, created Medicare and Medicaid. Medicare provides hospital and medical expense insurance protection to those aged 65 and older, to those of any age who suffer from chronic kidney disease, or to those who are receiving Social Security disability benefits. Medicaid, jointly funded by the states and the federal government, reimburses hospitals and physicians for providing care to needy and low-income people who cannot finance their own medical expenses. Medicaid is the main source of public assistance for nursing home costs. State workers' compensation laws require employers to provide benefits to employees for work-related injuries, illness, or death.

In this unit, we will look at Medicare and Medicaid, as well as workers' compensation programs. ■

MEDICARE

The original **Medicare** plan consists of two parts: **Medicare Part A** and **Medicare Part B**. **Medicare Part A** is compulsory hospitalization insurance (HI) that provides specified in-hospital and related benefits. It is compulsory in that all workers covered by Social Security finance its operation through a portion of their FICA taxes and automatically receive benefits once they qualify for Social Security benefits.

Medicare Part B is a voluntary program designed to provide supplementary medical insurance (SMI) to cover physician services, medical services, and supplies not covered under Part A. Those who desire the coverage must enroll and pay a monthly premium. Medicare Part B is financed by monthly premiums from those who participate and by tax revenues.

Medicare Part A Coverages

Medicare Part A provides coverage for inpatient hospitalization, posthospital skilled facility care, and home care. For the first 60 days of hospitalization during any one benefit period, Medicare pays for all covered services, except for an initial deductible ($1,216 in 2014). Covered services include semiprivate rooms, nursing services, and other inpatient hospital services.

For the 61st through the 90th day of hospitalization, Medicare pays a reduced amount of the covered services. The patient is responsible for a daily co-payment equal to one-fourth of the initial deductible figure.

This 90-day hospitalization coverage is renewed with each benefit period. A **benefit period** starts when a patient enters the hospital and ends when the patient has been out of the hospital for 60 days. If a patient reenters a hospital before the end of a benefit period, the deductible is not reapplied, and the 90-day hospital coverage period is not renewed. However, if the patient reenters a hospital after a benefit period ends, a new deductible is required and the 90-day hospital coverage period is renewed.

Medicare patients also have a **lifetime reserve** of 60 days of hospital coverage. If a patient is hospitalized longer than 90 days in a benefit period, he can tap into the 60-day reserve. The lifetime reserve is a one-time benefit; it does not renew with a new benefit period. If a patient is hospitalized and taps into the reserve days, he is required to pay a higher co-payment equal to half of the initial deductible figure. If a patient is hospitalized beyond the 60th lifetime reserve day, thereby exhausting the reserve, he is responsible for all hospital charges.

Medicare Part A is available when an individual turns 65 and is automatically provided when she applies for Social Security benefits.

Hospice care is a Medicare Part A benefit for terminally ill patients and their families. Included are skilled nursing either in a hospice facility or home setting, as well as medications for pain relief and symptom management. Respite for caregivers in a home setting and home health aides are also available. Hospice benefits are unlimited; but, to be eligible, a doctor must certify that the medical condition is terminal and that death is expected within seven months (210 days).

Home health benefits under Part A, which are limited to 20 service days per benefit period, provide intermediate care or physical, occupational, or speech therapy in a home setting. These benefits may also include home health aides, medical social services, medical supplies, and the rental of durable medical equipment.

In addition, Part A provides benefits to a limited degree, for inpatient psychiatric care. In all cases, Part A covers only those services that are medically necessary and only up to amounts deemed "reasonable" by Medicare.

Part A covers the costs of care in a skilled nursing facility as long as the patient was first hospitalized for three consecutive days. Treatment in a skilled nursing facility is covered in full for the first 20 days. From the 21st to the 100th day, the patient must pay the daily co-payment equal to one-eighth of the initial deductible figure. No Medicare benefits are provided for treatment in a skilled nursing facility beyond 100 days.

Medicare Part B Coverages

For those who desire, additional coverage is available under Medicare Part B for physician services, diagnostic tests, physical and occupational therapy, medical supplies, and the like. Part B participants are required to pay a monthly premium and are responsible for an annual deductible. After the deductible, Part B will pay 80% of covered expenses, subject to Medicare's standards for reasonable charges.

The Medicare Part B deductible is usually raised annually by the same percentage as the annual increase in the Medicare Part B premium. For example, if the annual Part B premium increases 3%, then the Part B deductible will also increase by 3%. After 2009, higher income Medicare beneficiaries pay higher premiums for Medicare Part B coverage, and the higher the income, the higher the premium.

ILLUSTRATION 20.1

What the Original Medicare Plan Covers

Part A	Part B
■ Inpatient hospital services, including semiprivate room and board and nursing services ■ Posthospital skilled nursing care, in an accredited care facility ■ Posthospital home health services, including nursing care, therapy, and part-time home health aides ■ Hospice benefits for the care of terminally ill patients (to the exclusion of all other Medicare benefits, except for physician services) ■ Inpatient psychiatric care, on a limited basis	■ Physicians' and surgeons' services, whether in a hospital, clinic, or elsewhere ■ Medical and health services, such as x-rays, diagnostic lab tests, ambulance services, medical supplies, medical equipment rental, and physical and occupational therapy

Exclusions under Medicare

Many people erroneously assume that Medicare pays all or most health-care expenses for participants. In addition to the out-of-pocket premiums, deductibles, and coinsurance, however, there are many common medical costs for older Americans that are not paid by Medicare and must be borne by the participants, such as:

■ private duty nursing;

■ private hospital rooms (unless medically necessary);

■ the first three pints of blood or blood products used;

■ skilled nursing after 100 days per benefit period;

■ physician charges outside those approved by Medicare;

■ care received outside the United States (limited availability in North America);

■ custodial care received at home; and

■ well care (eyesight care, hearing care, dental care, routine physical exams, immunizations, acupuncture, and so on).

Primary Payor and Secondary Payor

Anyone aged 65 who is eligible for Medicare and works for an employer of 20 or more employees is entitled to the same health insurance benefits as the employer offers to younger employees. In these cases, the employer-sponsored plan is the **primary payor** and Medicare is the **secondary payor**. This means that Medicare pays only those charges that the employer-sponsored plan does not cover. This also applies to any disabled Medicare enrollee who is also covered by an employer-provided health care plan as a current employee or as a family member of an employee, but only if the employer plan covers 100 or more employees.

Part C: Medicare Advantage

While Medicare is facing many challenges, the most pressing are the financial pressures resulting from changing demographics. Today and in the future, the number of people becoming eligible for Medicare will increase rapidly and the number of workers paying taxes to support Medicare will decrease.

In 1997, Congress passed a law to reduce the financial strain on Medicare funds and provide Medicare beneficiaries with a variety of new health plan options. The original Medicare Plan and Medicare supplement insurance (discussed in the next unit), which are purchased from private insurance companies, are still available. However, new options are available through **Medicare Part C**. These options include managed care plans, preferred provider organizations, private fee-for-service plans, and specialty plans.

Medicare's managed care system consists of a network of approved hospitals, doctors, and other health care professionals who agree to provide services to Medicare beneficiaries for a set monthly payment from Medicare. The health care providers receive the same fee every month regardless of the actual services provided. As a result of this arrangement, health care providers try to manage care in such a way that they achieve a balance between budgetary and healthcare concerns.

Preferred provider organization plans (PPOs) are similar to managed care plans. They differ in that beneficiaries don't need referrals to see specialist providers outside the network, and they can see any doctor or provider that accepts Medicare. Regional PPOs limit the maximum amount that members pay for care outside the network.

Another Medicare Advantage option is a **private fee-for-service plan (PFFS)**. This type of plan offers a Medicare-approved private insurance plan. Medicare pays the plan for Medicare-covered services while the PFFS plan determines, up to a limit, how much the care recipient will pay for covered services. The Medicare beneficiary is responsible for paying the difference between the amount Medicare pays and the PFFS charges.

Medicare Advantage specialty plans provide more focused health care for people with specific conditions. A person who joins one of these plans gets health care services as well as more focused care to manage a specific disease or condition.

To be eligible for any of the Medicare Advantage options, a Medicare beneficiary must be enrolled in both Medicare Part A and Part B. All programs are considered part of Medicare and will provide for all Medicare covered services. Medicare Advantage options do not replace the need for long-term care insurance.

Medicare Part D: Prescription Drug Plan

The Medicare Prescription Drug and Modernization Act of 2003 established a new Medicare Part D prescription drug benefit. Since January 2006, Medicare offers insurance coverage for prescription drugs to anyone who has

Medicare Part A or Part B. Prescription drug coverage is needed because medical practice today relies on drug therapies to treat chronic conditions. As a result, most Medicare beneficiaries sooner or later will need prescription drugs to stay healthy.

Under the standard benefit plan, Medicare beneficiaries pay a monthly premium and an annual deductible. Beneficiaries then pay 25% of prescription drug costs, and Medicare pays the other 75%. Coverage stops completely at a certain level. However, if a beneficiary's total drug costs are more than a second, higher amount, then catastrophic coverage starts and beneficiaries pay co-payments of $2.50 for generic drugs and $6.30 for brand name drugs or 5% of total costs, whichever is higher. (Nicknamed the *donut hole*, these dollar thresholds are scheduled to increase each year.) Although companies have considerable flexibility in designing their own plans, the overall value of the drug coverage offered must be the same or greater than the basic plan. Of course, companies that offer more benefits can charge higher premiums.

Coverage is available only through private plans that are either stand-alone prescription drug plans (PDPs) or Medicare private plans such as HMOs, PPOs, or PFFSs. A stand-alone plan only offers prescription drug benefits. People in these plans get other medical services through the Original Medicare Plan. Most Medicare private plans provide all Medicare-covered services, including prescription drug coverage. Individuals in private fee-for-service plans that don't offer drug coverage can enroll in a stand-alone prescription drug plan. However, individuals in HMOs or PPOs must receive all of their medical and drug coverage through these plans. The law provides federal subsidy payments to employers and unions that sponsor qualified retiree prescription drug plans.

However, if a Medicare beneficiary did not enroll during the initial enrollment period and decides to enroll later, the beneficiary will pay a 1% penalty for each month of delayed enrollment, unless that person has comparable coverage from another source, such as a private or group plan. For example, Medicare beneficiaries who receive drug coverage through a former employer or union may stay in that plan, and they will not have to pay the penalty if they later decide to sign up for the Medicare drug benefit.

Those who want to receive all of their medical and drug benefits from one source can join a Medicare Advantage plan and choose a prescription drug plan that will provide an integrated benefit covering their hospital, physician, and drug costs. All plans must offer basic drug coverage. Both PDPs and Medicare Advantage plans can offer enhanced coverage for an additional premium.

The law provides federal subsidy payments to employers and unions that sponsor qualified retiree prescription drug plans.

Three of the standardized Medigap benefit plans—H, I, and J (discussed in the next unit)—include coverage for prescription drugs. As of 2006, these Medigap policies may no longer be sold with prescription drug coverage. Beneficiaries who already have Medigap-with-drug policies and do not enroll in a Part D prescription drug plan can renew their policies. If these beneficiaries choose to enroll in a Part D prescription drug plan, they can keep their current Medigap policies but without the drug coverage and with the premium adjusted. These beneficiaries will have the option to switch to another

Medigap plan offered by the same insurer but only if they elect Part D during the initial enrollment period.

MEDICAID

Medicaid is a government-funded, means-tested program designed to provide health care to poor people of all ages. The goal of Medicaid is to offer medical assistance to those whose income and resources are insufficient to meet the costs of necessary medical care. Individuals claiming benefits must prove they do not have the ability or **means** to pay for their own medical care.

Applicants must complete a lengthy questionnaire, disclosing all assets and income. To qualify for Medicaid, a person must be poor or become poor. Such people frequently include children born to low-income mothers, babies born addicted to drugs, AIDS patients, and the indigent elderly.

Individual states design and administer the Medicaid programs under broad guidelines established by the federal government. On average, the federal government contributes about 56 cents for every Medicaid dollar spent; however, the amount contributed may be lower or higher. State governments contribute the balance and the extent of coverage and the quality of services vary widely from state to state.

Qualifying for Medicaid Nursing Home Benefits

Unlike Medicare, Medicaid does provide for custodial care or assisted care in a nursing home. However, as explained earlier, individuals claiming a need for Medicaid must prove they cannot pay for their own nursing home care. In addition, the potential recipient must:

- be at least age 65, blind, or disabled (as defined by the recipient's state);

- be a US citizen or permanent resident alien;

- need the type of care that is provided only in a nursing home; and

- meet certain asset and income tests.

People meeting these basic criteria will usually have their long-term nursing home care paid for by Medicaid. However, each state (and even some counties within certain states) evaluates an individual's ability to pay by looking at the nursing home resident's (and spouse's) income and assets. The specific limits for each of these sources vary by state and change annually.

Problems with Medicaid Estate Planning

In the past, some persons would take certain steps to meet the asset and income tests to become eligible for Medicaid. Their goal was to take countable assets (those that must be reduced to qualify for Medicaid) and make them exempt from consideration. This typically involved such steps as transferring assets to other individuals or to a Medicaid trust. However, there are now criminal penalties for transferring assets to qualify for Medicaid.

Perhaps the most common means of Medicaid planning was to transfer otherwise countable assets to family or friends. Once the assets were given away, they were not countable for the purposes of determining Medicaid eligibility. However, the government moved to close this loophole by providing that a person's Medicaid eligibility will be delayed if he transfers assets for less than their market value during a specific look-back period. Under the Deficit Reduction Act of 2005, this look-back period has been extended to five years. Also, the home equity exemption has been limited to $750,000.

The ineligibility period is determined by dividing the amount of the asset transfer by the figure Medicaid determines to be the average private cost of a nursing home in the state. The resulting number of ineligibility months begins when the applicant:

- is in the nursing home;

- has spent down the asset limit for Medicaid eligibility;

- has applied for Medicaid coverage; and

- has been approved for coverage, except for the transfer, as of the date of the initial asset transfer.

Medicaid Reform

The Deficit Reduction Act of 2005 (DRA) gave states new options by which to reform and modernize their Medicaid programs. These options include cost-sharing, flexible benefits, and health opportunity accounts (HOAs). HOAs are similar to consumer-controlled health savings accounts (HSAs) in that they give Medicaid beneficiaries a personal account that pays for health care services. These new options make the state's cost of the program more affordable while expanding coverage for the uninsured. Although these measures are intended to encourage beneficiaries' use of preventive care and slow increases in state Medicaid spending, they are not yet proven to work.

State legislators are interested in increasing consumer responsibility for the care they receive from the Medicaid program. By doing so, states hope to save money in the administration of their programs. Beneficiaries are encouraged to use more low-cost preventive services and avoid more expensive care that may later become necessary. They are encouraged to choose lower-cost alternatives for equivalent care, such as generic prescription drugs instead of brand-name drugs.

The states are taking different approaches to carry this out. Two models have appeared: the direct services model and the insurance model. In the direct services model, states give beneficiaries health spending accounts to buy a defined set of health care services. In the insurance model, Medicaid beneficiaries receive a fixed budget to buy a health insurance product of their choice. Some states are proposing programs that combine both models.

For instance, Florida's plan gives beneficiaries a risk-adjusted premium to buy a state-approved insurance product of their choice from a managed care organization (MCO).

Eligible beneficiaries can also open enhanced benefits accounts. These accounts draw from funds that the state sets aside to encourage recipients to practice healthy behavior (making and keeping all primary care appointments and childhood preventive care, for instance, as well as participating in a smoking cessation program if applicable or a documented exercise program). Beneficiaries earn credits from these funds by engaging in these healthy behaviors or completing health practices. Each credit has a dollar value that varies according to how often it may be earned, the value of the behavior or practice, and whether it can be verified or is reported only by the beneficiary. Beneficiaries can use these credits to buy health-related services and supplies.

Florida Healthy Kids Corporation

In an effort to help improve access to comprehensive health insurance for Florida's uninsured children, the state legislature established the Florida Healthy Kids Corporation as a combined public and private venture in 1990. Participation in the program is on a voluntary basis.

Through the corporation, uninsured children can obtain affordable health care coverage. The program serves as a source of funds by collecting local, state, federal, and family money to pay premiums to commercial health insurers who underwrite the risk. In this manner, families who would otherwise be unable to afford the desired coverage can obtain it while paying only a portion of the premium. Coverage can insure services ranging from preventive care to major surgery.

STATE WORKERS' COMPENSATION PROGRAMS

All states have **workers' compensation laws**, which were enacted to provide mandatory benefits to employees for work-related injuries, illness, or death. Employers are responsible for providing workers' compensation benefits to their employees and do so by purchasing coverage through state programs, private insurers, or by self-insuring.

Workers' compensation laws are designed to help injured workers recover and return to work. They are based on the principle that work-related injuries are compensable by the employer without regard to who was at fault. However, the amount of compensation payable is limited and fixed by law. Generally, such compensation encompasses medical care costs, disability income, rehabilitation benefits, and for certain specified injuries, specific lump-sum benefits. These benefits relieve injured workers of the burden of medical expenses, replace some of the wages lost due to the disability, and provide rehabilitation services to return the person to work. Because of the wide variation among state programs, the laws of each state must be examined to discover available coverages and benefits. See Unit 16 for a listing of common procedures, requirements, and benefits.

SUMMARY

The original **Medicare** plan provides hospital and medical expense insurance protection to those aged 65 and older, to those of any age who suffer from chronic kidney disease, or to those who receive Social Security disability benefits. **Medicare Advantage** plans are offered by private companies that sign a contract with Medicare. Medicare pays these companies a set amount of money for the services they provide to Medicare beneficiaries. **Medicare Part D** is a new prescription drug benefit. **Medicaid** is a joint federal and state program to pay health care expenses for the poor. To qualify for Medicaid benefits, an individual must meet certain asset and income limitation tests. However, even if a person qualifies for Medicaid, finding an adequate nursing home is difficult because Medicaid does not pay for the full cost of care. Medicaid patients are limited in their choice of nursing home.

KEY CONCEPTS

Students should be familiar with the following concepts:

Medicare   Medicare Part A

Medicaid   Medicare Part B

benefit period   Medicare Part C

Medicare Advantage   Medicare Part D

                                  lifetime reserve

UNIT TEST

1. Which of the following statements pertaining to Medicare is CORRECT?

   A. Bob is covered under Medicare Part B. He submitted a total of $1,100 of approved medical charges to Medicare after paying the required deductible. Of that total, Bob must pay $880.

   B. Each individual covered by Medicare Part A is allowed one 90-day benefit period per year.

   C. For the first 90 days of hospitalization, Medicare Part A pays 100% of all covered services, except for an initial deductible.

   D. Medicare Part A is automatically provided when a qualified individual applies for Social Security benefits.

2. Under Medicare Part B, the participant must pay all of the following EXCEPT

   A. an annual deductible
   B. a per benefit deductible
   C. 20% of covered charges above the deductible
   D. a monthly premium

3. Which of the following statements about Medicare Part B is NOT correct?

   A. It is a compulsory program.
   B. It covers services and supplies not covered by Part A.
   C. It is financed by monthly premiums.
   D. It is financed by tax revenues.

4. For how many days of skilled nursing facility care will Medicare pay benefits?

   A. 25
   B. 60
   C. 75
   D. 100

5. Which of the following statements concerning workers' compensation is NOT correct?

   A. Workers' compensation laws are designed to return injured persons to work.
   B. Benefits include medical care costs and disability income.
   C. A worker receives benefits only if the work-related injury was not her fault.
   D. All states have workers' compensation laws.

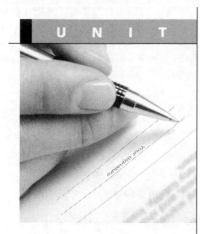

21

Private Insurance Plans for Seniors

■ Medicare Supplement Policies

■ Long-Term Care Insurance

In this unit, we will focus on two types of health care policies designed to protect elderly people from the high cost of health care. These two types of coverages, Medicare supplements and long-term care, have received a great deal of attention in recent years. Because of medical breakthroughs, individuals are living longer. However, as individuals live longer, they encounter more medical problems requiring more care. The cost of treating these problems has spiraled at a dizzying rate, leading to an ever-growing concern over how these costs will be paid. The concern is especially great for the elderly because, as a group, seniors are some of the heaviest users of medical and health care services. ■

MEDICARE SUPPLEMENT POLICIES

A **Medigap** policy is a Medicare supplement insurance policy sold by private insurance companies to fill "gaps" in Medicare Parts A and B. Medigap policies do not pay costs for Medicare Parts C and D. A person who has a Medicare Advantage plan does not need a Medigap policy because these plans generally cover many of the same benefits that a Medigap policy would cover. In fact, it is illegal for anyone to sell a Medigap policy to a person who is in a Medicare Advantage plan.

Prior to June 1, 2010, there were 12 standardized Medigap plans labeled Plan A through Plan L Some of these plans have been eliminated, and two new plans have been added. Plans purchased before June of 2010 will remain in force and are renewable for life.

As of June 2010, there are 10 standardized Medigap plans. Each of the 10 plans has a letter designation of A, B, C, D, F, G, K, L, M, or N. These policies were standardized by the National Association of Insurance Commissioners (NAIC) to help consumers understand and compare them and thus make informed buying decisions. These standards can be found in NAIC's Medicare Supplement Insurance Minimum Standards Model Act. The benefits in each plan may not be altered by insurers, nor may the letter designation be changed (although insurers may add names or titles to the letter designations).

Medigap Plan A covers basic benefits; Medigap Plans B, C, D, F, G, M, and N include the Plan A basic benefits and some extra benefits; Plans K and L offer different benefits than the other Medigap Plans and have lower premiums than those plans. However, Plans K and L require higher out-of-pocket costs from beneficiaries because these plans were designed to give beneficiaries an incentive to control costs. Although Plans K and L are similar, they differ in the percentage of coverage for claims and in the maximum amount of out-of-pocket costs. Note that insurance companies that sell Medigap policies don't have to offer every Medigap plan. Each insurance company decides which Medigap policies it wants to sell. The front of each Medigap policy must state that it is Medicare supplement insurance.

Each standardized Medigap policy must cover basic benefits. Plans A, B, C, D, F, G, M, and N have one set of basic benefits, and Plans K and L have different benefits.

The basic benefits policy covers 100% of the Part A hospital coinsurance amount for each day used from the 61st through the 90th day in any Medicare benefit period. It also covers:

- 100% of the Part A hospital coinsurance amount for each Medicare lifetime inpatient reserve day used from the 91st through the 150th day in any Medicare benefit period;

- 100% of the Part A-eligible hospital expenses for 365 additional days after all hospital benefits are exhausted;

- Part B coinsurance amount (generally 20% of Medicare-approved expenses) after the annual deductible is met; and

- the cost of the first three pints of blood each year and hospice Part A coinsurance.

The basic benefits under Plans K and L provide for different cost sharing for items and services than Plans A through J. Plan K pays:

- 100% of Part A hospitalization coinsurance plus coverage for 365 days after Medicare benefits end;

- 50% of hospice cost sharing;

- 50% of Medicare-eligible expenses for the first three pints of blood; and

- 50% of Part B coinsurance, except for 100% coinsurance for Part B preventive services.

Plan L pays:

- 100% of Part A hospitalization coinsurance plus coverage for 365 days after Medicare benefits end;

- 75% of hospice cost sharing;

- 75% of Medicare-eligible expenses for the first three pints of blood; and

- 75% of Part B coinsurance, except for 100% coinsurance for Part B preventive services.

ILLUSTRATION 21.1

Standardized Medicare Supplement Plans

Medicare Supplement Plans A–N (June 1, 2010 and later)										
	A	B	C	D	F	G	K	L	M	N
Medicare Part A Coinsurance and All Cost After Hospital Benefits are Exhausted	✓	✓	✓	✓	✓	✓	✓	✓	✓	✓
Medicare Part B Coinsurance or Copayment for Other Than Preventive Services	✓	✓	✓	✓	✓	✓	50%	75%	✓	Copayment: $20/$50
Blood (First 3 Pints)	✓	✓	✓	✓	✓	✓	50%	75%		✓
Hospice Care Coinsurance Or Copayment	✓	✓	✓	✓	✓	✓	50%	75%	✓	✓
Skilled Nursing Facility Care Coinsurance			✓	✓	✓	✓	50%	75%	✓	✓
Medicare Part A Deductible		✓	✓	✓	✓	✓	50%	75%	50%	✓
Medicare Part B Deductible			✓		✓					
Medicare Part B Excess Charges					✓	✓				
Foreign Travel Emergency (Up To Plan Limits) – $250 Deductible			✓	✓	✓	✓			✓	✓
Medicare Preventive Care Part B Coinsurance (After Part B Deductible)	✓	✓	✓	✓	✓	✓	✓	✓	✓	✓

In general, the following six minimum standards apply to all policies designated as Medicare Supplement Insurance.

- The policy must supplement both Part A and Part B of Medicare.

- The policy must automatically adjust its benefits to reflect statutory changes in Medicare.

- The policy must cover all expenses not covered by Part A from the 61st to the 90th day. Furthermore, it must cover the lifetime reserve co-payment and must provide full coverage for an additional 365 days after Medicare benefits are exhausted.

- If the policy excludes coverage for preexisting conditions, the exclusion cannot exist for longer than six months. That is, no coverage can be denied as a preexisting condition after the policy has been in effect for six months.

- Part B expenses not covered by Medicare (that is, the 20% co-payment) must be covered by the Medigap policy, up to a maximum of $5,000 per year. However, policies may include a deductible before this benefit becomes payable.

- The policy must include a minimum 30-day free-look provision.

LONG-TERM CARE INSURANCE

Americans are living longer and many can expect to live a substantial portion of their lives in retirement. That's the good news. The bad news is, although statistics regarding longevity for older Americans may be improving, many individuals over age 65 still have to deal with poor health during their retirement years. As people age, they consume a larger proportion of health care services because of chronic illness, such as Alzheimer's disease, heart disease, and stroke. The cost of the extended day-in, day-out care some older people need can be staggering: as much as $80,000 a year or more for nursing home care and upwards of $3,500 a month—or more—for home health care aides who come to one's home.

As beneficial as Medicare and Medicare supplement insurance are to the elderly in protecting them against the costs of medical care, neither of these programs covers long-term custodial or nursing home care. Medicaid covers some of the costs associated with long-term care, but a person is ineligible for Medicaid until he is practically destitute. How can these costs be paid? The solution for many is **long-term care insurance**.

What Is Long-Term Care?

You'll often see nursing home care referred to as *long-term care*. However, long-term care (LTC) refers to a broad range of medical, personal, and environmental services designed to assist individuals who have lost their ability to remain completely independent in the community. Although care may be provided for short periods of time while a patient is recuperating from an accident or illness, LTC refers to care provided for an extended period of time, normally more than 90 days. And, depending on the severity of the impairment, assistance may be given at home, at an adult care center, or in a nursing home.

A large percentage of the elderly population will spend time in a nursing home or at home requiring care. The national average cost of a semiprivate nursing home room rose 4.4% in 2011, to $78,110 (or $214 per day), according to a survey conducted by MetLife. Meanwhile, the cost for a home health aide remained steady, according to the same study, at $20 per hour or $38,400 per year.

What Is Long-Term Care Insurance?

Long-term care insurance is a relatively new type of insurance product. However, more and more insurance companies are beginning to offer this coverage as the need for it grows. It is similar to most insurance plans, in that the insured, in exchange for a certain premium, receives specified benefits in the event she requires long-term care, as defined by the policy. Most LTC policies pay the insured a fixed dollar amount for each day she receives the kind of care the policy covers, regardless of what the care costs. For example, if the fixed daily dollar amount is $225 and the facility charges $210 a day, the insurance company will pay the full $225 per day.

Insurers offer a wide range of benefit amounts, ranging from, for example, $40 a day to $300 a day for nursing home care. The daily benefit for at-home care is typically half the nursing home benefit. Many policies include an inflation rider or option to purchase additional coverage, enabling the policies to keep pace with increases in LTC costs.

Long-Term Care Coverages

As individuals age, they are likely to suffer from acute and chronic illnesses or conditions. An **acute illness** is a serious condition, such as pneumonia or influenza, from which the body can fully recover with proper medical attention. The patient may also need some assistance with chores for short periods of time until recovery and rehabilitation from the illness are complete.

Some people will suffer from **chronic conditions**, such as arthritis, heart disease, or hypertension, that are treatable but not curable illnesses. When chronic conditions such as diabetes or heart disease initially manifest, many people ignore the inconvenience or pain they cause. Over time, however, a chronic condition frequently goes beyond being a nuisance and begins to inhibit a person's independence.

Typically, the need for LTC arises when physical or mental conditions, whether acute or chronic, impair a person's ability to perform the basic activities of everyday life—feeding, toileting, bathing, dressing, and walking. This is the risk that long-term care insurance is designed to protect.

Long-term care defines three types of care based on frequency and type of provider:

- **Skilled nursing care** is continuous, around-the-clock care provided by licensed medical professionals under the direct supervision of a physician. Skilled nursing care is usually administered in nursing homes.

- **Intermediate nursing care** is provided by registered nurses, licensed practical nurses, and nurse's aides under the supervision of a physician. Intermediate care is provided in nursing homes for stable medical conditions that require daily, but not 24-hour, supervision.

■ **Custodial care** provides assistance in meeting daily living requirements, such as bathing, dressing, getting out of bed, toileting, and so on. Such care does not require specialized medical training, but it must be given under a doctor's order. Custodial care is usually provided by nursing homes but can also be given in adult day care centers, respite centers, or at home.

Broadly speaking, the kinds of services and support associated with long-term care are provided at three kinds of locations: **institutional care, home-based care,** and **community care**. Within each of these broad levels are many types of care, any or all of which may be covered by a long-term care insurance policy. Typical types of coverages are explained in the following.

Home and Community-Based Services

Home health care is care provided in the insured's home, usually on a part-time basis. It can include skilled care (e.g., nursing, rehabilitative, or physical therapy care ordered by a doctor) or unskilled care (e.g., help with cooking or cleaning).

Adult Day Care

Adult day care is designed for those who require assistance with various activities of daily living, while their primary caregivers (usually family or friends) are absent. These day care centers offer skilled medical care in conjunction with social and personal services, but custodial care is usually their primary focus.

Alternative Care

Alternative care is a package of home and community-based services, including trained caregivers, home-delivered meals, transportation services, adult day care, look-in and call-in services, and other community-based services. It is designed as a more desirable and less expensive alternative to traditional institutional care.

Respite Care

Respite care is designed to provide a short rest period for a family caregiver. There are two options: either the insured is moved to a full-time care facility or a substitute care provider moves into the insured's home for a temporary period, giving the family member a rest from his caregiving activities.

Continuing Care

A fairly new kind of LTC coverage, **continuing care** coverage, is designed to provide a benefit for elderly individuals who live in a continuing care retirement community. Retirement communities are geared to senior citizens' full-time needs, both medical and social, and are often sponsored by religious or nonprofit organizations. It provides independent and congregate living and personal, intermediate, and skilled nursing care and attempts to create an environment that allows each resident to participate in the community's life to whatever degree desired.

LTC Policy Provisions and Limits

As we have stated, there are a number of LTC policies on the market today, each characterized by some distinguishing feature or benefit that sets it apart from the rest. However, there are enough similarities to allow us to discuss the basic provisions of these policies and their typical limits or exclusions.

In addition, as a result of the passage of the Health Insurance Portability and Accountability Act (HIPAA) of 1996, all LTC policies must now contain certain provisions in order that their benefits qualify for tax-exempt treatment. These provisions include, for example, a definition of the types of services offered by the plan and when an individual becomes eligible for benefits under the plan. Both provisions, of course, must conform to qualifying standards under HIPAA. In addition, LTC policies must also adopt certain provisions of the NAIC's long-term care insurance model regulation. (See Illustration 21.2.)

ILLUSTRATION 21.2

NAIC Model LTC Regulations

The Health Insurance Portability and Accountability Act (HIPAA) of 1996 laid to rest concerns about how the benefits payable under a long-term care policy would be treated for tax purposes. Essentially, the question was, "Are such benefits taxable?" HIPAA determined that LTC policies are to be treated as other health insurance contracts—that benefits payable under LTC policies are considered reimbursement for expenses incurred for medical care—and are, therefore, not taxable to the insured. However, there is an important caveat: to be treated this way, the LTC policy must be "qualified." This means that the policy's provisions must conform to certain standards and guidelines as set forth by the Internal Revenue Code and HIPAA. Among the qualifying standards is the requirement to conform to the NAIC's long-term care insurance model regulations. In brief, the NAIC model addresses such things as:

- policy renewability (the policy must be guaranteed renewable);
- prohibitions on limits and exclusions;
- policy replacement;
- policy conversion;
- prohibition against post-claims underwriting;
- requirement to offer inflation-adjusted benefits;
- proper marketing standards;
- suitability and appropriateness of the recommended purchase; and
- a standard format for the outline of coverage.

LTC Services

Qualified LTC services are defined as diagnostic, preventive, therapeutic, curing, treating, mitigating and rehabilitative services, and maintenance or personal care services that are required by a chronically ill individual and are provided under a plan of care established by a licensed health care practitioner.

Qualifying for Benefits

When LTC policies were first introduced, insurers frequently required at least three days of prior hospitalization or skilled nursing home stays before the LTC policy benefits were triggered. The benefit trigger is an event or condition that must occur before policy benefits become payable. As a result of HIPAA, prior hospitalization can no longer be used as a benefit trigger; instead, the individual must be diagnosed as chronically ill.

Diagnosis of chronic illness can be made on two levels: physical and (or) cognitive. The physical diagnosis of a chronically ill individual is one who has been certified as being unable to perform at least two activities of daily living. (Activities of daily living, or ADLs, are eating, toileting, transferring, bathing, dressing, and continence.) A long-term care policy must take into account at least five of these ADLs. In addition, an individual would be considered chronically ill if she requires substantial supervision to protect her health or safety owing to severe cognitive impairment, and this condition was certified within the previous 12 months.

Benefit Limits

Almost all LTC policies set **benefit limits**, in terms of how long the benefits are paid or how much the dollar benefit will be for any one covered care service or a combination of services. Maximum dollar amounts vary considerably from policy to policy. Maximum coverage periods also vary.

In fact, with LTC policies, it is not unusual for one policy to include separate maximum coverage periods for nursing home care and home health care. Generally speaking, maximum coverage periods extend anywhere from two to six years. Some policies offer unlimited lifetime coverage.

Age Limits

LTC policies typically set **age limits** for issue, the average age being about 79. However, some newer policies can be sold to people up through age 89. Some policies also set a minimum purchase age.

Renewability

As a result of the 1996 Health Insurance Portability and Accountability Act, all long-term care policies sold today must be **guaranteed renewable**. This means the insurance company cannot cancel the policy and must renew coverage each year, as long as premiums are paid. A guaranteed renewable policy allows the insurer to raise premiums but only for entire classes of insureds.

Elimination Periods

LTC **elimination periods** can range from 0 to 365 days, and many insurers give the insured the option of selecting the period that best serves his needs. The elimination period may be thought of as a voluntary time deductible in which the longer the elimination period selected, the lower the LTC premium.

Specified Exclusions

While organic cognitive disorders, such as Alzheimer's disease, senile dementia, and Parkinson's disease, are almost always included in long-term care insurance policies, the following are excluded from most long-term care insurance policies: drug and alcohol dependency, acts of war, self-inflicted injuries, and nonorganic mental conditions.

Premiums

The cost for an LTC policy is based on a number of factors: the insured's age and health, the type and level of benefits provided, the inclusion or absence of an elimination period and the length of that period, and whether or not options or riders are included with the policy (such as the option to purchase additional coverage in the future or the inflation-adjustment rider, which automatically increases the policy's coverage to match inflation levels).

ILLUSTRATION 21.3

The Impairment Continuum—
Activities of Daily Living

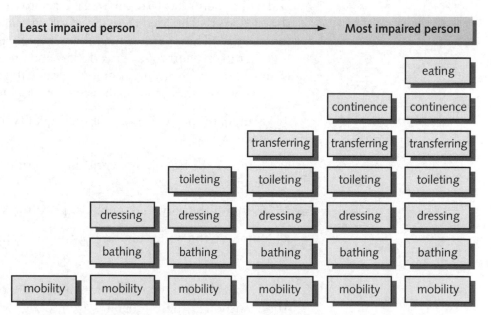

This illustration shows the progression of impairments included in the activities of daily living. Persons with a more severe impairment usually have all lesser impairments.

Group LTC

An increasing number of employers are offering group LTC plans or voluntary (employee-paid) LTC plans as part of their employment benefits package. The types of coverages and eligibility for benefits are usually similar to those discussed earlier in this unit. The advantages of group LTC include the absence of individual underwriting and a structure that allows benefits to be applied to more than one member of the family (spouse or children). Also, any contributions made by the employer are helpful, but most of these plans are currently voluntary (entirely employee-paid). One other distinction to group LTC is that, unlike most group products, the premiums may be equal to or even higher than comparable individual plans.

Taxation of LTC Benefits

As noted earlier, qualified LTC insurance contracts are treated in the same manner as accident and health insurance contracts. Consequently, amounts received under an LTC contract are excluded from income because they are considered amounts received for personal injuries and sickness. However, there is a limit on these amounts. These limits are adjusted for inflation annually.

State Partnership Programs for Long-Term Care

State partnership programs are a partnership between state governments and the insurance industry to contain Medicaid expenses and allow individuals to access Medicaid reimbursement without impoverishing themselves.

Under a partnership plan, insureds obtain a policy from an insurer which will give them a certain amount of long-term care insurance protection. If they collect maximum benefits under this coverage, they qualify for Medicaid and will be permitted to retain assets equal to the amount of insurance benefits they received. The Medicaid applicant must meet the income requirements for the state. These partnerships allow state governments and insurers to work together in an effort to save tax dollars and promote independence from government control by using insurance money to pay nursing home bills.

In general, these partnerships have four objectives:

- Stimulate the availability of high-quality, private, long-term care insurance

- Remove the fear of impoverishment resulting from a need for health care services

- Contain the growth of public expenditures

- Improve the understanding of the financing of long-term care through state counseling services

The plans were pioneered by California, Connecticut, Indiana, and New York. Although these programs were designed for people in the lower- to middle-income range, the majority of policyholders have significant assets to protect. Most participants have assets in excess of $350,000.

Many other states have since passed the required legislation or have it pending. The Deficit Reduction Act of 2005 encouraged all states to implement such programs. Florida and 41 other states already have enacted legislation to implement partnership programs.

The primary plan design allows the owner of a partnership plan to receive insurance benefits before applying for Medicaid. Under the plan, the insurer reimburses the insured for services that would have been covered by Medicaid if the insured had been an eligible Medicaid recipient. Those services include nursing home care, home health care, adult day care services, respite care, and supportive home care. The amount of benefits paid by the insurer are excluded from the applicant's total assets when applying for Medicaid. In other words, the state Medicaid program does not have to count this amount as part of the applicant's assets. The applicant still must have income levels below the state's Medicaid limits. Once qualified for Medicaid, persons receiving these types of services must contribute their income toward their care in the same way as required for other Medicaid recipients.

A second model of asset protection allows participants to keep all of their assets after receiving insurance benefits for three years of nursing home care, six years of home health care, or a combination of the two (in which two days of home care equal one day of nursing home care).

SUMMARY

Medicare supplement or **Medigap** policies are designed to make up for what Medicare doesn't cover and are also becoming increasingly popular. The NAIC has developed 10 Medicare standard supplement plans, ranging from the basic core policy, Plan A, to plans with more comprehensive coverage.

As beneficial as Medicare and Medicare supplement insurance are to the elderly in protecting them against the costs of medical care, **long-term care insurance** is still needed to offer a broad range of medical and personal services for individuals who need assistance with daily activities for an extended period of time.

KEY CONCEPTS

Students should be familiar with the following concepts:

Medicare supplement policies	continuing care
long-term care policies	acute illness
chronically ill	activities of daily living (ADLs)
skilled nursing care	intermediate nursing care
custodial care	home health care
adult day care	respite care

UNIT TEST

1. The core policy (Plan A) developed by the NAIC as a standard Medicare supplement policy includes all of the following EXCEPT

   A. the Medicare Part A deductible
   B. Part A coinsurance amounts
   C. the first 3 pints of blood each year
   D. the 20% Part B coinsurance amounts for Medicare-approved services

2. Which of the following is a serious condition from which a patient can fully recover with proper medical attention?

   A. Chronic illness
   B. Long-term illness
   C. Acute illness
   D. Severe illness

3. Skilled nursing care differs from intermediate care in which of the following ways?

   A. It must be performed by skilled medical professionals, whereas intermediate care does not require medical training.
   B. It must be available 24 hours a day, while intermediate care is daily but not 24-hour care.
   C. It is typically given in a nursing home, while intermediate care is usually given at home.
   D. It encompasses rehabilitation, while intermediate care is for meeting daily personal needs, such as bathing and dressing.

4. All of the following conditions are typically covered in a long-term insurance policy EXCEPT

   A. Alzheimer's disease
   B. senile dementia
   C. alcohol dependency
   D. Parkinson's disease

5. Which of the following statements about long-term care insurance policies is NOT correct?

   A. Maximum coverage periods generally extend from 2 to 6 years.
   B. Long-term care policies sold today must be guaranteed renewable.
   C. A long-term care policy with a long probationary period will have a lower premium than one with a shorter probationary period.
   D. Premiums for a long-term care policy are based solely on the insured's age, health, and the type of benefits provided.

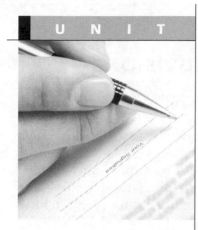

UNIT

22

Health Insurance Policy Provisions

- NAIC Model Health Insurance Policy Provisions
- Common Exclusions or Restrictions
- Renewability Provisions

To understand health insurance, one must have a firm knowledge of the contract provisions that distinguish it from other insurance policies. Health insurance, more so than life insurance, is characterized by a number of mandatory provisions that must be included in the contract. The 12 mandatory provisions and 11 optional provisions covered in this unit evolved for the purpose of adding a uniformity to contracts that present themselves as health insurance policies, thus elevating health insurance to a very high level of regulatory protection. ■

NAIC MODEL HEALTH INSURANCE POLICY PROVISIONS

Years ago, the National Association of Insurance Commissioners (NAIC) developed a model Uniform Individual Accident and Sickness Policy Provisions Law. Almost all states have adopted this model law or similar legislation or regulations.

The purpose of the NAIC law was to establish uniform or model terms, provisions, and wording standards for inclusion in all individual health insurance contracts or all contracts that provide insurance against loss "resulting from sickness or from bodily injury or death by accident or both." The result was **12 mandatory policy provisions** and **11 optional policy provisions**. The *mandatory provisions* predominantly protect the interests of insureds, while the *optional provisions* generally protect the interests of insurers. As a practical matter, however, both groups will usually appear in any health contract. Because these provisions are to be followed "in substance," insurers may employ different wording from that of the law, as long as the protection is provided and is no less favorable to the insured than the law stipulates.

Similar to a life insurance contract, a health insurance contract obligates the insurer to pay the insured (or a beneficiary) a stipulated benefit under circumstances specified in the contract. The specifics of the benefit and the requisite circumstances are set forth in the contract's provisions. Let's take a look at these provisions.

Twelve Mandatory Policy Provisions

In accordance with the NAIC model law, there are **12 mandatory provisions** that are required to be in all health insurance contracts. These are as follows.

1. Entire Contract

Like its counterpart in a life insurance policy, the **entire contract** provision in a health insurance policy protects the policyowner in two ways. First, it states that nothing outside of the contract (the contract includes the signed application and any attached policy riders) can be considered part of the contract; that is, nothing can be "incorporated by reference." Second, it assures the policyowner that no changes will be made to the contract after it has been issued, even if the insurer makes policy changes that affect all policy sales in the future.

2. Time Limit on Certain Defenses

Under the **time limit on certain defenses** provision, the policy is incontestable after it has been in force a certain period of time, usually two years. This is similar to the incontestable clause in a life insurance policy. However, unlike life policies, a fraudulent statement on a health insurance application is grounds for contest at any time, unless the policy is guaranteed renewable, in which case it cannot be contested for any reason after the contestable period expires.

Another part of this provision concerns any preexisting conditions (i.e., conditions that existed prior to the policy's effective date) an insured may have. Under the provision, the insurance company cannot deny a claim on the basis of a preexisting condition after expiration of the stated contestable period—unless such preexisting condition has been excluded specifically from the policy by name or description.

3. Grace Period

Per the **grace period** provision, the policyowner is given a number of days after the premium due date during which time the premium payment may be delayed without penalty and the policy continues in force. Depending on the state, the minimum grace periods that may be specified are typically seven days for policies with weekly premium payments (i.e., industrial policies), 10 days for policies with premiums payable on a monthly basis, and 31 days for other policies. Florida insurance law requires these minimum grace periods. (Some states, however, require a standard grace period of one month but not less than 31 days, regardless of the frequency of premium payment or policy term.)

The Affordable Care Act (ACA) provides that individuals who purchase coverage on the health insurance exchange/marketplace and who qualify for premium tax credits may have a 90-day grace period to pay outstanding premiums.

4. Reinstatement

Under certain conditions, a policy that has lapsed may be **reinstated**. Reinstatement is automatic if the delinquent premium is accepted by the company or its authorized agent and the company does not require an application for reinstatement.

If a company does require such an application, it may or may not approve the application. If it takes no action on the application for 45 days, the policy is reinstated automatically. To protect the company against **adverse selection**, losses resulting from sickness are covered only if the sickness occurs at least 10 days after the reinstatement date.

5. Notice of Claim

The **notice of claim** provision describes the policyowner's obligation to the insurer to provide notification of loss within a reasonable period of time. Typically, the period is 20 days after the occurrence or a commencement of the loss, or as soon thereafter as is reasonably possible. If the loss involves disability income payments that are payable for two or more years, the disabled claimant must submit proof of loss every six months. Such proof may be submitted to either the company or an authorized agent of the company.

6. Claim Forms

It is the company's responsibility to supply a **claim form** to an insured within 15 days after receiving notice of claim. If it fails to do so within the time limit, the claimant may submit proof of loss in any form, explaining the occurrence, the character, and the extent of the loss for which the claim is submitted.

7. Proof of Loss

After a loss occurs, or after the company becomes liable for periodic payments (e.g., disability income benefits), the claimant has 90 days in which to submit **proof of loss**. The claim will not be affected in any way, however, if it is not reasonably possible for the claimant to comply with the 90-day provision.

There is a time limit for submitting proof of loss—whether or not it is reasonably possible to do so—and that is one year after the company becomes liable for the loss. The only exception to the one-year limit is if the claimant does not have the legal capacity to comply.

8. Time of Payment of Claims

The **time of payment of claims** provision provides for immediate payment of the claim after the insurer receives notification and proof of loss. If the claim involves disability income payments, they must be paid at least monthly, if not at more frequent intervals specified in the policy. In some states, the time payment of claims is 60 days; in other states, it's 30 days. In Florida, the time payment of claims is 45 days after first received.

9. Payment of Claims

The **payment of claims** provision in a health insurance contract specifies how and to whom claim payments are to be made. Payments for loss of life are to be made to the designated beneficiary. If no beneficiary has been named, death proceeds are to be paid to the deceased insured's estate. Claims other than death benefits are to be paid to the insured.

In accordance with this required provision are two optional provisions that insurers may add. One gives the insurer the right to expedite payment of urgently needed claim funds and pay up to $3,000 in benefits to a relative or individual who is considered to be equitably entitled to payment. The other optional provision allows the insured to have medical benefits assigned—or paid directly—to the hospital or physician rendering the covered services.

10. Physical Exam and Autopsy

The **physical exam and autopsy** provision entitles a company, at its own expense, to make physical examinations of the insured at reasonable intervals during the period of a claim. In the case of death, the insurer has the right to conduct an autopsy on the body of the insured, provided it is not forbidden by state law.

11. Legal Actions

The insured cannot take **legal action** against the company in a claim dispute until after 60 days from the time the insured submits proof of loss. The same rule applies to beneficiaries. Also, if legal action is to be taken against the company, it must be done within a certain time after proof of loss is submitted. In Florida, a claimant must take legal action against the company within five years.

12. Change of Beneficiary

The insured, as policyowner, may change the **beneficiary designation** at any time, unless a beneficiary has been named irrevocably. So long as the insured reserves the right to change beneficiaries, she also may surrender or assign the policy without obtaining the consent of the beneficiary.

Eleven Optional Provisions

There are **11 optional** health policy provisions, and companies may ignore them or use only those that are needed in their policy forms. The provisions pertaining to "other insurance in this insurer," "insurance with other insurers," and "relation of earnings to insurance" seldom are used. They were intended to deal with the problem of overinsurance but generally proved to be ineffective.

1. Change of Occupation

The **change of occupation** provision sets forth the changes that may be made to premium rates or benefits payable should the insured change occupations. Many insurers include this provision in their disability income policies because an individual's occupation has a direct bearing on his risk profile and his risk profile has a direct bearing on premium charges. Consequently, this provision allows the insurer to reduce the maximum benefit payable under the policy if the insured switches to a more hazardous occupation or to reduce the premium rate charged if the insured changes to a less hazardous occupation. These benefit and premium changes take effect at the time the insured changes occupations; if a change in jobs is discovered after a disability begins, the changes are made retroactively.

2. Misstatement of Age or Sex

The **misstatement of age or sex** provision allows the insurer to adjust the benefit payable if the age or sex of the insured was misstated when application for the policy was made. Benefit amounts payable in such cases will be what the premiums paid would have purchased at the correct age or sex. As we know, the older the applicant, the higher the premium; therefore, if the insured was older at the time of application than is shown on the application, benefits would be reduced accordingly. The reverse would be true if the insured were younger than listed in the application. This provision is an exception to the Time Limit on Certain Defenses provision as it will be effected whenever the error is discovered, even beyond two years.

3. Other Insurance in This Insurer

The purpose of the **other insurance in this insurer** provision is to limit the company's risk with any individual insured. Under this provision, the total amount of coverage to be underwritten by a company for one person is restricted to a specified maximum amount, regardless of the number of policies issued. Premiums that apply to any such excess of coverage must be returned to the insured or the insured's estate.

4. Insurance with Other Insurer

In attempting to deal with the potential problem of overinsurance, the **insurance with other insurer** provision states that benefits payable for expenses incurred will be prorated in cases where the company accepted the risk without being notified of other existing coverage for the same risk. When premiums are paid that exceed the amount needed to cover what the company determines it will pay, the excess premiums must be refunded to the policyowner.

5. Insurance with Other Insurers

Similar to the previous, the **insurance with other insurers** provision calls for the prorating of benefits that are payable on any basis other than expenses incurred. It also provides for a return of premiums that exceed the amount needed to pay for the company's portion of prorated benefits.

6. Relation of Earnings to Insurance

If disability income benefits from *all* disability income policies for the same loss exceed the insured's monthly earnings at the time of disability (or the average monthly earnings for two years preceding disability), the **relation of earnings** provision states that the insurer is liable only for that *proportionate* amount of benefits as the insured's earnings bear to the total benefits under all such coverage.

In Florida, total indemnities payable to the insured may not be reduced below $500 or the sum total benefits under all applicable coverage, whichever is less. Any premiums paid for the excess coverage are refunded.

7. Unpaid Premiums

If there is an **unpaid premium** at the time a claim becomes payable, the amount of the premium is to be deducted from the sum payable to the insured or beneficiary. Or, if the premium is covered by a note when a claim is submitted, the note payment will be subtracted from the amount payable for the claim.

8. Cancellation

Though prohibited in a number of states, the provision for **cancellation** gives the company the right to cancel the policy at any time with 45 days' written notice to the insured. (This notice must also be given when the insurer refuses to renew a policy or change the premium rates.) If the cancellation is for nonpayment of premium, the insurer must give 10 days' written notice to the insured, unless the premiums are due monthly or more frequently. The cancellation provision also allows the insured to cancel the policy any time after the policy's original term has expired. Any unearned premium is to be refunded to the insured. If a claim is pending at the time of cancellation, the claim cannot be affected by the cancellation. (See also *Renewability Provisions* later in this unit.)

ILLUSTRATION 22.1

NAIC Uniform Health Insurance Policy Provisions

Mandatory Provisions	Optional Provisions
1. Entire contract	1. Change of occupation
2. Time limit on certain defenses	2. Misstatement of age
3. Grace period	3. Other insurance in this insurer
4. Reinstatement	4. Insurance with other insurer
5. Notice of claims	5. Insurance with other insurers
6. Claims forms	6. Relation of earnings to insurance
7. Proof of loss	7. Unpaid premiums
8. Time of payment of claims	8. Cancellation
9. Payment of claims	9. Conformity with state statutes
10. Physical exam and autopsy	10. Illegal occupation
11. Legal actions	11. Intoxicants and narcotics
12. Change of beneficiary	

9. Conformity with State Statutes

Any policy provision that is in conflict with **state statutes** in the state where the insured lives at the time the policy is issued is automatically amended to conform with the minimum statutory requirements.

10. Illegal Occupation

The **illegal occupation** provision specifies that the insurer is not liable for losses attributed to the insured's commission of, or being connected with, a felony or participation in any illegal occupation.

11. Intoxicants and Narcotics

The insurer is not liable for any loss attributed to the insured while **intoxicated** or under the influence of *narcotics*, unless such drugs were administered on the advice of a physician.

Other Health Insurance Policy Provisions

The 12 mandatory provisions and 11 optional provisions just described comprise the substantive elements of individual health insurance policies. However, there are a number of other very important clauses and provisions that should be noted.

Insuring Clause

Generally, the **insuring clause** is a broad statement on the first page of the health policy, stipulating conditions under which benefits are to be paid. While these critical provisions vary considerably in health insurance contracts, they basically represent a company's "promise to pay" benefits for specific kinds of losses resulting from sickness or accidents. They usually specify that benefits are subject to all provisions and exclusions stated in the policy.

Consideration Clause

The **consideration clause** states the amount and frequency of premium payments. If the first premium has not been paid—even though the application has been completed and signed by the applicant—the necessary consideration is partially lacking. As is the case with life insurance, the legal consideration for a health policy consists of the application and payment of the initial premium. A copy of the application is attached to the policy.

Frequently, the consideration clause also lists the effective date of the contract and defines the initial term of the policy. In addition, it may specify the insured's right to renew the policy.

Conversion Privilege for Dependents

A single health policy may insure one person or more than one if the applicant is an adult family member and the others to be covered are members of her family. Thus, additional persons who may be insured include the husband, wife, dependent children, or others dependent upon the adult applicant. To be eligible, children must meet certain age requirements.

Generally, children of the insured are eligible for coverage under a family policy until they attain a specified age. Beginning October 1, 2010, the Affordable Health Care Act mandated that all policies and plans must provide dependent coverage up to age 26. Florida currently requires insurers to provide the offer of dependent coverage up to age 30. Adopted children, stepchildren, and foster children usually are eligible for coverage. As long as a policy is in force, coverage for a child generally continues until the child marries or reaches the limiting age. However, a number of states have enacted special laws that require insurers to retain as insureds under the parent's individual or group health policy any child who reaches the limiting age but is dependent on the insured and incapable of self-support because of mental or physical impairment. In Florida, both individual and group policies must continue to provide coverage for a handicapped child when the child becomes an adult.

Attaining a minimum age, such as 14 days, may be required for coverage; however, legislation in most states mandates that health policies insuring family members also provide coverage for newborn children from the moment of birth. Typically, such legislation permits the insurer to require that notice of the child's birth be given and an application and additional premium be submitted within a specified period.

If the insurance on a covered individual is terminated because he no longer fits the policy definition of "family member," that person has a right to take out a **conversion policy** without evidence of insurability. For example, if Faye divorces Stanley and thus no longer can be covered under his family policy, she has a right to obtain a conversion policy. When their children reach the limiting age for children's coverage, they also will be eligible for a conversion policy.

Free-Look Provision

Florida mandates that health insurance policies contain a **free-look** provision permitting policyowners 10 days in which to examine their new policies at no obligation. If they decide not to keep their policies, they may return them within the prescribed time limit and receive full refunds of premiums paid. However, for Medicare supplement and long-term care policies, Florida requires a 30-day free look.

COMMON EXCLUSIONS OR RESTRICTIONS

Health insurance policies frequently cite a number of **exclusions** or conditions that are not covered. The common ones are injuries due to war or an act of war, **self-inflicted injuries** and those incurred while the insured is serving as a **pilot** or **crew member** of an aircraft.

Other exclusions are losses resulting from suicide, hernia (as an accidental injury), riots, or the use of drugs or narcotics. Losses due to injuries sustained while committing a felony, or attempting to do so, also may be excluded. Foreign travel may not be excluded in every instance, but extended stays overseas or foreign residence may cause a loss of benefits.

Maternity Benefits

Maternity benefits generally are handled differently in individual health policies than in group health policies. When available for individual policies, a maternity provision may provide a fixed amount for childbirth or a benefit based upon a specified multiple of the daily hospital room benefit. Frequently, the maternity benefit is available only as an added benefit for an additional premium.

Maternity coverage in group health plans is discussed in Unit 24.

Preexisting Conditions

As we have learned, medical expense and disability income policies usually exclude paying benefits for losses due to **preexisting conditions** pertaining to illness, disease, or other physical impairments. For purposes of issuing individual health policies, insurers consider a preexisting condition to be one that the insured contracted (or one that was manifested) prior to the policy's effective date. Consequently, in the event the insured did not specifically cite the condition on the application and the insurer did not expressly exclude the condition from coverage, the preexisting condition provision would serve to exclude the condition nonetheless. However, such exclusions are subject to the "time limit on certain defenses" provision.

Any preexisting condition that the insured has disclosed clearly in the application usually is not excluded or, if it is, the condition is named specifically in an excluding waiver or rider.

The treatment of preexisting conditions under group health plans is a little different and is discussed in Unit 26 and Unit 30, as it relates specifically to Florida.

Waivers for Impairments

The majority of health policies are standard and are issued as applied for. However, a few people have an existing impairment that increases the risk and so are required to pay an extra premium. A few people are uninsurable and must be declined. Others, however, fall in between and would not be able to obtain health insurance if waivers were not in use. Waivers usually are stated in simple language. For example: "This policy does not cover or extend to any disability resulting directly or indirectly from . . ." A waiver is dated and bears the signature of an officer of the company and, in many cases, the applicant. This is usually called an *impairment rider*.

If the insured's condition improves, the company may be willing to remove the waiver. Meanwhile, the person at least has health protection from other hazards that she otherwise could not obtain.

RENEWABILITY PROVISIONS

One of the distinguishing features of health insurance policies is the provisions they contain that allow the insurer to continue or discontinue coverage. Known as **renewability provisions**, they vary from policy to policy. Generally speaking, the more favorable the renewability provision is to the insured policyholder, the higher the premium.

Cancellable Policies

The renewability provision in a **cancellable** policy allows the insurer to cancel or terminate the policy at any time, simply by providing written notification to the insured and refunding any advance premium that has been paid. Cancellable policies also allow the insurer to increase premiums.

Optionally Renewable Policies

The renewability provision in an **optionally renewable** policy gives the insurer the option to terminate the policy on a date specified in the contract. Furthermore, this provision allows the insurer to increase the premium for any class of optionally renewable insureds.[1] Usually termination or premium increases take place on policy anniversary dates or premium due dates.

Conditionally Renewable Policies

A **conditionally renewable** policy allows an insurer to terminate the coverage but only in the event of one or more conditions stated in the contract. These conditions cannot apply to the insured's health; most frequently, they are related to the insured reaching a certain age or losing gainful employment. Usually, the premium for conditionally renewable policies may be increased, if such an increase applies to an entire class of policies.

Guaranteed Renewable Policies

The renewal provision in a **guaranteed renewable** policy specifies that the policy must be renewed, as long as premiums are paid, until the insured reaches a specified age, such as 60 or 65. Premium increases may be applied but only for the entire class of insureds; they cannot be assessed to individual insureds.

Noncancellable Policies

A **noncancellable** or "noncan" policy cannot be cancelled nor can its premium rates be increased under any circumstances; these rates are specified in the policy. The term of most noncancellable policies is to the insured's age 65. Noncan provisions are most commonly found in disability income policies; they are rarely used in medical expense policies.

SUMMARY

To protect the rights of individual health insurance policyholders, the NAIC developed a set of **12 mandatory** and **11 optional policy provisions**. These provisions help assure consumers that the health policies they buy will meet at least a minimum level of standards. Other provisions, though not categorized as "required" or "optional," are equally important. Of special note are *the* **renewability provisions**, absent from life insurance policies, but an essential feature of health policies.

---

1   A "class" of insureds includes all insureds of policies of a particular kind or all insureds of a specific group. For example, a class of insureds may be those of a particular age or in a specific geographic region.

KEY CONCEPTS

Students should be familiar with the following concepts:

entire contract	time limit on certain defenses
grace period	reinstatement
notice of claims	claims forms
proof of loss	time of payment of claims
payment of claims	physical examination and autopsy
legal actions	change of beneficiary
change of occupation	misstatement of age
other insurance in this insurer	relation of earnings to insurance
insurance with other insurer(s)	cancellation
unpaid premiums	illegal occupation
conformity with state statutes	insuring clause
intoxicants and narcotics	conversion privilege
consideration clause	exclusions and waivers
free look	cancellable
preexisting conditions	conditionally renewable
optionally renewable	noncancellable
guaranteed renewable	

UNIT TEST

1. A company may change the wording of a uniform policy provision in its health insurance policies only if the
   A. company's board of directors approves the change
   B. modified provision is not less favorable to the insurer
   C. applicant directs that it be changed
   D. modified provision is not less favorable to the insured

2. The Affordable Health Care Act mandates that children of the insured are eligible for health insurance coverage until they attain age
   A. 20
   B. 21
   C. 22
   D. 26

3. Which of the following statements pertaining to the grace period and reinstatement provisions in health insurance policies is NOT correct?
   A. Craig's health policy has a grace period of 31 days. He had a premium due June 15 while he was on vacation. He returned home July 7, mailed his premium the next day and the insurer received it July 10. His policy would have remained in force.
   B. Warren's medical expense policy was reinstated on September 30 and he became ill and entered the hospital on October 5. His hospital expense will not be paid by the insurer.
   C. Under a health policy's reinstatement terms, insured losses from accidental injuries and sickness are covered immediately after reinstatement.
   D. States may require grace periods of 7, 10, or 31 days, depending on the mode of premium payment or term of insurance; however, many states require a 31-day grace period in any case.

4. Which of the following is the usual grace period for a semiannual premium policy?
   A. 7 days
   B. 20 days
   C. 31 days
   D. 60 days

5. Diana, the beneficiary under her husband's AD&D policy, submits an accidental death claim on May 1, 2010, following his death. However, the company denies the claim on the basis that death was due to natural causes. She decides to talk to her attorney. What is the earliest date for taking legal action against the insurer?
   A. May 2, 2010
   B. June 1, 2010
   C. July 1, 2010
   D. May 1, 2011

6. All of the following are required uniform provisions in individual health insurance policies EXCEPT
   A. change of occupation
   B. grace period
   C. entire contract
   D. reinstatement

7. Under the misstatement of age provision in a health insurance policy, what can a company do if it discovers that an insured gave a wrong age at the time of application?
   A. Cancel the policy
   B. Increase the premium
   C. Adjust the benefits
   D. Assess a penalty

8. The conformity with state statutes provision in a health insurance policy stipulates that any policy provision that is in conflict with the statutes of the state where the insured resides is

   A. to be submitted to the chief financial officer for approval
   B. cause for the insured's policy to be voided
   C. automatically amended to conform to the minimum requirements of the state's statutes
   D. to be rewritten if the policy is returned to the company

9. Which section of a health insurance policy specifies the conditions, times, and circumstances under which the insured is NOT covered by the policy?

   A. Coinsurance provision
   B. Coverages
   C. Insuring clause
   D. Exclusions

10. Which kind of health insurance policy assures renewability up to a specific age of the insured, although the company reserves the right to change the premium rate on a class basis?

    A. Noncancellable
    B. Guaranteed renewable
    C. Optionally renewable
    D. Cancellable

11. According to the notice of claims provision in a health insurance policy, a claimant normally must notify the insurance company of loss within how many days after the loss occurs?

    A. 10
    B. 20
    C. 40
    D. 60

12. Which of the following types of health insurance policies prevents the company from changing the premium rate or modifying the coverage in any way?

    A. Optionally renewable
    B. Noncancellable
    C. Guaranteed renewable
    D. Cancellable

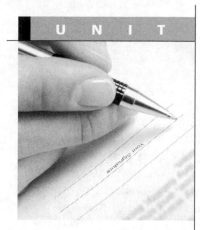
23

Health Insurance Underwriting and Premiums

- Risk Factors in Health Insurance
- Health Insurance Premium Factors
- Tax Treatment of Health Insurance Premiums and Benefits
- Managed Care

Health insurers are increasingly finding themselves in a tough position. The high cost of medical care requires them to charge premiums that adequately cover the correspondingly high level of health insurance claims, and yet public sentiment and even competition from within the industry pressure companies to keep rates as low as possible. Health insurers are reacting to these conflicting forces by tightening their underwriting requirements—becoming more selective in the risks they will accept—and controlling claims through innovative measures. This unit looks at the important topic of health insurance underwriting and covers the related subjects of health insurance premiums and tax treatment of premiums and benefits. Finally, we'll look at the emerging issues of cost control and case management. ■

RISK FACTORS IN HEALTH INSURANCE

While most of the underwriting factors that apply to life insurance are also applicable to health insurance, they take on greater significance in the context of health risks. With life insurance, there is but one death claim per insured. But with health insurance, multiple claims per insured is the rule rather than the exception. Thus, the classification of health insurance risks is critically important. Data accumulated over the years by insurance companies in underwriting health insurance serves as the primary basis for classifying risks.

Classifying risks for health insurance is more complex than simply deciding whether a risk is acceptable or not acceptable. The **degree of risk** is highly important when considering the probable future health of an individual applicant and the amount of premium to be charged, so home office underwriters are charged with the responsibility of scrutinizing health insurance applications with special care.

Many factors are reviewed in underwriting health insurance policies. Three of the most important factors are **physical condition, moral hazards,** and **occupation**.

Physical Condition

An applicant's present **physical condition** is of primary importance when evaluating health risks. For example, the underwriter must know whether the individual has been treated for any chronic conditions, and any physical impairments of the applicant are checked out carefully. Hernias or ulcers, for example, may require surgical correction or treatment in the future and, thereby, represent an additional risk. Persons with an unusual body build, including extreme weight or height, also represent higher risks to the insurer.

Moral Hazards

The **habits** or **lifestyles** of applicants also can flash warning signals that there may be additional risk for the insurer. Personalities and attitudes may draw attention in the underwriting process. Excessive drinking and the use of drugs represent serious moral hazards. Applicants who are seen as accident-prone or potential malingerers (feigning a continuing disability in order to collect benefits) likewise might be heavy risks, particularly those applying for disability income insurance. Other signals of high moral hazard can be a poor credit rating or dishonest business practices.

Occupation

A third significant factor involved with health insurance risks is the applicant's **occupation**. This is because occupation has a direct bearing on both the **probability of disability** and the **average severity of disability**.

Experience shows that disability benefit costs for insurers can vary considerably from occupation to occupation. There is little physical risk associated with professional persons, office managers, or office workers, but occupations involving heavy machinery, strong chemicals, or high electrical voltage, for example, represent a high degree of risk for the insurer.

Jobs requiring manual labor can also influence the length of recuperation periods for disabled workers and how soon they can return to work. Further, the sporadic nature of employment in certain occupations can have a bearing on claim costs because the number and size of such claims tend to rise when insureds are unemployed.

Some occupations involve irregular hours, uncertain earnings, and, in some cases, not even a definite place of business—all of which contribute to higher risks for insurers. Examples are entertainers and authors, who generally do not have regular business hours. In addition, disability benefit costs to insurers also can be influenced by the social and economic character of persons in some occupational classifications.

For underwriting purposes, many insurers divide occupations into five classes: AAA, AA, A, B, and C. The five classes range from the top classification (AAA), which includes professional and office workers, to more hazardous occupations in the lower (B and C) classes. Persons in a few occupations, such as steeplejacks, airplane test pilots, or stunt flyers, usually are uninsurable.

The applicant's occupation and the renewability factor of a policy also are connected from an underwriting standpoint. According to the change of occupation provision, if the insured changes to a less hazardous job, the insurer will return any excess unearned premium; however, if the change is to a more hazardous occupation, the benefits are reduced proportionately and the premium remains the same. The change of occupation clause generally is not included in guaranteed renewable policies, especially long-term disability income policies. Noncancellable policies are sold only to individuals in the higher occupational classes in which change of occupation is seldom a factor. Limited and industrial health policies usually are available at standard rates for all occupations, except those excluded by specific policy provisions.

Other Risk Factors

Additional health insurance risk factors include the applicant's **age, sex, medical and family history,** and **avocations.**

- **Age.** Generally, the older the applicant, the higher the risk he represents. Most individual health insurance policies limit the coverage to a specified age such as 60 or 65 (although some lifetime coverages are available).

- **Sex.** An applicant's sex is also an underwriting consideration. Men show a lower rate of disability than women, except at the upper ages.

- **History.** An applicant's medical history may point to the possibility of a recurrence of a certain health condition. Likewise, an applicant's family history may reflect a tendency she has toward certain medical conditions or health impairments.

- **Avocations.** Certain hobbies an applicant may have—such as skydiving or mountain climbing—may increase his risk to the insurer. An applicant's avocations are carefully evaluated.

Insurable Interest

Finally, when evaluating health insurance risks, the underwriter must determine whether an **insurable interest** exists between the applicant and the individual to be insured. In health insurance, an insurable interest exists if the applicant is in a position to suffer a loss should the insured incur medical expenses or be unable to work due to a disability. As with life insurance, insurable interest is a prerequisite for issuing a health insurance policy.

Classification of Applicants

Once an underwriter has reviewed the various risk factors associated with an individual applicant and has measured them against the company's underwriting standards, there are four ways to classify the applicant and her request for health coverage: as a **preferred risk**, a **standard risk**, a **substandard risk**, or an **uninsurable risk**.

Standard risk applicants are usually issued a policy at standard terms and rates. Preferred risks generally receive lower rates than standard risks, reflecting the fact that people in this class have a better-than-standard risk profile. Uninsurable applicants are usually rejected and denied coverage. Substandard risk applicants—those who pose a higher-than-average risk for one or more reasons—are treated differently. Substandard applicants may represent a very low risk on moral and occupational considerations and still pose a high risk because of their physical condition. Other substandard applicants may be in top physical condition but work at a hazardous occupation. Besides outright rejection, there are three techniques commonly used by insurers in issuing health insurance policies to substandard risks:

- Attaching an **exclusion** (or **impairment**) rider or waiver to a policy

- Charging an **extra premium**

- **Limiting the type** of policy

Exclusion or impairment riders rule out coverage for losses resulting from chronic conditions or physical impairments. With the questionable risks excluded, policies then are issued at standard rates. When some occupational hazard exists, applicants may be charged an extra premium to compensate for the additional risk. The same may be true when applicants are overweight, show signs of high blood pressure, and so on. Extra premiums may be charged only for a few years or on a permanent basis.

When applicants represent a substandard risk, the type of policy requested may be modified in some manner. For example, a policy may exclude all sickness or a specific kind of sickness but cover all losses due to accidental injuries. In other cases, a policy may provide protection for a lower amount than requested or provide a shorter benefit period. A provision may be inserted calling for a longer waiting period than indicated in the application.

Only a small percentage of applicants are classified as substandard risks. With years of experience to guide them, insurers today reject a smaller percentage of applicants for health insurance than in the past.

HEALTH INSURANCE PREMIUM FACTORS

Rate-making for health insurance policies is more complex than for life insurance, primarily because it involves more than one type of benefit. The average frequency of covered health insurance losses further complicates premium computations. There are a number of variables—primary and secondary—all insurers take into account when determining the premium rate for a particular health insurance product.

Primary Premium Factors

At the base level, there are three primary factors that affect health insurance premiums: **morbidity**, **interest**, and **expenses**. Note how closely these correspond to basic life insurance premium factors, except that morbidity is substituted for mortality.

Morbidity

Whereas mortality rates show the average number of persons within a larger group of people who can be expected to die within a given year at a given age, **morbidity** rates indicate the average number at various ages who can be expected to become **disabled** each year due to accident or sickness. Morbidity statistics also reveal the average duration of disability, so insurers can approximate not only how many in a large group will become disabled, but how long the disabilities can be expected to last.

Morbidity statistics, which are available to companies offering health insurance, have been collected over many, many years and reflect the disabilities of hundreds of thousands of people. They are compiled into morbidity tables.

Interest

Just as with life insurance, **interest** is a major element in establishing health insurance premiums. A large portion of every premium received is invested to earn interest. The interest earnings reduce the premium amount that otherwise would be required from policyowners.

Expenses

Every business has expenses that must be paid and the insurance business is no different. Each health insurance policy an insurer issues must carry its proportionate share of the costs for employees' salaries, agents' commissions, utilities, rent or mortgage payments, maintenance costs, supplies, and other administrative expenses.

Secondary Premium Factors

In addition to these three primary factors, the actual rate assigned to a specific health policy by the underwriter depends on several other factors, including the benefits provided under the policy, past **claims experience**, the **age** and **sex** of the insured, and the insured's **occupation** and **hobbies**.

Benefits

A health insurance policy may offer a specific type of benefit or a variety of benefits. For example, a hospital expense-only policy offers benefits to cover just hospitalization expenses while a comprehensive major medical policy covers a much broader range of medical expenses. The **number and kinds of benefits** provided by a policy affect the premium rate.

Another aspect is that, while two policies may provide identical types of benefits, the **amount of protection** or benefits in one policy may be higher than in another. So, the greater the benefits, the higher the premium, or, to state it another way, the greater the risk to the company, the higher the premium.

Claims Experience

Before realistic premium rates can be established for health insurance, the insurer must know what can be expected as to the dollar amount of the future claims. The most practical way to estimate the cost of future claims is to rely on claims tables based on **past claims experience**. For example, experience tables have been constructed for hospital expenses based on the amounts paid out in the past for the same types of expenses. Such tables, along with an added factor to account for rising hospital costs, enable companies to estimate the average amounts of future hospital expenses. Similarly, experience tables have been developed for surgical benefits, covering various kinds of surgery based on past experience. The same procedure is followed to estimate average claims expected in the future for other medical expenses. Such tables must be adjusted periodically, of course, to reflect more recent experience.

Age and Sex of the Insured

As discussed earlier, experience has shown that health insurance claims costs tend to increase as the age of the insured increases. For any given coverage, the older the insured, the higher the applicable premium rate.

Also, disabilities among women under age 55, on the average, have a greater frequency and longer duration than among men, so female premium rates for certain coverages are higher than the premium rates for males. At the older ages, however, that is generally not true.

Occupation and Hobbies

Because some types of work are more hazardous than others, the premium rates for a person's health insurance policy may be affected by his **occupation**. If an insured's occupation indicates a higher than normal risk to the company, the policy may carry an extra premium charge. (Insurers establish their own occupational classifications, which represent another element in the premium structure.) The same holds true for any dangerous **hobbies** in which the insured may participate.

TAX TREATMENT OF HEALTH INSURANCE PREMIUMS AND BENEFITS

The tax treatment of health insurance premiums and benefits depends, to a large degree, on the type of insurance in question.

Taxation of Disability Income Insurance

Premiums paid for personal disability income insurance are *not* deductible by the individual insured, but the disability benefits are **tax free** to the recipient.

When a group disability income insurance plan is paid for entirely by the employer and benefits are paid directly to individual employees who qualify, the premiums are **deductible** by the employer. The benefits, in turn, are **taxable** to the recipient. However, if an employee contributes to any portion of the premium, her benefit will be received tax free in proportion to the premium contributed. For example, if an employee pays 40% of the premium and the employer pays 60%, 40% of the benefit is tax free to the employee and 60% is taxable.

Persons under age 65 who are retired on permanent and total disability may be eligible for a tax credit on their disability income.

Taxation of Medical Expense Insurance

Incurred medical expenses that are reimbursed by insurance may not be deducted from an individual's federal income tax. Furthermore, incurred medical expenses that are not reimbursed by insurance may only be deducted to the extent they exceed 10% of the insured's adjusted gross income. For example, an individual who has an adjusted gross income of $35,000 would be able to deduct only the amount of unreimbursed medical expenses over $3,500.

For purposes of figuring any deductible medical expenses, prescription drugs, insulin, hospital expenses, physician and surgeon fees, nursing care, dental care, rehabilitative treatments, and medical insurance premiums (including long-term care insurance premiums, within limits) can all be considered.

Benefits received by an insured under a medical expense policy are not included in his gross income because they are paid to offset losses he incurred. However, medical expense insurance benefits must be included in gross income to the extent that reimbursement is received for medical expenses deducted in a prior year.

For self-employed individuals, the rules are slightly different. For them, all amounts paid for medical care (including insurance premiums) became fully deductible as of 2003.

Premiums paid for family members who are bona fide employees of the self-employed individual are fully deductible.

MANAGED CARE

With the support and involvement of government, business, and the insurance industry, managed care has become the key strategy for containing rising health care costs that were threatening the country's competitive position in global markets. The success of this strategy was revealed in a recent survey conducted by benefit consultants Foster Higgins. The survey found that insurers' costs for managed care grew at a consistently slower pace than traditional reimbursement costs.

Managed care organizations (MCOs) achieve these results because they integrate the financing and delivery of health care services to contain and control costs and to provide health care and services as efficiently as possible. Common techniques they use to achieve their objectives include selectively contracting with efficient and effective health care professionals and organizations; establishing financial incentives for members to use providers and procedures sanctioned by the plan; controlling expensive hospital admissions and lengths of stay; using utilization management tools such as utilization review, standardized medical practices guidelines, and clinical pathways to achieve better outcomes and case management; and emphasizing disease prevention and health promotion programs. These characteristics are typical of health maintenance organizations (HMOs), preferred provider organizations (PPOs), and exclusive provider organizations (EPOs), which were discussed in Unit 16.

Other important and related actions insurers are taking to contain health care costs address policy design and medical cost management techniques. The medical cost management techniques discussed in the following are common practices in managed care organizations.

Policy Design

The **design** or **structure** of a policy and its provisions can have an impact on an insurer's cost containment efforts. A **higher deductible** will help limit claims, for example, and in fact the average deductible has increased in recent years. Whereas the typical deductible was $100 for an individual and $300 for a family just a few years ago, it is more common now to find deductibles in the $300 to $500 range for an individual and $900 or higher for a family. **Coinsurance** is another important means of sharing the cost of medical care between the insured and the insurer. Shortened benefit periods can also prove beneficial from a cost containment standpoint, in that they can reduce the tendency some people have to seek medical attention for a condition that has long since been resolved.

Medical Cost Management

Medical cost management is being widely recognized and applauded as the most promising means of controlling claims expenses. Basically, it is the process of controlling how policyowners utilize their policies. There are four general approaches insurers use for cost management: **mandatory second opinions**, **precertification review**, **ambulatory surgery**, and **case management**.

Mandatory Second Opinions

In an effort to reduce unnecessary surgical operations, many health policies today contain a provision requiring the insured to obtain a **second opinion** before receiving non-life-threatening surgery. Benefits are often reduced if a second opinion is not obtained.

Precertification Review

To control hospital claims, many policies today require policyowners to **obtain approval** from the insurer before entering a hospital on a nonemergency basis. Even if the admission was on an emergency basis, most policies with this type of provision require the insured to notify the insurer within a short period of time (usually 24 hours) after being admitted. The insurer will then determine how much of the hospital stay it will cover, depending on the reason for the admission. If the insured wants to stay longer, the additional expense will be the responsibility of the insured, not the insurer.

Ambulatory Surgery

The advances in medicine now permit many surgical procedures to be performed on an **outpatient** basis where once an overnight hospital stay was required. To encourage insureds to utilize less expensive outpatient care, many policies offer some sort of inducement. For example, a policy may waive the deductible or coinsurance if the policyowner elects to be treated on an outpatient basis rather than as an admitted patient.

Case Management

Case management, as referred to here, involves a specialist within the insurance company, such as a registered nurse, who reviews a potentially large claim as it develops to discuss treatment alternatives with the insured. For example, the insured's policy might state that treatment for a kidney ailment can only be performed in a hospital or registered hemodialysis center. However, if it makes economic sense to the insurer—and practical sense to the insured—to have treatments conducted at the insured's home, the case manager might negotiate with the insured to allow treatment to be performed at home as long as certain conditions are met.

The purpose of case management is to let the insurer take an active role in the management of what could potentially become a very expensive claim.

SUMMARY

The escalating cost of medical care makes it imperative that insurers exercise precaution in their **underwriting**. A number of important factors come together during the health underwriting process. Preexisting medical conditions as well as circumstances that may affect future medical losses are reviewed carefully by health underwriters. Health insurance premium rates are affected not only by the three primary factors of **morbidity**, **interest**, and **expenses**, but by secondary factors as well, including the particular benefits provided by the policy and characteristics of the insured. As is true with all aspects of life and health insurance, the **tax treatment** of health insurance premiums and benefits is an important consideration from a personal financial standpoint. Typically, premiums paid for personal health insurance are not deductible and benefits received are not taxable. The exception is self-employed individuals, whose insurance is partly regarded as *employer-sponsored*. These individuals may deduct the cost of medical care up to certain limits.

In an effort to control health claims expenses, many insurers exercise some form of **cost management**, from requiring second surgical opinions to instituting full case management.

KEY CONCEPTS

Students should be familiar with the following concepts:

health insurance risk factors	substandard risks
health insurance premium factors	tax treatment of premiums and benefits
cost containment measures	

UNIT TEST

1. Susan is covered under her employer-sponsored disability group plan. The premium is $50 a month: Susan pays $10 and the employer pays $40. Assuming Susan were to become disabled and receive monthly disability benefits of $700 from the plan, how much, if any, of the monthly benefit would be taxable income?

   A. $0
   B. $70
   C. $140
   D. $560

2. Assume the following individuals are issued health insurance policies with varying renewability provisions. All other factors being equal, who would pay the highest premium?

   A. Dan—cancellable
   B. Jim—optionally renewable
   C. Henry—conditionally renewable
   D. Jack—noncancellable

3. Which of the following is the purpose of medical cost management?

   A. To influence hospital charges and doctors' fees
   B. To discourage individuals from utilizing health care services
   C. To control health claims expenses
   D. To encourage individuals to seek medical help only as a last resort

4. All of the following are primary risk factors in underwriting individual health insurance policies EXCEPT

   A. geographical location
   B. moral hazard
   C. occupation
   D. physical condition

5. Which of the following statements most aptly describes health insurance benefits?

   A. Each policy offers a single type of benefit.
   B. Claims, not benefits, affect premium rates.
   C. Policyowners who have policies with identical benefits pay the same premiums.
   D. The greater the benefits, the higher the premium.

6. Which of the following would probably NOT be considered in underwriting a health insurance risk?

   A. Personal habits
   B. Credit rating
   C. Medical history
   D. Marital status

7. All of the following factors would affect a health insurance policy's premium rate EXCEPT

   A. age of the insured
   B. occupation of the insured
   C. type of benefit provided
   D. residential address of the insured

8. Rick, who has no health insurance, experienced $3,000 in medical expenses this year. Assuming his adjusted gross income was $29,000, how much of those medical expenses can he deduct from his adjusted gross income, if any?

   A. $0
   B. $825
   C. $2,175
   D. $3,000

9. What kind of table reflects the average number of disabilities due to sickness or accidents at various ages?

   A. Mortality
   B. Morbidity
   C. Claims underwriting
   D. Underwriting

10. What is the effect of an impairment rider attached to a health insurance policy?

    A. To increase the premium rate charged
    B. To decrease the amount of benefits provided
    C. To exclude from coverage losses resulting from specified conditions
    D. To increase the policy's waiting period

UNIT

24

Group Health Insurance

- Nature of Group Health Insurance
- Group Health Insurance Coverages
- Tax Treatment of Group Health Plans

Most of our discussion of health and accident insurance so far has focused on individual coverage. However, 90% of those with private insurance are covered through group plans through their employers.

Group health insurance, like individual health insurance, can be tailored to meet the employer's needs. By its very nature, however, group insurance has several features that set it apart from individual plans, including the nature of the contract, the cost of the plan, the form of premium payments, and eligibility requirements. In this unit, we will examine the characteristics of this type of insurance protection and review the favorable tax treatment given to group plans. ■

NATURE OF GROUP HEALTH INSURANCE

In Unit 10, we introduced the subject of group life insurance and discussed its basic principles. Like group life, group health is a plan of insurance that an employer (or other eligible group sponsor) provides for its employees. The contract for coverage is between the insurance company and the employer, and a **master policy** is issued to the employer. The individual insureds covered by the policy are not given separate policies; instead, they receive **certificates of insurance** and an outline or booklet that describes their benefits. Generally speaking, the benefits provided under a group health plan are more extensive than those provided under an individual health plan. Group health plans typically have higher benefit maximums and lower deductibles.

Characteristics of Group Health Insurance

The characteristics of group health insurance are similar to those of group life. These include eligibility standards for groups and for individuals within the groups, method of premium payments (contributory versus noncontributory), lower cost, predetermined benefits, underwriting practices, conversion privileges, and preexisting conditions provisions. Let's briefly review each.

Eligible Groups

To qualify for group health coverage, the group must be a **natural group**. This means that it must have been formed for some reason other than to obtain insurance. Qualifying groups include employers, labor unions, trade associations, creditor-debtor groups, multiple employer trusts, lodges, and the like.

State laws specify the minimum number of persons to be covered under a group policy. One state may stipulate 15 persons as a minimum number, while another state may require a minimum of 10. (Ten lives is the most typical minimum requirement.) For instance, with respect to employee groups, Florida law does not specify a minimum number or percentage of participants for the issuance of a group health insurance policy. (This topic is fully discussed in Unit 29.)

Individual Eligibility

Like group life, group health plans commonly impose a set of **eligibility requirements** that must be met before an individual member is eligible to participate in the group plan. It is common to find the following requirements:

- Minimum of one to three months employment service

- Full-time employment status

Contributory Versus Noncontributory

Group health plans may be **contributory** or **noncontributory**. If the employer pays the entire premium, the plan is noncontributory; if the employees share a portion of the premium, it is contributory. Most noncontributory group health plans require 100% participation by eligible members, whereas contributory group health plans often require participation by 75% of eligible members. The reason for these minimum participation requirements is to protect the insurer against adverse selection and to keep administrative expenses in line with coverage units. Note, however, that under Florida law there is no specific minimum percentage participation for employees covered by group health insurance.

Lower Cost

Benefit for benefit, the cost of insuring an individual under a group health plan is less than the cost of insurance under an individual plan. This is because the administrative and selling expenses involved with group plans are far less.

Predetermined Benefits

Another characteristic of group health plans is that the benefits provided to individual insureds are predetermined by the employer in conjunction with the insurer's benefit schedules and coverage limits. For example, group disability benefits are tied to a position or earnings schedule, as are accidental death and dismemberment benefits.

Underwriting Practices

Generally speaking, the approach in underwriting group health plans is the same as underwriting group life plans: the insurer **evaluates the group as a whole**, rather than individuals within the group. Based on the group's risk profile, which is measured against the insurer's selection standards, the group is either accepted or rejected.

However, there are some changes taking place with regard to underwriting group medical expenses plans, especially for small groups. Whereas for large group medical plans it is common to accept all currently eligible members and new members coming into the group, this is not necessarily true any longer for smaller groups. In smaller groups the presence of even one bad risk can have a significant impact on the claims experience of the group. Consequently, most insurers today reserve the right to engage in **individual underwriting** to some degree with groups they insure.

As the term implies, individual underwriting is the process of reviewing a group member's individual risk profile. Most commonly this is done on two occasions: when a group is first taken on by an insurer and when a group member (e.g., an employee) tries to enter the plan after initially electing not to participate. In the latter case, the underwriter's objective is to reduce the risk of adverse selection. In the former case, individual underwriting is only done on members for whom the initial application indicates a potential risk problem (such as a preexisting condition). If the member is found to represent too great a risk, the insurer often retains the right to reject the member from participating in the plan or at least charge an increased premium (or exclude coverage for the specified condition). It is important to note that if an insurer does reserve this right of individual underwriting, most states require the insurer to explain, in the policy, how it will exercise this right.

Rarely is an entire group rejected on the basis of one bad risk, unless the group is very small. The underwriter reviews a number of factors to determine whether or not the group should be accepted. (See Illustration 24.1.)

ILLUSTRATION 24.1

General Group Underwriting Considerations

In spite of the many differences between types of groups, there are certain general underwriting considerations applicable to all or most types of groups:

- Reason for the group's existence (purchasing group insurance must be incidental to the group's formation, not the reason for it)
- Stability of the group (underwriters want to see a group of stable workers without an excessive amount of "turnover")
- Persistency of the group (groups that change insurers every year do not represent a good risk)
- Method of determining benefits (it must be by a schedule or method that prevents individual selection of benefits)
- How eligibility is determined (insurers want to see a sickness-related probationary period, for example, to reduce adverse selection)
- Source of premium payments, whether contributory or noncontributory (noncontributory plans are preferred because they require 100% participation, which helps spread the risk and reduces adverse selection)
- Prior claims experience of the group
- Size and composition of the group
- Industry or business with which the group is associated (hazardous industries are typified by higher-than-standard mortality and morbidity rates)

Under Florida law, insurers of large groups (at least 51 persons) must accept the entire group. If they believe an individual in the group poses too great a risk to insure the group, they can reject the entire group. Florida law does not permit individual risk "carve outs" in such cases.

Conversion Privilege

Group health plans that provide medical expense coverage universally contain a **conversion privilege** for individual insureds, which allows them to convert their group certificate to an individual medical expense policy with the same insurer, if and when they leave their employment. Insurers are permitted to evaluate the individual and charge the appropriate premium, be it a standard rate or substandard rate; however, an individual cannot be denied coverage, even if she has become uninsurable.

The conversion must be exercised within a given period of time, usually 30 or 31 days, depending on the state. During this time, the individual remains insured under the group plan, whether or not a conversion ultimately takes place. Conversion privileges generally are reserved for those who were active in the group plan during the preceding three months.

Preexisting Conditions

In the past, group health insurance plans typically excluded a person from coverage because of preexisting conditions. A **preexisting condition** was generally defined as any condition for which a participant received treatment at any time during the three months prior to the effective date of the group coverage. Group plans also specified when a condition would stop being considered preexisting.

However, the Health Insurance Portability and Accountability Act (HIPAA) has changed the rules governing preexisting conditions for group health plans. Beginning July 1, 1997, HIPAA limited the ability of employer-sponsored groups and insurers to exclude individuals on the basis of preexisting medical conditions. The exclusion for preexisting conditions is now limited to conditions for which medical advice or treatment was recommended or received within the six-month period ending on the enrollment date. However, the exclusion can extend for no more than 12 months (18 months for late enrollees).

GROUP HEALTH INSURANCE COVERAGES

All of the types of health insurance coverages discussed in this text—medical expense, disability income, and accidental death and dismemberment—are available for group plans. Rather than repeat the discussion of these policies—their purpose and functions are the same whether it's a group product or an individual product—let's focus on the features of these coverages when they are part of a group plan.

ILLUSTRATION 24.2

Dental and Vision Care—Popular Group Benefits

Relatively new to the array of health care benefits offered to groups are coverages for **dental care** and **vision care**.

Dental care coverage is designed to cover the costs associated with normal dental maintenance as well as oral surgery, root canal therapy, and orthodontia. The coverage may be on a "reasonable and customary charge" basis or on a dollar-per-service schedule approach. Deductible and coinsurance features are typical (though some policies will cover routine cleaning and exams at 100%), as are maximum yearly benefit amounts, such as $1,000 or $2,000.

Vision care coverage usually pays for reasonable and customary charges incurred during eye exams by opthalmologists and optometrists. Expenses for the fitting or cost of contact lenses or eyeglasses often are excluded.

Group Basic Medical Expense

The three standard forms of basic medical expense insurance—hospital, surgical, and physicians' expenses—are available for group insurance. In addition, a number of newer coverages have been developed in recent years, including dental and vision care, prescription drugs, home health care, extended care facilities, diagnostic x-rays, and laboratory services. In fact, some of these specified coverages, such as vision and dental care, are available only on a group basis.

A group basic medical expense plan can combine two or more of these coverages or it may consist of only one type of coverage, such as hospital expense only.

Group Major Medical Plans

Like individual major medical plans, group major medical plans may be offered as a single, extensive plan (**comprehensive major medical**) or superimposed over a group basic plan (**supplemental major medical**). Participants are usually required to satisfy an initial deductible with comprehensive plans and either a corridor or an integrated deductible with supplemental plans.

Benefits provided by group major medical plans are usually more extensive than those of individual plans. For example, it is not uncommon to find group plans that offer individual benefit maximums of $1 million; still others do not set any maximum benefit limits. Also, deductibles are usually lower for group plans, typically ranging from $250 to $500, whereas deductibles for individual policies can be $1,000 or more.

There are two other characteristics of group medical expense plans that distinguish them from individual plans. These are the **coordination of benefits provision** and the treatment of **maternity benefits**.

Coordination of Benefits

The purpose of the **coordination of benefits (COB) provision**, found only in group health plans, is to avoid duplication of benefit payments and overinsurance when an individual is covered under more than one group health plan. The provision limits the total amount of claims paid from all insurers covering the patient to no more than the total allowable medical expenses. For example, an individual who incurs $700 in allowable medical expenses would not be able to collect any more than $700, no matter how many group plans he is covered by.

The COB provision establishes which plan is the **primary plan**, or the plan that is responsible for providing the full benefit amounts as it specifies. Once the primary plan has paid its full promised benefit, the insured may submit the claim to the secondary provider for any additional benefits payable. In no case, however, will the total amount the insured receives exceed the costs incurred or the total maximum benefits available under all plans.

Coordinating benefits is appropriate for married couples, when each is covered by an employer group plan. For example, John and Cindy, a young married couple, each are participants in their own company's health plan and are also covered as dependents under their spouse's plan. John's plan would specify that it is the primary plan for John; Cindy's plan would be his secondary plan. Likewise, Cindy's plan would specify that it is the primary plan for Cindy; John's plan would be her secondary plan.

Subrogation

In most insurance policies, the insurer is given **subrogation** rights. The insured transfers the "right of recovery against others" to the insurer. In most cases, the insurer will pay any legitimate claim filed by the insured. However, if the insurer believes other individuals or insurers are legally liable to share or even assume the full responsibility for the loss, the insurer will sue or otherwise seek to recover the costs of the claim using these subrogation rights.

Maternity Benefits

Whereas it is common for individual health plans to exclude routine maternity care from coverage, group medical expense plans must provide **maternity benefits**. This is the result of a 1979 amendment to the Civil Rights Act, which requires plans covering 15 or more people to treat pregnancy-related claims no differently than any other allowable medical expense.

COBRA Continuation of Benefits

Participants in group medical expense plans are protected by a federal law that guarantees a continuation of their group coverage if their employment is terminated for reasons other than gross misconduct. Practically speaking, the law protects employees who are laid-off but not those who are fired "for cause." (The circumstances that qualify for this continued coverage are noted in Illustration 24.3.)

This law, known as the **Consolidated Omnibus Budget Reconciliation Act of 1985** (i.e., COBRA), requires employers with 20 or more employees to continue group medical expense coverage for terminated workers (as well as their spouses, divorced spouses, and dependent children) for up to 18 months (or 36 months, in some situations) following termination. (See Unit 29 for Florida's "mini-COBRA" law for employees with fewer than 20 employees.)

Some important points about this law should be noted. It is not the same as the policy conversion privilege by which an employee may convert a group certificate to an individual policy. COBRA permits the terminated employee to continue her group coverage.

ILLUSTRATION 24.3

COBRA Continued Coverage for Former Employees

The following events would qualify for extended medical expense coverage under COBRA for a terminated employee:

- Employment is terminated (for other than gross misconduct):
  18 months of continued coverage (or up to 29 months if disabled)
- Employee's hours are reduced (resulting in termination from the plan):
  18 months of continued coverage (or up to 29 months if disabled)
- Employee dies:
  36 months of continued coverage for dependents
- Dependent child no longer qualifies as "dependent child" under the plan:
  36 months of continued coverage
- Employee becomes eligible for Medicare:
  36 months of continued coverage
- Employee divorces or legally separates:
  36 months of continued coverage for former spouse

The law does not require the employer to pay the cost of the continued group coverage; the terminated employee can be required to pay the premium, which may be up to 102% of the premium that would otherwise be charged. (The additional 2% is allowed to cover the insurer's administrative expenses.) The schedule of benefits will be the same during the continuation period as under the group plan.

Group Disability Income Plans

Group disability income plans differ from individual plans in a number of ways. Individual plans usually specify a flat income amount, based on the person's earnings, determined at the time the policy is purchased. In contrast, group plans usually specify benefits in terms of a percentage of the individual's earnings.

Like individual plans, group disability can include short-term plans or long-term plans. The definitions of "short term" and "long term," however, are different for group and individual.

Group short-term disability plans are characterized by maximum benefit periods of rather short duration, such as 13 or 26 weeks. Benefits are typically paid weekly and range from 50% to 100% of the individual's income.

Group long-term disability plans provide for maximum benefit periods of more than two years, occasionally extending to the insured's retirement age. Benefit amounts are usually limited to about 60% of the participant's income.

If an employer provides both a short-term plan and long-term plan, the long-term plan typically begins paying benefits only after the short-term benefits cease. Often, long-term plans use an "own occupation" definition of total disability for the first year or two of disability and then switch to an "any occupation" definition.

Most group disability plans require the employee to have a minimum period of service, such as 30 to 90 days, before he is eligible for coverage. In addition, most group plans include provisions making their benefits supplemental to workers' compensation benefits, so that total benefits received do not exceed a specified percentage of regular earnings. In some cases, group disability plans actually limit coverage to nonoccupational disabilities because occupational disabilities normally qualify for workers' compensation benefits.

Group AD&D

Accidental death and dismemberment insurance is a very popular type of group coverage, frequently offered in conjunction with group life insurance plans. It may also be provided as a separate policy, in which case it is normally paid for entirely by the employee. Such employee-pay-all plans are called voluntary group AD&D because plan participation is voluntary. Benefits may be provided for both occupational and nonoccupational losses or for nonoccupational losses only. Voluntary group AD&D typically provides benefits for both types of losses.

Like individual AD&D, group AD&D pays a principal sum upon the insured's accidental death (or loss of any two body members). A capital sum is payable upon the accidental loss of one body member. Some group AD&D plans specify a higher death benefit if the insured dies while on company business.

Group AD&D, unlike group life and group medical, normally does not include a conversion privilege.

Other Types of Group Health Plans

In addition to the typical group health insurance plan—as would be utilized by an employer, for example—there are four additional types of plans worth noting: **blanket health insurance**, **franchise (or wholesale) health insurance**, **credit accident and health insurance**, and **health savings accounts**.

Blanket Health Plans

Blanket health insurance is issued to cover a group who may be exposed to the same risks, but the composition of the group—the individuals within the group—are constantly changing. A blanket health plan may be issued to an airline or a bus company to cover its passengers or to a school to cover its students.

Franchise Health Plans

Franchise health plans, sometimes called *wholesale plans*, provide health insurance coverage to members of an association or professional society. Individual policies are issued to individual members; the association or society simply serves as the sponsor for the plan. Premium rates are usually discounted for franchise plans.

Credit Accident and Health Plans

Like credit life plans, **credit accident and health plans** are designed to help the insured pay off a loan in the event she is disabled due to an accident or sickness. If the insured becomes disabled, the policy provides for monthly benefit payments equal to the monthly loan payments due.

Health Savings Accounts (HSAs)

The Medicare Prescription Drug and Modernization Act of 2003 established a new way for consumers to pay for medical expenses: health care savings accounts (HSAs). An HSA is a tax-favored vehicle for accumulating funds to cover medical expenses.

Eligibility. Individuals under age 65 and families are eligible to establish HSAs if they have a qualified high-deductible health plan. The specific minimum deductibles and out-of-pocket expense caps are indexed annually for inflation.

Contribution Limits. Annual contributions of up to 100% of an individual's health plan deductible can be made to an HSA. Individuals with HSAs who are age 55 and older may make an additional contribution of $1,000 in 2010 and thereafter.

Tax Treatment. Earnings in HSAs grow tax free, and account beneficiaries can make tax-free withdrawals to cover current and future qualified health care costs.

Qualified health care expenses include amounts paid for:

- doctors' fees;

- prescription and nonprescription medicines;

- necessary hospital services not paid for by insurance;

- retiree health insurance premiums;

- Medicare expenses (but not Medigap);

- qualified long-term care services; and

- COBRA coverage.

Qualified medical expenses are expenses incurred by the HSA owner, the spouse, and dependents. Nonqualified withdrawals are subject to income taxes and a 10% penalty. HSAs are fully portable, and assets can accumulate over the years. Upon death, HSA ownership may be transferred to a spouse tax free.

TAX TREATMENT OF GROUP HEALTH PLANS

As an incentive for employers to provide health insurance benefits to their employees, the federal government grants favorable tax treatment to group plans. Let's briefly review this treatment.

Taxation of Group Health Premiums

Employers are entitled to take a tax deduction for premium contributions they make to a group health plan, as long as the contributions represent an "ordinary and necessary business expense." By the same token, individual participants do not include employer contributions made on their behalf as part of their taxable income.

As a general rule, individual premium contributions to a group health plan are not tax deductible. Only when unreimbursed medical expenses—expenses that can include any individual contributions to a group medical plan—exceed 10% of an individual's adjusted gross income can a tax deduction be taken. The deduction is limited to the amount exceeding 10% of adjusted gross income. Any premiums the individual contributes for group disability or group AD&D coverage are not considered qualifying medical expenses when determining this excess.

Taxation of Group Health Benefits

Any benefits an individual receives under a medical expense plan are not considered taxable income because they are provided to cover losses the individual incurred. It is a somewhat different story with disability income plans, however. Disability benefit payments that are attributed to employee contributions are not taxable, but benefit payments that are attributed to employer contributions are taxable. Let's look at an example.

Anne is a participant in a contributory group disability income plan in which her employer pays two-thirds of the premium and Anne pays one-third. Her employer qualifies for a tax deduction for its share of the premium and, as is true with employer contributions to all group health plans, Anne is not taxed on those contributions. The premium portion that Anne pays does not qualify for a tax deduction for her.

Now assume Anne becomes disabled and receives disability income benefits of $900 a month. One-third of the monthly benefit—$300—would be tax free because it is attributed to the premium she paid; the remaining two-thirds of the payment—$600—would be taxable income because it is attributed to the premium her employer paid.

SUMMARY

Group health insurance—like group life insurance—is evidenced by one master contract that covers multiple lives. Virtually any health insurance product available as an individual contract is also available under the group umbrella. Thus, **medical expense insurance**, **disability income insurance**, and **accidental death and dismemberment insurance** are all common group plans. In addition, there are a number of coverages, like vision and dental care, that are only available to groups.

Of utmost concern to insurance regulators is that employees be protected from loss of their insurance coverage if their job is terminated. Accordingly, nearly all states have provisions in their insurance laws that require group life and medical expense policies to provide a **conversion option** to terminating participants. The federal government has also exercised its regulatory prerogative by passing laws that protect terminated employees (COBRA) and that guarantee maternity cases will be treated the same as any other medical condition.

KEY CONCEPTS

Students should be familiar with the following concepts:

master policy

contributory versus noncontributory plans

group major medical expense

group AD&D

conversion privilege

COBRA

HSA

certificate of insurance

group basic medical expense

group disability income

group health underwriting

preexisting conditions

taxation of group health insurance

UNIT TEST

1. Which of the following statements about group health insurance is CORRECT?

   A. A group health insurance contract is between the insurance company and the employee.
   B. Group health plans provide more extensive benefits than individual health plans.
   C. If a group plan provides medical expense benefits, it must be with a comprehensive policy.
   D. COBRA requirements are directed at employers with 20 or fewer employees.

2. Which type of group health coverage typically does NOT contain a conversion privilege?

   A. Basic medical expense
   B. Comprehensive medical expense
   C. Disability income
   D. Accidental death and dismemberment

3. Which of the following can an individual include as **qualifying expenses** for purposes of determining a medical tax deduction?

   A. Premium contributions paid by the employer to a group medical expense plan
   B. Premium contributions paid by the employer to a group disability plan
   C. Premium contributions paid by the individual to a group medical expense plan
   D. Premium contributions paid by the individual to a group disability plan

4. An individual purchased group credit accident and health insurance to cover a car loan. Following an accident, the individual was disabled for eight months. Which of the following benefits were paid under the policy?

   A. Monthly income benefits to the insured
   B. An amount equal to 8 months of the loan payment to the insured's creditor
   C. An amount equal to 10 months of the loan payment to the insured's creditor
   D. Monthly income benefits to the insured and an amount equal to 8 months of the loan payment to the insured's creditor

5. Dan is a participant in his company's group health plan. One of the plan's provisions specifies that, in the event he is eligible for benefits under another policy, his group plan will serve as the primary plan. What is this provision called?

   A. Excess coverage provision
   B. Coordination of benefits provision
   C. Other insurance with this insurer provision
   D. Double indemnity provision

6. A vacation cruise line that wants group health coverage for its passengers would purchase what kind of insurance?

   A. Franchise health insurance
   B. Wholesale health insurance
   C. Blanket health insurance
   D. Credit health insurance

7. The purpose of COBRA requirements concerns

   A. coordination of health benefits
   B. continuation of health insurance
   C. Medicare supplement coverage
   D. nondiscrimination in group health plans

8. Sally is covered by her employer's noncontributory group disability income plan, the premium for which is $50 a month. If she were to become disabled and receive $1,000 a month, how much of each benefit payment would be taxable income to her?

   A. $0
   B. $50
   C. $950
   D. $1,000

9. Which of the following statements regarding group disability income plans is NOT correct?

    A. Benefits are specified in terms of a percentage of the participant's earnings.
    B. Benefits paid under the group plan are supplemental to workers' compensation benefits.
    C. Employees covered under both a short-term and long-term plan collect benefits from each simultaneously.
    D. A minimum length of service may be required before an employee is eligible to participate in the plan.

10. Which of the following statements about COBRA is CORRECT?

    A. The premium for continued group medical coverage may be up to 102% of the premium that would otherwise be charged.
    B. The employer must pay the cost of the continued group coverage.
    C. The schedule of benefits during the continuation period may be different than those provided under the group plan.
    D. COBRA permits an employee to convert a group certificate to an individual policy.

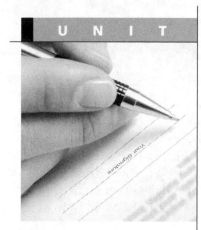

25

Uses of Health Insurance

- A Proper Health Insurance Program
- Individual Needs for Health Insurance
- Business Needs for Health Insurance

It may at first seem that the uses of health insurance are self-explanatory: one purchases health insurance to protect against the cost of health care—or, more accurately, health insurance provides protection against the costs associated with the loss of one's health. However, just as life insurance can be used creatively to meet a variety of needs, so too can the different types of health insurance plans be used in various ways to meet an individual's or business's unique needs.

Individuals, for example, need to have a comprehensive health insurance plan in place to insure against the financial consequences of illness or disability. Similarly, health insurance also is necessary to protect a business against the risks it faces, including losses due to a key employee's death or disability. Businesses also commonly offer health insurance as part of an employee benefits program. In this unit, we will take a closer look at some of the ways in which individuals and businesses use health insurance. ■

A PROPER HEALTH INSURANCE PROGRAM

What is a "proper" health insurance program? That question cannot be answered without first addressing several preliminary issues. Is the insurance for an individual only, a family, or a business? Is coverage currently available from a group plan or social insurance program? How willing is the policy-owner to assume some responsibility for medical care expenses (through policy deductibles and coinsurance) in exchange for reduced premiums? These and other questions must first be answered before reaching a conclusion as to the "right" health insurance program.

INDIVIDUAL NEEDS FOR HEALTH INSURANCE

At one time it was acceptable to expect one's family to provide support when illness or disability struck. Those days are now long past; today, we all must prepare for and assume the responsibility of covering the cost of medical care. However, unless one is independently wealthy, the prospect of covering costs out-of-pocket is not an attractive one; indeed, it can be downright terrifying.

The loss of one's health can have wide-ranging consequences. Not only does the cost of medical care come with a high price tag, but the loss of income that often accompanies a disabling illness or injury can compound the devastating effects of the health loss. Current demographics, which show that most families have both parents working, emphasize the need to consider both parents' income needs when designing a complete health insurance program.

Medical Expense Insurance Needs

While it is difficult to measure the importance of one type of insurance over another, it is fair to presume that a health insurance program must begin with an adequate amount of **medical expense insurance**. Without proper protection devoted to these potential costs, even the most basic medical care can quickly exhaust an individual's savings; a catastrophic claim can spell financial disaster.

At one time, most medical policies were the basic medical expense type. However, today it is more common to find most Americans covered under some form of a major medical policy or a service plan such as an HMO. If the policyowner can afford the cost, an ideal policy is a combination plan in which a basic plan is enhanced by a supplementary major medical plan. Under this approach, the insured obtains the "first dollar" benefits of the basic plan and also has the expansive protection offered by the major medical plan.

Most policyowners, of course, are concerned with the cost of their health insurance and find that some financial sacrifice may be required. For example, an individual major medical plan with a $100 individual deductible is going to cost more than a comparable plan with a $500 deductible. A plan with an 80/20 coinsurance provision will cost more than a comparable plan with a 75/25 coinsurance provision. The question the policyowner must answer is, "Am I willing to assume more of the cost risk of possible future claims in exchange for the *definite* cost savings offered by a plan with a higher deductible or coinsurance limit?"

Group Versus Individual Coverage

More Americans are protected under a group medical expense policy than an individual policy. The benefit to the group member, even assuming the plan is contributory, is the significantly less out-of-pocket cost than a comparable individual plan. The group plan participant can take comfort in knowing that even if he should terminate employment, continued coverage is guaranteed through the **conversion privilege** built into every group health policy.

Disability Income Insurance Needs

The importance of protecting one's earnings is sometimes overlooked in the insurance needs analysis process—a regrettable fact for the many people who become disabled every year. Americans too often assume that Social Security will provide the income necessary to survive if disability strikes. This is an unfortunate assumption; not only is the definition of "disabled" to qualify for Social Security benefits extremely narrow, but there is no assurance that the benefits will meet the disabled person's needs.

Social Security disability income should be viewed as a possible source of income to augment a personal plan. Whether the personal plan is based on a group policy or an individual policy, it should be regarded as the primary source of income if earnings are lost due to disability.

Policyowners can control the premium cost of a disability income plan by electing a longer elimination period than might otherwise be desired. The length of the benefit period also has a direct impact on the premium.

Because of the favorable tax treatment given to individually funded disability income policies, a plan that provides about 60% of predisability gross earnings can be considered sufficient. This is because disability income benefits are income tax free if the individual insured paid the premiums. An individual who earns $3,000 a month may only take home $2,000 after taxes. Consequently, a disability plan that provides a monthly tax-free benefit of $1,800 would likely be sufficient.

In the case of group disability income plans, the group member has little choice as to the level of benefits provided; the plan document must have a schedule of benefits that identifies what the participant will receive if disabled. However, the group member benefits to the extent the employer contributes to the disability income premiums.

If both parents in a family are actively employed, then disability income must be considered for each. If each parent's income is indispensable for the financial support of the family, then it is safe to assume that the loss of *either* income would present a financial problem.

BUSINESS NEEDS FOR HEALTH INSURANCE

Many health insurance producers have found a niche servicing the business market. There is a good, practical reason for this—the health insurance needs of the business market are as great as the needs of individuals.

Business uses of health insurance can be broadly divided into two categories: **employee benefit plans** and **business continuation plans**.

Employee Benefit Plans

While the term **employee benefit plan** can encompass a wide variety of benefit offerings—life insurance, a pension or profit-sharing plan, vacation pay, deferred compensation arrangements, funeral leave, sick time—it is rare when it does not include some kind of provision for health insurance or health benefits. The large and rapid increases in the cost of health care are likely the primary reasons for the popularity of employer-sponsored health plans, and many people rely on these plans as their sole source of health insurance.

Group Health Insurance

As we have learned, a **group health plan** can consist of medical insurance, disability income insurance, accidental death and dismemberment insurance—alone or in any combination. In fact, it is not uncommon to find all of these coverages included in a single group insurance plan.

By providing its employees with a plan for health insurance, an employer derives a number of benefits.

- The plan contributes to employee morale and productivity.

- The plan enables the employer to provide a needed benefit that employees would otherwise have to pay for with personal after-tax dollars (this helps hold down demands for wage increases).

- The plan places the employer in a competitive position for hiring and retaining employees.

- The employer can obtain a tax deduction for the cost of contributing to the plan.

- The plan enhances the employer's image in both public and employee relations.

Cafeteria Plans

Many times, employer-provided health insurance benefits are part of a **cafeteria plan**. As its name implies, cafeteria plans (also known as Section 125 plans) are benefit arrangements in which employees can pick and choose from a menu of benefits, thus tailoring their benefits package to their specific needs. Employees can select the benefits they value or need and forgo those of lesser importance to them. The employer allocates a certain amount of money to each employee to "buy" the benefits she desires; if the cost of the benefits exceeds the allocation, the employee may contribute the balance.

The types of flexible benefits usually available under a cafeteria plan include medical coverage, accidental death and dismemberment insurance, short-term and long-term disability, life insurance, and dependent care. Some plans provide for "choices within the choices": an employee may have the option of selecting from various levels of medical plans or choosing from among a variety of HMOs, for example.

Business Continuation Plans

Just as life insurance provides a way to help a business continue in the event an owner or key employee dies, health insurance also serves continuation purposes in the event of a disabling sickness or injury. It does so through the following plans.

Business Overhead Expense Insurance

Business overhead expense insurance is designed to reimburse a business for overhead expenses in the event a businessowner becomes disabled. It is sold on an individual basis to professionals in private practice, self-employed businessowners, partners, and occasionally close corporations.

Overhead expenses include such things as rent or mortgage payments, utilities, telephones, leased equipment, employees' salaries, and the like—all the expenses that would continue and must be paid, regardless of the owner's disability. Business overhead expense policies do not include any compensation for the disabled owner; they are designed to help the day-to-day operation of his business continue during the period of disability.

The benefits payable under these kinds of policies are limited to the covered expenses incurred or the maximum that is stated in the policy. For example, assume Dr. Miller is the insured under a business overhead expense policy that pays maximum monthly benefits of $4,500. If Dr. Miller became disabled and actual monthly expenses were $3,950, the monthly benefits paid would be $3,950. If Dr. Miller's actual expenses were $4,700, the benefits payable would be $4,500.

The premium for business overhead insurance is a legitimate, tax-deductible business expense. The benefits when paid, however, are treated as taxable income.

Disability Buy-Outs

A **disability buy-sell agreement** operates in much the same way as a life insurance buy-sell agreement; however, in this case, the plan sets forth the terms for selling and buying a partner's or stock owner's share of a business in the event she becomes disabled and is no longer able to participate in the business. It is a legal, binding arrangement, funded with a disability income policy.

Unlike typical disability income insurance plans that pay benefits in the form of periodic payments, the buy-out plan usually contains a provision allowing for a lump-sum payment of the benefit, thereby facilitating the buy-out of the disabled's interest. However, if the owners desire, the plan often permits the buy-out to occur through the use of periodic income payments.

Disability buy-out plans are characterized by lengthy elimination periods, often as long as two years. The reason for this is simple: because the plan involves the sale of a disabled partner's or owner's interest in the business, it is important to be quite sure that the disabled person will not be able to return to the business.

Considering the fact that a disabled partner can represent a double liability—the remaining partners must not only make up the slack left by the disabled partner's absence but usually must pay him an income as well—it is understandable why the disability buy-out plan is popular with businessowners.

Key Person Disability Insurance

Just as key person life insurance indemnifies the business for the lost services of a key person, so does a key person disability income policy. This type of coverage pays a monthly benefit to a business to cover expenses for additional help or outside services when an essential person is disabled. The key person could be a partner or working stockholder of the business. The key person could also be a management person who is personally responsible for some very important functions, such as a sales manager.

The key person's economic value to the business is determined in terms of the potential loss of business income that could occur, as well as the expense of hiring and training a replacement for the key person. The key person's value then becomes the disability benefit that will be paid to the business. The benefit amount may be paid in a lump sum or in monthly installments. Generally, the policy's elimination period will be 30 to 90 days, and the benefit period will be one or two years.

The business is the owner and premium payor of the policy. Benefits are received by the business tax free because the premium paid is not tax deductible.

SUMMARY

The uses of health insurance—notably medical expense and disability income—are as varied as the need for it is vital. Both the personal market and the business market have many uses for these important insurance products. Often the insured's concern is not "Should I have it?" but "How can I afford it?" Fortunately, every type of health insurance plan offers some way for the owner to reduce premium costs, including increasing the deductible or lengthening the elimination period.

KEY CONCEPTS

Students should be familiar with the following concepts:

individual versus group health insurance

employee benefit plans

business overhead expense insurance

key person disability insurance

disability buy-out insurance

UNIT TEST

1. All of the following are methods of keeping premium costs to a minimum in a health policy EXCEPT

    A. modifying benefit amounts
    B. increasing the deductible
    C. waiving the right to receive benefit payments when due
    D. extending the elimination period

2. Fred owns a small hardware store and is covered under a business overhead expense policy. If he becomes disabled, he can expect all the following expenses to be covered EXCEPT

    A. his employees' salaries
    B. his salary
    C. utility bills
    D. property and liability insurance premiums

3. Which of the following characteristics is associated with disability buy-out plans?

    A. A short elimination period
    B. The option to elect a lump-sum payment
    C. Provisions to cover the business's overhead expenses
    D. Irrevocable agreements

4. What is the income tax consequence if Marie's employer pays for her group disability income coverage?

    A. Marie must pay taxes on the premium payments.
    B. Marie can deduct the premium payments.
    C. The employer receives the disability income benefits tax free.
    D. The employer can deduct the premium payments.

5. With regard to health insurance policies, which of the following statements is CORRECT?

    A. A major medical plan with a $100 deductible is less expensive than one with a $500 deductible.
    B. More Americans are covered by an individual medical expense policy than a group policy.
    C. The appropriate benefit payable under a disability income policy should equal the insured's monthly gross income.
    D. A disability policy with a 6-month elimination period is less expensive than one with a 60-day elimination period, all other factors being equal.

Florida-Specific Laws and Rules

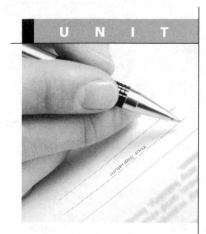

26

Florida Laws and Rules Pertinent to Life and Health Insurance

■ Financial Services Regulation

■ Licensing

■ Agent Responsibilities

■ Insurance Guaranty Fund

■ Marketing Practices

■ Rule 69B-215, F.A.C., Code of Ethics—NAIFA

This unit describes Florida's regulation of the life and health insurance business, its companies, and their marketing practices. Candidates for either the Life and Annuity Insurance Examination or the Health Insurance Examination, or both, will be tested on the various required laws and rules covered in this unit. ■

FINANCIAL SERVICES REGULATION

Chief Financial Officer (CFO)

The Chief Financial Officer is an independently elected official and a member of the Governor's cabinet. The CFO serves as head of the Department of Financial Services and as a member of the Financial Services Commission.

The CFO directly oversees 15 divisions and offices, including a Division of Accounting and Auditing (Bureau of Unclaimed Property), a Division of Insurance Agents and Agency Services, a Division of Insurance Fraud, a Division of Consumer Services, and the Office of the Insurance Consumer Advocate, all five of which have a role in regulating insurance. Therefore, regulation of insurance agents is directly administered by the CFO, as is insurance fraud and insurance consumer protection. The CFO, the Financial Services Commission, and the Commissioner of the Office of Insurance Regulation administer the insurance laws of Florida. [Sec. 20.121]

Financial Services Commission

The Financial Services Commission is composed of the Governor, the CFO, the Attorney General, and the Commissioner of Agriculture. This Commission in turn supervises the Office of Insurance Regulation and the Office of Financial Regulation. [Sec. 20.121]

Office of Financial Regulation

The Office of Financial Regulation (OFR) is responsible for all activities of the Financial Services Commission relating to the regulation of banks, credit unions, other financial institutions, finance companies, and the securities industry. The head of the office is the Director or Commissioner of Financial Regulation. The OFR includes a Bureau of Financial Investigations that may investigate suspected wrongdoing, both inside and outside of Florida, and may refer suspected violations of criminal law to state or federal law enforcement or prosecutorial agencies.

Office of Insurance Regulation

The Office of Insurance Regulation (OIR) is responsible for all activities of the Financial Services Commission relating to the regulation of insurers and other risk-bearing entities. The head of the office is the Director or Commissioner of Insurance Regulation. The specific duties of the office include the following:

- Rate-making supervision

- Policy forms approval

- Market conduct investigation

- Issuing insurer certificates of authority

- Assessing insurer solvency

- Regulating viatical settlements

- Regulating premium financing arrangements

- Administrative supervision

DEPARTMENT OF FINANCIAL SERVICES

The Department of Financial Services, headed by the Chief Financial Officer and the Commissioner of the Office of Insurance Regulation, oversees the insurance industry in accordance with the provisions of the Insurance Code. Members of the department have broad administrative, quasi-legislative (rule-making), and quasi-judicial powers in order to carry out their responsibilities.

General duties and powers

The department and respective offices have the following powers and duties. [Sec. 624.307]

- They enforce the Insurance Code and carry out those duties set forth by the code.

- Their powers and authority may be expressed or implied in the Insurance Code.

- They may conduct any investigation of insurance matters expressed in the code, determine if a person has violated the code, or obtain information to administer the code.

- They can collect, propose, publish, or disseminate information regarding the duties imposed upon it by the code.

- They shall have additional powers and duties as provided by other laws of the state.

- The department and office may each employ actuaries. Actuaries employed pursuant to this paragraph shall be members of the Society of Actuaries or the Casualty Actuarial Society.

Policyholders' rights

The principles expressed in the following statements serve as standards to be followed by the department, commission, and office in exercising their powers and duties, in exercising administrative discretion, in dispensing administrative interpretations of the law, and in adopting rules. [Sec. 626.9641]

- Policyholders shall have the right to competitive pricing practices and marketing methods that enable them to determine the best value among comparable policies.

- Policyholders shall have the right to obtain comprehensive coverage.

- Policyholders shall have the right to insurance advertising and other selling approaches that provide accurate and balanced information on the benefits and limitations of a policy.

- Policyholders shall have a right to an insurance company that is financially stable.

- Policyholders shall have the right to be serviced by a competent, honest insurance agent or broker.

- Policyholders shall have the right to a readable policy.

- Policyholders shall have the right to an insurance company that provides an economic delivery of coverage and that tries to prevent losses.

- Policyholders shall have the right to a balanced and positive regulation by the department, commission, and office.

OFFICE OF INSURANCE REGULATION

In addition to duties and powers listed previously, the Office of Insurance Regulation is responsible for the following areas.

Policy approval authority rates and forms

A basic insurance policy, annuity contract, application form, group certificate of insurance, rider, endorsement, or renewal certificate may not be delivered in Florida unless the form has been filed with the office and has been approved by the office. Each filing must be made at least 30 days in advance of any such use or delivery. At the expiration of the 30 days, the form filed will be deemed approved unless prior thereto it has been affirmatively approved or disapproved by order of the office.

In addition, an insurer may not deliver, issue for delivery, or renew in Florida any health insurance policy form until it has filed with the office a copy of every applicable rating manual, rating schedule, change in rating manual, and change in rating schedule.

The office may, for cause, withdraw a previous approval. [Sec. 624.302, 627.410, Rule 69O-149.002-023]

Market conduct examinations

The Office of Insurance Regulation may examine each insurer as often as may be warranted for the protection of the policyholders and in the public interest, and must examine each domestic insurer not less frequently than once every five years.

In lieu of making its own examination, the office may accept a full report of the last recent examination of a foreign insurer, certified by the insurance supervisory official of another state. The examination by the office of an alien insurer shall be limited to the alien insurer's insurance transactions and affairs in the United States, except as otherwise required by the office.

The examination may include examination of the affairs, transactions, accounts, and records relating directly or indirectly to the insurer and of the assets of the insurer's managing general agents and controlling or controlled person. To facilitate uniformity in examinations, the commission may use the methods in the Market Conduct Examiners Handbook and the Financial Condition Examiners Handbook of the National Association of Insurance Commissioners.

The office will examine each insurer applying for an initial certificate of authority to transact insurance in this state before granting the initial certificate. An examination must be conducted at least once every year with respect to a domestic insurer that has continuously held a certificate of authority for less than three years. The examination must cover the preceding fiscal year or the period since the last examination of the insurer. [Sec. 624.316, Rule 690-138.001]

Agency actions

The Office of Insurance Regulation major areas of responsibility are as follows:

- Organizing and licensing of companies, including establishment of the initial financial requirements for insurance companies

- Policing against unauthorized insurance activities

- Continuing regulation of insurance company activities, including policy forms and provisions and rates (although direct rate regulation is not applicable to life insurance)

- Supervising the methods of obtaining business, including licensing of agents and control of unfair trade and advertising practices

- Monitoring the financial condition of insurers, including specification of appropriate investment categories and appropriate methodology for developing liabilities

- Rehabilitating or liquidating insurers where necessary

Investigation

If the Department of Financial Services or Office of Insurance Regulation believes that any person has violated or is violating any provision the Insurance Code, it will conduct an investigation. The Department of Financial Services may investigate the accounts, records, documents, and transactions pertaining to insurance affairs of any general agent, surplus lines agent, adjuster, managing general agent, insurance agent, insurance agency, customer representative, service representative, unaffiliated agent, or other person subject to its jurisdiction.

The Office of Insurance Regulation will conduct such investigation as it deems necessary of the accounts, records, documents, and transactions pertaining to the insurance affairs of any: administrator, service company, person having a contract or power of attorney under which she or he enjoys in fact the exclusive or dominant right to manage or control an insurer; or person engaged in or proposing to be engaged in the promotion or formation of a domestic insurer, an insurance holding corporation, or a corporation to finance a domestic insurer or in the production of the domestic insurer's business.

During an examination or investigation, the department or office may administer oaths, examine witnesses, receive evidence, subpoena witnesses, compel their attendance and testimony, and require by subpoena the production of books, papers, records, files, correspondence, documents, or other evidence that is relevant to the inquiry.

Any individual who willfully obstructs the department, the office, or the examiner in the examinations or investigations authorized by this part is guilty of a misdemeanor. [Sec. 624.317, .318, .321, 626.601]

OFFICE OF FINANCIAL REGULATION

General duties and powers

In addition to other powers conferred by Florida statutes, the Office of Financial Regulation has the following general supervision over all state financial institutions, their subsidiaries, and service corporations. The office has access to all books and records of all persons over whom the office exercises general supervision as is necessary for the performance of its duties and functions. It has the power to issue orders and declaratory statements.

The office's purpose is to provide for and promote the safe and sound conduct of the business of financial institutions, as well as, maintain public confidence in the financial institutions subject to the financial institutions' codes. Its powers and duties help preserve the financial institution system in Florida and the protect the interests of the depositors and creditors of financial institutions [Sec. 655.012]

Agency Actions

In imposing any administrative remedy or penalty, the office will take into account the appropriateness of the penalty with respect to the size of the financial resources and good faith of the person charged, the gravity of the violation, the history of previous violations, and other matters as justice may require. [Sec 655.031]

Cease and desist orders

The office may issue and serve upon any state financial institution a complaint stating charges whenever the office has reason to believe that such state financial institution is engaging in or has engaged in conduct that is an:

■ unsafe or unsound practice;

■ violation of any law relating to the operation of a financial institution;

■ violation of any rule of the commission;

■ violation of any order of the office;

■ breach of any written agreement with the office;

■ prohibited act or practice pursuant to Sec. 655.0322; or

■ willful failure to provide information or documents to the office or any appropriate federal agency, or any of its representatives, upon written request. [Sec. 655.033]

The complaint must contain the statement of facts and notice of opportunity for a hearing. If no hearing is requested within the time allowed, or if a hearing is held and the office finds that any of the charges are true, the office may enter an order directing the state financial institution to cease and desist from engaging in the conduct complained of and to take corrective action. If the state financial institution fails to respond to the complaint within the time allotted, such failure constitutes a default and justifies the entry of a cease and desist order.

Whenever the office finds that the conduct is likely to cause insolvency, substantial dissipation of assets or earnings of the state financial institution or substantial prejudice to the depositors, members, or shareholders, it may issue an emergency cease and desist order requiring the state financial institution to immediately cease and desist from engaging in the conduct complained of and to take corrective action. The emergency order is effective immediately upon service of a copy of the order upon the state financial institution and remains effective for 90 days.

Injunctions

Whenever a violation of the financial institutions' codes is threatened or impending and such violation will cause substantial injury to a state financial institution or to the depositors, members, creditors, or stockholders thereof, the circuit court has jurisdiction to hear any complaint filed by the office and, upon proper proof, to issue an injunction restraining such violation or granting other such appropriate relief. [Sec. 655.034]

Investigations

The office may make investigations, within or outside this state, which it deems necessary to determine whether a person has violated or is about to violate any provision of the Florida financial institutions codes or of the rules adopted by the commission. In an investigation, the office has the power to administer oaths and affirmations, take testimony and depositions, and to issue subpoenas to require persons to be or appear before the office at a specific time and place, and to bring books, records, and documents for inspection.

In the event of noncompliance with a subpoena, the office may petition the circuit court for an order requiring the subpoenaed person to appear and testify and to produce such books, records, and documents. Failure to comply with an order granting a petition for enforcement of a subpoena is contempt of court. Reasonable and necessary investigation expenses incurred by the office are assessed against the person or entity being investigated. [Sec. 655.032]

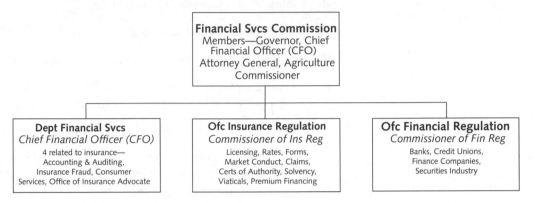

DEFINITIONS

The following definitions are in addition to the definitions described in units 1 and 3.

Insurance transaction. Any of the following would be examples of insurance transactions:

■ Solicitation or inducement to purchase insurance

■ Preliminary negotiations toward the sale of insurance

■ Effectuation of a contract of insurance

■ Transaction of matters subsequent to effectuation of a contract of insurance and arising out of it

Certificate of authority. No person may act as an insurer, directly or indirectly transacting insurance, in Florida except as authorized by a certificate of authority issued to the insurer by the office. Any person who acts as an insurer, transacts insurance, or otherwise engages in insurance activities without a certificate of authority in violation of this section commits a felony of the third degree.

Authorized and unauthorized companies/admitted and non-admitted companies. An authorized insurer is one duly authorized by a certificate of authority issued by the office to transact insurance in this state. An unauthorized insurer is an insurer that does not have a certificate of authority.

Unlicensed entities. No person may directly or indirectly act as agent for, or otherwise represent or aid on behalf of another, any insurer not authorized to transact insurance in Florida. If an unauthorized insurer fails to pay in full or in part any claim or loss within the provisions of any insurance contract that is entered into in violation of this section, any person who knew or reasonably should have known that such contract was entered into in violation of this section and who solicited, negotiated, took application for, or effectuated such insurance contract is liable to the insured for the full amount of the claim or loss not paid. A mail order insurance company is one that operates principally by mail without personal agent solicitation of prospects. Florida law prohibits unauthorized mail order insurers from soliciting in Florida. The transaction of insurance, including the application for insurance, must be taken by and the policy delivered through a licensed and appointed Florida agent.

Penalties for violation. In addition to any other penalties provided in the Insurance Code, any insurance agent licensed in Florida who knowingly represents or aids an unauthorized insurer commits a felony of the third degree.

LICENSING

Purpose

The purpose of the Florida licensing statutes is to help protect the general public by requiring a minimum level of insurance knowledge and competence of the licensee. In addition, licensees are expected to have an understanding of Florida insurance statutes and regulations. [Sec. 626.011–939]

License types

Agent means a general lines agent, life agent, health agent, or title agent. The term *agent* does not include a customer representative, limited customer representative, or service representative. [Sec. 626.015]

A **public adjuster** is any person, except a licensed attorney exempt under Florida law who, for compensation, prepares, completes, or files an insurance claim form for an insured or third-party claimant. The term also includes any person who, for compensation, acts on behalf of or aids an insured or third-party claimant in negotiating or effecting the settlement of claims for loss or damage covered by an insurance contract.

An **all-lines adjuster** is a person who is self-employed, employed by an insurer, or an independent adjusting firm, and who undertakes on behalf of an insurer to ascertain and determine the amount of any claim, loss, or damage payable under an insurance contract or undertakes to effect settlement of such claim, loss, or damage. [Sec. 626.851, .854, .8548]

Insurance agency means a business location at which an individual, firm, partnership, corporation, association, or other entity engages in any activity that by law may be performed only by a licensed insurance agent. The term *agency* does not include an insurer or an adjuster.

No individual, firm, partnership, corporation, association, or any other entity shall act in its own name or under a trade name, directly or indirectly, as an insurance agency, unless it possesses an insurance agency license for each place of business. [Sec. 626.015, .112]

An **unaffiliated agent** is a licensed agent, except a limited lines agent, who is not appointed by or affiliated with any insurer, but is self-appointed. This agent acts as an independent consultant in the business of analyzing insurance policies, providing insurance advice or counseling, or making specific recommendations or comparisons of insurance products for a fee. The fee must be established in advance by a written contract signed by the parties. Unaffiliated agents are prohibited from being affiliated with an insurer, insurer-appointed insurance agent, or insurance agency contracted with or employing insurer-appointed insurance agents. However, unaffiliated agents may continue to receive commissions on sales made before the date of appointment as an unaffiliated insurance agent as long as the agent discloses the receipt of commissions to the client when making recommendations or evaluating products of the entity from which commissions are received. Unaffiliated insurance agents will pay the same appointment fees required of agents appointed by insurers. [Sec. 626.015(18)]

Appointments

No person may act as an insurance agent unless she is currently licensed by the department and appointed by an insurer or other appropriate appointing entity. Unaffiliated agents, however, must appoint themselves and may not be appointed by an insurer. An individual who fails to maintain an appointment with an insurer or appointing entity during any 48-month period will not be granted an appointment by the department until he or she qualifies as a first-time applicant. [Sec. 626.112, .311, .381, .431, .471, .511, Rule 69B-211.004]

Term of appointment

New appointments or appointments being continued for natural persons, which are effectuated in a licensee's birth month, shall expire 24 months later on the last day of the licensee's birth month and shall be subject to renewal at that time by the entity for which they are appointed. In the case of entities other than natural persons, new appointments or appointments being continued, which are effectuated in the same month a licensee was first licensed as an insurance representative, shall expire 24 months later on the last day of the licensee's license issue month and shall be subject to renewal at that time by the entity for which they are appointed.

Appointments effectuated during any month other than the licensee's birth month in the case of natural persons, or during the license issue month in the case of entities other than natural persons, shall be valid for not less than 24 months and no longer than 36 months. This minimum and maximum number of months are necessary to convert the original issue month to the licensee's birth month or license issue month, whichever the case may be. Appointments renew every 24 months thereafter unless suspended, revoked, or otherwise terminated at an earlier date. [Rule 69B-211.004]

Appointment termination

Except when appointment termination is based on the suspension or revocation of an appointee's license, an appointing entity may terminate its appointment of any appointee at any time, with at least 60 days' advance written notice. Within 30 days after terminating the appointment of an appointee, the appointing entity must file written notice with the department including the reasons and facts involved in the termination. [Sec. 626.471, .511]

License requirements

Applicants for an insurance license must file a written application, completed under oath and signed by the applicant, meet the required qualifications, and pay all applicable fees in advance to the department. The application will require applicants to provide their full name, age, Social Security number, residence address, business address, mailing address, contact phone numbers, and email address. Applicants must also provide proof that they have completed, or are in the process of completing, any required prelicensing education. The requirement for life, health, or life and health licenses is 40 hours of approved prelicensing education. [Sec. 626.171 .191, .281, .7851, .8311]

Background check

The department or office may ask questions, in addition to those contained in the application, to any applicant for license or appointment, any license renewal, or license reinstatement, relating to the applicant's qualifications, residence, prospective place of business, and any other matter that, in the opinion of the department or office, is deemed necessary or advisable for the protection of the public and to ascertain the applicant's qualifications. The department or office may make these further investigation as it may deem advisable of the applicant's character, experience, background, and fitness for the license or appointment.

An inquiry or investigation of the applicant's qualifications, character, experience, background, and fitness must include submission of the applicant's fingerprints to the Department of Law Enforcement and the Federal Bureau of Investigation and consideration of any state criminal records, federal criminal records, or local criminal records obtained from these agencies or from local law enforcement agencies. [Sec. 626.201, .521, .621, .651; 624.34]

Credit or character report of license applicants

For each applicant who for the first time in this state is applying and qualifying for a license as agent, adjuster, service representative, customer representative, or managing general agent, the appointing insurer or agent will coincidentally with such appointment or employment secure and thereafter keep on file a full detailed credit and character report made by an established and reputable independent reporting service. If requested by the department, the insurer or agent will furnish to the department information as it reasonably requires regarding the applicant and investigation. [Sec. 626.521]

License Examination

Applicants for an agent, customer representative, or adjuster license must pass an examination that will test the applicant's ability, competence, and knowledge of the kinds of insurance to be handled under the license applied for (life, health, general lines, etc.). The exam will also cover the duties and responsibilities of a licensee and the pertinent provisions of Florida law. Within 30 days after the applicant has passed the license exam, the department will notify the applicant and issue the insurance license. For those applicants who have passed the examination prior to submitting the license application, the department will promptly issue the license as soon as the department approves the application. A passing grade on an examination is valid for a period of one year. The department will not issue a license to an applicant based on an examination taken more than one year prior to the date that an application for license is filed.

An examination is not necessary for any of the following:

- An applicant for renewal of appointment as an agent, customer representative, or adjuster, unless the department determines that an examination is necessary to establish the competence or trustworthiness of the applicant

- An applicant for a limited license as agent for travel insurance, motor vehicle rental insurance, credit insurance, in-transit and storage personal property insurance, or portable electronics insurance

- In the discretion of the department, an applicant for reinstatement of license or appointment as an agent, customer representative, or all-lines adjuster whose license has been suspended within the four years before the date of application or written request for reinstatement

- An applicant for a temporary license

- An applicant for a license as a life or health agent who has received the designation of Chartered Life Underwriter™ (CLU™) and has been engaged in the insurance business within the past four years (an applicant may be required to take an exam regarding Florida insurance laws and regulations)

- An applicant for license as a general lines agent, customer representative, or adjuster who has received the designation of Chartered Property Casualty Underwriter® (CPCU®) and has been engaged in the insurance business within the past four years (an applicant may be required to take an exam regarding Florida insurance laws and regulations)

- An applicant applying for a nonresident license, or a license transfer from another state if the applicant has successfully completed the prelicensing examination requirements in the applicant's previous home state, or meets the CLU or CPCU requirement previously described

Retaking the examination

An applicant for license or examination who has taken an examination and failed to make a passing grade may take additional examinations, after filing for reexamination together with applicable fees. Applicants may not take an examination for a license type more than five times in a 12-month period. [Sec. 626.281]

Maintaining a license

Continuing education

As described in the following, a licensee must complete a total of 24 hours of continuing education every two years. Each licensee except a title insurance agent must complete a five-hour law and ethics update course every two years that is specific to the license held by the licensee. A licensee who holds multiple insurance licenses must complete an update course that is specific to at least one of the licenses held. The course must be developed and offered by providers and approved by the department. The content of the course must address all lines of insurance for which examination and licensure are required and include the following subject areas:

- Insurance law updates

- Ethics for insurance professionals

- Disciplinary trends and case studies

- Industry trends

- Premium discounts

- Determining suitability of products and services

- Other similar insurance-related topics the department determines are relevant to legally and ethically carrying out the responsibilities of the license granted

Each licensee must also complete 19 hours of elective continuing education courses every two years, except in the following circumstances.

- A licensee who has been licensed for six or more years must complete a minimum of 15 hours of elective continuing education every two years.

- A licensee who has been licensed for 25 years or more and is a CLU or a CPCU or has a bachelor of science degree in risk management must complete a minimum of five hours of elective continuing education courses every two years.

- An individual who holds a license as a customer representative, limited customer representative, title agent, motor vehicle physical damage and mechanical breakdown insurance agent, or an industrial fire insurance or burglary insurance agent and who is not a licensed life or health agent, must complete a minimum of five hours of continuing education courses every two years.

■ Bail bond agents must complete the five-hour update course and a minimum of nine hours of elective continuing education courses every two years.

Licensees who are unable to comply with the continuing education requirements due to active duty in the military may submit a written request for a waiver to the department.

Excess hours accumulated during any two-year compliance period may be carried forward to the next compliance period.

A nonresident licensee who must complete continuing education requirements in her home state may use the home state requirements to also meet Florida's continuing education requirements if the licensee's home state recognizes reciprocity with Florida's continuing education requirements.

The following courses may be completed in order to meet the elective continuing education course requirements:

■ Any part of the Life Underwriter Training Council Life Course Curriculum: 24 hours; Health Course: 12 hours

■ Any part of the American College "CLU" diploma curriculum: 24 hours

■ Any part of the Insurance Institute of America's program in general insurance: 12 hours

■ Any part of the American Institute for Property and Liability Underwriters' Chartered Property Casualty Underwriter (CPCU) professional designation program: 24 hours

■ Any part of the Certified Insurance Counselor program: 21 hours

■ Any part of the Accredited Advisor in Insurance: 21 hours

The department may immediately terminate or refuse to renew the appointment of an agent or adjuster who has been notified by the department that his continuing education requirements have not been certified, unless the agent or adjuster has been granted an extension or waiver by the department. The department may not issue a new appointment of the same or similar type to a licensee who was denied a renewal appointment for failing to complete continuing education as required until the licensee completes his continuing education requirement.

Communicating with the department

Insurance companies, by statute, have 20 days to respond to the department once a consumer complaint has been filed. [Sec. 20.121]

Recordkeeping

A licensee must notify the department, in writing, within 30 days after a change of name, residence address, principal business street address, mailing address, contact telephone numbers, including a business telephone number, or email address. A licensee who has moved her principal place of residence and principal place of business from this state shall have her license and all appointments immediately terminated by the department. Failure to notify the department within the required time shall result in a fine not to exceed $250 for the first offense and a fine of at least $500 or suspension or revocation of the license for a subsequent offense. [Sec. 626.551]

Administrative action

Within 30 days after the final disposition of an administrative action taken against a licensee or insurance agency by a governmental agency or other regulatory agency in this or any other state or jurisdiction relating to the business of insurance, the sale of securities, or activity involving fraud, dishonesty, trustworthiness, or breach of a fiduciary duty, the licensee or insurance agency must submit a copy of the order, consent to order, or other relevant legal documents to the department. [Sec. 626.536]

Criminal action

An agent must report in writing to the department within 30 days if he has plead guilty or nolo contendere to, or has been convicted or found guilty of, a felony or a crime punishable by imprisonment of one year or more under any state law, federal law, or law of any other country. This written report is required whether or not the agent was convicted by the court having jurisdiction of the case. [Sec. 626.621]

Agents' additional appointments

At any time while a licensee's license is in force, an insurer may apply to the department for an additional appointment as a general lines agent or life or health agent. Upon receipt of the appointment and payment of the applicable appointment taxes and fees, the department may issue the additional appointment without further investigation concerning the applicant.

A life or health agent with an appointment in force may solicit applications for policies on behalf of an insurer for which she is not an appointed life or health agent if the agent simultaneously with the submission to such insurer of the application for insurance requests the insurer to appoint her as an agent. However, no commissions may be paid by such insurer to the agent until the additional appointment has been received by the department. [Sec. 626.341]

Excess or rejected business

A licensed agent is permitted to place business with another company if the agent's own company rejects the applicant or if the amount is in excess of that which the agent's own company will write. This is called *excess* or *rejected business*. No additional appointment is required, and commissions can be paid under what is known as a *single case agreement*. This is governed by Florida's exchange of business law. [Secs. 626.793, .837]

Insurance agency licensing

An insurance agency owned and operated by a single licensed agent who does business in her/his own name, and does not employ or use other licensees, is not required to obtain an insurance agency license.

An agency license will continue in force until canceled, suspended, revoked, or until it is otherwise terminated or it expires by operation of law. A branch place of business of a licensed insurance agency is not required to be licensed if it transacts business under the name and federal tax identification number as the licensed agency and has designated with the department a licensed insurance agent in charge of the branch. Effective October 15, 2015, all registered insurance agency "registrations" will be converted to agency licenses. [Sec. 626.112]

Florida law allows an insurance agency to permit a third party to complete, submit and sign the licensing application on the insurance agency's behalf. However, the agency will be responsible for ensuring that the information provided in the application is true and correct and the agency will be held accountable for any misstatements or misrepresentations.

Insurance agency applications must include the names of each owner, partner, officer, director, treasurer, and limited liability company member who directs or participates in the management or control of the agency whether by ownership of voting securities, by contract, by ownership of any agency bank account, or otherwise. The application must also include street and email addresses of the agency, any branch location(s), and the name of the agent in full-time charge of the agency and branch location(s). [Sec. 626.172, .311]

The licensed agent in charge of an insurance agency may also be the agent in charge of additional branch office locations of the agency if insurance activities requiring licensure as an insurance agent do not occur at any location when an agent is not physically present. Unlicensed employees at the location(s) shall not engage in insurance activities requiring licensure as an insurance agent or customer representative.

An insurance agency and each branch place of business of an insurance agency must file the name and license number of the agent in charge and the physical address of the insurance agency location with the department at the department's designated website. The designation of the agent in charge may be changed at the option of the agency. A change of the designated agent in charge is effective upon notification to the department, which shall be provided within 30 days after such change.

Residential business office

Florida resident property and casualty agents may maintain an office in their residence, if:

- a separate room is set aside by the agent and is actually used as, the office or place of business;

- such room is easily accessible to the public and is in fact used by the agent in her dealings with the public; and

- the existence of such place of business is suitably advertised, as determined by the department. [Sec. 626.749]

Prohibited practices

Temporary Suspension of agent license upon felony charge

The Department may temporarily suspend the license of an agent who has been charged with a felony. The suspension shall continue if the licensee is convicted or if adjudication of guilt is withheld. [Sec. 626.611]

Denial, suspension, revocation, or refusal to renew or continue license or appointment

The department may deny an application, suspend, revoke, or refuse to renew the license or appointment of any applicant, agent, adjuster, customer representative, service representative, or managing general agent if it finds that the applicant, licensee, or appointee has engaged in any one or more of the following:

- Violation of any provision of this code or of any other law applicable to the business of insurance

- Violation of any lawful order or rule of the department, commission, or office

- Failure to pay to any insurer any money belonging to the insurer

- Violation of the provision against twisting

- Engaging in unfair methods of competition or in unfair or deceptive acts or practices

- Willful overinsurance of any property or health insurance risk

- Having been found guilty of or having pleaded guilty or nolo contendere to a felony or a crime punishable by imprisonment of one year or more under the law of the United States of America or of any state thereof or under the law of any other country, without regard to whether a judgment of conviction has been entered by the court having jurisdiction of such cases

- If a life agent, violation of the code of ethics

- Cheating on an examination required for licensure

- Failure to inform the department in writing within 30 days after pleading guilty or nolo contendere to, or being convicted or found guilty of, any felony or a crime punishable by imprisonment of one year or more under the law of the United States or of any state thereof, or under the law of any other country without regard to whether a judgment of conviction has been entered by the court having jurisdiction of the case

- Knowingly aiding, assisting, procuring, advising, or abetting any person in the violation of, or to violate a provision of the insurance code or any order or rule of, the department, commission, or office.

- Has been the subject of or has had a license, permit, appointment, registration, or other authority to conduct business subject to any decision, finding, injunction, suspension, prohibition, revocation, denial, judgment, final agency action, or administrative order by any court of competent jurisdiction, administrative law proceeding, state agency, federal agency, national securities, commodities, or option exchange, or national securities, commodities, or option association involving a violation of any federal or state securities or commodities law or any rule or regulation adopted thereunder, or a violation of any rule or regulation of any national securities, commodities, or options exchange or national securities, commodities, or options association

- Failure to comply with any civil, criminal, or administrative action taken by the child support enforcement program to determine paternity or to establish, modify, enforce, or collect child support [Sec. 626.621]

AGENT RESPONSIBILITIES

Fiduciary capacity

A fiduciary is a person in a position of special trust and confidence. All premiums, return premiums, or other funds belonging to insurers or others received by an agent or insurance agency are trust funds received by the licensee in a fiduciary capacity. An agent or insurance agency must keep the funds belonging to each insurer for which an agent is not appointed, other than a surplus lines insurer, in a separate account so as to allow the department or office to properly audit such funds. The licensee in the applicable regular course of business shall account for and pay the premiums to the insurer, insured, or other person entitled to the premium. [Sec. 626.561]

The licensee must keep and make available to the department or office books, accounts, and records, as they will enable the department or office to determine whether the licensee is complying with the provisions of this code. Every licensee shall preserve books, accounts, and records pertaining to a premium payment for at least three years after payment. The three-year requirement does not apply to insurance binders when no policy is ultimately issued and no premium is collected. Any agent or insurance agency that diverts or misappropriates fiduciary funds commits the offense specified in the following:

- If the funds diverted or misappropriated are $300 or less, a misdemeanor of the first degree

- If the funds diverted or misappropriated are more than $300, but less than $20,000, a felony of the third degree

- If the funds diverted or misappropriated are $20,000 or more, but less than $100,000, a felony of the second degree

- If the funds diverted or misappropriated are $100,000 or more, a felony of the first degree

Commissions and compensation/charges for extra services

Agents are generally compensated by the payment of commissions that are a certain percentage of the initial (first year) and subsequent (renewal) premiums. Florida law specifies that no policy of life or health insurance may be issued for delivery in this state unless the application is taken by, and the policy delivered through, a licensed agent who will receive the usual commission. No person other than a licensed and appointed agent may accept any commission or other valuable compensation for soliciting or negotiating insurance. [Sec. 624.428, 626.572, .581, .794]

Commission for examining any group health insurance

Florida law was amended in 2004 to permit a licensed health agent to be compensated at rates other than that which an insurer files with the Office of Insurance Regulation. This alternative form of compensation is limited to providing advice, counsel, or recommendations regarding any group health insurance or group health benefit plans. Such compensation must be based upon a written contract between the agent and the party being charged the separately negotiated fee. Such written contract must clearly define the amount of compensation to be paid to the agent and must inform the person being charged that any commission received by the agent from the insurer will be rebated to that party within 30 days of receipt by the agent from the insurer. A copy of such contract must be retained by the licensed agent for three years after services have been fully performed. [Sec. 626.593]

Commission rebates

An insurance agency or agent may not rebate any portion of a commission except as follows.

- The rebate shall be available to all insureds in the same actuarial class.

- The rebate shall be in accordance with a rebating schedule filed by the agent with the insurer issuing the policy to which the rebate applies.

- The rebating schedule shall be uniformly applied in that all insureds who purchase the same policy through the agent for the same amount of insurance receive the same percentage rebate.

- Rebates shall not be given to an insured with respect to a policy purchased from an insurer that prohibits its agents from rebating commissions.

- The rebate schedule is prominently displayed in public view in the agent's place of doing business, and a copy is available to insureds on request at no charge.

- The age, sex, place of residence, race, nationality, ethnic origin, marital status, or occupation of the insured or location of the risk is not utilized in determining the percentage of the rebate or whether a rebate is available.

The insurance agency or agent must maintain a copy of all rebate schedules for the most recent five years and their effective dates. No rebate may be withheld or limited in amount based on factors that are unfairly discriminatory. No rebate may be given that is not reflected on the rebate schedule. No rebate may be refused or granted based upon the purchase or failure of the insured or applicant to purchase collateral business. [Sec. 626.572]

Commissions contingent on loss settlements prohibited

When agents of the insurer are acting as an adjuster of claims, it is unlawful for the insurer to enter into any agreement or understanding with its agents in Florida, which base the agents' commissions on Florida policies contingent upon savings in the settlement of claims. Nothing in this section will be construed to apply to any contingent commissions agreement under which agents do not pay claims arising under policies of the insurer. [Sec. 626.581]

Ethics

Scope

The business of life insurance is hereby declared to be a public trust in which all agents of all companies have a common obligation to work together in serving the best interests of the insuring public, by:

- understanding and observing the spirit and letter of the laws governing life insurance;

- presenting accurately and completely every fact essential to a client's decision;

- being fair in all relations with colleagues and competitors; and

- always placing the policyholder's interests first.
  [Rule 69B-215.210, F.A.C.]

Use of designations

The purpose of this rule is to set forth standards to protect consumers from dishonest, deceptive, misleading, and fraudulent trade practices with respect to the use of certifications and professional designations in the marketing, solicitation, negotiation, sale, or advice made in connection with an insurance transaction by any licensee. The department does NOT endorse any particular professional designation. For purposes of this rule, a **designation** is any combination of words, any acronym standing for a combination of words, or any job title that indicates or implies that a licensee has special knowledge or training in advising or servicing consumers beyond the knowledge or training required for the license held. A **certification** is any designation that indicates, implies, or recognizes that an individual or organization meets certain established criteria beyond the criteria required for the license held.

A designation may not be lawfully used under the Insurance Code unless the designation is obtained from an organization that has published standards and procedures for assuring the competency of its certificants or designees on specific subject matters. The organization or entity conferring the designation must approve any terminology, combination of words, and/or acronym to be used by the designee.

The prohibited use of any designation includes but is not limited to:

- use of a designation by a person who has not actually earned or is otherwise ineligible to use such designation;

- use of a nonexistent or self-conferred designation;

- use of a designation that indicates or implies a level of occupational qualifications obtained through education, training, or experience that the person using the designation does not have; and

- use of any designation not obtained in compliance with Florida law.

Codes of ethics establish a broad outline defining appropriate and inappropriate business behavior for insurance agents. They also establish the activities of agents as a matter of public trust. The Code of Ethics for the National Association of Financial and Insurance Advisors (NAIFA) follows.

NATIONAL ASSOCIATION OF INSURANCE AND FINANCIAL ADVISORS

Code of Ethics

PREAMBLE: Helping my clients protect their assets and establish financial security, independence and economic freedom for themselves and those they care about is a noble endeavor and deserves my promise to support high standards of integrity, trust and professionalism throughout my career as an insurance and financial professional. With these principles as a foundation, I freely accept the following obligations:

- To help maintain my clients' confidences and protect their right to privacy.

- To work diligently to satisfy the needs of my clients.

- To present, accurately and honestly, all facts essential to my clients' financial decisions.

- To render timely and proper service to my clients and ultimately their beneficiaries.

- To continually enhance professionalism by developing my skills and increasing my knowledge through education.

- To obey the letter and spirit of all laws and regulations which govern my profession.

- To conduct all business dealings in a manner which would reflect favorably on NAIFA and my profession.

- To cooperate with others whose services best promote the interests of my clients.

- To protect the financial interests of my clients, their financial products and my profession, through political advocacy.

Adopted July 2012, Board of Trustees

Reprinted with the permission of the National Association of Insurance and Financial Advisors. For more information about NAIFA, visit www. naifa.org. [Rule 69B-215.235, F.A.C.]

INSURANCE GUARANTY FUND

The Florida Life and Health Insurance Guaranty Association is a non-profit legal entity. All life, health, and annuity insurers are members of the association as a condition of their authority to transact insurance in Florida.

The association's purpose is to protect policyowners, insureds, beneficiaries, annuitants, payees, and assignees of insurance policies and contracts against the failure of an insurer to perform its contractual obligations due to its impairment or insolvency. [Sec. 631.711–.735]

Scope of provisions

Coverage from the association will be provided to life insurance, health insurance, and annuity policyowners, certificateholders, beneficiaries, and assignees who are residents of Florida. Residents of other states are covered, but only if:

- the insurers that issued such policies or contracts are domiciled in Florida;

- such insurers were not licensed in the states in which such persons reside at the time specified in a state's guaranty association law as necessary for coverage by that state's association;

- such other states have associations similar to the Florida association; and

- such persons are not eligible for coverage by such associations.

Association coverage does not apply to the following:

- That portion or part of a variable life insurance contract or variable annuity contract not guaranteed by an insurer

- That portion or part of any policy or contract under which the risk is borne by the policyholder

- Fraternal benefit societies as defined in § 632.601

- Health maintenance insurance

- Dental service plan insurance

- Pharmaceutical service plan insurance

- Optometric service plan insurance

- Ambulance service association insurance

- Preneed funeral merchandise or service contract insurance

- Prepaid health clinic insurance

- Any annuity contract or group annuity contract that is not issued to and owned by an individual, except to the extent of any annuity benefits guaranteed directly and not through an intermediary to an individual by an insurer under such contract or certificate

- The portion of a policy or contract that exceeds association limits for policies or contracts using a rate of interest, crediting rate, or similar factor based on an index or other external reference to determine returns or policy values

■ A policy or contract providing Medicare Part C or Part D health care benefits

■ Any policy or contract or part thereof assumed by the impaired or insolvent insurer under a contract of reinsurance, other than reinsurance for which assumption certificates have been issued

■ Any federal employees' group policy or contract that, under 5 U.S.C. § 8909(f), is prohibited from being subject to an assessment under § 631.718

Definitions

Impaired insurer means a member insurer deemed by the department to be potentially unable to fulfill its contractual obligations and not an insolvent insurer.

Insolvent insurer means a member insurer authorized to transact insurance in this state, either at the time the policy was issued or when the insured event occurred, and against which an order of liquidation with a finding of insolvency has been entered by a court of competent jurisdiction.

Establishment of association; separate accounts

The association performs its functions according to its plan of operation and exercises its powers through a board of directors. For purposes of administration and assessment, the association maintains three accounts:

■ The health insurance account

■ The life insurance account

■ The annuity account

Board of directors

The board of directors of the association must consist of not fewer than five nor more than nine member insurers, serving terms as established in the plan of operation. At all times, at least one member of the board must be a domestic insurer. The members of the board will be elected by member insurers subject to the approval of the department. In approving the election of members to the board, the department will consider, among other things, whether all member insurers are fairly represented.

Members of the board may be reimbursed from the assets of the association for expenses incurred by them as members of the board of directors, but members of the board shall not otherwise be compensated by the association for their services.

Powers and duties of association

The association's liability for the contractual obligations of the insolvent insurer will be no greater than the contractual obligations of the insurer in the absence of such insolvency. The aggregate liability of the association shall not exceed:

- $100,000 in net cash surrender and net cash withdrawal values for life insurance;

- $250,000 in net cash surrender and net cash withdrawal values for deferred annuity contracts; or

- $300,000 for all benefits including cash values, with respect to any one life. In no event shall the association be liable for any penalties or interest.

If a domestic insurer is an impaired insurer, the association may, subject to the approval of the impaired insurer and the department guarantee or reinsure, or cause to be guaranteed, assumed, or reinsured, any or all of the covered policies of the impaired insurer, and loan money to the impaired insurer.

If a domestic insurer is an insolvent insurer, the association shall, subject to the approval of the department guarantee, assume, or reinsure, or cause to be guaranteed, assumed, or reinsured, the covered policies of covered persons; and provide moneys, pledges, notes, guarantees, or other means that are proper and reasonably necessary to ensure payment of the contractual obligations of the insolvent insurer with regard to covered persons.

If a foreign or alien insurer is an insolvent insurer, the association shall, subject to the approval of the department guarantee, assume, or reinsure, or cause to be guaranteed, assumed, or reinsured, the covered policies of Florida residents; and provide moneys, pledges, notes, guarantees, or other means that are proper and reasonably necessary to ensure payment of the contractual obligations of the insolvent insurer with regard to covered persons. However, this subsection does not apply when the department has determined that the foreign or alien insurer's domiciliary jurisdiction provides, by statute, protection substantially similar to that provided by this part for Florida residents.

Assessments against member insurers

For the purpose of providing the funds necessary to carry out the powers and duties of the association, the board of directors shall assess the member insurers for each of the accounts referred to in (Sec. 631.715) at such time and for such amounts as the board finds necessary.

The total of all assessments upon a member insurer for each account may not in any one calendar year exceed 1% of the sum of the insurer's premiums written in this state regarding business covered by the account received during the three calendar years preceding the year in which the assessment is made, divided by three.

Powers and duties of department

The department shall, in any liquidation or rehabilitation proceeding involving a domestic insurer, be appointed as the liquidator or rehabilitator. If a foreign or alien member insurer is subject to a liquidation proceeding in its domiciliary jurisdiction or state of entry, the department shall be appointed conservator.

The office may suspend or revoke, after notice and hearing, the certificate of authority to transact insurance in this state of any member insurer that fails to pay an assessment when due or fails to comply with the approved plan of operation of the association.

Use of membership in advertising

A person may not make, publish, disseminate, circulate, or place before the public, or cause directly or indirectly to be made, published, disseminated, circulated, or placed before the public, in any publication, notice, circular, pamphlet, letter, or poster, or over any radio station or television station, any advertisement that uses the existence of the Insurance Guaranty Association of this state for the purpose of sales, solicitation, or inducement to purchase any form of insurance covered by the Florida Life and Health Insurance Guaranty Association Act.

MARKETING PRACTICES

Unfair methods of competition

The following are defined as unfair methods of competition and unfair or deceptive acts or practices [Sec. 626.9541]:

Sliding. This is the act or practice of:

- representing to the applicant that a specific ancillary coverage or product is required by law in conjunction with the purchase of insurance when such coverage or product is not required;

- representing to the applicant that a specific ancillary coverage or product is included in the policy applied for without an additional charge when such charge is required; or

- charging an applicant for a specific ancillary coverage or product, in addition to the cost of the insurance coverage applied for, without the informed consent of the applicant.

Boycott, coercion, and intimidation. Entering into any agreement to commit, or by any concerted action committing, any act of boycott, coercion, or intimidation resulting in, or tending to result in, unreasonable restraint of, or monopoly in, the business of insurance.

Misrepresentations and false advertising of insurance policies. Knowingly making, issuing, circulating, or causing to be made, issued, or circulated, any estimate, illustration, circular, statement, sales presentation, omission, comparison, or property and casualty certificate of insurance altered after being issued that does any of the following:

- Misrepresents the benefits, advantages, conditions, or terms of any insurance policy

- Misrepresents the dividends or share of the surplus to be received on any insurance policy

- Makes any false or misleading statements as to the dividends or share of surplus previously paid on any insurance policy

- Is misleading as to the financial condition of any person or as to the legal reserve system upon which any life insurer operates

- Uses any name or title of any insurance policy or class of insurance policies misrepresenting its true nature

- Is a misrepresentation for the purpose of inducing, or tending to induce, the lapse, forfeiture, exchange, conversion, or surrender of any insurance policy

- Is a misrepresentation for the purpose of effecting a pledge or assignment of, or effecting a loan against, any insurance policy

- Misrepresents any insurance policy as being shares of stock or misrepresents ownership interest in the company

- Uses any advertisement that would mislead or otherwise cause a reasonable person to believe mistakenly that the state or the federal government is responsible for the insurance sales activities of any person or stands behind any person's credit or that any person, the state, or the federal government guarantees any returns on insurance products or is a source of payment of any insurance obligation of or sold by any person

Defamation. Knowingly making, publishing, disseminating, or circulating, directly or indirectly, or aiding, abetting, or encouraging the making, publishing, disseminating, or circulating of, any oral or written statement, or any pamphlet, circular, article, or literature, that is false or maliciously critical of, or derogatory to, any person and that is calculated to injure such person.

False advertising. Knowingly making, publishing, disseminating, circulating, or placing before the public, or causing, directly or indirectly, to be made, published, disseminated, circulated, or placed before the public:

- in a newspaper, magazine, or other publication;

- in the form of a notice, circular, pamphlet, letter, or poster;

- over any radio or television station; or

- in any other way an advertisement, announcement, or statement containing any assertion, representation, or statement with respect to the business of insurance that is untrue, deceptive, or misleading.

Unfair discrimination. Knowingly making or permitting any unfair discrimination between individuals of essentially the same hazards, the same actuarial class, or equal life expectancy, in life or health insurance or annuity rates, dividends, benefits payable, or any other terms and conditions of the contract. Insurers may not discriminate based on race, color, creed, marital status, sex, or national origin.

An insurer or managed care provider may not refuse to issue or renew a policy, refuse to pay a claim, cancel a policy, or increase rates based upon the fact that an insured has made a claim or sought medical or psychological treatment in the past for abuse or protection from abuse. The insurer or managed care provider may not consider that a claim was caused in the past by, or might occur as a result of, any future assault, battery, or sexual assault by a family or household member upon another family or household member. A life insurer, health insurer, disability insurer, or managed care provider may refuse to underwrite, issue, or renew a policy based on the applicant's medical condition, but shall not consider whether such condition was caused by an act of abuse.

No insurer authorized to transact insurance in this state shall refuse to issue, nor charge a higher premium on a life or health insurance policy solely because the person to be insured has the sickle-cell trait. [Sec. 626.9706, .9707]

Other unfair practices

False statements and entries. This includes knowingly filing with any supervisory official or the general public any false material statement and knowingly making any false entry or omitting a material fact in any book, report, or statement of any person.

Failure to maintain complaint-handling procedures. This includes failure of any person to maintain a complete record of all the complaints received since the date of the last examination. A complaint is any written communication primarily expressing a grievance.

Advertising gifts permitted. An insurer or agent may give to insureds, prospective insureds, and others, for the purpose of advertising, any article of merchandise having a value of not more than $25.

Life insurance limitations based on past foreign travel experiences or future foreign travel plans. An insurer may not refuse life insurance, nor limit the amount, extent, or kind of life insurance coverage available to an individual based solely on the individual's past lawful foreign travel experiences.

An insurer may not refuse life insurance, nor limit the amount, extent, or kind of life insurance coverage available to an individual based solely on the individual's future lawful travel plans unless the insurer can demonstrate and the Office of Insurance Regulation determines that it is actuarially supported.

Loan or extension of credit; voluntary selection of insurer. No lender may require, as a condition to lending money or extension of credit, that the person purchase a policy through a particular insurer, agent, or broker.

Any person offering the sale of insurance at the time of and in connection with an extension must disclose in writing that the choice of an insurance provider will not affect the decision regarding the extension of credit or sale or lease of goods or services. [Sec. 626.9551]

Unfair claims practices

Unfair claims practices include attempting to settle claims on the basis of an application, or any other material document that was altered without knowledge or consent of, the insured. Also, a material misrepresentation made to an insured or any other person having an interest in the proceeds payable under a contract or policy, for the purpose of effecting settlement of such claims on less favorable terms than those provided in the contract or policy. Lastly, committing or performing with such frequency as to indicate a general business practice any of the following:

■ Failing to adopt and implement standards for the proper investigation of claims

■ Misrepresenting pertinent facts or insurance policy provisions relating to coverages at issue

■ Failing to acknowledge and act promptly upon communications with respect to claims

■ Denying claims without conducting reasonable investigations based upon available information

■ Failing to affirm or deny full or partial coverage of claims, and, as to partial coverage, the dollar amount or extent of coverage, or failing to provide a written statement that the claim is being investigated, upon the written request of the insured within 30 days after proof-of-loss statements have been completed

■ Failing to promptly provide a reasonable explanation in writing to the insured of the basis in the insurance policy, in relation to the facts or applicable law, for denial of a claim or for the offer of a compromise settlement

■ Failing to promptly notify the insured of any additional information necessary for the processing of a claim

■ Failing to clearly explain the nature of the requested information and the reasons why such information is necessary

Fraud

A person commits a fraudulent insurance act if during policy issuance or payment of a claim the person knowingly and with intent to defraud presents to an insurer, broker, or agent any written statement which the person knows contains materially false information concerning any material fact. Intentionally concealing a material fact for the purpose of misleading another is also a fraudulent act.

Fraudulent signatures on an application or policy-related document

This includes willfully submitting to an insurer on behalf of a consumer an insurance application or policy-related document bearing a false or fraudulent signature.

Proof of loss; fraud statement

All proof of loss statements must prominently display the following statement: "Pursuant to § 817.234, Florida Statutes, any person who, with the intent to injure, defraud, or deceive any insurer or insured, prepares, presents, or causes to be presented a proof of loss or estimate of cost or repair of damaged property in support of a claim under an insurance policy knowing that the proof of loss or estimate of claim or repairs contains any false, incomplete, or misleading information concerning any fact or thing material to the claim commits a felony of the third degree." [Sec. 626.8797]

Controlled business

The department will not grant, renew, continue, or permit to exist any license or appointment of a life or health agent if it finds that the licensee obtained a license not for the purpose of holding himself or herself out to the general public as a life or health insurance agent but principally for the purpose of soliciting, negotiating, or procuring controlled business. [Sec. 626.784, .830]

Controlled business means life or health insurance or annuity contracts covering the agent or family members; officers, directors, stockholders, partners, or employees of a business in which the agent or a family member is engaged; or the debtors of a firm, association, or corporation of which the agent is an officer, director, stockholder, partner, or employee.

A violation of this section shall be deemed to exist, if the department finds that during a 12-month period the premiums submitted on controlled business are in excess of the premiums submitted during the same period by the licensee on life or health insurance contracts to the general public.

Twisting

Twisting is knowingly making any misleading representations or incomplete or fraudulent comparisons or fraudulent material omissions of or with respect to any insurance policies or insurers for the purpose of inducing, any person to lapse, forfeit, surrender, terminate, retain, pledge, assign, borrow on, or convert any insurance policy or to take out a policy of insurance with another insurer.

Churning

Churning is the practice whereby policy values in an existing life insurance policy or annuity contract are directly or indirectly used to purchase another insurance policy or annuity contract with that same insurer for the purpose of earning additional premiums, fees, commissions, or other compensation:

■ without an objectively reasonable basis for believing that the replacement or extraction will result in a benefit to the policyholder;

■ in a fashion that is fraudulent, deceptive, or otherwise misleading or that involves a deceptive omission;

■ when the applicant is not informed that the policy values of the existing policy or contract will be reduced, forfeited, or used in the purchase of the replacing or additional policy or contract, if this is the case; or

■ without informing the applicant that the replacing or additional policy or contract will not be a paid-up policy or that additional premiums will be due, if this is the case. [FAC Rule 69B-151.202]

Unlawful rebates

Except as otherwise expressly provided by law, or in an applicable filing with the office, knowingly:

■ permitting, or offering to make, or making, any contract or agreement as to such contract other than as plainly expressed in the insurance contract issued thereon;

■ paying, allowing, or giving, or offering to pay, allow, or give, directly or indirectly, as inducement to such insurance contract, any unlawful rebate of premiums payable on the contract, any special favor or advantage in the dividends or other benefits thereon, or any valuable consideration or inducement not specified in the contract; or

■ giving, selling, or purchasing, or offering to give, sell, or purchase, as inducement to such insurance contract or in connection therewith, any stocks, bonds, or other securities of any insurance company or other corporation, association, or partnership, or any dividends or profits accrued thereon, or anything of value whatsoever not specified in the insurance contract.

The following are not considered unfair discrimination or unlawful rebates:

■ In the case of any contract of life insurance or life annuity, paying bonuses to all policyholders or otherwise abating their premiums in whole or in part out of surplus accumulated from nonparticipating insurance, provided that any such bonuses or abatement of premiums is fair and equitable to all policyholders and for the best interests of the company and its policyholders

■ In the case of life insurance policies issued on the industrial debit plan, making allowance to policyholders who have continuously for a specified period made premium payments directly to an office of the insurer in an amount that fairly represents the saving in collection expenses

■ Readjustment of the premium rate for a group insurance policy based on the loss or expense thereunder, at the end of the first or any subsequent policy year of insurance thereunder, which may be made retroactive only for such policy year

- Issuance of life insurance policies or annuity contracts at rates less than the usual rates of premiums for such policies or contracts, as group insurance or employee insurance as defined in this code

- Issuing life or disability insurance policies on a salary savings, bank draft, preauthorized check, payroll deduction, or other similar plan at a reduced rate reasonably related to the savings made by the use of such plan

General prohibition and penalties

Except as provided in the following, any person who engages in unfair methods of competition is subject to a fine in an amount not greater than $2,500 for each nonwillful violation and not greater than $20,000 for each willful violation. Fines under this subsection may not exceed an aggregate amount of $10,000 for all nonwillful violations arising out of the same action or an aggregate amount of $100,000 for all willful violations arising out of the same action. The fines may be imposed in addition to any other applicable penalty. [Sec. 626.9521]

If a person commits the offenses known as "twisting," or "churning," the person commits a misdemeanor of the first degree, punishable as provided in Florida criminal code, and an administrative fine not greater than $5,000 may be imposed for each nonwillful violation or an administrative fine not greater than $75,000 may be imposed for each willful violation. To impose an administrative fine for a willful violation under this paragraph, the practice of "churning" or "twisting" must involve fraudulent conduct.

If a person willfully submits fraudulent signatures on an application or policy-related document, the person commits a felony of the third degree, punishable as provided in Florida criminal code, and an administrative fine not greater than $5,000 may be imposed for each nonwillful violation or an administrative fine not greater than $75,000 may be imposed for each willful violation.

- Administrative fines for twisting, churning, or fraudulent signatures may not exceed an aggregate amount of $50,000 for all nonwillful violations arising out of the same action or an aggregate amount of $250,000 for all willful violations arising out of the same action.

Hearings and cease and desist orders

The department and office shall each have power within its respective regulatory jurisdiction to examine and investigate the affairs of every person involved in the business of insurance in this state in order to determine whether such person has been or is engaged in any unfair method of competition or in any unfair or deceptive act or practice. [Sec. 626.9561, .9571, 9581, .9601]

Hearing on misconduct

Whenever the department or office has reason to believe that any person has engaged, or is engaging, in this state in any unfair method of competition or any unfair or deceptive act, it may conduct a hearing.

Cease and desist order; penalties for violation of act

After the hearing, the department or office shall enter a final order in accordance with Florida law. If it is determined that the person charged has engaged in an unfair or deceptive act or practice or the unlawful transaction of insurance, the department or office will also issue an order requiring the violator to cease and desist from engaging in such method of competition, act, or practice or the unlawful transaction of insurance. The department or office may also, at its discretion, order suspension or revocation of the person's certificate of authority or license.

Any person who violates a cease and desist order may be subject to any one or more of the following:

- A monetary penalty of not more than $50,000 as to all matters determined in such hearing

- Suspension or revocation of such person's certificate of authority, license, or eligibility to hold such certificate of authority or license

LIFE INSURANCE, ANNUITY CONTRACTS, AND HEALTH INSURANCE ADVERTISING

Purpose

The purpose of the advertising rules is to provide prospective purchasers with clear and unambiguous statements in the advertisement of life insurance, annuity contracts, and health insurance. This purpose is accomplished by guidelines and standards of conduct in advertising to ensure that product descriptions are presented in a manner that prevents unfair, deceptive, and misleading advertising. [FAC Rule 69O-150.001, .003 .101, .103]

Advertisement includes any method of communication:

- in a newspaper, magazine, or other publication;

- in the form of a notice, circular, pamphlet, letter, or poster;

- over any radio or television station; or

- in any other way, advertisement, announcement, or statement containing any assertion, representation, or statement with respect to the business of insurance.

Advertisement does not include:

- material to be used solely for the training and education of an insurer's employees, agents, or brokers;

- internal communications within an insurer's own organization not intended for dissemination to the public;

- individual communications of a personal nature with current policy-holders regarding existing coverage other than material urging such policyholders to renew, increase, or expand coverages; or

- correspondence between a prospective group or blanket policyholder and an insurer in the course of negotiating a group or blanket contract.

Method of disclosure of required information

All required disclosures must be set out conspicuously and in close conjunction with the statements to which such information relates or under appropriate captions of such prominence that it must not be minimized, rendered obscure, or presented in an ambiguous fashion or intermingled with the context of the advertisement so as to be confusing or misleading. [FAC Rule 69O- 150.004]

Form and content of advertisements

The form and content of life insurance, annuity contracts, and health Insurance advertisements must be sufficiently complete and clear to avoid deception or the capacity to mislead or deceive. Whether an advertisement has a capacity to mislead or deceive will be determined by the Director from the overall impression that the advertisement may be reasonably expected to create upon a person of average education or intelligence, within the segment of the public to which it is directed. [FAC Rule 69O-150.005, .105]

An insurer must clearly identify its life insurance, annuity contracts, and health insurance as an insurance policy or annuity contract in its advertisements. The name of any policy must be followed by or include the words "Insurance Policy," "Annuity," or similar words clearly identifying, the fact that an insurance policy or annuity is being offered (e.g., whole life insurance policy, level term life insurance, deferred annuity, long-term care insurance policy, major medical insurance policy, or disability insurance policy).

Advertisements of benefits or proceeds payable or premiums payable

No advertisement may omit information or use words, phrases, statements, references, or illustrations if the omission or phraseology has the capacity to mislead purchasers as to the nature or extent of any policy benefit payable, loss covered, or premium payable. [FAC Rule 69O-150.006, .107]

Disclosing policy provisions relating to renewability, cancellability, and termination

An advertisement that is an invitation to contract must disclose the provisions relating to renewability. The advertisement must also disclose provisions relating to termination and modification of benefits, losses covered, or premiums because of age or for other reasons, in a manner that must not minimize or render obscure the qualifying conditions. [FAC Rule 69O-150.007, .108]

Testimonials

Testimonials and endorsements used in advertisements must be genuine, represent the current opinion of the author, be applicable to the policy advertised, and be accurately reproduced. The insurer, in using a testimonial or endorsement, makes as its own all of the statements contained therein, and the advertisement, including such statement is subject to all the provisions of the advertising rules. [FAC Rule 69O-150.008, .110]

Disparaging comparisons and statements

An advertisement must not directly or indirectly make unfair or incomplete comparisons of policies, contracts, or benefits. Advertisements must not disparage competitors, their policies, or contracts; services or business methods; and must not disparage or unfairly minimize competing methods of marketing insurance. [FAC Rule 69O-150.011, .112]

Identity of insurer

The name of the actual insurer must be stated in all of the insurer's advertisements. The form number or numbers of the policy advertised must be stated in any invitation to contract. An advertisement must not use a trade name, name of the parent company of the insurer, name of a particular division of the insurer, name of any reinsurer or any other party, service mark, slogan, symbol, or other device that would be misleading as to the true identity of the actual insurer.

No advertisement must use any combination of words, symbols, or physical materials that by their content, phraseology, shape, color, or other characteristics are so similar to combination of words, symbols, or physical materials used by agencies of the federal government or of the state of Florida, or otherwise appear to be of such a nature that it tends to confuse or mislead prospective insureds into believing that the solicitation is in some manner connected with an agency of the municipal, county, state, or federal government. Advertisements must not mislead the public into believing that the advertiser is the same as, is connected with, or is endorsed by such governmental entities.

All advertisements used by agents, producers, brokers, or solicitors of an insurer must have prior written approval or prior oral approval with subsequent written confirmation of approval by the insurer. [FAC Rule 69O-150.013, .114]

Statements about an insurer

An advertisement must not contain statements that are untrue or misleading, with respect to the assets, corporate structure, financial standing, age, or relative position of the insurer in the insurance business. [FAC Rule 69O-150.016, .117]

Advertising file

Each insurer must maintain at its home or principal office a complete file containing:

- every printed, published, or prepared advertisement of its individual policies;

- typical printed, published, or prepared advertisements of its blanket, franchise, and group policies disseminated in Florida; and

- a notation must be attached to each advertisement indicating the manner and extent of distribution and the form number of any policy advertised.

The file must specifically include those advertisements submitted to the insurer by agents, brokers, or others and approved by the insurer for use in Florida. The file must be available for inspection by the office.

All advertisements must be maintained in the file for a period of four years or until the filing of the next regular report or examination of the insurer, whichever is the longer period of time. [FAC Rule 69O-150.018, .119]

KEY CONCEPTS

Students should be familiar with the following concepts:

insurance regulatory agencies	Code of Ethics of the NAIFA
Chief Financial Officer	agent responsibilities
Office of Insurance Regulation	rebating
Insurance Code	misrepresentation
admitted versus nonadmitted insurers	defamation

U N I T   T E S T

1. The individual who sits on the Financial Services Commission and supervises the insurance function in Florida is called the

   A. Chief Insurance Commissioner
   B. Director of Financial Regulation
   C. Chief Financial Officer
   D. Director of Financial Regulation

2. The major areas of regulation by the Office of Insurance Regulation include which of the following?

   A. Policing against unauthorized insurance activities
   B. Proposing legislation to regulate the insurance industry
   C. Enacting new insurance laws
   D. Enforcing criminal penalties against those who violate the Insurance Code

3. The major difference between producers acting as agents and producers acting as brokers is that

   A. agents represent the client; brokers represent the company
   B. brokers are not subject to the same laws and regulations as agents
   C. agents represent the company; brokers represent the client
   D. only agents can solicit prospects for the purpose of selling insurance

4. The prelicensing education requirement for a life insurance agent's license is

   A. 30 hours
   B. 40 hours
   C. 20 hours
   D. 24 hours

5. Keeping premium money separate from personal accounts is a

   A. reinsurance regulation
   B. replacement regulation
   C. duty of the insurer
   D. fiduciary responsibility of the agent

6. The state Life and Health Guaranty Association covers all of the following insurance contracts EXCEPT

   A. annuity contracts
   B. health insurance contracts
   C. insurance contracts issued by fraternal benefit societies
   D. Medicare supplement contracts

7. To be licensed in Florida as a resident producer, all of the following must be completed EXCEPT

   A. a criminal background check
   B. paying an application fee that is refundable
   C. the prelicensing education requirements
   D. providing any other information required by the state

8. The definition of transacting insurance includes all of the following EXCEPT

   A. soliciting a contract of insurance
   B. negotiating a contract of insurance
   C. underwriting a contract of insurance
   D. effectuating a contract of insurance

9. Of the following terms, which best describes the act of replacing life insurance with a new life insurance policy based upon incomplete or incorrect representations?

   A. Twisting
   B. Rebating
   C. Embezzlement
   D. Concealment

10. All of the following activities could result in the suspension of an agent's license EXCEPT

    A. misrepresenting the financial condition of an insurer
    B. selling any replacement policy that causes an insured to lapse an existing policy
    C. attaining a license for the sole purpose of handling controlled business
    D. demonstrating incompetency to transact business as an insurance agent

11. Felony convictions on an applicant to be licensed as an agent may

    A. cause the licensing fee to be increased
    B. require the applicant to sign a nolo contendere plea
    C. cause the license application to be refused
    D. be disregarded if the applicant has a licensed sponsor approved by the state of Florida

12. All of the following activities violate the Florida insurance code EXCEPT

    A. dividing commission on a life insurance policy with any licensed agent
    B. dividing commission on a life insurance policy with a licensed health agent
    C. dividing commission on a life insurance policy with another agent who is licensed and appointed to sell the same line of insurance
    D. dividing commission on a life insurance policy with a licensed insurance broker who regularly transacts life insurance

13. Violation of the controlled business statute occurs if an agent sells most of her business to

    A. employees of a business owned by her father
    B. members of her civic club
    C. city and county employees
    D. members of the local medical society

14. Sliding consists of all the following activities EXCEPT

    A. telling an applicant that certain ancillary coverage is required by law when it is not
    B. advising a client that certain ancillary coverage is included at no additional charge when such a charge is required
    C. charging an applicant for ancillary coverage over the cost of coverage applied for without the applicant's consent
    D. recommending that a client take cash value from a policy to make other investments

15. Which of the following statements is CORRECT about the Department of Financial Services' right to examine an agent's records?

    A. An examination can be conducted at any time to discover any unfair trade practices.
    B. An agent's records involving a premium transaction are confidential and not subject to examination.
    C. The Chief Financial Officer may examine an agent's records only once per year, unless good cause is shown.
    D. The statutes do not give the Department the right to examine the affairs of insurance licensees to discover unfair trade practices.

16. Producers must retain records of insurance transactions pertaining to premium payments for at least

    A. 10 years
    B. 2 years
    C. 5 years
    D. 3 years

17. Which of the following activities is NOT a violation of the Insurance Code?

    A. Charging a fee that is more than the premium stated in the policy
    B. Collecting premiums and depositing them in the agent's personal account
    C. Writing as much non-controlled insurance business as controlled business
    D. Offering a premium rebate if the insured contracts for other insurance business

18. What is the professional organization whose code of ethics has been incorporated into Florida insurance law?

    A. National Association of Insurance and Financial Advisors (NAIFA-FL)
    B. National Association of Life Underwriters (NALU)
    C. Association of Chartered Life Underwriters (ACLU)
    D. National Association of Insurance Commissioners (NAIC)

19. How soon after an administrative action is taken against a licensee by any governmental or regulatory agency regarding fraud, dishonesty, or untrustworthiness, must the licensee submit copies of the report to the Department?

    A. Within 90 days
    B. Within 30 days
    C. Within 60 days
    D. Within 45 days

20. If an agent changes her residence address, she must notify the Department of Financial Services within

    A. 15 days
    B. 30 days
    C. 60 days
    D. A change of address does not require notification

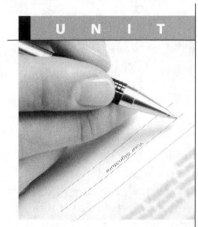

27

Florida Laws and Rules Pertinent to Life Insurance

- Marketing Practices
- Policy Replacement
- Individual Contracts
- Group Life
- Annuities

This unit outlines only those marketing practices, policies, and provisions of life insurance that are regulated by the state of Florida. Candidates for the Life Insurance Examination will be tested on their knowledge of the various required laws, rules, and regulations that are covered in this unit. ■

MARKETING METHODS AND PRACTICES

Agent Responsibilities

An agent must inform the prospective purchaser, before a life insurance sales presentation, that she is acting as a life insurance agent and must inform the prospective purchaser of the full name of the insurance company that the agent is representing. Terms such as financial planner, investment adviser, financial consultant, or financial counseling must not be used in such a way as to imply that the insurance agent is generally engaged in an advisory business in which compensation is unrelated to sales unless such is actually the case.

Any reference to policy dividends must include a statement that dividends are not guaranteed. A presentation of benefits must not display guaranteed and nonguaranteed benefits as a single sum unless they are shown separately in close proximity to each other

A system or presentation that does not recognize the time value of money through the use of appropriate interest adjustments must not be used for comparing the cost of two or more life insurance policies. Such a system may be used for the purpose of demonstrating the cash flow pattern of a policy if such presentation is accompanied by a statement disclosing that the presentation does not recognize that, because of interest, a dollar in the future has less value than a dollar today.

A statement regarding the use of the life insurance cost indexes must include an explanation to the effect that the indexes are useful only for the comparison of the relative costs of two or more similar policies. A life insurance cost index that reflects dividends or an equivalent level annual dividend must be accompanied by a statement that it is based on the insurer's current dividend scale and is not guaranteed. [Sec. 626.99]

Disclosure

The insurer shall provide to each prospective purchaser a Buyer's Guide and a Policy Summary prior to accepting the applicant's initial premium, unless the policy for which application is made provides an unconditional refund for at least 14 days. In these instances, the Buyer's Guide and Policy Summary must be delivered with the policy or before delivery of the policy. [Sec. 626.99]

Buyer's Guide

The purpose of the Buyer's Guide is to improve the buyer's ability to select the most appropriate plan of life insurance for his needs, improve the buyer's understanding of the basic features of the policy that has been purchased or that is under consideration, and improve the ability of the buyer to evaluate the relative costs of similar plans of life insurance.

Policy Summary

Policy Summary means a written statement describing the elements of the policy, including, but not limited to, the following:

■ A prominently placed title as follows: STATEMENT OF POLICY COST AND BENEFIT INFORMATION

■ The name and address of the insurance agent

■ The full name and home office address of the life insurance company

■ The generic name of the basic policy and of each rider

■ The following amounts, when applicable, for the first five policy years and representative policy years thereafter, sufficient to clearly illustrate the premium and benefit patterns, including, but not necessarily limited to, the years for which life insurance cost indexes are displayed and at least one age from 60 through 65, or maturity of the policy, whichever is earlier:

— The annual premium for the basic policy

— The annual premium for each optional rider

— The guaranteed amount payable upon death

— The total guaranteed cash surrender values

— The cash dividends payable at the end of the year, with values shown separately for the basic policy and each rider (dividends need not be displayed beyond the 20th policy year)

— The effective policy loan annual percentage interest rate, if the policy contains this provision, including the maximum annual percentage rate

— Life insurance cost indexes for 10 and 20 years, but in no case beyond the premium-paying period

■ The equivalent level annual dividend, in the case of participating policies, for the same durations at which life insurance cost indexes are displayed

■ For a Policy Summary that includes dividends, a statement that dividends are based on the company's current dividend scale and are not guaranteed

■ The date on which the Policy Summary is prepared

Advertising and sales

Advertising materials and other communications developed by insurers regarding insurance products must clearly indicate that the communication relates to insurance products. When soliciting or selling insurance products, agents must clearly indicate to prospective insureds that they are acting as insurance agents with regard to insurance products and identified insurers. [Sec. 626.9531]

Disclosure requirements for indeterminate value life annuity contract advertisements

Advertisements containing a rate to be earned, including interest rates, rates of return, or any other designation of earnings performance, are prohibited unless all limitations and conditions that affect the rate of return ultimately realized by the policyholder/certificateholder or annuitant are disclosed prominently with equal emphasis to describe the interest rate or rate of return. The disclosure shall include the following:

■ Premium expense charges, if any

■ Administrative charges, if any

■ The full surrender charge, year by year

■ Any policy fees

■ Free withdrawal provisions or bail-outs, if any

■ Market value adjustment, if any

■ Participation rates, if any

■ Any other provisions that affect the rate of return ultimately realized by the policyholder/certificateholder or annuitant, and how the return is affected

■ Guaranteed minimum interest rate during the accumulation period and the annuitization period, if any

An advertisement must not refer to an annuity as a CD annuity. All variable life and annuity advertisements shall clearly disclose whether the insured may realize positive or negative returns on the principal, including a potential loss of the original principal contribution. [FAC Rule 69O-150.106]

Advertisements of proceeds payable, premiums payable

Invitations to contract must clearly reflect the insurer, the agent, the policy form number(s), the type plan, premium payable, payment period, and if applicable, changes in face amounts and premiums. An advertisement of life insurance sold by direct response shall not contain the phrase "no salesman will call," or "no agent will call," or "by eliminating the agent and/or commission we can offer this low cost plan," or similar wording in a misleading manner.

An advertisement that also is an invitation to join an association, trust, or discretionary group must solicit insurance coverage on a separate and distinct application that requires separate signatures for each application. Any applicable membership fees or dues shall be disclosed on each application and must appear separately so as not to be construed as part of the premium for insurance coverage.

An advertisement must not refer to premium as a "deposit."

An advertisement containing an interest rate to be earned, rate of return to be earned, or yield to be earned is prohibited unless all limitations and conditions that affect the ultimate rate of return earned by the policyholder/insured/beneficiary are disclosed prominently and conspicuously with equal emphasis to describe the interest rate, rate of return, or yield. [FAC Rule 69O-150.107]

Dividends

An advertisement shall not be used that utilizes or describes dividends in a manner that is misleading. An advertisement shall not directly or indirectly state or imply that the amount of dividends or divisible surplus is guaranteed; nor shall such advertisement state or imply that a policyholder will profit by the growth of the company. Any comparison between participating and nonparticipating policies or contracts must be true and accurate. [FAC Rule 69O-150.109]

FLORIDA REPLACEMENT RULE

The purpose of Florida policy replacement rules are to: regulate the activities of insurers and agents with respect to the replacement of existing life insurance; and protect the interests of life insurance policyowners by establishing minimum standards of conduct to be observed in the replacement of existing life insurance by: ensuring that the policyowner receives information with which a decision can be made in her best interests; and reducing the opportunity for misrepresentation and incomplete disclosures. [FAC RULE 69B-151.001 - .008; 69O-151.001 - .008]

Replacement means any transaction in which new life insurance is to be purchased, and it is known or should be known to the proposing agent or to the proposing insurer that existing life insurance has been or is to be:

- lapsed, forfeited, surrendered, or otherwise terminated;

- converted to reduced paid-up insurance, continued as extended term insurance, or otherwise reduced in value by the use of nonforfeiture benefits or other policy values;

- amended so as to effect either a reduction in benefits or in the term for which coverage would otherwise remain in force or for which benefits would be paid;

- reissued with any reduction in cash value; or

- pledged as collateral or subjected to borrowing, whether in a single loan or under a schedule of borrowing over a period of time, for amounts in aggregate exceeding 25% of the loan value set forth in the policy.

Life insurance. For the purpose of replacement regulations, life insurance includes annuities, tax-sheltered annuities, or life insurance policies that qualify under the definition of tax-sheltered annuities.

Exemptions. These replacement regulations do not apply to:

- industrial insurance;

- group, franchise, and individual credit life insurance;

- group life insurance and life insurance policies issued in connection with a pension, profit sharing, or other benefit plan qualifying for tax deductibility of premiums;

- an application to the existing insurer that issued the existing life insurance where a contractual change or conversion privilege is being exercised;

- existing life insurance that is a nonconvertible term life insurance policy that will expire in five years or less and cannot be renewed, unless such policy has tabular cash values;

- proposed life insurance that is to replace existing life insurance issued under a binding or conditional receipt delivered by the same company; or

- variable life insurance or annuities under which the death benefits and cash values vary in accordance with unit values of investments held in a separate account.

Duties of agent

Each agent shall submit to the insurer with or as a part of each application for life insurance:

- a statement signed by the applicant as to whether or not the new insurance will replace existing life insurance; and

- a signed statement as to whether or not the agent knows a replacement is or may be involved in the transactions.

Where replacement is or may be involved, the agent must do the following.

- Have the applicant, not later than at the time of taking the application, sign a Notice to Applicant Regarding Replacement of Life Insurance form. The notice must also be signed by the agent and left with the applicant.

- Leave with the applicant the original or a copy of all sales proposals used for presentation to the applicant.

- Submit to the replacing insurer with the application, a completed copy of the "Notice to Applicant Regarding Replacement of Life Insurance" and a copy of all sales proposals used for presentation to the applicant.

Duties of replacing insurance company

The replacing insurer must inform its field representatives of the requirements of these rules. The following apply to instances in which a replacement is involved.

■ Require from the agent with the application for life insurance a completed copy of the Notice to Applicant Regarding Replacement of Life Insurance and a copy of all sales proposals used for presentation to the applicant.

■ Send to the applicant when requested in the notice, a completed Comparative Information Form containing complete information required by the form regarding the proposed insurance. This must be done within five working days of the date the application and the Notice to the Applicant Regarding Replacement of Life Insurance are received at its home or regional office.

■ Send to the existing insurer a copy of the Notice to the Applicant Regarding the Replacement of Life Insurance immediately upon receipt at its home or regional office.

■ Provide to each prospective purchaser a Buyer's Guide and a Policy Summary prior to accepting any applicant's initial premium or premium deposit, unless the policy for which application is made contains a provision for an unconditional refund for a period of at least 10 days, in which event the Buyer's Guide and Policy Summary must be delivered with the policy or prior to delivery of the policy.

■ Maintain copies of the Notice to Applicant Regarding Replacement of Life Insurance, requested Comparative Information Forms, and all sales proposals used, and a replacement register, cross indexed, by replacing agent and existing insurer to be replaced, for at least three years or until the conclusion of the next regular examination by the insurance department of its state of domicile, whichever is later.

Duties of the existing insurer

The existing insurer must inform its responsible personnel of the requirements of these rules. Each existing insurer must do the following.

■ Within 10 days from the date it receives the *Notice to the Applicant Regarding Replacement of Life Insurance*, furnish the policyowner when requested in the notice with a Comparative Information Form concerning the existing life insurance. The values shown in this Form shall be computed from the current policy year of the existing life insurance.

■ Maintain a file containing the following: Copies of the *Notice to the Applicant Regarding Replacement of Life Insurance* received from replacing insurers and copies of fully completed Comparative Information Forms.

■ This material shall be indexed by replacing insurer and held for three years or until the conclusion of the next regular examination conducted by the insurance department of its domicile, whichever is later.

Surrender recommendations

Insurance agents, insurers, or persons performing insurance agent activities under an exemption from licensure who recommend the surrender of an annuity or life insurance policy containing a cash value and do not recommend that the proceeds from the surrender be used to fund or purchase another annuity or life insurance policy, before execution of the surrender, must provide, on a form that satisfies DFS requirements, information relating to the annuity or policy to be surrendered. Such information must include, but is not limited to, the amount of any surrender charge, the loss of any minimum interest rate guarantees, the amount of any tax consequences resulting from the transaction, the amount of any forfeited death benefit, and the value of any other investment performance guarantees being forfeited as a result of the transaction. [Sec. 627.4553]

INDIVIDUAL CONTRACTS

Standard provisions

Protection of beneficiaries from creditors

At death of the insured, life insurance death benefits will be paid exclusively to the benefit of the named beneficiary as designated in the policy. The proceeds are exempt from the claims of creditors of the insured unless the insurance policy or a valid assignment provides otherwise.

Whenever the insurance, by designation or otherwise, is payable to the insured's estate, the insurance proceeds will become a part of the insured's estate for all purposes and will be administered by the personal representative of the estate of the insured in accordance with the probate laws of the state in like manner as other assets of the insured's estate. Therefore, the proceeds may be subject to the claims of the insured's creditors. [Sec. 222.13, .14]

Proceeds exempt from attachment

The cash surrender values of life insurance policies issued upon the lives of citizens or residents of the state and the proceeds of annuity contracts issued to citizens or residents of the state, upon whatever form, shall not in any case be liable to attachment, garnishment, or legal process in favor of any creditor of the person whose life is so insured or of any creditor of the person who is the beneficiary of such annuity contract, unless the insurance policy or annuity contract was effected for the benefit of such creditor. [Sec. 222.14]

Prohibited provisions

Policy loan. An insurance company can charge a fixed rate of no more than 10% annual interest subject to restrictions. The insurance company can also use an adjustable rate of interest with the limit based on the average monthly published interest rate determined by Moody's corporate bond index. [Sec. 627.4585]

Free look

An unconditional refund of premiums for life insurance must be available for a period of at least 14 days. An unconditional refund of premiums for a fixed annuity contract, including any contract fees or charges, must be available for a period of 21 days.

An unconditional refund for variable annuity contracts must also be available for a period of 21 days. The unconditional refund shall be equal to the cash surrender value provided in the annuity contract, plus any fees or charges deducted from the premiums or imposed under the contract; or a refund of all premiums paid. [Sec. 626.99]

Grace period

Every individual life insurance contract shall provide that the insured is entitled to a grace period of not less than 30 days within which payment of any premium may be made. The payment may, at the option of the insurer, be subject to an interest charge not in excess of 8% per year for the number of days of grace elapsing before the payment of the premium. If the policy becomes a claim during the grace period before the overdue premium is paid, the amount of such premium with interest may be deducted from the death benefit paid. [Sec. 627.453]

Designation of beneficiary

The owner of an insurance contract has the right at all times to change the beneficiary or beneficiaries unless the owner waives this right by specifically requesting in writing that the beneficiary designation be irrevocable.

Life agents as beneficiaries

A life insurance agent cannot be named as beneficiary of a life insurance policy covering the life of a person who is not a family member of the agent unless the agent has an insurable interest in the life of such person. Family member means father, mother, son, daughter, brother, sister, grandfather, grandmother, uncle, aunt, first cousin, nephew, niece, husband, wife, father-in-law, mother-in-law, brother-in-law, sister-in-law, stepfather, stepmother, stepson, stepdaughter, stepbrother, stepsister, half brother, or half sister. [Sec. 626.798]

Effect of divorce on death proceeds

Unless a specific exception applies, a beneficiary designation naming a former spouse is void at the time the policyholder's marriage is judicially dissolved, so long as the beneficiary designation was made prior to the court order. [Sec. 732.703]

Additional lapse notice and secondary addressee

Except as provided in this section, a contract for life insurance issued for delivery in Florida, covering a natural person 64 years of age or older, which has been in force for at least one year, may not be lapsed for nonpayment of premium unless, after expiration of the grace period, and at least 21 days before the effective date of any such lapse, the insurer has mailed a notification of the impending lapse in coverage to the policyowner and to a specified secondary addressee if such addressee has been designated in writing by name and address by the policyowner.

An insurer must notify the applicant of the right to designate a secondary addressee at the time of application for the policy, or at any time the policy is in force, by submitting a written notice to the insurer containing the name and address of the secondary addressee. This section does not apply to any life insurance contract under which premiums are payable monthly or more frequently and are regularly collected by a licensed agent, paid by credit card, or any preauthorized check. [Sec. 627.4555, .4556]

Conversion of industrial life

When an insured has industrial life policies with a single insurance company that total $3,000 or more in face value, the insured has the option to convert all of these policies into one ordinary life insurance policy without evidence of insurability. [Sec. 627.517]

Nonforfeiture options

Life insurance policies delivered in Florida must contain the following nonforfeiture options [Sec. 627.476]:

- Reduced paid-up life insurance
- Cash surrender value
- Extended term life insurance

Policy settlement

Every contract must provide that, when a policy becomes a claim by the death of the insured, settlement must be made upon receipt of proof of death and surrender of the policy. When a policy provides for payment of its death proceeds in a lump sum, the payment must include interest from the date the insurer receives written proof of death of the insured. If a policy provides for payment of its proceeds in installments, a table showing the amount and period of such installments must be included in the policy. [Sec. 627.461, .4615, .462]

GROUP LIFE

Standard provisions/required provisions

Group life insurance policies delivered in Florida must have the following provisions or provisions that are at least as favorable to the persons insured. [Sec. 627.558–.565]

There is no minimum number of members (lives) required for a group policy in Florida so long as the organization is one that is eligible for group life insurance. [Sec. 627.551]

Grace period

A group life insurance policy shall provide that the policyholder is entitled to a grace period of 31 days for the payment of any premium due except the first. If an insured dies during the grace period, the death benefit will be paid.

Incontestability

A group life insurance policy shall provide that the validity of the policy shall not be contested, except for nonpayment of premium, after it has been in force for two years from its date of issue.

Attachment of application to policy; representations in application

A group life insurance policy shall provide that a copy of the application, if any, of the policyholder be attached to the policy when issued, that all statements made by the policyholder or by the persons insured be deemed representations and not warranties, and that no statement made by any person insured be used in any contest unless a copy of the instrument containing the statement is or has been furnished to such person or to her or his beneficiary.

Evidence of individual insurability

A group life insurance policy must contain a provision setting forth the conditions, if any, under which the insurer reserves the right to require a person eligible for insurance to furnish evidence of individual insurability satisfactory to the insurer as a condition to part or all of her coverage.

Misstatement of age

A group life insurance policy shall contain a provision specifying an equitable adjustment of premiums or of benefits, or of both, to be made in the event the age of a person insured has been misstated. The provision shall contain a clear statement of the method of adjustment to be used.

Designated beneficiary; reimbursement for expenses

A group life insurance policy shall provide that any sum becoming due by reason of the death of the person insured be payable to the designated beneficiary. Subject to the provisions of the policy, in the event there is no designated beneficiary living at the time of the insured's death, all or any part of such sum shall be subject to any right reserved by the insurer in the policy and set forth in the certificate to pay at its option a part of the sum not exceeding $2,000 to any person appearing to the insurer to be equitably entitled thereto by reason of having incurred funeral or other expenses incident to the last illness or death of the person insured.

Individual certificates

A group life insurance insurer must issue to the policyholder for delivery to each person insured an individual certificate containing the group number and describing:

- the person insured;

- the insurance protection to which the certificateholder is entitled;

- to whom the insurance benefits are payable;

- any dependent's coverage included in the certificate;

- the rights and conditions; and

- the person to whom the insurance benefits are payable.

For employee groups, the certificate may, in lieu of including the name of the person insured and the person to whom benefits are payable, prominently display the following statement: *"This certificate provides life insurance for the employees and dependents, if applicable, of (employer's name and address) under (group contract number). The employee shall be given a copy of the group enrollment application. The benefits are payable to the beneficiaries of record designated by the employee."* Current records shall be maintained by the employer and the insurer of all insured persons and beneficiaries.

Notification of termination

Every insurance company shall notify each certificate holder (member) when the master policy has expired or has been canceled. The insurance company may take this action through the policyowner (i.e., employer) by notifying it and requesting that it notify the certificate holders. The policyowner shall advise each certificate holder, as soon as practicable, of the notice of expiration or cancellation. [Sec. 627.5725]

Conversion rights

Conversion on termination of group eligibility

A group life insurance policy must provide that, if the insurance on a person covered under the policy or on the dependent of a person covered ceases because of termination of employment, such person is entitled to have issued to him by the insurer, without evidence of insurability, an individual life insurance policy, without health or other supplementary benefits, provided application for the individual policy is made, and the first premium is paid to the insurer within 31 days after such termination.

In addition, the individual policy must be on any one of the forms then customarily issued by the insurer at the age and for the amount applied for, except that the group policy may exclude the option to elect term insurance. The premium on the individual policy will be at the insurer's then customary rate applicable to the form and amount of the individual policy, to the class of risk to which such person then belongs, and to such person's age attained on the effective date of the individual policy.

Conversion on policy termination

A group life insurance policy shall provide that, if the group policy terminates or is amended so as to terminate the insurance of any class of insured persons, every person insured on the date of such termination whose insurance terminates, including insured dependents, and who has been so insured for at least five years prior to such termination date is entitled to have issued to her an individual life insurance policy subject to the same conditions and limitations as are provided by Section 627.566, except that the group policy may provide that the amount of such individual policy shall not exceed the smaller of:

- the amount of the person's life insurance protection ceasing because of the termination or amendment of the group policy, less the amount of any life insurance for which she is or becomes eligible under any group policy issued or reinstated by the same or another insurer within 31 days after such termination; or

- $10,000.

Death pending conversion

A group life insurance policy must provide that, if a person insured under the policy dies during the conversion period and before an individual policy has become effective, the amount of life insurance that she would have been entitled to have issued under the individual policy shall be payable as a claim under the group policy. [Sec. 627.566 - .568]

Types of groups/eligible groups

Under the Florida law, the eligible groups are the following.

- **Employer-employee group.** The full-time employees of a single employer.

- **Labor union group.** Members of a particular labor union. The policy is held by the union because the members may work for several employers during the year.

- **Trustee group.** A group of the employees of two or more employers together. The trustee holds the policy for the members.

- **Debtor group.** Debtors of a single creditor. For example, those who purchase furniture from a particular store on the installment plan can obtain credit life insurance. If the debtor dies, the debt is paid by the insurance. The amount of insurance on the life of any debtor shall at no time exceed the amount owed by the debtor.

- **Association group.** Any association of professionals who are licensed by the state can obtain association group life insurance. The association must have been in existence for two years and formed for a purpose other than obtaining insurance. It must hold regular meetings at least on an annual basis. If the premium is contributory, at least 100 members must participate. If it is noncontributory, all members must be covered.

- **Credit union members.** Credit unions and their members are permitted to have a group life insurance policy, which provides coverage equal to the amount of share balance held by the member.

Dependent coverage

The dependent spouse and children of a member of a group may be covered up to an amount not to exceed the amount of insurance for which the employee or member is insured.

Employee life

The lives of a group of individual employees of an employer may be insured, for the benefit of persons other than the employer, under a group policy issued to the employer. The employees eligible for insurance under the policy must be all of the employees of the employer, or all of any classes of employees determined by conditions pertaining to their employment.

The term **employee** includes the employees of one or more subsidiary corporations, and includes the employees, individual proprietors, and partners, if the employer is an individual proprietor or a partnership. The policy may also provide that the term **employee** includes directors of a corporate employer, former employees, or retired employees.

The premium for the policy is be paid by the policyholder, either from the employer's funds, insured employee funds, or both. A policy on which no part of the premium is derived from funds contributed by the insured employees must insure all eligible employees, or all except any as to whom evidence of individual insurability is not satisfactory to the insurer, except those employees who reject coverage in writing. The amounts of insurance under the policy must be based upon some plan precluding individual selection either by the employees or by the employer.

Assignment of proceeds

A person insured under a group life insurance policy is allowed to make an assignment of all or part of his incidents of ownership under that policy. This includes but is not limited to the privilege of having an individual policy issued to him and the right to name a beneficiary. This assignment shall be made without prejudice to the insurer because of any payment it may make or individual policy it may issue in accordance with Florida statutes prior to receipt of notice of an assignment. [Sec. 627.552–.571]

ANNUITIES

Suitability

The purpose of this section is to require insurers to establish standards and procedures for making recommendations to consumers that result in transactions involving annuity products, and to establish a system for supervising such recommendations in order to ensure that the insurance needs and financial objectives of consumers are appropriately addressed at the time of the transaction. [Sec. 627.4554; FAC Rule 69B-162.011]

Recommendation means advice provided by an insurer or its agent to a consumer that would result in the purchase, exchange, or replacement of an annuity in accordance with that advice.

Replacement means a transaction in which a new policy or contract is to be purchased, and it is known or should be known to the proposing insurer or its agent that by reason of such transaction an existing policy or contract will be:

- lapsed, forfeited, surrendered or partially surrendered, assigned to the replacing insurer, or otherwise terminated;

- converted to reduced paid-up insurance, continued as extended term insurance, or otherwise reduced in value due to the use of nonforfeiture benefits or other policy values;

- amended so as to effect a reduction in benefits or the term for which coverage would otherwise remain in force or for which benefits would be paid;

- reissued with a reduction in cash value; or

- used in a financed purchase.

Suitability information means information related to the consumer that is reasonably appropriate to determine the suitability of a recommendation made to the consumer, including the following:

- Age

- Annual income

- Financial situation and needs, including the financial resources used for funding the annuity

- Financial experience

- Financial objectives

- Intended use of the annuity

- Financial time horizon

- Existing assets, including investment and life insurance holdings

- Liquidity needs

- Liquid net worth

- Risk tolerance

- Tax status

Duties of insurers and insurance representatives

When recommending the purchase or exchange of an annuity to a consumer that results in an insurance transaction or series of insurance transactions, the agent and insurer must have reasonable grounds for believing that the recommendation is suitable for the consumer, based on the consumer's suitability information, and that there is a reasonable basis to believe all of the following.

- The consumer has been reasonably informed of various features of the annuity, such as the potential surrender charge, potential tax penalties, and other fees.

- The consumer would benefit from certain features of the annuity, such as tax-deferred growth, annuitization, or the death or living benefit.

- The particular annuity as a whole is suitable.

- In the case of an exchange or replacement of an annuity, the exchange or replacement is suitable after considering whether the consumer:

  — will incur a surrender charge;

  — be subject to the commencement of a new surrender period;

  — lose existing benefits, such as death, living, or other contractual benefits; or be subject to increased fees, investment advisory fees, or charges for riders and similar product enhancements;

— would benefit from product enhancements and improvements; and

— has had another annuity exchange or replacement, including an exchange or replacement within the preceding 36 months.

Before executing a purchase, exchange, or replacement of an annuity resulting from a recommendation, an insurer or its agent must make reasonable efforts to obtain the consumer's suitability information. An insurer may not issue an annuity recommended to a consumer unless there is a reasonable basis to believe the annuity is suitable based on the consumer's suitability information. However, an insurer or its agent does not have an obligation to a consumer related to an annuity transaction if:

■ a recommendation has not been made;

■ a recommendation was made and is later found to have been based on materially inaccurate information provided by the consumer;

■ a consumer refuses to provide relevant suitability information and the annuity transaction is not recommended; or

■ a consumer decides to enter into an annuity transaction that is not based on a recommendation of an insurer or its agent.

Before executing a replacement or exchange of an annuity contract resulting from a recommendation, the agent must provide on form DFS-H1-1981 information that compares the differences between the existing annuity contract and the annuity contract being recommended in order to determine the suitability of the recommendation and its benefit to the consumer. An agent may not dissuade, or attempt to dissuade, a consumer from truthfully responding to an insurer's request for confirmation of suitability information; filing a complaint; or cooperating with the investigation of a complaint.

An insurer shall establish a supervision system that is reasonably designed to achieve the insurer's and its agent's compliance with this section. Such system must include, but is not limited to the following:

■ Maintaining reasonable procedures to inform its agents of the requirements of this section and incorporating those requirements into relevant agent training manuals

■ Providing product-specific training and training materials that explain all material features of its annuity products to its agents

■ Maintaining procedures for the review of each recommendation before issuance of an annuity that are designed to ensure that there is a reasonable basis for determining that a recommendation is suitable

■ Maintaining reasonable procedures to detect recommendations that are not suitable, such as confirmation of consumer suitability information, systematic customer surveys, consumer interviews, confirmation letters, and internal monitoring programs

■ Annually providing a report to senior managers, including the senior manager who is responsible for audit functions, which details a review, along with appropriate testing, which is reasonably designed to determine the effectiveness of the supervision system, the exceptions found, and corrective action taken or recommended, if any

Recordkeeping

Insurers and agents must maintain or be able to make available to the office or department records of the information collected from the consumer and other information used in making the recommendations that were the basis for insurance transactions for five years after the insurance transaction is completed by the insurer. An insurer may maintain the documentation on behalf of its agent.

Prohibited charges

An annuity contract issued to a senior consumer age 65 or older may not contain a surrender or deferred sales charge for a withdrawal of money from an annuity exceeding 10% of the amount withdrawn. The charge must be reduced so that no surrender or deferred sales charge exists after the end of the 10th policy year or 10 years after the date of each premium payment if multiple premiums are paid, whichever is later.

KEY CONCEPTS

Students should be familiar with the following concepts:

Florida Replacement Rule	other policy provisions
buyer's guide	lapse notification and additional addressee
policy summary	group life insurance
policy conversion	group conversion rights
policy assignment	annuity suitability

UNIT TEST

1. Which of the following is CORRECT about the replacement rule?

    A. The replacement rule only applies to health insurance.
    B. The agent has 90 days from the effective date to deliver a buyer's guide.
    C. The agent must leave a copy of all sales proposals used in the presentation with the applicant.
    D. Up to 30 days is allowed for a full refund of premium.

2. Which of the following is NOT considered to be an element of replacement?

    A. The agent knows a new policy will take the place of an existing policy.
    B. An existing policy is subjected to a loan of 10% of its value.
    C. An existing policy is allowed to lapse.
    D. An existing policy is reissued with a reduced cash value.

3. In which of the following ways is a beneficiary protected from the creditors of the deceased insured?

    A. The proceeds of a policy can always be claimed by the deceased insured's creditors.
    B. When the policy is made payable to the estate, the proceeds are protected from the creditors.
    C. If the policy is made payable to a named beneficiary, then the creditors can make no claim on the proceeds.
    D. The cash surrender value of a life insurance policy can be attached by an ordinary creditor.

4. All of the following are correct insurance agent marketing responsibilities EXCEPT

    A. an agent must inform a prospect, prior to the presentation, that she is a life insurance agent and provide the name of her insurer
    B. any reference to policy dividends must include a statement that such dividends are not guaranteed
    C. any presentation comparing two or more life policies must recognize the time value of money using interest adjustments
    D. a presentation may not include references to life insurance policy cost indexes

5. Which of the following applies when an insured wishes to convert industrial insurance policies into an ordinary policy?

    A. This is not permitted under Florida law.
    B. It is possible to convert $3,000 or more of industrial insurance.
    C. Any such conversion requires a physical examination.
    D. The multiple policies can only be reissued as one industrial policy.

6. At the time of an insurance sale, which of the following is NOT correct?

    A. Personal information about the client should never be released without prior approval from the client.
    B. A producer only needs to disclose to a prospect the information that the prospect requests.
    C. Precision and accuracy in completing the application are in the best interest of both the insurer and the prospective insured.
    D. A producer has ethical responsibilities to the client and insurer.

7. All of the following groups are eligible for group life insurance EXCEPT

    A. employer and employee groups
    B. labor unions
    C. trustee groups
    D. social clubs

8. Which of the following is the CORRECT number of lives required in Florida for a group insurance policy?

   A. 3
   B. 8
   C. 10
   D. No minimum

9. Which of the following is NOT required when a group insurance policy is canceled?

   A. The insurance company must notify the group policyowner.
   B. The policyowner must notify the Department of the cancellation.
   C. The insurance company must notify the group members (but may request this to be done by the policyowner).
   D. The policyowner must notify the group members.

10. Suitability information gathered from consumers must be retained for review by the Department

    A. for 3 years by agents only
    B. for 4 years by insurers only
    C. by neither agents nor insurers
    D. by both agents and insurers for 5 years

11. To comply with disclosure requirements, producers must deliver which of the following documents to all insurance applicants?

    A. Policy guidelines and proposal form
    B. Policy summary and policy receipt
    C. Buyer's Guide and policy summary
    D. Proposal form and Buyer's Guide

12. Which of the following must be given to an insured when a replacement occurs?

    A. Notice regarding replacement
    B. Valued policy provision
    C. Termination notice
    D. Notice regarding insurer solvency

13. All of the following information and much more must be gathered from an annuity applicant in order to determine the suitability of the sale EXCEPT

    A. general financial information, including income, assets, and net worth of the applicant
    B. tax status of the applicant
    C. personal information, including age and sex of the annuitants and dependents
    D. membership in any civic clubs or organizations by the applicant

14. For an individual life contract on an insured 64 years of age or older, the insurer must advise the applicant

    A. of their right to a large-print copy of the policy if required
    B. of their right to designate a secondary addressee to receive a copy of any policy lapse notice
    C. of an extended free-look period
    D. of their right to name a trustee to exercise ownership rights under the policy

15. Which of the following statements applies to the rights of a surviving spouse under a group insurance policy?

    A. Coverage continues at the same rate and premium.
    B. Conversion privileges must be provided for dependents.
    C. Conversion rights extend to the spouse but not to the children.
    D. Conversion rights of the surviving spouse are less than those the deceased employee possessed.

16. Which of the following rules would apply if an agent knows an applicant is going to cash in an old policy and use the funds to purchase new insurance?

    A. Conversion rule
    B. Disclosure rule
    C. Replacement rule
    D. Reinstatement rule

17. During what period is a new life insurance policy owner entitled to renew a policy and return it for a full refund?

   A. During the 14 days prior to its effective date
   B. Within 14 days after delivery of the policy
   C. Within 30 days of purchase
   D. After receipt, but only with the prior approval of the agent

18. All of the following statements regarding the life insurance policy summary are correct EXCEPT

   A. it must illustrate all guaranteed cash surrender values
   B. it must illustrate all guaranteed policy dividend values
   C. it must present the generic name of the policy as well as the company's name for it
   D. it must be given to each new policy owner no later than at policy delivery

19. All the following are correct about the policy loan interest rate EXCEPT

   A. an adjustable rate of interest may be charged
   B. an insurance company may charge affixed rate of up to 10%
   C. adjustable rates are based on a published index
   D. there are no restrictions or limitations on policy loan rates

20. An insurer must establish a suitability supervision system including all of the following EXCEPT

   A. reasonable procedures to inform agents of suitability requirements
   B. product-specific training for agents explaining all material annuity features
   C. limiting annuity replacements to agents with 2 or more years' field experience
   D. reasonable procedures to detect unsuitable recommendations

21. Which of the following actions accurately portrays the limit Florida insurance regulations set for the combining of advertising for insurance policies with an association membership?

   A. By forbidding these two to be advertised together
   B. By requiring the insurance solicitation to come at least 30 days after the association membership
   C. By requiring separate applications and separate signatures
   D. By requiring a signed statement of understanding by the applicant

22. Which of the following statements is CORRECT about group life insurance?

   A. It is written with a master policy for the benefit of qualified groups.
   B. A group member is prohibited from assigning incidents of Ownership
   C. Group life rates are generally higher than those for individual policies.

23. How will a beneficiary designation naming a former spouse on a preexisting insurance contract be changed by the divorce?

   A. The beneficiary designation is voided by the divorce.
   B. There will be no change allowed under Florida law.
   C. The beneficiary change requires a court decree.
   D. Insurer policy rules will determine the result.

24. All of the following are duties of a replacing insurer EXCEPT

   A. maintain copies of every Notice Regarding Replacement, all sales proposals, and a register cross-indexed by replacing agent and existing insurer for three years
   B. immediately send a copy of the Notice Regarding Replacement to the existing insurer.
   C. require a statement, signed by any replacing agent, acknowledging such replacement
   D. insure that all appointed agents take a 2-hour course on replacement annually

25. All of the following statements are correct about group life insurance EXCEPT
    A. a member may assign her incidents of ownership
    B. certificate holders need not be notified if the policy expires
    C. rates are typically more favorable than for individual policies
    D. it is typically written as a one-year renewable term plan

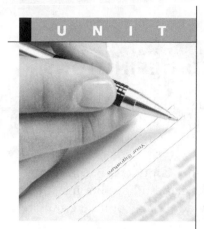

28

Florida Laws and Rules Pertinent to Variable Contracts

- Introduction to Variable Products and Definitions

- Annuities

- Variable Annuities

- Regulation and Licensing

- Marketing Practices and Suitability

The Florida insurance exam for variable insurance contracts contains several topics that are common to the life agent exam. In preparing for the variable insurance contracts exam, the student should review units 1, 8, 11, 12, 15, 26, and 27 in this manual in addition to this unit. ■

INTRODUCTION TO VARIABLE PRODUCTS AND DEFINITIONS

Variable insurance contracts, which include variable life insurance and variable annuities, are insurance contracts that derive their product values largely from the investment performance of a family of investment portfolios, called separate accounts. [Sec. 627.8015]

Indeterminate value contracts means annuity contracts, life insurance contracts, and contracts upon the lives of beneficiaries under life insurance contracts when such annuities or contracts provide variable or indeterminate benefits, values, or premiums.

Variable contracts means indeterminate value contracts for which assets are held in a separate account.

Separate account

A separate account is the central element in all variable products. Such an account may be created by either an insurer or an investment company.

In function, a separate account operates much like a family of mutual funds. The account contains a group of managed investment portfolios, each containing dozens of separate investments under the supervision of an investment manager. These portfolios each focus on a particular segment of the investment landscape, ranging from government or municipal bonds, through corporate bonds, to large, medium, and small-capitalization stock. There may also be foreign investment portfolios, as well as precious metals, and segments such as pharmaceuticals, technology, or manufacturing.

The variable contract owner may select a few of these portfolios, or many, from which to obtain the investment results that will determine their variable contract values. The variable contract owner may also change choice of portfolios at any time and at no cost in order to react to changing market conditions or simply to better reflect the owner's own changing investment preferences over time.

The net investment performance of the portfolios chosen by the variable contract owner will determine the variable cash value and variable death benefit of his variable life insurance, or the account value of his variable annuities. The separate account values will go up and down daily with market fluctuations, and the variable contract values will do the same. The variable contract owner has the opportunity to experience market-based gains, but also the owner bears the full market risk associated with market declines. [Sec. 627.802]

Fixed premium variable life

Fixed premium variable life insurance, also called scheduled premium variable life, variable whole life, or just plain variable life, is a variable insurance contract built on a whole life framework. This product has fixed, level, and required premiums, set by the insurer as to timing and amount. As with whole life, if a required premium is missed, the policy will lapse after the grace period.

Fixed premium variable life insurance also has a fixed and level death benefit, called the guaranteed minimum death benefit, which runs to age 100 like whole life. So long as the required premiums are paid, this death benefit will be payable no matter what the performance of the separate account may be.

If the policyowner wishes to access the cash values of the policy during the lifetime of the insured, she must execute a policy loan and pay interest. Remember as well that when a policy loan is executed, both the cash value and death benefit of the policy are reduced by the loan amount.

Flexible premium variable life

Flexible premium variable life insurance, also called variable universal life, is a variable life insurance contract built on a universal life framework. Variable universal policies are characterized by flexible premiums, which can be increased, decreased, or even omitted at will by the policyowner. Universal life policies do not lapse when a premium is missed like whole life as long as the cash value is sufficient to pay the monthly mortality expense charge, and monthly administrative fee.

Variable universal policies have adjustable death benefits that may be increased or decreased at will by the policyowner. Of course, as with other universal life policies, an increase to the death benefit must be accompanied by proof of insurability, and it will cause increased mortality charges. The cash value may be accessed using partial withdrawals or policy loans.

Lastly, variable universal life policies have the same dual death benefit options as other universal life policies. At the time of application, owners select option A (or 1) if they want a level death benefit equal to the face amount. If they select option B (or 2), the death benefit will equal the face amount plus the cash value at date of death. If owners select option B, they will incur a higher monthly mortality charge than they would have had with option A because of the higher death benefit.

ANNUITIES

Purpose and function

As you learned in the life insurance license unit, annuities are the savings vehicle of the insurance industry. Like stocks and bonds offered by the brokerage industry, or certificates of deposit offered by banks, annuities allow clients to build assets for the future. Annuities are sold by insurance agents, of course, but also by broker-dealers and bankers. There are, however, several features of annuities that are unique and that reflect their origin and close connection with life insurance companies. The financial aspects of an annuity closely parallel those of a life insurance contract, but they have opposite functions; the life insurance contract guards against dying too soon, while the annuity contract guards against living too long.

■ Annuities distribute back to the annuitant a stream of income that the insurance company guarantees will continue for the remaining lifetime of the annuitant, no matter how long that may be.

■ This guaranteed lifetime income stream is possible because insurers have mortality data that allows them to predict average life expectancy, and this feature of all annuities makes them uniquely valuable for retirement planning.

Structure and design

Individual annuities are the most common, and they are characterized by a single annuitant who creates the contract, makes the premium payments, and receives the distributions going forward. Interestingly, as this is the most common type of annuity ownership, the term "individual" is not included in the title on sales literature or brochures. Thus, a "deferred, single-premium, variable annuity" is understood to have an individual annuitant even though that term is not in the product title.

Joint and survivor annuities are annuities that are popular with married couples because they continue distributions until the second or last annuitant dies. A further decision must be made, when this type of annuity structure is selected, as to whether the surviving annuitant is to receive the same or a lessor distribution for the remainder of his or her life after the death of the first annuitant. If the same payment is to continue, it is called a "joint and 100% to the survivor" or "joint and full" arrangement. If the survivor payment is to be less, the percentage of the original payments that is to continue to the second annuitant is specified. Thus if John and Mary had a "joint and 50% to the survivor" annuity, and the payment while they were both alive was $1,000 per month, that payment would be reduced to $500 per month to the surviving spouse after the first death. The key to remember here is that the smaller the percentage to be paid to a survivor, the larger the payment that will be paid while they are both alive, so this is a means to "weight" the relative payments in whatever manner the annuitants may desire.

Joint life annuities have two or more annuitants. However, unlike joint and survivor the contract ends at the first death. This option is particularly useful with spouses or other annuitants who have substantial individual assets, or substantial insurance on each other, and who do not wish the annuity contract to continue after the first death, but rather wish to make new financial arrangements when the first annuitant dies.

Funding method

There are three typical arrangements in which payments may be made into an annuity.

Single premium annuity

A single premium annuity is funded entirely with one, single payment. Such payment arrangements are frequently chosen by annuitants who are at retirement age and selling a house, a business, or other assets, and who wish to convert the sales proceeds into a secure stream of retirement income for the remainder of their life. A single premium, immediate annuity will work well in this circumstance.

Flexible premium annuity

Conversely, younger annuitants often lack the ability to fund an annuity with a single premium payment. They might choose a flexible premium arrangement, which here means just what it does with flexible premium life insurance; that the annuitants may pay whatever they wish whenever they wish, typically over a span of years. The insurer will set an initial minimum premium requirement, such as $500, to start the annuity, but subsequently the annuitants may make truly flexible premium payments however and whenever they wish.

Periodic premium payments

Many annuitants want to create a structured annuity payment, using a draft from a bank account, in order to reinforce the discipline of retirement saving. Periodic premiums are a sub-set of a flexible premium annuity that are designed for such a circumstance. Because of the commitment on the part of the annuitant to systematic savings, the insurer will often have a lower initial premium requirement to start such an annuity. But also, since this is a sub-set arrangement, the annuitants may cancel the periodic payment commitment if they wish to at any point in the future, and the annuity will simply revert to flexible premiums thereafter.

Date income payments begin

A fourth annuity characteristic, or choice for the annuitant, is the matter of when benefits are to begin. All annuities have two phases: an accumulation phase and an annuitization phase. During the accumulation phase, the annuitant is making premium payments into the annuity. During the annuitization phase, the insurer is making payments out of the annuity to the annuitant. These two phases do not overlap. The annuitant decides when premiums are to end and distribution is to begin. Once the annuitization phase has started, no further premium payments may be made into the annuity.

Immediate annuity

An immediate annuity begins distribution to the annuitant immediately, which means on the next payment cycle. Payment cycles are based on the mode of distribution chosen by the annuitant. With a monthly mode, for instance, the first payment will be made in one month. On the other hand, a semiannual immediate annuity would make a first payment six months later and every six months thereafter. The longest interval for an immediate annuity is annually, with the first payment coming after one year. There is one other thing to remember: because an immediate annuity begins distribution immediately, there is only one method of premium payment possible—single premium.

Deferred annuity

With a deferred annuity, the annuitant has chosen to delay payout to some date beyond one year. The age or date need not be set at time of purchase. The term deferred simply means "delayed," and the annuitant may make premium payments of any type, single, flexible, or periodic, until he later decides that he wishes to start taking funds out. Remember, however, that once annuity distributions begin, no further premium payments may be made.

Payout options

The contract owner will choose the payout option at the start of the annuitization period. Three of the payout options are based on the annuitant's life expectancy. These types of payout involve the annuitant giving the entire account value of the annuity to the insurer in exchange for a contract to receive payments that will continue for the rest of the annuitant's life. As with life insurance, the insurer uses the mortality table and the concept of risk pooling to determine the amount it will pay for the life of the annuitant. For a retiree, this uniquely insurance-based type of payout removes a significant concern from the planning process: the risk of outliving her money.

Life only

Under the basic, or life only payout option, annuitants will continue to receive payments for as long as they live. The contract will be completed when the annuitant dies, whether that event occurs soon or much later. For this choice to make sense, annuitants must understand what life expectancy the insurer is basing payments on and what the likelihood is that they will live that long.

Annuities are unique from life insurance in that there is no medical underwriting by the insurer. The insurer makes its calculations based solely on the age and sex of the annuitant without considering that person's health. The annuitant, however, must take health into account to determine which payout option is likely to work best. These technical considerations of insurer mortality calculations and annuitant health underwriting are why an annuitant needs the services of a knowledgeable agent/retirement planner to assist in this decision-making process.

The life only payout option is also known as life income or life annuity, and you may see any of these names used on the exam. Also, the life only payout option will produce the largest monthly income guaranteed for life, which is a question both clients and the exam may well ask.

Life with period certain

If the health of the client suggests he may not live to the actuarial life expectancy used by the insurer, or if he is simply uncomfortable with the risk of not living long enough to experience a reasonable return on his annuity premium, the client may choose the life with period certain option. The insurer may offer several different time periods under this option (10, 15, or

20 years are common). Under this arrangement, the annuitant will receive payments for life, just as with the life only option. If the annuitant should die within the certain period, however, the insurer guarantees to continue the annuity payments to a named beneficiary for the balance of the certain period. The insurer is promising payments for life, but guaranteeing payments for a period of time, whether the annuitant lives that long or not.

Life with refund

The last of our three annuitization options, called life with refund, is similar to the previous one, except here the insurer guarantees payments for life, and if the annuitant dies before the payments they have received equals their basis (the total amount of premium they paid for the annuity), then the insurer agrees to pay out the remaining basis to a named beneficiary. As you will realize, this is a guarantee of a return of 100% of the annuitant's principal.

Annuities certain

Although the three choices related to annuitization uniquely allow an annuitant to be certain that her fixed or variable annuity income will extend for her remaining lifetime, and although these choices are also uniquely tax-advantaged as we will discuss later in this unit, these are certainly not the only ways to take distribution or even the most common. *Annuity certain* distributions allow an annuitant to dictate either the amount (*fixed amount option*) or the time period (*fixed period option*) of the distribution, which will then continue until the annuity is exhausted or the annuitant dies. If the annuitant dies before the distribution is completed, payments may then be made to a named beneficiary or to the annuitant's estate.

Partial withdrawals or lump sum

Under this arrangement, sometimes called the "no-plan" plan, the annuitant surrenders the annuity contract all at once or makes random withdrawals until the funds are exhausted. Although this approach is the antithesis of a planned or orderly distribution, it does demonstrate the flexibility of the annuity as a savings or investment vehicle.

Investment configuration

A significant decision that annuity purchasers must make revolves around how the annuity assets will be managed, and as a corollary, how much investment risk they wish to bear. We will examine three basic options here: fixed, indexed, and variable annuities.

Fixed annuities are managed entirely by the insurer, and the assets are held in the insurer's general account. They provide a guaranteed minimum rate of return, similar to that of whole life insurance, and, therefore, the insurer bears the entire investment risk. They will also pay a higher, "current" rate of return when the insurer's investments permit, but both the timing and the amount of these higher, current rates are entirely at the discretion of the insurer. When fixed annuities are annuitized, or converted to retirement income, they produce a fixed and level income for the life of the annuitant. The inherent downside of a fixed annuity is its inability to overcome inflation.

Indexed annuities are considered "fixed" and do not require securities registration for the agent selling them (just a life insurance license) because they always have a guaranteed minimum rate of return (sometimes 0%) that insures the client's principal investment is not at risk. The rate of return credited to an indexed annuity is tied to a market index, usually the S&P 500. This means the client has an opportunity to participate in equity market returns while being protected from a down-market loss by the minimum guarantee. The insurer does not credit the client in an indexed annuity with the full return earned by the index because there must be a margin to provide for expenses, profit, and to cover the cost of the guaranteed minimum rate the insurer will have to pay in an occasional down market. The methods that insurers use to make the tie between the investment return of the index and the crediting rate for the client are often extremely complex, but there are a few common terms used that we should know.

- **Participation rate** is the percentage of the index rate of return with which the client will be credited. Therefore, if the index made 8%, and the participation rate set in the contract was 80%, the client would be credited with 6.4% (80% × 8%).

- **Cap rate** is a maximum rate of return the contract will pay, and when higher returns are registered by the index, the insurer keeps those. In the preceding example, if the product had a 6% cap rate, then even though the participation calculation yielded 6.4%, the client would only be credited with 6%.

- **Floor rate** is a minimum rate that the insurer guarantees to pay on the contract no matter what occurs in the market. As mentioned earlier, this is often 0%, meaning that in a down market the client will not gain, but her current balance would be preserved.

- **Averaging interval and reset methodology** means the annuity contract will set a time interval to look at index results and credit them to the annuity, such as monthly or annually. The contract will also specify whether to use the ending rate of the index or an average rate over the period or some other methodology (and there are many).

Variable annuities are insurance contracts that function similar to fixed annuities insofar as the basic characteristics of premium payment options, number of annuitants, benefit start date choices, and payout options are concerned. These annuity characteristics were discussed in detail in unit 12. The distinction between variable and fixed annuities lies in the method by which variable annuities accumulate value.

As discussed previously, fixed annuity premiums accumulate inside the general account of the insurer, and the contract provides a guaranteed minimum rate of return regardless of the actual investment experience of the insurer. In addition, the insurer may pay a current rate of return above the guarantee. Under these terms, the insurer bears the market risk, and the annuity owner is fully protected against any loss of capital in a declining market.

Conversely, variable annuity values accumulate in a separate account, just as was described earlier. Under this arrangement, the owners of the variable annuity contract have a reasonable expectation that their account values will grow at market-based rates, and that the stream of retirement income once the product is annuitized will also continue to do so, overcoming the inflation risk. The investment performance of the separate account is in no way guaranteed, and the investment risk associated with the separate account is born by the contract owner.

VARIABLE ANNUITIES

The risk of living too long is the basic risk that is insured against by an annuity contract. An annuity is called the "opposite side of the coin" of a life insurance policy (risk of dying too soon). As discussed earlier, despite the interest rate guarantees of a fixed annuity, the risk assumed by the fixed annuity buyer is that the fixed dollar guaranteed payments may not maintain their purchasing power through time.

The variable annuity was developed to overcome the "purchasing power" shortcomings of fixed annuities. The variable annuity is an investment contract in which the purchaser's account value and annuity benefits increase or decrease according to the investment performance of an underlying portfolio of investments—oftentimes common stocks. The basic tenet of the investment base of variable annuities is that as common stock price levels fluctuate with general price levels, the annuity payments, which are determined by the common stock performance, will provide an effective long-run inflation hedge.

The values in a variable annuity are expressed in terms of units rather than dollars. There are two types of units: accumulation units and annuity units. The value of each type of unit is subject to daily fluctuation based upon the performance of the underlying separate account.

■ Common stocks represent ownership in the companies that issue them. They promise no fixed rate of return on investment. If the company prospers, its shares of common stock will increase in value; if the company does not prosper, its shares will generally decrease in value and may even become worthless. The market value of a stock freely traded in the market is determined solely by what the buyer is willing to pay and what the seller is willing to accept. Prices are not fixed or pegged by the company, the Exchange, or the seller. The price that people are willing to pay for stock is generally dependent on the company's earnings, dividends, and prospects for future earnings growth and dividend-paying ability.

■ Bonds, however, are instruments reflecting a debtor relationship. They carry a fixed coupon, or rate of return on investment, and generally have a fixed maturity date on which the principal amount will be repaid. The business success of the issuing company will have no effect on the value of its bonds so long as it is able to pay the fixed rate of interest and is able to repay the principal amount of the bond when due.

Accumulation units

In a deferred variable annuity, the period of time during which funds accumulate—that is, from the contract's issue date to the start of payments—is called the **accumulation period.** During the accumulation period, the value of each individual account rises or falls depending on the insurance company's investment results for the variable annuity separate account. Premiums paid into the company, less a deduction for expenses, are converted to **accumulation units** and credited to the individual's account. For example, if that person's net premium contribution is $100 and the cost of one accumulation unit is $10, the net contribution buys 10 accumulation units. If the net contribution to an individual account is $200 and the cost of one accumulation unit is $10, 20 accumulation units are assigned to the individual's account. Fractional units also may be assigned as necessary.

The value of one accumulation unit is found by dividing the total value of the insurance company's separate account by the total number of accumulation units outstanding. Thus, if a company had $20 million in its separate account and a total of four million accumulation units outstanding, the value of one accumulation unit would be $5. The company cannot guarantee an interest yield from investments because investment results may be geared to a portfolio of common stocks. So the value of the accumulation unit fluctuates accordingly.

Prior to retirement, most often the purchaser of a variable annuity pays a periodic premium amount. When these periodic premiums are paid, the purchaser is credited with a number of accumulation units, the actual number of units determined by the current value of one unit relative to the amount of premium paid. The set periodic premium will buy more units when unit values are low and less units when unit values are high. Thus, as periodic premiums continue to be paid, the purchaser acquires an increasing number of accumulation units. To find the dollar value of a person's variable annuity, the company multiplies the current value of one accumulation unit by the number of accumulation units in the individual account. Thus, if a person owns 3,200 accumulation units and each unit is valued at $4, the dollar value of the individual variable annuity is $12,800

Florida law provides that at least once each year the insurer must provide the contract owner with a report on an approved form that states the number of units credited to the contract and the dollar value of a unit as of a date not more than two months prior to the date the report is mailed. [F.A.C. Rule 69O-162.004, .013(2)]

Annuity units

Before variable annuity (VA) benefits can be paid out, the accumulation units in the participant's individual account must be converted into **annuity units. Annuity units** are the basic measure and method by which the purchaser's annuity income is determined. At the time of retirement, the annuity unit calculation is made and, from then on, the number of annuity units remains the same for that annuitant. The value of an annuity unit, however, can and does vary from month to month depending on investment results.

An annuity unit is used to calculate the amount of each payment made to an annuitant after retirement. To convert a lump sum in an individual's variable annuity account into annuity units, the company's annuity tables are used to determine the amount that applies to every $1,000 in the annuitant's account.

Suppose an individual beginning retirement is entitled to a $5.10 monthly income per thousand dollars of variable annuity funds, based on the company's annuity tables. If that person had accumulated $60,000 in variable annuity funds, the first monthly income payment would be $306 (60 × $5.10). If the value of one annuity unit were calculated by the company to be $2, the annuitant would have 153 annuity units. As has been pointed out, while the number of annuity units figured at the start of retirement stays the same, the value of the annuity unit may vary from month to month, based on the investment results of the separate account. Consequently, the dollar amount of each payment to the annuitant depends on the dollar value of the annuity unit when the payment is made. The theory is that the payout from a VA over a period of years will keep pace with the rate of inflation and thus maintain the annuitant's purchasing power at or above a constant level.

Assumed interest rate (AIR)

The assumed interest rate (AIR) is an arbitrary rate of return set by the insurer for any separate account it establishes. It is usually a low rate, perhaps around 2%, and it plays the role of an "artificial zero" for certain variable contract values. That is to say that a variable contract owner must experience a separate account net investment rate of return that exceeds the AIR in order for those product values to go up. In effect, the AIR serves as additional expense load for the benefit of the insurer. The AIR does not apply to all the values of a variable product.

For variable life, the AIR applies to the variable death benefit, but not to the variable cash value. So any separate account investment return above zero would increase the variable policy cash value, but only a separate account return above the AIR would increase the variable policy death benefit.

Similarly, with a variable annuity, the AIR applies to the variable annuity unit value and any payouts, but not to the variable accumulation value. Therefore, any separate account investment return above zero would increase the variable accumulation unit values, but only a separate account return above the AIR would increase the variable annuity unit values and payments.

Annuity guarantees

All annuities, including variable annuities, provide some guarantees such as the two discussed in the following. Most modern annuities will offer many additional guarantees either as contract provisions or as riders that can be added for an additional premium. However, as these other guarantees are not testable, we'll limit ourselves to these two.

Accumulation death benefit

All annuities, fixed, indexed, and variable, offer an accumulation death benefit guarantee. Although different insurers may structure it differently, it is basically a small life insurance commitment built into the annuity that says that should the contract owner die during the accumulation period the insurer guarantees to pay a named beneficiary the account value or the basis (sum of the premiums), whichever is larger. This, in effect, guarantees that the contract owners cannot suffer a loss of principal if they should die during the accumulation period. Recent VA designs can offer additional guarantees for an increased cost.

Maximum expenses and loads

The second guarantee provided in all annuities is the maximum expense and load guarantee, which is really a disclosure guarantee. It says that the insurer affirms that all expenses, loads, or other charges that may occur are disclosed in writing in the contract. The insurer can choose to charge less than the amounts disclosed, but never more.

REGULATION AND LICENSING

Companies that issue variable contracts may be chartered as life insurance companies or variable annuity companies and authorized to do business in Florida. Either way, such a company comes under the supervision of the state Office of Insurance Regulation.

Dual regulation

Government regulation of variable contracts takes place in two spheres. Although the United States had reserved insurance regulation as a matter for the states, variable contracts raised the question of whether such a contract is an insurance contract or a security, similar to shares in a mutual fund. The Supreme Court in 1959 held that federal law applied to insurers selling variable contracts. Thus, these insurers are subject to federal regulation by the SEC and by the state's Office of Insurance Regulation.

This dual regulation means that insurers issuing variable life insurance policies or variable annuities are still subject to regulation by the state Department of Financial Services and the Office of Insurance Regulation, but the separate account inside such contracts is regulated as a security. In addition to the separate account, the companies issuing variable contracts and the agents or registered representatives selling them fall under the supervision of the SEC and FINRA. [Rule 69O-162.014, F.A.C.; Sec. 627.805, F.S.]

Agent licensing

Agents who want to sell variable contracts must be properly licensed by the state after examination in both the life and variable contracts areas, and they must be appointed as a life including variable contracts insurance agent by the insurance company underwriting the risk. No person may sell variable contracts in Florida unless first duly licensed and appointed as a life including variable contracts agent. A life including variable contracts agent is one representing an insurer as to life insurance and variable insurance and annuity contracts. [Rule 69O-162.009, F.A.C.]

Group variable annuities

The SEC, by administrative action in 1963 and 1964, has permitted life insurance companies to sell certain types of group annuity contracts based on separate accounts, including variable annuity contracts, without registration as investment companies. The important restrictions are that the contracts must be used for qualified retirement plans that cover at least 25 employees and that no employee contributions may be allocated to the separate account invested primarily in common stocks.

The SEC has also authorized insurance companies to offer other forms of variable annuity contracts, both group and individual, provided the insurance company complies with the requirements of the Investment Company Act of 1940 and other securities acts.

Any group variable annuity contract forms used for qualified retirement plans established by associations of self-employed persons (under the Keogh Act) are required to be registered as securities. To issue such contracts, a company must file registration statements with the SEC and provide a prospectus. The company is not required to comply with all the requirements applicable to an investment company if it restricts its variable annuity activities to group contracts used for qualified pension and profit-sharing plans. The SEC has thus distinguished these group contracts from individual variable annuity contracts, for which full compliance with the Investment Company Act of 1940 is required.

MARKETING PRACTICES AND SUITABILITY

Prospectus

Before selling a variable life insurance policy or variable annuity, the agent must furnish the prospect with a prospectus. This document is prepared and furnished by the insurance company and reviewed by the SEC. A prospectus contains information about the nature and purpose of the insurance or annuity plan, the separate account, and the risk involved. It is a primary source of information for the prospect. All other materials, such as direct mail letters, brochures, and advertising, also must have prior approval by the SEC.

Agent's identification on annuity contracts

Florida law requires that an application for an insurance policy or an annuity contract display the name of the insuring entity prominently on the first page of the application. In addition, the law states the following [Sec. 627.4085, F.S.]:

> *Such applications shall also disclose the name and license identification number of the agent as shown on the agent's license issued by the department, which information may be typed, printed, stamped or handwritten if legible.*

Change of address

A licensee must notify the department, in writing, within 30 days after a change of name; residence address; principal business street address; mailing address; contact phone numbers, including a business phone number; or email address. Failure to comply with this 30-day rule can result in penalties of up to $250 for the first offense and at least $500 for subsequent violations, which can also result in the suspension or revocation of the license. [Sec. 626.551, F.S.]

Suitability

With regard to the sale or exchange of a fixed, indexed, or variable annuity, an agent is required to have a reasonable basis for believing the recommendation is suitable for the consumer based on facts provided by the consumer. The facts that must be collected from the consumer include, but are not limited to:

- personal information, including the age and sex of the parties to the annuity and the ages and number of any dependents;

- tax status of the consumer;

- investment objectives of the consumer;

- source of funds being used to purchase the annuity;

- the applicant's annual income;

- intended use of the annuity;

- the applicant's existing assets, including investment holdings;

- the applicant's liquid net worth and liquidity needs;

- the applicant's financial situation and needs;

- the applicant's risk tolerance; and

- such other information used or considered to be relevant by the insurance agent or insurer in making recommendations to the consumer regarding the purchase or exchange of an annuity contract.

This information must be collected on a form adopted by the Department of Financial Services and signed by the applicant and agent. If the consumer does not wish to provide all of this information, the agent must obtain from the consumer a signed verification form that the consumer refuses to provide the requested information and may be limiting protections regarding the suitability of the sale. An agent is prohibited from dissuading or attempting to dissuade a consumer from truthfully responding to the insurer's request for suitability information, from filing a complaint, or from cooperating with the investigation of a complaint. In the event that the consumer declines to follow an agent's advice, the agent must obtain a signed statement from the consumer acknowledging that the annuity transaction was not recommended.

An agent's recommendations must be recorded, and an agent must have a reasonable basis to believe that the consumer has been informed of relevant information, including annuity features, potential future tax penalties, applicable fees, features and charges for any riders, the annuity's insurance and investment components, and market risk. Where the consumer is exchanging or replacing an existing annuity, an agent must specifically consider whether the consumer will incur a surrender charge, be subject to commencement of a new surrender period, lose existing benefits, be subject to increased fees, benefit from product enhancements, or has recently had another annuity exchange or replacement.

An annuity policy sold to a senior (older than 65) consumer may not include a surrender charge or deferred sales charge for a withdrawal of money from an annuity in excess of 10% of the amount withdrawn with certain exceptions.

Replacement or exchange of an annuity contract

In transactions involving the replacement or exchange of an annuity contract, the agent must provide, on an approved form, information concerning differences between the existing annuity contract and the one being recommended, including:

- a comparison of the benefits, terms, and limitations;

- a comparison of any fees and charges;

- a written basis for the recommended exchange, including the overall advantages and disadvantages to the consumer; and

- such other information considered relevant by the agent or insurer in making recommendations to the consumer.

Before the purchase or exchange of an annuity contract, an agent must also disclose that there may be tax consequences as a result of the purchase or exchange and that the applicant should consult a tax advisor for more information. [Sec. 627.4554(4)(d)–(e)]

Penalties

If a consumer is harmed by an insurance company or agent who violates the laws relating to the sale of annuity products, the office may order an insurer to take reasonably appropriate corrective action, and may impose appropriate penalties and sanctions.

The department may order an insurance agent, MGA, or insurance agency that employs or contracts with an insurance agent to sell or solicit the sale of annuities to consumers to take reasonably appropriate corrective action. In addition to any other authorized penalty, the department shall order an insurance agent to pay restitution to a consumer who has been deprived of money by the agent's misappropriation, conversion, or unlawful withholding of moneys belonging to the consumer in the course of a transaction involving annuities. [Sec. 627.4554(7)]

Income tax treatment of benefits

For federal income tax treatment fixed and variable contracts are treated the same. As you learned in basic life insurance licensing, all insurance products enjoy significant tax advantages over other financial products.

- All cash value life insurance policies defer any taxes on the growth of cash value inside the policies. Additionally, when a partial withdrawal is contemplated, the FIFO (first in, first out) rule applies, which means any withdrawals are first taken from basis (after-tax premium) dollars and there is no tax liability. If a policy surrender is made, taxes are only due on the balance above the basis.

- With all annuities, income taxes are similarly deferred during the accumulation period. When annuities begin distribution, the method of taxation will depend on the type of distribution taken by the annuitant. If the distribution is of a lump sum, partial withdrawal, or annuity certain, then the method of taxation is called "last-in-first-out" (LIFO). As with life insurance, taxes will only be due on the gain above basis, but unlike life insurance, annuities use the LIFO approach, so the gain is required to be withdrawn and taxed before the basis can be taken. In addition, if the distribution is taken before age 59½, a 10% penalty for early withdrawal will be added to the taxes due.

- Gains distributed from life insurance cash value or annuity account value will be taxed as ordinary income in the year received.

Exclusion ratio

The basic theory underlying annuity taxation is that a taxpayer should be able to get back, income tax free, the amount that the taxpayer put into the annuity contract. If the distribution is annuitized (one of the three forms of payments for life discussed earlier) then the LIFO approach does not apply. Instead, each payment is taxed based on the exclusion ratio. Generally, this is accomplished by spreading tax free the return of premium (cost basis) over the anticipated life of the annuitant. A portion of each payment is considered to be a return of premium, and the rest is taxable income. The exclusion ratio is the ratio the aggregate premiums paid by the annuitant bears to the expected return over the annuitant's lifetime (ER = Basis / Expected Return). This ratio is applied to each payment to determine the tax-free portion. The balance is included in gross income for tax payment purposes.

Exclusion ratio in a variable annuity payout

If the annuity is a variable annuity, the application of a constant exclusion ratio to a substantially increased annuity payment would increase the tax-free portion of each payment. The Treasury Department has issued rules that prevent the exclusion ratio from operating to produce such an effect. The amount that can be received free of income tax in a taxable year is the portion of the premium (cost basis) in the contract that is allocated to that year. This is determined by dividing the premium (cost basis) by the number of years the annuitant is expected to live. For example, if the annuitant purchased a variable life annuity contract for $15,000 at age 65 and his life expectancy is 15 years, the annual tax-free portion is $1,000 ($15,000 divided by 15 years of life expectancy). The excess received each year is taxable income.

KEY CONCEPTS

Students should be familiar with the following concepts:

fixed premium variable life	separate account
flexible premium variable life	regulation and licensing requirements
variable annuity	role of the SEC
accumulation unit	exclusion ratio
annuity unit	

UNIT TEST

1. Variable life insurance and variable annuities contracts derive their product values largely from

   A. insurer guarantees
   B. general account performance
   C. separate account performance
   D. equity index performance

2. The period of time from a variable annuity's issue date until the start of payments is known as

   A. the deductible period
   B. the accumulation period
   C. the probationary period
   D. the funding period

3. Variable contracts include all of the following EXCEPT

   A. variable annuities
   B. variable term life
   C. variable whole life
   D. variable universal life

4. Separate account values and variable contract values fluctuate

   A. daily
   B. weekly
   C. monthly
   D. at the insurer's discretion

5. Which of the following statements regarding variable contracts are TRUE?

   A. The company cannot guarantee a specific interest yield from investments.
   B. Investment results principally derive from stock portfolios.
   C. Product and unit values fluctuate.
   D. All of the above statements are true.

6. Before variable annuity benefits can be paid out, the accumulation units in the participant's account must be converted to

   A. investment units
   B. statistical units
   C. annuity units
   D. income units

7. After retirement starts, which of the following is TRUE?

   A. The number of annuity units stays the same.
   B. The value of each annuity unit stays the same.
   C. The dollar amount of monthly payments stays the same.
   D. The value is adjusted to accommodate inflation.

8. If a consumer is harmed by an insurer or agent who violates Florida laws relating to annuity sales, all of the following actions may be ordered by the OIR EXCEPT

   A. immediate surrender of all licenses
   B. monetary restitution of all costs to the consumer by the agent
   C. contract rescission by the insurer
   D. refund of premiums or account value, whichever is larger

9. Which of the following statements regarding variable contracts is(are) TRUE?

   A. Insurers selling variable products are subject to regulation by the Office of Insurance Regulation (OIR).
   B. Variable annuities and variable life insurance policies are considered investments.
   C. The common stock and other assets of a separate account are under the supervision of the Securities and Exchange Commission (SEC).
   D. All of the statements are true.

10. An application for a variable annuity must show which of the following on the first page?

    A. Agent's name
    B. Agent's insurance license identification number
    C. Name of the insurer
    D. All of the above

11. Common stocks are predominantly used in the separate account portfolios because they
    A. usually provide a hedge against inflation
    B. guarantee a minimum rate of return
    C. are based on the full faith and credit of the insurer
    D. are insured by the federal government

12. Are investment gains in the separate account (and variable annuity and variable life accumulation values) subject to current income taxes?
    A. Yes, but only to the extent of the gain
    B. No, they are not currently taxable
    C. Yes, but the gain is paid by the insurer
    D. Yes, but taxable gains may be offset by losses

13. Florida law requires insurers to distribute to variable annuity owners an annual report containing which of the following?
    A. Dollar value of each unit
    B. Anticipated increase in number of units by the next anniversary
    C. Forecasted value of each unit by the next anniversary
    D. Taxable gain on each unit reported by the insurer to the IRS

14. Insurers selling variable contracts are subject to
    A. state insurance regulation
    B. federal securities regulation
    C. municipal regulation
    D. both A and B above

15. During the accumulation period of a deferred variable annuity, the value of individual accounts rises or falls based solely on
    A. variable premiums paid
    B. the number of annuitants
    C. investment performance
    D. company expense ratios

16. Before proposing any variable product the agent must provide the prospect with the
    A. outline of coverage
    B. prospectus
    C. consumer Buyer's Guide
    D. table of guaranteed values

17. The difference between scheduled premium and flexible premium variable life insurance policies will include
    A. the insurer expenses
    B. mortality rates
    C. different separate account portfolios to choose from
    D. a guaranteed minimum death benefit versus only a variable death benefit

18. A variable contracts agent must notify the Department within 30 days of any change in the following EXCEPT
    A. the agent's name
    B. the agent's insurer
    C. the agent's residence address
    D. the agent's mailing address

29

Florida Laws and Rules Pertinent to Health Insurance

- Standard Policy Provisions and Clauses
- Group Health
- Disclosure
- Medicare Supplements
- Long-term Care Policies
- Requirements for Small Employers
- Florida Healthy Kids Corporation
- Requirements relating to HIV/AIDs
- Plan Types
- Dread Disease Policy

This unit outlines only those marketing practices, policies, and provisions of health insurance that are regulated by the state of Florida. Candidates for the Health Insurance Examination will be tested on the various required laws and rules covered in this unit. ■

STANDARD POLICY PROVISIONS AND CLAUSES (INDIVIDUAL AND GROUP)

Minimum benefit standards

Free-look

The person to whom the health insurance policy is issued is permitted to return the policy within 10 days of delivery and to have a full refund of the premium paid if the purchaser is not satisfied with it for any reason.

Nongrandfathered health plan

Nongrandfathered health plan is a health insurance policy or health maintenance organization contract that is not a grandfathered health plan and is therefore subject to all the federal Patient Protection and Affordable Care Act (PPACA) requirements.

Grandfathered Health Plan

Grandfathered health plan has the same meaning as provided in the federal Patient Protection and Affordable Care Act. **Grandfathered health plan** coverage means coverage provided by a group health plan, or a group or individual health insurance issuer, in which an individual was enrolled on March 23, 2010, and has continuously covered someone since March 23, 2010 (not necessarily the same person, but at all times at least one person). Grandfathered plans may not have to meet all the requirements contained in PPACA. The following situations could cause a plan to lose grandfathered status. [Sec. 627.402]

- **Elimination of benefits.** The elimination of all or substantially all benefits to diagnose or treat a particular condition. For this purpose, the elimination of benefits for any necessary element to diagnose or treat a condition is considered the elimination of all or substantially all benefits to diagnose or treat a particular condition.

- **Increase in percentage cost-sharing requirement.** Any increase in a percentage cost-sharing requirement (such as an individual's coinsurance requirement).

- **Increase in a fixed-amount cost-sharing requirement other than a copayment.** Any increase in a fixed-amount cost-sharing requirement other than a copayment (e.g., deductible or out-of-pocket limit) if the total percentage increase in the cost-sharing requirement exceeds the maximum percentage increase allowed in federal regulations.

- **Increase in a fixed-amount copayment.** Any increase in a fixed-amount copayment causes a group health plan or health insurance coverage if the total increase in the copayment exceeds amounts allowed in federal regulations.

- **Decrease in contribution rate by employers and employee organizations.**

  - **Contribution rate based on cost of coverage.** If the employer or employee organization decreases its contribution rate based on cost of coverage by more than five percentage points below the contribution rate for the coverage period that includes March 23, 2010.

  - **Contribution rate based on a formula.** If the employer or employee organization decreases its contribution rate based on a formula by more than 5% below the contribution rate for the coverage period that includes March 23, 2010.

- Changes in annual limits.

  - **Addition of an annual limit.** A group health plan, or group or individual health insurance coverage, that on March 23, 2010, did not impose an overall annual or lifetime limit on the dollar value of all benefits ceases to be a grandfathered health plan if the plan or health insurance coverage imposes an overall annual limit on the dollar value of benefits.

  - **Decrease in limit for a plan or coverage with only a lifetime limit.** A group health plan, or group or individual health insurance coverage, that on March 23, 2010, imposed an overall lifetime limit on the dollar value of all benefits but no overall annual limit on the dollar value of all benefits ceases to be a grandfathered health plan if the plan or health insurance coverage adopts an overall annual limit at a dollar value that is lower than the dollar value of the lifetime limit on March 23, 2010.

  - **Decrease in limit for a plan or coverage with an annual limit.** A group health plan, or group or individual health insurance coverage, that on March 23, 2010, imposed an overall annual limit on the dollar value of all benefits ceases to be a grandfathered health plan if the plan or health insurance coverage decreases the dollar value of the annual limit (regardless of whether the plan or health insurance coverage also imposed an overall lifetime limit on March 23, 2010, on the dollar value of all benefits).

A group health plan that provided coverage on March 23, 2010, and has retained its status as a grandfathered health plan is a grandfathered health plan for new employees (whether newly hired or newly enrolled) and their families enrolling in the plan after March 23, 2010.

Patient Protection and Affordable Care Act (PPACA) provisions applicable to grandfathered health plans

Group health plans, and group and individual health insurance coverage:

- may not establish lifetime limits nor annual limits for essential benefits (however, a grandfathered individual health insurance policy may have annual limits);

- must continue dependent coverage for unmarried adult children until the child turns age 26 (the plan does not have to provide coverage for a child of the adult child receiving dependent coverage);

- may not establish waiting periods of more than 90 days (the term *waiting period* means the period of time that must pass with respect to the individual before the individual is eligible to be covered for benefits under the terms of the plan); and

- may not contain any preexisting conditions exclusions.

PPACA provisions NOT applicable to grandfathered health plans

Grandfathered group health plans and grandfathered group health insurance coverage do not have to provide free preventative care; and do not have to provide "essential health benefits" as defined in the law.

Disclosure of grandfather status

To maintain status as a grandfathered health plan, a plan or health insurance coverage must include a statement, in any plan materials describing the benefits provided under the plan or health insurance coverage, that the plan or coverage believes it is a grandfathered health plan within the meaning of section 1251 of the Patient Protection and Affordable Care Act.

Required and optional coverages

Medical providers

The words physician or medical doctor, when used in health insurance policies, include a dentist when the policy covers surgical procedures that are specified in the coverage or are performed in an accredited hospital in consultation with a licensed physician and are within the scope of a dentist's professional license.

Medical expense policies must also provide for payment to an optometrist chiropractor, or a podiatrist for procedures specified in the policy that are within the scope of their respective professional licenses. [Sec.627.419]

Diabetes coverage: equipment, supplies, and outpatient self-management training

Florida law requires health insurance policies and HMO contracts to provide coverage for all medically necessary equipment, supplies, and services used to treat diabetes when the patient's physician certifies that they are medically necessary. This includes outpatient self-management training and education services if medically necessary. [Sec. 627.6408]

Osteoporosis coverage

Health insurance policies and HMO contracts are required by Florida law to provide coverage for medically necessary diagnosis and treatment of osteoporosis for high-risk individuals. Specified accident, specified disease, hospital indemnity, Medicare supplement, long-term care health insurance, and the Florida state employee health program are not included in the requirement. Osteoporosis is a bone-thinning disease that increases the risk of bone fractures. [Sec. 627.6409]

Coverage for newborn children

Both individual and group health insurance policies that provide coverage for a family member of the insured must also provide that the health insurance benefits for children will be payable for a newborn child of the insured from the moment of birth. The law also requires that coverage be provided for a newborn child of a covered family member (e.g., the newborn of a covered daughter or son) for a period of 18 months.

The coverage for newborn children required by this section consists of coverage for injury or sickness, including the necessary care or treatment of medically diagnosed congenital defects, birth abnormalities, or prematurity, and transportation costs of the newborn to and from the nearest available facility appropriately staffed and equipped to treat the newborn's condition.

A policy may require the insured, or covered family member to notify the insurer of the birth of a child within a time period, as specified in the policy, of not less than 30 days after the birth. If timely notice is given, the insurer may not charge an additional premium for coverage of the newborn child for the duration of the notice period. If timely notice is not given, the insurer may charge an additional premium from the date of birth. The insurer may not deny coverage for a child due to the failure of the insured to timely notify the insurer of the birth of the child.

If the policy does not require the insured to notify the insurer of the birth of a child within a specified time period, the insurer may not deny coverage for such child or retroactively charge the insured an additional premium for such child. However, the insurer may prospectively charge the insured an additional premium for the child if the insurer provides at least 45 days' notice of the additional premium required.

This section does not apply to disability income or hospital indemnity policies or to normal maternity policy provisions applicable to the mother. [Sec. 627.641]

Coverage for adopted, foster, custodial care, and natural-born children

A health insurance policy that provides coverage for a family member of the insured must, as to the family member's coverage, provide that the health insurance benefits applicable to children of the insured also apply to an adopted child or a foster child of the insured placed in compliance with state law, prior to the child's 18th birthday, from the moment of placement in the residence of the insured. Except in the case of a foster child, the policy may not exclude coverage for any preexisting condition of the child. [Sec. 627.6415]

Child coverage

All health insurance policies providing coverage on an expense-incurred basis that provide coverage for a family member of the insured or subscriber must, as to such family member's coverage, also provide that the health insurance benefits applicable for children include coverage from the moment of birth to age 16 years for the following:

■ Medical history

■ Physical examination

■ Developmental assessment and anticipatory guidance

■ Appropriate immunizations and laboratory tests

Continued coverage for children with disabilities

Individual and group health insurance policies must continue to provide coverage of the child while the child continues to be both:

■ incapable of self-sustaining employment by reason of an intellectual or physical disability; and

■ chiefly dependent upon the employee or member for support and maintenance. [Sec. 627.6615, .6041]

Coverage for mastectomies

Florida law mandates coverage for prosthetic devices and reconstructive surgery following a mastectomy. In addition, Florida law:

■ mandates coverage for all surgeries necessary to reestablish symmetry between breasts;

■ prohibits inpatient hospital coverage for mastectomies from being limited to less than what is determined to be medically necessary by the physician after consultation with the patient;

■ requires that outpatient postsurgical care for mastectomies be comparable to inpatient postsurgical care for mastectomies;

■ prohibits a person from being denied or excluded from coverage for breast cancer, if the person has remained breast cancer free for two years; and

■ prohibits breast cancer follow-up care from being considered an evaluation for a preexisting condition, unless breast cancer is found. [Sec. 627.6417, .64171, .64172]

Coverage for mammograms

A health insurance policy delivered in Florida must provide coverage for at least the following:

- A baseline mammogram for any woman age 35 to 39

- A mammogram every two years for any woman age 40 to 49 or more frequently based on the patient's physician's recommendation

- A mammogram every year for any woman age 50 or older

- One or more mammograms a year, based upon a physician's recommendation, for any woman who is at risk for breast cancer because of a personal or family history of breast cancer [Sec. 627.6418]

Exclusion for fibrocystic condition prohibited

An insurer may not deny the issuance or renewal of a policy of health insurance, nor include any exception or exclusion of benefits in a policy solely because the insured has been diagnosed as having a fibrocystic condition, a nonmalignant lesion, a family history related to breast cancer, or any combination of these factors, unless the condition is diagnosed through a breast biopsy that demonstrates an increased disposition to developing breast cancer. [Sec. 627.6419]

Coverage for cleft lip and cleft palate of children

A health insurance policy that covers a child under the age of 18 must provide coverage for treatment of cleft lip and cleft palate for the child. The coverage must include medical, dental, speech therapy, audiology, and nutrition services only if such services are prescribed by the treating physician or surgeon and such physician or surgeon certifies that such services are medically necessary and consequent to treatment of the cleft lip or cleft palate. The coverage required by this section is subject to terms and conditions applicable to other benefits. This section does not apply to specified-accident, specified-disease, hospital indemnity, limited benefit disability income, or long-term-care insurance policies. [Sec. 627.64193]

Rebates for participation in wellness program

Individual health insurance policies filed with the office may provide for an appropriate rebate of premiums paid in the last year when the individual covered by such plan is enrolled in and maintains participation in any health wellness, maintenance, or improvement program approved by the health plan. The rebate may be based on premiums paid in the last calendar year or the last policy year. The individual must provide evidence of maintenance or improvement of the individual's health status as determined by assessments of agreed-upon health status indicators between the individual and the health insurer, including, but not limited to reduction in weight, body mass index, and smoking cessation.

The rebate may not exceed 10% of paid premiums. The premium rebate authorized by this section shall be effective for an insured on an annual basis, unless the individual fails to maintain or improve his or her health status while participating in an approved wellness program or the individual is not participating in the approved wellness program. [Sec. 627.6402]

Required health insurance policy provisions

Health insurance policies delivered or issued for delivery in Florida must contain the following required provisions. An insurer may substitute one or more corresponding provisions of different wording if approved by the commissioner, and they are not less favorable in any respect to the insured or the beneficiary. [Sec. 627.605– .617]

Entire contract clause

The clause states that the policy, its endorsements, and any attached materials, including the application, constitute the entire contract of insurance. This ensures that no other documents that are not actually a part of the contract can be used to deny claims or coverage. No change in the policy will be effective until approved by an officer of the insurer. No agent may change the policy or waive any of its provisions.

Time limit on defenses

This provision states in general that after two years, no misstatements except fraudulent ones, made by the applicant on the application, shall be used to void the policy or to deny a claim for loss incurred commencing after the end of such two-year period. It also provides that no claim for loss incurred after two years from the date of issue shall be denied on the grounds that a disease or physical condition, not specifically excluded by name, had existed prior to that date.

Grace period

The grace period is a stated period of time after the premium due date during which the policy remains in force even though the premium has not been paid. The grace period applies to premiums other than the initial premium. The law provides that there must be a grace period of not less than seven days on weekly premium policies, 10 days for monthly premium policies, and 31 days for all others.

Reinstatement

A policy lapses and insurance ceases when the premium is not paid when due nor within the grace period. If the insurer or agent completes a reinstatement application and issues a conditional receipt for the premium submitted, the policy will be reinstated upon approval of such application by the insurer, or on the 45th day following the date of the conditional receipt unless the insurer has previously notified the insured in writing of its disapproval of the application.

The reinstated policy will cover loss resulting from accidental injury immediately after reinstatement. Loss due to sickness will begin more than 10 days after the reinstatement date.

In all other respects, the insured and insurer will have the same rights as they had under the policy immediately prior to lapse, subject to any provisions endorsed in connection with the reinstatement. Any premium accepted in connection with a reinstatement will be applied to a period for which premium has not been previously paid, but not to any period more than 60 days prior to the date of reinstatement.

Notice of claim

Written notice of claim must be given within 20 days, giving the name of the insured and policy number. In the event it is not reasonably possible to give notice within this time, notice must be given as soon as reasonably possible.

Claim forms

The insurance company must furnish the claimant claim forms within 15 days. If it does not furnish the claimant with its forms, the claimant may present proof in any reasonably written manner showing the nature of loss, extent of loss, and other information.

Proof of loss

Written proof of loss must be given within 90 days after such loss. If it was not reasonably possible to give written proof in the time required, the insurer may not reduce or deny the claim for this reason if the proof is filed as soon as reasonably possible. In any event, the proof required must be given no later than one year from the time specified unless the claimant was legally incapacitated.

Time of payment of claims

Benefits payable under the policy for any loss, other than loss providing periodic payment, will be paid as soon as the insurer receives written proof of loss. For losses providing periodic payment, payments will be paid monthly.

Payment of claims

Benefits will be paid to the insured. Death benefits are payable in accordance with the beneficiary designation in effect at the time of payment. If none is then in effect, the death benefits will be paid to the insured's estate.

Physical examinations and autopsy

The insurer at its expense has the right to have the insured examined as often as reasonably necessary while a claim is pending. It may also have an autopsy made unless prohibited by law.

Legal actions

No legal action may be brought to recover on a health insurance policy within 60 days after written proof of loss has been given. No such action may be brought after five years of furnishing proof of loss to the insurance company.

Change of beneficiary

The insured can change the beneficiary at any time by giving the insurer written notice. The beneficiary's consent is not required for this or any other change in the policy, unless the designation of the beneficiary is irrevocable.

Optional health insurance provisions [Sec. 627.619–.629]

Health insurance policies delivered or issued for delivery in Florida may contain the following optional health insurance provisions. [Sec. 627.619–.629]

Change of occupation

If the insured is injured or contracts sickness after having changed his or her occupation to one classified by the insurer as more hazardous than that stated in the policy, the insurer will pay only such portion of the benefits provided in the policy as the premium paid would have purchased at the rates and within the limits fixed by the insurer for such more hazardous occupation.

If the insured changes his or her occupation to one classified by the insurer as less hazardous than that stated in the policy, the insurer, upon receipt of proof of such change of occupation, will reduce the premium rate accordingly, and will return the excess pro rata unearned premium from the date of change of occupation or from the policy anniversary date immediately preceding receipt of such proof, whichever is the more recent.

Misstatement of age or sex

If the age or sex of the insured has been misstated, all amounts payable under the policy will be such as the premium paid would have purchased according to the correct age or sex.

Other insurance with insurer

If two or more health insurance policies, exclusive of guaranteed-issue policies, are issued by the insurer covering the same insured, the insurer shall pay the total benefits payable under all policies issued; provided that when guaranteed-issue policies are in force concurrently either with or without other health insurance policies, resulting in coverage in excess of covered claims, the excess insurance provided under such guaranteed-issue policies shall be void, and all premiums paid for such excess shall be returned to the insured or to the insured's estate; provided further that full payment of all covered claims is made.

Insurance with other insurers: expense-incurred basis

If there is other valid coverage, with a different insurer, providing benefits for the same loss on an expense-incurred basis and of which the insurer has not been given written notice prior to the occurrence of loss, the only liability under any expense-incurred coverage of the policy will be for such proportion of the loss as the amount which would otherwise have been payable plus the total of the like amounts under all such other valid coverages for the same loss of which the insurer had notice bears to the total like amounts under all valid coverages for such loss, and for the return of such portion of the premiums paid as will exceed the pro rata portion for the amount so determined.

Insurance with other insurers: other than expense-incurred basis

If there is other valid coverage, with a different insurer, providing benefits for the same loss on other than an expense-incurred basis and of which the insurer has not been given written notice prior to the occurrence of loss, the only liability for such benefits under the policy shall be for such proportion of the indemnities otherwise provided hereunder for such loss as the like indemnities of which the insurer had notice (including the indemnities under the policy) bear to the total amount of all like indemnities for such loss, and for the return of such portion of the premium paid as shall exceed the pro rata portion for the indemnities thus determined.

Relation of earnings to insurance; valid loss-of-time coverage

If the total monthly amount of loss-of-time benefits promised for the same loss under all valid loss-of-time coverage upon the insured exceeds the monthly earnings of the insured at the time disability commenced or her average monthly earnings for the period of two years immediately preceding a disability, whichever is the greater, the insurer will be liable only for such proportionate amount of such benefits under the policy as the amount of such monthly earnings bears to the total amount of monthly benefits for the same loss under all such coverage upon the insured at the time such disability commences. The insurer must return premiums paid during such two years that exceed the pro rata amount of the premiums for the benefits actually paid. This provision shall not operate to reduce the total monthly amount of benefits payable under all such coverage upon the insured below the sum of $500 or the sum of the monthly benefits specified in such coverages, whichever is the lesser, nor shall it operate to reduce benefits other than those payable for loss of time.

Unpaid premium

Upon the payment of a claim under this policy, any premium then due and unpaid may be deducted from the claim payment.

Prohibited cancellation for HIV or AIDS

Notwithstanding any other provision of law to the contrary, no insurer shall cancel or nonrenew the health insurance policy of any insured because of diagnosis or treatment of human immunodeficiency virus infection or acquired immune deficiency syndrome.

Conformity with state statutes

Any provision of the policy which, on its effective date, is in conflict with the statutes of the state in which the insured resides on such date is hereby amended to conform to the minimum requirements of such statutes.

Illegal occupation

The insurer will not be liable for any loss that results from the insured committing or attempting to commit a felony or from the insured being engaged in an illegal occupation.

Intoxicants and narcotics

The insurer will not be liable for any loss resulting from the insured being drunk or under the influence of any narcotic unless taken on the advice of a physician.

GROUP HEALTH INSURANCE

Group health insurance may be issued to eligible groups in Florida insuring more than one individual. [Sec. 627.651–.6699]

Eligible groups (employer based, fraternal, assoc., blanket) [Sec. 627.6516–.656]

Trustee group policy

A group of employees of employers or members of labor unions may be insured for the benefit of persons other than the employers or unions under a policy issued to the trustees of a fund. The trustees are the policyholders. The premium may be paid by the policyholder, employer(s), union(s), or insured persons.

The policy must cover at date of issue not less than five persons, other than individual proprietors or partners, from each employer unit unless certain conditions apply. The amounts of insurance under the policy must be based upon some plan precluding individual selection either by the insured persons or by the policyholder, employer, or unions.

Employee group policy

A group of individual employees (and their dependents) of an employer may be insured, for the benefit of persons other than the employer, under a policy issued to the employer. The employer is the policyholder. Employees insured under the policy may include any of the following:

■ Directors of a corporate employer, former employees, or retired employees

■ The individual proprietor or partners if the employer is a proprietor or partnership

■ Elected or appointed officials if the policy is issued to insure employees of a public body

■ Employees of one or more entities under common control

A policy may not be issued unless all employees of the employer are declared eligible and acceptable to the insurer at the time of issuance. If class of employees determines eligibility, all members of any class must be declared eligible and acceptable to the insurer at the time of issuance. The classes must be determined by conditions pertaining to their employment but not determined so as to exclude those in more hazardous employment solely because of their hazardous employment. A policy may insure the spouse or dependent children with or without the employee being insured.

A group, blanket, or franchise health insurance policy issued or delivered in Florida that provides coverage to an employer for the benefit of its employees shall include in the definition of **full-time employee** an employee who has a normal workweek of 25 or more hours. This section does not prohibit an insurer from excluding coverage for a temporary or substitute employee.

Associations, labor unions, and small employer health alliances

A group of individuals may be insured under a policy issued to an association, including a labor union, if:

■ the association has a constitution and bylaws;

■ the association has not less than 25 individual members;

■ the association has been organized and has been maintained in good faith for a period of one year for purposes other than that of obtaining insurance;

■ the association is the policyholder; and

■ at least 15 individual members of the association enroll in the plan.

No policy may be issued to the association unless all individual members of the association, or all of any classes, are declared eligible and acceptable to the insurer at the time of the policy issuance. A policy may insure the spouse or dependent children with or without the member being insured. A single master policy issued to an association may include more than one health plan from the same insurer or affiliated insurer group as alternatives for an employer, employee, or member to select.

Debtor group policy

A group of individual debtors of a creditor may be insured under a policy issued to a creditor. The creditor is the policyholder. The debtors are indemnified in connection with a specific loan or credit transaction against loss of time resulting from bodily injury or sickness. Two types of insurance may be used to insure against the occurrence of disability of the lives of a group of individual debtors.

Credit disability insurance is for all of the debtors of the creditor, or all members of any class or classes of debtors of the creditor. A policy may insure the debtors of one or more subsidiary or affiliated entities under common control. However, a credit disability policy may be issued only if the group of eligible debtors is then receiving new entrants at the rate of at least 100 persons yearly, or may reasonably be expected to receive at least 100 new entrants during the first policy year. The insurer has the right to require evidence of individual insurability if less than 75% of the new entrants become insured.

Mortgage insurance is for all of the debtors of the creditor, or all of any class or classes of debtors of the creditor. The term **debtors** includes borrowers of money in connection with an indebtedness of more than 10 years' duration, and is secured by a first real estate mortgage.

Blanket health insurance

Blanket health insurance is a form of health insurance that covers special groups of individuals, including policies owned by and issued to the following:

■ Any common carrier covering passengers on such common carrier

■ A school, district school system, college, university, or other institution of learning, or to the official or officials of such institution insuring the students and teachers (Any such policy issued may insure the spouse or dependent children of the insured student.)

■ Any volunteer fire department or first aid group or other such volunteer group covering all of the members of such department or group

■ An organization, or branch thereof, such as the Boy Scouts of America, the Future Farmers of America, religious or educational bodies, or similar organizations, holding or operating meetings such as summer camps or other meetings for religious, instructive, or recreational purposes (The policy covers all those attending such camps or meetings, including counselors, instructors, and persons in other administrative positions.)

■ A newspaper covering independent contractor newspaper delivery persons

■ A health care provider covering patients (This coverage may be offered to patients of a health care provider but may not be made a condition of receiving care. The benefits provided under such policy or contract shall not be assignable to any health care provider.)

■ Any HMO covering the subscribers of the health maintenance organization (Payment may be made directly to the health maintenance organization by the blanket health insurer for health care services rendered by providers pursuant to the health care delivery plan.)

Continuation

The purpose and intent of the Florida Health Insurance Coverage Continuation Act ("Mini-COBRA") is to ensure continued access to affordable health insurance coverage for employees of small employers and their dependents and other qualified beneficiaries not currently protected by the Consolidated Omnibus Budget Reconciliation Act (COBRA) of 1985. This section does not apply if continuation of coverage benefits is available to covered employees or other qualified beneficiaries COBRA. [Sec. 627.6692]

Definitions

Small employer means any person who meets the definition of *small employer* as set forth in Florida insurance statutes who for purposes of this section employs fewer than 20 employees.

Group health plan means any small employer health benefit plan, which provides health care benefit to the employer's employees or former employees, or for the dependents of such employees or former employees.

Qualified beneficiary means any individual who, on the day before the qualifying event for the covered employee, is a beneficiary under the group health plan by virtue of the individual being:

■ The covered employee, except if the employee is terminated for gross misconduct

■ The spouse of the covered employee

■ The dependent child of the covered employee

Qualifying event means any of the following events that, but for the election of continuation coverage, would result in a loss of coverage to a qualified beneficiary:

■ The death of the covered employee

■ The termination or reduction of hours of the covered employee's employment

■ The divorce or legal separation of the covered employee from the covered employee's spouse

■ A dependent child ceasing to be a dependent child under the generally applicable requirements of the group health plan

Continuation of coverage under group health plans

A group health plan issued to a small employer must provide that each qualified beneficiary who would lose coverage under the group health plan because of a qualifying event is entitled, without evidence of insurability, to elect, within the election period, to continuation coverage under the employer's group health plan.

A qualified beneficiary must give written notice to the insurance carrier within 63 days after the occurrence of a qualifying event. Within 14 days after the receipt of the qualified beneficiary's written notice, the insurance carrier shall send each qualified beneficiary by certified mail an election and premium notice form.

A covered employee or other qualified beneficiary who wishes continuation of coverage must pay the initial premium and elect such continuation in writing to the insurance carrier within 30 days after receiving notice from the insurance carrier. The insurance carrier will process all elections promptly. Coverage and premium due will be retroactively to the date coverage would otherwise have terminated.

After the election, the insurance carrier must bill the qualified beneficiary monthly, with a due date on the first of the month and allowing a 30-day grace period. The premium paid for continuation of coverage may not exceed 115% of the applicable group premium.

Coverage under the group health plan must, at a minimum, extend from the date of the qualifying event and ending not earlier than the earliest of the following:

■ 18 months after the qualifying event

■ A qualified beneficiary who is determined, under Social Security, to have been disabled at the time of a qualifying event, may be eligible to continue coverage for an additional 11 months (29 months total). The qualified beneficiary must provide the written determination of disability from the Social Security Administration to the insurance carrier within 60 days of the date of determination of disability and prior to the end of the 18-month continuation period.

— The insurance carrier can charge up to 150% of the group rate during the 11-month disability extension.

■ The date on which coverage ceases due to nonpayment of premium

■ The date a qualified beneficiary becomes covered under any other group health plan, if the qualified beneficiary will not be subject to any exclusion or limitation because of a preexisting condition of that beneficiary

■ The date a qualified beneficiary is entitled to benefits under either Medicare part A or part B

■ The date on which the employer terminates coverage under the group health plan for all employees

Conversion

A group policy delivered or issued for delivery in Florida that provides hospital, surgical, or major medical expense insurance on an expense-incurred basis must provide that an employee or member whose insurance under the group policy has been terminated for any reason, including discontinuance of the group policy in its entirety, and who has been continuously insured under the group policy for at least three months immediately prior to termination, must be entitled to have issued to him by the insurer a policy or certificate of health insurance, referred to as a *converted policy*. The employee or member will not be issued a *converted policy* if:

■ termination of his group insurance occurred because he failed to pay the premium; or

■ because the discontinued group coverage was replaced by similar group coverage within 31 days after discontinuance.

Written application for the *converted policy* must be made and the first premium must be paid to the insurer, not later than 63 days after termination of the group policy. The *converted* policy must be issued without evidence of insurability.

The premium for the *converted policy* may not exceed 200% of the standard risk rate as established by the Florida Office of Insurance Regulation. The office will annually determine standard risk rates, using reasonable actuarial techniques and standards. The effective date of the *converted policy* will be the day following the termination of insurance under the group policy. The insurer may elect to provide group insurance coverage instead of issuing a converted individual policy.

Coordination of benefits

A group hospital, medical, or surgical expense policy, delivered or issued for delivery in Florida must contain a provision for coordinating its benefits with any similar benefits provided by any other group hospital, medical, or surgical expense policy, for the same loss. A policy may contain a provision whereby the insurer may reduce or refuse to pay benefits otherwise payable thereunder solely on account of the existence of similar benefits provided under insurance policies issued by the same or another insurer only if, as a condition of coordinating benefits with another insurer, the insurers together pay 100% of the total reasonable expenses actually incurred.

If a claim is submitted and the policy includes a coordination-of-benefits provision and the claim involves another policy or plan that has a coordination-of-benefits provision, the following rules determine the order in which benefits under the respective health policies or plans will be determined:

■ The benefits of a policy or plan that covers the person as an employee, member, or subscriber, other than as a dependent, are determined before those of the policy or plan that covers the person as a dependent.

■ If the person is also a Medicare beneficiary, and if the rule established under Social Security makes Medicare secondary to the plan covering the person as a dependent of an active employee, the order of benefit determination is:

— first, benefits of a plan covering a persons as an employee, member, or subscriber;

— second, benefits of a plan of an active worker covering a person as a dependent; and

— third, Medicare benefits.

■ If two or more policies or plans cover the same child as a dependent of different parents:

— the benefits of the policy or plan of the parent whose birthday, excluding year of birth, falls earlier in a year are determined before the benefits of the policy or plan of the parent whose birthday falls later in that year;

— if both parents have the same birthday, the benefits of the policy or plan that covered the parent for a longer period of time are determined before those of the policy or plan that covered the parent for a shorter period of time.

■ If two or more policies or plans cover a dependent child of divorced or separated parents, benefits for the child are determined in this order:

— First, the policy or plan of the parent with custody of the child

— Second, the policy or plan of the spouse of the parent with custody of the child

— Third, the policy or plan of the parent not having custody of the child

Coordination of benefits is not permitted against an indemnity-type policy, an excess insurance policy, a policy with coverage limited to specified illnesses or accidents, or a Medicare supplement policy. [Sec. 627.4235]

ERISA preemption and state insurance regulation

Employer-based health plans may be subject to federal regulation under Employee Retirement Income Security Act of 1974 (ERISA), as well as, state insurance regulations. As stated in a previous unit, the purpose of ERISA is to protect the rights of workers covered under employer-sponsored benefit plans. Despite the similarity of benefits afforded by an ERISA employee benefit plan and by a health insurer, a genuine single-employer ERISA plan is not subject to direct state insurance regulation.

The concept of *preemption* refers to language within federal ERISA statutes, that states: ERISA "supersede(s) any and all state laws insofar as they . . . relate to any employee benefit plan . . ." The scope of preemption is much narrower because of another ERISA provision, usually referred to as the savings clause. It provides in part, that nothing in ERISA ". . . shall be construed to exempt or relieve any person from any law of any state which regulates insurance, banking, or securities." The savings clause makes clear that ERISA does not preempt any state law that regulates insurance. To clarify the intended scope of ERISA, that being to regulate the employer-based plan itself, the deemer clause was included. It provides, in part, that no employee benefit plan or trust ". . . shall be deemed to be an insurance company or other insurer . . . or to be engaged in the business of insurance . . ." The net effect of the statutory provisions is that while ERISA governs an employee benefit plan, its jurisdiction is not exclusive. For example, state insurance regulation still applies to the insurer that is financially responsible for the payment of claims in an insured ERISA plan and to the forms utilized by that insurer to provide the insurance.

The MEWA issue. MEWA is the abbreviation for a type of risk-bearing entity called a **Multiple-Employer Welfare Arrangement**. MEWAs are regulated as risk-bearing entities by the Florida Insurance Code. They require a Certificate of Authority from the Office of Insurance Regulation. In general, the Florida Insurance Code defines a MEWA as an employee welfare benefit plan or other arrangement that is established or maintained to provide one or more of various insurance benefits (including health insurance) to the employees of two or more employers. According to this definition, a MEWA cannot be a single-employer plan. Therefore, MEWAs are not exempt from state insurance regulation. ERISA also defines and recognizes MEWAs. Therefore, there is concurrent state and federal regulatory authority over most employee welfare benefit plans that are MEWAs.

Special rules of preemption apply to MEWAs that meet the ERISA definition and that are also employee welfare benefit plans.

- If fully insured, the MEWA remains subject to state insurance laws that provide standards for the maintenance of specific levels of reserves and contributions so as to ensure the ability to pay benefits when due and laws that enforce those standards.

- If not fully insured, the MEWA is subject to all state insurance laws not inconsistent with Title I of ERISA unless exempted from them pursuant to other regulations of the U.S. Department of Labor. If the MEWA is so exempted, it is subject to state insurance regulation in the same manner as a fully insured MEWA.

- If the MEWA is not an employee benefit plan, there is no preemption at all. It is subject to full state insurance regulation.

Union plans can be an exception to the MEWA definition (that is, not constitute a MEWA) and therefore are not subject to state insurance regulations. However, for the exception to apply, the U.S. Department of Labor must make an express finding that the collective bargaining agreements between that union and the employers are bona fide. Absent such an express finding, the plan remains subject to state regulation as a MEWA. [Sec. 624.401, .436 - 446]

DISCLOSURE

Outline of Coverage

No individual or family accident and health insurance policy may be delivered, or issued for delivery, in Florida unless it is accompanied by an appropriate outline of coverage. An outline of coverage is completed and delivered to the applicant at the time of application, and an acknowledgment of receipt or certificate of delivery of such outline is provided to the insurer with the application. The outline of coverage must contain the following:

- A statement identifying the applicable category of coverage afforded by the policy

- A brief description of the principal benefits and coverage provided in the policy

- A summary statement of the principal exclusions and limitations or reductions contained in the policy, including, but not limited to, pre-existing conditions, probationary periods, elimination periods, deductibles, coinsurance, and any age limitations or reductions

- A summary statement of the renewal and cancellation provisions, including any reservation of the insurer of a right to change premiums

- A statement that the outline contains a summary only and that the issued policy should be referred to for the actual provisions

- When home health care coverage is provided, a statement that such benefits are provided in the policy [Sec. 627.642]

Renewal Agreements/Nonrenewal and Cancellation

Except as provided in this section, an insurer that provides individual or group health insurance coverage must renew the coverage at the option of the individual, or group policyholder. [Sec. 627.6425, .6571, 636.028, 641.31074]

Individual health insurance

At the time of coverage renewal, an insurer may modify the health insurance coverage for a policy form offered to individuals in the individual market as long as the modification is consistent with the laws of Florida and effective on a uniform basis among all individuals with that policy form. An insurer may nonrenew or discontinue an individual health insurance policy for one or more of the following reasons:

- Nonpayment of premiums

- Individual has performed an act or practice that constitutes fraud or made an intentional misrepresentation of material fact under the terms of the coverage

- Insurer is ceasing to offer coverage in the individual market in accordance with state law

- In the case of a health insurer that offers health insurance coverage in the market through a network plan, the individual no longer resides, lives, or works in the service area, or in an area for which the insurer is authorized to do business, but only if such coverage is terminated under this paragraph uniformly without regard to any health status–related factor of covered individuals

- In the case of health insurance coverage that is made available in the individual market only through one or more bona fide associations, and the individual ceases to be a member, but only if such coverage is terminated under this paragraph uniformly without regard to any health status–related factor of covered individuals

If an insurer decides to discontinue offering a particular health insurance policy form offered in the individual market, coverage under such form may be discontinued by the insurer only if the insurer provides notice to each covered individual at least 90 days before the date of nonrenewal. The insurer must also offer to each individual the option to purchase any other individual health insurance coverage currently being offered by the insurer for individuals in the state.

If an insurer elects to discontinue offering all health insurance coverage in the individual market in Florida, health insurance coverage may be discontinued by the insurer only if the insurer provides notice to the office and to each individual at least 180 days prior to the date of the nonrenewal. When the insurer discontinues all individual health insurance policies in the state, the insurer may not write individual health insurance coverage in Florida during the five-year period beginning on the date the last health insurance coverage was not renewed.

Group health insurance

At the time of coverage renewal, an insurer may modify the health insurance coverage for a product offered in the small-group or large-group market if the modification is consistent with Florida law and effective on a uniform basis among group health plans with that product. An insurer may nonrenew a group health insurance policy for one or more of the following reasons.

- Nonpayment of premiums occurs.

- The policyholder has performed an act or practice that constitutes fraud or made an intentional misrepresentation of material fact under the terms of the policy.

- The policyholder has failed to comply with a material provision of the plan that relates to rules for employer contributions or group participation.

- The insurer is ceasing to offer a particular type of coverage in a market.

■ In the case of an insurer that offers health insurance coverage through a network plan, there is no longer any enrollee in connection with such plan who lives, resides, or works in the service area of the insurer or in the area in which the insurer is authorized to do business.

■ In the case of health insurance coverage that is made available only through one or more bona fide associations and the employer ceases to be a member, but only if such coverage is terminated under this paragraph uniformly without regard to any health status–related factor that relates to any covered individuals.

An insurer may discontinue offering a particular policy form of group health insurance coverage offered in the small-group market or large-group market only if the insurer provides notice to each policyholder, and to covered participants and beneficiaries, at least 90 days before the date of nonrenewal. The insurer must offer to each policyholder the option to purchase all, or in the case of the large-group market, any other health insurance coverage currently being offered by the insurer in such market. Also, in exercising the option to discontinue coverage and in offering the coverage options listed, the insurer must act uniformly without regard to the claims experience of those policyholders or any health status–related factor that relates to any participants or beneficiaries covered or new participants or beneficiaries who may become eligible for coverage.

In any case in which an insurer elects to discontinue offering all health insurance coverage in the small-group market, large-group market, or both, health insurance coverage may be discontinued by the insurer only if the insurer provides notice to the office and to each policyholder, and covered participants and beneficiaries at least 180 days prior to the date of nonrenewal. When the insurer discontinues all health insurance policies in the state, the insurer may not write health insurance coverage in Florida during the five-year period beginning on the date the last health insurance coverage was not renewed.

Advertising

Advertising materials and other communications developed by insurers regarding insurance products must clearly indicate that the communication relates to insurance products. When soliciting or selling insurance products, agents must clearly indicate to prospective insureds that they are acting as insurance agents with regard to insurance products and identified insurers. [Sec. 626.9531; Rule 69O-150.001–.021]

Advertisements of benefits payable, losses covered, or premiums payable

No advertisement may use words or phrases such as "all," "full," "complete," "comprehensive," "unlimited," "up to," "as high as," or similar words and phrases, in a manner that exaggerates any benefits beyond the terms of the policy.

An advertisement that is also an invitation to join an association must solicit insurance coverage on a separate and distinct application that requires separate signatures for each application. Any applicable membership fees must be disclosed on each application and must appear separately so as not to be construed as part of the premium for insurance coverage.

An advertisement must not contain descriptions of a policy limitation, exception, or reduction, worded in a positive manner to imply that it is a benefit, such as describing a waiting period as a "benefit builder," or stating "even preexisting conditions are covered after a limited period of time." Words and phrases used in an advertisement to describe such policy limitations, exceptions, and reductions must fairly and accurately describe the negative features of such limitations, exceptions, and reductions of the policy offered.

No advertisement of a benefit for which payment is conditional upon confinement in a hospital or similar facility may use words or phrases such as "tax free," "extra cash," "extra income," "extra pay," in a manner that would have the capacity, or effect of misleading the public into believing that the policy advertised will, in some way, enable them to make a profit from being hospitalized or disabled.

An advertisement for a policy providing benefits for specified illnesses only, such as cancer, or for specified accidents, such as automobile accidents, or for a limited benefit, such as nursing home coverage only, must clearly and conspicuously in prominent type state the limited nature of the policy. The statement must be worded in language identical to, or substantially similar to the following: "THIS IS A LIMITED POLICY," "THIS IS A CANCER ONLY POLICY," "THIS IS AN AUTOMOBILE ACCIDENT ONLY POLICY," "THIS IS A NURSING HOME COVERAGE ONLY POLICY."

An advertisement that is an invitation to contract must disclose exceptions, reductions, and limitations affecting the basic provisions of the policy. The advertisement must disclose the existence of a waiting period, elimination period, or probationary period. An invitation to contract for health benefits must also, in negative terms, disclose the extent to which any loss is not covered if the cause of such loss is traceable to a condition existing prior to the effective date of the policy. The term "preexisting condition" without an appropriate definition or description must not be used.

Certificate of coverage

Each group health insurance policy must contain a provision that the insurer will furnish to the policyholder, for delivery to each employee or member of the insured group, a certificate containing the group number and setting forth the essential features of the insurance coverage and to whom benefits are payable. If dependents are included in the coverage, only one certificate is needed for each family unit. [Sec. 627.657]

Group blanket health

Blanket health insurance is that form of health insurance that covers special groups of individuals, including policies owned by and issued to the following.

■   Any common carrier covering passengers on such common carrier is included.

■ A school, district school system, college, university, or other institution of learning, or to the official or officials of such institution insuring the students and teachers. Any such policy issued may insure the spouse or dependent children of the insured student.

■ Any volunteer fire department or first aid group or other such volunteer group covering all of the members of such department or group.

■ An organization, or branch thereof, such as the Boy Scouts of America, the Future Farmers of America, religious or educational bodies, or similar organizations, holding or operating meetings such as summer camps or other meetings for religious, instructive, or recreational purposes. The policy covers all those attending such camps or meetings, including counselors, instructors, and persons in other administrative positions.

■ A newspaper covering independent contractor newspaper delivery persons is included.

■ A health care provider covering patients. This coverage may be offered to patients of a health care provider but may not be made a condition of receiving care. The benefits provided under such policy or contract may not be assignable to any health care provider.

■ Any HMO covering the subscribers of the health maintenance organization. Payment may be made directly to the health maintenance organization by the blanket health insurer for health care services rendered by providers pursuant to the health care delivery plan. [Sec. 627.659]

Required provisions

Blanket policy provisions relative to payment of claim, notice of claim, proof of loss, time for paying benefits, or legal actions must be at least as favorable to the individuals insured as would be permitted by the comparable provisions required for individual health insurance policies. An individual application is not required from a person covered under a blanket health insurance policy. The insurer is not required to furnish a certificate of coverage to persons covered, except for blanket policies issued to schools, colleges, universities, and other institutions of learning. [Sec. 627.660]

MEDICARE SUPPLEMENT INSURANCE

Required provisions (Minimum standards)

Preexisting condition may not be defined to limit or preclude liability under a policy for a period longer than six months because of a condition for which medical advice was given or treatment was recommended by or received from a physician within six months before the effective date of the coverage.

A Medicare supplement policy may not exclude benefits based on a pre-existing condition if the individual has a continuous period of creditable coverage of at least six months as of the date of application for coverage. [Sec. 627.6741; FAC Rule 69O-156.009]

Free look. Medicare supplement policies and certificates must have a notice prominently printed on the first page of the policy or certificate stating in substance that the policyholder or certificateholder has the right to return the policy or certificate within 30 days of its delivery and to have the premium refunded if, after examination of the policy or certificate, the insured person is not satisfied for any reason.

A policy filed with the office as a Medicare supplement policy must do the following:

- Have a definition of "Medicare eligible expense" that is not more restrictive than health care expenses of the kinds covered by Medicare or to the extent recognized as reasonable by Medicare

- Provide that benefits designed to cover cost-sharing amounts under Medicare will be changed automatically to coincide with any changes in the applicable Medicare deductible amount and copayment percentage factor

- Be written in simplified language, be easily understood by purchasers [Sec. 627.674; 69O- 156.003, .014]

Open enrollment periods

65 and over. A Medicare supplement insurer may not deny any application for a Medicare supplement policy, nor discriminate in the pricing of such a policy because of the health status, claims experience, receipt of health care, or medical condition of an applicant if the application is submitted prior to or during the six-month period beginning with the first day of the first month in which an individual is both 65 years of age or older and is enrolled for benefits under Medicare Part B. Each Medicare supplement policy currently available from an insurer must be made available to all applicants who qualify under this rule without regard to age.

Under 65. A Medicare supplement insurer must offer the opportunity of enrolling in a Medicare supplement policy, without conditioning the issuance of the policy on, and without discriminating in the price of the policy based on, the medical or health status or receipt of health care by the individual:

- to any Florida resident who is under age 65 and eligible for Medicare by reason of disability or end-stage renal disease, upon the request of the individual during the six-month period beginning with the first month the individual is eligible for Medicare by reason of a disability or end-stage renal disease, and is enrolled in Medicare Part B; or

■ to any Florida resident who is under 65 years of age and eligible for Medicare by reason of a disability or end-stage renal disease, and who is enrolled in Medicare Part B, upon the request of the individual during the two-month period following termination of coverage under a group health insurance policy.

Advertising and marketing standards

Every insurer, health care service plan, or other entity marketing Medicare supplement insurance coverage in this state, directly or through its producers, must abide by the following standards.

■ Establish marketing procedures to ensure that any comparison of policies by its agents or other producers will be fair and accurate.

■ Establish marketing procedures to ensure excessive insurance is not sold or issued.

■ Display prominently by type, stamp, or other appropriate means, on the first page of the outline of coverage and policy, the following:

"Notice to buyer: This policy may not cover all of the costs associated with medical care incurred by the buyer during the period of coverage. The buyer is advised to review carefully all policy limitations."

■ Inquire and otherwise make every reasonable effort to identify whether a prospective applicant or enrollee for Medicare supplement insurance already has accident and sickness insurance and the types and amounts of any such insurance.

■ Every insurer or entity marketing Medicare supplement insurance must establish auditable procedures for verifying compliance with Florida law.

■ In recommending the purchase or replacement of any Medicare supplement policy or certificate, an agent must make reasonable efforts to determine the appropriateness of a recommended purchase or replacement.

■ Any sale of Medicare supplement policy or certificate that will provide an individual with more than one Medicare supplement policy or certificate is prohibited.

■ An issuer must not issue a Medicare supplement policy or certificate to an individual enrolled in Medicare Part C unless the effective date of the Medicare supplement coverage is after the termination date of the individual's Part C coverage.

In addition to previously identified unfair practices prohibited, the following acts and practices are prohibited:

■ **Twisting** Knowingly making any misleading representation or incomplete or fraudulent comparison of any insurance policies or insurers for the purpose of inducing, or tending to induce, any person to lapse, forfeit, surrender, terminate, retain, pledge, assign, borrow on, or convert any insurance policy or to take out a policy of insurance with another insurer.

■ **High-pressure tactics** Employing any method of marketing having the effect of or tending to induce the purchase of insurance through force, fright, threat whether explicit or implied, or undue pressure to purchase or recommend the purchase of insurance.

■ **Cold lead advertising** Making use directly or indirectly of any method of marketing that fails to disclose in a conspicuous manner that a purpose of the method of marketing is solicitation of insurance and that contact will be made by an insurance agent or insurance company. [Sec. 627.6743; FAC Rule 69O-156.017]

Permitted compensation arrangements

An insurer or other entity may provide compensation to an agent or other representative for the sale of a Medicare supplement policy or certificate only if the first year compensation is no more than 200% of the compensation paid for selling or servicing the policy or certificate in the second year or period. However, an issuer on entry, who restricts first agent commission or compensation to 15% or less of the policy premium, may elect not to pay any commission or other compensation to an agent or other representative for the renewal or replacement of a Medicare supplement policy or certificate. For purposes of this rule, "compensation" includes pecuniary or nonpecuniary remuneration of any kind relating to the sale or renewal of the policy or certificates including but not limited to bonuses, gifts, prizes, awards and finder's fees.

The commission or other compensation provided in subsequent (renewal) years must be the same as that provided in the second year or period and must be provided for no fewer than five renewal years. No issuer or other entity may provide compensation to its agents or other producers and no agent or producer may receive compensation greater than the renewal compensation payable by the replacing insurer on renewal policies or certificates if an existing policy or certificate is replaced. [Sec. 627.6742; FAC Rule 69O-156.013]

Multiple policies

Medicare supplement insurance may not be issued or sold to an individual if:

■ the sale of Medicare supplement coverage will provide an individual more than one Medicare supplement policy or certificate; or

■ an individual's written statement indicates that the individual is entitled to Medicaid, unless this state's Medicaid plan under Title XIX pays the premiums for the policy, or pays less than an individual's full liability for Medicare cost sharing as defined under the federal Medicare law.

This section does not prohibit the sale of a Medicare supplement policy to an individual who has another Medicare supplement policy if:

- the individual indicates in writing that the policy replaces the other policy and indicates an intent to terminate the policy being replaced when the new policy becomes effective; and

- the insurer providing the replacement policy forwards the statement to the insurer whose policy is being replaced. [Sec. 627.6744]

Disclosure

Buyer's Guide

Except in the case of a direct response insurer, delivery of a Buyer's Guide must be made at the time of application, and acknowledgment of receipt or certification of delivery of the Buyer's Guide must be provided to the insurer. Direct response insurers must deliver the Buyer's Guide upon request, but not later than at the time the policy is delivered. The Medicare Supplement Buyer's Guide is developed jointly by the National Association of Insurance Commissioners and the Health Care Financing Administration of the United States Department of Health and Human Services. [Sec. 627.674]

Outline of coverage

A Medicare supplement outline of coverage must be delivered to the applicant at the time application is made, and, except for the direct response policy, acknowledgment of receipt of the outline of coverage must be provided to the insurer. The following language must be printed on or attached to the first page of the outline of coverage delivered in conjunction with an individual policy of hospital confinement insurance, indemnity insurance, specified disease insurance, specified accident insurance, supplemental health insurance other than Medicare supplement insurance, or nonconventional health insurance coverage, as defined by law in this state, to a person eligible for Medicare [Sec. 627.674]:

> *"This policy IS NOT A MEDICARE SUPPLEMENT policy. If you are eligible for Medicare, review the Medicare Supplement Buyer's Guide available from the company."*

Replacement/replacement forms

Replacement is any transaction wherein new Medicare supplement insurance is to be purchased and it is known to the agent, broker, or insurer at the time of application that, as a part of the transaction, existing accident and health insurance has been or is to be lapsed or the benefits thereof substantially reduced.

Application forms must include statements and questions designed to elicit information as to whether, as of the date of the application, the applicant currently has Medicare supplement, or Medicare Advantage, Medicaid coverage, or another health insurance policy or certificate in force or whether a Medicare supplement policy or certificate is intended to replace any other accident and sickness policy or certificate presently in force.

If the sale will involve replacement of Medicare supplement coverage, any issuer or its agent, other than a direct response issuer, must furnish the applicant, prior to issuance or delivery of the Medicare supplement policy or certificate, a **Notice Regarding Replacement of Medicare Supplement Coverage**. One copy of the notice signed by the applicant and the agent, except where the coverage is issued without an agent, must be provided to the applicant and an additional signed copy will be retained by the issuer. A direct response issuer must deliver to the applicant at the time of the issuance of the policy the notice regarding replacement of Medicare supplement coverage.

Within five working days from the receipt of an application at its policy issuance office, the replacing insurer must furnish a copy of such notice to the existing insurer whose policy is being replaced.

If a Medicare supplement policy or certificate replaces another Medicare supplement policy or certificate or other creditable coverage, the replacing insurer must waive any time periods applicable to preexisting conditions, waiting periods, elimination periods, and probationary periods in the new Medicare supplement policy for similar benefits to the extent such time was spent under the original policy. Therefore, if a Medicare supplement policy or certificate replaces another Medicare supplement policy or certificate that has been in effect for at least six months, the replacing policy may not provide any time period applicable to preexisting conditions, waiting periods, elimination periods, and probationary periods for benefits similar to those contained in the original policy or certificate. [69O-156.003, .015, .019]

Duplication of benefits

No Medicare supplement policy or certificate in force in the state must contain benefits that duplicate benefits provided by Medicare. [FAC Rule 69O-156.005]

Standardized policy benefits (A–N)

The following standards are applicable to all 2010 Standardized Medicare supplement policies or certificates delivered or issued for delivery in Florida with an effective date for coverage on or after June 1, 2010.

Note: Specific coverages by plan are discussed in unit 21, Private Insurance Plans for Seniors, in this manual.

■ Medicare supplement policies must be guaranteed renewable.

■ No policy or certificate may be advertised, solicited, delivered, or issued for delivery in this state as a Medicare supplement policy or certificate unless it complies with these benefit standards.

■ A Medicare supplement policy or certificate must not indemnify against losses resulting from sickness on a different basis than losses resulting from accidents.

■ A Medicare supplement policy or certificate must provide that benefits designed to cover cost sharing amounts under Medicare will be changed automatically to coincide with any changes in the applicable Medicare deductible, co-payment, or coinsurance amounts. Premiums may be modified to correspond with such changes. The premium changes must be submitted to and approved by the office.

- No Medicare supplement policy or certificate must provide for termination of coverage of a spouse solely because of the occurrence of an event specified for termination of coverage of the insured, other than the nonpayment of premium.

- Outpatient prescription drugs A Medicare supplement policy with benefits for outpatient prescription drugs in existence prior to January 1, 2006, may be renewed for current policyholders who do not enroll in Part D at the option of the policyholder.

A Medicare supplement policy with benefits for outpatient prescription drugs may not be issued after December 31, 2005.

LONG-TERM CARE POLICIES

Disclosure

Outline of coverage

A long-term care insurance outline of coverage must be delivered to an applicant for an individual long-term care insurance policy at the time of application. In the case of direct response solicitations, the insurer must deliver the outline of coverage upon the applicant's request, but regardless of request must make such delivery no later than at the time of policy delivery. The outline of coverage must include:

- a description of the principal benefits and coverage provided in the policy;

- a statement of the principal exclusions, reductions, and limitations contained in the policy;

- a statement of the renewal provisions, including any reservation in the policy of a right to change premiums;

- a statement that the outline of coverage is a summary of the policy issued or applied for and that the policy should be consulted to determine governing contractual provisions;

- a graphic comparison of the benefit levels of a policy that increases benefits over the policy period and a policy that does not increase benefits, showing benefit levels over a period of at least 20 years; and

■ any premium increases or additional premiums required for automatic or optional benefit increases. If the amount of premium increases or additional premiums depends on the age of the applicant at the time of the increase, the insurer must also disclose the amount of the increased premiums or additional premiums for benefit increases that would be required of the applicant at the ages of 75 and 85 years. [Sec. 627.9407; 69O-157.120]

Buyer's Guide

A long-term care insurance shopper's guide in the format developed by the National Association of Insurance Commissioners (2001) must be provided to all prospective applicants of a long-term care insurance policy or certificate. An agent must deliver the shopper's guide prior to the presentation of an application or enrollment form. In the case of direct response solicitations, the shopper's guide must be presented in conjunction with any application or enrollment form. Life insurance policies or riders containing accelerated long-term care benefits are not required to furnish the above-referenced guide, but shall furnish the Policy Summary required under Florida law. [69O-157.121]

Advertising and Marketing

The commission has adopted rules and standards for the advertising, marketing, and sale of long-term care insurance policies in order to protect applicants from unfair or deceptive sales or enrollment practices. An insurer must file with the office any long-term care insurance advertising material intended for use in Florida, whether through written, radio, television, electronic, or other medium for review or approval by the office. The insurer may immediately begin using material upon filing, subject to subsequent disapproval by the office. Following receipt of a notice of disapproval or a withdrawal of approval, the insurer must immediately cease use of the disapproved material.

A qualified long-term care insurance policy must include a disclosure statement within the policy and within the outline of coverage that the policy is intended to be a qualified long-term contract. A long-term care insurance policy that is not intended to be a qualified long-term care insurance contract must include a disclosure statement within the policy and within the outline of coverage that the policy is not intended to be a qualified long-term care insurance contract. The disclosure must be prominently displayed and must read as follows:

> "This long-term care insurance policy is not intended to be a qualified long-term care insurance contract. You need to be aware that benefits received under this policy may create unintended, adverse income tax consequences to you. You may want to consult with a knowledgeable individual about such potential income tax consequences."

Prohibition against post-claims underwriting

All applications for long-term care insurance policies or certificates except those that are guaranteed issue must contain clear and unambiguous questions designed to ascertain the health condition of the applicant. Except for policies or certificates that are guaranteed issue, the following language must be set out conspicuously and in close conjunction with the applicant's signature block on an application for a long-term care insurance policy or certificate:

"Caution: If your answers on this application are incorrect or untrue, [company] may have the right to deny benefits or rescind your policy."

The following language, or language substantially similar to the following, must be set out conspicuously on the long-term care insurance policy or certificate at the time of delivery:

"Caution: The issuance of this long-term care insurance [policy] [certificate] is based upon your responses to the questions on your application. A copy of your [application] [enrollment form] [is enclosed] [was retained by you when you applied]. If your answers are incorrect or untrue, the company may have the right to deny benefits or rescind your policy. The best time to clear up any questions is now, before a claim arises! If, for any reason, any of your answers are incorrect, contact the company at this address: [insert address]."

Requirements for replacements

Applications must include questions designed to elicit information as to whether, as of the date of the application, the applicant has another long-term care insurance policy or certificate in force or whether a long-term care policy or certificate is intended to replace any other accident and sickness or long-term care policy or certificate presently in force. Agents must list any other health insurance policies they have sold to the applicant.

If the sale will involve replacement, an insurer (other than a direct response insurer), or its agent; must furnish the applicant prior to issuance or delivery of the individual long-term care insurance policy a **Notice Regarding Replacement of Accident and Sickness or Long-Term Care Coverage**. One copy of the notice must be retained by the applicant, and an additional copy signed by the applicant must be retained by the insurer.

The replacing insurer must notify in writing the existing insurer of the proposed replacement within five working days from the date the application is received by the insurer or the date the policy is issued, whichever is sooner.

Prohibition against preexisting conditions and probationary periods in replacement policies or certificates

If a long-term care insurance policy or certificate replaces another long-term care policy or certificate, the replacing insurer must waive any time periods applicable to time limit on certain defenses, preexisting conditions, and probationary periods in the new long-term care policy for similar benefits to the extent that similar exclusions have been satisfied under the original policy.

Producer training

Insurers providing long-term care insurance must maintain records that before any producer sells, solicits, or negotiates a long-term care insurance policy, that they receive necessary and sufficient training to understand partnership policies and their relationship to public and private coverage for long-term care.

Suitability

Every insurer marketing long-term care insurance must develop and use suitability standards to determine whether the purchase or replacement of long-term care insurance is appropriate for the needs of the applicant. To determine whether the applicant meets the standards developed by the insurer, the agent and insurer must develop procedures that take the following into consideration:

■ The ability to pay for the proposed coverage and other pertinent financial information related to the purchase of the coverage

■ The applicant's goals or needs with respect to long-term care and the advantages and disadvantages of insurance to meet these goals or needs

■ The values, benefits, and costs of the applicant's existing insurance, if any, when compared to the values, benefits, and costs of the recommended purchase or replacement

The insurer and the agent must make reasonable efforts to obtain suitability information. This includes presentation to the applicant, at or prior to application, the Long-Term Care Personal Worksheet. A completed personal worksheet must be sent to the insurer prior to the insurer's consideration of the applicant for coverage, except the personal worksheet need not be returned for sales of employer group long-term care insurance to employees and their spouses. At the same time the personal worksheet is provided to the applicant, the disclosure form titled "Things You Should Know Before You Buy Long-Term Care Insurance" must be provided.

If the insurer determines that the applicant does not meet its financial suitability standards, or if the applicant has declined to provide the information, the insurer may reject the application. [Sec. 627.9407; FAC Rule 69O-157.109, .110, .115–.116]

Policy standards

Free look. An individual long-term care insurance policyholder has the right to return the policy within 30 days after its delivery and to have the premium refunded if, after examination of the policy, the policyholder is not satisfied for any reason.

A policy issued to an individual must not contain renewal provisions other than "guaranteed renewable" or "noncancellable."

Preexisting conditions. A long-term care insurance policy or certificate may not use a definition of "preexisting condition" that is more restrictive than the following: Preexisting condition means a condition for which medical advice or treatment was recommended by or received from a provider of health care services within six months preceding the effective date of coverage of an insured person. The definition of preexisting condition does not prohibit an insurer from using an application form designed to elicit the complete health history of an applicant, and, on the basis of the answers on that application, from underwriting in accordance with that insurer's established underwriting standards.

A long-term care insurance policy or certificate may not exclude coverage for a loss or confinement that is the result of a preexisting condition unless such loss or confinement begins within six months following the effective date of coverage of an insured person. A long-term care insurance policy or certificate may not exclude or use waivers or riders of any kind to exclude, limit, or reduce coverage or benefits for specifically named or described preexisting diseases or physical conditions.

Limitations and exclusions

A policy may not be delivered or issued for delivery in Florida as long-term care insurance if the policy limits or excludes coverage by type of illness, treatment, medical condition, or accident, except as follows:

- Preexisting conditions or diseases

- Mental or nervous disorders; however, this does not permit exclusion or limitation of benefits on the basis of Alzheimer's disease

- Alcoholism and drug addiction

- War or act of war (whether declared or undeclared)

- Participation in a felony, riot, or insurrection

- Service in the armed forces or units auxiliary thereto

- Suicide (sane or insane), attempted suicide, or intentionally self-inflicted injury

- Aviation (this exclusion applies only to non-fare-paying passengers)

- Treatment provided in a government facility (unless otherwise required by law)

- Services for which benefits are available under Medicare or other governmental program (except Medicaid)

- Any state or federal workers' compensation, employer's liability or occupational disease law, or any motor vehicle no-fault law

- Services provided by a member of the covered person's immediate family

- Services for which no charge is normally made in the absence of insurance

A long-term care insurance policy may not do the following:

■ Be canceled, nonrenewed, or otherwise terminated on the grounds of the age or the deterioration of the mental or physical health of the insured individual or certificateholder

■ Contain a provision establishing a new waiting period in the event existing coverage is converted to or replaced by a new or other form within the same insurer or any affiliated insurer, except with respect to an increase in benefits voluntarily selected by the insured individual or group policyholder

■ Restrict its coverage to care only in a licensed nursing home or provide significantly more coverage for such care than coverage for lower levels of care

■ Contain an elimination period in excess of 180 days; as used in this paragraph, the term " elimination period " means the number of days at the beginning of a period of confinement for which no benefits are payable

■ Condition eligibility for benefits on a prior hospitalization requirement.

The premium rate schedule must be based on the issue age of the insured. A long-term care insurance policy may not be issued if the premiums to be charged are calculated to increase based solely on the age of the insured. Any premium increase for existing insureds must not result in a premium charged to the insureds that would exceed the premium charged on a newly issued insurance policy, except to reflect benefit differences

Any long-term care insurance policy or certificate issued or renewed, at the option of the policyholder or certificateholder must make available to the insured the contingent benefit upon lapse as provided in the Long-Term Care Insurance Model Regulation adopted by the National Association of Insurance Commissioners in the second quarter of the year 2000. [Sec. 627.9407; FAC Rule 69O-157.104]

Home care coverage

A long-term care insurance policy, certificate, or rider that contains a home health care benefit must meet or exceed the minimum standards specified in this section. The policy, certificate, or rider may not exclude benefits by any of the following means [Sec. 627.94071]:

■ Providing that home health care cannot be covered unless the insured would, without the home health care, require skilled care in a skilled nursing facility

■ Requiring that the insured first or simultaneously receive nursing or therapeutic services in a home setting or community setting before home health care services are covered

■ Excluding coverage for personal care services provided by a home health aide

- Requiring that the provision of home health care services be at a level of certification of licensure greater than that required by the eligible service

- Requiring that the insured/claimant have an acute condition before home health care services are covered

- Limiting benefits to services provided by Medicare-certified agencies or providers

- Excluding coverage for adult day care services

Inflation protection

An insurer that offers a long-term care insurance policy, certificate, or rider must offer, in addition to any other inflation protection, the option to purchase a policy that provides that benefit levels increase with benefit maximums or reasonable durations, to account for reasonably anticipated increases in the costs of services covered by the policy. The inflation protection option required by this paragraph must be no less favorable to the policyholder than one of the following [Sec. 627.94072]:

- A provision that increases benefits annually at a rate of not less than 5%, compounded annually

- A provision that guarantees to the insured person the right to periodically increase benefit levels without providing evidence of insurability or health status, if the option for the preceding period has not been declined. The total amount of benefits provided under this option must be equal to or greater than the existing benefit level increased by 5% compounded annually for the period beginning with the purchase of the existing benefits and ending with the year in which the offer is accepted

- A provision that covers a specified percentage of actual or reasonable charges and does not include a specified indemnity amount or limit

Nonforfeiture benefits

An insurer that offers a long-term care insurance policy, certificate, or rider must offer a nonforfeiture protection provision providing reduced paid-up insurance, extended term, shortened benefit period, or any other benefits approved by the office if all or part of a premium is not paid. The nonforfeiture protection provision providing a shortened benefit period must, at a minimum, provide the same benefits, amounts, and frequency in effect at the time of lapse be payable for a qualifying claim, but the lifetime maximum dollars or days of benefits are determined by the following.

- The standard nonforfeiture credit must be equal to 100% of the sum of all premiums paid, including the premiums paid prior to any changes in benefits. The insurer may offer additional shortened benefit period options, as long as the benefits for each duration equal or exceed the standard nonforfeiture credit for that duration. However, the minimum nonforfeiture credit must not be less than 30 times the daily nursing home benefit at the time of lapse.

■ At the time of lapse, or upon request, the insurer must disclose to the insured the insured's then-accrued nonforfeiture values. At the time the policy is issued, the insurer must provide to the policyholder schedules demonstrating estimated values of nonforfeiture benefits; however, such schedules must state that the estimated values are not to be construed as guaranteed nonforfeiture values. [Sec. 627.94072]

Contingent benefit on lapse

If the offer to purchase nonforfeiture benefits is rejected, for individual and group policies without nonforfeiture benefits the insurer must include in the policy, or as a rider or endorsement to the policy, the contingent benefit upon lapse. The contingent benefit on lapse will be triggered every time an insurer increases the premium rates to a level that results in a cumulative increase of the annual premium equal to or exceeding the percentage of the insured's initial annual premium as set forth in Florida law, and the policy or certificate lapses within 120 days of the due date of the premium so increased. On or before the effective date of a substantial premium increase, the insurer must:

■ offer to reduce policy benefits provided by the current coverage without the requirement of additional underwriting so that required premium payments are not increased; or

■ offer to convert the coverage to a paid-up status with a shortened benefit period in accordance with the terms of the shortened benefit period nonforfeiture benefit. This option may be elected at any time during the 120-day period referenced above. [FAC Rule 69O-157.118]

Grace period and unintentional lapse

A long-term care policy must provide that the insured is entitled to a **grace period** of not less than 30 days, within which payment of any premium after the first may be made. If the policy becomes a claim during the grace period before the overdue premium is paid, the amount of such premium or premiums with interest not in excess of 8% per year may be deducted from the claim.

Unintentional lapse. As part of the application process, the applicant may designate a *secondary addressee* who, in addition to the applicant, is to receive a notice of lapse or termination of the policy for nonpayment of premium. If a policy is canceled due to nonpayment of premium, the policyholder is entitled to have the policy reinstated if, within a period of not less than five months after the date of cancellation, the policyholder or any secondary addressee demonstrates that the failure to pay the premium was unintentional and due to the policyholder's cognitive impairment, loss of functional capacity, or continuous confinement in a hospital, skilled nursing facility, or assisted living facility for a period in excess of 60 days. Policy reinstatement must be subject to payment of overdue premiums. The standard of proof of cognitive impairment or loss of functional capacity must not be more stringent than the benefit eligibility criteria for cognitive impairment or the loss of functional capacity, if any, contained in the policy and certificate. [Sec. 627.94073]

Conditions for determination of benefit payments

A long-term care insurance policy may condition the payment of benefits on a determination of the insured's ability to perform activities of daily living and on cognitive impairment. Eligibility for the payment of benefits must not be more restrictive than requiring either a deficiency in the ability to perform not more than three of the activities of daily living or the presence of cognitive impairment. Activities of daily living must include at least the following. [Sec. 627.94074]

- **Bathing** means washing oneself by sponge bath or in either a tub or shower, including the task of getting into or out of the tub or shower.

- **Continence** means the ability to maintain control of bowel and bladder function, or, when unable to maintain control of bowel or bladder function, the ability to perform associated personal hygiene, including caring for catheter or colostomy bag.

- **Dressing** means putting on and taking off all items of clothing and any necessary braces, fasteners, or artificial limbs.

- **Eating** means feeding oneself by getting food into the body from a receptacle, such as a plate, cup, or table, or by a feeding tube or intravenously.

- **Toileting** means getting to and from the toilet, getting on and off the toilet, and performing associated personal hygiene.

- **Transferring** means moving into or out of a bed, chair, or wheelchair.

The determination of a deficiency due to loss of functional capacity or cognitive impairment must not be more restrictive than:

- requiring the hands-on assistance of another person to perform the prescribed activities of daily living, meaning physical assistance, minimal, moderate, or maximal, without which the individual would not be able to perform the activity of daily living; or

- due to the presence of a cognitive impairment, requiring supervision, including verbal cueing by another person in order to protect the insured or others.

Assessment of activities of daily living and cognitive impairment must be performed by licensed or certified professionals, such as physicians, nurses, or social workers. Long-term care insurance policies must include a clear description of the process for appealing and resolving the benefit determinations.

Required provisions (Minimum standards)

All long-term care policies must provide coverage for at least one type of lower level of care, in addition to coverage for care in a nursing home. A long-term care policy may not provide significantly more coverage for care in a nursing home than coverage for lower levels of care. Benefits for all lower levels of care in the aggregate, as determined by the insured for each policy, must provide a level of benefits equivalent to at least 50% of the benefits provided for nursing home coverage (i.e., if the nursing home benefit amount is $100 per day, then the required lower level of care benefit amount must be at least $50 per day). For the purposes of this rule, "lower level(s) of care" means the following:

■ Nursing service

■ Assisted living facility

■ Home health services

■ Adult day care center

■ Adult foster home

■ Community care for the elderly

■ Personal care and social services

Riders and Endorsements

Except for riders or endorsements requested in writing by the insured, all riders or endorsements added to an individual long-term care insurance policy after date of issue or at reinstatement or renewal that reduce or eliminate benefits in the policy must require signed acceptance by the individual insured. After the date of policy issue, any rider or endorsement that increases benefits with a corresponding increase in premium during the policy term must be agreed to in writing and signed by the insured, except if the increased benefits are required by law. [FAC Rule 69O-157.106]

Other provisions

Group long-term care

The sponsoring policyholder of a group policy is not required to contribute premiums; however, if the sponsoring policyholder does contribute any premium, all members of the group, or all of any class or classes thereof, must be declared eligible and acceptable to the insurer at the time of issuance of the policy. A certificate issued pursuant to a group long-term care insurance policy must include the following:

■ A description of the principal benefits and coverage provided in the policy

- A statement of the principal exclusions, reductions, and limitations contained in the policy

- A statement that the description of principal benefits is a summary of the policy and that the group master policy should be consulted to determine governing contractual provisions

- Person insured

- Person to whom benefits are payable

- Group contract number

- Certificate number

- Effective date

- Time certificate is effective

Group long-term care continuation or conversion

Group long-term care insurance must provide covered individuals with a basis for continuation or conversion of coverage. "A basis for continuation of coverage" means a policy provision that maintains coverage under the existing group policy when the coverage would otherwise terminate and that is subject only to the continued timely payment of premium when due.

"A basis for conversion of coverage" means a policy provision that an individual whose coverage under the group policy would otherwise terminate, and who has been continuously insured under the group policy, for at least six months immediately prior to termination, must be entitled to convert to an individual policy issued by the insurer, without evidence of insurability. The policy and rate schedule for the converted policy must be a policy that is available, at the time of conversion, for general sales by the insurer. Written application for the converted policy must be made and the first premium due, if any, must be paid not later than 31 days after termination of coverage under the group policy. The premium for the converted policy must be calculated on the basis of the insured's age and risk class at inception of coverage under the group policy from which conversion is made.

Terminology

Long-term care insurance policy means any insurance policy or rider advertised, marketed, offered, or designed to provide coverage on an expense-incurred, indemnity, prepaid, or other basis for one or more necessary or medically necessary diagnostic, preventive, therapeutic, curing, treating, mitigating, rehabilitative, maintenance, or personal care services provided in a setting other than an acute care unit of a hospital. Long-term care insurance must not include any insurance policy that is offered primarily to provide basic Medicare supplement coverage, basic hospital expense coverage, basic medical-surgical expense coverage, hospital confinement indemnity coverage, major medical expense coverage, disability income protection coverage, accident only coverage, specified disease or specified accident coverage, or limited health insurance coverage not otherwise defined as long-term care insurance.

Chronically ill means certified by a licensed health care practitioner as:

■ being unable to perform, without substantial assistance from another individual, at least two activities of daily living for a period of at least 90 days due to a loss of functional capacity; or

■ requiring substantial supervision for protection from threats to health and safety due to severe cognitive impairment.

Cognitive impairment means a deficiency in a person's short-term or long-term memory, orientation as to person, place, and time, deductive or abstract reasoning, or judgment as it relates to safety awareness.

Qualified long-term care services means necessary diagnostic, preventive, curing, treating, mitigating, and rehabilitative services, and maintenance or personal care services that are required by a chronically ill individual and are provided pursuant to a plan of care prescribed by a licensed health care practitioner.

Adult day care center means a program for six or more individuals of social and health-related services provided during the day in a community group setting for the purpose of supporting frail, impaired elderly or other disabled adults who can benefit from care in a group setting outside the home.

Assisted living facility must be defined in the policy and must be defined in relation to the services and facilities required to be available and the licensure or degree status of those providing or supervising the services.

Home health services means medical and nonmedical services provided to ill, disabled, or infirm persons in their residences. Such services may include homemaker services, assistance with activities of daily living, and respite care services.

Nursing home facility means any appropriately licensed facility that provides nursing services for the care and comfort of individuals.

Personal care means the provision of hands-on services to assist an individual with activities of daily living.

Waiting period or probationary period as used in a long-term care policy means that period of time that follows the date a person is initially insured under the policy before the coverage or coverages of the policy must become effective as to that person.

Long-term care partnership

Florida's Long-term Care Partnership Program is a partnership program between Medicaid and private long-term care insurers designed to encourage individuals to purchase private long-term care insurance. Long-term Care Partnership provides dollar-for-dollar asset protection in the event the policyholder needs to apply for long-term care Medicaid assistance. For every dollar that a partnership policy pays out in benefits, a dollar of assets can be protected from Medicaid spend-down requirements. A policy or certificate marketed as an approved long-term care partnership program policy must meet the following criteria:

■ Be a qualified long-term care insurance policy

- Be issued to a Florida resident or another state that has entered into a reciprocal agreement with Florida when coverage first became effective under the policy

- Be issued with and retain inflation coverage that meets the inflation standards based on the insured's then-attained age. Policies or certificates issued to an individual who has not yet attained age 61 must contain annual compound inflation coverage.

- Policies or certificates issued to an individual who has attained age 61 but has not attained age 76 must contain annual inflation coverage. [FAC Rule 69O-157.201]

An insurer issuing or marketing policies that qualify as partnership policies must provide a disclosure notice, on the insurer's letterhead, indicating that at the time of coverage issue, the policy is an approved long-term care partnership policy. The insurer may use Form OIR-B2-1786 (1/2007), Partnership Status Disclosure Notice. This notice must be provided to the insured no later than the time of policy or certificate delivery.

When an insurer is made aware that the policyholders or certificateholders have taken an action that will result in the loss of partnership status, the insurer must provide a written explanation of how such action may impact the insured, and how to retain partnership status.

REQUIREMENTS FOR SMALL EMPLOYERS

The purpose and intent of the Florida Employee Health Care Access Act is to promote the availability of health insurance coverage to small employers regardless of their claims experience or their employees' health status, and to improve the overall fairness and efficiency of the small-group health insurance market. [SEC. 627.6699]

Definitions

Dependent means the spouse or child of an eligible employee, subject to the applicable terms of the health benefit plan covering that employee.

Eligible employee means an employee who works full time, having a normal workweek of 25 or more hours, and who has met any applicable waiting period requirements or other requirements of this act. The term includes a self-employed individual, a sole proprietor, a partner of a partnership, or an independent contractor, if the sole proprietor, partner, or independent contractor is included as an employee under a health benefit plan of a small employer, but does not include a part-time, temporary, or substitute employee.

Guaranteed-issue basis means an insurance policy that must be offered to an employer, employee, or dependent of the employee, regardless of health status, preexisting conditions, or claims history.

Small employer means, in connection with a health benefit plan with respect to a calendar year and a plan year, a person, sole proprietor, self-employed individual, independent contractor, firm, corporation, partnership, or association that is actively engaged in business, has its principal place of business in Florida, and employed an average of at least one but not more than 50 eligible employees on business days during the preceding calendar year, the majority of whom were employed in Florida.

Small employer carrier means a carrier that offers health benefit plans covering employees of one or more small employers.

Special provisions

For employers who have fewer than two employees, a late enrollee may be excluded from coverage for no longer than 24 months if he or she was not covered by creditable coverage continually to a date not more than 63 days before the effective date of his or her new coverage.

Any requirement used by a small employer carrier in determining whether to provide coverage to a small employer group, including requirements for minimum participation of eligible employees and minimum employer contributions, must be applied uniformly among all small employer groups having the same number of eligible employees applying for coverage from the small employer carrier. A small employer carrier may vary application of minimum participation requirements and minimum employer contribution requirements only by the size of the small employer group. In applying minimum participation requirements with respect to a small employer, a small employer carrier shall not consider as an eligible employee employees or dependents who have qualifying existing coverage in an employer-based group insurance plan or an ERISA-qualified self-insurance plan in determining whether the applicable percentage of participation is met.

A small employer carrier may count eligible employees and dependents who have coverage under another health plan that is sponsored by that employer. A small employer carrier shall not increase any requirement for minimum employee participation or any requirement for minimum employer contribution applicable to a small employer at any time after the small employer has been accepted for coverage, unless the employer size has changed, in which case the small employer carrier may apply the requirements that are applicable to the new group size.

If a small employer carrier offers coverage to a small employer, it must offer coverage to all the small employer's eligible employees and their dependents. A small employer carrier may not offer coverage limited to certain persons in a group or to part of a group, except with respect to late enrollees. A small employer carrier may not modify any health benefit plan issued to a small employer with respect to a small employer or any eligible employee or dependent through riders, endorsements, or otherwise to restrict or exclude coverage for certain diseases or medical conditions otherwise covered by the health benefit plan.

An initial enrollment period of at least 30 days must be provided. An annual 30-day open enrollment period must be offered to each small employer's eligible employees and their dependents.

Disclosure requirements

In connection with the offering of a health benefit plan to a small employer, a small employer carrier must make a reasonable disclosure to such employer, as part of its solicitation and sales materials, of the availability of information regarding:

- the provisions of such coverage concerning an insurer's right to change premium rates and the factors that may affect changes in premium rates;

- the provisions of such coverage that relate to renewability of coverage;

- the provisions of such coverage that relate to any preexisting condition exclusions; and

- the benefits and premiums available under all health insurance coverage for which the employer is qualified.

This section applies to a health benefit plan that provides coverage to employees of a small employer, unless the coverage is marketed directly to the individual employee, and the employer does not contribute directly or indirectly to the premiums or facilitate the administration of the coverage in any manner. For the purposes of this subparagraph, an employer is not deemed to be contributing to the premiums or facilitating the administration of coverage if the employer does not contribute to the premium and merely collects the premiums for coverage from an employee's wages or salary through payroll deduction and submits payment for the premiums of one or more employees in a lump sum to a carrier.

Denial/termination/nonrenewal

A small employer carrier need not offer coverage or accept applications to:

- a small employer if the small employer is not physically located in an established geographic service area of the small employer carrier, provided such geographic service area shall not be less than a county;

- an employee if the employee does not work or reside within an established geographic service area of the small employer carrier; or

- a small employer group within an area in which the small employer carrier reasonably anticipates, and demonstrates to the satisfaction of the office, that it cannot, within its network of providers, deliver service adequately to the members of such groups because of obligations to existing group contract holders and enrollees.

A small employer carrier may deny health insurance coverage in the small-group market if the carrier has demonstrated to the office that:

- it does not have the financial reserves necessary to underwrite additional coverage; and

- it is applying this sub-subparagraph uniformly to all employers in the small-group market in the state without regard to the claims experience of those employers and their employees and their dependents or any health status–related factor that relates to such employees and dependents.

A small employer carrier, upon denying health insurance coverage in connection with health benefit plans in accordance with sub-subparagraph, may not offer coverage in connection with group health benefit plans in the small-group market for a period of 180 days after the date such coverage is denied or until the insurer has demonstrated to the office that the insurer has sufficient financial reserves to underwrite additional coverage, whichever is later.

Fair marketing standards

Each small employer carrier shall actively market health benefit plan coverage, including the basic and standard health benefit plans to eligible small employers in the state. Small employer carriers must offer and issue all plans on a guaranteed-issue basis. No small employer carrier or agent shall, directly or indirectly, engage in the following activities:

- Encouraging or directing small employers to refrain from filing an application for coverage with the small employer carrier because of the health status, claims experience, industry, occupation, or geographic location of the small employer

- Encouraging or directing small employers to seek coverage from another carrier because of the health status, claims experience, industry, occupation, or geographic location of the small employer

- These provisions do not apply with respect to information provided by a small employer carrier or agent to a small employer regarding the established geographic service area or a restricted network provision of a small employer carrier.

No small employer carrier may, directly or indirectly, enter into any contract, agreement, or arrangement with an agent that provides for or results in the compensation paid to an agent for the sale of a health benefit plan to be varied because of the health status, claims experience, industry, occupation, or geographic location of the small employer except if the compensation arrangement provides compensation to an agent on the basis of percentage of premium. The percentage shall not vary because of the health status, claims experience, industry, occupation, or geographic area of the small employer.

No small employer carrier shall terminate, fail to renew, or limit its contract or agreement of representation with an agent for any reason related to the health status, claims experience, occupation, or geographic location of the small employers placed by the agent with the small employer carrier unless the agent consistently engages in unfair marketing practices.

No small employer carrier or agent shall induce or otherwise encourage a small employer to separate or otherwise exclude an employee from health coverage or benefits provided in connection with the employee's employment.

Denial by a small employer carrier of an application for coverage from a small employer shall be in writing and shall state the reason or reasons for the denial.

Benefit plans offered

A small employer carrier must file with the office a standard health care plan, a high-deductible plan that meets the federal requirements of a health savings account plan or a health reimbursement arrangement, and a basic health care plan to be used by the carrier. The small employer carrier may not use any policy, contract, form, or rate under this section, including applications, enrollment forms, policies, contracts, certificates, evidences of coverage, riders, amendments, endorsements, and disclosure forms, until the insurer has filed it with the office and the office has approved it.

Standard, basic, high-deductible, and limited health benefit plans. The Chief Financial Officer appoints a health benefit plan committee composed of four representatives of carriers that includes at least two representatives of HMOs, two representatives of agents, four representatives of small employers, and one employee of a small employer. The plans will comply with all of the requirements of this subsection and must be filed with and approved by the office to issuance or delivery by any small employer carrier.

Each small employer carrier issuing new health benefit shall offer to any small employer, upon request, a standard health benefit plan, a basic health benefit plan, and a high-deductible plan. A small employer carrier may include the following managed care provisions in the policy or contract to control costs:

- A preferred provider arrangement or exclusive provider organization or any combination thereof

- A procedure for utilization review by the small employer carrier or its designees

- Policy or contract managed care and cost containment provisions that have potential for controlling costs in a manner that do not result in inequitable treatment of insureds or subscribers (the carrier may use such provisions to the same extent as authorized for group products that are not issued to small employers)

The standard health benefit plan must include:

- coverage for inpatient hospitalization;

- coverage for outpatient services;

- coverage for newborn children;

- coverage for child care supervision services pursuant as required by Florida law;

- coverage for adopted children upon placement in the residence;

- coverage for mammograms;

- coverage for handicapped children;

- emergency or urgent care out of the geographic service area; and

- coverage for services provided by a hospice in cases where such coverage would be the most appropriate and the most cost-effective method for treating a covered illness.

The standard health benefit plan and the basic health benefit plan may include a schedule of benefit limitations for specified services and procedures. The basic health benefit plan must include all of the benefits specified previously; however, the basic health benefit plan places additional restrictions on the benefits and utilization and may also impose additional cost containment measures.

The high-deductible plan associated with a health savings account or a health reimbursement arrangement must include all the benefits specified previously.

If a small employer rejects, in writing, the standard health benefit plan, the basic health benefit plan, and the high-deductible health savings account plan or a health reimbursement arrangement, the small employer carrier may offer the small employer a limited benefit policy or contract.

Upon offering coverage under a standard health benefit plan, a basic health benefit plan, or a limited benefit policy or contract for a small employer group, the small employer carrier shall provide such employer group with a written statement that contains, at a minimum:

- an explanation of those mandated benefits and providers that are not covered by the policy or contract;

- an explanation of the managed care and cost control features of the policy or contract, along with all appropriate mailing addresses and telephone numbers to be used by insureds in seeking information or authorization; and

- an explanation of the primary and preventive care features of the policy or contract.

Before a small employer carrier issues a standard health benefit plan, a basic health benefit plan, or a limited benefit policy or contract, the carrier must obtain from the prospective policyholder a signed written statement in which the prospective policyholder:

- certifies as to eligibility for coverage under the standard health benefit plan, basic health benefit plan, or limited benefit policy or contract;

- acknowledges the limited nature of the coverage and an understanding of the managed care and cost control features of the policy or contract;

- acknowledges that if misrepresentations are made regarding eligibility for coverage under a standard health benefit plan, a basic health benefit plan, or a limited benefit policy or contract, the person making such misrepresentations forfeits coverage provided by the policy or contract; and

■   if a limited plan is requested, acknowledges that the prospective policyholder had been offered, at the time of application for the insurance policy or contract, the opportunity to purchase any health benefit plan offered by the carrier and that the prospective policyholder rejected that coverage.

A copy of such written statement must be provided to the prospective policyholder by the time of delivery of the policy or contract, and the original of such written statement must be retained in the files of the small employer carrier for the period of time that the policy or contract remains in effect or for five years, whichever is longer.

Small Employer Rating, Renewability, and Portability Act

The commission may establish regulations to ensure that rating practices used by small employer carriers are consistent with the purpose of this section, including assuring that differences in rates charged for health benefit plans are reasonable.

Small employer carriers must use a modified community rating methodology in which the premium for each small employer is determined solely on the basis of the eligible employee's and eligible dependent's gender, age, family composition, tobacco use, or geographic area. A small employer carrier is not required to use gender as a rating factor for a nongrandfathered health plan. Rating factors related to age, gender, family composition, tobacco use, or geographic location may be developed by each carrier to reflect the carrier's experience. The factors used by carriers are subject to office review and approval.

Small employer carriers may not modify the rate for a small employer for 12 months from the initial issue date or renewal date, unless the composition of the group changes or benefits are changed. Any adjustments in rates for claims experience, health status, or duration of coverage may not be charged to individual employees or dependents. Any adjustment must be applied uniformly to the rates charged for all employees and dependents of the small employer. For a small employer's policy, adjustments may not result in a rate for the small employer that deviates more than 15% from the carrier's approved rate. A small employer carrier may make an adjustment to a small employer's renewal premium, up to 10% annually, due to the claims experience, health status, or duration of coverage of the employees or dependents of the small employer.

A carrier may issue a group health insurance policy to a small employer health alliance or other group association with rates that reflect a premium credit for expense savings attributable to administrative activities being performed by the alliance or group association if such expense savings are specifically documented in the insurer's rate filing and are approved by the office.

A health benefit plan that is subject to this section is renewable for all eligible employees and dependents.

Guaranteed issue

Beginning January 1, 1993, every small employer carrier issuing new health benefit plans to small employers in Florida must, as a condition of transacting business in this state, offer all small employer health benefit plans on a guaranteed-issue basis to every eligible small employer with 2 to 50 eligible employees a standard health benefit plan and a basic health benefit plan. Such a small employer carrier must issue a standard health benefit plan or a basic health benefit plan to every eligible small employer that elects to be covered under such plan, agrees to make the required premium payments under such plan, and to satisfy the other provisions of the plan.

Small employer access program

The 2004 legislature determined that increased access to health care coverage for small employers with up to 25 employees could improve employees' health and reduce the incidence of costs of illness and disabilities among residents of Florida. As a result, the legislature created the Small Employers Access Program, which includes the creation of the Small Business Health Plan. This plan is intended to provide small employers the option and ability to provide health care benefits to their employees through the creation of purchasing pools. These pools may consist not only of employers with up to 25 employees but any municipality, county, school district, or hospital employer located in rural areas, as well as any nursing home employer regardless of the number of employees. Insurers wishing to provide such coverage must be selected by the Office of Insurance Regulation through a competitive bidding process and must offer basic, standard, and high-deductible plans. Selected insurers must maintain public awareness programs, encourage the effective use of health saving accounts, and demonstrate the ability to deliver cost-effective health care services.

FLORIDA HEALTHY KIDS CORPORATION

In an effort to help improve access to comprehensive health insurance for Florida's uninsured children, the state legislature established the Florida Healthy Kids Corporation as a combined public and private venture in 1990. Participation in the program is on a voluntary basis. Through the corporation, uninsured children can obtain affordable health care coverage. The program serves as a source of funds by collecting local, state, federal, and family money to pay premiums to commercial health insurers who underwrite the risk. In this manner, families who would otherwise be unable to afford the desired coverage can obtain it while paying only a portion of the premium. Coverage can insure services ranging from preventive care to major surgery.

The Florida Healthy Kids Corporation is one of several providers of services to children eligible for medical assistance under Title XXI of the Social Security Act. Although the corporation may serve other children, the primary recipients of services provided through the corporation are school-age children with a family income below 200% of the federal poverty level, who do not qualify for Medicaid. [Sec. 624.91]

REQUIREMENTS RELATED TO HIV/AIDS

HIV testing; AIDS exclusion clauses

Prior to testing for HIV/ AIDS, the insurer must disclose its intent to test the person for HIV and must obtain the person's written informed consent to administer the test. The written informed consent must include an explanation of the test, including its purpose, potential uses, and limitations, and the meaning of its results and the right to confidential treatment of information. An applicant shall be notified of a positive test result by a physician designated by the applicant or, in the absence of such designation, by the Department of Health.

An insurer may inquire whether a person has been tested positive for exposure to the HIV infection or been diagnosed as having ARC or AIDS caused by the HIV infection or other sickness or conditions derived from such infection. Sexual orientation may not be used in the underwriting process or in the determination of which applicants may be tested for exposure to the HIV infection. The marital status, living arrangements, occupation, gender, beneficiary designation, or ZIP code or other territorial classification of an applicant may not be used to establish the applicant's sexual orientation.

Insurers shall maintain strict confidentiality regarding medical test results with respect to exposure to the HIV infection or a specific sickness or medical condition derived from such exposure. The insurer may not disclose information regarding specific test results outside of the insurance company or its employees, insurance affiliates, agents, or reinsurers, except to the person tested and to persons designated in writing by the person tested. The insurer may not furnish specific test results for exposure to the HIV infection to an insurer industry data bank if a review of the information would identify the individual and the specific test results. [Sec. 627.429]

Restrictions on coverage exclusions and limitations

Subject to the total benefits limits in a health insurance policy, no health insurance policy may contain an exclusion or limitation with respect to coverage for exposure to the HIV infection or a specific sickness or medical condition derived from such infection, except as provided in a preexisting condition clause.

Benefits under a life insurance policy may not be denied or limited based on the fact that the insured's death was caused, directly or indirectly, by exposure to the HIV infection or a specific sickness or medical condition derived from such infection.

Prohibited cancellation for HIV or AIDS

No insurer shall cancel or nonrenew the health insurance policy of any insured because of diagnosis or treatment of HIV or AIDS. [627.6265, .6646]

PLAN TYPES

Health maintenance organization (HMO)

A health maintenance organization is a health care delivery system that provides comprehensive health care services for its members. The members are typically enrolled on a group basis by their employer. The employer pays a fixed periodic contribution in advance for the services of participating physicians and cooperating hospitals. The employee may also contribute to the prepayment in some groups. A major difference is that the HMO provides medical service while emphasizing preventive medicine and early treatment through routine physical examinations and diagnostic screening techniques. At the same time, the HMOs also provide complete hospital and medical care for sickness and injury.

Traditional health insurance plans are designed to provide reimbursement for medical costs incurred in the treatment of sickness or injury. These plans emphasize curative rather than preventive medicine and contribute toward the cost of medical services rather than delivering the service.

Preferred provider organization (PPO)

Following the passage of legislation in 1983, insurance companies were authorized to enter into "alternative rates of payment" agreements with licensed health care providers. Those entering into the agreements are called preferred provider organizations (PPOs). The concept is that if one provider or a group of providers has a large volume of business from a group of insureds, it can afford to give them health care at lower guaranteed costs. This savings in health care costs can then be used to prevent health insurance premiums from increasing for that particular group of insureds. If a patient uses a provider within the network, the provider will get paid for the services directly from the insurer. The PPO provider is prohibited from charging any additional amount to the patient above what the provider is paid from the insurer, except for the coinsurance amount that is based on the network discounted fee that the provider agreed to accept. If the patient uses an out-of-network provider, the insurer must also pay the provider directly for the services, but in this case, the provider can charge the patient any difference between what is paid by the insurer and the amount the provider charges for services. [Sec. 627.6471, F.S.]

Exclusive provider organization (EPO)

An EPO, or exclusive provider organization, is a type of entity authorized by the 1992 Legislature. It is a provider that has entered into a written agreement with a health insurance company to provide health care services for certain insureds. It can offer these services through its own facilities or a network of health care professionals, or it may use another facility, such as an HMO. The agreement provides reasonable access to these services in the service area. Strict criteria are established under law, and EPO agreements must be approved, inspected, and monitored by the office. Because these are actually health insurance policies, they may only be written by licensed health insurance agents appointed to represent the insurer. [Sec. 627.6472, F.S.]

Multiple employer welfare arrangement (MEWA)

A MEWA is a type of MET. It consists of small employers who have joined to provide health benefits for their employees, often on a self-insured basis. They are tax-exempt entities. Employees covered by a MEWA are required by law to have an employment-related common bond.

Prepaid limited health service organization (PLHSO)

A PLHSO is any person, corporation, partnership, or any other entity that, in return for a prepayment, undertakes to provide or arrange for, or provide access to, the provision of a limited health service to enrollees through an exclusive panel of providers for the following services:

Ambulance services	Substance abuse services
Dental care services	Chiropractic services
Vision care services	Podiatric care services
Mental health services	Pharmaceutical services

Indemnity plan

A hospital indemnity or fixed-rate policy simply provides a daily, weekly, or monthly payment of a specified amount based on the number of days the insured is hospitalized. For example, such a plan may provide the insured $100 a day for every day he is confined in a hospital. This insurance has been available for many years but has been promoted more heavily in recent years largely due to skyrocketing health care costs. Many companies can offer high benefit fixed-rate plans at reasonable premiums because underwriting and administration are greatly simplified and claim costs are not affected by increases in medical costs. Benefits may run as high as $4,500 per month, based on a daily hospital confinement benefit of $150, and some are even higher. Maximum benefit periods range from about six months to several years or up to a lifetime. Benefits are payable directly to the insureds and may be used for any purpose. Hospital fixed-rate policies usually are exempt from most state laws that apply to specific kinds of insurance contracts.

Discount medical plan

A discount medical plan is an arrangement or contract in which a person, in exchange for fees or other consideration, provides access for plan members to the services of medical service providers at a discount. Although organizations offering such plans must be licensed by the Office of Insurance Regulation, such plans are not considered insurance. Such organizations may not use in their advertisements the terms "health plan," "coverage," "co-pay," "preexisting conditions," "guaranteed issue," "premium," and certain other terms typically associated with insurance products. Marketers of such plans are not required to be licensed as insurance agents. [Secs. 636.202, .204, .210, F.S.]

DREAD DISEASE POLICY

Policies that provide medical expense coverage for specific kinds of illnesses are known as **limited risk**, **dread disease**, or **critical illness** policies. They are available primarily due to the high costs associated with certain illnesses, such as cancer or heart disease. Such policies will frequently pay a single, lump-sum amount to help defray medical costs associated with a specific medical diagnosis. Limited risk policies that cover specified accidents are also available.

KEY CONCEPTS

Students should be familiar with the following concepts:

grandfathered plans	community health purchasing
free-look privilege	Medicare supplements
required coverages	required contract provisions
preexisting conditions	HMOs
Florida Employer Health Care Access Act	EPOs
Florida Health Insurance Coverage Continuation Act	PLHSOs
guarantee-issue basis	group health insurance
small employer	long-term care
portability	

UNIT TEST

1. Legal action may not be taken after how many years from filing a health insurance claim proof of loss?

   A. One year
   B. Four years
   C. Five years
   D. Two years

2. Which of the following applies to the 10-day free-look privilege in a health insurance contract?

   A. It permits the insured to reject the policy within 10 days of policy delivery and receive a full refund.
   B. It allows the insured an additional 10 days to pay the initial premium.
   C. It can be waived only by the insurance company.
   D. It is granted only at the option of the agent.

3. All of the following statements about the Outline of Coverage for health insurance policies are correct EXCEPT

   A. it must be provided at time of application or delivery of policy
   B. principal benefits also shown in the policy need not be included
   C. it is to include a summary statement of principal exclusions
   D. it must include any right the insurer reserves to change premiums

4. If a health insurance company tests a person for AIDS/HIV which of the following must be signed?

   A. notice of informed consent
   B. AIDS/HIV rate disclosure form
   C. AIDS/HIV underwriting disclosure form
   D. outline of coverage

5. All of the following provisions are required by Florida law for group health insurance policies EXCEPT

   A. coverage for mental and nervous disorders must be available to the group policyholder
   B. a newborn child is to be provided coverage from the moment of birth
   C. coverage must continue until age 25 for a handicapped child that is a family member
   D. a newborn child of a covered family member is to be provided coverage for 18 months

6. All of the following statements regarding group health insurance are correct EXCEPT

   A. coordination of benefits is required between group policies and Medicare supplements
   B. coordination of benefits helps to reduce costs
   C. duplication of benefits results in overpayment
   D. coordination of benefits is permitted so long as the insured is completely reimbursed for covered expenses

7. Which of the following statements is CORRECT about a group health insurance policy?

   A. It cannot exclude coverage from an occupational accident.
   B. It can exclude newborn children from coverage.
   C. It cannot exclude coverage for VA hospital treatment.
   D. It can provide coverage for handicapped children.

8. In which of the following situations is a group health insurance policy NOT required to provide coverage?

   A. Qualified services performed in an ambulatory surgical center
   B. Outpatient services that would have been paid if rendered for an inpatient
   C. Specified services by a licensed podiatrist
   D. Treatment for an occupational illness or injury

9. All of the following are correct about the required provisions of a health insurance policy EXCEPT

   A. a grace period of 31 days is found in an annual pay policy
   B. the entire contract clause means the policy, endorsements, and attachments constitute the entire contract
   C. a reinstated policy provides immediate coverage for an illness
   D. proof-of-loss forms must be sent to the insured within 15 days of notice of claim

10. The notice to the insurance company of a health insurance claim must include

    A. estimated amount of claim
    B. name of the insured
    C. nature of sickness or injury
    D. date of loss

11. A health insurance proof-of-loss form must be given to the insurer within how many days after a loss?

    A. Immediately
    B. 20 days
    C. 90 days
    D. 15 days

12. At what point in time can a policyholder file suit against a health insurance company for failure to pay a claim?

    A. 60 days from date of loss
    B. 120 days from date of loss
    C. 60 days after filing proof of loss
    D. 120 days after filing proof of loss

13. If a health insurance policyowner changes jobs to a more hazardous occupation, which of the following could apply?

    A. Benefits could be increased if the policy so provides.
    B. Premiums would be increased and collected from date of change to more hazardous occupation.
    C. Premiums would be decreased and refunded from date of change to more hazardous occupation.
    D. Benefits could be reduced if the policy so provides.

14. A health maintenance organization provides which of the following?

    A. Free health care for Medicare patients
    B. Preventive health care for its members
    C. A program of "pay as you go" medicine
    D. An extension of VA hospital treatment for veterans

15. A grandfathered health plan means a health plan that was issued on or prior to

    A. March 23, 2011
    B. March 23, 2013
    C. March 23, 2012
    D. March 23, 2010

16. A group credit disability policy may be issued to a creditor if the expected new entrants into the plan

    A. are more than 25
    B. are at least 100 persons yearly
    C. are about the same each year
    D. are subject to insurability

17. Florida's "mini-COBRA" applies to employers with?

    A. five or more employees
    B. 20 or more employees
    C. less than 20 employees
    D. less than five employees

18. All of the following provisions are required by the Florida Employee Health Care Access Act EXCEPT

    A. coverage must always be renewed by carriers
    B. carriers must use a "modified community rating" methodology
    C. all small group health benefit plans must be issued on a "guarantee-issue" basis
    D. small employer means an employer with 1–50 employees

19. Which of the following statements is CORRECT about coverage for a handicapped family member who reaches adulthood?

    A. Coverage ceases for the family member at the limiting age in the policy.
    B. Coverage continues if the member is chiefly dependent on the policyholder.
    C. Group health policies must continue coverage, unlike individual policies.
    D. Coverage automatically ceases when the family member obtains employment.

20. Group health insurance policies are required to provide all of the following EXCEPT

    A. coverage for hospitalization during disability
    B. coverage for a newborn child of a family member
    C. coverage for a newborn child from the moment of birth
    D. coverage for dental expenses

21. Individual and group health insurance policies and HMO contracts can be canceled for all of the following reasons EXCEPT

    A. failure to pay premiums
    B. the insured develops a serious illness
    C. the insurer ceases to offer coverage in the market
    D. fraud or intentional misrepresentation of a material fact

22. Florida's Long-Term Care Partnership Program provides which of the following?

    A. Asset protection
    B. Medicare coverage
    C. Inpatient hospital treatment
    D. Medicaid medical expense coverage

23. Which of the following practitioners is NOT defined as a "physician" under Florida law?

    A. Surgeon in an ambulatory surgical center
    B. Dentist performing surgery in an office
    C. Optometrist rendering services at an eye clinic
    D. Sports therapist performing services in a health club

24. All of the following provisions are mandatory in health insurance policies EXCEPT

    A. time limit on certain defenses
    B. grace period
    C. change of occupation
    D. time of claims payment

25. Florida's Long-Term Care Partnership Program must provide which of the following coverage?

    A. Medical expense coverage
    B. Disability coverage
    C. Inflation coverage
    D. Outpatient hospital treatment

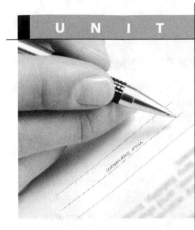

30

Florida Laws and Rules Pertinent to Health Maintenance Organizations

■ Purpose of Health Maintenance Organizations

■ How an HMO Operates

■ Definitions

■ Regulation and Licensing

■ Marketing Practices

■ Required Benefits

One of the biggest problems facing our state and our nation today is to furnish quality health care to our citizens while trying to control spiraling costs. The development of health maintenance organizations, or HMOs as they are commonly called, is one method of addressing this challenge. In Unit 16, we gave a brief overview of HMOs. Here, we will look more closely at these organizations in the context of Florida statutes and the rules and regulations of the Office of Insurance Regulation. ■

PURPOSE OF HEALTH MAINTENANCE ORGANIZATIONS

The reason for the existence of HMOs is clearly expressed in the legislative intent section of the enabling legislation known as the Health Maintenance Organization Act, Florida Statute 641.18. It states:

> *Faced with the continuation of mounting costs of health care coupled with the state's interest in high quality care, the Legislature has determined that there is a need to explore alternative methods for the delivery of health care services, with a view toward achieving greater efficiency and economy in providing these services.*

To paraphrase the language of the act, the policy of the state of Florida is to eliminate legal barriers to the promotion and expansion of comprehensive prepaid health plans and to ensure that these comprehensive plans deliver high quality health care without impeding the present health care delivery system in the state. [Sec. 641.18, F.S.]

Comprehensive Health Care

According to Florida law, **comprehensive health care services** means "services, medical equipment and supplies furnished by a provider, which may include, but are not limited to:

- medical, surgical, and dental care;

- psychological, optometric, optical, chiropractic, podiatric, nursing, physical therapy and pharmaceutical services;

- health education, preventive medical, rehabilitative and home health services;

- inpatient and outpatient hospital services;

- extended care, nursing home care and convalescent institutional care;

- technical and professional clinical pathology laboratory services;

- laboratory and ambulance services;

- appliances, drugs, medicines and supplies; and

- any other care, service or treatment of disease or correction of defects for human beings." [Sec. 641.19(4), F.S.]

History of HMOs in Florida

The original act empowering providers to form health maintenance organizations was passed in 1972. Shortly thereafter, the first Florida HMO was licensed. Appropriately enough, the first certificate of authority was issued to an organization founded by a Cuban family that had fled to Miami from Communist Cuba. Prepaid health care through a clinic arrangement had been popular in Cuba prior to the Castro regime, and the large Hispanic population in the Miami area was a natural market for the HMO concept.

At the same time, a group of physicians in Volusia county had their HMO plan approved and licensed. From these beginnings, the HMO movement has grown to its present status.

HOW AN HMO OPERATES

At the present time, HMOs operate almost exclusively through the **group enrollment system**. Each member of the group pays a premium—a fixed sum per month—whether or not the person uses the services of the HMO. By having the services prepaid, the individual is encouraged to see a doctor early so that preventive measures may be taken. By encouraging preventive medicine, it is expected that the general health of all HMO subscribers will benefit from early detection and treatment. Furthermore, many of the costly procedures that become necessary when a condition is discovered too late to cure easily can be avoided.

In contrast to the traditional fee-for-service method of health care delivery, HMOs offer savings based on early prevention and detection, volume discount arrangements with hospitals and providers, and agreements with physicians and other health care professionals to provide service on a prearranged per capita basis.

DEFINITIONS

Health maintenance contract is the term used to delineate the arrangement between the subscriber or group of subscribers and the HMO. It sets forth the services to be provided and the fixed fee or premium to be paid. It is the equivalent of **the policy** in traditional health care terminology. [Sec. 641.19(11), F.S.]

Insolvency means that all the assets of the HMO, if made immediately available, would not be enough to discharge all of its liabilities; the HMO is unable to pay its debts as they occur in the ordinary course of business. [Sec. 641.19(13), F.S.]

Provider is any physician, hospital, organization, or other person or institution that furnishes health care services and is licensed or otherwise authorized to practice in Florida. [Sec. 641.19(14), F.S.]

Subscriber is the person or entity who has a health maintenance contract with the HMO, pays the fee, and uses the services of the HMO. [Sec. 641.19(18), F.S.]

Capitation is the fixed amount paid by the HMO to a health care physician or provider in exchange for the medical services rendered by that provider. [Sec. 641.19(3), F.S.]

Co-payment is the specified dollar amount that the HMO subscriber must pay for certain covered health care services. These amounts are typically small and must be approved by the Office of Insurance Regulation. [Sec. 641.19(5), F.S.]

A **prepaid health clinic** is an organization that delivers basic medical services at a specified location for the members of a group who make regular premium payments in exchange for those services. They differ from HMOs in that the requirements, both financial and otherwise, are much less stringent and they are limited only to the delivery of basic health services.

Basic health services are defined under the law as being restricted to "emergency care, physician care other than hospital inpatient physician services, ambulatory diagnostic treatment, and preventive health care services."

Prepaid health clinics may not use the word "HMO" or any derivative thereof, or any term such as "insurance," "surety," "mutual," or "casualty" and should not be confused with an HMO that delivers the full range of services.

Prepaid health clinics are supervised by the Office of Insurance Regulation and are subject to many of the same reporting requirements and rules of conduct applicable to insurers and HMOs. [Secs. 641.402, .403, .405, .408, .41, .437, F.S.]

REGULATION AND LICENSING

An HMO can offer not offer insurance. An HMO can offer only HMO contracts approved by the Office of Insurance Regulation and cannot engage in any other type of activity, including insurance. However, an insurance company or service corporation can own or sponsor an HMO. [Secs. 641.2017, .21, .234, .31, F.S.]

An HMO must obtain a Certificate of Authority from the Office of Insurance Regulation. The office will not issue a certificate unless the HMO first receives a valid Health Care Provider Certificate from the Agency for Health Care Administration of Florida and has met the other requirements set forth in Florida statutes. These requirements include capital and surplus minimums, rate filings, contract and forms submissions, bylaws, marketing procedures, experience, and a host of other criteria established by the Legislature. Before final approval, the HMO must also pay all required fees, make a deposit of $10,000 to the Rehabilitation Administration Expense Fund and become a member of the Florida Health Maintenance Organization Consumer Assistance Plan (CAP). [Secs. 641.21, .22, .225, .227, .228, F.S.]

Each HMO is required to file a report of its activities within three months of the end of each fiscal year. The office may require reports more frequently if it is deemed necessary. In addition, the office can and does conduct on-site visits. A complete examination of all of an HMO's affairs is conducted at least every five years. In this way, the office can monitor every HMO and require any organization to take corrective action if it is deemed necessary to protect the interests of Florida consumers. [Secs. 641.26, .27, F.S.]

MARKETING PRACTICES

With respect to an HMO contract, no person, unless licensed and appointed as a health insurance agent, may:

- solicit contracts or procure applications; or

- engage or hold himself as engaging in the business of analyzing or abstracting health maintenance organization contracts, unless he is an actuary or a full-time employee giving advice to an employer regarding such contracts. [Sec. 641.386, F.S.]

HMO contracts may be sold only by a licensed and appointed health insurance agent or a full-time salaried employee or officer of an HMO who devotes most of her services to activities other than soliciting HMO contracts from the public and who receives no commission or compensation for procuring such contracts. [Sec. 641.386, F.S.]

Unfair trade practices

Similar to insurance laws and regulations the following are defined as HMO unfair trade practices:

- Misrepresentation and false advertising of HMO contracts

- False information and false advertising in general

- Defamation

- False statements and entries

- Unfair claim settlement practices

- Failure to maintain claim handling procedures

- Operating without a subsisting certificate of authority

- Misrepresentations in HMO applications

- Twisting

- Illegal dealing in premiums

- False claims; obtaining money dishonestly

- Prohibited discriminatory practices

- Misrepresentation in availability of providers

- Adverse action against a provider [Sec. 641.3903, F.S.]

- Rebating (An HMO issuing group or individual health benefit plans may offer rewards and incentives for participation in a voluntary wellness or health improvement program.) [Sec 641.9303, F.S.]

Defamation is making any oral or written statement or any pamphlet, circular, article, or literature that is false or maliciously critical of any person and that is calculated to injure such person. [Sec. 641.3903(3), F.S.]

Misrepresentation is knowingly making a false or fraudulent representation on or relative to an application for an HMO contract, for the purpose of obtaining a fee, commission, money, or other benefit from any HMO, agent or representative, broker, or individual. [Sec. 641.3903(8), F.S.]

Twisting is knowingly making any misleading representations or incomplete or fraudulent comparisons of any HMO contract or HMO organization or any insurance policy or insurer for the purpose of inducing any person to lapse, forfeit, terminate, surrender, retain, or convert any insurance policy or HMO contract or to purchase an insurance policy or HMO contract with another insurance company or HMO. [Sec. 641.3903(9), F.S.]

The penalty for violating the Unfair Trade Practices Act may include probation, or suspension or revocation of license or the HMO Certificate of Authority. The maximum fine is up to $200,000. If the violation is determined to be criminal, it can result in imprisonment. [Secs. 624.15, 641.3909, .3913, 775.082, F.S.]

Special procedures for Medicare beneficaries

There are special laws pertaining to the role of HMO contracts to this class of citizens. The HMO must establish marketing procedures that assure that any comparisons between Medicare and its HMO contract or any other HMO contract are fair and accurate.

Subscribers must be told that when they enroll in an HMO, they are disenrolled from Medicare. The following notice must be printed, typed, or stamped on the first page of the application and on the contract:

> **Notice to Buyer**: *When you enroll in this HMO, you will be disenrolled from Medicare. The buyer should be aware that in order to receive payment or coverage for services, such services must be rendered by physicians, hospitals and other health care providers designated by the HMO. If the services are rendered by a nonparticipating physician, hospital or other health care provider, the purchaser may be liable for payment for such services except in very limited circumstances.*

The agent must inquire if the prospective Medicare participant has previously been enrolled in the same or any other HMO as a Medicare participant. The agent can not use fraud, deceit, force, fright, threat (whether implied or explicit), intimidation, harassment, or undue pressure in the sales process.

Further, the 1992 Legislature passed a law that requires the agent to ask each person solicited if he is covered under a health insurance policy, continuing care, or health maintenance contract or a Medicare supplement insurance policy. The agent must then explain the extent to which the proposed coverage will overlap or duplicate the existing coverage. The office may require agents to have appropriate forms signed when the application is taken or before it is processed and to retain such forms in the agent's file. [Secs. 626.8373, 641.309, F.S.]

HMO Consumer Assistance Plan (CAP)

CAP was established to protect the subscribers of HMOs against the failure of the HMO to perform its contractual obligations due to its insolvency. The law specifically prohibits the use of the CAP in any way in the sale of an HMO contract, even if it is for the purpose of reassuring the prospect. [Sec. 631.827, F.S.]

REQUIRED BENEFITS

HMO Contract

The HMO contract, certificate, or member's handbook must be delivered within 10 working days after approval of the enrollment by the HMO. The contract must contain all of the provisions and disclosures required by law. [Sec. 641.31, 641.3107, F.S.]

- The rates charged shall not be excessive, inadequate, or unfairly discriminatory, as determined by the Office of Insurance Regulation. The rate of payment must be clearly stated. For plan year 2015, rates charged must also be approved by HHS.

- The contract must not exclude coverage for HIV infection or contain limitations on HIV or AIDS coverage that are different from those that apply to any other sickness or medical condition.

- It must not exclude or limit benefits because the subscriber has been diagnosed as having a fibrocystic condition, unless the condition is diagnosed through a breast biopsy that demonstrates an increased disposition to developing breast cancer.

- It must clearly state all services covered by the contract and any limitations placed on these services.

- A statement outlining procedures to be followed for emergency treatment outside the HMO's geographic area must be included.

- Special provisions pertaining to disenrollment and reenrollment in Medicare, if applicable, must be noted.

- A grace period of not less than 10 days must be expressly included.

- Any restrictions regarding preexisting conditions must be noted.

- A statement delineating immediate coverage for newborn children must be included.

- Each contract providing family coverage must cover adopted children.

- Preexisting conditions in children may not be excluded.

- If maternity services are included, they must allow the options of nurse-midwives, midwives, or birth centers, if located within the service area.

- Ocular services, if provided, may be furnished by an ophthalmologist, or optometrist, if within the scope of her license.

- Anesthesia may be performed by a medical doctor or by a nurse-anesthetist.

- A statement of time limit on certain defense clause must be included. It must provide that after a period of two years, only fraudulent statements may be used to void a contract or deny payment for a claim. (See also Unit 29 on the Florida Employee Health Care Access Act.)

The contract, certificate, or member handbook must be accompanied by an identification card that contains, at a minimum, the following:

- The name of the organization offering or administering the contract

- The name of the subscriber

- A statement that the health plan is a health maintenance organization

- The member identification number, contract number, and group number

- A contact phone number or email address for authorizations and admission certifications

- A phone number or address that can be used by hospitals, physicians, or any other person rendering services to obtain benefits verification to estimate patient financial responsibility

- The national plan identifier

Extension of benefits

Every HMO contract must provide an **extension of benefits** that if the HMO terminates the contract, it will be without prejudice to any continuous loss that commenced while the contract was in force. This applies until the earliest of the following:

- 12 months have expired

- The member is no longer totally disabled

- Another carrier assumes coverage

- Maximum benefits under the contract have been paid [Sec. 641.3111, F.S.]

Open enrollment

The law requires that each HMO that offers a group plan within Florida must have an open enrollment period of not less than 30 days during every 18-month period. During that time, each eligible group member may enroll regardless of health history. [Sec. 641.31(22), F.S.]

Conversion of HMO contracts

If a subscriber has been enrolled for at least three months prior to termination of a group HMO plan, he is entitled to a **converted contract**. This applies to termination for any reason, except the following:

- Failure to pay premiums

- Fraud in applying for benefits

- Replacement by similar coverage within 30 days

- Disenrollment for cause (disruptive, unruly, abusive, or uncooperative)

- Willful and knowing misuse of the HMO ID membership card by a subscriber

- Willful and knowing furnishing to the organization by the subscriber of incorrect or incomplete information for the purpose of fraudulently obtaining coverage or benefits

- The subscriber has left the geographic area of the HMO with the intent to relocate or establish a new residence outside the HMO's geographic area [Sec. 641.3921(5), (6), (7), F.S.]

Direct access to dermatologists

HMOs and EPOs must give subscribers/members direct access to dermatologists under contract with the HMO or EPO for office visits, minor procedures, and testing without the need for the subscriber/member to go through a primary care physician. Direct access is the ability of an insured to obtain such services without a referral or other authorization before receiving services. The number of visits to a dermatologist without prior authorization may be limited to five office visits within a 12-month period. [Secs. 627.6472, 641.31, F.S.]

Newborn child coverage

Contracts that provide coverage for a family member of the insured must also provide that the health insurance benefits for children will be payable for a newborn child of the insured from the moment of birth.

The law also requires that coverage be provided for a newborn child of a covered family member (e.g., the newborn of a covered daughter or son) for a period of 18 months. [Sec. 641.31(9), F.S.]

HMO claim payments to providers

An HMO must pay benefits directly to any contracted hospital, ambulance provider, physician, or dentist to which a subscriber has specifically authorized benefits if any benefits are due to the subscriber under her contract with the HMO. An HMO cannot prohibit direct payment of benefits to a licensed hospital, ambulance provider, physician, or dentist for emergency services provided. A subscriber can submit the attestation of assignment of benefits in writing or electronic form.

The HMO has 12 months after payment of a claim to submit a claim for overpayment to the provider. Likewise, a provider has 12 months after payment of a claim by an HMO to submit a claim for underpayment.

Florida Statute requires a health maintenance organization (HMO) to reimburse all claims or any portion of any claim made by a contract provider for services or goods provided under a contract with the HMO within 20 days after the receipt of the claim by the HMO, unless the HMO contests or denies the claim. If the claim or a portion of a claim is contested by the HMO, the HMO is required to formally notify the contract provider within 20 days after receipt of the claim. Such notification must identify the contested portion of the claim and the specific reason for contesting or denying the claim, and may include a request for additional information.

If the HMO requests additional information, the provider must provide the information within 35 days of the receipt of such request. Upon receipt of the additional information requested from the contract provider, the HMO must pay or deny the contested claim or portion of the contested claim within 90 days after receipt of the claim. In any event, an insurer must pay or deny any claim no later than 120 days after receiving the claim. [Sec. 641.3155, F.S.]

KEY CONCEPTS

Students should be familiar with the following concepts:

health maintenance organization	unfair claim settlement practice
health maintenance contract	twisting
provider	HMO Consumer Assistance Plan
subscriber	extension of benefits
defamation	open enrollment

UNIT TEST

1. HMOs are known for stressing
   - A. preventive care and early intervention
   - B. state-sponsored health plans
   - C. outpatient care and services
   - D. coverage for government employees

2. The Legislature stated that the purpose of HMOs is to do all of the following EXCEPT
   - A. deliver high-quality health care
   - B. provide an alternative method of health care
   - C. replace the existing system of health care delivery
   - D. control the escalating cost of health care

3. Savings of the HMO system are based on all of the following EXCEPT
   - A. keeping the premium high enough to net a profit
   - B. volume discounts with hospitals
   - C. capitation arrangements with physicians
   - D. encouraging members to see their doctors early

4. All of the following are considered unfair trade practices with regard to HMOs EXCEPT
   - A. defamation
   - B. misrepresentation
   - C. conversion
   - D. twisting

5. The written agreement between the subscriber and the HMO is called
   - A. a health care contract
   - B. a health insurance policy
   - C. a health maintenance agreement
   - D. a health maintenance contract

6. The term *capitation* means
   - A. the premium for the HMO coverage
   - B. the amount paid to the physician for each member
   - C. the amount of capital the HMO possesses
   - D. the value of the HMO capital improvements and buildings

7. The term *co-payment* means
   - A. a fixed amount per visit or per service the subscriber must pay
   - B. the amount the HMO pays the subscriber if he secures service outside the service area
   - C. the amount the physician receives from the HMO for each patient treated
   - D. the premium the subscriber pays

8. The Office of Insurance Regulation will NOT issue a Certificate of Authority to an HMO until it has
   - A. 500 prospective members
   - B. deposited capital and surplus in the amount of $1 million
   - C. received a valid Health Care Provider Certificate from the Agency for Health Care Administration of Florida
   - D. been inspected and approved by the Florida Medical Association

9. The Florida HMO Consumer Assistance Plan
   - A. helps low-income families secure HMO coverage
   - B. assists consumers in understanding their HMO coverage
   - C. adjudicates contested claims by subscribers against HMOs
   - D. provides coverage for subscribers to HMOs that become insolvent

10. How often must HMOs file a report of their activities to the Office of Insurance Regulation?
    - A. Every 3 years
    - B. Every 3 months
    - C. Within 3 months after the close of a fiscal year
    - D. At the end of each calendar year

11. Which of the following persons may solicit applications for HMO coverage?
    - A. Licensed health agent
    - B. Consulting actuary
    - C. Company attorney
    - D. Financial adviser

12. In order to sell HMO contracts, an agent must do all of the following EXCEPT

    A. keep and renew her appointment
    B. maintain a bond of not less than $10,000
    C. abide by the Unfair Trade Practices Act
    D. obey all regulations of the Department of Financial Services

13. If an agent signs up an HMO subscriber who is eligible for Medicare

    A. Medicare will pay what the HMO does not
    B. the subscriber is disenrolled from Medicare
    C. the subscriber becomes eligible for Medicaid
    D. the subscriber can decide whether or not to keep both HMO and Medicare coverage

14. What is the grace period for paying premiums on an HMO contract?

    A. There is a 10-day grace period.
    B. There is a 30-day grace period.
    C. There is a 60-day grace period.
    D. There is no grace period for HMO contracts.

15. In what way must the Notice to Buyer be conveyed to an HMO subscriber who is eligible for Medicare?

    A. Printing, typing, or stamping the notice on the first page of the HMO contract
    B. Stamping the notice on the application
    C. Typing the notice on the first page of the application and the contract
    D. Reading the notice to the subscriber and having the subscriber sign an acknowledgment form

16. An HMO contract must contain all of the following EXCEPT

    A. a listing of the surgical schedules by which surgeons are paid
    B. the premium because it is subject to change
    C. the length of the grace period
    D. procedures to be followed for emergencies

17. HMOs offering group coverage must have an open enrollment at least

    A. once a year
    B. for 18 days every 30 months
    C. for 1 month every 3 years
    D. for 30 days every 18 months

18. An individual who buys a membership in a prepaid health clinic because the premium is less than an HMO should be aware that the clinic cannot provide

    A. outpatient service
    B. emergency care
    C. hospitalization
    D. ambulatory diagnostic services

Glossary

A

absolute assignment Policy assignment under which the assignee (person to whom the policy is assigned) receives full control over the policy and also full rights to its benefits. Generally, when a policy is assigned to secure a debt, the owner retains all rights in the policy in excess of the debt, even though the assignment is absolute in form. (See **assignment**) 119

accelerated benefits rider A life insurance rider that allows for the early payment of some portion of the policy's face amount should the insured suffer from a terminal illness or injury. 120

acceptance (See **offer and acceptance**) 34

accidental bodily injury provision Disability income or accident policy provision that requires that the injury be accidental in order for benefits to be payable. 313

accidental death and dismemberment (AD&D) Insurance providing payment if the insured's death results from an accident, if the insured accidentally severs a limb above the wrist or ankle joints, or totally and irreversibly loses eyesight. 321–323

accidental death benefit rider A life insurance policy rider providing for payment of an additional benefit when death occurs by accidental means. 129

accidental dismemberment Often defined as "the severance of limbs at or above the wrists or ankle joints, or the entire irrevocable loss of sight." Loss of use in itself may or not be considered dismemberment. 322

accidental means provision Unforeseen, unexpected, unintended cause of an accident. Requirement of an accident-based policy that the cause of the mishap must be accidental for any claim to be payable. 313

accident and health insurance Insurance under which benefits are payable in case of disease, accidental injury, or accidental death. Also called health insurance, personal health insurance, and sickness and accident insurance. 324

accumulation unit Premiums an annuitant pays into a variable annuity are credited as accumulation units. At the end of the accumulation period, accumulation units are converted to annuity units. 214

acquired immune deficiency syndrome (AIDS) A life-threatening condition brought on by the human immunodeficiency virus; insurers must adhere to strict underwriting and claims guidelines in regard to AIDS risks and AIDS-related conditions. 164, 333

acute illness A serious condition, such as pneumonia, from which the body can fully recover with proper medical attention. 343

adhesion A life insurance policy is a contract of adhesion because buyers must adhere to the terms of the contract already in existence. They have no opportunity to negotiate terms, rates, values, and so on. 36

adjustable life insurance Combines features of both term and whole life coverage with the length of coverage and amount of accumulated cash value as the adjustable factors. Premiums may be increased or decreased to fit the specific needs. Such adjustments are not retroactive and apply only to the future. 99

administrative-services-only (ASO) plan Arrangement under which an insurance company or an independent organization, for a fee, handles the administration of claims, benefits, and other administrative functions for a self-insured group. 290

admitted insurer An insurance company that has met the legal and financial requirements for operation within a given state.

adult day care Type of care (usually custodial) designed for individuals who require assistance with various activities of daily living, while their primary caregivers are absent. Offered in care centers. 348

adverse selection Selection "against the company." Tendency of less favorable insurance risks to seek or continue insurance to a greater extent than others. Also, tendency of policyowners to take advantage of favorable options in insurance contracts. 353, 379, 380

Advertising Code Rules established by the National Association of Insurance Commissioners (NAIC) to regulate insurance advertising. 26

agency Situation wherein one party (an agent) has the power to act for another (the principal) in dealing with third parties. 40

agent Anyone not a duly licensed broker who solicits insurance or aids in placing risks, delivering policies, or collecting premiums on behalf of an insurance company. 40

agent's report The section of an insurance application where the agent reports personal observations about the applicant. 176

aleatory Feature of insurance contracts in that there is an element of chance for both parties and that the dollar given by the policyholder (premiums) and the insurer (benefits) may not be equal. 35

alien insurer Company incorporated or organized under the laws of any foreign nation, providence, or territory. 24

ambulatory surgery Surgery performed on an outpatient basis. 372

amount at risk Difference between the face amount of the policy and the reserve or policy value at a given time. In other words, the dollar amount over what the policyowner has contributed of cash value toward payment of the policyowner's own claim. Because the cash value increases every year, the net amount at risk naturally decreases until it finally reaches zero when the cash value or reserve become the face amount.

annually renewable term (ART) A form of renewable term insurance that provides coverage for one year and allows the policyowner to renew coverage each year without evidence of insurability. Also called yearly renewable term (YRT). 87

annuitant One to whom an annuity is payable, or a person upon the continuance of whose life further payment depends. 206

annuity A contract that provides a stipulated sum payable at certain regular intervals during the lifetime of one or more persons, or payable for a specified period only. 206

annuity unit The number of annuity units denotes the share of the funds an annuitant will receive from a variable annuity account after the accumulation period ends and benefits begin. A formula is used to convert accumulation units to annuity units. 214

any occupation A definition of total disability that requires that for disability income benefits to be payable, the insured must be unable to perform any job for which the insured is "reasonably suited by reason of education, training, or experience." 311

apparent authority The authority an agent appears to have, based on the principal's (the insurer's) actions, words, deeds, or because of circumstances the principal (the insurer) created. 41

application Form supplied by the insurance company, usually filled in by the agent and medical examiner (if applicable) on the basis of information received from the applicant. It is signed by the applicant and is part of the insurance policy if it is issued. It gives information to the home office underwriting department, so it may consider whether an insurance policy will be issued and, if so, in what classification and at what premium rate. 175

appointment The authorization or certification of an agent to act for or represent an insurance company. 20

approval receipt Rarely used today, a type of conditional receipt that provides that coverage is effective as of the date the application is approved (before the policy is delivered). 183

assessment mutual insurer An insurance company characterized by member-insureds who are assessed an individual portion of each loss that occurs. No premium payment is payable in advance. 16

assignee Person (including corporation, partnership, or other organization) to whom a right or rights under a policy are transferred by means of an assignment. 119

assignment provision (health contracts) Commercial health policy provision that allows the policyowner to assign benefit payments from the insurer directly to the health care provider. 279

assignment Signed transfer of benefits of a policy by an insured to another party. The company does not guarantee the validity of an assignment. 119

assignor Person (including corporation, partnership, or other organization or entity) who transfers a right or rights under an insurance policy to another by means of an assignment. 119

attained age With reference to an insured, the current insurance age. 87

authority The actions and deeds an agent is authorized to conduct on behalf of an insurance company, as specified in the agent's contract. 41

authorized company Company duly authorized by the insurance department to operate in the state. 24

automatic premium loan provision Authorizes insurer to automatically pay any premium in default at the end of the grace period and charge the amount so paid against the life insurance policy as a policy loan. 121

average indexed monthly earnings (AIME) The basis used for calculating the primary insurance amount (PIA) for Social Security benefits. 228

average monthly wage (AMW) The average wage base for computing virtually all Social Security benefits prior to 1979. 228

aviation exclusion Either attached by rider or included in standard policy language excepting from coverage certain deaths or disabilities due to aviation, such as "other than a fare-paying passenger." 122

B

backdating The practice of making a policy effective at an earlier date than the present. 185

basic medical expense policy Health insurance policy that provides "first dollar" benefits for specified (and limited) health care, such as hospitalization, surgery, or physician services. Characterized by limited benefit periods and relatively low coverage limits. 299

beneficiary Person to whom the proceeds of a life or accident policy are payable when the insured dies. The various types of beneficiaries are primary beneficiaries (those first entitled to proceeds), secondary beneficiaries (those entitled to proceeds if no primary beneficiary is living when the insured dies), and tertiary beneficiaries (those entitled to proceeds if no primary or secondary beneficiaries are alive when the insured dies). 137

benefit May be either money or a right to the policyowner upon the happening of the conditions set out in the policy. 160

benefit period Maximum length of time that insurance benefits will be paid for any one accident, illness, or hospital stay. 314

Best's Insurance Report A guide, published by A.M. Best, Inc., that rates insurers' financial integrity and managerial and operational strengths. 27

binding receipt Given by a company upon an applicant's first premium payment. The policy, if approved, becomes effective from the date of the receipt. 184

blackout period Period following the death of a family breadwinner during which no Social Security benefits are available to the surviving spouse. 262

blanket policy Covers a number of individuals who are exposed to the same hazards, such as members of an athletic team, company officials who are passengers in the same company plane, and so on. 200

broker Licensed insurance representative who does not represent a specific company, but places business among various companies. Legally, the broker is usually regarded as a representative of the insured rather than the company. 19, 40

business continuation plan Arrangements between the business owners that provide that the shares owned by any one of them who dies or becomes disabled shall be sold to and purchased by the other co-owners or by the business. 394, 395

business overhead expense insurance A form of disability income coverage designed to pay necessary business overhead expenses, such as rent, should the insured business owner become disabled. 395

buyer's guides Informational consumer guide books that explain insurance policies and insurance concepts; in many states, they are required to be given to applicants when certain types of coverages are being considered. 181

buy-sell agreement Agreement that a deceased business owner's interest will be sold and purchased at a predetermined price or at a price according to a predetermined formula. 264

C

cafeteria plan Employee benefit arrangements in which employees can select from a range of benefits. 394

cancellable contract Health insurance contract that may be terminated by the company or that is renewable at its option. 357

capital sum Amount provided for accidental dismemberment or loss of eyesight. Indemnities for loss of one member or sight of one eye are percentages of the capital sum. 322

career agency system A method of marketing, selling, and distributing insurance, it is represented by agencies or branch offices committed to the ongoing recruitment and development of career agents. 20

case management The professional arrangement and coordination of health services through assessment, service plan development, and monitoring. 373

cash or deferred arrangements A qualified employer retirement plan under which employees can defer amounts of their salaries into a retirement plan. These amounts are not included in the employee's gross income and so are tax deferred. Also called 401(k) plans. 243

cash refund annuity Provides that, upon the death of an annuitant before payments totaling the purchase price have been made, the excess of the amount paid by the purchaser over the total annuity payments received will be paid in one sum to designated beneficiaries. 215

cash surrender option A nonforfeiture option that allows whole life insurance policyowners to receive a payout of their policy's cash values. 123

cash surrender value Amount available to the owner when a life insurance policy is surrendered to the company. During the early policy years, the cash value is the reserve less a "surrender charge"; in later policy years, it usually equals or closely approximates the reserve value at time of surrender. 89, 123

cash value The equity amount or "savings" accumulation in a whole life policy. 89, 122

churning The practice by which policy values in an existing life insurance policy or annuity contract are used to purchase another policy or contract with that same insurer for the purpose of earning additional premiums or commissions without an objectively reasonable basis for believing that the new policy will result in an actual and demonstrable benefit.

class designation   A beneficiary designation. Rather than specifying one or more beneficiaries by name, the policyowner designates a class or group of beneficiaries. For example, "my children." 140

classification   Occupational category of a risk. 180

close corporation   A corporation owned by a small group of stockholders, each of whom usually has a voice in operating the business. 267

COBRA   Consolidated Omnibus Budget Reconciliation Act of 1985, extending group health coverage to terminated employees and their families for up to 18 or 36 months. 383

coinsurance (percentage participation)   Principle under which the company insures only part of the potential loss, the policyowners paying the other part. For instance, in a major medical policy, the company may agree to pay 75% of the insured expenses, with the insured to pay the other 25%. 301

collateral assignment   Assignment of a policy to a creditor as security for a debt. The creditor is entitled to be reimbursed out of policy proceeds for the amount owed. The beneficiary is entitled to any excess of policy proceeds over the amount due the creditor in the event of the insured's death. 119

combination company   Company whose agents sell both weekly premium life and health insurance and ordinary life insurance. Also called a multi-line company. 16

commercial health insurers   Insurance companies that function on the reimbursement approach, which allows policyowners to seek medical treatment then submit the charges to the insurer for reimbursement. 286

commissioner   Head of a state insurance department; public officer charged with supervising the insurance business in a state and administering insurance laws. Called "superintendent" in some states, "director" in others. 23

Commissioner's Standard Ordinary (CSO) Table   Table of mortality based on intercompany experience over a period of time, which is legally recognized as the mortality basis for computing maximum reserves on policies issued within past years. The 1980 CSO Table replaced the 1958 CSO Table. 153

common disaster provision   Sometimes added to a policy and designed to provide an alternative beneficiary in the event that the insured as well as the original beneficiary dies as the result of a common accident. 144

competent parties   To be enforceable, a contract must be entered into by competent parties. A competent party is one who is capable of understanding the contract being agreed to. 35

comprehensive major medical insurance   Designed to give the protection offered by both a basic medical expense and major medical policy. It is characterized by a low deductible amount, coinsurance clause, and high maximum benefits. 298

concealment   Failure of the insured to disclose to the company a fact material to the acceptance of the risk at the time application is made. 38

conditional contract   Characteristic of an insurance contract in that the payment of benefits is dependent on or a condition of the occurrence of the risk insured against. 37

conditionally renewable contract   Health insurance policy providing that the insured may renew the contract from period to period, or continue it to a stated date or an advanced age, subject to the right of the insurer to decline renewal only under conditions defined in the contract. 361

conditional receipt   Given to the policyowners when they pay a premium at time of application. Such receipts bind the insurance company if the risk is approved as applied for, subject to any other conditions stated on the receipt. 183

consideration clause   The part of an insurance contract setting forth the amount of initial and renewal premiums and frequency of future payments. 115, 358

consideration   Element of a binding contract; acceptance by the company of payment of the premium and statements made by the prospective insured in the application. 34

contestable period   Period during which the company may contest a claim on a policy because of misleading or incomplete information in the application. 352

contingent beneficiary   Person(s) named to receive proceeds in case the original beneficiary is not alive. Also referred to as secondary or tertiary beneficiary. 144

continuing care   Type of health or medical care designed to provide a benefit for elderly individuals who live in a retirement community; addresses full-time needs, both social and medical. Also known as residential care. 344

contract   An agreement enforceable by law whereby one party binds itself to certain promises or deeds. 34

contract of agency   A legal document containing the terms of the contract between the agent and company, signed by both parties. Also called agency agreement. 40

contributory plan   Group insurance plan issued to an employer under which both the employer and employees contribute to the cost of the plan. Generally, 75% of the eligible employees must be insured. (See **noncontributory plan**) 379

conversion factor A stated dollar-per-point amount used to determine benefit amounts paid for the cost of a procedure under a health insurance plan. For example, a plan with a $5-per-point conversion factor would pay $1,000 for a 200-point-procedure. 296

conversion privilege Allows the policyowner, before an original insurance policy expires, to elect to have a new policy issued that will continue the insurance coverage. Conversion may be effected at attained age (premiums based on the age attained at time of conversion) or at original age (premiums based on age at time of original issue). 358, 380, 393

convertible term Contract that may be converted to a permanent form of insurance without medical examination. 87

coordination of benefits (COB) provision Designed to prevent duplication of group insurance benefits. Limits benefits from multiple group health insurance policies in a particular case to 100% of the expenses covered and designates the order in which the multiple carriers are to pay benefits. 382

corridor deductible In superimposed major medical plans, a deductible amount between the benefits paid by the basic plan and the beginning of the major medical benefits. 299

cost of living (COL) rider A rider available with some policies that provides for an automatic increase in benefits (typically tied to the Consumer Price Index), offsetting the effects of inflation. 130, 316

coverage requirements Standards of coverage that prevent retirement plans from discriminating in favor of highly compensated employees. A plan must pass an IRS coverage test to be considered qualified. 240

credit accident and health insurance If the insured debtor becomes totally disabled due to an accident or sickness, the policy premiums are paid during the period of disability or the loan is paid off. May be individual or group policy. 385

credit life insurance Usually written as decreasing term on a relatively small decreasing balance install-ment loan that may reflect direct borrowing or a bal-ance due for merchandise purchased. If borrower dies, benefits pay balance due. May be individual or group policy. 99, 199

credit report A summary of an insurance applicant's credit history, made by an independent organization that has investigated the applicant's credit standing. 178

cross-purchase plan An agreement that provides that upon a business owner's death, surviving owners will purchase the deceased's interest, often with funds from life insurance policies owned by each principal on the lives of all other principals. 266–267

currently insured Under Social Security, a status of limited eligibility that provides only death benefits. 227

custodial care Level of health or medical care given to meet daily personal needs, such as dressing, bath-ing, getting out of bed, and so on. Though it does not require medical training, it must be administered under a physician's order. 344

D

death rate Proportion of persons in each age group who die within a year; usually expressed as so many deaths per thousand persons. (See **expected mortality**) 152

debit insurer (See **home service insurer**) 18

decreasing term insurance Term life insurance on which the face value slowly decreases in scheduled steps from the date the policy comes into force to the date the policy expires, while the premium remains level. The intervals between decreases are usually monthly or annually. 85

deductible Amount of expense or loss to be paid by the insured before a health insurance policy starts paying benefits. 299

deferred annuity Provides for postponement of the commencement of an annuity until after a specified period or until the annuitant attains a specified age. May be purchased either on single-premium or flexible premium basis. 210

deferred compensation plan The deferral of an employee's compensation to some future age or date. These plans are frequently used to provide fringe ben-efits, such as retirement income, to selected personnel. 244

defined benefit plan A pension plan under which benefits are determined by a specific benefit formula. 240

defined contribution plan A tax-qualified retirement plan in which annual contributions are determined by a formula set forth in the plan. Benefits paid to a par-ticipant vary with the amount of contributions made on the participant's behalf and the length of service under the plan. 240

delayed disability provision A disability income policy provision that allows a certain amount of time after an accident for a disability to result, and the insured remains eligible for benefits. 315

dental insurance A relatively new form of health insurance coverage typically offered on a group basis, it covers the costs of normal dental maintenance as well as oral surgery and root canal therapy. 381

dependency period Period following the death of the breadwinner up until the youngest child reaches maturity. 262

deposit term Has modest endowment feature. Normally is sold for 10-year terms with a higher first-year premium than for subsequent years. If policy lapses, insured forfeits the "deposit" and receives no refund. 88

disability buy-sell agreement An agreement between business co-owners that provides that shares owned by any one of them who becomes disabled shall be sold to and purchased by the other co-owners or by the business using funds from disability income insurance. 395

disability income insurance A type of health insurance coverage, it provides for the payment of regular, periodic income should the insured become disabled from illness or injury. 279, 310, 384

disability income rider Typically a rider to a life insurance policy, it provides benefits in the form of income in the event the insured becomes totally disabled. 315

disability Physical or mental impairment making a person incapable of performing one or more duties of that person's occupation. 311

dividend options The different ways in which the insured under a participating life insurance policy may elect to receive surplus earnings: in cash, as a reduction of premium, as additional paid-up insurance, left on deposit at interest, or as additional term insurance. 126

dividend Policyowner's share in the divisible surplus of a company issuing insurance on the participating plan. 125

domestic insurer Company within the state in which it is chartered and in which its home office is located. 24

dread disease policy (See **limited risk policy**) 304

E

elimination period Duration of time between the beginning of an insured's disability and the commencement of the period for which benefits are payable. 314

employee benefit plans Plans through which employers offer employees benefits such as coverage for medical expenses, disability, retirement, and death. 269, 394

endowment Contract providing for payment of the face amount at the end of a fixed period, at a specified age of the insured, or at the insured's death before the end of the stated period. 94

endowment period Period specified in an endowment policy during which, if the insured dies, the beneficiary receives a death benefit. If the insured is still living at the end of the endowment period, the insured receives the endowment as a living benefit. 94

enhanced whole life A whole life insurance policy issued by a mutual insurer, in which policy dividends are used to provide extra death benefits or to reduce future premiums. 109

enrollment period Period during which new employees can sign up for coverage under a group insurance plan. 196

entire contract provision An insurance policy provision stating that the application and policy contain all provisions and constitute the entire contract. 115, 352

entity plan An agreement in which a business assumes the obligation of purchasing a deceased owner's interest in the business, thereby proportionately increasing the interests of surviving owners. 266

errors and omissions insurance Professional liability insurance that protects an insurance producer against claims arising from service the producer rendered or failed to render. 42

estate Most commonly, the quantity of wealth or property at an individual's death. 139

estate tax Federal tax imposed on the value of property transferred by an individual at death. 139

estoppel Legal impediment to denying the consequences of one's actions or deeds if they lead to detrimental actions by another. 43

evidence of insurability Any statement or proof regarding a person's physical condition, occupation, and so forth, affecting acceptance of the applicant for insurance. 86

examiner Physician authorized by the medical director of an insurance company to make medical examinations. Also, person assigned by a state insurance company to audit the affairs of an insurance company. 177

excess interest Difference between the rate of interest the company guarantees to pay on proceeds left under settlement options and the interest actually paid on such funds by the company. 162

exclusions Specified hazards listed in a policy for which benefits will not be paid. 122, 347, 359

expected mortality Number of deaths that theoretically should occur among a group of insured persons during a given period, according to the mortality table in use. Normally, a lower mortality rate is anticipated and generally experienced. 153

experience rating Review of the previous year's claims experience for a group insurance contract in order to establish premiums for the next period. 194

express authority The specific authority given in writing to the agent in the contract of agency. 41

extended term insurance   Nonforfeiture option providing for the cash surrender value of a policy to be used as a net single premium at the insured's attained age to purchase term insurance for the face amount of the policy, less indebtedness, for as long a period as possible, but no longer than the term of the original policy. 124

extra percentage tables   Mortality or morbidity tables indicating the percentage amount increase of premium for certain impaired health conditions. 156

F

face amount   Commonly used to refer to the principal sum involved in the contract. The actual amount payable may be decreased by loans or increased by additional benefits payable under specified conditions or stated in a rider. 152

facility-of-payment provision   Clause permitted under a uniform health insurance policy provision allowing the company to pay up to $1,000 of benefits or proceeds to any relative appearing entitled to it if there is no beneficiary or if the insured or beneficiary is a minor or legally incompetent. 146

Fair Credit Reporting Act   Federal law requiring an individual to be informed if she is being investigated by an inspection company. 22, 178

family plan policy   All-family plan of protection, usually with permanent insurance on the primary wage earner's life and with spouse and children automatically covered for lesser amounts of protection, usually term, all included for one premium. 97

FICA   Contributions made by employees and employers to fund Social Security benefits (OASDI). 227

fiduciary   Person in a position of special trust and confidence (e.g., in handling or supervising affairs or funds of another). 41

final expense fund   Basic use for life insurance; reserve to cover costs of last illness, burial, legal and administrative expenses, mis-cellaneous outstanding bills, and so on. Also called cleanup fund. 261

fixed-amount settlement option   A life insurance settlement option whereby the beneficiary instructs that proceeds be paid in regular installments of a fixed dollar amount. The number of payment periods is determined by the policy's face amount, the amount of each payment, and the interest earned. 162

fixed annuity   A type of annuity that provides a guaranteed fixed benefit amount, payable for the life of the annuitant. 213

fixed-period settlement option   A life insurance settlement option in which the number of payments is fixed by the payee, with the amount of each payment determined by the amount of proceeds. 162

flat deductible   Amount of covered expenses payable by the insured before medical benefits are payable. 299

Florida Viatical Settlement Act   State law that provides for regulation of viatical settlement contracts and providers by the Department of Insurance.

foreign insurer   Company operating in a state in which it is not chartered and in which its home office is not located. 24

franchise insurance   Life or health insurance plan for covering groups of persons with individual policies uniform in provisions, although perhaps different in benefits. Solicitation usually takes place in an employer's business with the employer's consent. Generally written for groups too small to qualify for regular group coverage. May be called wholesale insurance when the policy is life insurance. 385

fraternal benefit insurer   Nonprofit benevolent organization that provides insurance to its members. 18

fraud   An act of deceit; misrepresentation of a material fact made knowingly, with the intention of having another person rely on that fact and consequently suffer a financial hardship. 44

free look   Provision required in most states whereby policyholders have either 10 or 20 days to examine their new policies at no obligation. 115, 359

fully insured   A status of complete eligibility for the full range of Social Security benefits: death benefits, retirement benefits, disability benefits, and Medicare benefits. 227

funding   In a retirement plan, the setting aside of funds for the payment of benefits. 239

G

general agent   Independent agent with authority, under contract with the company, to appoint soliciting agents within a designated territory and fix their compensation. 20

government insurer   An organization that, as an extension of the federal or state government, provides a program of social insurance. 19, 279

grace period   Period of time after the due date of a premium during which the policy remains in force without penalty. 116, 353

graded premium whole life   Variation of a traditional whole life contract providing for lower than normal premium rates during the first few policy years, with premiums increasing gradually each year. After the preliminary period, premiums level off and remain constant. 93

gross premium   The total premium paid by the policyowner, it generally consists of the net premium plus the expense of operation minus interest. 154

group credit insurance   A form of group insurance issued by insurance companies to creditors to cover the lives of debtors for the amounts of their loans. 199

group insurance   Insurance that provides coverage for a group of persons, usually employees of a company, under one master contract. 84, 194

guaranteed insurability (guaranteed issue)   Arrangement, usually provided by rider, whereby additional insurance may be purchased at various times without evidence of insurability. 127, 317

guaranteed renewable contract   Health insurance contract that the insured has the right to continue in force by payment of premiums for a substantial period of time during which the insurer has no right to make unilaterally any change in any provision, other than a change in premium rate for classes of insureds. 361

guaranty association   Established by each state to support insurers and protect consumers in the case of insurer insolvency, guaranty associations are funded by insurers through assessments. 27

H

hazard   Any factor that gives rise to a peril. 9

health insurance   Insurance against loss through sickness or accidental bodily injury. Also called accident and health, accident and sickness, sickness and accident, or disability insurance. 4, 278

health maintenance organization (HMO)   Health care management stressing preventive health care, early diagnosis, and treatment on an outpatient basis. Persons generally enroll voluntarily by paying a fixed fee periodically. 18, 287

Holocaust Victims Insurance Act   Requires insurers that receive claims from Holocaust victims or beneficiaries, descendents, or heirs, to allow, investigate, and pay their rightful claims under the policy regardless of any statute of limitations. Claimants must have submitted their claims within 10 years of the effective date of the law or by July 1, 1998.

home health care   Skilled or unskilled care provided in an individual's home, usually on a part-time basis. 344

home service insurer   Insurer that offers relatively small policies with premiums payable on a weekly basis, collected by agents at the policyowner's home. 18

hospital benefits   Payable for charges incurred while the insured is confined to, or treated in, a hospital, as defined in a health insurance policy. 295

hospital expense insurance   Health insurance benefits subject to a specified daily maximum for a specified period of time while the injured is confined to a hospital, plus a limited allowance up to a specified amount for miscellaneous hospital expenses, such as operating room, anesthesia, laboratory fees, and so on. Also called hospitalization insurance. (See **medical expense insurance**) 295

hospital indemnity   Form of health insurance providing a stipulated daily, weekly, or monthly indemnity during hospital confinement; payable on an unallocated basis without regard to actual hospital expense. 304

human life value   An individual's economic worth, measured by the sum of the individual's future earnings that is devoted to the individual's family. 11, 259

I

immediate annuity   Provides for payment of annuity benefit at one payment interval from date of purchase. Can only be purchased with a single payment. 209

implied authority   Authority not specifically granted to the agent in the contract of agency, but which common sense dictates the agent has. It enables the agent to carry out routine responsibilities. 41

incontestable clause   Provides that, for certain reasons such as misstatements on the application, the company may void a life insurance policy after it has been in force during the insured's lifetime, usually one or two years after issue. 117

increasing term insurance   Term life insurance in which the death benefit increases periodically over the policy's term. Usually purchased as a cost of living rider to a whole life policy. (See **cost of living rider**) 86

indemnity approach   A method of paying health policy benefits to insureds based on a predetermined, fixed rate set for the medical services provided, regardless of the actual expenses incurred. 37, 297

independent agency system   A system for marketing, selling, and distributing insurance in which independent brokers are not affiliated with any one insurer but represent any number of insurers. 20

indexed annuity   A fixed deferred annuity that offers the traditional guaranteed minimum interest rate and an excess interest feature that is based on the performance of an external equities market index. 216

indexed whole life   A whole life insurance policy whose death benefit increases according to the rate of inflation. Such policies are usually tied to the Consumer Price Index (CPI). 94

individual insurance   Policies providing protection to the policyowner, as distinct from group and blanket insurance. Also called personal insurance. 84

individual retirement account (IRA) A personal qualified retirement account through which eligible individuals accumulate tax-deferred income up to a certain amount each year, depending on the person's tax bracket. 219, 245

industrial insurance Life insurance policy providing modest benefits and a relatively short benefit period. Premiums are collected on a weekly or monthly basis by an agent calling at insured's homes. (See **home service insurer**) 84

inspection receipt A receipt obtained from an insurance applicant when a policy (upon which the first premium has not been paid) is left with the applicant for further inspection. It states that the insurance is not in effect and that the policy has been delivered for inspection only. 186

inspection report Report of an investigator providing facts required for a proper underwriting decision on applications for new insurance and reinstatements. 178

installment refund annuity An annuity income option that provides for the funds remaining at the annuitant's death to be paid to the beneficiary in the form of continued annuity payments. 211

insurability All conditions pertaining to individuals that affect their health, susceptibility to injury, or life expectancy; an individual's risk profile. 175

insurability receipt A type of conditional receipt that makes coverage effective on the date the application was signed or the date of the medical exam (whichever is later), provided the applicant proves to be insurable. 183

insurable interest Requirement of insurance contracts that loss must be sustained by the applicant upon the death or disability of another and loss must be sufficient to warrant compensation. 39, 174, 368

insurance code The laws that govern the business of insurance in a given state.

insurance Social device for minimizing risk of uncertainty regarding loss by spreading the risk over a large enough number of similar exposures to predict the individual chance of loss. 4

insurer Party that provides insurance coverage, typically through a contract of insurance. 16

insuring clause Defines and describes the scope of the coverage provided and limits of indemnification. 115, 358

integrated deductible In superimposed major medical plans, a deductible amount between the benefits paid by the basic plan and those benefits paid by the major medical. All or part of the integrated deductible may be absorbed by the basic plan. 300

interest adjusted net cost method A method of comparing costs of similar policies by using an index that takes into account the time value of money. 69

interest-only option (interest option) Mode of settlement under which all or part of the proceeds of a policy are left with the company for a definite period at a guaranteed minimum interest rate. Interest may either be added to the proceeds or paid annually, semi-annually, quarterly, or monthly. 161

interest-sensitive whole life Whole life policy whose premiums vary depending upon the insurer's underlying death, investment and expense assumptions. 99

interim term insurance Term insurance for a period of 12 months or less by special agreement of the company; it permits a permanent policy to become effective at a selected future date. 185

intermediate nursing care Level of health or medical care that is occasional or rehabilitative, ordered by a physician, and performed by skilled medical personnel. 343

irrevocable beneficiary Beneficiary whose interest cannot be revoked without the beneficiary's written consent, usually because the policyowner has made the beneficiary designation without retaining the right to revoke or change it. 143

J

joint and last survivor policy A variation of the joint life policy that covers two lives but pays the benefit upon the death of the second insured. 98

joint and survivor annuity Covers two or more lives and continues in force so long as any one of them survives. 212

joint life policy Covers two or more lives and provides for the payment of the proceeds at the death of the first among those insured, at which time the policy automatically terminates. 98

juvenile insurance Written on the lives of children who are within specified age limits and generally under parental control. 98

K

Keogh plans Designed to fund retirement of self-employed individuals; name derived from the author of the Keogh Act (HR-10), under which contributions to such plans are given favorable tax treatment. 244

key-person insurance Protection of a business against financial loss caused by the death or disablement of a vital number of the company, usually individuals possessing special managerial or technical skill or expertise. 268

L

lapse   Termination of a policy upon the policyowner's failure to pay the premium within the grace period. 116, 353

law of large numbers   Basic principle of insurance that the larger the number of individual risks combined into a group, the more certainty there is in predicting the degree or amount of loss that will be incurred in any given period. 7

legal purpose   In contract law, the requirement that the object of, or reason for, the contract must be legal. 34

legal reserve   Policy reserves are maintained according to the standard levels established through the insurance laws of the various states. 158

level premium funding method   The insurance plan (used by all regular life insurance companies) under which, instead of an annually increasing premium that reflects the increasing chance of death, an equivalent level premium is paid. Reserves that accumulate from more than adequate premiums paid in the early years supplement inadequate premiums in later years. 88, 91, 157

level term insurance   Term coverage on which the face value remains unchanged from the date the policy comes into force to the date the policy expires. 85

license   Certification issued by a state insurance department that an individual is qualified to solicit insurance applications for the period covered; usually issued for one year, renewable on application without need to repeat the original qualifying requirements. 23

licensed insurer   (See **admitted insurer**)

lien system   Plan for issuing coverage for substandard risks. A standard premium is paid, but there is a lien against the policy to reduce the amount of insurance if the insured dies from a cause that resulted in the substandard rating. 157

life annuity   Payable during the continued life of the annuitant. No provision is made for the guaranteed return of the unused portion of the premium. 210

life expectancy   Average duration of the life remaining to a number of persons of a given age, according to a given mortality table. Not to be confused with "probable lifetime," which refers to the difference between a person's present age and the age at which death is most probable (i.e., the age at which most deaths occur). 152

life income settlement option   A settlement option providing for life insurance or annuity proceeds to be used to buy an annuity payable to the beneficiary for life-often with a specified number of payments certain or a refund if payments don't equal or exceed premiums paid. 163, 210

life insurance   Insurance against loss due to the death of a particular person (the insured) upon whose death the insurance company agrees to pay a stated sum or income to the beneficiary. 4

limited pay life insurance   A form of whole life insurance characterized by premium payments only being made for a specified or limited number of years. 91

limited policies   Restrict benefits to specified accidents or diseases, such as travel policies, dread disease policies, ticket policies, and so forth. 305, 324

limited risk policy   Provides coverage for specific kinds of accidents or illnesses, such as injuries received as a result of travel accidents or medical expenses stemming from a specified disease. (See **special risk policy**) 305, 323

Lloyd's of London   An association of individuals and companies that underwrite insurance on their own accounts and provide specialized coverages. 17

loading   Amount added to net premiums to cover the company's operating expenses and contingencies; includes the cost of securing new business, collection expenses, and general management expenses; excess of gross premiums over net premiums. 154

loan value   Determinable amount that can be borrowed from the issuing company by the policyowner using the value of the life insurance policy as collateral. 117

long-term care policy   Health insurance policies that provide daily indemnity benefits for extended care confinement. 343

long-term care   Refers to the broad range of medical and personal services for individuals (often the elderly) who need assistance with daily activities for an extended period of time. 342

loss sharing   (See **risk pooling**) 7

lump sum   Payment of entire proceeds of an insurance policy in one sum. The method of settlement provided by most policies unless an alternate settlement is elected by the policyowner or beneficiary. 161

M

major medical expense policy   Health insurance policy that provides broad coverage and high benefits for hospitalization, surgery, and physician services. Characterized by deductibles and coinsurance cost-sharing. 297

managed care   A system of delivering health care and health care services, characterized by arrangements with selected providers, programs of ongoing quality control, and utilization review and financial incentives for members to use providers and procedures covered by the plan. 372

mandatory second opinion To control costs, many health policies provide that, in order to be eligible for benefits, insureds must get a second opinion before receiving non-life-threatening surgery. 372

master contract Issued to the employer under a group plan; contains all the insuring clauses defining employee benefits. Individual employees participating in the group plan receive individual certificates that outline highlights of the coverage. Also called master policy. 194

maturity value Proceeds payable on an endowment contract at the end of the specified endowment period, or payable on an ordinary life contract at the last age of the mortality table if the insured is still living at that age. Maturity value of a policy is the same as the face amount of the policy and is equal to the reserve value of the contract on this maturity date. Actual amount payable by the company may be increased by dividend additions or accumulated dividend deposits or decreased by outstanding loans. 90, 95

McCarran-Ferguson Act Also known as Public Law 15, the 1945 act exempting insurance from federal antitrust laws to the extent insurance is regulated by states. 22

Medicaid Provides medical care for the needy under joint federal-state participation (Kerr-Mills Act). 279, 288, 333

medical cost management The process of controlling how policyholders utilize their policies. (See **mandatory second opinion, precertification, ambulatory surgery, and case management**) 372

medical examination Usually conducted by a licensed physician; the medical report is part of the application, becomes part of the policy contract, and is attached to the policy. A "nonmedical" is a short-form medical report filled out by the agent. Various company rules, such as amount of insurance applied for or already in force, or applicant's age, sex, past physical history, and data revealed by inspection report, and so on, determine whether the examination will be "medical" or "nonmedical." 176

medical expense insurance Pays benefits for nonsurgical doctors' fees commonly rendered in a hospital; sometimes pays for home and office calls. 294

Medical Information Bureau (MIB) A service organization that collects medical data on life and health insurance applicants for member insurance companies. 177

medical report A document completed by a physician or other approved examiner and submitted to an insurer to supply medical evidence of insurability (or lack of insurability) or in relation to a claim. 176

Medicare Federally sponsored health insurance and medical program for persons age 65 or older; administered under provisions of the Social Security Act. 279, 288, 328

Medicare Part A Compulsory hospitalization insurance that provides specified in hospital benefits and related benefits. All workers covered by Social Security finance its operation through a portion of their FICA tax. 328

Medicare Part B Voluntary program designed to provide supplementary medical insurance to cover physician services, medical services, and supplies not covered under Medicare Part A. 328

Medicare Part C Medicare Part C is called Medicare Advantage. The program offers a variety of managed care plans, a private fee-for-service plan, and Medicare specialty plans. These specialty plans provide services that focus care on the management of a specific disease or condition. 331

Medicare Part D A program that offers a prescription drug benefit to help Medicare beneficiaries pay for the drugs they need. The drug benefit is optional and is available to anyone who is entitled to Medicare Part A or enrolled in Part B. This benefit is available through private prescription drug plans (PDPs) or Medicare Advantage (PPO) plans. 331

Medicare supplement policy Health insurance that provides coverage to fill the gaps in Medicare coverage. 340

minimum deposit insurance A cash value life insurance policy having a first-year loan value that is available for borrowing immediately upon payment of the first-year premium. 94

minimum premium plan (MPP) Designed to support a self-insured plan, a minimum premium plan helps insure against large, unpredictable losses that exceed the self-insured level. 290

miscellaneous expenses Hospital charges, other than for room and board (e.g., x-rays, drugs, laboratory fees, and so forth), in connection with health insurance. 295

misrepresentation Act of making, issuing, circulating, or causing to be issued or circulated, an estimate, illustration, circular, or statement of any kind that does not represent the correct policy terms, dividends, or share of the surplus or the name or title for any policy or class of policies that does not in fact reflect its true nature.

misstatement of age or sex provision If the insured's age or sex is misstated in an application for insurance, the benefit payable usually is adjusted to what the premiums paid should have purchased. 120, 355

misuse of premium Improper use of premiums collected by an insurance producer. 79

modified endowment contract (MEC)   A life insurance policy under which the amount a policyowner pays in during the first years exceeds the sum of net level premiums that would have been payable to provide paid-up future benefits in seven years. 96

modified whole life   Whole life insurance with premium payable during the first few years, usually five years, only slightly larger than the rate for term insurance. Afterwards, the premium is higher for the remainder of life than the premium for ordinary life at the original age of issue, but lower than the rate at the attained age at the time of charge. 93

money purchase plan   A type of qualified plan under which contributions are fixed amounts or fixed percentages of the employee's salary. An employee's benefits are provided in whatever amount the accumulated or current contributions will produce for the employee. 241

morale hazard   Hazard arising from indifference to loss because of the existence of insurance. 9

moral hazard   Effect of personal reputation, character, associates, personal living habits, financial responsibility, and environment, as distinguished from physical health, upon an individual's general insurability. 9, 366

morbidity rate   Shows the incidence and extent of disability that may be expected from a given large group of persons; used in computing health insurance rates. 369

morbidity   The relative incidence of disability due to sickness or accident within a given group. 369

mortality table   Listing of the mortality experience of individuals by age; permits an actuary to calculate, on the average, how long a male or female of a given age group may be expected to live. 153

mortality   The relative incidence of death within a group. 152

mortgage insurance   A basic use of life insurance, so-called because many family heads leave insurance for specifically paying off any mortgage balance outstanding at their death. The insurance generally is made payable to a family beneficiary instead of to the mortgage holder. 261

multiple employer trust (MET)   Several small groups of individuals that need life and health insurance but do not qualify for true group insurance band together under state trust laws to purchase insurance at a more favorable rate. 290

multiple employer welfare arrangement (MEWA)   Similar to a multiple employer trust (MET) with the exception that in a MEWA, a number of employers pool their risks and self-insure. 291

multiple protection policy   A combination of term and whole life coverage that pays some multiple of the face amount of the basic whole life portion (such as $10 per month per $1,000) throughout the multiple protection period (such as to age 65). 98

mutual insurer   An insurance company characterized by having no capital stock; it is owned by its policyowners and usually issues participating insurance. 16

N

National Association of Health Underwriters (NAHU)   NAHU is an organization of health insurance agents that is dedicated to supporting the health insurance industry and to advancing the quality of service provided by insurance professionals. 27

National Association of Insurance and Financial Advisors (NAIFA)   NAIFA is an organization of life insurance agents that is dedicated to supporting the life insurance industry and advancing the quality of service provided by insurance professionals. 27

National Association of Insurance Commissioners (NAIC)   Association of state insurance commissioners active in insurance regulatory problems and in forming and recommending model legislation and requirements. 26

natural group   A group formed for a reason other than to obtain insurance. 195, 378

needs approach   A method for determining how much insurance protection a person should have by analyzing a family's or business's needs and objectives should the insured die, become disabled, or retire. 260

net premium   Calculated on the basis of a given mortality table and a given interest rate, without any allowance for loading. 154

nonadmitted insurer   An insurance company that has not been licensed to operate within a given state. 24

noncancellable and guaranteed renewable contract   Health insurance contract that the insured has the right to continue in force by payment of premiums set forth in the contract for a substantial period of time, during which the insurer has no right to make unilaterally any change in any contract provision. 361

noncontributory plan   Employee benefit plan under which the employer bears the full cost of the employees' benefits; must insure 100% of eligible employees. 379

nondisabling injury   Requires medical care, but does not result in loss of time from work. 315

nonduplication provision   Stipulates that insureds shall be ineligible to collect for charges under a group health plan if the charges are reimbursed under their own or spouse's group plan. 382

nonforfeiture options Privileges allowed under terms of a life insurance contract after cash values have been created. 123

nonforfeiture values Those benefits in a life insurance policy that by law, the policyowner does not forfeit even if the policyowner discontinues premium payments: usually cash value, loan value, paid-up insurance value, and extended term insurance value. 123

nonmedical insurance Issued on a regular basis without requiring a regular medical examination. In passing on the risk, the company relies on the applicant's answers to questions regarding the applicant's physical condition and on personal references or inspection reports. 176

nonparticipating Insurance under which the insured is not entitled to share in the divisible surplus of the company. 280

nonqualified plan A retirement plan that does not meet federal government requirements and is not eligible for favorable tax treatment. 238

notice of claims provision Policy provision that describes the policyowner's obligation to provide notification of loss to the insurer within a reasonable period of time. 353

O

offer and acceptance The offer may be made by the applicant by signing the application, paying the first premium, and if necessary, submitting to a physical examination. Policy issuance, as applied for, constitutes acceptance by the company. Or, the offer may be made by the company when no premium payment is submitted with application. Premium payment on the offered policy then constitutes acceptance by the applicant. 34

Old-Age, Survivors, Disability, and Hospital Insurance (OASDI) Retirement, death, disability income, and hospital insurance benefits provided under the Social Security system. 226

optionally renewable contract Health insurance policy in which the insurer reserves the right to terminate the coverage at any anniversary or, in some cases, at any premium due date, but does not have the right to terminate coverage between such dates. 361

ordinary insurance Life insurance of commercial companies not issued on the weekly premium basis; amount of protection usually is $1,000 or more. 84

other insureds rider A term rider, covering a family member other than the insured, that is attached to the base policy covering the insured. 131

overhead insurance Type of short-term disability insurance reimbursing the insured for specified, fixed, monthly expenses; normal and customary in operating the insured's business. 395

overinsurance An excessive amount of insurance; an amount of insurance that would result in payment of more than the actual loss or more than incurred expenses. 356, 382

own occupation A definition of total disability that requires that in order to receive disability income benefits the insured must be unable to work at the insured's own occupation. 311

P

paid-up additions Additional life insurance purchased by policy dividends on a net single premium basis at the insured's attained insurance age at the time additions are purchased. 125

paid-up policy No further premiums are to be paid and the company is held liable for the benefits provided by the contract. 91

parol evidence rule Rule of contract law that brings all verbal statements into the written contract and disallows any changes or modifications to the contract by oral evidence. 43

partial disability Illness or injury preventing insured from performing at least one or more, but not all, of the insured's occupational duties. 312

participating physician A doctor or physician who accepts Medicare's allowable or recognized charges and will not charge more than this amount. 328

participating Plan of insurance under which the policyowner receives shares (commonly called dividends) of the divisible surplus of the company. 280

participation standards Rules that must be followed for determining employee eligibility for a qualified retirement plan. 239

partnership A business entity that allows two or more people to strengthen their effectiveness by working together as co-owners. 265

payor rider Available under certain juvenile life insurance policies, upon payment of an extra premium. Provides for the waiver of future premiums if the person responsible for paying them dies or is disabled before the policy becomes fully paid or matures as a death claim, or as an endowment, or the child reaches a specific age. 129

per capita rule Death proceeds from an insurance policy are divided equally among the living primary beneficiaries. 141

peril The immediate specific event causing loss and giving rise to risk. 9

period certain annuity An annuity income option that guarantees a definite minimum period of payments. 212

permanent flat extra premium A fixed charge added per $1,000 of insurance for substandard risks. 156

personal producing general agency (PPGA) A method of marketing, selling, and distributing insurance in which personal producing general agents (PPGAs) are compensated for business they personally sell and business sold by agents with whom they subcontract. Subcontracted agents are considered employees of the PPGA, not the insurer. 20

per stirpes rule Death proceeds from an insurance policy are divided equally among the named beneficiaries. If a named beneficiary is deceased, the beneficiary's share then goes to the living descendants of that individual. 141

policy In insurance, the written instrument in which a contract of insurance is set forth. 34

policy loan In life insurance, a loan made by the insurance company to the policyowner, with the policy's cash value assigned as security. One of the standard nonforfeiture options. 116

policyowner (policyholder) These terms are used interchangeably to describe the person who pays for an insurance contract. This person is usually, but not necessarily, the applicant as well. 114

policy provisionsThe term or conditions of an insurance policy as contained in the policy clauses. 119, 352

precertification The insurer's approval of an insured's entering a hospital. Many health policies require precertification as part of an effort to control costs. 373

preexisting condition An illness or medical condition that existed before a policy's effective date; usually excluded from coverage, through the policy's standard provisions or by waiver. 302, 360, 381

preferred provider organization (PPO) Association of health care providers, such as doctors and hospitals, that agree to provide health care to members of a particular group at fees negotiated in advance. 287

preferred risk A risk whose physical condition, occupation, mode of living, and other characteristics indicate a prospect for longevity for unimpaired lives of the same age. 180

preliminary term insurance Term insurance attached to a newly issued permanent life insurance policy extending term coverage of a preliminary period of 1 to 11 months, until the permanent insurance becomes effective. The purpose is to provide full life insurance premium and the anniversary to a later date. 186

premium factors The three primary factors considered when computing the basic premium for insurance: mortality, expense, and interest. 155, 369

premium The periodic payment required to keep an insurance policy in force. 152, 353

prescription drug coverage Usually offered as an optional benefit to group medical expense plans, this coverage covers some or all of the cost of prescription drugs. 381

presumptive disability benefit A disability income policy benefit that provides that if an insured experiences a specified disability, such as blindness, the insured is presumed to be totally disabled and entitled to the full amount payable under policy, whether or not the insured is able to work. 311

primary beneficiary In life insurance, the beneficiary designated by the insured as the first to receive policy benefits. 140

principal An insurance company that, having appointed someone as its agent, is bound to the contracts the agent completes in its behalf. 40

principal sum The amount under an AD&D policy that is payable as a death benefit if death is due to an accident. 322

private insurer An insurer that is not associated with federal or state government. 16

probationary period Specified number of days after an insurance policy's issue date during which coverage is not afforded for sickness. Standard practice for group coverages. 314

proceeds Net amount of money payable by the company at the insured's death or at policy maturity. 160

producer A general term applied to an agent, broker, personal producing general agent, solicitor, or other person who sells insurance. 20, 24

professional liability insurance (See **errors and omissions insurance**) 42

profit-sharing plan Any plan whereby a portion of a company's profits is set aside for distribution to employees who qualify under the plan. 241

proof of loss A mandatory health insurance provision stating that the insured must provide a completed claim form to the insurer within 90 days of the date of loss. 354

proper solicitation High professional standards that require an agent to identify himself properly as an agent soliciting insurance on behalf of an insurance company. 180

pure endowment Contract providing for payment only upon survival of a certain person to a certain date and not in the event of that person's prior death. This type of contract is just the opposite of a term contract, which provides for payment only in the event the injured person dies within the term period specified. 94

pure risk Type of risk that involves the chance of loss only; there is no opportunity for gain; insurable. 9

Q

qualified plan   A retirement or employee compensation plan established and maintained by an employer that meets specific guidelines spelled out by the IRS and consequently receives favorable tax treatment. 219

R

rate-up in age   System of rating substandard risks that assumes the insured to be older than the insured really is and charging a correspondingly higher premium. 156

rating   The making of insurance also creates the premium classification given an applicant for life or health insurance. 156

reasonable and customary charge   Charge for health care service consistent with the going rate of charge in a given geographical area for identical or similar services. 296

rebating   Returning part of the commission or giving anything else of value to the insured as an inducement to buy the policy. It is illegal and cause for license revocation in most states. In some states, it is an offense by both the agent and the person receiving the rebate.

reciprocal insurer   Insurance company characterized by the fact its policyholders insure the risks of other policyholders. 17

recurrent disability provision   A disability income policy provision that specifies the period of time during which the reoccurrence of a disability is considered a continuation of a prior disability. 315

reduced paid-up insurance   A nonforfeiture option contained in most life insurance policies providing for the insured to elect to have the cash surrender value of the policy used to purchase a paid-up policy for a reduced amount of insurance. 123

re-entry option   An option in a renewable term life policy under which the policyowner is guaranteed, at the end of the term, to be able to renew the policyowner's coverage without evidence of insurability, at a premium rate specified in the policy. 87

refund annuity   Provides for the continuance of the annuity during the annuitant's lifetime and, in any event, until total payment equal to the purchase price has been made by the company. 215

reimbursement approach   Payment of health policy benefits to insured based on actual medical expenses incurred. 281

reinstatement   Putting a lapsed policy back in force by producing satisfactory evidence of insurability and paying any past-due premiums required. 116, 353

reinsurance   Acceptance by one or more insurers, called reinsurers, of a portion of the risk underwritten by another insurer who has contracted for the entire coverage. 17

relative value scale   Method for determining benefits payable under a basic surgical expense policy. Points are assigned to each surgical procedure and a dollar per point amount, or conversion factor, is used to determine the benefit. 296

renewable option   An option that allows the policyowner to renew a term policy before its termination date without having to provide evidence of insurability. 87

renewable term   Some term policies prove that they may be renewed on the same plan for one or more years without medical examination, but with rates based on the insured's advanced age. 87

replacement   Act of replacing one life insurance policy with another; may be done legally under certain conditions. (See **twisting**)

representation   Statements made by applicants on their applications for insurance that they represent as being substantially true to the best of their knowledge and belief, but that are not warranted as exact in every detail. (See **warranties**) 38

reserve basis   Refers to mortality table and assumed interest rate used in computing rates. 158

reserve   Fund held by the company to help fulfill future claims. 158, 281

residual disability benefit   A disability income payment based on the proportion of income the insured has actually lost, taking into account the fact that the insured is able to earn some income. 312

respite care   Type of health or medical care designed to provide a short rest period for a caregiver. Characterized by its temporary status. 344

results provision   (See **accidental bodily injury provision**) 313

revocable beneficiary   Beneficiary whose rights in a policy are subject to the policyowner's reserved right to revoke or change the beneficiary designation and the right to surrender or make a loan on the policy without the beneficiary's consent. 142

rider   Strictly speaking, a rider adds something to a policy. However, the term is used loosely to refer to any supplemental agreement attached to and made a part of the policy, whether the policy's conditions are expanded and additional coverages added or a coverage of conditions is waived. 126

risk pooling   A basic principle of insurance whereby a large number contribute to cover the losses of a few. (See **loss sharing**) 7

risk selection   The method of a home office underwriter used to choose applicants that the insurance company will accept. The underwriter must determine whether risks are standard, substandard, or preferred and adjust the premium rates accordingly. 173

risk   Uncertainty regarding loss; the probability of loss occurring for an insured or prospect. 7, 366

rollover IRA   An individual retirement account established with funds transferred from another IRA or qualified retirement plan that the owner had terminated. 251

S

salary continuation plan   An arrangement whereby an income, usually related to an employee's salary, is continued upon employee's retirement, death, or disability. 270

salary reduction SEP   A qualified retirement plan limited to companies with 25 or fewer employees. It allows employees to defer part of their pretax income to the plan, lowering their taxable income. (See **simplified employee pension plan**) 245

savings incentive match plan for employees (SIMPLE)   A qualified employer retirement plan that allows small employers to set up tax-favored retirement savings plans for their employees. 245

schedule   List of specified amounts payable, usually for surgical operations, dismemberment, fractures, and so forth. 296

secondary beneficiary   An alternative beneficiary designated to receive payment, usually in the event the original beneficiary predeceases the insured. 140

Section 457 plans   Deferred compensation plans for employees of state and local governments in which amounts deferred will not be included in gross income until they are actually received or made available. 244

Self-Employed Individuals Retirement Act   Passed by Congress in 1962, this Act enables self-employed persons to establish qualified retirement plans similar to those available to corporations. 244

self-insurance   Program for providing insurance financed entirely through the means of the policyowner, in place of purchasing coverage from commercial carriers. 19, 290

self-insured plan   A health insurance plan characterized by an employer (usually a large one), labor union, fraternal organization, or other group retaining the risk of covering its employees' medical expenses. 290

service insurers   Companies that offer prepayment plans for medical or hospital services, such as health maintenance organizations. 18

service providers   An organization that provides health coverage by contracting with service providers to provide medical services to subscribers who pay in advance through premiums. Examples of such coverages are HMOs and PPOs. 18, 286

settlement options   Optional modes of settlement provided by most life insurance policies in lieu of lump-sum payment. Usual options are lump-sum cash, interest-only, fixed-period, fixed-amount, and life income. 161

simplified employee pension plan (SEP)   A type of qualified retirement plan under which the employer contributes to an individual retirement account set up and maintained by the employee. 245

single dismemberment   Loss of one hand or one foot, or the sight of one eye. 323

single-premium whole life insurance   Whole life insurance for which the entire premium is paid in one sum at the beginning of the contract period. 92

skilled nursing care   Daily nursing care ordered by a doctor; often medically necessary. It can only be performed by or under the supervision of skilled medical professionals and is available 24 hours a day. 343

sliding   The act of telling an insurance applicant that the law requires the applicant to buy a specific ancillary coverage or product with the purchase of insurance when that coverage or product is not required. It is also the act of telling an applicant that a policy includes a specific ancillary coverage or product without additional charge when such a charge is required. Sliding also occurs when an insurer charges for a specific ancillary coverage or product, in addition to the cost of the coverage applied for, without the applicant's informed consent.

Social Security   Programs first created by Congress in 1935 and now composed of Old-Age, Survivors, and Disability Insurance (OASDI), Medicare, Medicaid, and various grants-in-aid, which provide economic security to nearly all employed people. 226

special agent   An agent representing an insurance company in a given territory. 40

special class   Applicants who cannot qualify for standard insurance but may secure policies with riders waiving payment for losses involving certain existing health impairments. 126

special questionnaires   Forms used when, for underwriting purposes, the insurer needs more detailed information from an applicant regarding aviation or avocation, foreign residence, finances, military service, or occupation. 178

special risk policy   Provides coverage for unusual hazards normally not covered under accident and health insurance, such as a concert pianist insuring his hands for a million dollars. (See **limited risk policy**) 324

speculative risk   A type of risk that involves the chance of both loss and gain; it is not insurable. 8

spendthrift provision   Stipulates that, to the extent permitted by law, policy proceeds shall not be subject to the claims of creditors of the beneficiary or policyowner. 145

split-dollar life insurance   An arrangement between two parties where life insurance is written on the life of one party who names the beneficiary of the net death benefits (death benefits less cash value), and the other party is assigned the cash value, with both sharing premium payments. 269

spousal IRA   An individual retirement account that persons eligible to set up IRAs for themselves may set up jointly with a non-working spouse. 251

standard provisionsForerunners of the Uniform Policy Provisions in health insurance policies today. 114

standard risk   Person who, according to a company's underwriting standards, is entitled to insurance protection without extra rating or special restrictions. 180, 368

stock bonus plan   A plan under which bonuses are paid to employees in shares of stock. 241

stock insurers   An insurance company owned and controlled by a group of stockholders whose investment in the company provides the safety margin necessary in issuance of guaranteed, fixed premium, nonparticipating policies. 16

stock redemption plan   An agreement under which a close corporation purchases a deceased stockholder's interest. 267

stop-loss provision   Designed to stop the company's loss at a given point, as an aggregate payable under a policy, a maximum payable for any one disability, or the like; also applies to individuals, placing a limit on the maximum out-of-pocket expenses an insured must pay for health care, after which the health policy covers all expenses. 301

straight life income annuity (straight life annuity, life annuity)   An annuity income option that pays a guaranteed income for the annuitant's lifetime, after which time payments stop. 210

straight whole life insurance   (See **whole life insurance**) 91

Stranger-Originated Life Insurance (STOLI)   Life insurance arrangements where investors persuade consumers to take out new life insurance policies, with the investors named as beneficiary. Investors loan money to the insured to pay the premiums and the insured ultimately assigns ownership of the policy to the investors, who receive the death benefit when the insured dies. Because the investors are the constructive applicants, owners, and beneficiaries of the policies, and they have no insurable interest in the insureds, many states view STOLI arrangements as fraudulent. 39

subscriber   Policyowner of a health care plan underwritten by a service insurer. 286

substandard risk   Person who is considered an under-average or impaired insurance risk because of physical condition, family or personal history of disease, occupation, residence in unhealthy climate, or dangerous habits. (See special class) 156, 180, 368

successor beneficiary   (See **secondary beneficiary**) 140

suicide provision   Most life insurance policies provide that if the insured commits suicide within a specified period, usually two years after the issue date, the company's liability will be limited to a return of premiums paid. 120

supplemental accident coverage   Often included as part of a group basic or major medical plan, this type of coverage is designed to cover expenses associated with accidents to the extent they are not provided under other coverages. 323

supplementary major medical policy   A medical expense health plan that covers expenses not included under a basic policy and expenses that exceed the limits of a basic policy. 298, 382

surgical expense insurance   Provides benefits to pay for the cost of surgical operations. 295

surgical schedule   List of cash allowances payable for various types of surgery, with the respective maximum amounts payable based upon severity of the operations; stipulated maximum usually covers all professional fees involved (e.g., surgeon, anesthesiologist). 296

surrender value   (See **cash surrender value**) 89

T

taxable wage base   The maximum amount of earnings upon which FICA taxes must be paid. 227

tax-sheltered annuity   An annuity plan reserved for nonprofit organizations and their employees. Funds contributed to the annuity are excluded from current taxable income and are only taxed later, when benefits begin to be paid. Also called tax-deferred annuity and 403(b) plan. 219

temporary flat extra premium   A fixed charge per $1,000 of insurance added to substandard risks for a specified period of years. 156

temporary insurance agreement   (See **binding receipt**) 183

term insurance   Protection during limited number of years; expiring without value if the insured survives the stated period, which may be one or more years, but usually is 5 to 20 years because such periods generally cover the needs for temporary protection. 84

term of policy   Period for which the policy runs. In life insurance, this is to the end of the term period for term insurance, to the maturity date for endowments, and to the insured's death (or age 100) for permanent insurance. In most other kinds of insurance, it is usually the period for which a premium has been paid in advance; however, it may be for a year or more, even though the premium is paid on a semiannual or other basis. 84, 90

tertiary beneficiary   In life insurance, a beneficiary designated as third in line to receive the proceeds or benefits if the primary and secondary beneficiaries do not survive the insured. 140

third-party administrator (TPA)   An organization outside the members of a self-insurance group which, for a fee, processes claims, completes benefits paperwork, and often analyzes claims information. 290

third-party applicant   A policy applicant who is not the prospective insured. 174

time limit on certain defenses   A provision stating that an insurance policy is incontestable after it has been in force a certain period of time. It also limits the period during which an insurer can deny a claim on the basis of a preexisting condition. 352

total disability   Disability preventing insureds from performing any duty of their usual occupations or any occupation for remuneration; actual definition depends on policy wording. 312

traditional net cost method   A method of comparing costs of similar policies that does not take into account the time value of money. 69

transacting insurance   The transaction of any of the following, in addition to other acts included under applicable provisions of the state code: solicitation or inducement, preliminary negotiations, effecting a contract of insurance, and transacting matters subsequent to effecting a contract of insurance and arising out of it.

travel-accident policies   Limited to indemnities for accidents while traveling, usually by common carrier. 323

trust   Arrangement in which property is held by a person or corporation (trustee) for the benefit of others (beneficiaries). The grantor (person transferring the property to the trustee) gives legal title to the trustee, subject to terms set forth in a trust agreement. Beneficiaries have equitable title to the trust property. 138

trustee   One holding legal title to property for the benefit of another; may be either an individual or a company, such as a bank and trust company. 139

twisting   Practice of inducing a policyowner with one company to lapse, forfeit, or surrender a life insurance policy for the purpose of taking out a policy in another company. Generally classified as a misdemeanor, subject to fine, revocation of license, and sometimes imprisonment. (See **misrepresentation**)

U

underwriter   Company receiving premiums and accepting responsibility for fulfilling the policy contract. Company employee who decides whether or not the company should assume a particular risk. The agent who sells the policy. 174

underwriting   Process through which an insurer determines whether, and on what basis, an insurance application will be accepted. 173, 365

Unfair Trade Practices Act   A model act written by the National Association of Insurance Commissioners (NAIC) and adopted by most states empowering state insurance commissioners to investigate and issue cease and desist orders and penalties to insurers for engaging in unfair or deceptive practices, such as misrepresentation or coercion. 26

Uniform Individual Accident and Sickness Policy Provisions Law   NAIC model law that established uniform terms, provisions, and standards for health insurance policies covering loss "resulting from sickness or from bodily injury or death by accident or both." 352

Uniform Simultaneous Death Act   Model law that states when an insured and beneficiary die at the same time, it is presumed that the insured survived the beneficiary. 145

unilateral   Distinguishing characteristic of an insurance contract in that it is only the insurance company that pledges anything. 36

uninsurable risk   One not acceptable for insurance due to excessive risk. 173

universal life Flexible premium, two-part contract containing renewable term insurance and a cash value account that generally earns interest at a higher rate than a traditional policy. The interest rate varies. Premiums are deposited in the cash value account after the company deducts its fee and a monthly cost for the term coverage. 100

utilization review A technique used by health care providers to determine after the fact if health care was appropriate and effective. 372

V

valued contract A contract of insurance that pays a stated amount in the event of a loss. 37, 281

variable life insurance Provides a guaranteed minimum death benefit. Actual benefits paid may be more, however, depending on the fluctuating market value of investments behind the contract at the insured's death. The cash surrender value also generally fluctuates with the market value of the investment portfolio. 109

variable universal life insurance A life insurance policy combining characteristics of universal and variable life policies. A VUL policy contains unscheduled premium payments and death benefits and a cash value that varies according to the underlying funds whose investment portfolio is managed by the policyowner. 109

vesting Right of employees under a retirement plan to retain part or all of the annuities purchased by the employer's contributions on their behalf or, in some plans, to receive cash payments or equivalent value, on termination of their employment, after certain qualifying conditions have been met. 239

viatical broker An insurance producer licensed to solicit viatical settlement agreements between providers and policyowners of life insurance contracts. 168

viatical provider A company that buys a life insurance policy from a policyowner who is suffering from a terminal illness or a severe chronic illness.

viatical settlement contract An agreement under which the owner of a life insurance policy sells the policy to another person in exchange for a bargained-for payment, which is generally less than the expected death benefit under the policy. 164

viator An individual suffering from a terminal illness or severe chronic illness who sells her life insurance policy to a viatical company. The company becomes the policyowner and assumes responsibility for paying premiums. When the insured dies, the company receives the death benefits. 168

vision insurance Optional coverage available with group health insurance plans; vision insurance typically pays for charges incurred during eye exams; eyeglasses and contact lenses are usually excluded. 381

voidable contract A contract that can be made void at the option of one or more parties to the agreement. 43

void contract An agreement without legal effect: an invalid contract. 43

voluntary group AD&D A group accidental death and dismemberment policy paid for entirely by employees, rather than an employer. 384

W

waiting period (See **elimination period**) 314

waiver Agreement waiving the company's liability for a certain type or types of risk ordinarily covered in the policy; a voluntary giving up of a legal, given right. 43, 360

waiver of premium Rider or provision included in most life insurance policies and some health insurance policies exempting the insured from paying premiums after the insured has been disabled for a specified period of time, usually six months in life policies and 90 days or six months in health policies. 127, 316

war clause Relieves the insurer of liability, or reduces its liability, for specified loss caused by war. 122

warranties Statements made on an application for insurance that are warranted to be true; that is, they are exact in every detail as opposed to representations. Statements on applications for insurance are rarely warranties, unless fraud is involved. (See **representation**) 38

whole life insurance Permanent level insurance protection for the "whole of life," from policy issue to the death of the insured. Characterized by level premiums, level benefits, and cash values. 89

workers' compensation Benefits paid to workers for injury, disability, or disease contracted in the course of their employment. Benefits and conditions are set by law, although in most states the insurance to provide the benefits may be purchased from regular insurance companies. A few states have monopolistic state compensation funds. 289, 335

Y

yearly renewable term insurance (YRT) (See **annually renewable term**) 87

QUESTIONS FOR REVIEW ANSWER KEY

Unit 1

1. D
2. D
3. C
4. B
5. A
6. C
7. B
8. B
9. C
10. B

Unit 2

1. C
2. D
3. A
4. C
5. A
6. A
7. B
8. C
9. C
10. B
11. D

12. C
13. D
14. B
15. D

Unit 3

1. B
2. C
3. B
4. B
5. D
6. B
7. C
8. B
9. B
10. D
11. B
12. D
13. B
14. C
15. A

Unit 4

1. D
2. B

3.	B	3.	C
4.	A	4.	C
5.	C	5.	A
6.	D	6.	C
7.	C	7.	C
8.	A	8.	C
9.	C	9.	B
10.	B	10.	C
11.	B	11.	C
12.	C	12.	B
13.	B	13.	C
14.	B	14.	C
15.	D	15.	C
16.	B	16.	D
17.	B	17.	A
18.	B		

Unit 6

19.	C	1.	D
20.	B	2.	C
21.	A	3.	A
22.	C	4.	D
23.	D	5.	A
24.	D	6.	B

Unit 5

		7.	C
1.	C	8.	C
2.	B	9.	D

10.	B	10.	D
11.	D	11.	C
12.	D	12.	A
13.	B	13.	C
14.	C	14.	B
15.	B	15.	A
16.	C		

Unit 8

17.	D	1.	C
18.	A	2.	C
19.	A	3.	B
20.	D	4.	C
21.	D	5.	D
22.	A	6.	A
23.	B	7.	D
24.	B	8.	A

Unit 7

		9.	B
1.	D	10.	D
2.	B	11.	B
3.	C	12.	C
4.	C	13.	C
5.	D	14.	B
6.	B	15.	A
7.	C	16.	C
8.	C		
9.	D		

Unit 9

1. D
2. A
3. B
4. C
5. A
6. A
7. B
8. B
9. B
10. B

Unit 10

1. C
2. B
3. B
4. A

Unit 11

1. A
2. B
3. B
4. B
5. A
6. B
7. B
8. B

9. C
10. C
11. D
12. C

Unit 12

1. D
2. B
3. C
4. C
5. C
6. A
7. D
8. A

Unit 13

1. C
2. D
3. D
4. C
5. C
6. B
7. D
8. D
9. A
10. D
11. C

12. **D**

13. **C**

Unit 14

1. **D**

2. **A**

3. **C**

4. **D**

5. **C**

6. **B**

7. **C**

8. **B**

9. **A**

10. **D**

Unit 15

1. **D**

2. **B**

3. **C**

4. **C**

5. **B**

Unit 16

1. **A**

2. **B**

3. **C**

4. **C**

5. **B**

6. **D**

7. **D**

8. **B**

Unit 17

1. **C**

2. **B**

3. **C**

4. **A**

5. **C**

6. **C**

7. **C**

8. **B**

9. **D**

10. **C**

Unit 18

1. **B**

2. **D**

3. **B**

4. **B**

5. **C**

6. **D**

7. **C**

8. **A**

9. **B**

10. **B**

Unit 19

1. D
2. C
3. B
4. A

Unit 20

1. D
2. B
3. A
4. D
5. C

Unit 21

1. A
2. C
3. B
4. C
5. D

Unit 22

1. D
2. D
3. C
4. C
5. C
6. A
7. C

8. C
9. D
10. B
11. B
12. B

Unit 23

1. D
2. D
3. C
4. A
5. D
6. D
7. D
8. B
9. B
10. C

Unit 24

1. B
2. D
3. C
4. B
5. B
6. C
7. B
8. D

9. C

10. A

Unit 25

1. C

2. B

3. B

4. D

5. D

Unit 26

1. C

2. A

3. C

4. B

5. D

6. C

7. B

8. C

9. A

10. B

11. C

12. C

13. A

14. D

15. A

16. D

17. C

18. A

19. B

20. B

Unit 27

1. C

2. B

3. C

4. D

5. B

6. B

7. D

8. D

9. B

10. D

11. C

12. A

13. D

14. B

15. B

16. C

17. B

18. B

19. D

20. C

21. C

22. A

23. A

24. D

25. B

Unit 28

1. C

2. B

3. B

4. A

5. D

6. C

7. A

8. A

9. D

10. D

11. A

12. B

13. A

14. D

15. C

16. B

17. D

18. B

Unit 29

1. C

2. A

3. B

4. A

5. C

6. A

7. D

8. D

9. C

10. B

11. C

12. C

13. D

14. B

15. D

16. B

17. C

18. A

19. B

20. D

21. B

22. A

23. D

24. C

25. C

Unit 30

1. **A**

2. **C**

3. **A**

4. **C**

5. **D**

6. **B**

7. **A**

8. **C**

9. **D**

10. **C**

11. **A**

12. **B**

13. **B**

14. **A**

15. **C**

16. **A**

17. **D**

18. **C**

Final Exam Review

This is not a sample of the official state insurance licensing exam and is not intended to replace any other final exams that schools or educational providers administer for their courses.

General Principles

1. In the insurance business, risk can best be defined as

    A. sharing the possibility of a loss
    B. uncertainty regarding the future
    C. uncertainty regarding financial loss
    D. uncertainty regarding when death will occur

2. Which of the following risks is insurable?

    A. Pure risks
    B. Gambling
    C. Speculative risks
    D. Investing

3. Buying insurance is one of the most effective ways of

    A. avoiding risk
    B. transferring risk
    C. reducing risk
    D. retaining risk

4. Which of the following best describes the function of insurance?

    A. It is a form of legalized gambling.
    B. It spreads financial risk over a large group to minimize the loss to any one individual.
    C. It protects against living too long.
    D. It creates and protects risks.

5. All of the following are elements of an insurable risk EXCEPT

    A. the loss must be due to chance
    B. the loss must be predictable
    C. the loss must be catastrophic
    D. the loss must have a determinable value

6. The amount of money an insurer sets aside to pay future claims is called

    A. a premium
    B. a reserve
    C. a dividend
    D. an accumulated interest

7. Which of the following constitutes an insurable interest?

    A. The policyowner must expect to benefit from the insured's death.
    B. The policyowner must expect to suffer a loss when the insured dies or becomes disabled.
    C. The beneficiary, by definition, has an insurable interest in the insured.
    D. The insured must have a personal or business relationship with the beneficiary.

8. Which of the following statements describes the parol evidence rule?

    A. A written contract cannot be changed once it is signed.
    B. An oral contract cannot be modified by written evidence.
    C. A written contract cannot be changed by oral evidence.
    D. An oral contract takes precedence over any earlier written contracts.

9. Which of the following factors determines whether policy dividends will be paid on a participating policy?

    A. Reserves and experience
    B. Expenses and claims costs
    C. Interest and benefits
    D. Premiums and renewability

10. A licensed agent legally represents

    A. the insurer
    B. the applicant/insured
    C. the state insurance department
    D. himself or herself

11. All of the following statements regarding policy replacement are correct EXCEPT

    A. replacement involves convincing a policyholder to lapse or terminate an existing policy and to purchase another
    B. interrupting one cash value insurance plan to begin another could cause serious financial problems for the policyowner
    C. even if the customer wants to replace his or her existing policy, an agent can effect a policy replacement only by following the replacement regulations in the agent's state
    D. premiums for replacement policies are generally lower than premiums for the existing policies they replace

12. With regard to insurable risks, which of the following statements is NOT correct?

    A. Only pure risks are insurable.
    B. An insurable risk must involve loss that is within the insured's control.
    C. Insurers will not insure risks that are catastrophic in nature.
    D. An insurable risk must be measurable.

13. On August 9, Albert made an application for life insurance that his agent submitted a day later without a premium payment. On August 21, the insurer issued the policy as applied for and on August 24, the agent delivered the policy and collected the initial premium. On what day was the contract offer made?

    A. August 9
    B. August 10
    C. August 21
    D. August 24

14. All statements made by an applicant in an application for life insurance are considered to be

    A. warranties
    B. affirmations
    C. representations
    D. declarations

15. Which of the following legal terms indicates that a life insurance contract contains the enforceable promises of only one party?

    A. Adhesion
    B. Unilateral
    C. Conditional
    D. Aleatory

16. Which of the following types of agent authority is specifically set forth in writing in the agent's contract?

    A. Express
    B. Implied
    C. Apparent
    D. Personal

17. Assume a home catches fire after it is struck by lightning and the fire destroys its structure and contents. By insurance definition, the fire is

    A. the risk
    B. the hazard
    C. the peril
    D. the proximate cause

18. What constitutes "consideration" for a life insurance policy?

    A. Application and initial premium
    B. Agent's commission
    C. Adhesion feature of the contract
    D. Policy's benefits

19. Statements made by an applicant for life insurance that are guaranteed to be true are

    A. warranties
    B. material statements
    C. representations
    D. declarations

20. Which of the following insurance companies is owned by its policyholders?

    A. Service insurer
    B. Stock insurer
    C. Reinsurer
    D. Mutual insurer

Principles of Life Insurance

21. With regard to life insurance, all of the following statements are correct EXCEPT
    A. all individuals are considered to have insurable interests in themselves
    B. spouses are automatically considered to have insurable interests in each other
    C. a creditor has an insurable interest in a debtor
    D. insurable interest must be maintained throughout the life of the contract

22. A life insurance company is organized in Orlando where it maintains its home office. In Florida, the company is classified as
    A. a domestic company
    B. a local company
    C. a foreign company
    D. a preferred company

23. A life insurance company organized in Illinois, with its home office in Philadelphia, is licensed to conduct business in Wisconsin. In Wisconsin, this company is classified as
    A. a domestic company
    B. an alien company
    C. a foreign company
    D. a regional company

24. To whom does the cash value of a life insurance policy belong?
    A. Policyowner
    B. Insured
    C. Insurer
    D. Beneficiary

25. Frank is the insured in a $40,000, 5-year level term policy issued in 2003. He died in 2009. His beneficiary received
    A. nothing
    B. $20,000
    C. $40,000
    D. the cash value of the policy

26. All of the following statements regarding assignment of a life insurance policy are correct EXCEPT
    A. to secure a loan, the policy can be transferred temporarily to the lender as security for the loan
    B. the policyowner must obtain approval from the insurance company before a policy can be assigned
    C. the life insurance company assume no responsibility for the validity of an assignment
    D. the life insurance company must be notified in writing by the policyowner of any assignment

27. After a family's breadwinner dies, the "blackout period" generally can be defined as the period
    A. during which children are living at home
    B. that begins when the youngest child turns 16 and ends when the surviving parent retires
    C. during which children are in school
    D. from the surviving parent's retirement to death

28. A company with 3 partners is considering a buy-sell plan. All of the following statements pertaining to buy-sell plans and this partnership are correct EXCEPT
    A. an insured entity buy-sell agreement designates the partnership as the beneficiary
    B. if they choose a cross-purchase plan, each partner would have to purchase 2 policies for a total of 6 plans
    C. no benefits will accrue to the partnership from the buy-sell agreement until one of the partners dies
    D. if they choose an entity buy-sell agreement, the business would be party to the agreement

29. Bill names his church as the beneficiary of his $300,000 life insurance policy. When Bill dies, who is responsible for the income taxes payable on the lump-sum proceeds received by the church?
    A. Bill's estate is responsible.
    B. Bill's church is responsible.
    C. No income tax is payable on the death proceeds.
    D. Bill's estate and Bill's church split the tax.

30. Which provision of a life insurance policy states that the application is part of the contract?

    A. Consideration clause
    B. Insuring clause
    C. Entire contract clause
    D. Incontestable clause

31. Ron, the insured, dies during the grace period for his $100,000 life insurance policy. Considering that the premium on the policy has not been paid, what happens?

    A. The premium is canceled because the insured died during the grace period.
    B. The amount of the premium is deducted from the policy proceeds paid to the beneficiary.
    C. The premium due, plus a 10% penalty, is charged against the policy.
    D. The beneficiary must pay the premium after the death claim is paid.

32. Which of the following is stated in the consideration clause of a life insurance policy?

    A. Insured's risk classification
    B. Insured's general health condition
    C. Amount and frequency of premium payments
    D. Benefits payable upon the insured's death

33. John stopped paying premiums on his permanent life insurance policy 8 years ago though he never surrendered it. He is still insurable and has no outstanding loan against the policy. The company probably will decline to reinstate the policy because the time limit for reinstatement has expired. The limit usually is

    A. 6 months
    B. 1 year
    C. 2 years
    D. 3 years or as long as 7 years

34. All of the following statements pertaining to reinstatement of a life insurance policy are correct EXCEPT

    A. a suicide exclusion period is renewed with a reinstated policy
    B. when reinstating a policy, the insurer may charge the policyowner for past-due premiums
    C. when reinstating a policy, the insurer may charge the policyowner for interest on past-due premiums
    D. a new contestable period usually becomes effective in a reinstated policy

35. Leland elects to surrender his whole life policy for a reduced paid-up policy. The cash value of his new policy will

    A. continue to increase
    B. decrease gradually
    C. remain the same as in the old policy
    D. decrease by 50% immediately

36. Kevin, the insured in a $200,000 life insurance policy, and his sole beneficiary, Lynda, are killed instantly in a car accident. Under the Uniform Simultaneous Death Act, to whose estate will the policy proceeds be paid?

    A. The policy proceeds will be paid to Lynda's estate.
    B. The policy proceeds will be paid to Kevin's estate.
    C. The policy proceeds will be paid to equally to both Kevin's and Lynda's estate.
    D. The proceeds will escheat to the state.

37. When a policyowner cannot exercise rights of ownership without the policy beneficiary's consent, the beneficiary is designated

    A. vested
    B. contractual
    C. irrevocable
    D. primary

38. All of the following statements about term insurance are correct EXCEPT

    A. it pays a benefit only if the insured dies during a specified period
    B. level, decreasing, and increasing are basic forms of term insurance
    C. cash values build during the specified period
    D. it provides protection for a temporary period of time

39. Bob purchases a $50,000, 5-year level term policy. All of the following statements about Bob's coverage are correct EXCEPT

    A. the policy provides a straight, level $50,000 of coverage for 5 years
    B. if the insured dies at any time during the 5 years, his beneficiary will receive the policy's face value
    C. if the insured dies after the specified 5 years, only the policy's cash value will be paid
    D. if the insured lives beyond the 5 years, the policy expires and no benefits are payable

40. Mrs. Williamson purchases a 5-year, $50,000 term policy with an option to renew. Which of the following statements about the policy's renewability is CORRECT?

    A. The premium for the renewal period will be the same as the initial period.
    B. The premium for the renewal period will be higher than the initial period.
    C. The premium for the renewal period will be the same as the initial period, but a one-time service charge will be assessed upon renewal.
    D. The premium for the renewal period will be lower than the initial period.

41. Joanna and her husband, Tom, have a $40,000 annuity that pays them $200 a month. Tom dies and Joanna continues receiving the $200 monthly check as long as she lives. When Joanna dies, the company ceases payment. This is an example of

    A. an installment refund annuity
    B. a joint and full survivor annuity
    C. a life annuity
    D. a cash refund annuity

42. Each of the following statements about the incontestable clause in a life insurance policy is correct EXCEPT

    A. the clause gives people assurance that when their policies become claims, they will be paid without delays or protests
    B. the incontestable clause means that after a certain period, an insurer cannot refuse to pay the proceeds of a policy or void the contract
    C. incontestable clauses usually become effective two years from the issue date of the policy
    D. insurers can void a contract even after the specified period provided they can prove the policy was purchased fraudulently

43. All of the following statements correctly describe the purpose of Social Security EXCEPT

    A. to provide basic protection against financial problems accompanying death, disability, and retirement
    B. to augment a sound personal insurance plan
    C. to provide a source of income for a meaningful standard of living
    D. to protect workers, their spouses, and dependent children

44. Ralph owns a $50,000 nonpar whole life policy. Its cash value has accumulated to $15,000, and he has paid a total of $9,500 in premiums. If he surrenders the policy for its cash value, how will it be taxed?

    A. Ralph will receive the $15,000 tax free.
    B. Ralph will receive $5,500 tax free; the $9,500 balance is taxable as income.
    C. Ralph will receive $9,500 tax free; the $5,500 balance is taxable as income.
    D. Ralph will receive the $15,000 as taxable income.

45. Which of the following would NOT apply when a life insurance policy is reinstated after a lapse?

    A. All back premiums must be paid.
    B. All outstanding loans must be paid.
    C. A new contestable period goes into effect.
    D. A new suicide exclusion period goes into effect.

46. Jane, age 35, has just purchased a 20-pay whole life policy. When she turns 55, she will
    A. receive the policy's face amount benefit
    B. have a fully matured policy
    C. cease paying premiums
    D. no longer be covered by the policy

47. If a life insurance applicant is given a binding receipt, when does the applicant's coverage become effective?
    A. The date the policy is issued
    B. The date the applicant proves to be insurable
    C. The date the receipt is given
    D. The date the policy is delivered

48. Who performs the function of risk selection in determining an individual's insurability for policy issue?
    A. Actuary
    B. Agent
    C. Fiduciary
    D. Underwriter

49. Regular notices sent to policyowners for payment of their life insurance policy premiums reflect
    A. gross premium
    B. net level premium
    C. net single premium
    D. none of the above

50. In which of the following situations would the premium payor of a life insurance policy be able to deduct the premium payments for tax purposes?
    A. Joe, the sole proprietor of a grocery store, purchases and pays premiums on a $75,000 term life policy on his life and names his wife as beneficiary.
    B. Leland, a local board member of the United Way, assigns his $25,000 whole life policy to that organization, but continues to make the premium payments.
    C. Michelle, the legal guardian of 5-year-old Angela, makes the premium payments on Angela's $5,000 juvenile life insurance policy.
    D. Bob takes over the premium payments on his son's $30,000 whole life policy after his son declares bankruptcy.

51. At what point does a whole life policy mature or endow?
    A. When the policy's cash value equals the face amount
    B. When premiums paid equal the policy's face amount
    C. When premiums paid equal the policy's cash value
    D. When the policy's cash value equals the loan amount

52. Assume 4 individuals, all age 30, purchase the following life insurance policies. If all policies are still in force 10 years later, who will have the largest cash value in his policy?

    Bob $100,000 straight whole life
    Dennis $100,000 life paid-up at 65
    Ralph $100,000 20-pay life
    Jack $100,000 life paid-up at 55

    A. Bob
    B. Dennis
    C. Ralph
    D. Jack

53. Who designates the beneficiary of a life insurance policy?
    A. Insured
    B. Policyowner
    C. Underwriter
    D. Fiduciary

54. A retirement plan that is not employer-sponsored allows single workers who earn up to $25,000 a year to contribute up to $5,000 every year and deduct the contribution from their taxes. The plan described is
    A. a 401(k) plan
    B. an SEP plan
    C. an HR-10 plan
    D. an IRA plan

55. When an insured dies, who stands first to receive the policy's proceeds?
    A. Policyowner
    B. Primary beneficiary
    C. Insured's creditors
    D. Insured's estate

56. What is the basic source of information for life insurance underwriting and policy issue?

   A. Consumer reports
   B. Medical Information Bureau
   C. Application
   D. Physician reports

57. Jerry has just purchased a life insurance policy and is taking time to review the policy's provisions. He will find that his policy excludes death by all of the following means EXCEPT

   A. suicide
   B. accident
   C. aviation
   D. war

58. A universal life policy expires when

   A. an outstanding loan equals the death benefit
   B. a regularly scheduled premium payment is missed
   C. the cash value becomes too small to pay the cost of insurance
   D. the cash value equals the death benefit

59. Randy's premium payment was due on June 1, but the company did not receive it until June 28. Which policy provision kept Randy's policy from lapsing?

   A. Reinstatement
   B. Facility-of-payment
   C. Grace period
   D. Automatic premium loan

60. Which of the following statements regarding policy assignments is CORRECT?

   A. The policyowner must notify the insurer of the assignment and receive the insurer's permission.
   B. The procedure required for policy assignment is explained in the policy's insuring clause.
   C. A policy that has named an irrevocable beneficiary cannot be assigned without that beneficiary's agreement.
   D. Insurable interest must exist between the insured and the assignee at the time of assignment.

Principles of Health Insurance

61. On August 1, Roger completed an application for a major medical policy, gave his agent a check for the initial premium, and received an insurability receipt from the agent. No medical examination was required. On August 3, the agent submitted Roger's application and premium to the insurance company. On August 6, Roger was involved in an accident and admitted to a hospital. On August 12, the agent received Roger's policy from the insurance company. Which of the following statements concerning this situation is CORRECT?

   A. Roger's coverage will begin when he receives the policy from the agent.
   B. Roger's coverage began when he received the insurability receipt.
   C. Roger's coverage began the day the insurance company received the application and premium from the agent.
   D. Roger's coverage began the day the agent sent the application and premium to the insurance company.

62. Beth's health insurance policy contains a provision that allows her to renew coverage up to age 65. However, the policy also states that should Beth lose her job, the insurance company will cancel the policy, regardless of Beth's age. In terms of renewability, what type of policy does Beth have?

   A. Cancelable
   B. Optionally renewable
   C. Guaranteed renewable
   D. Conditionally renewable

63. Health maintenance organizations are known for stressing the provision of

   A. preventive care
   B. health care and services on a fee-for-services-rendered basis
   C. health care and services in hospital settings
   D. health care and services to government employees

64. All of the following statements are true of preferred provider organizations EXCEPT
    A. a PPO is a group of health care providers, such as doctors, hospitals, and ambulatory health care organizations, that contract with a group to provide their services
    B. PPOs operate on a prepaid basis
    C. PPO members select from among the preferred providers for needed services
    D. groups that contract with PPOs are employers, insurance companies, or other health insurance benefits providers

65. All of the following benefits are available under Social Security EXCEPT
    A. welfare benefits
    B. death benefits
    C. old-age or retirement benefits
    D. disability benefits

66. Medicaid provides
    A. funds to states for the provision of medical care to the aged
    B. funds to states to assist their medical public assistance programs
    C. funds to charitable organizations for providing medical benefits to poor people
    D. medical benefits to those who contributed to Medicare funding through payroll taxes

67. Mr. Ritchie, a taxidermist, is insured under a business overhead expense policy that pays maximum monthly benefits of $2,000. Mr. Ritchie becomes disabled. His actual monthly expenses are $2,700. The monthly benefit payable under his policy will be
    A. $1,300
    B. $2,000
    C. $2,350
    D. $2,700

68. All of the following statements about Medicare supplement (Medigap) policies are correct EXCEPT
    A. Medigap policies supplement Medicare benefits
    B. Medigap policies cover the cost of extended nursing home care
    C. Medigap policies pay most, if not all, Medicare deductibles and copayments
    D. Medigap policies pay for some health care services not covered by Medicare

69. Which of the following is NOT a typical type of long-term care coverage?
    A. Skilled nursing care
    B. Home health care
    C. Hospice care
    D. Residential care

70. All of the following are mandatory provisions in health insurance policies EXCEPT
    A. proof of loss
    B. entire contract
    C. change of beneficiary
    D. misstatement of age

71. Under the notice of claims provision of a health insurance policy, a policyowner must provide notification of loss within a reasonable period of time, usually
    A. 10 days after an occurrence or a commencement of a loss
    B. 20 days after an occurrence or a commencement of a loss
    C. 1 month after an occurrence or a commencement of a loss
    D. no later than 3 months after an occurrence or a commencement of a loss

72. Paul is hospitalized with a back injury and, upon checking his disability income policy, learns that he will not be eligible for benefits for at least 60 days. This would indicate that his policy probably has a 60-day
    A. elimination period
    B. probationary period
    C. disability period
    D. blackout period

73. Major risk factors in health insurance underwriting include all of the following EXCEPT

    A. physical condition
    B. habits or lifestyle
    C. marital status
    D. occupation

74. Which of the following is known for stressing preventive health care?

    A. Administrative-services-only providers
    B. Lloyd's of London
    C. Health maintenance organizations
    D. Commercial insurers

75. Leonard owns a major medical health policy which requires him to pay the first $200 of covered expenses each year before the policy pays its benefits. The $200 is the policy's

    A. coinsurance amount
    B. deductible
    C. stop-loss amount
    D. annual premium

76. Basic hospital expense insurance provides coverage for all of the following EXCEPT

    A. hospital room and board
    B. anesthesia and use of the operating room and supplies
    C. physician services
    D. drugs and x-rays

77. All of the following approaches are used by insurers to determine benefits payable under basic surgical expense insurance EXCEPT

    A. relative value scale approach
    B. traditional net cost method
    C. reasonable and customary approach
    D. surgical schedule method

78. Basic surgical expense policies generally provide coverage for all of the following EXCEPT

    A. anesthesiologist services
    B. surgeon services
    C. postoperative care
    D. miscellaneous expenses, such as lab fees and x-rays

79. A waiver of premium provision may be included with which kind of health insurance policy?

    A. Hospital indemnity
    B. Major medical
    C. Disability income
    D. Basic medical

80. The minimum number of persons to be insured under a group health insurance plan is established by

    A. the NAIC
    B. state law
    C. federal law
    D. the employer

81. Alice has a major medical policy with a $500 deductible and an 80/20 coinsurance provision. If she receives a hospital bill for $7,500 of covered expenses, how much of that bill will she have to pay?

    A. $1,400
    B. $1,900
    C. $2,000
    D. $2,400

82. Which of the following reimburses its insureds for covered medical expenses?

    A. Health maintenance organizations
    B. Preferred provider organizations
    C. Commercial insurers
    D. Service providers

83. Individual health insurance policies are typically written on which basis?

    A. Participating
    B. Nonparticipating
    C. Experience-rated
    D. Claims-rated

84. Workers' compensation covers income loss resulting from

    A. work-related disabilities
    B. plant and office closings
    C. job layoffs
    D. job terminations

85. As it pertains to group health insurance, COBRA stipulates that

    A. retiring employees must be allowed to convert their group coverage to individual policies
    B. terminated employees must be allowed to convert their group coverage to individual policies
    C. group coverage must be extended for terminated employees up to a certain period of time at the employee's expense
    D. group coverage must be extended for terminated employees up to a certain period of time at the employer's expense

86. Which of the following statements regarding morbidity tables is CORRECT?

    A. They indicate the average number of individuals from a given group who will die in a given year.
    B. They indicate the average number of individuals from a given group who will become disabled.
    C. They indicate the number of males and females from a given group who will die in a given year.
    D. They indicate and number of males and females from a given group who will become disabled in a given year.

87. All of the following are primary health insurance premium factors EXCEPT

    A. interest
    B. expense
    C. policy benefits
    D. morbidity

88. When a group disability insurance plan is paid entirely by the employer, benefits paid to disabled employees are

    A. taxable income to the employee
    B. deductible income to the employee
    C. deductible business expenses to the employer
    D. taxable income to the employer

89. Harry, the owner of a convenience store, is the insured under a business overhead policy. Were Harry to become disabled, the policy would cover all of the following EXCEPT

    A. Harry's salary
    B. the store manager's salary
    C. the rent
    D. utility bills

90. All of the following are mandatory health insurance policy provisions EXCEPT

    A. change of occupation
    B. entire contract
    C. grace period
    D. reinstatement

91. Which renewability provision allows an insurer to terminate a health insurance policy on any date specified in the policy and to increase the premium for any class of insureds?

    A. Conditionally renewable
    B. Optionally renewable
    C. Guaranteed renewable
    D. Cancelable

92. The time of payment of claims provision requires that

    A. claims must be paid after the insurer is notified of a loss
    B. claims must be paid after the insurer is notified and receives proof of loss
    C. the insured must submit proof of loss within a specified time, or the claim may be denied
    D. the insured must periodically submit proof of loss in order to receive the claim

93. By most insurers' definitions, "partial disability" is

    A. the loss of one or more limbs
    B. the ability of a disabled insured to work at any job for which the insured is reasonably suited
    C. the inability of the insured to work at the insured's own job
    D. the inability of the insured to perform certain important duties of the insured's own job

94. The period of time immediately following a disability during which benefits are not payable is

    A. the elimination period
    B. the probationary period
    C. the residual period
    D. the short-term disability period

95. All of the following are characteristics of group health insurance plans EXCEPT

    A. their benefits are more extensive than those under individual plans
    B. the parties to a group health contract are the employer and the employees
    C. employers may require employees to contribute to the premium payments
    D. the cost of insuring an individual is less than what would be charged for comparable benefits under an individual plan

96. Bill's medical expense policy states that it will pay him a flat $50 a day for each day he is hospitalized. The policy pays benefits on which basis?

    A. Reimbursement
    B. Indemnity
    C. Service
    D. Partial

97. After a week in the hospital, Lola receives a bill for $9,000 of covered expenses. Her major medical policy has a $250 deductible and a 75/25 coinsurance feature. How much of the total expense will Lola's policy cover?

    A. $2,063
    B. $6,063
    C. $6,563
    D. $8,753

98. A basic surgical expense policy that covers surgeons' fees per a schedule approach

    A. bases its benefits on what is customary for a particular area
    B. assigns a set of points to each surgical procedure
    C. assigns a dollar amount to each surgical procedure
    D. bases its benefits on a percentage of hospital room and board expenses

99. A stop-loss feature in a major medical policy specifies the maximum

    A. benefit amount the policy provides each year
    B. benefit amount the policy provides in a lifetime
    C. amount the insured must pay in premiums
    D. amount the insured must pay toward covered expenses

100. Which of the following is a standard optional provision for health policies?

    A. Grace period
    B. Physical exam and autopsy
    C. Change of beneficiary
    D. Misstatement of age

Final Exam Review
Answers and Rationales

General Principles

1. **C.** The concept of insurance developed from the need to minimize the adverse effects of risk associated with the probability of financial loss.

2. **A.** Only pure risks are insurable because they involve only the chance of loss. They are pure in the sense that they do not mix both profits and losses. Insurance is concerned with the economic problems created by pure risks.

3. **B.** Buying insurance is one of the most effective ways of transferring risk. Through the insurance contract, the burden of carrying the risk and indemnifying the financial loss is transferred from the individual to the insurance company.

4. **B.** The function of insurance is to safeguard against financial loss by having the losses of few paid by the contributions of many who are exposed to the same risk.

5. **C.** One of the criteria for an insurable risk is that it *not* be catastrophic. A principle of insurance holds that only a small portion of a given group will experience loss at any one time. Risks that would adversely affect large numbers of people or large amounts of property—wars or floods, for example—are typically not insurable.

6. **B.** Reserves can be defined as the amounts that are set aside to fulfill the insurance company's obligation to pay future claims. The reserve is compiled from past premium payments and interest.

7. **B.** Insurable interest requires the policyowner to benefit from the insured's continuing to live or enjoy good health or to suffer a loss when the insured dies or is disabled.

8. **C.** The parol evidence rule states that when parties put their agreement in writing, all previous verbal statements come together in that writing, and a written contract cannot be changed or modified by parol (oral) evidence.

9. **B.** If expenses and claims costs are less than expected, dividends are likely to be paid.

10. **A.** An agent is an individual who has been authorized by an insurer to be its representative to the public and to offer for sale its goods and services.

11. **D.** The new policy will probably be at a higher premium rate because it will be based on the insured's then-attained age.

12. **B.** To be insurable, a risk must involve the chance of loss that is fortuitous and outside the insured's control.

13. **C.** If an applicant does not submit an initial premium with the application, the applicant is inviting the insurance company to make a contract offer. The insurer can respond by issuing a policy (the offer) that the applicant can accept by paying the premium when the policy is delivered.

14. **C.** Most states require that life insurance policies contain a provision that all statements made in the application be deemed representations, not warranties. A representation is a statement made by the applicant that the applicant believes to be true. A warranty is a statement made by the applicant that is guaranteed to be true. If an insurance company rejects a claim on the

basis of a representation, the company bears the burden of proving materiality.

15. **B.** Insurance contracts are unilateral in that only one party—the insurer—makes any kind of enforceable promise.

16. **A.** Express authority is the authority a principal gives to its agent. Express authority is granted by means of the agent's contract, which is the principal's appointment of the agent to act on its behalf.

17. **C.** A peril is the immediate specific event causing loss and giving rise to risk. When a building burns, fire is the peril.

18. **A.** Consideration is the value given in exchange for the promises sought. In an insurance contract, consideration is given by the applicant in exchange for the insurer's promise to pay benefits, and it consists of the application and the initial premium.

19. **A.** A warranty in insurance is a statement made by the applicant that is guaranteed to be true. It becomes part of the contract and, if found to be untrue, can be grounds for revoking the contract. Warranties are presumed to be material because they affect the insurer's decision to accept or reject an applicant.

20. **D.** Mutual insurers are owned by the policyholders. Anyone purchasing insurance from a mutual insurer is both a customer and an owner.

Principles of Life Insurance

21. **D.** Insurable interest is required only when a contract is issued; it does not have to be maintained throughout the life of the contract, nor is it necessary at the time of claim.

22. **A.** An insurer is termed "domestic" in a state when it is incorporated in that state.

23. **C.** A foreign company operates within a state in which it is not chartered and in which its home office is not located.

24. **A.** The accumulation that builds over the life of a policy is called the "cash value," and it belongs to the policyowner, who may or may not be the insured.

25. **A.** In this case, the insured died after his term policy had expired. As a result, his beneficiary received nothing.

26. **B.** Policyowners actually own their policies and may do with them as they please. They can even give them away, just as they can give away any other kind of property they own. Nevertheless, they must notify the insurance company in writing of any transfers of ownership (assignments). The company must then accept the validity of the assignments without question.

27. **B.** The "blackout period" is the time during which no Social Security benefits are payable to a surviving spouse. This period begins when the youngest child reaches age 16 and continues until the spouse retires.

28. **C.** A buy-sell plan offers several advantages to the partners while they are all living. The partners know they will have a legal right to buy a deceased partner's share of the business, and the family and heirs of the partners know that the partnership interest will be disposed of at a fair price. Further, the money needed to purchase the deceased partner's interest will be available when needed. All this adds up to security and peace of mind for all involved, including employees of the business.

29. **C.** Lump-sum proceeds payable upon the death of the insured are not subject to income tax, no matter who the beneficiary is.

30. **C.** The entire contract clause states that the policy document; the application, which is attached to the policy; and any attached riders constitute the entire contract. The policy cannot refer to any outside documents as being part of the contract.

31. **B.** If the premium of a policy has not been paid and the insured dies during the grace period, the policy benefit is payable. However, the premium amount due is deducted from the benefits paid to the beneficiary.

32. **C.** The consideration clause specifies the amount and frequency of premium payments that the policyowner must make to keep the insurance in force.

33. **D.** There is a limited period of time in which policies may be reinstated after lapse. This period is usually 3 years, but may be as long as 7 years, in some cases.

34. **A.** When reinstating a life policy, no new suicide exclusion period goes into effect.

35. **A.** When Leland surrenders his whole life policy for a reduced paid-up policy, the face value is reduced but the cash value continues to increase.

36. **B.** Under the Uniform Simultaneous Death Act, if the insured and primary beneficiary are killed in the same accident and there is not sufficient evidence to show who died first, the policy proceeds are to be distributed as if the insured died last. Kevin's estate would receive the proceeds because Lynda, the beneficiary, was deemed to have predeceased Kevin, and no other beneficiary was named.

37. **C.** If a beneficiary is named irrevocable, the policyowner gives up the right to change that beneficiary, and unless otherwise specified in the policy, the owner cannot take any action that would affect the right of that beneficiary to receive the full amount of the insurance at the insured's death. This includes taking out a policy loan or surrendering the policy.

38. **C.** There are no cash values in term policies.

39. **C.** If the insured lives beyond the 5-year period, the policy expires and no benefits are payable. There are no cash values in term policies.

40. **B.** Premiums for the renewal period will be higher because of the insured's advanced age and, thus, increased risk.

41. **B.** The joint and full survivor option provides for payment of the annuity to two people. If either person dies, the same income payments continue to the survivor for life. When the surviving annuitant dies, no further payments are made to anyone.

42. **D.** After the policy has been in force for the specified period, the company cannot contest a death claim or refuse payment of the proceeds even on the basis of a material misstatement, concealment, or fraud.

43. **C.** The purpose of the Social Security system is to provide a basic floor of protection to augment—not replace—a sound personal insurance plan. Many expect Social Security to fulfill all their financial needs and to provide a meaningful standard of living. The consequences of this misunderstanding have been disillusionment by many Americans who found they were inadequately covered when they needed life insurance, disability income, or retirement income.

44. **C.** A policyowner is allowed to receive tax free an amount equal to what the policyowner paid into the policy over the years in the form of premiums.

45. **D.** There is no new suicide exclusion period when a policy is reinstated.

46. **C.** Limited pay whole life policies have level premiums that are limited to a certain

period (less than life), after which no more premiums are owed.

47. **C.** Under a binding receipt (or temporary insurance agreement), coverage is guaranteed at the time of application for the amount of insurance applied for. The temporary coverage continues until the policy is issued as requested, until the company offers a different policy or until the company rejects the application, but in no event for more than 60 days from the date the agreement was signed.

48. **D.** Who is qualified to purchase life insurance and who is not? The process of answering this question is called risk selection, a function that is performed by insurance company underwriters.

49. **A.** Gross premium equals net single premium plus expense. The gross premium is what the policyowners are required to pay.

50. **B.** Premiums paid for life insurance owned by a qualified charitable organization are deductible.

51. **A.** Whole life insurance is designed to mature at age 100. At age 100, the cash value of the policy has accumulated to the point that it equals the face amount of the policy, as it was actuarially designed to do. At that point, the policy has completely matured or endowed. No more premiums are owed; the policy is completely paid up.

52. **C.** The larger the face amount of the policy, the larger the cash values; the shorter the premium-payment period, the quicker the cash values grow; and the longer the policy has been in force, the greater the build-up in cash values.

53. **B.** One of the rights of owning a life insurance policy is the right to designate and change the beneficiary of the policy proceeds.

54. **D.** Anyone under the age of 70½ who has earned income may open an IRA and

contribute each year an amount up to $5,000 or 100% of compensation, whichever is less. Contributions grow tax free until they are withdrawn.

55. **B.** A primary beneficiary is the party designated to receive the proceeds of a life insurance policy when they become payable.

56. **C.** The application for insurance is the basic source of insurability information. It is the first source of information to be reviewed, and it is reviewed thoroughly.

57. **B.** Most life insurance policies exclude the following risks: war, aviation, hazardous occupation or hobbies, commission of a felony, and suicide.

58. **C.** Universal life premiums are flexible and deposited into the policy cash value account along with interest credited by the insurer. Increasing monthly mortality charges are deducted from the cash value account. If the cash value account is insufficient to pay the monthly mortality charges at any point, the policy lapses.

59. **C.** If policyowners forget or neglect to pay their premiums by the date they are due, the grace period allows an extra 30 days or 1 month during which premiums may be paid to keep policies in force.

60. **C.** When beneficiaries are designated irrevocable, the policyowner gives up the right to change them. Irrevocable beneficiaries have a vested right in the policy, and the policyowner cannot exercise rights of ownership without the beneficiary's consent.

Principles of Health Insurance

61. **B.** The insurability type of conditional receipt provides that when an applicant pays the initial premium, coverage is effective—on the condition that the applicant proves to be insurable—either on the date the

application was signed or the date of the medical examination, if one is required.

62. **D.** A conditionally renewable policy allows an insurer to terminate the coverage, but only in the event of one or more conditions stated in the contract. These conditions cannot apply to the insured's health. Most frequently, they are related to the insured reaching a certain age or losing gainful employment.

63. **A.** HMOs stress preventive care to reduce the number of unnecessary hospital admissions and duplication of services.

64. **B.** Unlike HMOs, preferred provider organizations usually operate on a fee-for-service-rendered basis, not on a prepaid basis.

65. **A.** Social Security provides death benefits, old-age or retirement benefits, and disability benefits to eligible workers. Social Security is an entitlement program, not a welfare program.

66. **B.** Medicaid provides matching federal funds to states for their medical public assistance programs to help needy persons, regardless of age.

67. **B.** Business overhead expense insurance reimburses business for the covered expenses incurred or the maximum that is stated in the policy. If Mr. Ritchie's monthly expenses were $1,700, his plan would have paid a monthly benefit of $1,700. However, because Mr. Ritchie's expenses exceeded his maximum coverage, the policy pays the maximum benefit stated in the policy, $2,000.

68. **B.** Medigap policies do not cover the cost of extended nursing home care.

69. **C.** Long-term care services are designed for senior citizens, while hospice services are for terminally ill persons and their families.

70. **D.** Misstatement of age is an optional provision of health insurance policies.

71. **B.** Under the notice of claims provision, an insured must provide notification of loss 20 days after an occurrence or a commencement of a loss.

72. **A.** Similar in concept to a deductible, the elimination period is the time immediately following the start of a disability when benefits are not payable.

73. **C.** Physical condition, habits or lifestyle (moral hazards), and occupation are major risk factors in health insurance. Marital status is not a risk factor.

74. **C.** Health maintenance organizations stress preventive care to promote patient health and to control the use of health care resources, particularly expensive resources like hospitals.

75. **B.** A *deductible* is a stated initial dollar amount that the individual insured is required to pay before insurance benefits are paid.

76. **C.** Physicians' services are not covered under a basic hospital expense policy, even in the case of surgery. The cost for a physician is covered under a basic surgical expense or basic physician's (nonsurgical) expense policy.

77. **B.** The traditional net cost method is a way of comparing costs of similar policies.

78. **D.** Miscellaneous expenses are covered under basic hospital expense policies. These "extras" include drugs, x-rays, anesthesia, lab fees, dressings, use of the operating room, and supplies.

79. **C.** A **waiver of premium** rider generally is included with guaranteed renewable and noncancelable individual disability income policies. It is a valuable provision because it exempts the policyowner from paying the

policy's premiums during periods of total disability.

80. **B.** State laws specify the minimum number of persons to be covered under a group policy. One state may stipulate 15 persons as a minimum number, while another state may require a minimum of 10. (The most typical minimum requirement is 10 lives.)

81. **B.**

Total expenses	$ 7,500
Deductible Alice pays	− 500
Basis for insurer's payment	$ 7,000
	× .80
Amount insurer pays	$ 5,600
Coinsurance amount Alice pays	$ 1,400
Deductible	+ 500
Total Alice pays	$ 1,900

82. **C.** Commercial insurance companies function on the reimbursement approach. Policyowners obtain medical treatment from whatever source they feel is most appropriate and, per the terms of their policy, submit their charges to their insurer for reimbursement.

83. **B.** Most individual health insurance is issued on a nonparticipating basis.

84. **A.** All states have workers' compensation laws, which were enacted to provide mandatory benefits to employees for work-related injuries, illness, or death.

85. **C.** COBRA requires employers with 20 or more employees to continue group medical expense coverage for terminated workers (as well as their spouses, divorced spouses, and dependent children) for up to 18 months (or 36 months, in some situations) following termination. However, the terminated employee can be required to pay the premium, which may be up to 102% of the premium that would otherwise be charged.

86. **B.** Whereas mortality rates show the average number of persons within a larger group of people who can be expected to die within a given year at a given age, morbidity tables indicate the average number of individuals at various ages who can be expected to become disabled each year due to accident or sickness. They also reveal the average duration of disability.

87. **C.** There are three primary factors that affect health insurance premiums: morbidity, interest, and expenses.

88. **A.** Disability benefit payments that are attributed to employee contributions are not taxable, but benefit payments that are attributed to employer contributions are taxable.

89. **A.** Business overhead expense policies do not include any compensation for the disabled owner.

90. **A.** Change of occupation is an optional provision.

91. **B.** The renewability provision in an optionally renewable policy gives the insurer the option to terminate the policy on the date specified in the contract. Furthermore, this provision allows the insurer to increase the premium for any class of optionally renewable insureds.

92. **B.** The time of payment of claims provision provides for immediate payment of the claim after the insurer receives notification and proof of loss.

93. **D.** By most definitions, partial disability is the inability of the insured to perform one or more important duties of the insured's job.

94. **A.** The elimination period is the time immediately following the start of a disability when benefits are not payable. Elimination periods eliminate claims for short-term disabilities for which the insured can usually manage without financial

hardship and save the insurance company from the expense of processing and settling small claims.

95. **B.** The contract for coverage is between the insurance company and the employer, and a master policy is issued to the employer.

96. **B.** Indemnity medical expense policies do not pay expenses or bills; they merely provide the insured with a stated benefit amount for each day the insured is confined to a hospital as an in-patient. The money may be used by the insured for any purpose.

97. **C.** Responsibility for payment would be as follows:

Total expenses	$ 9,000
Deductible Lola pays	− 250
Basis for insurer's payment	$ 8,750
	× .75
Amount insurer pays	$ 6,563
Coinsurance Lola pays	$ 2,187

98. **C.** Under the surgical schedule method, every surgical procedure is assigned a dollar amount by the insurer. When a claim is submitted to the insurer, the claims examiner reviews the policy to determine what amount is payable; if the surgeon's bill is more than the allowed charge set by the insurer, it is up to the insured to pay the surgeon the difference. If the surgeon's bill is less than the allowed charge, the insurer will pay only the full amount billed; the claim payment will never exceed the amount charged.

99. **D.** To provide a safeguard for insureds, many major medical policies contain a stop-loss feature that limits the insured's out-of-pocket expenses. This means that once the insured has paid a specified amount toward the insured's covered expenses—usually $1,000 to $2,000—the company pays 100% of covered expenses after that point.

100. **D.** Misstatement of age is 1 of 11 optional policy provisions. Companies may ignore them or use them in their policy forms.

Notes

Notes

Notes

Notes

Notes